The Hallmark Features

A COMPLETE LEARNING PACKAGE

Discover Sociology: Core Concepts explores sociology as a discipline of curious minds, with the theoretical, conceptual, and empirical tools needed to understand, analyze, and even change the world—all in a more streamlined format. Adapted from *Discover Sociology, Third Edition*, the core version offers in-depth coverage of 12 high-priority topics that are at the heart of almost all introductory sociology courses. **Core Concepts** maintains its reader-friendly narrative and the hallmark themes of the parent book:

- **INEQUALITY MATTERS** explores a crucial theme of sociology—power and its unequal distribution in society, probing manifestations of and explanations for power and resource disparities.
- **PRIVATE LIVES, PUBLIC ISSUES** develops sociological imaginations, illustrating how our individual lives and social forces shape each other.
- **WHAT CAN I DO WITH A SOCIOLOGY DEGREE?** links the skills learned in sociology courses to potential careers. This feature highlights how sociology graduates use their degree in the work they do, as well as a short U.S. Bureau of Labor Statistics overview of the occupational field, its educational requirements, median income, and expected growth potential.

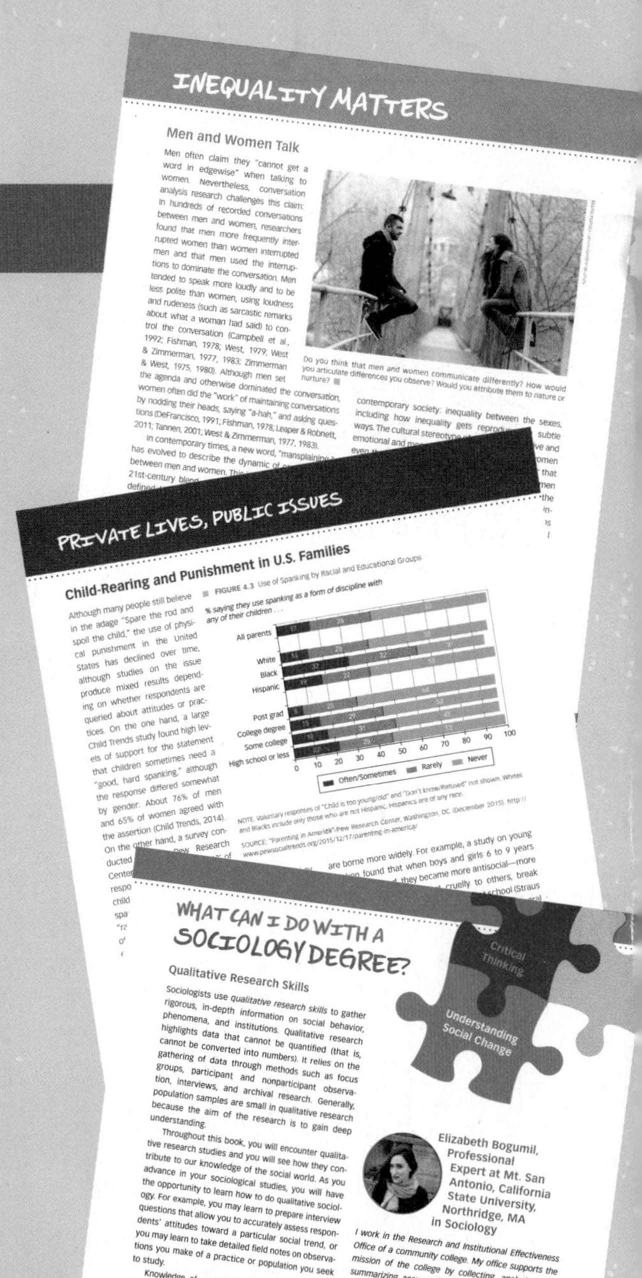

INEQUALITY MATTERS

Men and Women Talk

Men often claim they "cannot get a word in edgewise" when talking to women. Nevertheless, conversation analysis research challenges this claim: In hundreds of recorded conversations between men and women, researchers found that men more frequently interrupted women than women interrupted men and that men used the interruptions to dominate the conversation. Men tended to speak more loudly and to be less polite than women, using loudness and rudeness (such as sarcastic remarks about what a woman had said) to control the conversation (Campbell et al., 1992; Fishman, 1978; West, 1979; West & Zimmerman, 1977, 1983; Zimmerman & West, 1975, 1980). Although men set the agenda and otherwise dominated the conversation, women often did the "work" of maintaining conversations by nodding their heads, saying "a-hah," and asking questions (DeFrancisco, 1991; Fishman, 1978; Leaper & Robnett, 2011; Tannen, 2001; West & Zimmerman, 1977, 1983).

In contemporary times, a new word, "mansplaining," has evolved to describe the dynamic of ... between men and women. This ... 21st-century blend ... defined ...

Do you think that men and women communicate differently? How would you articulate differences you observe? Would you attribute them to nature or nurture?

contemporary society: inequality between the sexes, including how inequality gets reprodu... subtle ways. The cultural stereotype ... emotional and ... ve and even ... omen ... that ... men ... the ... in- ... is

PRIVATE LIVES, PUBLIC ISSUES

Child-Rearing and Punishment in U.S. Families

Although many people still believe in the adage "Spare the rod and spoil the child," the use of physical punishment in the United States has declined over time, although studies on the issue produce mixed results depending on whether respondents are queried about attitudes or practices. On the one hand, a large Child Trends study found high levels of support for the statement that children sometimes need a "good, hard spanking," although the response differed somewhat by gender: About 76% of men and 65% of women agreed with the assertion (Child Trends, 2014). On the other hand, a survey conducted ... Pew Research Center ... respo... child... spa... "r... o...

FIGURE 4.3 Use of Spanking by Racial and Educational Groups

% saying they use spanking as a form of discipline with any of their children . . .

	Often/Sometimes	Rarely	Never
All parents	17	28	53
White	14	28	57
Black	32	32	35
Hispanic	19	22	55
Post grad	8	25	66
College degree	15	29	53
Some college	18	31	47
High school or less	22	25	52

NOTE: Voluntary responses of "Child is too young/old" and "Don't know/Refused" not shown. Whites and Blacks include only those who are not Hispanic. Hispanics are of any race.

SOURCE: "Parenting in America". Pew Research Center, Washington, DC (December 2015). http://www.pewsocialtrends.org/2015/12/17/parenting-in-america/

... are borne more widely. For example, a study on young ... found that when boys and girls 6 to 9 years ... they became more antisocial—more ... cruelly to others, break ... school (Straus ...

WHAT CAN I DO WITH A SOCIOLOGY DEGREE?

Critical Thinking

Understanding Social Change

Qualitative Research Skills

Sociologists use *qualitative research skills* to gather rigorous, in-depth information on social behavior, phenomena, and institutions. Qualitative research highlights data that cannot be quantified (that is, cannot be converted into numbers). It relies on the gathering of data through methods such as focus groups, participant and nonparticipant observation, interviews, and archival research. Generally, population samples are small in qualitative research because the aim of the research is to gain deep understanding.

Throughout this book, you will encounter qualitative research studies and you will see how they contribute to our knowledge of the social world. As you advance in your sociological studies, you will have the opportunity to learn how to do qualitative sociology. For example, you may learn to prepare interview questions that allow you to accurately assess respondents' attitudes toward a particular social trend, or you may learn to take detailed field notes on observations you make of a practice or population you seek to study.

Knowledge of qualitative research methods is a beneficial skill in today's job market. Learning to collect data through observation, interviews, and focus groups, for instance, prepares you to do a wide variety of job tasks, including survey development, questionnaire design, data collection and reporting, and market research. Furthermore, qualitative research experience fosters communication competencies through the processes of small-group management and rapport building, as well as through negotiation with study participants.

Elizabeth Bogumil, Professional Expert at Mt. San Antonio, California State University, Northridge, MA in Sociology

I work in the Research and Institutional Effectiveness Office of a community college. My office supports the mission of the college by collecting, analyzing, and summarizing accurate, timely, and reliable data. We work with various departments, centers, and projects across the college campus to determine and document the effectiveness of programs and services. Our office focuses on both qualitative and quantitative research, and stresses the collaborative nature of every stage of the research process. One does not often hear about institutional research in higher education; however, every university and community college has institutional researchers providing insight, data, and support to the administrative services, the instructional services, the student services, human resources, and the office of the college or university president.

Why Study Socialization and Social Interaction?

123

DISCOVER
SOCIOLOGY
CORE CONCEPTS

The Core Concepts edition of Discover Sociology *is dedicated to my colleagues at The George Washington University. It is a privilege to work in a rigorous intellectual environment that also offers fulfilling academic collaborations and friendships.*

As always, I am grateful for the support of my family: my patient and wonderful husband, Joe, and my two children, Niklavs and Anna, who have grown into thoughtful and amazing young adults.

—DSE

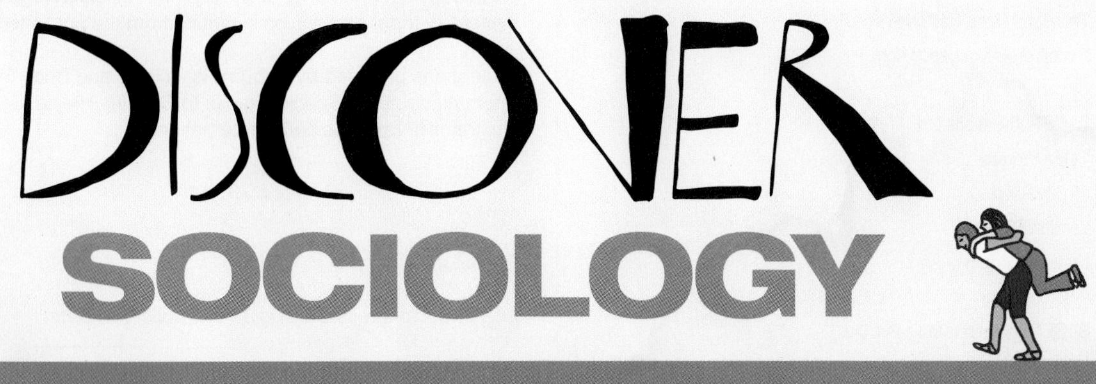

CORE CONCEPTS

Daina S. Eglitis | William J. Chambliss

George Washington University

Los Angeles | London | New Delhi
Singapore | Washington DC | Melbourne

FOR INFORMATION:

SAGE Publications, Inc.
2455 Teller Road
Thousand Oaks, California 91320
E-mail: order@sagepub.com

SAGE Publications Ltd.
1 Oliver's Yard
55 City Road
London EC1Y 1SP
United Kingdom

SAGE Publications India Pvt. Ltd.
B 1/I 1 Mohan Cooperative Industrial Area
Mathura Road, New Delhi 110 044
India

SAGE Publications Asia-Pacific Pte. Ltd.
3 Church Street
#10-04 Samsung Hub
Singapore 049483

Acquisitions Editor: Jeff Lasser
Content Development Editors: Nancy Matuszak, Sarah Dillard
Editorial Assistant: Adeline Wilson
Production Editor: Kelly DeRosa
Copy Editor: Sheree Van Vreede
Typesetter: C&M Digitals (P) Ltd.
Proofreader: Susan Schon
Indexer: Robie Grant
Cover Designer: Scott Van Atta
Marketing Manager: Kara Kindstrom

Illustrations provided by Auburn Associates and Body Scientific International, LLC. Special thanks to Carolina Hrejsa, Senior Medical Illustrator of Body Scientific International.

Printed in Canada

Library of Congress Cataloging-in-Publication Data

Names: Eglitis, Daina S., author. | Chambliss, William J., author.

Title: Discover sociology : core concepts / Daina S. Eglitis, George Washington University, William J. Chambliss, George Washington University.

Description: Los Angeles : SAGE, [2019] | Includes bibliographical references and index.

Identifiers: LCCN 2017037616 | ISBN 9781506347431 (pbk. : alk. paper)

Subjects: LCSH: Sociology.

Classification: LCC HM585 .E438 2019 | DDC 301—dc23
LC record available at https://lccn.loc.gov/2017037616

This book is printed on acid-free paper.

18 19 20 21 22 10 9 8 7 6 5 4 3 2 1

BRIEF CONTENTS

Preface xvii

Acknowledgments xxi

About the Authors xxv

Chapter 1: Discover Sociology 1

Chapter 2: Discover Sociological Research 34

Chapter 3: Culture and Mass Media 62

Chapter 4: Socialization and Social Interaction 94

Chapter 5: Groups, Organizations, and Bureaucracies 126

Chapter 6: Deviance and Social Control 156

Chapter 7: Social Class and Inequality 190

Chapter 8: Race and Ethnicity 228

Chapter 9: Gender and Society 264

Chapter 10: Families and Society 306

Chapter 11: Education and the Economy 342

Chapter 12: Social Movements and Social Change 378

Glossary 409

References 419

Index 449

DETAILED CONTENTS

Preface xvii

Acknowledgments xxi

About the Authors xxv

Chapter 1: Discover Sociology 1

Artur Debat/Getty Images

A Curious Mind 2
The Sociological Imagination 3
Critical Thinking 6

DISCOVER & DEBATE: What Is a Debate? 8

The Development of Sociological Thinking 9
The Birth of Sociology: Science, Progress, Industrialization, and Urbanization 9
19th-Century Founders 11

PRIVATE LIVES, PUBLIC ISSUES: Why Do Couples Get Divorced? 14

Significant Founding Ideas in U.S. Sociology 17

SOCIAL LIFE, SOCIAL MEDIA: Capturing the World in 140 Characters 18

Women in Early Sociology 21
Sociology: One Way of Looking at the World—or Many? 22
The Functionalist Paradigm 23

INEQUALITY MATTERS: Why Are Some People Poor and Others Rich? 24

GLOBAL ISSUES: Local Consumption, Global Production 26

The Social Conflict Paradigm 27
Principal Themes in This Book 29
Power and Inequality 29
Globalization and Diversity 30
Technology and Society 30
Why Study Sociology? 30

WHAT CAN I DO WITH A SOCIOLOGY DEGREE? An Introduction 31

Chapter 2: Discover Sociological Research 34

©iStockphoto.com/themacx

No Roof Overhead: Researching Eviction in America 36
Sociology and Common Sense 37
Research and the Scientific Method 39
Relationships Between Variables 40
Testing Theories and Hypotheses 42
Validity and Reliability 43
Objectivity in Scientific Research 44
Doing Sociological Research 45
Sociological Research Methods 45
Survey Research 45
Fieldwork 47

BEHIND THE NUMBERS: What Factors Affect Survey Responses? 48

Experimentation 50
Working With Existing Information 50
Participatory Research 51

DISCOVER & DEBATE: Discover Sociological Research 52
Doing Sociology: A Student's Guide to Research 53
Frame Your Research Question 53
SOCIAL LIFE, SOCIAL MEDIA: Does Technology Affect Studying? 54
Review Existing Knowledge 55
Select the Appropriate Method 55
Weigh the Ethical Implications 56
Collect and Analyze the Data 56
Share the Results 56
PRIVATE LIVES, PUBLIC ISSUES: Zimbardo's Experiment: The Individual and the Social Role 57
Why Learn to Do Sociological Research? 58
WHAT CAN I DO WITH A SOCIOLOGY DEGREE? Quantitative Research Skills 59
Career Data: Statistician 59

Chapter 3: Culture and Mass Media 62

Zombie Apocalypse 64
Culture: Concepts and Applications 65
Material and Nonmaterial Culture 66
Ideal and Real Culture in U.S. Society 70
PRIVATE LIVES, PUBLIC ISSUES: Media, Markets, and the Culture of Thinness in America 72
Ethnocentrism 74
Subcultures 75
Culture and Language 76
Language and Social Integration 77
Culture and Mass Media 79
GLOBAL ISSUES: Language, Resistance, and Power in Northern Ireland 80
SOCIAL LIFE, SOCIAL MEDIA: Music, Money, and Marketing 82
Culture, Media, and Violence 83
Culture, Class, and Inequality 85
Culture and Globalization 86
DISCOVER & DEBATE: Culture and Mass Media 88
Why Study Culture and Media Through a Sociological Lens? 90
WHAT CAN I DO WITH A SOCIOLOGY DEGREE? Critical Thinking 90
Career Data: Market Research Analyst 91

Chapter 4: Socialization and Social Interaction 94

Selfie and Society 96
The Birth of the Social Self 97
Behaviorism and Social Learning Theory 99
Socialization as Symbolic Interaction 100
Stages of Development: Piaget and Kohlberg 102
Biological Needs Versus Social Constraints: Freud 103
Agents of Socialization 104
The Family 104
Teachers and School 105
PRIVATE LIVES, PUBLIC ISSUES: Child-Rearing and Punishment in U.S. Families 106
Peers 107
Organized Sports 109
Religion 109
Mass Media and Social Media 110
Work 111
GLOBAL ISSUES: When Is Dinner? 113
Socialization and Aging 114
Total Institutions and Resocialization 115
Social Interaction 116
DISCOVER & DEBATE: Socialization and Social Interaction 117
Studies of Social Interaction 118

Joel Ryan/Invision/AP Photo

©iStockphoto.com/hadynyah

The Dramaturgical Approach: Erving Goffman 119
Ethnomethodology and Conversation Analysis 120
INEQUALITY MATTERS: Men and Women Talk 121
Why Study Socialization and Social Interaction? 122
WHAT CAN I DO WITH A SOCIOLOGY DEGREE? Qualitative Research Skills 123
Career Data: Operations Research Analyst 124

Chapter 5: Groups, Organizations, and Bureaucracies 126

David Ramos/Stringer/Getty Images

Marooned: Group Dynamics on a Deserted Island 128
The Nature of Groups 129
The Power of Groups 130
The Effects of Size 130
PRIVATE LIVES, PUBLIC ISSUES: Individuals, Groups, and Academic Achievement 132
Types of Group Leadership 134
Conformity to Groups 135
Economic, Cultural, and Social Capital 138
Organizations 139
Types of Formal Organizations 139
SOCIAL LIFE, SOCIAL MEDIA: Charity Organizations and Social Media 140
Bureaucracies 141
Written Rules and Regulations 142
Bureaucracies: A Critical Evaluation 143
DISCOVER & DEBATE: Groups, Organizations, and Bureaucracies 144
Bureaucracy and Democracy 146
The Global Organization 147
International Governmental Organizations 147
GLOBAL ISSUES: International Organizations, Disaster, and Development: Rebuilding Haiti After the 2010 Earthquake 148
International Nongovernmental Organizations 150
Why Study Groups and Organizations? 151
WHAT CAN I DO WITH A SOCIOLOGY DEGREE? Leadership Skills and Teamwork 151
Career Data: Training and Development Specialist 152

Chapter 6: Deviance and Social Control 156

Ken Kaminesky/Getty Images

The Death of Len Bias 158
What Is Deviant Behavior? 160
How Do Sociologists Explain Deviance? 161
Biological Perspectives 161
Functionalist Perspectives 162
GLOBAL ISSUES: Globalization and Criminal Opportunities 164
Conflict Perspectives 165
Interactionist Perspectives 168
DISCOVER & DEBATE: Deviance and Social Control 170
Types of Deviance 171
Everyday Deviance 171
Sexual Deviance 171
Deviance of the Powerful 171
Crime 172
BEHIND THE NUMBERS: Counting Crime in the United States 174
Social Control of Deviance 178
Schools and Discipline: Is There a School to Prison Pipeline? 179
Imprisonment in the United States 180
INEQUALITY MATTERS: The Stigma of Imprisonment 182
The Death Penalty in the United States 183
Why Study Deviance? 185
WHAT CAN I DO WITH A SOCIOLOGY DEGREE? Written Communication Skills 186
Career Data: Private Detectives and Investigators 187

Chapter 7: Social Class and Inequality 190

Yong Kim/The Philadelphia Inquirer via AP

Poverty and Prosperity in the United States Today 192
Stratification in Traditional and Modern Societies 193
Caste Societies 193
Class Societies 194
Sociological Building Blocks of Social Class 194
Income 197
Wealth 197
Occupation 198
Status 198
Political Voice 199
Class and Inequality in the United States: Dimensions and Trends 199
Income Inequality 199
Wealth Inequality 201
Other Gaps: Inequalities in Health Care, Health, and Access to Consumer Goods 202
SOCIAL LIFE, SOCIAL MEDIA: New Research on Food Deserts in the United States 204
Why Has Inequality Grown? 205
At the Bottom of the Ladder: Poverty in the United States 207
The Problem of Neighborhood Poverty 208
BEHIND THE NUMBERS: Calculating U.S. Poverty 209
Why Do Stratification and Poverty Exist and Persist in Class Societies? 211
The Functionalist Explanation 211
The Social Conflict Explanation 212
Dimensions of Global Inequality and Poverty 213
Hunger, Mortality, and Fertility in Poor Countries 215
Education Matters 217
INEQUALITY MATTERS: Wealth and Poverty on the Road 218
Theoretical Perspectives on Global Inequality 219
Applying the Theories: The Case of Nigerian Oil Wealth 221
DISCOVER & DEBATE: Class and Inequality 223
Why Study Inequality in the United States and Around the World? 224
WHAT CAN I DO WITH A SOCIOLOGY DEGREE? Community Resource and Service Skills 224
Career Data: Health Educator/ Community Health Worker 225

Chapter 8: Race and Ethnicity 228

Robert Alexander/Contributor/Getty Images

Athletes Stand for Racial Equality 230
The Social Construction of Race and Ethnicity 231
Race 231
Ethnicity 232
Minorities 232
Minority and Dominant Group Relations 232
Expulsion 233
Segregation 233
BEHIND THE NUMBERS: Counting—and Not Counting—Hate Crimes in the United States 234
Assimilation and Cultural Pluralism 237
Theoretical Approaches to Ethnicity, Racism, and Minority Status 238
The Functionalist Perspective 238
The Conflict Perspective 238
The Symbolic Interactionist Perspective 239
Prejudice, Stereotyping, and Discrimination 240
PRIVATE LIVES, PUBLIC ISSUES: Locked Out: Poor Black Women and the Struggle of Eviction 242
Prison, Politics, and Power 244
Consequences of Prejudice and Discrimination: Race and Health 245

Technologies of Discrimination 246
Race and Ethnicity in Hollywood—and on Broadway 246
Racial and Ethnic Groups in the United States 247
American Indians 248
African Americans 249
INEQUALITY MATTERS: Who Has the Power to Name? 250
Latinos/Latinas 251
Asian Americans 252
Arab Americans 253
White Ethnic Americans 254
Multiracial Americans 255
Race and Ethnicity From a Global Perspective 256
Genocide: The Mass Destruction of Societies 256
DISCOVER & DEBATE: Race and Ethnicity 258
What Explains Genocide? 259
Why Study Race and Ethnicity From a Sociological Perspective? 260
WHAT CAN I DO WITH A SOCIOLOGY DEGREE? Making an Evidence-Based Argument 261
Career Data: Social Science Research Assistant 262

Chapter 9: Gender and Society 264

LWA/Dann Tardif/Getty Images

The College Gap: Women and Men on Campus 266
Concepts of Sex, Gender, and Sexuality 267
Constructing Gendered Selves 269
The Roots of Gender: The Family 270
Gender Among Friends: Peer Influences 271
Media Power: Reflecting and Reinforcing Gender 272
Gender in the Classroom: Schools and Socialization 273
Doing Gender 274
Gender and Society 275
Gender and Family Life 275
Gender in High School: Why Do Boys Outscore Girls on the SAT? 276
Gender and Higher Education 277
Gender and Economics: Men, Women, and the Gender Wage Gap 281
SOCIAL LIFE, SOCIAL MEDIA: Technology Takes on the Wage Gap 284
Classical Theories, Feminist Thought, and the Sociology of Masculinities 286
Classical Sociological Approaches to Gender 286
INEQUALITY MATTERS: The Internet Haters: Movies, Journalism, Misogyny 288
Contemporary U.S. Feminist Thinking on Gender 290
Feminist Perspectives on Doing Sociology 292
The Sociology of Masculinities 293
Women's Lives in a Global Perspective 295
Mothers and Children: The Threat of Maternal Mortality 295
GLOBAL ISSUES: Fighting Sextortion Around the World 296
The Price of (Being) a Girl 297
Women and Conflict: Rape in War 298
Change Happens: Women's Empowerment 299
DISCOVER & DEBATE: Equal Gender Representation 300
Why Study Gender From a Sociological Perspective? 302
WHAT CAN I DO WITH A SOCIOLOGY DEGREE? Ethical Decision-Making 302
Career Data: Urban and Regional Planner 303

Chapter 10: Families and Society 306

Hill Street Studios/Getty Images

Millennials and Marriage 308
How Do Sociologists Study the Family? 309
Families and the Work of Raising Children 311

Theoretical Perspectives on Families 311
The Functionalist Perspective 312
The Feminist Approach: A Conflict Perspective . . . and Beyond 312
U.S. Families Yesterday and Today 315
Marriage and Divorce in the Modern United States 316
Who's Minding the Children? Child Care in the United States Today 319
Immigration and Family Patterns 321
America's First Nations: Native American Families 322
GLOBAL ISSUES: Functional Alternatives to the Family in Modern Japan 323
Deaf Culture and Family Life 324
Violence and the Family 325
Socioeconomic Class and Family in the United States 326
Social Class and Child Rearing 326
DISCOVER & DEBATE: Sociology of the Family 327
Economy, Culture, and Family Formation 329
Family Life in the Middle Class 331
PRIVATE LIVES, PUBLIC ISSUES: Parenting in Poverty 332
Globalization and Families 333
International Families and the Global Woman 334
Why Study Family Through a Sociological Lens? 335
PRIVATE LIVES, PUBLIC ISSUES: Son Preference and the Problem of Marriage in China and India 336
WHAT CAN I DO WITH A SOCIOLOGY DEGREE? Problem Solving 338
Career Data: Social and Community Service Manager 339

Chapter 11: Education and the Economy 342

iStock Photo/kali9

Robots and the Future of Work 344
Education, Industrialization, and the "Credential Society" 345
Theoretical Perspectives on Education 347
The Functionalist Perspective 347
The Conflict Perspective 348
Education, Opportunity, and Inequality 351
INEQUALITY MATTERS: American Indian Schools 352
Word Poverty and Adult Illiteracy 353
School Segregation 354
Dropping In, Dropping Out: Why Are College Dropout Rates So High? 356
Education, Employment, and Earnings 359
The Economy in Historical Perspective 361
DISCOVER & DEBATE: Education and the Economy 362
The Agricultural Revolution and Agricultural Society 363
The Industrial Revolution and Industrial Society 363
Postindustrial Society 365
BEHIND THE NUMBERS: Unemployment, Employment, and Underemployment in the United States 368
The Technological Revolution and the Future of Work 369
Big Names, Few Workers: Digital Networking Companies in the Contemporary Economy 370
Rise of the Robots? 370
Why Study Education and the Economy? 372
GLOBAL ISSUES: The Digital Sweatshop 373
WHAT CAN I DO WITH A SOCIOLOGY DEGREE? The Global Perspective 374

Chapter 12: Social Movements and Social Change 378

AP Photo/Eric Gay

Students and Social Movements 380
Sociological Perspectives on Social Change 381

The Functionalist Perspective 381
The Conflict Perspective 382
Rise-and-Fall Theories of Social Change 384
Sources of Social Change 385
Collective Behavior 385
INEQUALITY MATTERS: Sports and Social Change 386
How Do Crowds Act? 389
Social Movements 391
DISCOVER & DEBATE: Social Movements and Social Change 392
Types of Social Movements 394
BEHIND THE NUMBERS: There Were Millions . . . Or Not 395
Why Do Social Movements Arise? 398
Micromobilization Contexts for Building Social Movements 402
New Social Movements 402
Why Study Social Change? 403
SOCIAL LIFE, SOCIAL MEDIA: Technology, Dystopia, and Social Change 404
WHAT CAN I DO WITH A SOCIOLOGY DEGREE? Understanding and Fostering Social Change 405
Career Data: Public Relations Specialist 406

Glossary 409
References 419
Index 449

PREFACE

The brilliant German physicist Albert Einstein wrote that "the important thing is not to stop questioning. Curiosity has its own reason for existing." Indeed, *curiosity* is the bedrock of all scientific inquiry because curiosity underlies the motivation and passion to seek answers to hard questions—and then to find new questions! But curiosity is not enough. To be a component of good sociology, curiosity must be disciplined: Answers must be sought within the scientific tradition of gathering data through systematic observations and explaining the findings with carefully constructed explanations or theories. In this text, our goal is to pique students' curiosity about the social world—and then to give them the academic tools to understand that world, analyze it, and maybe even change it.

There are many introductory sociology textbooks, some of which are very good. We believe that our contribution to the marketplace of sociological texts and ideas is a book that engages the sociology student's curious mind—and then offers him or her the theoretical, conceptual, and empirical tools to analyze and understand the issues that affect our world, both local and global. We have written this book in a way that we hope will encourage students to keep reading, not only because of assigned pages but also because, with the encouragement of the instructor and the text, they have a desire to know more! We also endeavor to show the discipline of sociology as a source of critical skills valued in the job market and in graduate and professional education. We are delighted that the first three editions of *Discover Sociology* have been well received, and it is our goal in the core concepts edition to keep the best of those editions in a volume that features a smaller number of chapters for instructors in institutions that use a trimester or other system with fewer weeks than a traditional semester or who seek a book that focuses largely on the sociological basics. Below we review some of the key features in this core concepts edition.

CHAPTER OPENERS THAT SPEAK TO STUDENTS

In this book, you will find chapters that begin with openers drawn from contemporary issues and events and that endeavor to speak to readers and to the kinds of experiences or concerns they have as students, as well as in other roles in the family or at work. From the questions of why more women than men are enrolled in college and how artificial intelligence is bringing important changes to the labor market, to the discussion of the sociological significance of zombie movies and the "selfie," the book's openers offer instructors a terrific way to begin discussions to which students will eagerly contribute. The beginning of each chapter also features "What do you think?" questions to engage students' curiosity and give a small preview of interesting issues that will be covered in the chapter.

SOCIOLOGY IS A SCIENTIFIC DISCIPLINE

Every chapter in the book integrates empirical research from sociology, highlighting the point that sociology is about the *scientific understanding* of the social world—rigorous research can illuminate the sociological roots of diverse phenomena and institutions, ranging from poverty and deviance to capitalism and the nuclear family. Research may also result in conflicting or ambiguous conclusions. Students learn that social life is complex and that sociological research is an ongoing effort to explain why things are as they are—and how they might change.

KEY THEMES AND BOXED FEATURES

Each chapter has a mixture of boxed features that highlight key themes in this book:

- The **sociological imagination**, of course, is a foundational concept in the discipline. It is important throughout the book, and we also feature **Private Lives, Public Issues** boxes that illustrate the relationship between our individual lives and the social forces that shape them.
- Second, **power** is a key theme in sociology—and in this text. Sociologists want to know how power

is distributed, how it is reproduced, and how it is exercised in social relationships and institutions. The unequal distribution of power is one important topic of sociological inquiry, and this text offers **Inequality Matters** boxes that probe manifestations of and explanations for power and resource disparities.

- Third, we emphasize the importance of being a **critical consumer of information.** We are surrounded by sources of data that stream into our lives from the Internet, newspapers, peers and colleagues, friends and family, and academic studies. Sociology asks us to look carefully at information and to understand its sources and assumptions in order to ascertain what it illuminates and what it obscures. To this end, we include **Behind the Numbers** boxes to give students the opportunity to look critically and carefully at statistical information on social problems such as unemployment and poverty, among others.
- Fourth, contemporary life, from politics to popular culture to personal interactions, is increasingly structured and influenced by social media. Social science is only beginning to grasp the significance of these dramatic developments. The book's **Social Life, Social Media** boxes endeavor to provide a sociological perspective on social media's functions, contributions, and consequences.
- Finally, the book highlights **globalization** and **global perspectives** in an effort to help students develop a fuller understanding of the place of their lives, their communities, and their country in an interconnected, interdependent, and multicultural international environment—and to enable them to see how other countries around the world are experiencing societal changes and challenges. The book's **Global Issues** boxes are part of this effort.

All of the boxed features include questions for students to help them reflect on the material and link it back to the chapter's larger themes.

NEW IN THE CORE CONCEPTS EDITION

An important goal of the core concepts edition of *Discover Sociology* is to reduce the total number of chapters to meet demand for shorter texts, while retaining the most widely used introductory chapters and bringing in some fresh material that we hope will be well received by readers of our book. This edition features updated social indicators, bringing in the latest data available from the U.S. Census Bureau, the Bureau of Labor Statistics, the Centers for Disease Control and Prevention, and the Pew Research Center, among others, as well as a revised **What Can I Do with a Sociology Degree?** feature and a fully new feature titled **Discover & Debate.**

CONNECTING SOCIOLOGY AND CAREER SUCCESS

As an instructor of introductory sociology, you are probably frequently asked by students, "What can I do with a sociology degree?" This is an important question for students (and, often, their parents) and instructors. This book offers instructors and students a unique feature that speaks directly and specifically to this question. This edition features some revised and updated career content. Although there are fewer total essays than there were in the full-length third edition, additional essays have been moved online, where students and instructors can access a range of career-related content.

In the core concepts edition of *Discover Sociology*, all of the chapters beginning with Chapter 2 feature an essay that accomplishes two major tasks. First, every essay *highlights specific skills students learn as sociology majors and describes those skills in ways that provide students a vocabulary that they can use in the job market.* Second, each essay profiles a graduate with a degree in sociology who is putting his or her skills to work in an interesting occupation or workplace. Graduates share in their own words what they learned from sociology and how it has contributed to their skills, knowledge, and career.

This feature helps students make a strong link between sociological skills and future careers in a wide array of occupational fields. It is important to note that this feature is not only for sociology majors! Sociology is often among the general education courses completed by students across a variety of disciplines, and it can help all students develop important skills, such as critical thinking, data literacy, and written communication, that they will need in the workplace. A *Washington Post* report on technology jobs, for instance, notes:

> As tech jobs evolve at the pace of light through fiber-optic cable, . . . leaders of tech firms such as

> Mozilla, Reddit and Tumblr say students should consider schools that not only will teach them traditional skills like coding, but also the softer skills that aren't listed in the course guide but are essential to the 21st-century workplace: working with others, problem-solving, the ability to pick up enough from disciplines other than their own to create products users believe are indispensable to their lives. (Lednicer, 2014, para. 5)

Clearly, for students across disciplines, there is value in understanding and naming the skills that they gain when they study sociology. We encourage all students to take advantage of this valuable feature.

DISCOVER & DEBATE

In *Discover Sociology: Core Concepts*, we are pleased to introduce a new feature, *Discover & Debate*. This feature goes beyond discussion questions and the pro/con approach to controversial issues. Rather, it highlights compelling sociological issues and offers a discussion model for instructors and students that takes the form of debate. A basic understanding of debate and, in particular, of the construction and evaluation of reasoned arguments, is vital to civic life, civil interaction, and even social change. In a society that often addresses vital issues in soundbites and tweets, it is especially challenging but important to develop the skills and knowledge to evaluate positions on issues critically and to build evidence-based arguments.

Beginning with Chapter 2, every chapter includes a *Discover & Debate* essay that presents a motion for debate, basic background on a current social issue, and an introduction to key arguments from the two sides. It also includes questions to consider when evaluating each position and a debate tip to help students build debate skills. We hope you will find this feature to be a valuable addition to the *Discover Sociology*.

PHOTOS AND GRAPHICS

The photographs in this edition have been carefully selected to help students put images together with ideas, events, and phenomena. A good photo can engage a student's curiosity and give him or her a visual vehicle for remembering the material under discussion. This has been our goal in choosing the photos included here. We have also carefully prepared visually appealing graphics, including tables, figures, and maps, to attract students' attention and enhance learning.

GLOSSARIES FOR LEARNING

This book features marginal glossaries, offering students easy access to definitions of key concepts, phenomena, and institutions. Additionally, key terms are bolded in the text, and a comprehensive glossary is available at the end of the book.

CHAPTER REVIEW

Every chapter ends with a summary of key learning points and a set of discussion questions to review what students have learned and to foster critical thinking about the materials.

DIGITAL RESOURCES

Discover Sociology includes a comprehensive ancillary package that uses new media and a wide range of instructional technologies designed to support instructor course preparation and student learning.

STUDENT STUDY SITE

An open-access student study site, available at **http://edge.sagepub.com/eglitis**, provides a variety of additional resources to build students' understanding of the book content and extend their learning beyond the classroom. Students will have access to the following features for each chapter:

- An online Action Plan includes tips and feedback on progress through the course and materials, which allows students to individualize their learning.
- SAGE Journal Articles: *Exclusive!* Certain full-text journal articles have been carefully selected for each chapter. Each article supports and expands on the concepts presented in the chapter. This feature also provides questions to focus and guide student interpretation. Combine cutting-edge academic journal scholarship with the topics in your course for a robust classroom experience.

- **Reference, *CQ Researcher,* and *Pacific Standard* magazine links:** Each chapter includes links to relevant articles from SAGE handbooks and encyclopedias, as well as links to articles from *CQ Researcher* and *Pacific Standard* magazine.
- **Video, Audio, and Web Links:** These carefully selected, Web-based resources feature relevant interviews, lectures, personal stories, inquiries, and other content for use in independent or classroom-based explorations of key topics.
- **eFlashcards and Web Quizzes:** These mobile-friendly resources reinforce understanding of key terms and concepts that have been outlined in the chapters.
- And much more!

INSTRUCTOR TEACHING SITE

A password-protected instructor teaching site, available at **http://edge.sagepub.com/eglitis**, provides integrated sources for all instructor materials, including the following key components for each chapter:

- The **Microsoft Word test bank** contains multiple-choice, true/false, short-answer, and essay questions for each chapter. The test bank provides you with a diverse range of prewritten options as well as with the opportunity to edit any question and/or insert your own personalized questions to assess students' progress and understanding effectively.
- The **Diploma electronic test bank** can be used on PCs and Macs. Containing multiple-choice, true/false, short-answer, and essay questions per chapter, the test bank provides you with a diverse range of prewritten options as well as with the opportunity to edit any questions and/or insert your own personalized questions to assess students' progress and understanding effectively. Diploma is also compatible with many popular learning management systems, so you can easily get your test questions into your online course.
- Editable, chapter-specific Microsoft **PowerPoint slides** offer you complete flexibility in easily creating a multimedia presentation for your course. Highlight essential content, features, and artwork from the book.
- **Lecture notes** summarize key concepts on a chapter-by-chapter basis to help with preparation for lectures and class discussions.
- **Sample course syllabi** for semester and quarter courses provide suggested models for use in the creation of syllabi for your courses.
- **Chapter-specific discussion questions** can help you launch classroom interaction by prompting students to engage with the material and by reinforcing important content.
- Lively and stimulating **ideas for class activities** can be used in class to reinforce active learning. The activities apply to individual or group projects.
- And much more!

INTERACTIVE E-BOOK

Discover Sociology is also available as an interactive e-book, which can be packaged free with the book or purchased separately. This interactive e-book offers links to Web, audio, and video resources, as well as to original author video.

ACKNOWLEDGMENTS

I am grateful to the terrific editors and staff at SAGE, including Jeff Lasser, Nancy Matuszak, Kara Kindstrom, Gabrielle Piccininni, Sarah Dillard, Scott Van Atta, Sheree Van Vreede, Kelly DeRosa, and Adeline Wilson. It is a privilege to work with such a creative, supportive, and smart group. Many thanks as well to SAGE's amazing sales staff, some of whom I have had the privilege to meet in Thousand Oaks. I am particularly grateful to sales representative Mariam Joan, who planted the seeds of the idea that blossomed into our new Discover & Debate feature.

I am also indebted to colleagues and graduate students who have helped over all four editions of the book. Among those who contributed ideas and assistance are the Department of Sociology at GWU's Michelle Kelso, Steven Tuch, Greg Squires, Ivy Ken, Antwan Jones, Hiromi Ishizawa, Fran Buntman, Emily Morrison, Michael Wenger, and Richard Zamoff. In addition, I owe a big debt of gratitude to Ann Scammon of the GWU Career Center for her contributions to the materials on career development in the first and second editions and to Carolyn Vasques Scalera for her terrific work on "What Can I Do With a Sociology Degree?" in the third edition. I would like to extend special thanks to the excellent research assistants who have supported this book: for the core edition, Srushti Upadhyay; for the third edition, Marwa Moaz and Anna Eglitis; for the second edition, Ann Horwitz and Chris Moloney; for the first edition, Chris Moloney, Jee Jee Kim, Claire Cook, Scott Grether, Ken Leon, Ceylan Engin, and Adam Bethke. Finally, for their patience and support, I also thank the Sociology Department office staff, particularly Octavia Kelsey. This project could not have been brought to completion without the valuable help and skills of all of the people named.

I am so grateful to my family, particularly my husband, Joseph Burke, my children, Niklavs and Anna Eglitis, and my mother, Silvia Stukuls. They continue to be the heart of this project and everything I do.

Finally, I thank all of the reviewers listed below, who contributed to *Discover Sociology* with excellent suggestions, creative insights, and helpful critiques.

REVIEWERS FOR THE CORE CONCEPTS EDITION

Michael Bourgoin, CUNY, Queens College

Gerri Brown, Copiah-Lincoln Community College

Marianne Cutler, East Stroudsburg University of Pennsylvania

Kellie J. Hagewen, College of Southern Nevada

Mark Killian, Whitworth University

Rosalind Kopfstein, Western Connecticut State University

Ryan Jerome LeCount, Hamline University

Ho Hon Leung, SUNY Oneonta

Sherry N. Mong, Capital University

Kaitlyne A. Motl, University of Kentucky

Susan B. Murray, San Jose State University

Carolyn Pevey, Germanna Community College

Thomas Piñeros Shields, University of Massachusetts at Lowell

Karen Platts, Bucks County Community College

Frank A. Salamone, Westchester Community College

Kamesha Spates, Kent State University

Jennifer Valentine, Tidewater Community College

Abraham Waya, Boston University

Lia Chervenak Wiley, The University of Akron

REVIEWERS FOR THE THIRD EDITION Laura Chambers Atkins, Jacksonville University; Marian Colello, Strayer University; Leslie Elrod, University of Cincinnati; Matthew Green, College of DuPage; Othello Harris, Miami University; Belinda Hartnett, Strayer University; Rick Jones, Marquette University; Lauren Kempton, University of New Haven; Veena S. Kulkarni, Arkansas State University; Elaine Leeder, Sonoma State University; Olena Leipnik, Sam Houston State University; Peter LeNeyee, Strayer University; Robert Sean Mackin, Texas A&M University; Aurelien Mauxion, Columbia College; Debra M. McCoy, Strayer University; Virginia Merlini, Strayer University; Allan Mooney, Strayer University; Andrew J. Prelong, University of Northern Colorado; Angela Primm-Bethea, Strayer University; Terri Slonaker, San Antonio College; Lia Chervenak Wiley, The University of Akron; Susan L. Wortmann, Nebraska Wesleyan University.

REVIEWERS FOR THE SECOND EDITION Dianne Berger-Hill, Old Dominion University; Alison J. Bianchi, University of Iowa; Michael Bourgoin, Queens College, The City University of New York; Paul E. Calarco Jr., Hudson Valley Community College; Nicolette Caperello, Sierra College; Susan E. Claxton, Georgia Highlands College; Sonya R. De Lisle, Tacoma Community College; Heather A. Downs, Jacksonville University; Leslie Elrod, University of Cincinnati; S. Michael Gaddis, University of Michigan; Cherly Gary-Furdge, North Central Texas College; Louis Gesualdi, St. John's University; Todd Goodsell, University of Utah; Matthew Green, College of DuPage; Ashley N. Hadden, Western Kentucky University; Othello Harris, Miami University; Michael M. Harrod, Central Washington University; Sarah Jacobson, Harrisburg Area Community College; Kimberly Lancaster, Coastal Carolina Community College; Katherine Lawson, Chaffey Community College; Jason J. Leiker, Utah State University; Kim MacInnis, Bridgewater State University; Barret Michalec, University of Delaware; Amanda Miller, University of Indianapolis; Christine Mowery, Virginia Commonwealth University; Scott M. Myers, Montana State University; Frank A. Salamone, Iona College; Bonita A. Sessing-Matcha, Hudson Valley Community College; Richard States, Allegany College of Maryland; Myron T. Strong, Community College of Baltimore County; Heather Laine Talley, Western Carolina University; PJ Verrecchia, York College of Pennsylvania; Jerrol David Weatherly, Coastal Carolina Community College; Debra L. Welkley, California State University, Sacramento; and Luis Zanartu, Sacramento City College.

REVIEWERS FOR THE FIRST EDITION Kristian P. Alexander, Zayed University; Lori J. Anderson, Tarleton State University; Shannon Kay Andrews, University of Tennessee at Chattanooga; Joyce Apsel, New York University; Gabriel Aquino, Westfield State College; Janet Armitage, St. Mary's University; Dionne Mathis Banks, University of Florida; Michael S. Barton, University at Albany; Jeffrey W. Basham, College of the Sequoias; Paul J. Becker, University of Dayton; Alison J. Bianchi, University of Iowa; Kimberly Boyd, Piedmont Virginia Community College; Mariana Branda, College of the Canyons; Jennifer Brennom, Kirkwood Community College; Denise Bump, Keystone College; Nicolette Caperello, Sierra College; Michael J. Carter, California State University, Northridge; Vivian L. Carter, Tuskegee University; Shaheen A. Chowdhury, College of DuPage; Jacqueline Clark, Ripon College; Susan Eidson Claxton, Georgia Highlands College; Debbie Coats, Maryville University; Angela M. Collins, Ozarks Technical Community College; Scott N. Contor, Idaho State University; Denise A. Copelton, The College at Brockport, State University of New York; Carol J. Corkern, Franklin University; Jennifer Crew Solomon, Winthrop University; William F. Daddio, Georgetown University; Jeffrey S. Debies-Carl, University of New Haven; Melanie Deffendall, Delgado Community College; Marc Jung-Whan de Jong, State University of New York, Fashion Institute of Technology; David R. Dickens, University of Nevada, Las Vegas; Keri Diggins, Scottsdale Community College; Amy M. Donley, University of Central Florida; Amanda Donovan, Bristol Community College; Heather A. Downs, Jacksonville University; Daniel D. Doyle, Bay College; Dorothy E. Everts, University of Arkansas–Monticello; Gary Feinberg, St. Thomas University; Bernie Fitzpatrick, Western Connecticut State University; Tonya K. Frevert, University of North Carolina at Charlotte; Cherly Furdge, North Central Texas College; S. Michael Gaddis, University of North Carolina at Chapel Hill; Robert Garot, John Jay College of Criminal Justice; Todd A. Garrard, University of Texas at San Antonio; Cherly Gary-Furdge, North Central Texas College; Marci Gerulis-Darcy, Metropolitan State University; Louis Gesualdi, St. John's University; Jennifer E. Givens, University of Utah; John Glass, Collin College; Malcolm Gold, Malone University; Thomas B. Gold, University of California, Berkeley; Matthew Green, College of DuPage; Johnnie M. Griffin, Jackson State University; Randolph M. Grinc, Caldwell College; Greg Haase, Western State College of Colorado; Dean H. Harper, University of Rochester; Anne S. Hastings, University of North Carolina at Chapel Hill; Anthony L. Haynor, Seton Hall University; Roneiko Henderson-Beasley, Tidewater Community College; Marta T. Henriksen, Central New Mexico Community College; Klaus Heyer, Nunez Community College; Jeremy D. Hickman, University of Kentucky; Bonniejean Alford

Hinde, College of DuPage; Joy Crissey Honea, Montana State University, Billings; Caazena P. Hunter, University of North Texas; John Iceland, Pennsylvania State University; Robert B. Jenkot, Coastal Carolina University; Wesley G. Jennings, University of South Florida; Audra Kallimanis, Wake Technical Community College; Ali Kamali, Missouri Western State University; Leona Kanter, Mercer University; Earl A. Kennedy, North Carolina State University; Lloyd Klein, York College, The City University of New York; Julie A. Kmec, Washington State University; Todd M. Krohn, University of Georgia; Veena S. Kulkarni, Arkansas State University; Karen F. Lahm, Wright State University; Amy G. Langenkamp, Georgia State University; Barbara LaPilusa, Montgomery College; Jason LaTouche, Tarleton State University; Ke Liang, Baruch College, The City University of New York; Carol S. Lindquist, Bemidji State University; Travis Linnemann, Kansas State University; Stephen Lippmann, Miami University; David G. LoConto, Jacksonville State University; Rebecca M. Loew, Middlesex Community College; Jeanne M. Lorentzen, Northern Michigan University; Betsy Lucal, Indiana University South Bend; George N. Lundskow, Grand Valley State University; Crystal V. Lupo, Auburn University; Brian M. Lynch, Quinebaug Valley Community College; Kim A. MacInnis, Bridgewater State University; Mahgoub El-Tigani Mahmoud, Tennessee State University; Lori Maida, The State University of New York; Hosik Min, Norwich University; Madeline H. Moran, Lehman College, The City University of New York; Amanda Moras, Sacred Heart University; Rebecca Nees, Middle Georgia College; Christopher Oliver, University of Kentucky; Sophia M. Ortiz, San Antonio College; Kathleen N. Overmiller, Marshall University; Josh Packard, Midwestern State University; Marla A. Perry, Nashville State Community College; Daniel Poole, Salt Lake Community College; Shana L. Porteen, Finlandia University; Eric Primm, University of Pikeville; Jeffrey Ratcliffe, Drexel University; Jo Reger, Oakland University; Daniel Roddick, Rio Hondo College; David Rohall, Western Illinois University; Olga I. Rowe, Oregon State University; Josephine A. Ruggiero, Providence College; Frank A. Salamone, Iona College; Stephen J. Scanlan, Ohio University; Michael D. Schulman, North Carolina State University; Maren T. Scull, University of Colorado, Denver; Shane Sharp, Northern Illinois University; Mark Sherry, The University of Toledo; Amber M. Shimel, Liberty University; Vicki Smith, University of California, Davis; Dan Steward, University of Illinois at Urbana-Champaign; Myron T. Strong, Community College of Baltimore County; Richard Sullivan, Illinois State University; Sara C. Sutler-Cohen, Bellevue College; Joyce Tang, Queens College, The City University of New York; Debra K. Taylor, Metropolitan Community College–Maple Woods; Richard Tewksbury, University of Louisville; Kevin A. Tholin, Indiana University–South Bend; Brian Thomas, Saginaw Valley State University; Lorna Timmerman, Indiana University East; Cynthia Tooley-Heddlesten, Metropolitan Community Colleges–Blue River; Okori Uneke, Winston-Salem State University; Paula Barfield Unger, McLennan Community College; PJ Verrecchia, York College of Pennsylvania; Joseph M. Verschaeve, Grand Valley State University; Edward Walker, University of California, Los Angeles; Tom Ward, New Mexico Highlands University; Lisa Munson Weinberg, Florida State University; Casey Welch, Flagler College; Shonda Whetstone, Blinn College; S. Rowan Wolf, Portland Community College; Loreen Wolfer, University of Scranton; Jason Wollschleger, Whitworth University; and Kassia R. Wosick, New Mexico State University.

ABOUT THE AUTHORS

Daina S. Eglitis (PhD, University of Michigan—Ann Arbor) is an associate professor of sociology and international affairs and the director of undergraduate studies in the Department of Sociology at The George Washington University. Her scholarly interests include class and social stratification, historical sociology, contemporary theory, gender, and culture. She is the author of *Imagining the Nation: History, Modernity, and Revolution in Latvia* (Penn State Press, 2002), as well as of numerous articles on social life and social change in postcommunist Latvia. She has held two Fulbright awards in Latvia and is a past recipient of research fellowships and awards from the U.S. Holocaust Memorial Museum, the American Council of Learned Societies, the National Council for Eurasian and East European Research, the International Research and Exchanges Board, and the Woodrow Wilson International Center for Scholars. Dr. Eglitis is the author of "The Uses of Global Poverty: How Economic Inequality Benefits the West," an article widely used by undergraduate students. At GWU, she teaches courses in contemporary sociological theory, class and inequality, and introduction to sociology, among others. She presents and writes on the topic of teaching and learning and is the author of the *Teaching Sociology* articles "Performing Theory: Dramatic Learning in the Theory Classroom" (2010) and "Social Issues and Problem-Based Learning in Sociology: Opportunities and Challenges in the Undergraduate Classroom" (2016). Outside the classroom, Dr. Eglitis is an avid reader of fiction (recent discoveries include *News of the World*, *An Orphan's Tale*, and *Purple Hibiscus*) and loves to travel to new places (especially if they include a beach).

William J. Chambliss (PhD, Indiana University) was a professor of sociology at The George Washington University from 1986 until his passing in 2014. During his long and distinguished career, he wrote and edited close to two dozen books and produced numerous articles for professional journals in sociology, criminology, and law. The integration of the study of crime with the creation and implementation of criminal law was a central theme in his writings and research. His articles on the historical development of vagrancy laws, the legal process as it affects different social classes and racial groups, and his efforts to introduce the study of state-organized crimes into the mainstream of social science research are among the most recognized achievements of his career. Dr. Chambliss was the recipient of numerous awards and honors, including a doctorate of laws *honoris causa*, University of Guelph, Guelph, Ontario, Canada, 1999; the 2009 Lifetime Achievement Award, Sociology of Law, American Sociological Association; the 2009 Lifetime Achievement Award, Law and Society, Society for the Study of Social Problems; the 2001 Edwin H. Sutherland Award, American Society of Criminology; the 1995 Major Achievement Award, American Society of Criminology; the 1986 Distinguished Leadership in Criminal Justice, Bruce Smith Sr. Award, Academy of Criminal Justice Sciences; and the 1985 Lifetime Achievement Award, Criminology, American Sociological Association. Professor Chambliss also served as president of the American Society of Criminology and the Society for the Study of Social Problems.

DISCOVER SOCIOLOGY

1.1 Describe the sociological imagination

1.2 Understand the significance of critical thinking in the study of sociology

1.3 Trace the historical development of sociological thought

1.4 Identify key theoretical paradigms in the discipline of sociology

1.5 Identify the three main themes of this book

Artur Debat/Getty Images

WHAT DO YOU THINK?

1. Can societies be studied scientifically? What does the scientific study of societies entail?
2. What is a theory? What role do theories play in sociology?
3. In your opinion, what social issues or problems are most interesting or important today? What questions about those issues or problems would you like to study?

©iStockphoto.com/Leonardo Patrizi

A goal of this book is to take you on a sociological journey. But let's begin with a basic question: *What is sociology?* First of all, sociology is a discipline of and for curious minds. Sociologists are deeply committed to answering the question, "Why?" Why are some people desperately poor and others fabulously wealthy? Why does racial segregation in housing and public education exist, and why does it persist half a century after civil rights laws were enacted in the United States? What accounts for the decline of marriage among the poor and the working class—as well as among the millennial generation? Why are the poor more likely to be overweight or obese than their middle-class counterparts? Why is the proportion of women entering and completing college rising while men's enrollment has fallen? Why, despite this, do men as a group still earn higher incomes than do women as a group? And how is it that social media is simultaneously praised as a vehicle of transformational activism and criticized as a cause of social alienation and civic disengagement? Take a moment to think about some *why* questions you have about society and social life: As you look around you, hear the news, and interact with other people, what strikes you as fascinating—but perhaps difficult to understand? What are you curious about?

Sociology is an academic discipline that takes a scientific approach to answering the kinds of questions our curious minds imagine. When we say that sociology is **scientific**, we mean that it is *a way of learning about the world that combines logically constructed theory and systematic observation.* The goal of sociological study and research is to base answers to questions like those above on careful examination of the roots of social phenomena such as poverty, segregation, and the wage gap. Sociologists do this with *research methods*—surveys, interviews, observations, and archival research, among others—which yield data that can be tested, challenged, and revised. In this text, you will see how sociology is done—and you will learn how to do sociology yourself.

Concisely stated, **sociology** is *the scientific study of human social relations, groups, and societies.* Unlike *natural sciences* such as physics, chemistry, and biology, sociology is one of several *social sciences* engaged in the scientific study of human beings and the social worlds they consciously create and inhabit. The purpose of sociology is to understand and generate new knowledge about human behavior, social relations, and social institutions on a larger scale. The sociologist adheres to the principle of **social embeddedness**: the idea that *economic, political, and other forms of human behavior are fundamentally shaped by social relations.* Thus, sociologists pursue studies on a wide range of issues occurring within, between, and among families, communities, states, nations, and the world. Other social sciences, some of which you may be studying, include anthropology, economics, political science, and psychology.

Sociology is a field in which students have the opportunity to build strong core knowledge about the social world with a broad spectrum of important skills, ranging from gathering and analyzing information to identifying and addressing social problems to effective written and oral communication. Throughout this book, we draw your attention to important skills you can gain through the study of sociology and the kinds of jobs and fields in which these skills can be put to work.

Doing sociology requires that you build a foundation for your knowledge and understanding of the social world. Some key foundations of sociology are the *sociological imagination* and *critical thinking.* We turn to these below. ■

Sociology seeks rigorous research and understanding of societies, social groups, and social relationships. A new area of interest is the way social media is changing social interactions. ■

THE SOCIOLOGICAL IMAGINATION

As we go about our daily lives, it is easy to overlook the fact that large-scale economic, political, and cultural forces shape even the most personal aspects of our lives. When parents divorce, for example, we tend to focus on individual explanations: A father was devoted more to his work than to his family; a mother may have felt trapped in an unhappy marriage but stuck with it for the sake of young children. Yet even though personal issues are inevitable parts of a breakup, they can't tell the whole story. When many U.S. marriages end in divorce, forces larger than incompatible personalities or marital discord are at play. But what are those greater social forces, exactly?

As sociologist C. Wright Mills (1916–1962) suggested half a century ago, uncovering the relationship between what he called *personal troubles* and *public issues* calls for a **sociological imagination** (1959/2000b). The

Scientific: A way of learning about the world that combines logically constructed theory and systematic observation.

Sociology: The scientific study of human social relations, groups, and societies.

Social embeddedness: The idea that economic, political, and other forms of human behavior are fundamentally shaped by social relations.

Sociological imagination: The ability to grasp the relationship between individual lives and the larger social forces that help to shape them.

sociological imagination is the ability to grasp the relationship between individual lives and the larger social forces that shape them—that is, to see where biography and history intersect.

In a country like the United States, where individualism is part of the national heritage, people tend to believe that each person creates his or her life's path and largely disregards the social context in which this happens. When we cannot get a job, fail to earn enough to support a family, or experience marital separation, for example, we tend to see it as a personal trouble. We do not necessarily see it as a public issue. The sociological imagination, however, invites us to make the connection and to step away from the vantage point of a single life experience to see how powerful social forces—for instance, changes in social norms, ethnic or sex discrimination, large shifts in the economy, or the beginning or end of a military conflict—shape the obstacles and opportunities that contribute to the unfolding of our life's story. Among Mills's (1959/2000b) most often cited examples is the following:

> When, in a city of 100,000, only one man is unemployed, that is his personal trouble, and for its relief we properly look to the character of the man, his skills, and his immediate opportunities. But when in a nation of 50 million employees, 15 million men are unemployed, that is an issue, and we may not hope to find its solution within the range of opportunities open to any one individual. The very structure of opportunities has collapsed. Both the correct statement of the problem and the range of possible solutions require us to consider the economic and political institutions of the society, and not merely the personal situation and character of a scatter of individuals. (p. 9)

To apply the idea to contemporary economic conditions, we might look at recent college graduates. If many of the young adults graduating from college today are finding employment in fields of interest to them, they may account for their success by citing personal effort and solid academic qualifications. These are, of course, very important! The sociological imagination, however, suggests that there are also larger social forces at work. The recent economic recovery in the United States has manifested in the form of growing job creation and more hiring: The official unemployment rate for all college graduates with

FIGURE 1.1 Unemployment Rate of Young College Graduates, by Gender, 1989–2017

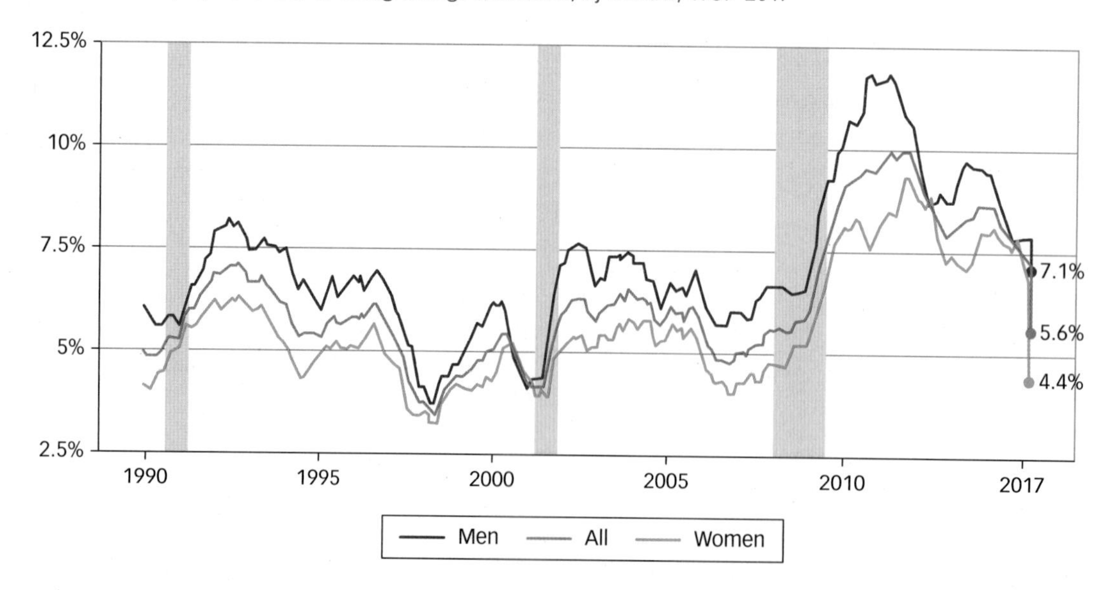

SOURCE: "The Class of 2017," by Teresa Kroeger and Elise Gould, May 4, 2017. Washington, DC: Economic Policy Institute. http://www.epi.org/publication/the-class-of-2017/. Reprinted with permission.

a bachelor's degree in 2016 was 2.7% (U.S. Bureau of Labor Statistics, 2017a). A review of 2016 figures shows that the rate of unemployment of young college graduates (ages 21–24) was higher, at 5.9%, although this also represented a significant drop after the postrecession high of nearly 10% (Figure 1.1). If your friends or relatives who graduated during the economic crisis or even the first years following that period encountered difficulties securing a job after graduation, this suggests that personal effort and qualifications are only part of the explanation for the success of one class of college completers and the frustration of another.

C. Wright Mills highlighted the use of the sociological imagination in studying social issues. When 16% of urban residents are poor by the government's official measure, we cannot assume the sole cause is personal failings but must ask how large-scale social and economic forces are implicated in widespread socioeconomic disadvantage experienced in many communities. ■

Understanding this relationship is particularly critical for people in the United States, who often regard individuals as fully responsible for their social, educational, and economic successes and failures. For instance, it is easy to fault the poor for their poverty, assuming they only need to work harder and "pull themselves up by their bootstraps." We may neglect the powerful role of social forces like racial or ethnic discrimination, the outsourcing or automation of manufacturing jobs that used to employ those with less education, or the dire state of public education in many economically distressed rural and urban areas. The sociological imagination implores us to seek the intersection between private troubles, such as a family's poverty, and public issues, such as lack of access to good schooling and jobs paying a living wage, to develop a more informed and comprehensive understanding of the social world and social issues.

It is useful, when we talk about the sociological imagination, to bring in the concepts of agency and structure. Sociologists often talk about social actions—individual and group behavior—in these terms. **Agency** can be understood as the ability of individuals and groups to exercise free will and to make social changes on a small or large scale. **Structure** is a complex term but may be defined as patterned social arrangements that have effects on agency—structure may enable or constrain social action. For example, sociologists talk about the class structure, which is composed of social groups who hold varying amounts of resources such as money, political voice, and social status. They also identify normative structures—for instance, they might analyze patterns of social norms regarding "appropriate" gender behaviors in different cultural contexts.

Sociologists take a strong interest in the relationship between structure and agency. Consider that, on one hand, we all have the ability to make choices—we have free will and we can opt for one path over another. On the other hand, the structures that surround us impose obstacles on us or afford us opportunities to exercise agency: We can make choices, but they may be enabled or constrained by structure. For instance, in the early 1900s, we would surely have found bright young women in the U.S. middle class who wanted to study to be doctors or lawyers. The social norms of the time, however, held that young women of this status

Agency: The ability of individuals and groups to exercise free will and to make social changes on a small or large scale.

Structure: Patterned social arrangements that have effects on agency.

FIGURE 1.2 Structure and Agency

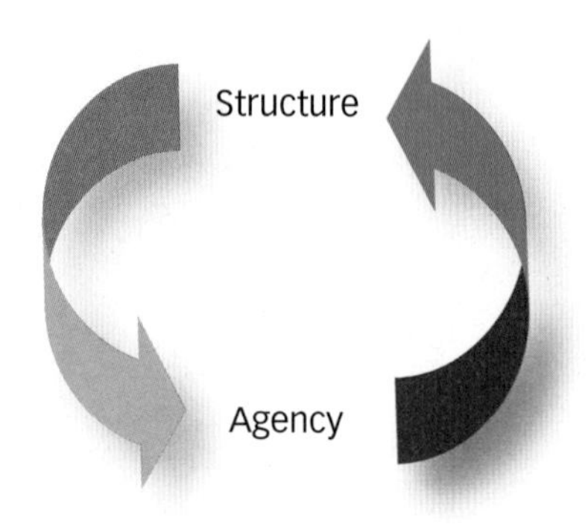

were better off marrying and caring for the husband, home, and children. There were also legal constraints to women's entry into higher education and the paid labor force. So although the women in our example might have individually argued and pushed to get an education and have professional careers, the dreams of this group were constrained by powerful normative and legal structures that identified women's place as being in the home.

Consider as well the relationship between the class structure and individual agency as a way of thinking about social mobility in U.S. society. If, for instance, a young man today whose parents are well educated and whose family is economically prosperous wishes to go to college and study to be an architect, engineer, or college professor, his position in the class structure (or the position of his family) is *enabling*—that is, it raises the probability that he will be able to make this choice and realize it. If, however, a young man from a poor family with no college background embraces these same dreams, his position in the class structure is likely to be *constraining*: Not only does his family have insufficient economic means to pay for college, but he may also be studying in an underfunded or underperforming high school that cannot provide the advanced courses and other resources he needs to prepare for college. A lack of college role models may also be a factor. This does not mean that inevitably the first young man will go to college and realize his hopes and the second will not; it does, however, suggest that structural conditions favor the first college aspirant over the second.

Critical thinking: The ability to evaluate claims about truth by using reason and evidence.

To understand why some students go to college and others do not, sociologists would say that we cannot rely on individual choice or will (agency) alone—structures, whether subtly or quite obviously, exercise an influence on social behavior and outcomes. At the same time, we should not see structures as telling the whole story of social behavior because history shows the power of human agency in making change even in the face of obstacles. Agency itself can transform structures (for example, think about the ways women's historical activism has helped to transform limiting gender norms for women today). Sociologists weigh both agency and structure and continue to study how the two intersect and interact. For the most part, sociologists understand the relationship as reciprocal—that is, it goes in both directions, as structure affects agency and agency, in turn, can change the dimensions of a structure (Figure 1.2).

CRITICAL THINKING

Applying the sociological perspective requires more than an ability to use the sociological imagination. It also entails **critical thinking**, the ability to evaluate claims about truth by using reason and evidence. In everyday life, we frequently accept things as "true" because they are familiar, feel right, or are consistent with our beliefs. Critical thinking takes a different approach—recognizing poor arguments, rejecting statements not supported by evidence, and questioning our assumptions. One of the founders of modern sociology, Max Weber, captured the spirit of critical thinking in two words when he said that a key task of sociological inquiry is to acknowledge "inconvenient facts."

Critical thinking requires us to be open-minded, but it does not mean that we must accept all arguments as equally valid. Those supported by logic and backed by evidence are clearly preferable to those that are not. For instance, we may passionately agree with Thomas Jefferson's famous statement, "That government is best that governs least." Nevertheless, as sociologists we must also ask, "What evidence backs up the claim that less government is better under all circumstances?"

To think critically, it is useful to follow six simple rules (adapted from Wade & Tavris, 1997):

1. **Be willing to ask any question, no matter how difficult.** The belief in small government is a cherished

U.S. ideal. But sociologists who study the role of government in modern society must be willing to ask whether there are circumstances under which more—not less—government is better. Government's role in areas such as homeland security, education, and health care has grown in the past several years—what are the positive and negative aspects of this growth?

2. **Think logically and be clear.** Logic and clarity require us to define concepts in a way that allows us to study them. "Big government" is a vague concept that must be made more precise and measurable before it provides for useful research. Are we speaking of federal, state, or local government, or all of these? Is "big" measured by the cost of government services, the number of agencies or offices within the government, the number of people working for it, or something else? What did Jefferson mean by "best," and what would that "best" government look like? Who would have the power to define this notion in any case?

3. **Back up your arguments with evidence.** Founding Father Thomas Jefferson is a formidable person to quote, but quoting him does not prove that smaller government is better in the 21st century. To find evidence, we need to seek out studies of contemporary societies to see whether there is a relationship between a population's well-being and the size of government or the breadth of services it provides. Because studies may offer contradictory evidence, we also need to be able to assess the strengths and weaknesses of arguments on different sides of the issue.

4. **Think about the assumptions and biases—including your own—that underlie all studies.** You may insist that government has a key role to play in modern society. On the other hand, you may believe with equal passion that big government is one root of the problems in the United States. Critical thinking requires that we recognize our beliefs and biases. Otherwise we might unconsciously seek out only evidence that supports our argument, ignoring evidence to the contrary. Passion has a role to play in research: It can motivate us to devote long hours to studying an issue. But passion should not play a role when we are weighing evidence and drawing conclusions.

5. **Avoid anecdotal evidence.** It is tempting to draw a general conclusion from a single experience or anecdote, but that experience may illustrate the exception rather than the rule. For example, you may know someone who just yesterday received a letter mailed 2 years ago, but that is not evidence that the U.S. Postal Service is inefficient or does not fulfill its mandates. To determine whether this government agency is working well, you would have to study its entire mail delivery system and its record of work over time.

Another well-known quote from Thomas Jefferson is, "The tree of liberty must be refreshed from time to time with the blood of patriots and tyrants." Taking a critical perspective, how might we evaluate the meaning and applicability of the quote to the United States today?

6. **Be willing to admit when you are wrong or uncertain about your results.** Sometimes we expect to find support for an argument only to find that things are not so clear. For example, consider the position of a sociologist who advocates small government and learns that Japan and Singapore initially became economic powerhouses because their governments played leading roles in promoting growth, or a sociologist who champions an expanded role for government but learns from the downturn of the 1990s in the Asian economies that some societal needs can be better met by private enterprise. Empirical evidence may contradict our beliefs: We learn from recognizing erroneous assumptions and having a mind open to new information.

DISCOVER & DEBATE

What Is Discover & Debate?

In *Discover Sociology: Core Concepts*, we are pleased to introduce a new feature, **Discover & Debate**. This feature offers not just discussion questions for the classroom but also a discussion model for instructors and students that takes the form of debate. A basic understanding of debating and, in particular, of the construction and evaluation of reasoned arguments is vital to civic life, civil interaction, and even social change. In a society that often addresses vital issues in sound bites and "tweets," it is particularly challenging but important to have the skills and knowledge to evaluate positions on issues critically and to build evidence-based arguments.

What Is a Debate?

According to the *Oxford English Dictionary*, debate is a "formal discussion on a particular matter in a public meeting or legislative assembly, in which opposing arguments are put forward and which usually ends with a vote" (2010). Although most commonly associated with electoral politics, debates are also used in high schools and universities to help students learn to gather and evaluate information and to build evidence-based arguments.

Debate is a form of public speaking; it is a formal, oral contest between teams or individuals on an assigned proposition or "motion" for the debate. It is an idea, statement, or policy that the teams formally argue. A typical debate comprises two teams—the Affirmative side and the Opposition side. The Affirmative side speaks for the motion, meaning they advocate and speak in favor of it, whereas the Opposition speaks against the motion.

What is the difference between a debate and an argument? Debates are structured arguments, where each participant is given a specific amount of time to present and defend his or her arguments. The motion is announced prior to the debate, and each team is randomly assigned a side. This aspect of academic debate is notable because it underscores the importance of understanding and recognizing the strengths and weaknesses of both sides of an issue. Debaters are given preparation time to develop arguments using empirical data. The first speakers on each team introduce their side of the argument and present the order in which team members will discuss the motion. The opening Opposition rebuts the argument presented by the opening Affirmative speaker. This format continues throughout the debate. The Affirmative side presents their argument, whereas the Opposition side following them rebuts it and presents their side.

In competitive debating, a panel of judges evaluates speakers on the substantive content of arguments, time management, style, and delivery and determines a winner. The judges' goal is not to label one side as right or wrong—assigned issues are normally too complex to categorize with such simple labels. This is important because it highlights the point that on a significant number of controversial and frequently debated issues in society, culture, economics, and politics, a strong supporting argument can be made for all sides of an issue. Being a good debater does not mean choosing a "right" side and labeling the opposing side as "wrong," but it means constructing a well-reasoned argument based on empirical evidence and an understanding of the strengths and weaknesses of all arguments.

A serious debate is fundamentally about presenting, defending, and challenging ideas with reasoned arguments. Constructing a strong argument is dependent on information literacy and on the ability to discern facts from opinions and evidence from ideology—skills from which we as engaged citizens and sociologists also benefit. Being a competent debater entails understanding all sides of an issue. Our goal with this feature is to help students develop skills to engage in well-informed and well-reasoned debate, whether that debate takes place in an academic or a political setting or in a less formal setting.

Each chapter contains a **Discover & Debate** feature that presents a motion for debate, basic background on a current social issue, and an introduction to key arguments from two sides. It also includes questions to consider when evaluating each position and a debate tip to help you build debate skills and win your argument.

What Are Sociological Debates?

Sociology is a discipline with a broad reach. Sociologists may debate issues related to media and violence, the labor market and economy, gender roles and status, crime and punishment, and many others. In the chapters that follow, we will introduce motions for debate on contemporary social issues and provide you with a discussion model to build strong arguments and counterarguments. The next time you see or hear these issues discussed, you will be better prepared to evaluate the positions presented and form your own arguments.

Critical thinking also means becoming "critical consumers" of the information—news, social media, surveys, texts, magazines, and scientific studies—that surrounds us. To be a good sociologist, it is important to look beyond the commonsense understanding of social life and develop a critical perspective. Being critical consumers of information entails paying attention to the sources of information we encounter and asking questions about how data were gathered. In this text, *Behind the Numbers* boxes will look critically at data on issues like unemployment, poverty, and high school dropouts, helping us to understand what is illuminated and what is obscured by these commonly cited social indicators.

THE DEVELOPMENT OF SOCIOLOGICAL THINKING

Humans have been asking questions about the nature of social life as long as people have lived in societies. Aristotle and Plato wrote extensively about social relationships more than 2,000 years ago. Ibn Khaldun, an Arab scholar writing in the 14th century, advanced several sociological concepts we recognize today, including ideas about social conflict and cohesion. Yet modern sociological concepts and research methods did not emerge until the 19th century, after the Industrial Revolution, and then largely in those European nations undergoing dramatic societal changes like industrialization and urbanization.

THE BIRTH OF SOCIOLOGY: SCIENCE, PROGRESS, INDUSTRIALIZATION, AND URBANIZATION

We can trace sociology's roots to four interrelated historical developments that gave birth to the modern world: the *scientific revolution, the Enlightenment, industrialization, and urbanization*. Since these developments initially occurred in Europe, it is not surprising that sociological perspectives and ideas evolved there during the 19th century. By the end of the 19th century, sociology had taken root in North America as well; somewhat later, it gained a foothold in Central and South America, Africa, and Asia. Sociology throughout the world initially bore the stamp of its European and North American origins, although recent decades have brought a greater diversity of perspectives to the discipline.

THE SCIENTIFIC REVOLUTION The rise of modern natural and physical sciences, beginning in Europe in the 16th century, offered scholars a more advanced understanding of the physical world. The success of natural science contributed to the belief that science could be fruitfully applied to

The harnessing of waterpower and the development of the steam engine helped give rise to the industrial era and to factories, immortalized by writers such as Charles Dickens, in which men, women, and even children toiled for hours in wretched working conditions. Poet William Blake called these workplaces the "dark satanic mills." ■

human affairs, thereby enabling people to improve society or even perfect it. Auguste Comte (1798–1857) coined the term "sociology" to characterize what he believed would be a new "social physics"—that is, the scientific study of society.

THE ENLIGHTENMENT Inspired in part by the success of the physical sciences, French philosophers in the 18th century such as Voltaire (1694–1778), Montesquieu (1689–1755), Diderot (1719–1784), and Rousseau (1712–1778) promised that humankind could attain lofty heights by applying scientific understanding to human affairs. Enlightenment ideals such as equality, liberty, and fundamental human rights found a home in the emerging social sciences, particularly sociology. Émile Durkheim (1858–1917), considered by many to be the first modern sociologist, argued that sociological understanding would create a more egalitarian, peaceful society, in which individuals would be free to realize their full potential. Many of sociology's founders shared the hope that a fairer and more just society would be achieved through the scientific understanding of society.

Norms: Accepted social behaviors and beliefs.

Anomie: A social condition of normlessness; a state of normative uncertainty that occurs when people lose touch with the shared rules and values that give order and meaning to their lives.

THE INDUSTRIAL REVOLUTION The Industrial Revolution, which began in England in the mid-to-late 18th century and soon spread to other countries, dramatically changed European societies. Traditional agricultural economies and the small-scale production of handicrafts in the home gave way to more efficient, profit-driven manufacturing based in factories. For instance, in 1801 in the English city of Leeds, there were about 20 factories manufacturing a variety of goods. By 1838, Leeds was home to 106 woolen mills alone, employing 10,000 people.

Small towns, including Leeds, were transformed into bustling cities, showcasing extremes of wealth and poverty as well as opportunity and struggle. In the face of rapid social change and growing inequality, sociologists sought to gain a social scientific perspective on what was happening and how it had come about. German theorist and revolutionary Karl Marx (1818–1883), who had an important impact on later sociological theorizing about modern societies and economies, predicted that industrialization would make life increasingly intolerable for the masses. He believed that private property ownership by the wealthy allowed for the exploitation of working people and that its elimination, and revolution would bring about a utopia of equality for all.

URBANIZATION: THE POPULATION SHIFT TOWARD CITIES Industrialization fostered the growth of cities as people streamed from rural fields to urban factories in search of work. By the end of the 19th century, more than 20 million people lived in English cities. The population of London alone exceeded 7 million by 1910.

Early industrial cities were often fetid places, characterized by pollution and dirt, crime, and crowded housing tenements. In Europe, sociologists lamented the passing of communal village life and its replacement by a savage and alienating urban existence. Durkheim, for example, worried about the potential breakdown of stabilizing beliefs and values in modern urban society. He argued that whereas traditional communities were held together by shared culture and **norms**, or *accepted social behaviors and beliefs*, modern industrial communities were threatened by **anomie**, or a *state of normlessness that occurs when people lose sight* *of the shared rules and values that give order and meaning to their lives*. In a state of anomie, individuals often feel confused and anxious because they do not know how to interact with each other and their environment. Durkheim raised the question of what would hold societies and communities together as they shifted from homogeneity and shared cultures and values to heterogeneous masses of diverse cultures, norms, and occupations.

Interestingly, Harriet Martineau translated into English the work of Auguste Comte, who dismissed women's intellect, saying, "Biological philosophy teaches us that . . . radical differences, physical and moral, distinguish the sexes . . . biological analysis presents the female sex . . . as constitutionally in a state of perpetual infancy, in comparison with the other" (Kandal, 1988, p. 75).

19TH-CENTURY FOUNDERS

Despite its largely European origins, early sociology sought to develop universal understandings that would apply to other peoples, times, and places. The discipline's principal acknowledged founders—Auguste Comte, Harriet Martineau, Émile Durkheim, Karl Marx, and Max Weber—left their marks on sociology in different ways.

AUGUSTE COMTE Auguste Comte (1798–1857), a French social theorist, is credited with founding modern sociology, naming it, and establishing it as the scientific study of social relationships. The twin pillars of Comte's sociology were the study of **social statics**, the way society is held together, and the analysis of **social dynamics**, the laws that govern social change. Comte believed social science could be used effectively to manage the social change resulting from modern industrial society but always with a strong respect for traditions and history.

Comte proclaimed that his new science of society was **positivist**. This meant that it was to be based on facts alone, which should be determined scientifically and allowed to speak for themselves. Comte argued that this purely factual approach was the proper method for sociology. He argued that all sciences—and all societies—go through three stages. The first stage is a theological one, in which key ways of understanding the world are framed in terms of superstition, imagination, and religion. The second stage is a metaphysical one, characterized by abstract speculation but framed by the basic belief that society is the product of natural rather than of supernatural forces. The third and last stage is one in which knowledge is based on scientific reasoning "from the facts." Comte saw himself as leading sociology toward its final positivist stage.

Comte left a lasting mark on modern sociology. The scientific study of social life continues to be the goal of

As a founding figure in the social sciences, Auguste Comte is associated with positivism or the belief that the study of society must be anchored in facts and the scientific method.

Social statics: The way society is held together.

Social dynamics: The laws that govern social change.

Positivist: Science that is based on facts alone.

Émile Durkheim pioneered some of sociology's early research on such topics as social solidarity and suicide. His work continues to inform sociological study and understanding of social bonds and the consequences of their unraveling.

sociological research. His belief that social institutions have a strong impact on individual behavior—that is, that our actions are the products of personal choices and the surrounding social context—remains at the heart of sociology.

HARRIET MARTINEAU Harriet Martineau (1802–1876) was an English sociologist who, despite deafness and other physical challenges, became a prominent social and historical writer. Her greatest handicap was being a woman in male-dominated intellectual circles that failed to value female voices. Today she is frequently recognized as the first major woman sociologist.

Deeply influenced by Comte's work, Martineau translated his six-volume treatise on politics into English. Her editing helped make Comte's esoteric prose accessible to the English-speaking world, ensuring his standing as a leading figure in sociology. Martineau was also a distinguished scholar in her own right. She wrote dozens of books, more than 1,000 newspaper columns, and 25 novels, including a three-volume study, *Society in America* (1837), based on observations of the United States that she made during a tour of the country.

Martineau, like Comte, sought to identify basic laws that govern society. She derived three of her four "laws" from other theorists. The fourth law, however, was her own and reflected her progressive (today we might say "feminist") principles: For a society to evolve, it must ensure social justice for women and other oppressed groups. In her study of U.S. society, Martineau treated slavery and women's experience of dependence in marriage as indicators of the limits of the moral development of the United States. In her view, the United States was unable to achieve its full social potential while it was morally stunted by persistent injustices like slavery and women's inequality. The question of whether the provision of social justice is critical to societal development remains a relevant and compelling one today.

ÉMILE DURKHEIM Auguste Comte founded and named the discipline of sociology, but French scholar Émile Durkheim (1858–1917) set the field on its present course. Durkheim established the early subject matter of sociology, laid out rules for conducting research, and developed an important theory of social change.

For Durkheim, sociology's subject matter was **social facts**, *qualities of groups that are external to individual members yet constrain their thinking and behavior*. Durkheim argued that such social facts as religious beliefs and social duties are external—that is, they are part of the social context and are larger than our individual lives. They also have the power to shape our behavior. You may feel compelled to act in certain ways in different contexts—in the classroom, on a date, at a religious ceremony—even if you are not always aware of such social pressures.

Durkheim also argued that only social facts *can explain other social facts*. For example, there is no scientific evidence that men have an innate knack for business compared with women—but in 2012, women headed just 18 of the *Fortune* 500 companies. A Durkheimian approach would highlight women's experience in society—where historically they have been socialized into more domestic values or

Social facts: Qualities of groups that are external to individual members yet constrain their thinking and behavior.

restricted to certain noncommercial professions—and the fact that the social networks that foster mobility in the corporate world today are still primarily male to help explain why men dominate the upper ranks of the business world.

Durkheim's principal concern was explaining the impact of modern society on **social solidarity**, *the bonds that unite the members of a social group*. In his view, in traditional society, these bonds are based on similarity—people speak the same language, share the same customs and beliefs, and do similar work tasks. He called this *mechanical solidarity*. In modern industrial society, however, bonds based on similarity break down. Everyone has a different job to perform in the industrial division of labor, and modern societies are more likely to be socially diverse. Nevertheless, workers in different occupational positions are dependent on one another for things like safety, education, and the provision of food and other goods essential to survival. The people filling these positions may not be alike in culture, beliefs, or language, but their dependence on one another contributes to social cohesion. Borrowing from biology, Durkheim called this organic solidarity, suggesting that modern society functions as an interdependent organic whole, like a human body.

Yet organic solidarity, Durkheim argued, is not as strong as mechanical solidarity. People no longer necessarily share the same norms and values. The consequence, according to Durkheim, is anomie. In this weakened condition, the social order disintegrates and pathological behavior increases (Durkheim, 1922/1973a).

Consider whether the United States, a modern and diverse society, is held together primarily by organic solidarity, or whether the hallmark of mechanical solidarity, a **collective conscience**—the common beliefs and values that bind a society together—is in evidence. Do public demonstrations of patriotism on nationally significant anniversaries such as September 11 and July 4 indicate mechanical solidarity built on a collective sense of shared values, norms, and practices? Or do the deeply divisive politics of recent years suggest social bonds based more fully on practical interdependence?

KARL MARX The extensive writings of Karl Marx (1818–1883) influenced the development of economics and political science as well as sociology. They also shaped world politics and inspired communist revolutions in Russia (later the Soviet Union), China, and Cuba, among others.

Marx's central idea was deceptively simple: Almost all societies throughout history have been divided into economic classes, with one class prospering at the expense of others. All human history, Marx believed, should be understood as the product of **class conflict**, competition between social classes over the distribution of wealth, power, and other valued resources in society (Marx & Engels, 1848/1998).

In the period of early industrialization in which he lived, Marx condemned capitalism's exploitation of working people, the **proletariat**, by the ownership class,

Karl Marx was a scholar and critic of early capitalism. His work has been thoroughly studied and critiqued around the world.

Social solidarity: The bonds that unite the members of a social group.

Collective conscience: The common beliefs and values that bind a society together.

Class conflict: Competition between social classes over the distribution of wealth, power, and other valued resources in society.

Proletariat: The working class; wage workers.

Why Do Couples Get Divorced?

Until about the middle of the 20th century, most marriages were "'til death do us part." In 1940, the rate of divorce in the United States was 2.0 per 1,000 population. In 1960, it was still 2.2 per 1,000, but it rose consistently through the 1970s, peaking in 1981 at 5.3 per 1,000 before dropping back to 3.2 per 1,000 in 2014 (Figure 1.3). What accounts for the shifting landscape of marital breakup in the United States?

The sociological imagination suggests to us that marriage and divorce, seemingly the most private of matters, are public issues as well as personal ones. Certainly, the end of a marriage is a profoundly personal experience and rooted in disagreements, conflicts, or crisis faced by a couple. At the same time, researchers recognize that there are structural and normative shifts that are important for understanding the context in which marriages are made, experienced, and ended.

Consider the fact that when wages for the working class began to stagnate in the mid-1970s, growing numbers of women went to work to help their families make ends meet. More women also went to college and pursued careers as a path to financial stability and personal fulfillment, a path enabled in part by the 1972 passage of Title IX, a federal law prohibiting discrimination on the basis of sex in any educational program receiving federal financial support. In fact, today more

FIGURE 1.3 144 Years of Marriage and Divorce in the United States

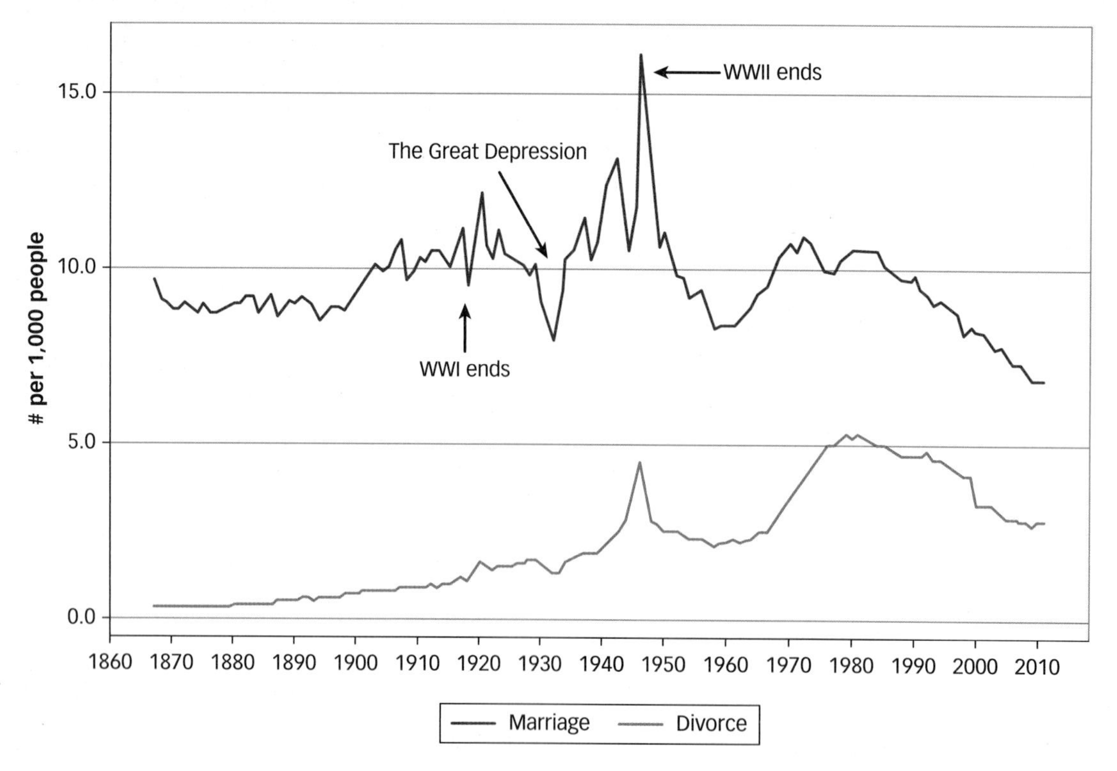

SOURCE: Reprinted with permission from Randal S. Olson.

women than men finish undergraduate degrees (a topic we cover in depth in Chapter 11), and women have a higher measure of economic independence than ever before. The combination of educational attainment and satisfying careers reinforces women's autonomy, making it easier for those who are in unhappy marriages to leave them. Greater social acceptance of divorce has also removed much of the stigma once associated with a failed marriage.

After rising to its peak in 1981, the divorce rate in the United States began to decline again, falling to and staying below 4.0 per 1,000 in 2000. Can we find the roots of this shift in sociological phenomena as well? Arguably, several more recent societal changes could be implicated in a dropping divorce rate. For example, as we will see in Chapter 10, fewer people today are marrying at all: The decline has been particularly notable among millennials, as well as among the poor and the working class, shrinking the pool from which divorced couples could emerge. More couples today are also cohabiting: Some break up before marriage, whereas others may discover compatibility that translates into a durable marriage. Furthermore, a trend toward later marriage, when careers have already been established, may mean that couples are likely to marry for love rather than for economic stability and are more likely to stay together. Economic stability, in fact, continues to be an important variable in the sociological picture: One demographic category where divorce remains high is among less-educated, low-income couples.

Charles Gullung/Photonica/Getty Images

Societal changes can be implicated in the rise—and decline—of divorce in the United States. The sociological imagination helps us to see that this *private trouble* is in many respects influenced by *public issues,* including women's growing economic independence, the dynamism of cultural norms related to marriage and divorce, and financial stresses experienced by less-educated and lower-income couples. Social research methods, which we will discuss in the next chapter, can help us learn to ask and study the kinds of sociological questions that will help us understand these trends more fully.

THINK IT THROUGH

- What other "private troubles" might sociologists identify as "public issues"? Can you use the sociological imagination to discuss any of the social issues and problems of interest to you?

the **bourgeoisie**. As we will see in later chapters, Marx's views on conflict and inequality are still influential in contemporary sociological thinking, even among sociologists who do not share his views on society.

Marx focused his attention on the emerging capitalist industrial society (Marx, 1867/1992a, 1885/1992b, 1894/1992c). Unlike his contemporaries in sociology, however, Marx saw capitalism as a transitional stage to a final period in human history in which economic classes and the unequal distribution of rewards and opportunities linked to class inequality would disappear and be replaced by a utopia of equality.

Although many of Marx's predictions have not proved to be correct, his critical analysis of the dynamics of capitalism proved insightful. Among other things, Marx argued that capitalism would lead to accelerating technological change, the replacement of workers by machines, and the growth of monopoly capitalism.

Marx also presciently predicted that ownership of the **means of production**, the sites and technology that produce the goods (and sometimes services) we need and use, would come to be concentrated in fewer and fewer hands. As a result, he believed, a growing wave of people would be thrust down into the proletariat, which owns only its own labor power. In modern society, large corporations have progressively swallowed up or pushed out smaller businesses; where small lumberyards and pharmacies used to serve many communities, corporate giants such as Home Depot, CVS, and Best Buy have moved in, putting locally owned establishments out of business.

In many U.S. towns, small business owners have joined forces to protest the construction of "big box" stores like Walmart (now the largest private employer in the United States), arguing that these enormous establishments, although they offer cheap goods, wreak havoc on local retailers and bring only the meager economic benefit of masses of entry-level, low-wage jobs. From a Marxist perspective, we might say that the local retailers, in resisting the incursion of the big box stores into their communities, are fighting their own "proletarianization." Even physicians, many of whom used to own their own means of production in the form of private medical practices, have increasingly been driven by economic necessity into working for large health maintenance organizations (HMOs), where they are salaried employees.

Unlike Comte and Durkheim, Marx thought social change would be revolutionary, not evolutionary, and would be the product of oppressed workers rising up against a capitalist system that exploits the many to benefit the few.

MAX WEBER Max Weber (1864–1920), a German sociologist who wrote at the beginning of the 20th century, left a substantial academic legacy. Among his contributions are an analysis of how Protestantism fostered the rise of capitalism in Europe (Weber, 1904–1905/2002) and insights into the emergence of modern bureaucracy (Weber, 1919/1946). Weber, like other founders of sociology, took up various political causes, condemning injustice wherever he found it. Although pessimistic about capitalism, he did not believe, as did Marx, that some alternative utopian form of society would arise. Nor did he see sociologists enjoying privileged insights into the social world that would qualify them to wisely counsel rulers and industrialists, as Comte (and, to some extent, Durkheim) had envisioned.

Weber believed that an adequate explanation of the social world begins with the individual and takes into account the meaning of what people say and do. Although he argued that research should be scientific and value free, Weber also believed that to explain what people do, we must use a method he termed **Verstehen**, the German word for interpretive understanding. This methodology, rarely used by sociologists today, sought to explain social relationships by having the sociologist/observer imagine how the subjects being studied might have perceived and interpreted the situation. Studying social life, Weber felt, is not like studying plants or chemical reactions because human beings act on the basis of meanings and motives.

Weber's theories of social and economic organization have also been highly influential (Weber, 1921/2012). Weber argued that the modern Western world showed an ever-increasing reliance on logic, efficiency, rules, and reason. According to him, modern societies are characterized by the development and growing influence of **formal rationality**, a context in which people's pursuit of goals is increasingly shaped by rules, regulations, and larger social structures. One of Weber's most widely known illustrations of formal rationality comes from his study of **bureaucracies**, formal organizations characterized by written rules, hierarchical authority, and paid staff, intended to promote organizational efficiency. Bureaucracies, for Weber, epitomized formally rational systems: On the one hand, they

Bourgeoisie: The capitalist (or property-owning) class.

Means of production: The sites and technology that produce the goods we need and use.

Verstehen: The German word for interpretive understanding; Weber's proposed methodology for explaining social relationships by having the sociologist imagine how subjects might perceive a situation.

Formal rationality: A context in which people's pursuit of goals is shaped by rules, regulations, and larger social structures.

Bureaucracies: Formal organizations characterized by written rules, hierarchical authority, and paid staff, intended to promote organizational efficiency.

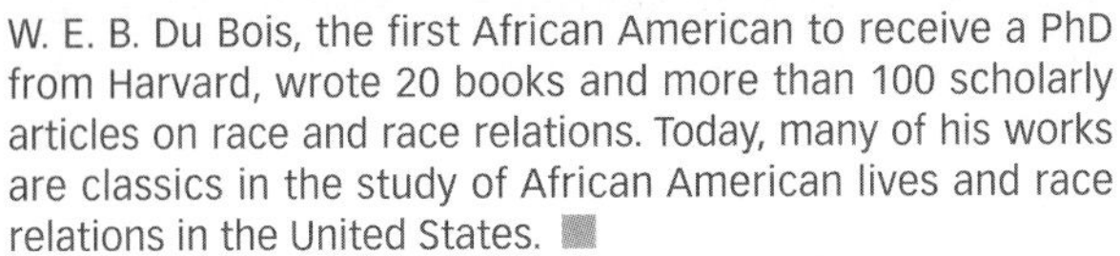

W. E. B. Du Bois, the first African American to receive a PhD from Harvard, wrote 20 books and more than 100 scholarly articles on race and race relations. Today, many of his works are classics in the study of African American lives and race relations in the United States. ■

Max Weber made significant contributions to the understanding of how capitalism developed in Western countries and its relationship to religious beliefs. His work on formal rationality and bureaucracy continues to influence sociologists' study of modern society. ■

offer clear, knowable rules and regulations for the efficient pursuit of particular ends, like obtaining a passport or getting financial aid for higher education. On the other hand, he feared, the bureaucratization of modern society would also progressively strip people of their humanity and creativity and result in an iron cage of rationalized structures with irrational consequences.

Weber's ideas about bureaucracy were remarkably prescient in their characterization of our bureaucratic (and formally rationalized) modern world. Today we are also confronted regularly with both the incredible efficiency and the baffling irrationality of modern bureaucratic structures. Within moments of entering into an efficiently concluded contract with a wireless phone service provider, we can become consumers of a cornucopia of technological opportunities, with the ability to chat on the phone or receive text messages from almost anywhere, post photographs or watch videos online, and pass the time on social media platforms. Should we later be confused by a bill and need to speak to a company representative, however, we may be shuttled through endless repetitions of an automated response system that never seems to offer us the option of speaking with another human being. Today, Weber's presciently predicted irrationality of rationality is alive and well.

SIGNIFICANT FOUNDING IDEAS IN U.S. SOCIOLOGY

Sociology was born in Europe, but it took firm root in U.S. soil, where it was influenced by turn-of-the-century industrialization and urbanization, as well as by racial strife and discrimination. Strikes by organized labor, corruption in government, an explosion of European immigration, racial

SOCIAL LIFE, SOCIAL MEDIA

Capturing the World in 140 Characters

What is Twitter? Just over a decade ago, no such question could have been asked. To "twitter" meant only to chatter (or to impart a "short burst of inconsequential information; Johnson, 2013), and "tweeting" was for the birds. Today, the social media platform Twitter is a significant and ubiquitous form of communication used by social activists, politicians, celebrities and fans, the news media, sports teams, advertisers, and friend groups. Social media reaches across the globe: According to a recent analysis, of the world's 7.3 million inhabitants, about 3.4 billion are Internet users and 2.3 billion are "active social media users." Both figures rose by 10% in the last year alone and are expected to grow (Chaffey, 2016). The rise of users in the United States has been dramatic. According to the Pew Research Center, in 2005, about 7% of the U.S. population used social media. In 2017, it had reached 69% (Pew Research Center, 2017b). Globally, Twitter is the third most popular social media platform on the planet (Figure 1.4), finding its most avid users in Indonesia, Turkey, Saudi Arabia, India, and the Philippines (Chaffey, 2015).

The Twitter social media site (https://about.twitter.com/company) was created by Jack Dorsey, Evan Williams, and Biz Stone. On March 21, 2006, Jack Dorsey (@Jack) sent out the first tweet. It said, "just setting up my twttr." Today, Twitter has over 310 million "monthly active users," tweeting in over 40 languages. A company that had eight employees in 2008 has grown to 3,800 worldwide. At this point, then, we can return to our opening question: What is Twitter? Novelist David Foster Wallace has been quoted as saying that Twitter is "the bathroom wall of the American psyche." The magazine *The New Yorker* responded to Wallace's characterization by asking its readers to use their own tweets to define Twitter. Among their entries:

- "Alone Together" (@dnahinga)
- "Communicative disease" (@Wodespain)

FIGURE 1.4 Top 10 Countries for Traffic on Twitter

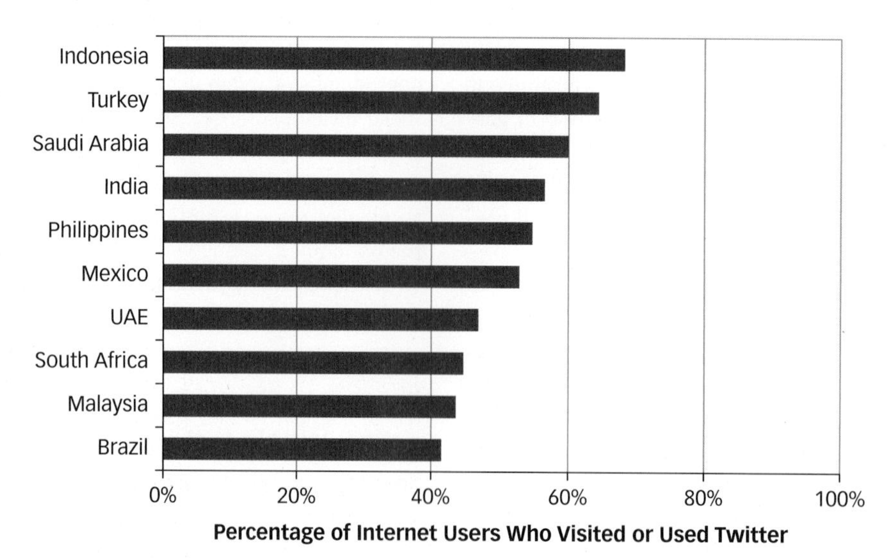

SOURCE: Adapted from Chart 9 in "Global social media research summary 2016," by Dave Chaffey, August 8, 2016, Smart Insights.

- "the carrier pigeon of the 21st century" (@Rajiv_Narayan)
- "Twitter is the dimestore in the marketplace of ideas" (@anglescott)
- "an infinite orchestra hall, where everyone has a kazoo solo anytime they want for 140 seconds" (@Shan19the6man6). ("Questioningly winner," 2012, para. 2–4)

Are you a Twitter user or follower? How would you define it in 140 characters or less?

From a sociological perspective, the key question that follows is this: What is the sociological significance of Twitter? The social media platform has been credited with contributing to scientific and medical knowledge, as well as to investment wisdom. *Social Media Today* points out that the U.S. Geological Survey has used tweets to track earthquakes: "[T]he USGS had found that by tracking mentions of the term 'earthquake', within specific parameters which they'd defined, they could better track seismic activity across the globe than they'd been able to via their previous measurement systems" (Hutchinson, 2016, "Health and Safety," para. 1). It has also been used to track influenza outbreaks. The same article notes that a small number of financial services companies "are using Twitter data to deliver better predictive results" with monitoring of information and conversations available on the site (Hutchinson, 2016, "Off to Market," para. 2). The sociological significance is more challenging to assess. Twitter has been at the forefront of social protest organizing across the globe. It has been used by politicians and celebrities to share news and to energize supporters and fans. It has also been used as a platform to spread rumors, conspiracy theories, and fear. Pressing social and political issues can't be debated in 140 characters without missing important complexities. In this book's *Social Life, Social Media* boxes, we look at the spectrum of ways Twitter—and other key social media platforms—reflects, affects, and shapes our social world in positive and problematic ways.

THINK IT THROUGH

▶ To what extent do social media platforms like Twitter simply provide a medium for sharing opinions, ideas, and information? To what extent are they also powerful media for shaping people's perspectives and practices?

Follow us on Twitter to keep up with current sociological stories and research! We're at @DiscoverSoc1.
Share your own ideas at #DiscoverSociology.

segregation, and the growth of city slums all helped mold early sociological thought in the United States. By the late 1800s, numerous universities in the United States were offering sociology courses. The first faculties of sociology were established at the University of Kansas (1889), the University of Chicago (1892), and Atlanta University (1897). Below, we look at a handful of sociologists who have had an important influence on modern sociological thinking in the United States. Throughout the book, we will learn about more U.S. sociologists who have shaped our perspectives today.

ROBERT EZRA PARK The sociology department at the University of Chicago, which gave us what is often known as the "Chicago School" of sociology, dominated the new discipline in the United States at the start of the 20th century. Chicago sociologist Robert Ezra Park (1864–1944) pioneered the study of urban sociology and race relations. Once a muckraking journalist, Park was an equally colorful academic, reportedly coming to class in disheveled clothes and with shaving soap still in his ears. But his students were devoted to him, and his work was widely recognized. His 1921 textbook *An Introduction to the Science* *of Sociology*, coauthored with his Chicago colleague Ernest Burgess, helped shape the discipline. The Chicago School studied a broad spectrum of social phenomena, from hoboes and flophouses (inexpensive dormitory-style housing) to movie houses, dance halls, and slums, and from youth gangs and mobs to residents of Chicago's ritzy Gold Coast.

Park was a champion of racial integration, having once served as personal secretary to the African American educator Booker T. Washington. Yet racial discrimination was evident in the treatment of Black sociologists, including W. E. B. Du Bois, a contemporary of many of the sociologists working in the Chicago School.

W. E. B. DU BOIS A prominent Black sociologist and civil rights leader at the African American Atlanta University, W. E. B. Du Bois (1868–1963) developed ideas that were considered too radical to find broad acceptance in the sociological community. At a time when the U.S. Supreme Court had ruled that segregated "separate but equal" facilities for Blacks and Whites were constitutional and when lynching of Black Americans had reached an all-time high, Du Bois condemned the deep-seated racism of White society. Today, his writings on race relations and the lives of U.S. Blacks are classics in the field.

Du Bois sought to show that racism was widespread in U.S. society. He was also critical of Blacks who had "made it" and then turned their backs on those who had not. One of his most enduring ideas is that in U.S. society, African Americans are never able to escape a fundamental awareness of race. They experience a **double consciousness**, as he called it—*an awareness of themselves both as Americans and as Blacks, never free of racial stigma*. He wrote, "The Negro is sort of a seventh son . . . gifted with second-sight . . . this sense of always looking at one's self through the eyes of others" (Du Bois, 1903/2008, p. 12). Today as in Du Bois's time, physical traits such as skin color may shape people's perceptions and interactions in significant and complex ways.

CHARLOTTE PERKINS GILMAN Charlotte Perkins Gilman (1860–1935) was a well-known novelist, feminist, and sociologist of her time. Because of her family's early personal and economic struggles, she had only a few years of formal schooling in childhood, although she would later enroll at the Rhode Island School of Design. She read widely, however, and she was influenced by her paternal aunts, who included suffragist Isabella Beecher Stowe and writer Harriet Beecher Stowe, author of *Uncle Tom's Cabin* (1852), an anti-slavery novel.

Gilman's most prominent publication was her semiautobiographical short story, *The Yellow Wallpaper* (1892), which follows the decline of a married woman shut away in a room (with repellent yellow wallpaper) by her husband, ostensibly for the sake of her health. Gilman used the story to highlight the consequences of women's lack of autonomy in marriage. She continued to build this early feminist thesis in the book *Women and Economics: A Study of the Economic Relation Between Men and Women as a Factor in Social Evolution* (1898/2006), which includes this memorable quote:

> The labor of women in the house, certainly, enables men to produce more wealth than they otherwise could; and in this way women are economic factors in society. But so are horses. The labor of horses enables men to produce more wealth than they otherwise could. The horse is an economic factor in society. But the horse is not economically independent, nor is the woman. (p. 7)

Gilman's work represents an early and notable effort to look at sex roles in the family not as natural and inevitable, as many saw them at the time, but as social constructions that had the potential to change and to bring greater autonomy to women in the home and society.

ROBERT K. MERTON After World War II, sociology began to apply sophisticated quantitative models to the study of social processes. There was also a growing interest in the grand theories of the European founders. At Columbia University, Robert K. Merton (1910–2003) undertook wide-ranging studies that helped further establish sociology as a scientific discipline. Merton is best known for his theory of deviance (Merton, 1938), his work on the sociology of science (Merton, 1996), and his iteration of the distinction between manifest and latent functions as a means for more fully understanding the relationships between and roles of sociological phenomena and institutions in communities and society. (Merton, 1968). He emphasized the development of theories in what he called the "middle range"—midway between the grand theories of Weber, Marx, and Durkheim and quantitative studies of specific social problems.

Double consciousness: Among African Americans, an awareness of being both American and Black, never free of racial stigma.

C. WRIGHT MILLS Columbia University sociologist C. Wright Mills (1916–1962) is best known in the discipline for describing the "sociological imagination," the imperative in sociology to seek the nexus between private troubles and public issues. In his short career, Mills was prolific. He renewed interest in Max Weber by translating many of his works into English and applying his ideas to the contemporary United States. But Mills, who also drew on Marx, identified himself as a "plain Marxist." His concept of the sociological imagination can be traced in part to Marx's famous statement that "man makes history, but not under circumstances of his own choosing," meaning that even though we are agents of free will, the social context has a profound impact on the obstacles or opportunities in our lives.

Mills synthesized Weberian and Marxian traditions, applying sociological thinking to the most pressing problems of the day, particularly inequality. He advocated an activist sociology with a sense of social responsibility. Like many sociologists, he was willing to turn a critical eye on "common knowledge," including the belief that the United States is a democracy that represents the interests of all the people. In a provocative study, he examined the workings of the "power elite," a small group of wealthy businessmen, military leaders, and politicians who Mills believed ran the country largely in their own interests (Mills, 1956/2000a).

Fritz Goro/The LIFE Picture Collection/Getty Images

The "sociological imagination" involves viewing seemingly personal issues through a sociological lens. C. Wright Mills is best known for coining this catchy and popular term. ■

WOMEN IN EARLY SOCIOLOGY

Why did so few women social scientists find a place among sociology's founders? After all, the American (1776) and French (1789) revolutions elevated such lofty ideals as freedom, liberty, and equality. Yet long after these historical events, women and minorities were still excluded from public life in Europe and North America. Democracy—which gives people the right to participate in their governance—was firmly established as a principle for nearly a century and a half in the United States before women achieved the right to vote in 1920. In France, it took even longer—until 1945.

Sociology as a discipline emerged during the first modern flourishing of feminism in the 19th century. Yet women and people of non-European heritage were systematically excluded from influential positions in the European universities where sociology and other modern social sciences originated. When women did pursue lives as scholars, the men who dominated the social sciences largely ignored their writings. Feminist scholar Julie Daubié won a prize from the Lyon Academy for her essay "Poor Women in the Nineteenth Century," yet France's public education minister denied her a diploma on the grounds that he would be "forever holding up his ministry to ridicule" (Kandal, 1988, pp. 57–58). Between 1840 and 1960, almost no women held senior academic positions in the sociology departments of any European or U.S. universities, with the exception of exclusively women's colleges.

Several woman scholars managed to overcome the obstacles to make significant contributions to sociological inquiry. For example, in 1792, the British scholar Mary Wollstonecraft published *A Vindication of the Rights of Women*, arguing that scientific progress could not occur unless women were allowed to become men's equals by means of universal education. In France in 1843, Flora Tristan called for equal rights for women workers, "the last remaining slaves in France." Also in France, Aline Valette published *Socialism and Sexualism* in 1893, nearly three quarters of a century before the term "sexism" found its way into spoken English (Kandal, 1988).

An important figure in early U.S. sociology is Jane Addams (1860–1935). Addams is best known as the founder of Hull House, a settlement house for the poor, sick, and

Underappreciated during her time, Jane Addams was a prominent scholar and early contributor to sociology. She is also known for her political activism and commitment to social reform. ■

aged that became a center for political activists and social reformers. Less well known is the fact that under Addams's guidance, the residents of Hull House engaged in important research on social problems in Chicago. *Hull-House Maps and Papers*, published in 1895, pioneered the study of Chicago neighborhoods, helping to shape the research direction of the Chicago School of sociology. Following Addams's lead, Chicago sociologists mapped the city's neighborhoods, studied their residents, and helped create the field of community studies. Despite her prolific work—she authored 11 books and hundreds of articles and received the Nobel Peace Prize for her dedication to social reform in 1931—she never secured a full-time position at the University of Chicago, and the school refused to award her an honorary degree.

Sociological theories: Logical, rigorous frameworks for the interpretation of social life that make particular assumptions and ask particular questions about the social world.

As Harriet Martineau, Jane Addams, Julie Daubié, and others experienced, early female sociologists were not accorded the same status as their male counterparts. Only recently have many of their writings been "rediscovered" and their contributions acknowledged in sociology.

SOCIOLOGY: ONE WAY OF LOOKING AT THE WORLD—OR MANY?

Often, multiple sociologists look at the same events, phenomena, or institutions and draw different conclusions. How can this be? One reason is that they may approach their analyses from different theoretical perspectives. In this section, we explore the key theoretical paradigms in sociology and look at how they are used as tools for the analysis of society.

Sociological theories are *logical, rigorous frameworks for the interpretation of social life that make particular assumptions and ask particular questions about the social world*. The word "theory" is rooted in the Greek word *theoria*, which means "a viewing." An apt metaphor for a theory is a pair of glasses. You can view a social phenomenon such as socioeconomic inequality or poverty, deviance, or consumer culture, or an institution like capitalism or the family, using different theories as lenses.

As you will see in the next section, in the discipline of sociology, several major categories of theories seek to examine and explain social phenomena and institutions. Imagine the various sociological theories as different pairs of glasses, each with colored lenses that change the way you see an image: You may look at the same institution or phenomenon as you put on each pair, but it will appear different depending on the glasses you are wearing. Keep in mind that sociological theories are not "truths" about the social world. They are logical, rigorous analytical tools that we can use to inquire about, interpret, and make educated predictions about the world around us. From the vantage point of any sociological theory, some aspects of a phenomenon or an institution are illuminated while others are obscured. In the end, theories are more or less useful depending on how well *empirical data*—that is, knowledge gathered by researchers through scientific methods—support their analytical conclusions. Below, we outline the basic theoretical perspectives that we will be using in this text.

The three dominant theoretical perspectives in sociology are *structural functionalism, social conflict theory*, and *symbolic interactionism*. We outline their basic characteristics below and will revisit them again throughout the book.

TABLE 1.1 The Three Principal Sociological Paradigms

Theoretical Perspective and Founding Theorist(s)	Structural Functionalism Émile Durkheim	Social Conflict Karl Marx	Symbolic Interactionism Max Weber, George Herbert Mead
Assumptions about self and society	Society is a system of interdependent, interrelated parts, like an organism, with groups and institutions contributing to the stability and equilibrium of the whole social system.	Society consists of conflicting interests, but only some groups have the power and resources to realize their interests. Some groups benefit from the social order at the expense of other groups.	The self is a social creation; social interaction occurs by means of symbols such as words, gestures, and adornments; shared meanings are important to successful social interactions.
Key focus and questions	Macrosociology: What keeps society operating smoothly? What functions do different societal institutions and phenomena serve for society as a whole?	Macrosociology: What are the sources of conflict in society? Who benefits and who loses from the existing social order? How can inequalities be overcome?	Microsociology: How do individuals experience themselves, one another, and society as a whole? How do they interpret the meanings of particular social interactions?

Symbolic interactionism shares with the functionalist and social conflict paradigms an interest in interpreting and understanding social life. Nevertheless, the first two are **macro-level paradigms**, *concerned with large-scale patterns and institutions*. Symbolic interactionism is a **micro-level paradigm**—that is, it is *concerned with small-group social relations and interactions*.

Structural functionalism, social conflict theory, and symbolic interactionism form the basic foundation of contemporary sociological theorizing (Table 1.1). Throughout this book, we will introduce variations on these theories, as well as new and evolving theoretical ideas in sociology.

THE FUNCTIONALIST PARADIGM

Structural functionalism (or functionalism—the term we use in this book) *seeks to explain social organization and change in terms of the roles performed by different social structures, phenomena, and institutions*. Functionalism characterizes society as made up of many interdependent parts—an analogy often cited is the human body. Each part serves a different function, but all parts work together to ensure the equilibrium and health of the entity as a whole. Society too is composed of a spectrum of different parts with a variety of different functions, such as the government, the family, religious and educational institutions, and the media. According to the theory, together these parts contribute to the smooth functioning and equilibrium of society.

The key question posed by the functionalist perspective is, "What function does a particular institution, phenomenon, or social group serve for the maintenance of society?" That is, what contribution does a given institution, phenomenon, or social group make to the equilibrium, stability, and functioning of the whole? Note the underlying assumption of functionalism: Any existing institution or phenomenon does serve a function; if it served no function, it would evolve out of existence. Consequently, the central task of the functionalist sociologist is to discover what function an institution or a phenomenon—for instance, the traditional family, capitalism, social stratification, or deviance—serves in the maintenance of the social order.

Émile Durkheim is credited with developing the early foundations of functionalism. Among other ideas, Durkheim observed that all known societies have some degree of deviant behavior, such as crime. The notion that deviance is functional for societies may seem counterintuitive: Ordinarily, we do not think of deviance as beneficial or necessary to society. Durkheim, however, reasoned that since deviance is universal, it must serve a social function—if it did not serve a function, it would cease to exist. Durkheim concluded that one function of deviance—specifically, of society's labeling of some acts as deviant—is to remind members of society what is "normal" or "moral"; when a society punishes deviant behavior, it reaffirms people's beliefs in what is right and good.

Talcott Parsons (1902–1979) expanded functionalist analysis by looking at whole social systems such as

Macro-level paradigms: Theories of the social world that are concerned with large-scale patterns and institutions.

Micro-level paradigm: A theory of the social world that is concerned with small-group social relations and interactions.

Structural functionalism: A theory that seeks to explain social organization and change in terms of the roles performed by different social structures, phenomena, and institutions; also known as functionalism.

Why Are Some People Poor and Others Rich?

The concentration of wealth at the top of the economic ladder and the widespread struggle of millions of others to make do with scant resources are critical issues on both the domestic and global levels. One common explanation of the stark economic disparities in the United States is that they are the outcome of individual differences in talent, ambition, and work ethic. Although personal effort is very important, the fact that more than 12.7% of the population lives below the official poverty line, including disproportionate numbers of Blacks (22%), Hispanics (19.4%), and children 18 and under (18%; Semenga, Fontent, & Kollar, 2017), should lead our sociological imaginations to recognize social and economic forces that underlie what we see in the data—and around us.

What are some of the sociological factors we might study to understand the existence and persistence of poverty in a wealthy country (Figure 1.5)? Consider the argument that educational opportunity is not equally distributed: In most U.S. states, schools are still funded primarily by local property taxes. Consequently, school districts sited in areas with high property values have more assets to tax than low-value areas. This means more money to spend on teachers, textbooks, and technology, as well as on the maintenance of schools, playgrounds, and athletic facilities. Even within districts,

FIGURE 1.5 Number in Poverty and Poverty Rate: 1959 to 2016

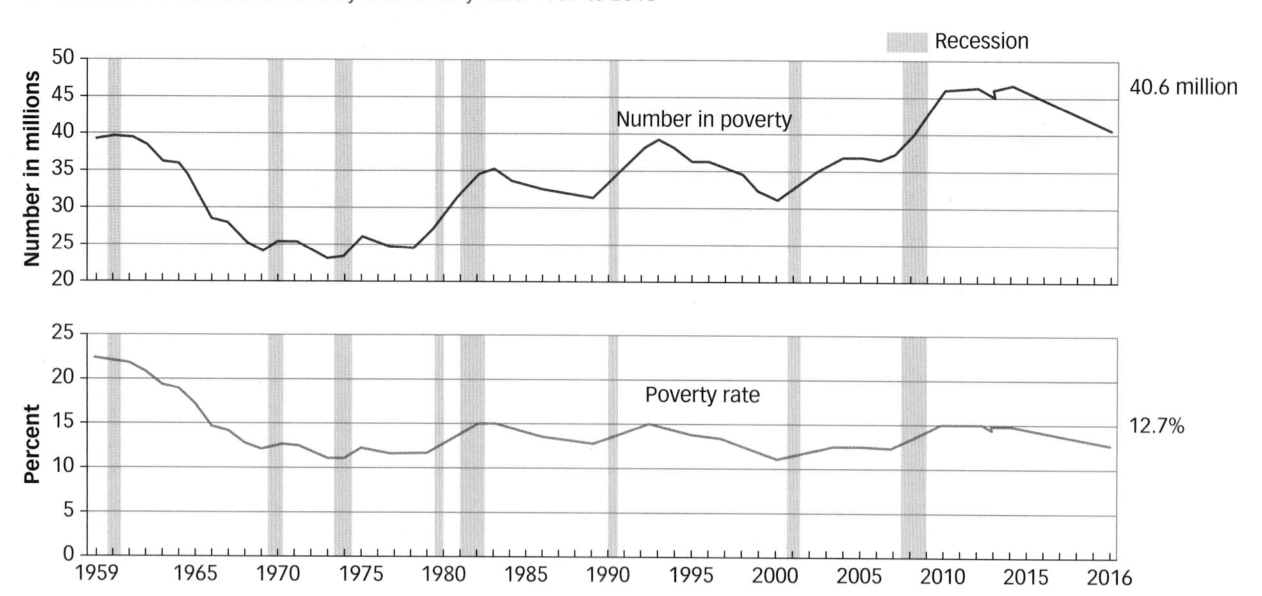

NOTE: The 2013 data reflect the implementation of the redesigned income questions. The data points are placed at the midpoints of the respective years. For information on confidentiality protection, sampling error, nonsampling error, and definitions, see <ftp://ftp2.census.gov/programs-surveys/cps/techodocs/cpsmar15.pdf>

SOURCE: Semenga, Fontent, & Kollar. (2017). Income and poverty in the United States. https://www.census.gov/content/dam/Census/library/publications/2017/demo/P60-259.pdf

individual schools in wealthier neighborhoods benefit from greater parental resources like donated funds and volunteer hours. Without a strong educational foundation that prepares them for a competitive economy, already poor children are at greater risk of remaining poor as adults, a topic we take up in Chapter 11. Recent social mobility research, in fact, suggests that there is a good probability that a family's economic status is reproduced in the next generation.

Macro-level economic changes affecting the U.S. labor market have also had a significant effect on many families and communities, a subject we'll explore in both Chapters 7 and 11. Automation and the movement abroad of manufacturing jobs since the 1970s have reduced the availability of jobs for less educated workers that pay a middle-class wage. Service jobs, including restaurant and retail work, have expanded as the manufacturing sector has contracted, but these positions are less secure and more poorly paid—they are far less likely to give workers a lift into the middle class. This makes a solid education more critical than ever, but as we noted above, young people growing up in low-income areas have fewer opportunities to access such an education.

Wealth, poverty, and inequality are complex sociological phenomena. In these boxes, and throughout the book, we seek to help you more fully understand their roots, manifestations, and consequences.

Lauri Lyons/Photonica World/Getty Images

Why are children of poor parents more likely to be poor as adults? This is a question of fundamental interest to sociologists. ■

THINK IT THROUGH

- If, as our sociological imaginations suggest, poverty is both a private trouble and a public issue, what are public issues other than those identified in this essay that may contribute to the existence and persistence of poverty in some families, communities, and regions?

government, the economy, and the family and how they contribute to the functioning of the whole social system (Parsons, 1964/2007, 1967). For example, he wrote that traditional sex roles for men and women contribute to stability on both the micro familial level and the macro societal level. Parsons argued that traditional socialization produces instrumental or rational and work-oriented males and expressive or sensitive, nurturing, and emotional females. Instrumental males, he reasoned, are well suited for the competitive world of work, whereas their expressive female counterparts are appropriately prepared to care for the family. According to Parsons, these roles are complementary and positively functional, leading men and women to inhabit different spheres of the social world. Complementary rather than competing roles contribute to solidarity in a marriage by reducing competition between husband and wife. Critics have rejected this idea as a justification of inequality.

GLOBAL ISSUES

Local Consumption, Global Production

REUTERS/Andrew Biraj

Try this at home: Walk through your dorm room, apartment, or house and make a list of the places of manufacture of some of the products you find. Be sure to check electronic equipment such as your laptop and smartphone. Go through your closets and drawers and look at some labels on your clothing and footwear. Can you locate where other household items like your microwave oven or coffeemaker were manufactured? Take a look at your list: What countries do you find there? It is likely that you will find that people who live outside the United States produced many of the necessities and luxuries of your everyday life. Even a U.S.-manufactured car is likely to have parts that have passed through the hands of workers abroad.

When you checked your closet, did you find any clothing made in the United States? If not, you are not alone. In 1950, about 95% of clothing purchased in this country was made domestically. By 1980, the share fell to 70%. Today, an estimated 2% of our clothing is manufactured in the United States (Vatz, 2013). The rest is manufactured in factories around the globe: Just after the turn of the millennium, the clothing chain The Gap was ordering its goods from about 1,200 factories across 42 countries (Cline, 2013). What are some of the sociological effects of this shift?

U.S. consumption of goods grew in the latter half of the 20th century. This came about as appetites were whetted by new advertising campaigns and credit options increased (although wages were stagnating by the mid-1970s). Notably as well, as more goods were manufactured abroad, they also became less expensive:

> In 1960, an average American household spent over 10 percent of its income on clothing and shoes—equivalent to roughly $4,000 today. The average person bought fewer than 25 garments each year . . .
>
> Today, the average American household spends less than 3.5 percent of its budget on clothing and shoes—under $1,800. Yet, we buy more clothing than ever before: nearly 20 billion garments a year, close to 70 pieces of clothing per person, or more than one clothing purchase per week. (Vatz, 2013, para. 1)

The falling costs of goods for consumers, however, have come at a price. As clothing and other manufacturers have shifted production abroad, there have been dramatic disruptions in the labor market. As we will see in Chapter 11, outsourcing abroad, as well as increased automation of production, have contributed to declining wages and lost jobs for manufacturing workers in the United States. Furthermore, millions of workers around the world are today employed in factories that are poorly regulated and operate largely outside the view of the consumers who buy their products. These poor conditions were highlighted in 2013 when 1,135 garment workers producing high-end clothing in a factory in Dhaka, Bangladesh, were killed when their building collapsed; despite a building evacuation conducted after cracks were detected in the building on the previous day, workers were ordered to come to work ("Rana Plaza collapse," 2016).

On the one hand, even with these risks, many workers in developing countries leave their rural homes to seek out opportunities to earn and learn in new urban factories, just as they did in the early decades of the Industrial Revolution in Western Europe. On the other hand, the world's low-wage workers, many of whom are women, are vulnerable to exploitation, and their hours are long and their work sites can be unpleasant or, as the incident in Dhaka demonstrated, even deadly. The conditions under which some workers toil today recall the 19th-century English factories that inspired Marx to write his powerful critique of capitalism's darker sides. Can the needs and desires of consumers and workers around the globe be reconciled? What do you think?

THINK IT THROUGH

- The cheap and ample fashion options that fill U.S. malls are often made by poorly compensated female labor abroad. Do labor conditions matter to U.S. consumers? Should they matter?

As this example suggests, functionalism is conservative in that it tends to accept rather than question the status quo; it holds that any given institution or phenomenon exists because it is functional for society, rather than asking whether it might benefit one group to the detriment of others, as critics say Parsons's position on gender roles does. One of functionalism's long-standing weaknesses is a failure to recognize inequalities in the distribution of power and resources and how those affect social relationships.

Merton attempted to refine the functionalist paradigm by demonstrating that not all social structures work to maintain or strengthen the social organism, as Durkheim and other early functionalists seemed to suggest. According to Merton, a social institution or phenomenon can have both positive functions and problematic dysfunctions. Merton broadened the functionalist idea by suggesting that **manifest functions** are the *obvious and intended functions of a phenomenon or institution*. **Latent functions**, by contrast, are *functions that are not recognized or expected.* He used the famous example of the Hopi rain dance, positing that although the manifest function of the dance was to bring rain, a no less important latent function was to reaffirm social bonds in the community through a shared ritual. Consider another example: A manifest function of war is usually to vanquish an enemy, perhaps to defend a territory or to claim it. Latent functions of war—those that are not the overt purpose but may still have powerful effects—may include increased patriotism in countries engaged in the war, a rise in the profits of companies manufacturing military equipment or contracting workers to the military, and changes in national budgetary priorities.

THE SOCIAL CONFLICT PARADIGM

In contrast to functionalism, the **social conflict paradigm** (which we refer to in this book as conflict theory) seeks to explain social organization and change in terms of the conflict built into social relationships. Conflict theory is rooted in ideas about class and power put forth by Marx.

Manifest functions: Functions of an object, an institution, or a phenomenon that are obvious and intended.

Latent functions: Functions of an object, an institution, or a phenomenon that are not recognized or expected.

Social conflict paradigm: A theory that seeks to explain social organization and change in terms of the conflict that is built into social relations; also known as *conflict theory.*

REUTERS/Alessandro Bianchi

The manifest function of a vehicle is to transport a person efficiently from point A to point B. One latent function is to say something about the status of the driver. ■

Although Durkheim's structural functionalist lens asked how different parts of society contribute to stability, Marx asked about the roots of conflict. Conflict theorists pose the questions, "Who benefits from the way social institutions and relationships are structured?" and "Who loses?" The social conflict paradigm focuses on what divides people rather than on what unites them. It presumes that group interests drive relationships, and that various groups in society (for instance, social classes, ethnic and racial groups, women and men) will act in their own interests. Conflict theory thus assumes not that interests are shared but that they may be different and irreconcilable and, importantly, that only some groups have the power and resources to realize their interests. As a result, conflict is—sooner or later—inevitable.

From Marx's perspective, the bourgeoisie benefits directly from the capitalist social order. If, as Marx suggests, the capitalist class has an interest in maximizing productivity and profit and minimizing costs (like the cost of labor in the form of workers' wages), and the working class has an interest in earning more and working less, then the interests of the two classes are difficult to reconcile. The more powerful group in society generally has the upper hand in furthering its interests.

After Marx, the body of conflict theory expanded tremendously. In the 20th century and today, theorists have extended the reach of the perspective to consider, for instance, how control of culture and the rise of technology (rather than just control of the means of production) underpins class domination (Adorno, 1975; Horkheimer, 1947), as well as how the expanded middle class can be accommodated in a Marxist perspective (Wright, 1998). Many key ideas in feminist theory take a conflict-oriented perspective, although the focus shifts from social class to gender power and conflict (Connell, 2005), as well as ways in which race is implicated in relations of power (Collins, 1990).

Recall Durkheim's functionalist analysis of crime and deviance. According to this perspective, society defines crime to reaffirm people's beliefs about what is right and dissuade them from deviating. A conflict theorist might argue that dominant groups in society define the behaviors labeled criminal or deviant because they have the power to do so. For example, street crimes such as robbery and carjacking are defined and punished as criminal behavior. They are also represented in reality television programs, movies, and other cultural products as images of criminal deviance. On the other hand, corporate or white-collar crime, which may cause the loss of money or even lives, is less likely to be clearly defined, represented, and punished as criminal. From a conflict perspective, white-collar crime is more likely to be committed by members of the upper class (for instance, business or political leaders or financiers) and is less likely to be punished harshly compared with street crime, which is associated with the lower income classes, although white-collar crime may have even greater economic and health consequences. A social conflict theorist would draw our attention to the fact that the decision makers who pass our laws are mostly members of the upper class and govern in the interests of capitalism and their own socioeconomic peers.

A key weakness of the social conflict paradigm is that it overlooks the forces of stability, equilibrium, and consensus in society. The assumption that groups have conflicting, even irreconcilable, interests and that those interests are realized by those with power at the expense of those with less power fails to account for forces of cohesion and stability in societies.

SYMBOLIC INTERACTIONISM **Symbolic interactionism** argues that *both the individual self and society as a whole are the products of social interactions based on language and other symbols*. The term "symbolic interactionism" was coined by U.S. sociologist Herbert Blumer (1900–1987) in 1937, but the approach originated in the lectures of George Herbert Mead (1863–1931), a University of Chicago philosopher allied with the Chicago School of sociology. The symbolic interactionist paradigm argues that people acquire their sense of who they are only through interaction with others. They do this by means of **symbols**, *representations of things that are not immediately present to our senses*. Symbols include such things as words, gestures, emoticons, and tattoos, among others.

Recall our earlier discussions of the theoretical interpretations of deviance and crime. A symbolic interactionist might focus on the ways in which people label one another as deviant (a symbolic act that uses language), the factors that make such a label stick, and the meanings underlying such a label. If you are accused of committing a crime you did not commit, how will the label of "criminal" affect the way others see you? How will it affect the way you see yourself, and will you begin to act differently as a result? Can being labeled "deviant" be a self-fulfilling prophecy? For the symbolic interactionist, sociological inquiry is the study of how people interact and how they create and interpret symbols in the social world.

Although symbolic interactionist perspectives draw our attention to important micro-level processes in society, they may miss the larger structural context of those processes, such as discovering who has the power to make laws defining what or who is deviant. For this reason, many sociologists seek to use both macro- and micro-level perspectives when analyzing social phenomena such as deviance.

The three paradigms described above lead to diverse images of society, research questions, and conclusions about the patterns and nature of social life. Each "pair of glasses" can provide a different perspective on the social world. Throughout this text, the three major theoretical paradigms—and some new ones we will encounter in later chapters—will help us understand key issues and themes of sociology.

PRINCIPAL THEMES IN THIS BOOK

We began this chapter with a list of *why* questions with which sociologists are concerned—and about which any one of us might be curious. Behind these questions, we find several major themes, which are also some of the main themes in this book. Three important focal points for sociology—and for us—are (1) power and inequality and the ways in which the unequal distribution of social, economic, and political resources shape opportunities, obstacles, and relationships; (2) the societal changes occurring as a result of globalization and the growing social diversity of modern communities and societies; and (3) the powerful impact of technological change on modern lives, institutions, and states.

POWER AND INEQUALITY

As we consider broad social topics such as gender, race, social class, and sexual orientation and their effects on social relationships and resources, we will be asking who has **power**—*the ability to mobilize resources and achieve goals despite the resistance of others*—and who does not. We will also ask about variables that influence the uneven distribution of power, and how some groups use power to create advantages for themselves (and disadvantages for others) and how disadvantaged groups mobilize to challenge the powerful.

Power is often distributed unequally and can be used by those who possess it to marginalize other social groups.

Symbolic interactionism: A microsociological perspective that posits that both the individual self and society as a whole are the products of social interactions based on language and other symbols.

Symbols: Representations of things that are not immediately present to our senses.

Power: The ability to mobilize resources and achieve goals despite the resistance of others.

Inequality refers to *differences in wealth, power, political voice, educational opportunities, and other valued resources*. The existence of inequality not only raises moral and ethical questions about fairness, but also it can tear at the very fabric of societies, fostering social alienation and instability. Furthermore, it may have negative effects on local and national economies. Notably, economic inequality is increasing both within and between many countries around the globe, a fact that makes understanding the roots and consequences of this phenomenon—that is, asking the why questions—ever more important.

GLOBALIZATION AND DIVERSITY

Globalization is *the process by which people all over the planet become increasingly interconnected economically, politically, culturally, and environmentally*. Globalization is not new. It began nearly 200,000 years ago when humans first spread from their African cradle into Europe and Asia. For thousands of years, humans have traveled, traded goods, and exchanged ideas over much of the globe, using seaways or land routes such as the famed Silk Road, a stretch of land that links China and Europe. But the rate of globalization took a giant leap forward with the Industrial Revolution, which accelerated the growth of global trade. It made another dramatic jump with the advent of the Information Age, drawing together individuals, cultures, and countries into a common global web of information exchange. In this book, we consider a spectrum of manifestations, functions, and consequences of globalization in areas like the economy, culture, and the environment.

Growing contacts between people and cultures have made us increasingly aware of social diversity as a feature of modern societies. **Social diversity** *is the social and cultural mixture of different groups in society and the societal recognition of difference as significant*. The spread of culture through the globalization of media and the rise of migration has created a world in which almost no place is isolated. As a result, many nations today, including the United States, are characterized by a high degree of social diversity.

Inequality: Differences in wealth, power, political voice, educational opportunities, and other valued resources.

Globalization: The process by which people all over the planet become increasingly interconnected economically, politically, culturally, and environmentally.

Social diversity: The social and cultural mixture of different groups in society and the societal recognition of difference as significant.

Ethnocentrism: A worldview whereby one judges other cultures by the standards of one's own culture and regards one's own way of life as "normal" and better than others.

Social diversity brings a unique set of sociological challenges. People everywhere have a tendency toward **ethnocentrism**, a *worldview whereby they judge other cultures by the standards of their own culture* and regard their own way of life as "normal"—and often superior to others. From a sociological perspective, no group can be said to be more human than any other. Yet history abounds with examples of people lashing out at others whose religion, language, customs, race, or sexual orientation differed from their own.

TECHNOLOGY AND SOCIETY

Technology is the practical application of knowledge to transform natural resources for human use. The first human technology was probably the use of rocks and other blunt instruments as weapons, enabling humans to hunt large animals for food. Agriculture—planting crops such as rice or corn in hopes of reaping a yearly harvest—represents another technological advance, one superior to simple foraging in the wild for nuts and berries. The use of modern machinery, which ushered in the Industrial Revolution, represents still another technological leap, multiplying the productivity of human efforts. Today we are in the midst of another revolutionary period of technological change: the information revolution. Thanks to the microchip, the Internet, and mobile technology, an increasing number of people around the world now have instant access to a mass of information that was unimaginable just 10 or 20 years ago. The information revolution is creating postindustrial economies based far more heavily on the production of knowledge than on the production of goods, as well as new ways of communicating that have the potential to draw people around the world together—or tear them apart.

WHY STUDY SOCIOLOGY?

A sociological perspective highlights the many ways that we both influence and are powerfully influenced by the social world around us: Society shapes us, and we, in turn, shape society. A sociological perspective enables us to see the social world through a variety of different lenses (recall the glasses metaphor we used when talking about theory): Sociologists might explain class differences and why they persist, for instance, in many different ways. Different theories illuminate different aspects of a sociological phenomenon or institution, enabling us to assemble a fuller, more rigorous perspective on social life.

Why are the issues and questions posed by sociology incredibly compelling for all of us to understand? One reason is that, as we will see throughout this book, many of the social issues sociologists study—marriage, fertility, poverty, unemployment, consumption, discrimination, and many others—are related to one another in ways we may not immediately see. *A sociological perspective helps us to make connections between diverse social phenomena*. When we understand these connections, we are better able to understand social issues, to address social problems, and to make (or vote for) policy choices that benefit society.

For example, a phenomenon like the *decline of marriage among the working class*, which we mentioned at the start of the chapter, is related to growing globalization, declining employment in the manufacturing sector, and the persistently high rate of poverty among single mothers. Consider these social phenomena as pieces of a puzzle. One of the defining characteristics of economic globalization is the movement of manufacturing industries away from the United States to lower wage countries. As a result, jobs in U.S. manufacturing, an economic sector dominated by men, have been declining since the 1970s. The decreasing number of less educated men able to earn a wage high enough to support a family in turn is related to a decline in marriage among the working class. Even as marriage rates fall, however, many women still desire to have families, so the proportion of nonmarital births rises. Single mothers with children are among the demographic groups in the United States most likely to be poor, and their poverty rate has remained high even in periods of economic prosperity.

Although the relationships between sociological factors are complex and sometimes indirect, when sociology helps us fit them together, we gain a better picture of the issues confronting all of us—as well as of U.S. society and the larger world. Let's begin our journey.

WHAT CAN I DO WITH A SOCIOLOGY DEGREE?

An Introduction

Have you ever wondered what you could do with a sociology degree, or how you can take the skills you'll learn in this major and use them in your career? This book can help you answer that question: Near the end of each chapter, we feature a short essay that links your study of sociology to potential career fields. In the *What Can I Do with a Sociology Degree?* feature, we highlight the professional skills and core knowledge that the study of sociology helps you develop. This set of skills and competencies, which range from critical thinking and written communication skills to aptitude in qualitative and quantitative research, to the understanding of diversity, prepares you for the workforce, as well as for graduate and professional school.

In every chapter that follows, this feature describes a specific skill that you can develop through the study of sociology. Each chapter also profiles a sociology graduate who shares what he or she learned through the study of sociology and how that particular skill has been valuable in his or her job. A short U.S. Bureau of Labor Statistics overview of the occupational field in which the graduate is working, its educational requirements, median income, and expected growth potential is also included to provide key information on each occupation.

Although this feature highlights sociology majors and graduates, it also speaks to students taking sociology who are majoring in other disciplines—being aware of your skills and able to articulate them precisely and clearly is important no matter what your chosen field of study or career path.

SUMMARY

- **Sociology** is the scientific study of human social relationships, groups, and societies. Its central task is to ask what the dimensions of the social world are, how they influence our behavior, and how we in turn shape and change them.
- Sociology adheres to the principle of **social embeddedness**, the idea that economic, political, and other forms of human behavior are fundamentally shaped by social relationships. Sociologists seek to study through scientific means the social worlds that human beings consciously create.
- The **sociological imagination** is the ability to grasp the relationship between our individual lives and the larger social forces that help to shape them. It helps us see the connections between our private lives and public issues.
- **Critical thinking** is the ability to evaluate claims about truth by using reason and evidence. Often we accept things as true because they are familiar, seem to mesh with our own experiences, and sound right. Critical thinking instead asks us to recognize poor arguments, reject statements not supported by evidence, and even question our own assumptions.
- Sociology's roots can be traced to the scientific revolution, the Enlightenment, industrialization and the birth of modern capitalism, and the urbanization of populations. Sociology emerged in part as a tool to enable people to understand dramatic changes taking place in modern societies.
- Sociology generally traces its classical roots to Auguste Comte, Émile Durkheim, Max Weber, and Karl Marx. Early work in sociology reflected the concerns of the men who founded the discipline.
- In the United States, scholars at the University of Chicago focused on reforming social problems stemming from industrialization and urbanization. Women and people of color worked on the margins of the discipline because of persistent discrimination.
- Sociologists base their study of the social world on different theoretical perspectives that shape theory and guide research, often resulting in different conclusions. The major sociological paradigms are **structural functionalism**, the **social conflict paradigm**, and **symbolic interactionism**.
- Major themes in sociology include the distribution of **power** and growing inequality, **globalization** and its accompanying social changes, the growth of **social diversity**, and the way advances in technology have changed communication, commerce, and communities.
- The early founders of sociology believed that scientific knowledge could lead to shared social progress. Some modern sociologists question whether such shared scientific understanding is indeed possible.

KEY TERMS

scientific, 2
sociology, 3
social embeddedness, 3
sociological imagination, 3
agency, 5
structure, 5
critical thinking, 6
norms, 10
anomie, 10
social statics, 11
social dynamics, 11
positivist, 11
social facts, 12
social solidarity, 13
collective conscience, 13
class conflict, 13
proletariat, 13
bourgeoisie, 15
means of production, 16
Verstehen, 16
formal rationality, 16
bureaucracies, 16
double consciousness, 20

sociological theories, 22

macro-level paradigms, 23

micro-level paradigm, 23

structural functionalism, 23

manifest functions, 27

latent functions, 27

social conflict paradigm, 27

symbolic interactionism, 29

symbols, 29

power, 29

inequality, 30

globalization, 30

social diversity, 30

ethnocentrism, 30

DISCUSSION QUESTIONS

1. Think about Mills's concept of the sociological imagination and its ambition to draw together what Mills called *private troubles* and *public issues.* Think of a private trouble that sociologists might classify as also being a public issue. Share your example with your classmates.
2. What is critical thinking? What does it mean to be a critical thinker in our approach to understanding society and social issues or problems?
3. In the chapter, we asked why women's voices were marginal in early sociological thought. What factors explain the dearth of women's voices? What about the lack of minority voices? What effects do you think these factors may have had on the development of the discipline?
4. What is theory? What is its function in the discipline of sociology?
5. Recall the three key theoretical paradigms discussed in this chapter—structural functionalism, conflict theory, and symbolic interactionism. Discuss the ways these diverse "glasses" analyze deviance, its labeling, and its punishment in society. Try applying a similar analysis to another social phenomenon, such as class inequality or traditional gender roles.

edge.sagepub.com/eglitis

Want a better grade?

Get the tools you need to sharpen your study skills. Access practice quizzes, eFlashcards, video and multimedia at **https://edge.sagepub.com/eglitis**.

DISCOVER SOCIOLOGICAL RESEARCH

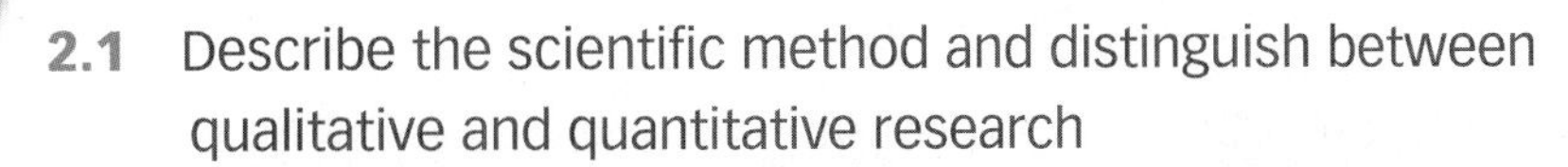

LEARNING OBJECTIVES

2.1 Describe the scientific method and distinguish between qualitative and quantitative research

2.2 Explain the components that comprise a scientific theory and how it is tested

2.3 Identify key methods of sociological research and when it is appropriate to use them

2.4 Discuss the major steps in sociological research

2.5 Summarize the importance of learning to do sociological research

©iStockphoto.com/themacx

WHAT DO YOU THINK?

1. What kinds of research questions could one pose to gain a better understanding of sociological phenomena like long-term poverty, cyberbullying, teen pregnancy, or the high dropout rate in some high schools? What kinds of research methods would be appropriate for studying these issues?

2. What factors could affect the honesty of people's responses to survey questions?

3. What makes a sociological research project ethical or unethical?

Andrew Lichtenstein/Contributor/Getty Images

NO ROOF OVERHEAD: RESEARCHING EVICTION IN AMERICA

In *Evicted: Poverty and Profit in the American City*, sociologist Matthew Desmond (2016a) writes that "millions of Americans are evicted every year because they can't make rent. . . . In 2013, 1 in 8 poor renting families nationwide were unable to pay all of their rent, and a similar number thought it would be likely they would be evicted soon" (pp. 4–5). Desmond argues in the book that eviction is not only a consequence of poverty but also a cause because the lack of a stable home undermines the ability of the poor to get and keep a job and to establish children in good schools, and it can lead to stress, depression, and even suicide. As a *New York Times* book review of *Evicted* poignantly notes, "Living in extreme poverty in the United States means waging an almost gladiatorial battle for creature comforts that luckier people take for granted. And of all those comforts, perhaps the most important is a stable, dignified home" (Senior, 2016, para. 4).

Desmond builds his research around a powerful, on-the-ground ethnographic account of the lives of eight Milwaukee families caught in a web of destitution and despair as they try to navigate the private rental market in that city. They include Arleen and her two young sons, fighting to find safe haven as Arleen struggles with money, depression, and the behavioral troubles of her boys. He also offers an account of the multigenerational Hinkston family, including young teenager Ruby, whose efforts at the public library to construct a bright, pleasant virtual home with a free online computer game are a grim contrast to her own living conditions in low-rent housing, which are characterized by instability, cockroaches, and chronically clogged plumbing.

Desmond points out that their stories are not isolated accounts; rather, in 2013, 67% of poor renting families received no housing assistance—demand for housing help far outpaces the availability of subsidized apartments or housing vouchers. This leaves families to seek what they hope will be permanent shelter in a private low-rent housing market that is rife with dismal, dirty, and even dangerous living conditions. Significantly, even the worst housing may stretch the resources of many families beyond their means: The majority of poor families today spend over half their income on rent, whereas about one quarter spend over 70% (Desmond, 2016a, p. 4). An unanticipated expense, a dispute with a landlord, or the loss of a job can easily put families on the street. The lack of resources and an eviction record can keep them there for a significant period of time.

Desmond's work is a good example of qualitative sociological research, and he recognizes its significance to academic and policy debates. By using a scientific approach and rigorous field research, Desmond casts light on the little-examined but significant problem of evictions. He recognizes the struggles of those who are most at risk of eviction—low-income minority women: "Women living in black neighborhoods in Milwaukee represent 9.6% of the population, but 30% of evictions" (Desmond, 2015, pp. 3–4). Importantly, he also sees that there is "profit" to be made from the misery of others, and he documents the multitude of ways in which landlords exploit the low-end market for their benefit, skimping on repairs, failing to provide even basic appliances (apparently a legal action), and keeping even low rents high enough that if tenants fail to pay, the landlord can evict them, keep the deposit, and move on to a new renter (Desmond, 2016a). As a sociologist, Desmond has described and defined his problem, examined its causes and consequences, and provided policy prescriptions to address it. ■

In this chapter, we examine the ways sociologists like Matthew Desmond study the social world. First, we distinguish between sociological understanding and common sense. Then we discuss the key steps in the research process itself. We examine how sociologists test their theories using a variety of research methods, and finally, we consider the ethical implications of doing research on human subjects.

SOCIOLOGY AND COMMON SENSE

Science is a unique way of seeing and investigating the world around us. The essence of the **scientific method** is straightforward: It is *a process of gathering empirical (scientific and specific) data, creating theories, and rigorously testing theories.* In sociological research, theories and empirical data exist in a dynamic relationship (Figure 2.1). Some sociological research begins from general theories, which offer "big picture" ideas: **Deductive reasoning** *starts from broad theories about the social world but proceeds to break them down into more specific and testable hypotheses.* Sociological **hypotheses** are *ideas about the world that describe possible relationships between social phenomena.* Some research begins from the ground up: **Inductive reasoning** *starts from specific data, such as interviews, observations, or field notes, which may focus on a single community or event, and endeavors to identify larger patterns from which to derive more general theories.*

Sociologists employ the scientific method in both quantitative and qualitative research. **Quantitative research**, which is often done through methods such as large-scale surveys, *gathers data that can be quantified and offers insight into broad patterns of social behavior* (for example, the percentage of U.S. adults who use corporal punishment like spanking with their children) *and social attitudes*

Scientific method: A way of learning about the world that combines logically constructed theory and systematic observation to provide explanations of how things work.

Deductive reasoning: The process of taking an existing theory and logically deducing that if the theory is accurate, we should discover other patterns of behavior consistent with it.

Hypotheses: Ideas about the world, derived from theories, which can be disproved when tested against observations.

Inductive reasoning: The process of generalizing to an entire category of phenomena from a particular set of observations.

Quantitative research: Research that gathers data that can be quantified and offers insight into broad patterns of social behavior and social attitudes.

FIGURE 2.1 The Relationship Between Theory and Research

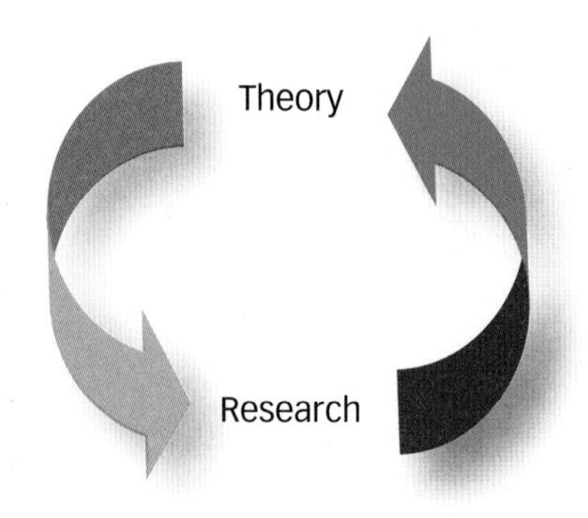

(for example, the percentage of U.S. adults who approve of corporal punishment) without necessarily delving into the meaning of or reasons for the identified phenomena. **Qualitative research**, such as that conducted by Matthew Desmond, is *characterized by data that cannot be quantified (or converted into numbers), focusing instead on generating in-depth knowledge of social life, institutions, and processes* (for example, why parents in particular demographic groups are more or less likely to use spanking as a method of punishment). It relies on the gathering of data through methods such as focus groups, participant and nonparticipant observation, interviews, content analysis, and archival research. Generally, population samples in qualitative research are small because they focus on in-depth understanding.

Personal experience and common sense about the world are often fine starting points for sociological research. They can, however, mislead us. In the 14th century, common sense suggested to people that the earth was flat; after all, it *looks* flat. Today, influenced by stereotypes and media portrayals of criminal behaviors, many people believe Black high school and college students are more likely than their White counterparts to use illegal drugs such as marijuana, cocaine, crack, and heroin. But common sense misleads on both counts. The earth is not flat (as you know!), and Black high school and college students are slightly *less* likely than White students to use illegal drugs (Table 2.1).

TABLE 2.1 Annual Prevalence Rate of Drug Use by 12th Graders, 2014

	Marijuana	Cocaine	Crack	LSD	Ecstasy
White	35.1	2.3	0.8	2.4	3.9
Black	35.9	1.6	1.3	1.1	1.7
Hispanic	37.1	3.6	1.7	2.0	3.9

Johnston, L. D., O'Malley, P. M., Bachman, J. G., Schulenberg, J. E., & Miech, R.A. (2014). Demographic subgroup trends among adolescents in the use of various licit and illicit drugs, 1975–2014. *Monitoring the Future Occasional Paper No. 83*. Ann Arbor, MI: Institute for Social Research.

Qualitative research: Research that is characterized by data that cannot be quantified (or converted into numbers), focusing instead on generating in-depth knowledge of social life, institutions, and processes.

Consider the following ideas, which many believe to be true, although all are false:

COMMON WISDOM *I know women who earn more than their husbands or boyfriends. The gender wage gap is no longer an issue in the United States.*

SOCIOLOGICAL RESEARCH Data show that men as a group earn more than women as a group. For example, in 2016, men had a weekly median income of $915 compared with $749 for women for all full-time occupations (U.S. Bureau of Labor Statistics, 2017e). There is some statistical variation, but data suggest that women as a group earn between 79 and 83 cents to a dollar that men earn (American Association of University Women [AAUW], 2016; U.S. Bureau of Labor Statistics, 2017e). These figures compare all men and all women who work full time and year round. Reasons for the gap include worker characteristics (such as experience, education, and ability to negotiate salary), job characteristics (such as hours required), devaluation of "women's work" by society, and pay discrimination against female workers (AAUW, 2016; Cabeza, Johnson, & Tyner, 2011; Reskin & Padavic, 2002). So although some women, of course, earn more than some men, the overall pattern of men outearning women remains in place today. This topic is discussed in greater detail in Chapter 9.

COMMON WISDOM *Homeless people lack adequate shelter because they do not work.*

SOCIOLOGICAL RESEARCH Finding safe permanent housing is a challenge for many U.S. residents, even those who work for pay. Low wages and poor benefits in the service industry, where many less educated people work, as well as a shortage of adequate housing options for low-income families, can make finding permanent shelter a challenge. As we saw in the opening story, many poor families are subject to the vagaries of a rental market that prices low-wage workers out: when tenants fail to make the rent, they can be put out on the street (Desmond, 2016a). Some homeless, particularly those who are part of the small population of the long-term homeless, do not work: "Nearly all of the long-term homeless have tenuous family ties and some kind of disability, whether it is a drug or alcohol addiction, a mental illness, or a physical handicap" (Culhane, 2010, para. 4). Alas, this is a group that would benefit from housing in facilities that can treat their ailments so they can attain self-sufficiency. These topics are discussed more fully in Chapter 7.

Bettman/Bettman/Getty Images

The Metropolitan Washington Council of Governments distinguishes between the "permanently supported homeless," who have housing but are at risk as a result of extreme poverty and/or disability, and the "chronically homeless," who are continually homeless for a year or more at least four times in three years. Do you think that these categories fully encompass the homeless population?

COMMON WISDOM *Education is the great equalizer. All children in the United States have the opportunity to get a good education. Low academic achievement is a personal failure.*

SOCIOLOGICAL RESEARCH Public education is free and open to all in the United States, but the quality of education can vary dramatically. Consider the fact that in many U.S. states and localities, a major source of public school funding is local property taxes, which constitute an average of about 45% of funding (state and federal allocations make up the rest; National Public Radio, 2016). As such, communities with high property values have richer sources of funding from which to draw educational resources, whereas poor communities—even those with high tax rates—have more limited pools. As well, high levels of racial segregation persist in U.S. schools. A recent U.S. Government Accountability Office report found that the proportion of U.S. schools that are highly segregated by race and class—that is, where more than 75% of children get free or reduced-price lunch and more than 75% are Black or Hispanic—is rising, climbing from 9% to 16% of schools between 2001 and 2014. It is also significant that students in the high-poverty and majority-Black or Hispanic schools were less likely to have access to the range of math and science courses available to their peers in better-off schools and to be subject to harsher disciplinary measures (U.S. Government Accountability Office, 2016). Research also shows a relationship between academic performance and class and racial segregation: Students who are not isolated in poor, racially segregated schools perform better on a variety of academic measures than those who are (Condron, 2009; Logan, Minca, & Adar, 2012). The problem of low academic achievement is complex, and no single variable can explain it. At the same time, the magnitude and persistence of this problem suggests that we are looking at a phenomenon that is a public issue rather than just a personal trouble. We discuss issues of class, race, and educational attainment further in Chapter 11.

Even deeply held and widely shared beliefs about society and social groups may be inaccurate—or more nuanced and complex than they appear on the surface. Until it is tested, common sense is merely conjecture. Careful research allows us to test our beliefs to gauge whether they are valid or merely anecdotal. From a sociological standpoint, empirical evidence is granted greater weight than common sense. By basing their decisions on scientific evidence rather than on personal beliefs or common wisdom, researchers and students can draw informed conclusions and policy makers can ensure that policies and programs are data driven and maximally effective.

RESEARCH AND THE SCIENTIFIC METHOD

Scientific theories *answer questions about how and why scientific observations are as they are.* A good scientific theory has the following characteristics:

Scientific theories: Explanations of how and why scientific observations are as they are.

- *It is logically consistent.* One part of the theory does not contradict another part.
- *It can be disproved.* If the findings contradict the theory, then we can deduce that the theory is wrong. Although we can say that testing has failed to disprove the theory, we cannot assume the theory is "true" if testing confirms it. Theories are always subject to further testing, which may point to needed revisions, highlight limitations, or strengthen conclusions.

Theories are made up of **concepts**, *ideas that summarize a set of phenomena.* Concepts are the building blocks of research and prepare a solid foundation for sociological work. Some key concepts in sociology are *social stratification, social class, power, inequality,* and *diversity,* which we introduced in the opening chapter.

To gather data and create viable theories, we need to define concepts in ways that are precise and measurable. A study of social class, for example, would need to begin with a working definition of that term. An **operational definition** of a concept *describes the concept in such a way that we can observe and measure it.* Many sociologists define social class in terms of dimensions such as income, wealth, education, occupation, and consumption patterns. Each of these aspects of class has the potential to be measurable. We may construct operational definitions in terms of *qualities* or *quantities* (Babbie, 1998; Neuman, 2000). In terms of qualities, we might say, for instance, that the "upper-middle class" is composed of working professionals who have completed advanced degrees, even though there may be a broad income spread between those with a master's degree in fine arts and those with a master's degree in business administration. This definition is based on an assumption of class as a social position that derives from educational attainment. Alternatively, by using quantity as a key measure, we might operationally define "upper class" as households with an annual income greater than $150,000 and "lower class" as households with an annual income of less than $20,000. This definition takes income as the preeminent determinant of class position, irrespective of education or other variables.

Concepts: Ideas that describe several things that have something in common.

Operational definition: A definition of a concept that allows the concept to be observed and measured.

Variable: A concept or its empirical measure that can take on multiple values.

Quantitative variables: Factors that can be counted.

Some research on bullying relies on self-reports, whereas other data come from peer reports. Research (Branson & Cornell, 2009) suggests that more than twice as many students (11%) were labeled bullies in peer reports than in self-reports (5%), highlighting the fact that any method of data collection has limitations.

Consider a social issue of contemporary interest—bullying. Imagine that you want to conduct a research study of bullying to determine how many female middle schoolers have experienced bullying in the past academic year. You would need to begin with a clear definition of bullying that operationalizes the term. That is, to measure how many girls have experienced bullying, you would need to articulate *what constitutes bullying.* Would you include physical bullying? If so, how many instances of being pushed or punched would constitute bullying? Would you include cyberbullying? What kinds of behaviors would be included in that category? To study a phenomenon like bullying, it is not enough to assume that "we know it when we see it." Empirical research relies on the careful and specific definition of terms and the recognition of how definitions and methods affect research outcomes.

RELATIONSHIPS BETWEEN VARIABLES

In studying social relationships, sociologists also need *variables.* A **variable** is *a concept that can take on two or more possible values.* For instance, sex can be male or female, work status can be employed or unemployed, and geographic location can be inner-city, suburbs, or rural area. We can measure variables both *quantitatively* and *qualitatively.* **Quantitative variables** include *factors we can count,* such as unemployment rates, victimization rates, and drug use frequency. **Qualitative variables** are *variables that express qualities and do not have numerical values.* Qualitative variables might include physical characteristics, such as gender or eye color, or attitudinal characteristics, such as a parent's preference for a private or public school or a commuter's preference for riding public transportation or driving to work.

Sociological research often tries to establish a relationship between two or more variables. Suppose you want to find out whether more education is associated with higher earnings. After asking people about their years of schooling and their annual incomes, both of which are quantitative variables, you could estimate the degree of *correlation* between the two. **Correlation**—literally, "co-relationship"—is *the degree to which two or more variables are associated with one another.* Correlating the two variables "years of education" and "annual income" demonstrates that the greater the education, the higher the income (Figure 2.2). (Do you see the exception to that relationship? How might you explain it?)

FIGURE 2.2 Correlation Between Education and Median Weekly Earnings in the United States, 2016

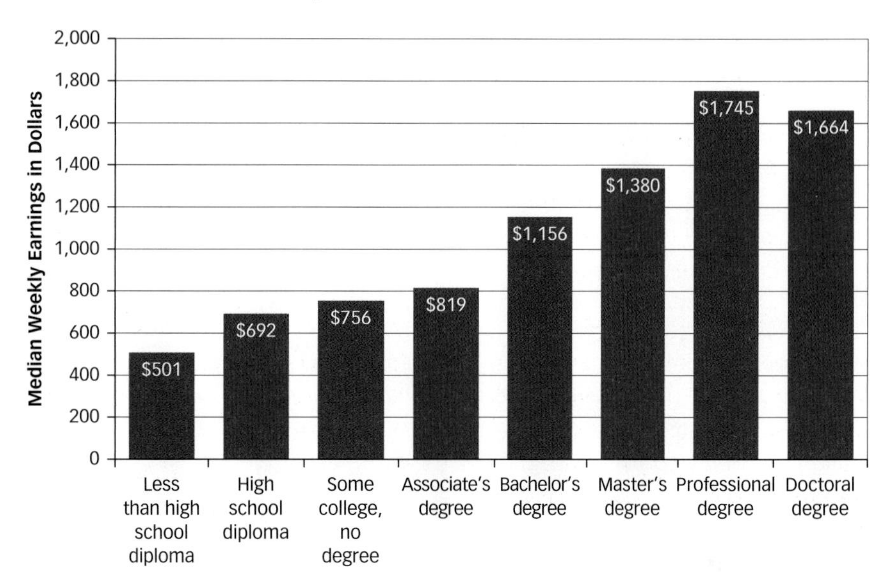

SOURCE: DeNavas-Walt and Proctor (2015). Centers for Disease Control and Prevention (2015), "Adult Obesity Prevalence Maps."

When two variables are correlated, we are often tempted to infer a **causal relationship**, *a relationship between two variables in which one is the cause of the other.* Nevertheless, just because two variables are correlated, we cannot assume that one causes the other. For example, ice cream sales rise during the summer, as does the homicide rate. These two events are correlated in the sense that both increase during the hottest months. Yet, because the sharp rise in ice cream sales does not *cause* rates of homicide to increase (nor, clearly, does the rise in homicide rates cause a spike in ice cream consumption), these two phenomena do not have a causal relationship. *Correlation does not equal causation.*

Sometimes an observed correlation between two variables is the result of a **spurious relationship**—that is, a *correlation between two or more variables caused by another factor that is not being measured.* In the example above, the common factor missed in the relationship is, in fact, the temperature. When it's hot, more people want to eat ice cream. Studies also show that rising temperatures are linked to an increase in violent crimes—although after a certain temperature threshold (about 90 degrees), crimes wane again (Gamble & Hess, 2012). Among the reasons more violent crimes are committed in the warm summer months is the fact that people spend more time outdoors in social interactions, which can lead to confrontations.

Let's take another example: Imagine that your school newspaper publishes a study concluding that coffee drinking causes poor test grades. The story is based on a survey of students that found those who reported drinking a lot of coffee the night before an exam scored lower than did their peers who had consumed little or no coffee. Having studied sociology, you wonder whether this relationship might be spurious. What is the "something else" that is not being measured here? Could it be that students who did not study in the days and weeks prior to the test and

Qualitative variables: Variables that express qualities and do not have numerical values.

Correlation: The degree to which two or more variables are associated with one another.

Causal relationship: A relationship between two variables in which one variable is the cause of the other.

Spurious relationship: A correlation between two or more variables that is the result of something else that is not being measured, rather than a causal link between the variables themselves.

FIGURE 2.3 Correlation Between Percentage in Poverty and Self-Reported Rates of Obesity, 2015

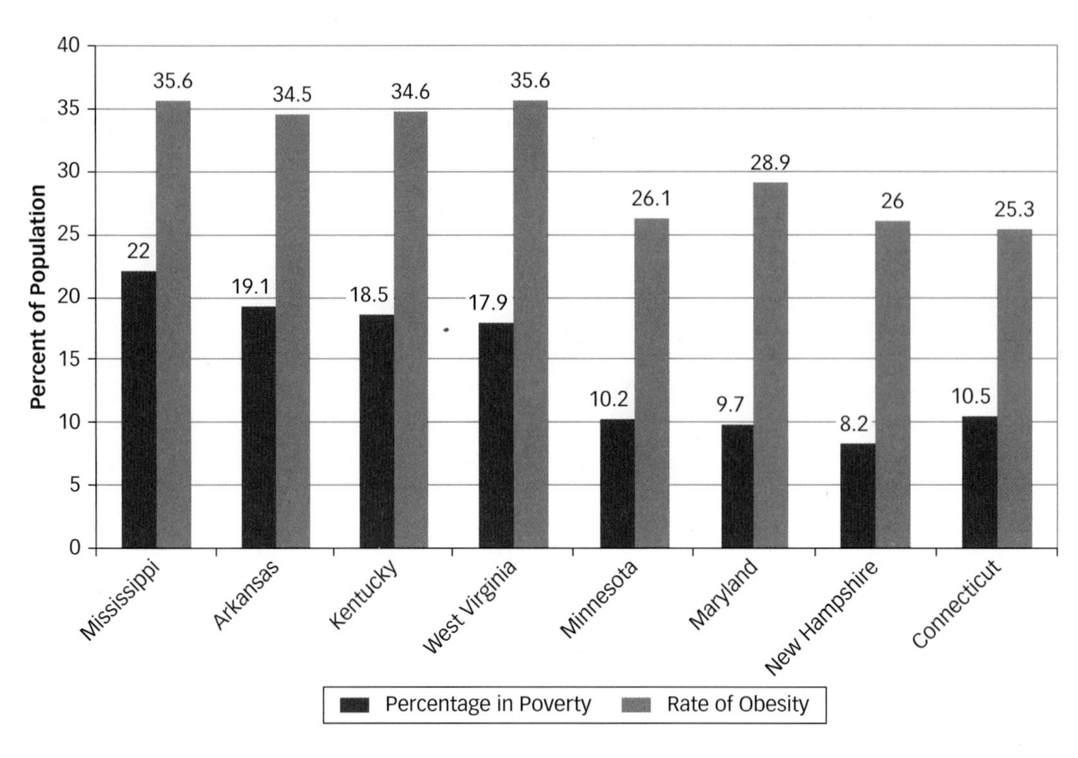

SOURCE: DeNavas-Walt and Proctor (2015); Centers for Disease Control and Prevention (2015), "Adult Obesity Prevalence Maps."

stayed up late the night before cramming—probably consuming a lot of coffee as they fought sleep—earned lower test grades than did peers who studied earlier and got adequate sleep the night before the test? The overlooked variable, then, is the amount of studying students did in the weeks preceding the exam, and we are likely to find a positive correlation and evidence of causation in looking at time spent studying and grade outcomes.

Sociologists attempt to develop theories systematically by offering clear operational definitions, collecting unbiased data, and identifying evidence-based relationships between variables. Sociological research methods usually yield credible and useful data, but we must always critically analyze the results to ensure their validity and reliability and to check that hypothesized relationships are not spurious.

TESTING THEORIES AND HYPOTHESES

Once we have defined concepts and variables with which to work, we can endeavor to test a theory by positing a hypothesis. Hypotheses enable scientists to check the accuracy of their theories. For example, data show that some positive correlation exists between obesity and poverty rates at the state level: for example, Mississippi, West Virginia, Kentucky, and Arkansas, which are among the poorest states in the country, are also among the states with the highest obesity rates (Figure 2.3). As well, four of the ten wealthiest states in the United States are among those with the lowest obesity rates. A positive correlation is *a relationship showing that as one variable rises or falls, the other does as well.* As we noted above, sociologists are quick to point out that correlation does not equal causation. Researchers are interested in creating and testing hypotheses to explain cases of positive correlation—they are also interested in explaining exceptions to the pattern of correlation between two (or more) variables.

In fact, researchers have explored and hypothesized the relationship between poverty and obesity. (See Figure 2.3.) Among the conclusions they have drawn is that living in poverty—and living in poor neighborhoods—puts people at higher risk of obesity, although the risk is pronounced for women and far less clear for men (Centers for Disease Control and Prevention, 2012; Hedwig, 2011; Smith, 2009). Among the factors that researchers have identified as contributing to a causal path between poverty and obesity are the lack of access to healthy food choices, the lack of access to safe and

Getting enough sleep can help students maintain good grades in college. How would you design a research study to examine the question of which factors correlate most strongly with solid grades? ■

nearby spaces for physical exercise, and a deficit of time to cook healthy foods and exercise. They have also cited the stress induced by poverty. Although the data cannot lead us to conclude decisively that poverty is a cause of obesity, research can help us to gather evidence that supports or refutes a hypothesis about the relationship between these two variables.

In the case of a **negative correlation**, *one variable increases as the other decreases.* As we discuss later in Chapter 10, which focuses on the family and society, researchers have found a negative correlation between male unemployment and rates of marriage. That is, as rates of male unemployment in a community rise, rates of marriage in the community fall. Observing this relationship, sociologists have conducted research to test explanations for it (Edin & Kefalas, 2005; Wilson, 2010).

Keep in mind that we can never prove theories to be decisively right—we can only prove them wrong. Proving a theory right would require the scientific testing of absolutely every possible hypothesis based on that theory—a fundamental impossibility. In fact, good theories are constructed in a way that makes it logically possible to prove them wrong. This is Karl Popper's (1959) famous **principle of falsification**, or **falsifiability**, which holds that *to be scientific, a theory must lead to testable hypotheses that can be disproved if they are wrong.*

VALIDITY AND RELIABILITY

For theories and hypotheses to be testable, both the concepts used to construct them and the measurements used to test them must be accurate. When our observations adequately reflect the real world, our findings have **validity**—that is, *the concepts and measurements accurately represent what they claim to represent.* For example, suppose you want to know whether the crime rate in the United States has gone up or down. For years sociologists depended on police reports to measure crime. Nevertheless, researchers could assess the validity of these tallies only if subsequent surveys were administered nationally to victims of crime. If the victim tallies matched those of the police reports, then researchers could say the police reports were a valid measure of crime in the United States. The National Crime Victimization Survey enables researchers to assess validity because it offers data on victimization, even for crimes that have not been reported to authorities.

Sociologists are also concerned with the reliability of their findings. **Reliability** is the extent to which the findings are consistent with the findings of different studies of the same phenomenon, or with the findings of the same study over time. Sociological research may suffer from problems of validity and reliability because of **bias**, a characteristic of results that systematically misrepresent the full dimensions of what is being studied. Bias can creep into research as a result of the use of inappropriate measurement instruments. For example, suppose the administrator of a city wants to know whether homelessness has risen in recent years. She operationally defines "the homeless" as those who sleep in the street or in shelters and dispatches her team of researchers to city shelters to count the number of people occupying shelter beds or sleeping on street corners or park benches. A sociologist reviewing the research team's results might question the administrator's operational definition of what it means to be homeless and, by extension, her findings. Are the homeless solely those spending nights in shelters or on the streets? What about those who stay

Negative correlation: A relation between two variables in which one increases as the other decreases.

Principle of falsification: The principle, advanced by philosopher Karl Popper, that a scientific theory must lead to testable hypotheses that can be disproved if they are wrong.

Falsifiability: The ability for a theory to be disproved; the logical possibility for a theory to be tested and proved false.

Validity: The degree to which concepts and their measurements accurately represent what they claim to represent.

Reliability: The extent to which researchers' findings are consistent with the findings of different studies of the same thing, or with the findings of the same study over time.

Bias: A characteristic of results that systematically misrepresent the true nature of what is being studied.

TABLE 2.2 How Truthful Are Survey Respondents? (in percentages)

	Threat of Validation		No Threat of Validation	
Survey Question	*Anonymous*	*Named*	*Anonymous*	*Named*
Ever smoked?	63.5	72.9	60.5	67.8
Smoked in the last month?	34.5	39.5	25.9	21.8
Smoked in the last week?	26.0	25.5	14.4	17.6

SOURCE: Adams, J., Parkinson, L., Sanson-Fisher, R. W., & Walsh, R. A. (2008). Enhancing self-report of adolescent smoking: The effects of bogus pipeline and anonymity. *Addictive Behaviors, 33*(10), 1291–1296.

with friends after eviction or camp out in their cars? In this instance, a sociologist might suggest that the city's measure is biased because it misrepresents (and undercounts) the homeless population by failing to define the concept in a way that captures the broad manifestations of homelessness.

Bias can also occur in research when respondents do not tell the truth (see Table 2.2). A good example of this is a study in which respondents were asked whether they used illegal drugs or had driven while impaired. All were asked the same questions, but some were wired to a machine they were told was a lie detector. The subjects who thought their truthfulness was being monitored by a lie detector reported higher rates of illegal drug use than did subjects who did not. Based on the assumption that actual drug use would be about the same for both groups, the researchers concluded that the subjects who were not connected to the device were underreporting their actual illegal drug use and that simply asking people about drug use would lead to biased findings because respondents would not tell the truth. Do you think truthfulness of respondents is a general problem, or is it one researchers are likely to encounter only where sensitive issues such as drug use or racism are at issue?

OBJECTIVITY IN SCIENTIFIC RESEARCH

Even if sociologists develop theories based on good operational definitions and collect valid and reliable data, like all human beings, they have passions and biases that may color their research. For example, criminologists long ignored the criminality of women because they assumed that women were not disposed toward criminal behavior. Researchers therefore did not have an accurate picture of women and crime until this bias was recognized and rectified.

Personal values and beliefs may affect a researcher's **objectivity** or *ability to represent the object of study accurately.* In the 19th century, sociologist Max Weber argued that for scientific research to be objective, it has to have **value neutrality**—that is, *the course of the research must be free of the influence of personal beliefs and opinions.* The sociologist should acknowledge personal biases and assumptions, make them explicit, and prevent them from getting in the way of observation and reporting.

How can we best achieve objectivity? First, recall Karl Popper's principle of falsification, which proposes that the goal of research is not to prove our ideas correct but to find out whether they are wrong. To accomplish this, researchers must be willing to accept that the data they collect might contradict their most passionate convictions. Research should deepen human understanding, not prove a particular point of view.

A second way we can ensure objectivity is to invite others to draw their own conclusions about the validity of our data through **replication**, *the repetition of a previous study using a different sample or population to verify or refute the original findings.* For research to be replicated, the original study must spell out in detail the research methods employed. If potential replicators cannot conduct their studies exactly as the original study was performed, they might accidentally introduce unwanted variables. To ensure the most accurate replication of their work, researchers should archive original materials such as questionnaires and field notes and allow replicators access to them.

Popper (1959) describes scientific discovery as an ongoing process of "confrontation and refutation." Sociologists usually subject their work to this process by publishing their results in scholarly journals. Submitted research undergoes a rigorous process of peer review, in which other experts in the field of study examine the work before the results are finalized and published. Once research has been published in a reputable journal such as the *American Sociological Review* or the *Journal of Health and Social Behavior,* other scholars read it with a critical eye. The study may then be replicated in different settings.

Objectivity: The ability to represent the object of study accurately.

Value neutrality: The characteristic of being free of personal beliefs and opinions that would influence the course of research.

Replication: The repetition of a previous study using a different sample or population to verify or refute the original findings.

DOING SOCIOLOGICAL RESEARCH

Sociological research requires careful preparation and a clear plan that guides the work. The purpose of a sociological research project may be to obtain preliminary knowledge that will help formulate a theory or to evaluate an existing theory about society and social life. As part of the strategy, the researcher selects from a variety of **research methods**—*specific techniques for systematically gathering data.* In the following sections, we look at a range of research methods and examine their advantages and disadvantages. We also discuss how you might prepare a sociological research project of your own.

SOCIOLOGICAL RESEARCH METHODS

Sociologists employ a variety of methods to learn about the social world (Table 2.3). Since each has strengths and weaknesses, a good research strategy may be to use several different methods. If they all yield similar findings, the researcher is more likely to have confidence in the results. The principal methods are the survey, fieldwork (either participant observation or detached observation), experimentation, working with existing information, and participatory research.

SURVEY RESEARCH

A **survey** *relies on a questionnaire or interviews with a group of people in person or by telephone or e-mail to determine their characteristics, opinions, and behaviors.* Surveys are versatile, and sociologists often use them to test theories or simply to gather data. Some survey instruments, such as National Opinion Research Center questionnaires, consist of *closed-ended questions* that respondents answer by choosing from among the responses presented. Others, such as the University of Chicago's Social Opportunity Survey, consist of open-ended questions that permit respondents to answer in their own words.

An example of survey research conducted for data collection is the largest survey in the nation, the U.S. Census, which is conducted every 10 years. The census is not designed to test any particular theory. Rather, it gathers voluminous data about U.S. residents that researchers, including sociologists, use to test and develop a variety of theories. In this text, you will find U.S. Census data in many chapters.

Usually, a survey is conducted on *a small number of people,* a **sample**, selected to represent a **population**, *the whole group of people to be studied.* The first step in designing a survey is to identify the population of interest. Imagine that you are doing a study of sociological factors that affect grades in college. Who would you survey? Members of a certain age group only? People in the airline industry? Pet owners? To conduct a study well, we need to identify clearly the survey population that will most effectively help us answer the research question. In your study, you would most likely choose to survey students now in college because they offer the best opportunity to correlate grades with circumstances and behaviors.

Once we have identified a population of interest, we need to select a sample, as we are unlikely to have the time or money to talk to all the members of a given population, especially if it is a large one. Other things being equal, larger samples better represent the population than do smaller ones. Nevertheless, with proper sampling techniques, sociologists can use small (and therefore inexpensive) samples to represent large populations. For instance, a well-chosen sample of 1,000 U.S. consumers can be used to represent 100,000 U.S. consumers with a fair degree of accuracy, enabling surveys to make predictions about economic behavior with reasonable confidence. Sampling is also used for looking at social phenomena such as marriages and online dating in a population: A recent report suggests that 32% of people who met their partners online eventually married, compared with 67% of people who met their partners offline, based on a 4,002-adults sample surveyed at Stanford University (Rosenfeld, Thomas, & Falcon, 2015).

Ideally, a sample should reflect the composition of the population we are studying. For instance, if you want to be able to use your research data about college students to generalize about the entire college student population of the United States, you would need to collect proportional samples from 2-year colleges, 4-year colleges, large universities, community colleges, online schools, and so on. It would not be adequate to survey only students at online colleges or only female students at private 4-year schools.

Research methods: Specific techniques for systematically gathering data.

Survey: A research method that uses a questionnaire or interviews administered to a group of people in person or by telephone or e-mail to determine their characteristics, opinions, and behaviors.

Sample: A portion of the larger population selected to represent the whole.

Population: The whole group of people studied in sociological research.

TABLE 2.3 Key Sociological Research Methods

Research Method	Appropriate Circumstances
Survey research	When basic information about a large population is desired. Sociologists usually conduct survey research by selecting samples that are representative of the entire populations of interest.
Fieldwork	When detailed information is sought, and when surveys are impractical for getting the information desired (for example, in studying youth gangs or gamblers). Fieldwork usually relies on small samples, especially compared to surveys.
Detached observation	When researchers desire to stay removed from the people being studied and must gather data in a way that minimizes impact on the subjects. Detached observations are often supplemented with face-to-face interviews.
Participant observation	When firsthand knowledge of the subjects' direct experience is desired, including a deeper understanding of their lives.
Experimentation	When it is possible to create experimental and control groups that are matched on relevant variables but provided with different experiences in the experiment.
Use of existing information	When direct acquisition of data is either not feasible or not desirable because the event studied occurred in the past or because gathering the data would be too costly or too difficult.
Participatory research	When a primary goal is training people to gain political or economic power and acquire the necessary skills to do the research themselves.

To avoid bias in surveys, sociologists may use **random sampling**, whereby *everyone in the population of interest has an equal chance of being chosen for the study*. Typically, they make or obtain a list of everyone in the population of interest. Then they draw names or phone numbers, for instance, by chance until the desired sample size is reached (today, most such work is done by computers). Large-scale random sample surveys permit researchers to draw conclusions about large numbers of people on the basis of small numbers of respondents. For our survey of college students, we could (theoretically) take all U.S. college students as our starting point and sample randomly from that group. We might also choose to use a stratified sample: In **stratified sampling**, *researchers divide a population into a series of subgroups (for instance, students at 4-year public universities, students at 2-year colleges, students at online schools, etc.) and take random samples from within each group. This can be used to ensure representation from all subgroups (like college students at different types of schools) in the final research sample*.

Researchers may assemble survey respondents through other sampling means. For example, they may use convenience sampling or snowball sampling. Imagine you are doing a survey of college students to learn what factors students consider when they choose a major. You may opt for a *convenience sample* of students at your school: This could include students in your classes, friends from clubs or organizations on campus, or if you live on campus, people in your dormitory. The term "convenience sample" suggests that the selection is driven by convenience rather than by systematic sampling.

You might use *snowball sampling* if you know a lot of students in your major but not in other majors. In such a case, if you wanted a wider sample, you could ask a few people you do know in other majors to refer classmates from those majors. From those classmates, you could expand your reach still further into other majors. Your sample then expands like a snowball, building from a core group outward through recruitment. Researchers sometimes rely on snowball sampling when they are trying to access a group that is insular or difficult to reach, such as sex workers or drug addicts.

Nonrandom samples like those gathered through convenience or snowball sampling can be suggestive of findings, but they are rarely generalizable by themselves and must be used with care.

In constructing surveys, sociologists are also concerned with ensuring that the questions and their possible responses will capture the respondents' points of view. The wording of questions is an important factor; poor wording can produce misleading results, as the following example illustrates. In 1993, an American Jewish Committee/Roper poll was taken to examine public attitudes and beliefs about the Holocaust. To the astonishment of many, the results indicated that fully 22% of survey respondents expressed a belief the Holocaust had never happened. Not immediately noticed was the fact that the survey contained some very awkward wording, including the question "Does it seem possible or does it seem impossible to you that the Nazi extermination of the Jews never happened?" Can you see why such a question might produce a questionable result? The question's compound structure and double-negative wording almost certainly confused many respondents.

Random sampling: Sampling in which everyone in the population of interest has an equal chance of being chosen for the study.

Stratified sampling: Dividing a population into a series of subgroups and taking random samples from within each group.

The American Jewish Committee released a second survey with different wording: "Does it seem possible to you that the Nazi extermination of the Jews never happened, or do you feel certain that it happened?" The results of the second poll were quite different. Only about 1% of respondents thought it was possible the Holocaust never happened, while 8% were unsure (Kagay, 1994). Despite the follow-up poll that corrected the mistaken perception of the previous poll's results, the new poll was not as methodologically rigorous as it could have been; a single survey question should ask for only one type of response. The American Jewish Committee's second survey contained a question that attempted to gauge two different responses simultaneously.

Sociologists may use snowball sampling in their research. Snowball sampling involves using a core group of known respondents as sources to contact new respondents, expanding the core group outward like a snowball. ■

A weakness of surveys is that they may reveal what people say rather than what they do. Responses are sometimes self-serving, intended to make the interviewee look good in the eyes of the researcher. As we saw in an earlier example, a respondent may not wish to reveal his or her drinking or drug habits. A well-constructed survey, however, can overcome these problems. Assuring the respondent of anonymity, assigning interviewers with whom respondents feel comfortable, and building in questions that ask for the same information in different ways can reduce self-serving bias in survey research.

FIELDWORK

Fieldwork is *a method of research that uses in-depth and often extended study to describe and analyze a group or community.* Sometimes called *ethnography,* it takes the researcher into the "field," where he or she directly observes—and sometimes interacts with—subjects in their social environment. Social scientists, including sociologists and anthropologists, have employed fieldwork to study everything from hoboes and working-class gangs in the 1930s (Anderson, 1940; Whyte, 1943) to prostitution and drug use among inner-city women (Maher, 1997) and Vietnam veterans motorcycling across the country to the Vietnam Veterans Memorial in Washington, D.C. (Michalowski & Dubisch, 2001). Matthew Desmond's (2016a) work on poor families experiencing eviction is another example of the use of fieldwork in sociological research.

Most fieldwork combines several different methods of gathering information. These include interviews, detached observation, and participant observation.

An **interview** is *a detailed conversation designed to obtain in-depth information about a person and his or her activities.* When used in surveys, interview questions may be either open-ended or closed-ended. They may also be formal or informal. In fieldwork, the questions are usually open-ended to allow respondents to answer in their own words. Sometimes the interviewer prepares a detailed set of questions; at other times, the best approach is simply to have a list of relevant topics to cover.

Good researchers guard against influencing respondents' answers. In particular, they avoid the use of **leading questions**—that is, *questions that tend to elicit particular responses.* Imagine a question on attitudes toward the marine environment that reads "Do you believe tuna fishing with broad nets, which leads to the violent deaths of dolphins, should be regulated?" The bias in this question is obvious—the stated association of broad nets with violent dolphin deaths creates a bias in favor of a yes answer. Accurate data depend on good questions that do not lead respondents to answer in particular ways.

Sometimes a study requires that researchers in the field keep a distance from the people they are studying and

Fieldwork: A research method that relies on in-depth and often extended study of a group or community.

Interview: A detailed conversation designed to obtain in-depth information about a person and his or her activities.

Leading questions: Questions that tend to elicit particular responses.

BEHIND THE NUMBERS

What Factors Affect Survey Responses?

If you are a follower of the news—whether on television, in newspapers, or online—you know that survey results are a popular media topic. We commonly hear about surveys asking respondents to indicate their support or rejection of particular public policies that seek to determine whether people believe or do not believe in climate change or support same-sex marriage or limitations on gun ownership, or that are gathering information on health behaviors like exercise and diet. In an election season, we read nearly every day about polling on the popularity (or lack thereof) of leading candidates for office.

Survey research is an important part of learning more about societal attitudes, ideologies, and behaviors. It is useful, for this reason, to understand some of its strengths and limitations. Research *about* survey research suggests that factors we might not consider can affect responses. In this essay, we discuss two such factors: *question order effects* and *social desirability bias*.

Question order can affect survey findings in part because respondents have a desire to be consistent in their responses (a "consistency effect"; Schuman & Presser, 1981). A study (Wilson, et al., 2008) on the issue of question order noted that "public opinion polls show that the public expresses greater support for gender-targeted AA [affirmative action] than race-targeted AA, but no research has addressed the extent to which expressed support for one group influences expressed support toward the other" (p. 514). The authors thus set out to find if asking respondents about one or the other affirmative-action target group would affect their stated attitudes about the other. In fact, they found that question order affected responses. Specifically, respondents who were asked about affirmative action for women *first* were much more likely to favor it than to oppose it: That is, about 63% supported affirmative action for women and 29% rejected it. When respondents were asked about affirmative action for women *after* being asked about such programs for racial minorities, support dropped: 57% supported affirmative action for women and 34% rejected it. Similarly, a greater percentage of respondents expressed support for racially targeted affirmative action when the question was asked after a question about affirmative action for women (57%) than when it was asked first (50%). The authors write that "results suggest that for the American public as a whole, support for one type of AA program is indeed affected by whether that program is considered by itself or in the context of both types of AA programs" (p. 518).

A second factor that may affect survey responses is social desirability bias, "the tendency of respondents to give answers they perceive to be socially desirable regardless of their own true positions" (Powell, 2013, p. 1054). An example of this can be found in measures on voter turnout. Because voting is a "socially desirable" behavior, research suggests that self-reported voting behavior may not match up with actual voter turnout: That is, there is a tendency for people to say they voted in an election even if they did not (Presser, 1990). The respondent's "bias" toward choosing a response that he or she believes will be perceived as socially acceptable by the interviewer may also affect survey findings on political candidates or social issues. For example, as racism has become socially unacceptable in the United States, some polls on Black candidates in political races have shown evidence of social desirability bias: "[S]ome individuals who favor the White candidate will actually express support for the Black candidate in an apparent attempt to appear racially tolerant to the interviewer" (Powell, 2013, p. 1055).

Recent research has shown declining effects of social desirability bias on mixed-race election polling (Hopkins, 2009), but other work finds a continued effect on some social issues, including same-sex marriage. In research conducted before the U.S. Supreme Court

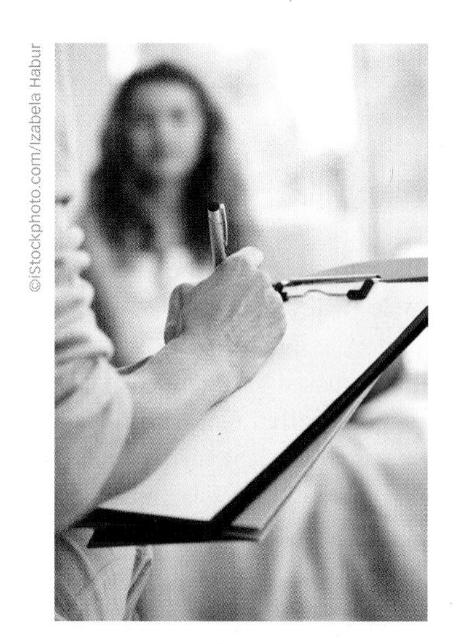

©iStockphoto.com/Izabela Habur

legalized same-sex marriage nationally, Powell (2013) found that there was a gap between public support expressed in preelection surveys for local or state ballot initiatives legalizing same-sex marriage and actual voting-day support. He determined that "other things equal, election day opposition to same-sex marriage is between 5% and 7% greater than found in preelection polls" (p. 1065). The wish to avoid stigma by voicing a position perceived to be socially acceptable to the interviewer may, thus, have an effect on survey responses to socially sensitive issues.

THINK IT THROUGH

- Survey researchers seek to gather accurate and unbiased data on attitudes and actions, but responses can be affected by a variety of factors, including question order and social desirability bias. Can you think of other factors—perhaps mentioned in the body of the chapter—that could affect survey outcomes? How can these problems in survey research be addressed?

simply observe without getting involved. The people being observed may or may not know they are being observed. This approach is called *detached observation.* In his study of two delinquent gangs (the "Saints" and the "Roughnecks"), William J. Chambliss, coauthor of this text, spent many hours observing gang members without being involved in what they were doing. With the gang members' permission, he sat in his car with the window rolled down so he could hear them talk and watch their behavior while they hung out on a street corner. At other times, he would observe them playing pool while he played at a nearby table. Chambliss sometimes followed gang members in his car as they drove around in theirs and sat near enough to them in bars and cafés to hear their conversations. Through his observations at a distance, he was able to gather detailed information on the kinds of delinquencies the gang members engaged in. He was also able to unravel some of the social processes that led to their behavior and observe other people's reactions to it.

Detached observation is particularly useful when the researcher has reason to believe other forms of fieldwork might influence the behavior of the people to be observed. It is also helpful for checking the validity of what the researcher has been told in interviews. A great deal of sociological information about illegal behavior has been gathered through detached observation.

One problem with detached observation is that the information gathered is likely to be incomplete. Without talking to people, we are unable to check our impressions against their experiences. For this reason, detached observation is usually supplemented by in-depth interviews. In his study of the delinquent gang members, Chambliss (1973, 2001) periodically interviewed them to complement his findings and check the accuracy of his detached observations.

Another type of fieldwork is *participant observation,* a mixture of active participation and detached observation. Participant observation can sometimes be dangerous. Chambliss's (1988b) research on organized crime and police corruption in Seattle, Washington, exposed him to threats from the police and organized crime network members who feared he would reveal their criminal activities. Desmond's (2016a) work also included participant observation; he spent significant amounts of time with the Milwaukee residents he studied, seeking to carefully document their voices and experiences.

Barbara Castello/Godong/Photononstop/Getty Images

When looking at the relationship between violent video games and violent behavior, researchers must account for many variables. What variables would you choose to study and why? ■

EXPERIMENTATION

Experiments are *research techniques for investigating cause and effect under controlled conditions.* We construct experiments to measure the effects of **independent or experimental variables**, *variables we change intentionally,* on **dependent variables**, which *change as a result of our alterations to the independent variables.* To put it another way, researchers modify one controllable variable (such as diet or exposure to violent movie scenes) to see what happens to another variable (such as willingness to socialize or the display of aggression). Some variables, such as sex, ethnicity, and height, do not change in response to stimuli and thus do not make useful dependent variables.

In a typical experiment, researchers select participants who share characteristics such as age, education, social class, or experiences that are relevant to the experiment. The participants are then randomly assigned to two groups. The first, called the *experimental group,* is exposed to the independent variable—the variable the researchers hypothesize will affect the subjects' behavior. The second group is assigned to the *control group.* These subjects are not exposed to the independent variable—they receive no special attention. The researchers then measure both groups for the dependent variable. For example, if a neuroscientist wanted to conduct an experiment on whether listening to classical music affects performance on a math exam, he or she might have an experimental group listen to Mozart, Bach, or Chopin for an hour before taking a test. The control group would take the same test but would not listen to any music beforehand. In this example, exposure to classical music is the independent variable, and the quantifiable results of the math test are the dependent variable.

To study the relationship between violent video game play and aggression, researchers took a longitudinal approach by examining the sustained violent video game play and aggressive behavior of 1,492 adolescents in grades 9 through 12 (Willoughby, Adachi, & Good, 2012). Their results showed a strong correlation between playing violent video games and being more likely to engage in, or approve of, violence. This body of literature represents another example of the importance of research methodology; the same researchers, in a separate study, found that the level of competitiveness in a video game, and not the violence itself, had the greatest influence on aggressive behavior (Adachi & Willoughby, 2011). More research on this topic may help differentiate between the effects of variables and avoid conclusions based on spurious relationships.

Experiments: Research techniques for investigating cause and effect under controlled conditions.

Independent or experimental variables: Variables that cause changes in other variables.

Dependent variables: Variables that change as a result of changes in other variables.

WORKING WITH EXISTING INFORMATION

Sociologists frequently work with existing information and data gathered by other researchers. Why would researchers choose to reinterpret existing data? Perhaps they want to do a secondary analysis of statistical data collected by an agency such as the U.S. Census Bureau, which makes its materials available to researchers studying issues ranging broadly from education to poverty to racial residential segregation. Or they may want to work with archival data to examine the cultural products—posters, films, pamphlets, and such—used by an authoritarian regime in a given period to legitimate its power or disseminated by a social movement like the civil rights movement to spread its message to the masses.

Statistical data include quantitative information obtained from government agencies, businesses, research studies, and other entities that collect data for their own or others' use. The U.S. Bureau of Justice Statistics, for example, maintains a rich storehouse of information on several criminal justice social indicators, such as prison populations, incidents of crime, and criminal justice expenditures. Many other government agencies routinely conduct surveys of commerce, manufacturing, agriculture, labor, and housing. International organizations such as the United Nations and the World Bank collect annual data on the health, education, population, and economies of nearly all countries in the world. Many businesses publish annual reports that yield basic statistical information about their financial performance.

Document analysis is the examination of written materials or cultural products: previous studies, newspaper reports, court records, campaign posters, digital reports, films, pamphlets, and other forms of text or images produced by individuals, government agencies, private organizations, and others. Nevertheless, because such documents are not always compiled with accuracy in mind, good researchers exercise caution in using them. People who keep records are often aware that others will see the records and take pains to avoid including anything unflattering. The diaries and memoirs of politicians are good examples of documents that are invaluable sources of data but that must be interpreted with great caution. The expert researcher looks at such materials with a critical eye, double-checking with other sources for accuracy where possible.

This type of research may include *historical research,* which entails the analysis of historical documents. Often such research is comparative, examining historical events in several different countries for similarities and differences. Unlike historians, sociologists usually identify patterns common to different times and places; historians tend to focus on particular times and places and are less likely to draw broad generalizations from their research. An early master of the sociological approach to historical research was Max Weber (1919/1946, 1921/1979), who contributed to our understanding of—among many other things—the differences between religious traditions in the West and those in East Asia.

Content analysis is the systematic examination of forms of documented communication. A researcher can take a content analysis approach by coding and analyzing patterns in cultural products like music, laws, tweets, blogs, and works of art. An exciting aspect of social science research is that your object of curiosity can become a research question. In 2009, sociologists conducted a content analysis of 403 gangsta rap songs to assess whether rap's reputation of being misogynistic (hostile to women) was justified (Weitzer & Kubrin, 2009). The analysis found that although only about a fifth of the songs in the sample contained lyrics that were notable for their "objectification, exploitation, and victimization" of women (p. 25), most portrayals of women were still gender stereotypical and disempowering.

PARTICIPATORY RESEARCH

Although sociologists usually try to avoid having an impact on the people they study, one research method is employed specifically to foster change. *Participatory research* supports an organization or community trying to improve its situation when it lacks the necessary economic or political power to do so by itself. The researcher fully participates by training the members to conduct research on their own while working with them to enhance their power (Freire, 1972; Park, 1993; Whyte, 1991). Such research might be part of, for instance, empowering a community to act against the threat of HIV/AIDS, as has been done in places like San Francisco and Nairobi, Kenya. Participatory research is an effective way of conducting an empirical study while also furthering a community or organizational goal that will benefit from the results of the study.

Statistical data: Quantitative information obtained from government agencies, businesses, research studies, and other entities that collect data for their own or others' use.

Document analysis: The examination of written materials or cultural products: previous studies, newspaper reports, court records, campaign posters, digital reports, films, pamphlets, and other forms of text or images produced by individuals, government agencies, or private organizations.

DISCOVER & DEBATE

Discover Sociological Research

Motion: Polling is an accurate way of gauging public attitudes about politics and society.

Background

In a democracy, the public's voice matters. President Abraham Lincoln said that, "What I want to get done is what the people desire to have done, and the question for me is how to find that out exactly." But how do we know what "the people" are thinking, how they are voting, and how they assess the direction of politics, the economy, and social life? Survey research, specifically public opinion polling, offers a means of looking into the public mind. Large-scale, social, scientifically based polling began in the United States early in the 20th century. In 1948, the *Chicago Tribune* famously published the headline, "Dewey Defeats Truman," when, in fact, Harry S. Truman had defeated Thomas Dewey to win the presidential race; this represents a well-known failure of political polling, although most later presidential polls have been accurate in predicting winners. The 2016 presidential contest, however, for which most polls predicted a win for Hillary Clinton over Donald Trump, has raised new questions about polling approaches and accuracy.

Affirmative Arguments

- Reputable polling organizations use scientifically selected samples to represent a population of interest as closely as possible. This enables them to learn about the attitudes and practices of a large population with a small number of respondents.
- Historically, preelection polling, particularly for presidential contests, has a strong record of accuracy.
- Because they endeavor to maintain reputations for accuracy, scientific polling organizations recognize errors and adjust for them in future polls. For example, in the 2016 presidential election, assumptions about who were "likely voters" did not correspond fully with actual voters: Because educated voters were more likely to respond to polls, the preferences of less-educated voters were only partially captured in polls, particularly in the Midwestern states that played a decisive role in the election.

Opposition Arguments

- Bias can be introduced into surveys by factors like interviewer effects, question order effects, and social desirability bias, which may cause respondents to give responses that do not correspond to their actual beliefs or actions.
- Shifts in technology use may affect participation and representativeness of samples. For example, as fewer people use landline phones and more have only cell phones, survey organizations may have difficulty reaching prospective respondents and, hence, assembling a representative population sample.
- A lack of trust in media and polling organizations may affect the willingness of some people to participate in polls, potentially skewing the sample.

Questions for Consideration

- How should pollsters address the problem of declining response rates in political polling?
- What kinds of messages about polling are present in the U.S. political environment? How might these affect participation rates?
- Are polls of people's attitudes toward issues other than politics, such as education funding, same-sex marriage, U.S. military involvement abroad, or how to address the opioid epidemic, important? If yes, why are they important?

Debate Tip

▶ Follow the model used by academic debaters, which foresees the development of a debate position in five steps.

1. Introduce your debate topic. Tell why it is important to you and to the audience.
2. State your main argument about the topic. You may break down the thesis of the argument into smaller parts.
3. Support your points with credible evidence.
4. Recognize and acknowledge a possible challenge to your argument, and briefly address it.
5. Finish with a statement that wraps up your argument and guides your audience to a conclusion.

DOING SOCIOLOGY: A STUDENT'S GUIDE TO RESEARCH

Sociological research seldom follows a formula that indicates exactly how to proceed. Sociologists often have to feel their way as they go, responding to the challenges that arise during research and adapting new methods to fit the circumstances. Thus, the stages of research can vary even when sociologists agree about the basic sequence. At the same time, for student sociologists, it is useful to understand the key building blocks of good sociological research. As you read through the following descriptions of the stages, think about a topic of interest to you and how you might use that as the basis for an original research project.

FRAME YOUR RESEARCH QUESTION

"Good research," Thomas Dewey observed, "scratches where it itches." Sociological research begins with the formulation of a question or questions to be answered. Society offers an endless spectrum of compelling issues to study: Does exposure to violent video games affect the incidence of aggressive behavior in adolescents? Does religious faith affect voting behavior? Is family income a good predictor of performance on standardized college entrance tests like the ACT or SAT? Beyond the descriptive aspects of social phenomena, sociologists are also interested in *how* relationships between the variables they examine can be explained.

Formulating a research question precisely and carefully is one of the most important steps toward ensuring a successful research project. Research questions come from many sources. Some arise from problems that form the foundation of sociology, including an interest in socioeconomic inequalities and their causes and effects, or the desire to understand how power is exercised in social relationships. Sociologists are also mindful that solid empirical data are important to public policies on issues of concern such as poverty, occupational mobility, and domestic violence.

Keep in mind that you also need to define your terms. Recall our discussion of operationalizing concepts. For example, if you are studying middle school bullying, you need to make explicit your definition of bullying and how that will be measured. The same holds true if you are studying a topic such as illiteracy or aggressive behavior.

Does Technology Affect Studying?

Has technology helped or hindered your studying in college? Does it mostly offer research help—or additional distractions? ■

In 2011, the National Survey of Student Engagement (NSSE) surveyed about 416,000 U.S. students at 673 institutions of higher education, asking about student relationships with faculty, engagement in class and on campus, and access to support. It also asked about a new topic—hours spent studying by major. Consistent with the results of other recent surveys, the NSSE found that students are spending far fewer hours studying than did their counterparts in previous decades. If in 1961 the average student reported studying about 24 hours per week, by 2011, the average student reported about 14 hours of study time (Babcock & Marks, 2010; NSSE, 2012). Within this figure are variations by major, ranging from about 24 hours per week for architecture majors to 10 for speech majors. Sociology majors reported studying an average of 13.8 hours per week (de Vise, 2012).

This study presents several interesting research questions, few of which are answered by the NSSE, which collected quantitative data but did not analyze the results. What factors might be behind the precipitous decline in self-reported hours spent studying?

Some existing hypotheses implicate modern technology for at least two reasons. First, it has been suggested that students study less because they are spending substantial time using social media such as Facebook. One pilot study at Ohio State University concluded that students who used Facebook had poorer grades than those who did not (Karpinski & Duberstein, 2009). Another study, however, found that most students (92%) used Facebook: Even though Facebook use had a negatively predictive impact on students' grade point average, the effect was very slight unless students were heavy users (Junco, 2012). These data suggest that another study could profitably look for correlations between social media use and study time—and to seek what those correlations mean.

Second, students may be reporting less study time because technology has cut the hours of work needed for some tasks. Although preparing a research paper in the past may have demanded hours in the library stacks or in pursuit of an expert to interview, today an online search engine can bring up a wealth of data earlier generations could not have imagined. Far fewer students consult research librarians or use library databases today. Notably, however, a recent study suggests that the quality of data students have the skills to find in their searches is mixed and often low (Kolowich, 2011).

Technology is only one possible factor in the decline in the time U.S. students spend studying. Two economists, for instance, suggest that studying time has decreased as achievement standards have fallen (Babcock & Marks, 2010). But there is no denying that one of the most dramatic differences between the

1960s and today is the proliferation of social media and technology, which suggests that an explanatory relationship may exist.

THINK IT THROUGH

▶ Imagine that your final paper for this semester involves answering the research question, "What is the impact of social media on students' studying in college?" How would you go about answering this question? How would you collect data for your project?

Follow us on Twitter to keep up with current sociological stories and research! We're at @DiscoverSoc1.
Share your own ideas at #DiscoverSociology.

REVIEW EXISTING KNOWLEDGE

Once you identify the question you want to ask, you need to conduct a review of the existing literature on your topic. The literature may include published studies, unpublished papers, books, dissertations, government documents, newspapers and other periodicals, and increasingly, data disseminated on the Internet. The key focus of the literature review, however, is usually published and peer-reviewed research studies. Your purpose in conducting the literature review is to learn about studies that have already been done on your topic of interest so that you can set your research in the context of existing studies. You will also use the literature review to highlight how your research will contribute to this body of knowledge.

FIGURE 2.4 Sociological Research Formula

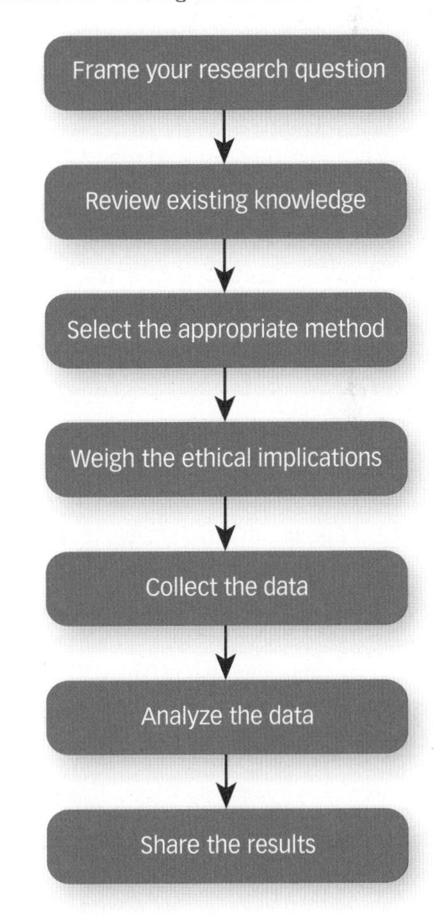

SELECT THE APPROPRIATE METHOD

Now you are ready to think about how your research question can best be answered. Which of the research methods described earlier (1) will give the best results for the project and (2) is most feasible for your research circumstances, experience, and budget?

If you wish to obtain basic information from a relatively large population in a short period of time, then a survey is the best method to use. If you want to obtain detailed information about a smaller group of people, then interviews might be most beneficial. Participant observation and detached observation are ideal research methods for verifying data obtained through interviews or, for the latter, when the presence of a researcher might alter the research results. Document analysis and historical research are good choices for projects focused on inaccessible subjects and historical sociology. Remember, sociological researchers often use multiple methods.

TABLE 2.4 The Nuremberg Code

	Directives for Human Experimentation
1.	The voluntary consent of the human subject is absolutely essential.
2.	The experiment should be such as to yield fruitful results for the good of society.
3.	The experiment should be so designed and based on the results of animal experimentation and a knowledge of the natural history of the disease.
4.	The experiment should be so conducted as to avoid all unnecessary physical and mental suffering and injury.
5.	No experiment should be conducted where there is an a priori reason to believe that death or disabling injury will occur.
6.	The degree of risk to be taken should never exceed that determined by the humanitarian importance of the problem to be solved by the experiment.
7.	Proper preparations should be made and adequate facilities provided to protect the experimental subject against even remote possibilities of injury, disability, or death.
8.	The experiment should be conducted only by scientifically qualified persons.
9.	During the course of the experiment the human subject should be at liberty to bring the experiment to an end.
10.	During the course of the experiment the scientist in charge must be prepared to terminate the experiment at any stage, if he has probable cause to believe, in the exercise of the good faith, superior skill, and careful judgment required of him that a continuation of the experiment is likely to result in injury, disability, or death to the experimental subject.

SOURCE: The Nuremberg Code, United States Holocaust Memorial Museum, https://www.ushmm.org/information/exhibitions/online-exhibitions/special-focus/doctors-trial/nuremberg-code.

WEIGH THE ETHICAL IMPLICATIONS

Research conducted on other human beings—as much of sociological research is—poses certain ethical problems. An outpouring of outrage after the discovery of gruesome experiments conducted by the Nazis during World War II prompted the adoption of the Nuremberg Code, a collection of ethical research guidelines developed to help prevent such atrocities from ever happening again (Table 2.4). In addition to these basic guidelines, scientific societies throughout the world have adopted their own codes of ethics to safeguard against the misuse and abuse of human subjects.

Before you begin your research, it is important that you familiarize yourself with the American Sociological Association's Code of Ethics (www.asanet.org/about/ethics.cfm), as well as with the standards of your school, and carefully follow both. Ask yourself whether your research will cause the subjects any emotional or physical harm. How will you guarantee their anonymity? Does the research violate any of your own ethical principles?

Most universities and research institutes require researchers to complete particular forms before undertaking experiments using human subjects, describing the research methods to be used and the groups of subjects who will take part. Depending on the type of research, a researcher may need to obtain written agreement from the subjects for their participation. Today, a study like that conducted by Philip Zimbardo in the 1970s at Stanford University (described in the *Private Lives, Public Issues* box) would be unlikely to be approved because of the stress put on the experiment's subjects in the course of the research. Approval of research involving human subjects is granted with an eye to both fostering good research and protecting the interests of those partaking in the study.

COLLECT AND ANALYZE THE DATA

Collecting data is the heart of research. It is time-consuming but exciting. During this phase, you will gather the information that will allow you to make a contribution to the sociological understanding of your topic. If your data set is qualitative—for example, open-ended responses to interview questions or observations of people—you will proceed by carefully reviewing and organizing your field notes, documents, and other sources of information. If your data set is quantitative—for example, completed closed-ended surveys—you will proceed by entering data into spreadsheets, comparing results, and analyzing your findings using statistical software.

Your analysis should offer answers to the research questions with which you began the study. Be mindful in interpreting your data, and avoid conclusions that are speculative or not warranted by the actual research results. Do your data support or contradict your initial hypothesis? Or are they simply inconclusive? Report *all* of your results. Do your findings have implications for larger theories in the discipline? Do they suggest the need for further study of another dimension of the issue at hand? Good research need not have results that unequivocally support your hypothesis. A finding that refutes the hypothesis can be instructive as well.

SHARE THE RESULTS

However fascinating your research may be to you, its benefits are amplified when you take advantage of opportunities to share it with others. You can share your findings with the sociological community by publishing the results in academic journals. Before submitting research for publication, you must learn which journals cover your topic areas and

PRIVATE LIVES, PUBLIC ISSUES

Zimbardo's Experiment: The Individual and the Social Role

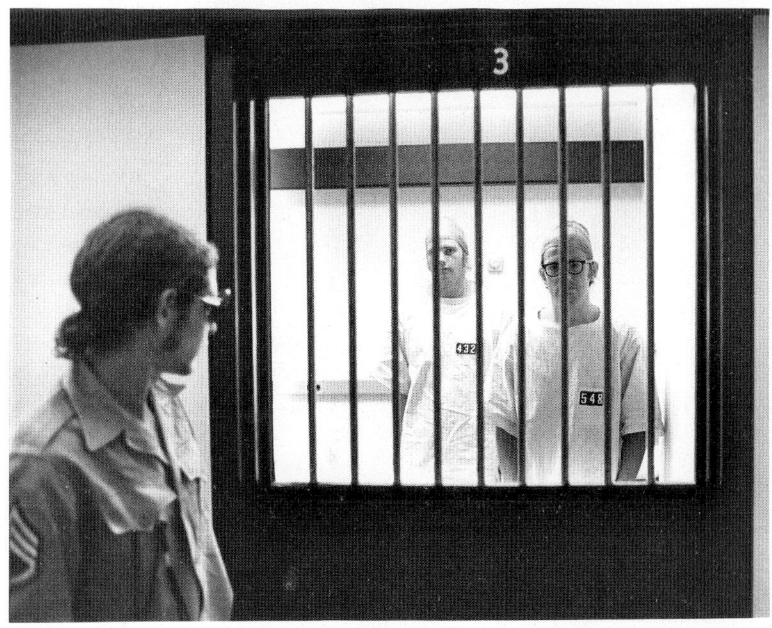

Stanford University Archives

Despite questions about the ethics of Philip Zimbardo's experiment, sociologists still study his work. Is it wrong to use research data gathered by means we now consider unethical? Do the results of research ever justify subjecting human beings to physical or psychological discomfort, invasion of privacy, or deception?

Social psychologist Philip Zimbardo (1974; Haney, Banks, & Zimbardo, 1973) wanted to investigate how role expectations shape behavior. He was intrigued by the possibility that the frequently observed cruelty of prison guards was a consequence of the institutional setting and role, not of the guards' personalities.

In an experiment that has since become well known, Zimbardo converted the basement of a Stanford University building into a makeshift prison. A newspaper ad seeking young men to take part in the experiment for pay drew 70 subject candidates, who were given a battery of physical and psychological tests to assess their emotional stability and maturity. The most mature 24 were selected for the experiment and randomly assigned to roles as "guards" or "prisoners." Those assigned to be prisoners were "arrested," handcuffed, and taken to the makeshift prison by the Palo Alto police. The behavior of the guards and the prisoners was filmed. Within a week, the prison setting took on many of the characteristics of actual prisons. The guards were often aggressive and seemed to take pleasure in being cruel. The prisoners began planning escapes and expressed hostility and bitterness toward the guards.

The subjects in the experiment so identified with their respective roles that many of them displayed signs of depression and anxiety. As a result, some were released early, and the experiment was canceled before the first week was over. Since the participants had all been screened for psychological and physical problems, Zimbardo concluded that the results could not be attributed to their personalities. Instead, the prison setting itself (the *independent variable*) appeared to be at the root of the guards' brutal behavior and the prisoners' hostility and rebelliousness (the *dependent variable*). Zimbardo's research shows how profoundly private lives are shaped by the behavioral expectations of the roles we occupy in social institutions.

THINK IT THROUGH

- Zimbardo's experiment could not be repeated today as it would violate guidelines for ethical research with human subjects. How might a researcher design an ethical experiment to test the question of the circumstances under which apparently "normal" individuals will engage in violent or cruel acts?

During the Nuremberg Trials, which brought key figures of the Nazi Party of Germany to justice, the practices of some Nazi medical personnel were found to be unethical and even criminal. The Nuremberg Code, which emerged from these trials, established principles for any type of human experimentation.

review those journals' standards for publication. Some colleges and universities sponsor undergraduate journals that offer opportunities for students to publish original research.

Other outlets for publication include books, popular magazines, newspapers, video documentaries, and websites. Another way to communicate your findings is to give a presentation at a professional meeting. Many professional meetings are held each year; at least one will offer a panel suited to your topic. In some cases, high-quality undergraduate papers are selected for presentation. If your paper is one, relevant experts at the meeting will likely help you interpret your findings further.

WHY LEARN TO DO SOCIOLOGICAL RESEARCH?

The news media provide us with an immense amount of round-the-clock information. Some of it is very good; some of it is misleading. Reported "facts" may come from sources that have agendas or are motivated by self-interest, such as political interest groups, lobbying groups, media outlets, and even government agencies. Perhaps the most problematic are "scientific" findings that are agenda driven, not scientifically unbiased. In particular, because we live in a time of information saturation, it is important that we learn to be critical consumers of information and to ask questions about the quality of the data presented to us. Carefully gathered and precise data are important not only as sources of information but also as the basis of informed decision-making on the part of elected officials and others in positions of power.

Because you now understand how valid and reliable data are gathered, you can better question the veracity and reliability of others' claims. For example, when a pollster announces that 80% of the "American people" favor Joe Conman for Congress, you can ask, "What was the size of the sample? How representative is it of the population? How was the survey questionnaire prepared? Exactly what questions were asked?" If it turns out that the data are based on the responses of 25 residents of a gated Colorado community or that a random sample was used but the survey included leading questions, you know the results do not give an accurate picture.

Similarly, your grasp of the research process allows you to have greater confidence in research that was conducted properly. You should put more stock in the results of a nationwide Centers for Disease Control and Prevention survey of college students' drug use or safe-sex choices that used carefully prepared questionnaires tested for their validity and reliability and less stock in data gathered by a reporter untrained in scientific methods who interviewed a small, nonrandom sample of students on a single college campus.

You have also taken the first step in learning how to gather and evaluate data yourself. Realizing the value of theories that can be tested and proved false if they are wrong is the first step in developing your own theories and hypotheses. By using the concepts, processes, and definitions introduced in this chapter, you can conduct research that is valid, appropriate, and even publishable.

In short, these research tools will help you be a more critical consumer of information and enhance your understanding of the social world around you. Other benefits of learning sociology will become apparent throughout the following chapters as you discover how the research process is applied to cultures, societies, and the institutions that shape your life.

WHAT CAN I DO WITH A SOCIOLOGY DEGREE?

Quantitative Research Skills

Sociologists use *quantitative research skills* to conduct systematic empirical investigations of social phenomena using statistical methods. Quantitative research encompasses those studies in which data are expressed in terms of numbers. Important sources of quantitative data include surveys and observations. The objective of quantitative research in sociology is to gather rigorous data and to use numerical data to characterize the dimensions of an issue or the extent of a problem (this could include, for instance, the collection of statistical data on rates of obesity and poverty in neighborhoods or states and the calculation of the correlation of the two phenomena). Data may be used to develop or test hypotheses about the roots of a sociological phenomenon or problem.

Knowledge of quantitative methods is a valuable skill in today's job market. Learning to collect and analyze quantitative data, which is an important part of a sociological education, prepares you to do a wide variety of job tasks, including survey development, questionnaire design, market research, brand health tracking, and financial quantitative modeling and analysis.

Amber Henderson, Survey Statistician, U.S. Census Bureau

The George Washington University, MA in Sociology

I work in the Center for Survey Measurement as a statistician at the U.S. Census Bureau. The goal of the Census Bureau is to provide timely, accurate, and quality data while minimizing the various sources of survey error. When fielding a survey, it must go through all of the phases of what we call the survey life cycle. This includes tasks such as project planning, data collection, data analyses, and reporting. During my first year at Census, I used statistical software packages to manipulate, edit, and analyze data for surveys on education. Statistical software is a valuable tool for those who work with data. I used it frequently to run basic descriptive statistics and to check the data for error. For example, if a respondent gave a date of birth that indicated they were 12 years of age and listed his or her marital status as "married," I would flag these data points for potential inconsistencies.

In my current role at Census, I do a lot more survey research where I specialize in structured cognitive interviewing and develop survey questions. The core sociology courses I took both during undergraduate and graduate school prepared me for my career at Census. I use a lot of what I learned in my courses on sociological research methods and data analysis to choose the best research method and work effectively and accurately with the Census Bureau's survey data. People often look puzzled when they learn you want to study sociology, but what they do not realize is that it's a multidimensional field. Sociology and my professors taught me both the qualitative and quantitative skills I needed to land my dream job. I wouldn't change a thing!

Career Data: Statistician

- 2016 Median Pay: $80,500
- Typical Entry-Level Education: Master's degree
- Projected Job Growth by 2024: 34% (Much faster than average)

SOURCE: Bureau of Labor Statistics, Occupational Outlook Handbook, 2016.

SUMMARY

- Unlike commonsense beliefs, sociological understanding puts our biases, assumptions, and conclusions to the test.
- As a science, sociology combines logically constructed theory and systematic observation to explain human social relations.
- **Inductive reasoning** generalizes from specific observations; **deductive reasoning** consists of logically deducing the empirical implications of a particular theory or set of ideas.
- A good theory is logically consistent, testable, and valid. The **principle of falsification** holds that if theories are to be scientific, they must be formulated in such a way that they can be disproved if wrong.
- Sociological **concepts** must be operationally defined to yield measurable or observable variables. Often, sociologists operationally define variables so they can measure these in quantifiable values and assess **validity** and **reliability**, to eliminate **bias** in their research.
- Quantitative analysis permits us to measure correlations between variables and identify **causal relationships**. Researchers must be careful not to infer causation from correlation.
- Qualitative analysis is often better suited than **quantitative research** to producing a deep understanding of how the people being studied view the social world. On the other hand, it is sometimes difficult to measure the reliability and validity of **qualitative research**.
- Sociologists seek **objectivity** when conducting their research. One way to help ensure objectivity is through the **replication** of research.
- Research strategies are carefully thought-out plans that guide the gathering of information about the social world. They also suggest the choice of appropriate **research methods**.
- Research methods in sociology include **survey** research (which often relies on random sampling), **fieldwork** (including participant observation and detached observation), **experiments**, working with existing information, and participatory research.
- Sociological research typically follows seven steps: framing the research question, reviewing the existing knowledge, selecting appropriate methods, weighing the ethical implications of the research, collecting data, analyzing data, and sharing the results.
- To be ethical, researchers must be sure their research protects the privacy of subjects and does not cause them unwarranted stress. Scientific societies throughout the world have adopted codes of ethics to safeguard against the misuse and abuse of human subjects.

KEY TERMS

scientific method, 37
deductive reasoning, 37
hypotheses, 37
inductive reasoning, 37
quantitative research, 37
qualitative research, 38
scientific theories, 39
concepts, 40
operational definition, 40
variable, 40
quantitative variables, 40
qualitative variables, 41
correlation, 41
causal relationship, 41
spurious relationship, 41
negative correlation, 43
principle of falsification, 43
falsifiability, 43

validity, 43
reliability, 43
bias, 43
objectivity, 44
value neutrality, 44
replication, 44
research methods, 45
survey, 45
sample, 45
population, 45
random sampling, 46
stratified sampling, 46
fieldwork, 47
interview, 47
leading questions, 47
experiments, 50
independent or experimental variables, 50
dependent variables, 50
statistical data, 51
document analysis, 51

DISCUSSION QUESTIONS

1. Think about a topic of contemporary relevance in which you may be interested (for example, poverty, juvenile delinquency, teen births, or racial neighborhood segregation). Using what you learned in this chapter, create a simple research question about the topic. Match your research question to an appropriate research method. Share your ideas with classmates.
2. What is the difference between quantitative and qualitative research? Give an example of each from the chapter. In what kinds of cases might one choose one or the other research method to effectively address an issue of interest?
3. Sociologists often use interviews and surveys as methods for collecting data. What are potential problems with these methods of which researchers need to be aware? What steps can researchers take to ensure that the data they are collecting are of good quality?
4. Imagine that your school has recently documented a dramatic rise in plagiarism reported by teachers. Your sociology class has been invited to study this issue. Consider what you learned in this chapter about survey research and design a project to assess the problem.
5. In this chapter, you learned about the issue of ethics in research and read about the Zimbardo prison experiment. How should knowledge collected under unethical conditions (whether it is sociological, medical, psychological, or other scientific knowledge) be treated? Should it be used just like data collected under ethically rigorous conditions?

edge.sagepub.com/eglitis

Want a better grade?

Get the tools you need to sharpen your study skills. Access practice quizzes, eFlashcards, video and multimedia at **https://edge.sagepub.com/eglitis**.

CULTURE AND MASS MEDIA

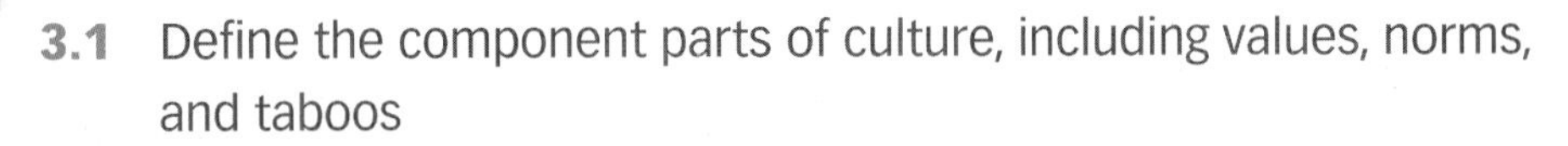

LEARNING OBJECTIVES

3.1 Define the component parts of culture, including values, norms, and taboos

3.2 Recognize the significance of language in representing culture

3.3 Discuss the relationship between culture and mass media and the debate over mass culture and violence

3.4 Explain how sociologists theorize the relationship between culture and social class

3.5 Apply functionalist and conflict perspectives to the phenomenon of global culture

Joel Ryan/Invision/AP Photo

WHAT DO YOU THINK?

1. In U.S. culture, a common expression is "don't judge a book by its cover." At the same time, research and many of our own experiences suggest that people are routinely evaluated based on their appearance. What explains this cultural inconsistency?

2. What is the relationship between popular culture and violence? Do cultural representations of violence in films, television, music, and video games have an effect on attitudes and behaviors?

3. Does a shared "global culture" exist? What are its key characteristics?

Awakening/Getty Images

ZOMBIE APOCALYPSE

In October 2016, about 17 million viewers tuned in to watch the first episode of season 7 of the television series *The Walking Dead.* The program follows a small band of human survivors trying to evade flesh-eating zombies who have taken over. The main character, Rick, and his compatriots fight for survival against the fearsome "walkers," who relentlessly hunt human and beast. The undead have not only overrun the planet on this TV show, however, but they also appear to have made some headway in taking over U.S. popular culture in recent years. Along with following the adventures of *The Walking Dead,* consumers of horror can read zombie books (such as *World War Z,* which was also made into a movie, and *The Zombie Survival Guide*), play zombie video games (for instance, *Resident Evil* and *House of the Dead*), and watch zombie films (like *Maze Runner: The Scorch Trials, I Am Legend,* and *28 Days Later*). In 2014, the Centers for Disease Control and Prevention even used the public interest in zombies to launch a disaster preparedness campaign, offering the U.S. public tips for surviving an onslaught of the undead. According to Dr. Ali Khan, the architect of the campaign, "If you are generally well equipped to deal with a zombie apocalypse, you will be prepared for a hurricane, pandemic, earthquake, or terrorist attack" (http://www.cdc.gov/phpr/zombies.htm).

Why have zombies become a cultural phenomenon in the 21st-century United States? Some writers suggest that films, television, and other cultural forms are a mirror of social anxieties: As sociologist Robert Wuthnow (1989) has written, "If cultural products do not articulate closely enough with their social settings, they are likely to be regarded . . . as irrelevant, unrealistic, artificial, and overly abstract" (p. 3). In the post–World War II period of the 1940s and 1950s, Americans were dogged by fears of technology run amok (particularly nuclear fears after the first use of an atomic weapon) and the threat of communist infiltration or invasion (Booker, 2001). Popular science fiction films like *The Day the Earth Stood Still* (1951) and *Invasion of the Body Snatchers* (1956) captured paranoia about alien beings who possessed powerful weapons and could arrive at any moment to destroy society and the state. The fear of communism and the concern about proliferation of destructive technology were embodied in otherworldly creatures who could enter a community undetected and crush resistance with deadly force.

Is the cultural proliferation of zombies a window into contemporary fears? Kyle W. Bishop (2010) writes that the rise of zombie popularity after traumatic societal events like the terrorist attacks on New York City and Washington, D.C., on September 11, 2001; the disease fears generated by deadly outbreaks of viruses like SARS; and even Hurricane Katrina is not a coincidence. Rather, zombie stories resonate with a public that is anxious about the threat of societal calamity, whether natural or human-made. Zombies evoke, Bishop (2009) suggests, a fear response, although the object of fear is not necessarily the zombie itself: "Because the aftereffects of war, terrorism, and natural disasters so closely resemble the scenarios of zombie cinema . . . [these films have] all the more power to shock and terrify a population that has become otherwise jaded by more traditional horror films" (p. 18).

In an entertainment publication article on *The Walking Dead*, the author observed that "there's a fascinating question critics should be answering: What is it about a show that is so relentlessly bleak that allows it to still resonate at such unexpected scale? What does it say about America? . . . it's the polar opposite of the escapist fare that typically serves as popular entertainment, a dystopian nightmare if there ever was one" (Wallenstein, 2014, para. 18). If critics don't have an answer, then sociologists might: Cultural products are more than just entertainment—they are a mirror of society. Popular culture in the form of films or television may capture our utopian dreams, but it is also a net that catches and reflects pervasive societal fears and anxieties. ■

In this chapter, we will consider the multitude of functions of culture and media, which is a key vehicle of culture, and we will seek to understand how culture both constructs and reflects society in the United States and around the globe. We begin our discussion with an examination of the basic concept of culture, taking a look at material and nonmaterial culture as well as ideal and real culture in the United States. We then explore contemporary issues of language and its social functions in a changing world. The chapter also addresses issues of culture and media, asking how media messages may reflect and affect behaviors and attitudes. We then turn to the topic of culture and class and the sociological question of whether culture and taste are linked to class identity and social reproduction. Finally, we examine the evolving relationship between global and local cultures, in particular, the influence of U.S. mass media on the world.

CULTURE: CONCEPTS AND APPLICATIONS

What is culture? The word "culture" might evoke images of song, dance, and literature—the beat of Latin salsa, Polish folk dances performed by girls with red ribbons braided into their hair, or the latest in a popular series of fantasy novels. It might remind you of a dish from the Old Country made by a beloved grandparent, or a spicy Indian meal you ate with friends from New Delhi.

Culture, from a sociological perspective, comprises *the beliefs, norms, behaviors, and products common to the members of a particular group.* Culture is integral to our social experience of the world. It offers diversion and entertainment, but it also helps form our identities and gives meaning to the artifacts and experiences of our lives. Culture shapes and permeates material objects like folk costumes, rituals like nuptial and burial ceremonies, and language as expressed in conversation, poetry, stories, and music. As social beings we make culture, but culture also makes us in ways that are both apparent and subtle.

Culture: The beliefs, norms, behaviors, and products common to the members of a particular group.

MATERIAL AND NONMATERIAL CULTURE

Every culture has both material and nonmaterial aspects. We can broadly define **material culture** as the *physical objects created, embraced, or consumed by society that help shape people's lives.* Material culture includes television programs, computer games, software, and other artifacts of human creation. It also emerges from the physical environment inhabited by the community. For example, in the countries surrounding the Baltic Sea, including Poland, Latvia, and Lithuania, amber—a substance created when the resin of fallen seaside pines is hardened and smoothed by decades or centuries in the salty waters—is an important part of local cultures. It is valued both for its decorative properties in jewelry and for its therapeutic properties; it is said to relieve pain. Amber has become a part of the material culture in these countries rather than elsewhere because it is a product of the physical environment in which these communities dwell.

Material culture also includes the types of shelters that characterize a community. For instance, in seaside communities, homes are often built on stilts to protect against flooding. The materials used to construct homes have historically been those available in the immediate environment—wood, thatch, or mud, for instance—although the global trade in timber, marble, granite, and other components of modern housing has transformed the relationship between place and shelter in many countries.

Nonmaterial culture is composed of the *abstract creations of human cultures, including ideas about behavior and living.* Nonmaterial culture encompasses aspects of the social experience, such as behavioral norms, values, language, family forms, and institutions. It also reflects the natural environment in which a culture has evolved.

Although material culture is concrete and nonmaterial culture is abstract, the two are intertwined: Nonmaterial culture may attach particular meanings to the objects of material culture. For example, people will go to great lengths to protect an object of material culture such as a national flag, not because of what it is—imprinted cloth—but because of the nonmaterial culture it represents, including ideals about freedom and patriotic pride. To grasp the full extent of nonmaterial culture, you must first understand three of the sociological concepts that shape it: *beliefs, norms,* and *values* (Table 3.1).

TABLE 3.1 Cultural Concepts and Characteristics

Concept	Characteristics
Values	General ideas about what is good, right, or just in a culture
Norms	Culturally shared rules governing social behavior ("oughts" and "shoulds")
Folkways	Conventions (or weak norms), the violation of which is not very serious
Mores	Strongly held norms, the violation of which is very offensive
Taboos	Very strongly held norms, the violation of which is highly offensive and even unthinkable
Laws	Norms that have been codified
Beliefs	Particular ideas that people accept as true

BELIEFS We broadly define **beliefs** as *particular ideas that people accept as true.* We can believe based on faith, superstition, science, tradition, or experience. To paraphrase the words of sociologists W. I. Thomas and D. S. Thomas (1928), beliefs may be understood as real when they are real in their consequences. They need not be objectively true. For example, during the witch hunts in early colonial America, rituals of accusation, persecution, and execution could be sustained in communities such as Salem, Massachusetts, because there was a shared belief in the existence of witches and diabolical power. From 1692 through 1693, more than 200 people were accused of practicing witchcraft; of these, 20 were executed, 19 by hanging and 1 by being pressed to death between heavy stones. Beliefs, like other aspects of culture, are dynamic rather than static: When belief in the existence of witchcraft waned, so did the witch hunts. In 1711, a bill was passed that restored "the rights and good names" of those who had been accused, and in 1957, the state of Massachusetts issued a formal apology for the events of the past (Blumberg, 2007).

NORMS In any culture, a set of ideas exists about what is right, just, and good, as well as about what is wrong and unjust. Norms, as we noted in Chapter 1, are *accepted social behaviors and beliefs,* or the common rules of a culture that govern the behavior of people belonging to that culture.

Material culture: The physical objects that are created, embraced, or consumed by society that help shape people's lives.

Nonmaterial culture: The abstract creations of human cultures, including language and social practices.

Beliefs: Particular ideas that people accept as true.

Todd Maisel/NY Daily News Archive via Getty Images

Many people find flag burning offensive because the flag, an object of material culture, is a symbol of the country and its ideals. The Supreme Court, however, has held in a series of cases that symbolic expression is protected by the First Amendment, which explicitly protects free speech.

Max Mumby/Indigo/Contributor/Getty Images

The marriage of James Matthews and Pippa Middleton in May 2017 captured worldwide attention. Celebrity weddings are often an object of intense public interest.

Sociologist Robert Nisbet (1970) writes, "The moral order of society is a kind of tissue of 'oughts': negative ones which forbid certain actions and positive ones which [require certain] actions" (p. 226). We can think of norms as representing a set of "oughts" and "ought nots" that guide behavioral choices such as where to stand relative to others in an elevator, how long to hold someone's gaze in conversation, how to conduct the rites of passage that mark different stages of life, and how to resolve disagreements or conflicts. Some norms are enshrined in legal statutes; others are inscribed in our psyches and consciences. Weddings bring together elements of both.

The wedding ceremony is a central ritual of adult life with powerful social, legal, and cultural implications. It is also significant economically: The term *wedding industrial complex* (Ingraham, 1999) has been used to describe a massive industry that generates over $72 billion in revenues and employs over a million people (IBISWorld, 2017). This comes as little surprise when we consider that in 2016, the estimated average amount spent on a wedding was just over $35,000 (Vasel, 2017). The wedding as a key cultural image and icon is cultivated in families, religions, and the media. Wedding images are used to sell products ranging from cosmetics to furniture, and weddings constitute an important theme in popular movies, including *My Big Fat Greek Wedding* (2002) and *My Big Fat Greek Wedding 2* (2016), *The Wedding Crashers* (2005), *Bridesmaids* (2011), and *Mike and Dave Need Wedding Dates* (2016). Popular television series such as *The Office, Sex and the City,* and *Nashville* have used weddings as narratives for highly anticipated season finales or premiers. Today, the reality program *Say Yes to the Dress* enthralls viewers with the drama of choosing a wedding gown and *Four Weddings* pits four brides against one another to pull off the "perfect wedding," while *90 Day Fiancé* follows long-distance couples who must decide whether or not to wed before the foreign partner's visa expires. The wedding ritual is a powerful artifact of our culture. In light of this, a sociologist might ask, "What are the cultural components of the ritual of entering matrimony, the wedding ceremony?"

Sociologist William Graham Sumner (1906–1959) distinguished among several different kinds of norms, each of which can be applied to weddings. **Folkways** are *fairly weak norms that are passed down from the past, the violation of which is generally not considered serious within a particular culture.* A folkway that has been part of many U.S. wedding rituals is the "giving away" of the bride: The father of the bride symbolically gives his daughter to the groom, signaling a change in the woman's identity from daughter to wife. Some couples

Folkways: Fairly weak norms that are passed down from the past, the violation of which is generally not considered serious within a particular culture.

Hopper Stone/ABC via Getty Images

In the years before the U.S. Supreme Court legalized same-sex marriage, public attitudes about marriage were shifting. According to one poll, watching television programs like *Modern Family*, which feature same-sex couples, made some viewers more likely to support same-sex marriage (Appelo, 2012).

FIGURE 3.1 Political Party Affiliation and Support for Social Welfare

Percent who agree that the government should . . .

Take care of people who can't take care of themselves

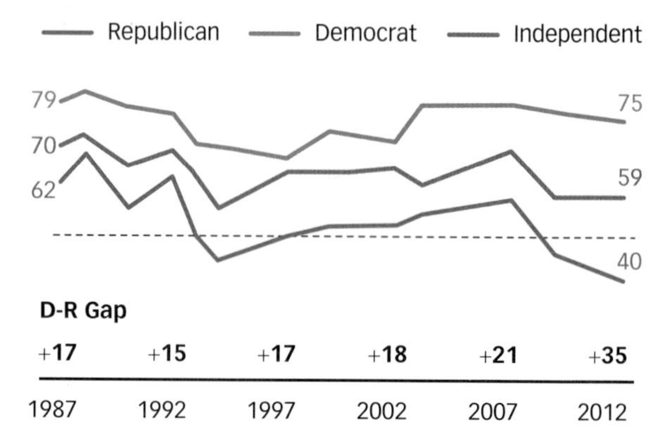

Help more needy people, even if it means going deeper in debt

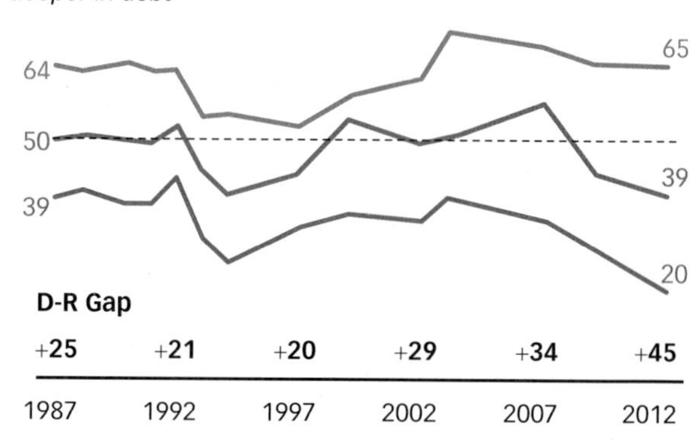

SOURCE: Pew Research Center, 2012.

today reject this ritual as patriarchal because it recalls earlier historical periods when a woman was treated as chattel given—literally—to her new husband by her previous keeper, her father.

Some modern couples are choosing to walk down the aisle together to signal an equality of roles and positions. Although the sight of a couple going to the altar together might raise a few eyebrows among more traditional guests, this violation of the "normal" way of doing things does not constitute a serious cultural transgression and, because culture is dynamic, may in time become a folkway itself.

Mores (pronounced "MOR-ays") are strongly held norms, the violation of which seriously offends the standards of acceptable conduct of most people within a particular culture. In a typical American wedding, the person conducting the ceremony plays an important role in directing the events, and the parties enacting the ritual are expected to respond in conventional ways. For instance, when the officiant asks the guests whether anyone objects to the union, the convention is for no one to object. When an objector surfaces (more often in television programs and films than in real life), the response of the guests is shock and dismay: The ritual has been disrupted and the scene violated.

Taboos are *powerful mores, the violation of which is considered serious and even unthinkable within a particular culture.* The label of taboo is commonly reserved for behavior that is extremely offensive: Incest, for example, is a nearly universal taboo. There may not be any taboos associated with the wedding ritual itself in the United States, but there are some relating to marital relationships. For instance, while in some U.S. states it is not illegal to marry a first cousin, in most modern communities, doing so violates a taboo against intermarriage in families.

Laws are *codified norms or rules of behavior.* Laws formalize and institutionalize society's norms. There are laws that govern marriage: For instance, until very recently, in many states, marriage was legally open only to heterosexual

Mores: Strongly held norms, the violation of which seriously offends the standards of acceptable conduct of most people within a particular culture.

Taboos: Powerful mores, the violation of which is considered serious and even unthinkable within a particular culture.

Laws: Codified norms or rules of behavior.

FIGURE 3.2 Political Party Affiliation and Attitude Toward Wealth and Poverty

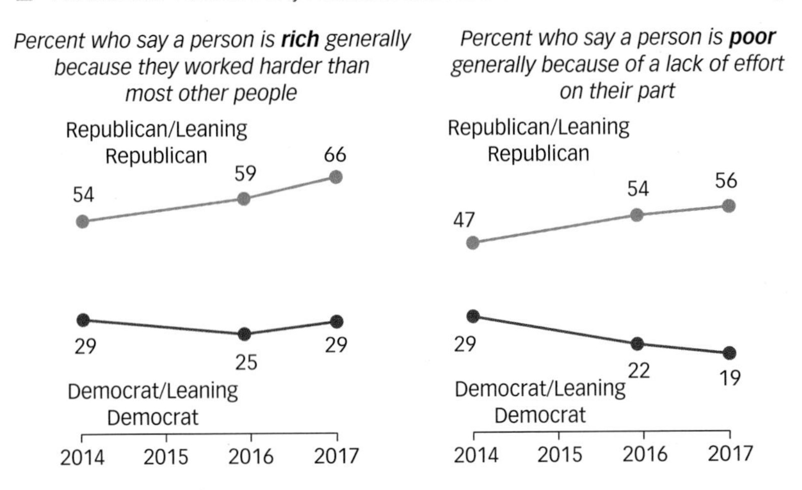

SOURCE: "Widening Gap Between Republicans and Democrats on Why People Are Rich And Poor," by the Pew Research Center, May 2, 2017 (www.pewresearch.org/fact-tank/2017/05/02/why-people-are-rich-and-poor-republicans-and-democrats-have-very-different-views/ft_17-05-02_richpoor_2/).

adults who are not already married to other people. In many respects, this was consistent with long-standing societal norms. Over time, however, the normative climate shifted and a majority of Americans expressed support for same-sex marriage. In June 2015, the Supreme Court of the United States ruled in *Obergefell v. Hodges* that state-level bans on same-sex marriage are not constitutional. Today, marriage is legally open to both heterosexual and homosexual couples, although there have been instances of county clerks in some states refusing to grant marriage licenses to same-sex couples because they claim it violates their beliefs.

VALUES Like norms, values are components of nonmaterial culture in every society. **Values** are *the abstract and general standards in society that define ideal principles, like those governing notions of right and wrong.* Sets of values attach to the institutions of society at multiple levels. You may have heard about national or patriotic values, community values, and family values. These can all coexist harmoniously within a single society. Because we use values to legitimate and justify our behavior as members of a country or community, or as individuals, we tend to staunchly defend the values we embrace (Kluckhohn & Strodtbeck, 1961).

Is there a specific set of values we can define as "American"? According to a classic study by Robin M. Williams Jr. (1970), "American values" include personal achievement, hard work, material comfort, and individuality. U.S. adults value science and technology, efficiency and practicality, morality and humanitarianism, equality, and "the American way of life." A joint 1998 study on American values by Harvard University, the *Washington Post,* and the Kaiser Family Foundation identified similar points—hard work, self-reliance, tolerance, and the embrace of equal rights—although respondents also voiced important disagreements about such issues as the ideal size of the U.S. government and the degree to which the government should promote economic equality (Kaiser Family Foundation, 1998).

Interestingly, researchers have identified a widening split in political values in the U.S. population, most acutely along partisan lines: That is, there are growing differences in expressed attitudes about issues ranging from social welfare to traditional family values. Although there are many shared values across race, gender, class, and other demographic characteristics, there are stark and growing differences along party lines. According to the Pew Research Center (2012), between 1987 and 2012, there was a dramatic split in the share of Republicans, Democrats, and independents who agreed that "the government should take care of people who can't take care of themselves" (see Figure 3.1). A more recent study suggests one possible explanation for this split: Republican respondents are likely to attribute poverty to "lack of effort," while their Democratic counterparts are more likely to attribute it to "circumstances beyond a person's control" (see Figure 3.2; Smith, 2017).

The 2012 Pew survey also asked respondents about values they attribute to others: Respondents were asked to indicate whether they believed that "in the last 10 years, values held by the middle class and poor people have gotten more similar, more different, or have had no change." About 47% of respondents said that they believed values between the social classes had gotten "more similar," while 41% suggested they had gotten "more different" (the remaining respondents indicated "no change" or "don't know"). Pew did not specify particular values. Hence, respondents were left to interpret the meaning of the question. How would you interpret this question on shifting values? How would you respond? How might we explain Pew's results?

Values: The general standards in society that define ideal principles, like those governing notions of right and wrong.

The "ugly step-sisters" Anastasia and Drizella from the story of Cinderella are just two of many children's story characters who combine an unattractive appearance with flawed personalities. How do we reconcile the idea that "beauty is only skin deep" with the images of popular culture? ■

Structural functionalists including Talcott Parsons (1951) have proposed that values play a critical role in the social integration of a society. Nevertheless, values do not play this role by themselves. They are abstract—vessels into which any generation or era pours its meanings in a process that can be both dynamic and contentious. For instance, equality is a value that has been strongly supported in the United States since the country's founding. The pursuit of equality was a powerful force in the American Revolution, and the Declaration of Independence declares that "all men are created equal" (Wood, 1993). Yet, equality has been defined differently across various eras of U.S. history. In the first half of the country's existence, "equality" did not include women or African Americans, who were by law excluded from its benefits. Over the course of the 20th century, equality became *more* equal as the rights of all citizens of the United States, regardless of race, gender, or class status, were formally recognized as equal before the law.

IDEAL AND REAL CULTURE IN U.S. SOCIETY

Beauty is only skin deep. Don't judge a book by its cover. All that glitters is not gold. These bits of common wisdom are part of U.S. culture. We rarely recall where we first heard them; we simply know them because they are part of the cultural framework of our lives. These three statements represent a commitment of sorts that society will value our inner qualities more than our outward appearances. They are also examples of **ideal culture**, *the values, norms, and behaviors that people in a given society profess to embrace,* even though the actions of the society may often contradict them.

Real culture consists of *the values, norms, and behaviors that people in a given society actually embrace and exhibit.* In the United States, for instance, empirical research shows that conventional attractiveness offers consistent advantages (Hamermesh, 2011). From childhood onward, the stories our parents, teachers, and the media tell us seem to sell the importance of beauty. Stories such as *Snow White, Cinderella,* and *Sleeping Beauty* connect beauty with morality and goodness, and unattractiveness with malice, jealousy, and other negative traits. The link between unattractive (or unconventional) appearance and unattractive behavior is unmistakable, especially in female figures. Think of other characters many American children are exposed to early in life, such as nasty Cruella de Vil in *101 Dalmatians,* the dastardly Queen of Hearts of *Alice in Wonderland,* and the angry octopod Ursula in *The Little Mermaid.*

On television, another medium that disseminates important cultural stories, physical beauty, and social status are powerfully linked. Overweight or average-looking characters populate television shows featuring working- or lower middle-class people, for example, *Family Guy* and *The Office.* Programs such as *Modern Family* and *Mike & Molly* offer leading characters who are pleasant and attractive—and often overweight. In the latter, for instance, Mike is a police officer and Molly is an elementary school teacher (she later becomes an author). They have not broken the glass ceiling of high-status jobs that remain largely reserved for their thinner prime-time peers. Characters such as those we encounter on *Scandal, Mad Men, Empire, House of Cards,* and *Sex and the City* are almost invariably svelte and stylish—and occupy higher rungs on the status hierarchy.

There is a clear **cultural inconsistency**, *a contradiction between the goals of ideal culture and the practices of real culture,* in our society's treatment of conventional attractiveness. Do we "judge a book by its cover"? Studies suggest this is precisely what many of us do in a variety of social settings:

- In the workplace, conventionally attractive job applicants appear to have an advantage in securing jobs (Hamermesh, 2011; Marlowe, Schneider,

Ideal culture: The values, norms, and behaviors that people in a given society profess to embrace.

Real culture: The values, norms, and behaviors that people in a given society actually embrace and exhibit.

Cultural inconsistency: A contradiction between the goals of ideal culture and the practices of real culture.

& Nelson, 1996; Shahani-Denning, 2003; Tews, Stafford, & Zhu, 2009). Women in one study who were an average of 65 pounds heavier than the norm of the study group earned about 7% less than their slimmer counterparts did, an effect equivalent to losing about one year of education or two years of experience. The link between obesity and a “pay penalty” has been confirmed by other studies (Harper, 2000; Lempert, 2007). Interestingly, some research has not found strong evidence that weight affects the wages of African American or Hispanic female workers (Cawley, 2001; DeBeaumont, 2009).

- In the courtroom, some defendants who do not meet conventional standards of attractiveness are disadvantaged (DeSantis & Kayson, 1997; Gunnell & Ceci, 2010; Taylor & Butcher, 2007). Mazzella and Feingold (1994) note that defendants charged with certain crimes, such as rape and robbery, benefit from being attractive. This is consistent with the “beautiful is good” hypothesis (Dion, Berscheid, & Walster, 1972), which attributes a tendency toward leniency to the belief that attractive people have more socially desirable characteristics. Ahola, Christianson, and Hellstrom (2009) suggest that female defendants in particular are advantaged by attractive appearance.
- Studies of college students have found that they are likely to perceive attractive people as more intelligent than unattractive people (Chia, Allred, Grossnickle, & Lee, 1998; Poteet, 2007). This bias has also been detected in students’ evaluations of their instructors: A pair of economists found that the independent influence of attractiveness gives some instructors an advantage on undergraduate teaching evaluations (Hamermesh & Parker, 2005).
- Social media is routinely used to shame both public and private figures who do not “fit” the mold of conventional body acceptability. For example, after hosting a 2012 presidential debate on television, veteran CNN correspondent Candy Crowley was mocked on Twitter with comments about her weight. In 2013, Buzzfeed reported that a blog called Return of Kings sponsored a “fat shaming week” on Twitter (Okun, 2013). In 2016, Facebook rejected an ad featuring plus-size model Tess Holliday wearing a modest bikini, arguing that it violated the company’s “health and fitness policy” for ads. Facebook later apologized (Hillin, 2016).

CBS Photo Archive/Contributor/Getty Images

ABC Photo Archives/Contributor/Getty Images

The Granger Collection, NYC — All rights reserved.

Mike and Molly, *Roseanne*, and *The Honeymooners* are examples of sitcoms that feature main characters who are working-class people who also happen to be overweight. The next time you’re flipping through the channels or watching a movie, take note of the relationship between socioeconomic status and appearance.

Another example of cultural inconsistency can be seen in our purported commitment to the ideal that “honesty is the best policy.” We find an unambiguous embrace of

Media, Markets, and the Culture of Thinness in America

Whether you are male or female, you may sometimes experience feelings of inadequacy as you leaf through magazines like *Cosmopolitan, GQ,* and *Vogue* or follow your favorite celebrities on Instagram. You may get a sense that, in this media-constructed universe, your face, hair, body, and clothing do not fit the masculine or feminine ideal. You may wish that you had the "right look" or that you were thinner. You would not be alone.

REUTERS/Fred Prouser

This billboard in Hollywood, California, features excessively thin models. The models are selling clothing, but they are also sending a message to viewers about thinness and glamour. How significant is this message in U.S. culture? What might be its consequences?

One survey of college-age women found that 83% desired to lose weight. Among these, 44% of women of normal weight intentionally ate less than they wanted, and most of the women did not have healthy dieting habits (Malinauskas, Raedeke, Aeby, Smith, & Dallas, 2006). A study examining the characteristics of college students who identify themselves as underweight or about the right weight, but still report trying to lose weight, found that "individuals who perceive themselves as under- or about the right weight and also indicate that they are trying to lose weight are more likely to be female, in a fraternity/sorority, and have a lower BMI" (Latimer, Velazquez, & Pasch, 2013, p. 256). According to a Canadian study, chronic dieters' sense of identity is often frail and reflects others' perceptions of them (Polivy & Herman, 2007). Indeed, a study examining body weight perceptions among college students found that women with exaggerated body weight perceptions were more likely to engage in unhealthy weight management strategies and were more depressed than those women with accurate perceptions of their weight (Harring, Montgomery, & Hardin, 2011).

Using our sociological imagination, we can deduce that the weight concerns many people experience as personal troubles are in fact linked to public issues: Worrying about (and even obsessing over) weight is a widely shared phenomenon. Millions of women diet regularly, and some manifest extreme attention to weight in the form of eating disorders. By one estimate, fully 9 million people in the United States are afflicted with eating disorders over the courses of their lives (Hudson, Hiripi, Pope, & Kessler, 2007), most of them women. The National Institute of Mental Health (2010) has reported that "women are three times as likely to experience anorexia (0.9 percent of women vs. 0.3 percent of men) and bulimia (1.5 percent of women vs. 0.5 percent of men) during their life. They are also 75 percent more likely to have a binge eating disorder (3.5 percent of women vs. 2.0 percent of men)."

The U.S. diet industry remains highly profitable, taking in an estimated $64 billion in 2014, although it has seen some contraction as a result of greater consumer interest in fresh food over processed food and diet drinks (Kell, 2015). The fashion industry (among others) primarily employs models who are abnormally thin and whose images are airbrushed or digitally altered to "perfection." Psychologist Sarah Grogan (2008) asserts that the dieting, fashion, cosmetic surgery, and advertising industries are fueled by the successful manipulation and oppression of women. That is, manufacturers and marketers create a beauty culture based on total but artificial perfection and then sell products to "help" women achieve a look that is unachievable.

As individuals, we experience the consequences of this artificially created ideal as a personal trouble—unhappiness about our appearance—but the deliberate construction and dissemination of an unattainable ideal for the purpose of generating profits is surely a public issue. Reflecting a conflict perspective, psychologist Sharlene Hesse-Biber (1997) has suggested that to understand the eating disorders and disordered eating so common among U.S. women, we ought to ask not "'What can women do to meet the ideal?' but 'Who benefits from women's excessive concern with thinness?'" (p. 32). This is the sociological imagination at work.

THINK IT THROUGH

- How would you summarize key factors that explain the broad gap between ideal culture, which entreats us not to judge a book by its cover, and real culture, which pushes women and men to pursue unattainable physical perfection?

honesty in the stories of our childhood. Think of *Pinocchio*: Were you warned as a child not to lie because it might cause your nose to grow? Did you ever promise a friend that you would not reveal his or her secret with a pinky swear and the words "Cross my heart and hope to die; stick a needle in my eye"? Yet most people do lie.

Why is this so? We may lie to protect or project a certain image of ourselves. Sociologist Erving Goffman (1959), a symbolic interactionist, called this *misrepresentation*. Goffman argued that all of us, as social actors, engage in this practice because we are concerned with "defining a situation"—whether it be a date or a job interview or a meeting with a professor or boss—in a manner favorable to ourselves. It is not uncommon for job seekers to pad their résumés, for instance, to leave the impression on potential employers that they are qualified or worthy. A CareerBuilder survey recently found that about 56% of employers had detected lying on a résumé. Common lies included misrepresentations of educational credentials, skill sets, dates of employment, and prior job responsibilities. According to the same survey, about 70% of employers spend under 5 minutes reviewing a résumé and half spend less than 2 minutes (CareerBuilder, 2015), suggesting that some dishonesty probably goes unnoticed. Lying in politics is so common that the *Washington Post* newspaper features a near-daily "fact checker" that rates statements with zero to four "Pinocchios" for veracity, and the Internet is home to a variety of sites like Politifact.com that are solely devoted to evaluating statements on the "Truth-O-Meter."

Studies also suggest that cheating and plagiarism are common among high school students (Table 3.2). In one study of 23,000 high school students, about half reported that they had cheated on a test in the past year. Just under a third also responded that they had used the Internet to plagiarize assigned work (Josephson Institute Center for Youth Ethics, 2012). Interestingly, a 2009 study suggests that about half of teens age 17 and younger believe cheating is necessary for success (Josephson Institute of Ethics, 2009).

TABLE 3.2 Ethical and Unethical Behavior Among High School Students in 2012 (in percentages)

	Never	Once	Two or More Times
Copied an Internet document for a class assignment	45	26	29
Cheated on a test	49	24	28
Lied to a teacher about something significant	45	26	29

SOURCE: Josephson Institute Center for Youth Ethics. (2012). *2012 Report Card on the Ethics of American Youth.*

Why do you think there is such a big gap between what we say and what we do? Do you think most people are culturally inconsistent? What about you?

ETHNOCENTRISM

Much of the time, a community's or society's cultural norms, values, and practices are internalized to the point where they become part of the natural order. Sociologist Pierre Bourdieu (1977) describes these internalized beliefs as **doxic**: *To a member of a given community or cultural group, common norms and practices appear as a part of the social order—just the way things are.* But the social organization of our lives is not natural, although it comes to appear that way. Instead, norms, values, and practices are *socially constructed.* That is, they are the products of decisions and directions chosen by groups and individuals (often, a conflict theorist would argue, those with the most power). And although all human societies share certain similarities, different societies construct different norms, values, and practices and then embrace them as "just the way things are."

Because we tend to perceive our own culture as "natural" and "normal," it emerges as the standard by which we tend to judge everything else. This is indicative of ethnocentrism, which, as noted in Chapter 1, is *a worldview whereby we judge other cultures by the standards of our own.* That which deviates from our own "normal" social order can appear exotic, even shocking. Other societies' rituals of death, for example, can look astonishingly different from those to which we are accustomed. This description of an ancient burial practice from the North Caucasus provides an illustration:

> Scythian-Sarmatian burials were horrible but spectacular. A royal would be buried in a *kurgan* [burial mound] alongside piles of gold, weapons, horses, and, Herodotus writes, "various members of his household: one of his concubines, his butler, his cook, his groom, his steward, and his chamberlain—all of them strangled." A year later, 50 fine horses and 50 young men would be strangled, gutted, stuffed with chaff, sewn up, then impaled and stuck around the *kurgan* to mount a ghoulish guard for their departed king. (Smith, 2001, pp. 33–34)

Let's interpret this historical fragment using two different cultural perspectives. From an **etic perspective**—that is, *the perspective of the outside observer*—the burial ritual looks bizarre and shockingly cruel. Nevertheless, to understand it fully and avoid a potentially ethnocentric perspective, we need to call on an **emic perspective**, *the perspective of the insider,* and ask, "What did people in this period believe about the royals? What did they believe about the departed and the experience of death itself? What did they believe about the utility of material riches in the afterlife and the rewards the afterlife would confer on the royals and those loyal to them?" Are there death rituals in the U.S. cultural repertoire that might appear exotic or strange to outsiders even though we see them as "normal"?

Putting aside the ethnocentric perspective allows us to embrace **cultural relativism**, a worldview whereby we understand the practices of another society sociologically, in terms of that society's own norms and values and not our own. In this way we can come closer to an understanding of cultural beliefs and practices such as those that surround the end of life. Whether the body of the departed is viewed or hidden, buried or burned, feasted with or feasted for, danced around or sung about, a culturally relativist perspective allows the sociologist to conduct his or her examination of the roots of these practices most rigorously.

We may also call on cultural relativism to help us understand the rituals of another people, the Nacirema, described here by anthropologist Herbert Miner (1956):

> Nacirema culture is characterized by a highly developed market economy which has evolved in a rich natural habitat. Although much of the people's time is devoted to economic pursuits, a large part of the fruits of these labors and a considerable portion of the day are spent in ritual activity. The focus of this activity is the human body, the appearance and health of which loom as a dominant concern in the ethos of the people. . . .
>
> The fundamental belief underlying the whole system appears to be that the human body is ugly and that its tendency is to debility and disease. Incarcerated in such a body, man's only hope is to avert these characteristics through the use of powerful influences of ritual and ceremony. Every household has one or more shrines devoted to this

Doxic: Taken for granted as "natural" or "normal" in society.

Etic perspective: The perspective of the outside observer.

Emic perspective: The perspective of the insider, the one belonging to the cultural group in question.

Cultural relativism: A worldview whereby the practices of a society are understood sociologically in terms of that society's norms and values, and not the norms and values of another society.

Luciano Lepre/AGF/UIG via Getty Images

SONNY TUMBELAKA/AFP/GETTY IMAGES

Bob Sacha/Corbis Documentary/Getty Images

In the Tibetan sky burial, the body is left on a mountaintop exposed to the elements. This once-common practice of "giving alms to the birds" represented belief in rebirth and the idea that the body is just an unneeded empty shell. In Indonesia, mass cremations take place where bodies are placed in sarcophagi of various sizes with animal representations. In New Orleans, a casket is paraded through the street. Death and burial rituals are components of culture.

> purpose. The more powerful individuals in this society have several shrines in their houses. . . .
>
> The focal point of the shrine is a box or chest which is built into the wall. In this chest are kept many charms and magical potions without which no native believes he could live. These preparations are secured from a variety of specialized practitioners. . . . However, the medicine men do not provide the curative potions for their clients, but decide what the ingredients should be and then write them down in an ancient and secret language. This writing is understood only by the medicine men and by the herbalists who, for another gift, provide the required charm. (pp. 503–504)

What looks strange here, and why? Did you already figure out that *Nacirema* is *American* spelled backward? Miner invites his readers to see American rituals linked to the body and health not as natural but as *part of a culture.* Can you think of other norms or practices in the United States that we could view from this perspective? What about the all-American game of baseball, the high school graduation ceremony, the language of texting, or the cultural obsession with celebrities or automobiles?

SUBCULTURES

When sociologists study culture, they do not presume that in any given country—or even community—there is a single culture. They may identify a dominant culture within any group, but significant cultural identities exist in addition to, or sometimes in opposition to, the dominant one. These are **subcultures**, *cultures that exist together with a dominant culture but differ from it in some important respects.*

Subcultures: Cultures that exist together with a dominant culture but differ in some important respects from that dominant culture.

Some subcultures, including ethnic subcultures, may embrace most of the values and norms of the dominant culture while simultaneously choosing to preserve the values, rituals, and languages of their (or their parents' or grandparents') cultures of origin. Members of ethnic subcultures such as Armenian Americans and Cuban Americans may follow political events in their heritage countries or prefer their children to marry within their groups. It is comfort in the subculture rather than rejection of the dominant culture that supports the vitality of many ethnic subcultures.

In a few cases, however, ethnic and other subcultures do reject the dominant culture surrounding them. The Amish choose to elevate tradition over modernity in areas such as transportation (many still use horse-drawn buggies), occupations (they rely on simple farming), and family life (women are seen as subordinate to men), and they lead a *retreatist* lifestyle in which their community is intentionally separated from the dominant culture.

Sociologists sometimes also use the term *counterculture* to designate subcultural groups whose norms, values, and practices deviate from those of the dominant culture. The hippies of the 1960s, for example, are commonly cited as a counterculture to mainstream "middle America," although many of those who participated in hippie culture aged into fairly conventional middle-class lives.

Even though there are exceptions, most subcultures in the United States are permeated by the dominant culture, and the influence runs both ways. What, for example, is an "all-American" meal? Your answer may be a hamburger and fries. But what about other U.S. staples, such as Chinese takeout and Mexican burritos? Mainstream culture has also absorbed the influence of the United States' multicultural heritage: Salsa music, created by Cuban and Puerto Rican American musicians in 1960s New York, is widely popular, and world music, a genre that reflects a range of influences from the African continent to Brazil, has a broad United States following. Some contemporary pop music, as performed by artists such as Lady Gaga, incorporates elements of British glam, U.S. hip-hop, and central European dance. The influence is apparent in sports as well: Soccer, now often the youth game of choice in U.S. suburbs, was popularized by players and fans from South America and Europe. Mixed martial arts, a combat sport popularized by the U.S. organization Ultimate Fighting Championship, incorporates elements of Greco-Roman wrestling, Japanese karate, Brazilian jujitsu, and muay Thai (from Thailand).

CULTURE AND LANGUAGE

Well over a billion people on our planet speak a dialect of Chinese as their first language. English and Spanish are the first languages of another 300 million people each. More than 182 million people speak Hindi, the primary official language of India, as a first language. In contrast, the world's 3,500 least widely spoken languages share just 8.25 million speakers. Aka, another language of India, has between 1,000 and 2,000 native speakers. The Mexican language of Seri has between 650 and 1,000. Euchee, a Native American language, has four fluent speakers left. According to an article in *National Geographic,* "one language dies every 14 days," and we can expect to lose about half the 7,000 languages spoken around the world by the end of the 21st century (Rymer, 2012). What is the significance of language loss for human culture?

Symbols, like the names we assign to the objects around us, are *cultural representations of social realities* or, as we put it in Chapter 1, representations of things that are not immediately present to our senses. They may take the form of letters or words, images, rituals, or actions. When we use language, we imbue these symbols with meaning. **Language** is *a symbolic system, composed of verbal, nonverbal, and sometimes written representations that are vehicles for conveying meaning.* Language is thus a key vehicle of culture.

In the 1930s, Edward Sapir and Benjamin Whorf developed the *Sapir–Whorf hypothesis,* which posits that our understandings and actions emerge from language—that is, the words and concepts of our own languages structure our perceptions of the social world. Language is also closely tied to cultural objects and practices. Consider that the Aka language has more than 26 words to describe beads, a rich vocabulary suited for a culture in which beads not only are decorative objects but also convey status and facilitate market transactions. In the Seri language, to inquire where someone is from you ask, "Where is your placenta buried?" This question references a historical cultural practice of burying a newborn's afterbirth by covering it with sand, rocks, and ashes (Rymer, 2012).

As languages like Aka and Seri die out, usually replaced by dominant tongues like Spanish, English, Chinese, Arabic, and Russian, we lose the opportunity to more fully

Language: A system of symbolic verbal, nonverbal, and written representations rooted within a particular culture.

■ **FIGURE 3.3** Endangered Languages Worldwide

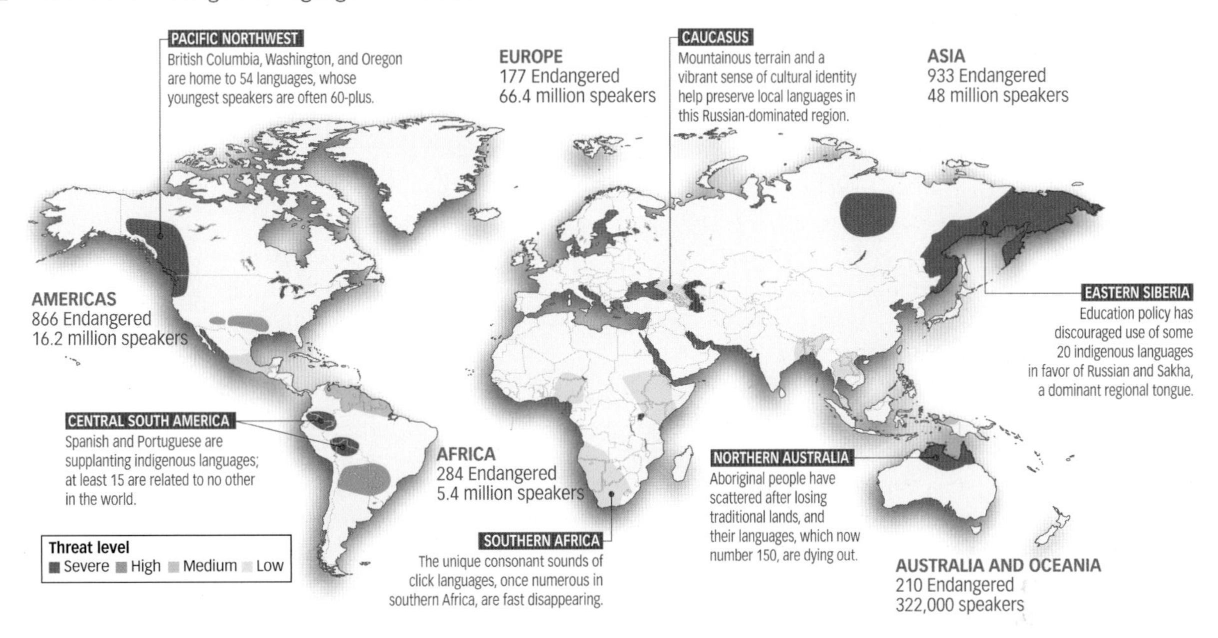

SOURCE: Mason, Virginia W. National Geographic Creative. Reprinted with permission.

understand the historical and contemporary human experience and the natural world (see Figure 3.3). For instance, the fact that some small languages have no words linked to specific numbers and instead use only relative designations like "few" or "many" opens the possibility that our number system may be a product of culture rather than of innate cognition as many believe. Or consider that the Seri culture, based in the Sonoran Desert, has names for animal species that describe behaviors that natural scientists are only beginning to document (Rymer, 2012). Language is a cultural vehicle that enables communication, illuminates beliefs and practices, roots a community in its environment, and contributes to the cultural richness of our world. Each language lost represents the erasure of cultural history, knowledge, and human diversity (Living Tongues Institute for Endangered Languages, n.d.).

LANGUAGE AND SOCIAL INTEGRATION

Conflict theorists focus on disintegrative forces in society, while functionalists study integrative forces. Where social conflict theorists see culture as serving the interests of the elite, functionalists argue that shared values and norms maintain social bonds both between individuals and between people and society (Parsons & Smelser, 1956). By serving as a vehicle for the dissemination of these values and norms, culture functions to keep society stable and harmonious and gives people a sense of belonging in a complex, even alienating, social world (Smelser, 1962). To illustrate, consider the issue of language use in the United States.

In part as a response to the increased use of Spanish and other languages spoken by members of the nation's large immigrant population, an English-only movement has arisen that supports the passage of legislation to make English the only official language of the United States and its government. Proponents argue that they want to "restore the great American melting pot," although the movement has roots in the early 20th century, when President Theodore Roosevelt wrote, "We have room for but one language in this country, and that is the English language, for we intend to see that the crucible turns our people out as Americans . . . and not as dwellers in a polyglot boarding house." Like today, Roosevelt's era was characterized by high rates of immigration to the United States.

How would a functionalist analyze the English-only movement? He or she might highlight language as a vehicle of social integration and a form of social glue. Indeed, the English-only movement focuses on the function of language as an integrative mechanism. For example, the organization ProEnglish states on its website (www.proenglish.org),

FIGURE 3.4 Percentage of U.S. Population Speaking a Language Other Than English at Home, 2010*

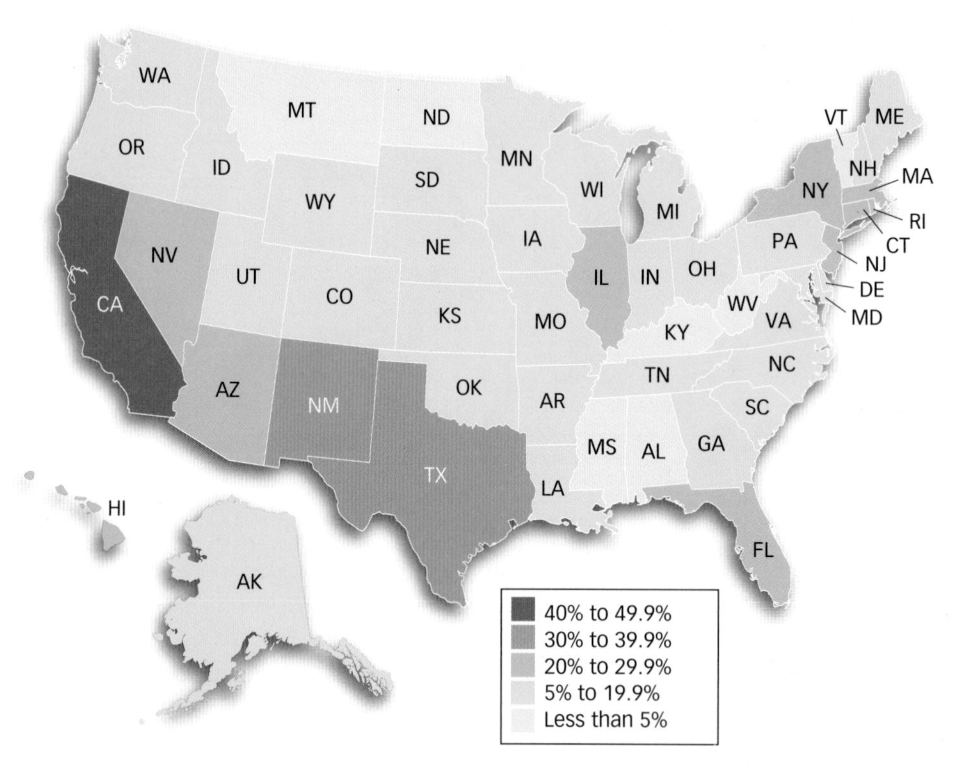

SOURCE: U.S. Census Bureau. (2010). "Population 5 Years and Older Who Spoke a Language Other Than English at Home by Hispanic Origin and Race: 2009." *American Community Survey Briefs.*

*Most recent data available.

"We work through the courts and in the court of public opinion to defend English's historic role as America's common, unifying language, and to persuade lawmakers to adopt English as the official language at all levels of government." The organization points out that 31 U.S. states have legislation declaring English the official language. From this perspective, the use of different primary languages in a single country is dysfunctional to the extent that it undermines the common socialization that comes from a shared language and culture.

A substantial proportion of U.S. residents support legislation making English the official language: A 2014 Huffington Post/YouGov survey found that 70% of respondents agreed with this position (Swanson, 2014). At the same time, most homes and residents are already active users of English even if one fifth also use another home language. Interestingly, a 2013 Gallup poll found that about half of respondents agreed that it is "essential" (20%) or "important" (50%) for Americans to learn a second language, although only about a third are conversant in a second language (Jones, 2013).

Many people embrace cultural diversity and emphasize the value of **multiculturalism**, *a commitment to respecting cultural differences rather than submerging them into a larger, dominant culture.* Multiculturalism recognizes that the country is as likely to be enriched by its differences as it is to be divided by them. In a globalizing world, knowledge of other cultures and proficiency in languages other than English is important. In fact, a functionalist might also regard the U.S. Census data cited above as indicative of *both* the common language that proponents of official English see as crucial to national unity and the cultural diversity that enriches the country and allows it to incorporate a variety of languages in its national and global political, cultural, and economic dealings—which is also positively functional for the country (Figure 3.4).

Multiculturalism: A commitment to respecting cultural differences rather than trying to submerge them into a larger, dominant culture.

CULTURE AND MASS MEDIA

From a sociological perspective, we are all *cultured* because we all participate in and identify with a culture or cultures. In one conventional use of the term, however, some classes of people are considered *more cultured* than others. We refer to people who attend the symphony, are knowledgeable about classic literature and fine wines, and possess a set of distinctive manners as cultured, and we often assume a value judgment in believing that being cultured is better than being uncultured.

We commonly distinguish between high culture and popular culture. **High culture** consists of *music, theater, literature, and other cultural products that are held in particularly high esteem in society.* It can also encompass a particular body of literature or a set of distinctive tastes. High culture is usually associated with the wealthier, more educated classes in society, but this association can shift over time. William Shakespeare's plays were popular with the English masses when they were staged in open public theaters during his lifetime. Lobster was a meal of the poor in colonial America. This suggests that high culture's association with educated and upper income elites may be more a function of accessibility—the prohibitive cost of theater tickets and lobster meat today, for instance—than with "good taste" as such.

Popular culture encompasses *the entertainment, culinary, and athletic tastes shared by the masses.* It is more accessible than high culture because it is widely available and less costly to consume. Popular culture can include music that gets broad airplay on the radio, television shows and characters that draw masses of viewers (for example, *The Walking Dead, Game of Thrones, Lost,* and *Homeland*), blockbuster films such as the *Hunger Games, X-Men,* or *Captain America* series, Oprah's Book Club, and spectator sports such as professional wrestling and baseball. Because it is an object of mass consumption, popular culture plays a key role in shaping values, attitudes, and consumption in society. It is an optimal topic of sociological study because, as we noted in our opening story about zombies, it not only *shapes* but also *is shaped by* society.

Mass media are *media of public communication intended to reach and influence a mass audience.* The mass media constitute a vehicle that brings us culture, in particular—although certainly not exclusively—popular culture. Although mass media permeate our lives today, their rise is more recent than we may realize. Theorist Jürgen Habermas (1962/1989) points out that the *public sphere* as a fundamental part of social life emerged only with the rise of industrial society; that is, prior to the development of printing presses and the spread of literacy, most communication was oral and local. The appearance of mass-circulation newspapers in the 1700s and the growth of literate populations spurred the growth of a public sphere in which information could be widely circulated and, as Habermas points out, public attitudes shaped. In the 20th century, mass media gained influence through the adoption of electronic means of communication ranging from the radio to television to the Internet.

Marshall McLuhan (1964) sought to understand the influence of mass media on society, suggesting that "the medium is the message"—that is, the medium itself has an influence on how the message is received and perceived. Television, for instance, is fundamentally different from print in how it communicates information. In looking at only a particular message, in other words, we may miss the power of the messenger itself and how that transforms social life. McLuhan also asserted that electronic media like television were constructing a *global village* in which people around the world, who did not and never would know one another, could be engaged with the same news event. For example, it was reported by FIFA, the world's governing body of soccer, that in the summer of 2014, more than a billion people (about a seventh of the world's population) tuned in for the final game between Germany and Argentina (Associated Press, 2015).

From a sociological perspective, the function of the mass media can be paradoxical. On the one hand, mass media are powerful and effective means for conveying information and contributing to the development of an informed citizenry: Mass-circulation newspapers, television networks like CNN and BBC, and radio news programs inform us about and help us understand important issues. On the other hand, some sociologists argue that mass media promote not active engagement in society but rather disengagement and distraction. Habermas (1962/1989), for instance, writes of the salons and coffeehouses of major European cities, where the exchange of informed opinions formed a foundation for later public

High culture: The music, theater, literature, and other cultural products that are held in particularly high esteem in society.

Popular culture: The entertainment, culinary, and athletic tastes shared by the masses.

Mass media: Media of public communication intended to reach and influence a mass audience.

Language, Resistance, and Power in Northern Ireland

Jim Richardson/National Geographic Creative

This chapter raises the problem of language loss—that is, the persistent and expanding extinction of small languages across our planet. In a few places, however, little-used languages are being revived for reasons that range from cultural to economic to political. In some instances, as in the case of Northern Ireland, language revival fits into all three categories.

The dominant language in the country of Northern Ireland has long been English, but there is a growing campaign to revive the Irish language, a tongue with little in common with English (consider the Irish word for independence: *neamhspleáchas*). The Irish language (also known as Irish Gaelic or *Gaeilge*) is a minority language in Northern Ireland. As of the country's 2001 census, 167,487 people (10.4% of the population) had "some knowledge of Irish" (Zenker, 2010). The use of Irish in Northern Ireland had nearly died out by the middle of the 20th century, but today efforts are under way to bring the language back to education, commerce, and political life ("In the trenches," 2013).

Northern Ireland has a history of violent conflict with its British neighbor. Early in the 20th century, Ireland was shaken by conflict between the Irish Catholic majority and the Protestant minority, who supported British rule and feared the rule of the Catholic majority. In 1920, the British Parliament passed the Government of Ireland Act, which sought to pacify the parties with the separation of Ireland into a free state of southern counties. In 1922, the larger part of Ireland seceded from the United Kingdom to become the independent Irish Free State (after 1937, this became the current state of Ireland). The six northeastern counties, together known as Northern Ireland, remained within the United Kingdom. Northern Ireland has since been the site of sporadic conflict between (mainly Catholic) nationalists and (mainly Protestant) unionists (Kennedy-Pipe, 1997).

The area remained largely peaceful until the late 1960s, when violence broke out in Londonderry and Belfast, foreshadowing three decades of armed conflict between British troops stationed in Northern Ireland and the rebellious Irish Republican Army (IRA), which represented primarily the interests of the Irish Catholic population. The violent conflicts over home versus British rule, which included terrorism committed by the IRA against British interests and populations, resulted in more than 3,000 deaths in this period (BBC, 2014b). A U.S.-brokered agreement helped to quell the violence in 1998, though sporadic problems remained. Nearly a decade later, in 2007, key parties to the conflict, including leaders of the Catholic and Protestant factions, took the reins of the country in a power-sharing agreement.

The interest in revival of the language dates back to the period of conflict, known locally as "the Troubles." In the 1960s, a small number of language enthusiasts set up a tiny Irish-speaking community in a Belfast neighborhood. By the 1970s, with the conflict in progress, Irish nationalist prisoners being held by the British in Maze Prison also began learning Irish, calling out words between cells and scrawling their words on the prison walls (Feldman, 1991). The effort spread to neighborhoods where families of the prisoners resided and, according to author Feargal Mac Ionnrachtaigh (2013), it became part of an "anti-colonial struggle."

Today, Irish nationalists, some of them veterans of the war against British rule, have taken up the mantle of Irish language revival, and the language is now the medium of instruction for about 5,000 schoolchildren in the country. Although this is just a tiny fraction of the total school population, supporters of language revival occupy some key governmental positions in Northern Ireland, and there has been an effort to enact the Irish Language Act, which would establish new rights to the use of the language in official business, thus creating new job opportunities for fluent speakers ("In the trenches," 2013).

Today Northern Ireland is peaceful. The Irish language, a part of the local heritage, is being revived. It remains to be seen, however, whether this will serve to draw together two communities with a long history of conflict (the country is about evenly split between the Catholic and Protestant communities) or will deepen the divide as the nationalist Catholic population embraces Irish while the pro-British Protestants resist.

THINK IT THROUGH

- Why does language matter to communities large and small? What does the Irish language revival movement share with movements like the official English movement in the United States, which supports a powerful and widespread language? How is it different?

political debates. He suggests, however, that the potential for the development of an active public sphere has been largely quashed by the rise of media that have substituted mass entertainment for meaningful debate, elevating sound bites over sound arguments.

Douglas Kellner (1990) has written that modern technology and media—and television in particular—constitute a threat to human freedom of thought and action in the realm of social change. Kellner suggests that the television industry "has the crucial ideological functions of legitimating the capitalist mode of production and delegitimating its opponents" (p. 9). That is, mainstream television appears to offer a broad spectrum of opinions, but in fact it systematically excludes opinions that seem to question the fundamental values of capitalism (for example, the right to accumulate unlimited wealth and power) or to critique not individual politicians, parties, and policies but the system within which they operate. Because television is such a pervasive force in our lives, the boundaries it draws around debates on capitalism, social change, and genuine democracy are significant.

Karl Marx wrote that the ruling ideas of any society are those of the ruling class. Arguably, many of those ideas are conveyed through television. Does television, which delivers images and messages to our homes as we watch for an average of 7 hours a day, foster passivity and make us vulnerable to manipulation? What about the Internet? How does it expand human creativity, freedom, and action? How does it limit them?

The mass media bring us the key forms of modern entertainment that constitute popular culture. Although some researchers theorize the effects of mass media on the public sphere, others look at how these media shape attitudes and practices—sometimes in negative ways. In the section that follows, we turn our attention to another dimension of culture: the controversial relationship between culture, mass media, and the negative but pervasive phenomenon of sexual violence against women.

Music, Money, and Marketing

Tomas/IMAGES/Getty Images

William Shakespeare famously wrote that "if music be the food of love, play on." Bono, the lead singer of the globally recognized pop group U2, has said that "music can change the world because it can change people," a sentiment echoed by renowned guitarist Jimi Hendrix, who asserted that "music doesn't lie. If there is something to be changed in this world, then it can only happen through music." Indeed, music is widely seen as a salve for emotional wounds (Michael Jackson called it "a mantra that soothes the soul"), a soundtrack for real-life romance and heartbreak, a vehicle of release from stress, and even a carrier of powerful messages of societal transformation.

But music today is also a significant marketing tool, and a report in *The Atlantic Monthly* magazine (Brennan, 2015) points out that more brands are paying for product placement in pop songs. The article quotes Adam Kluger, CEO of the Kluger Agency, which specializes in "lyrical product placements," as saying that a brand placement in a hit single "can easily offset the entire production and marketing budget" for the song (p. 40). Brand references in music are growing. According to William Brennan's calculation, these references appeared 109 times in the top 30 *Billboard* songs in 2012 compared with 47 times in 2002—and zero times in 1962. The popular song "I am the one," by DJ Khalid featuring Justin Bieber, Chance The Rapper, Lil Wayne, and Quavo references two fashion brands ("Chanel" and "Gucci"). The song also talks about "Netflix." Similarly, in "Closer," the Chainsmokers, a DJ duo, sing to their love interest, asking her to meet "in the backseat of (her) Rover."

Product placement may be even more overt: Justin Bieber's 2016 *Purpose* world tour featured backup dancers outfitted in Calvin Klein apparel, as well as video footage of the singer from his global advertising campaign with Calvin Klein (Business Wire, 2016). The merger between the pop culture icon and the brand was further underscored in Bieber's tweets, which featured him posing in #mycalvins and earning the admiration of his legion of fans.

The melding of advertising and culture is a topic in which sociologists have taken an interest. Critical theorists Theodor Adorno and Max Horkheimer (Horkheimer, 1947; Horkheimer & Adorno, 1944/2007) write of the "culture industry." They distinguish between *culture*, which, they suggest, retains the potential to be a vehicle for creativity, critique, and social change, and the *culture industry*, which encompasses mass culture and its creation and distribution. By contrast to culture, the culture industry "aborts and silences criticism" (Bottomore, 2002, p. 19) and engages in a "mass deception" by manufacturing homogenized, predictable, and banal cultural products that function to pacify and sell rather than inform and provoke. Indeed, the two theorists judge the culture industry to be one that promises an "escape from reality but it really offers an escape from the last thought of resisting that reality" (Horkheimer & Adorno, 1944/2007, p. 116). The road to happiness, as told by the culture industry, is through consumption and conformity. The magic (or deception) of the culture industry is rendered all the more powerful for the fact that its coercion and the "unfreedom" it peddles are "pleasant" to the masses (Marcuse, 1964).

From the perspective of the critical theorists, the marriage of music and marketing is utterly predictable, the outcome of a process of pacification and consumerization of culture that characterize modern capitalism. Can music be independent of the market? Should it strive to be? What do you think?

THINK IT THROUGH

- Can popular music play a role as both a progressive force and a marketing tool? Can you think of examples of artists or songs that occupy one or both roles?

Follow us on Twitter to keep up with current sociological stories and research! We're at @DiscoverSoc1.
Share your own ideas at #DiscoverSociology.

CULTURE, MEDIA, AND VIOLENCE

Statistics suggest that rape and sexual assault devastate the lives of thousands of U.S. women every year. According to the National Crime Victimization Survey, in 2013, there were 431,840 rapes, attempted rapes, or sexual assaults in the United States (Truman & Morgan, 2016). Men and boys also fall prey to these crimes, but women are the most commonly victimized.

One explanation for this number might be that sexual assaults are perpetrated by thousands of deviant individuals and are the outcomes of particular and individual circumstances. Applying the sociological imagination, however, means recognizing the magnitude of the problem and considering the idea that examination of individual cases alone, while important, is inadequate for fully understanding the phenomenon of rape and sexual assault in the United States. To paraphrase C. Wright Mills, it is clearly a personal trouble *and* a public issue.

Some researchers have posited the existence of a **rape culture**, *a social culture that provides an environment conducive to rape* (Boswell & Spade, 1996; Buchwald, Fletcher, & Roth, 2005; Sanday, 1990). According to some scholars, rape culture has been pervasive in the U.S. legal system. Feminist theorist and legal scholar Catharine MacKinnon (1989) argues that legislative and judicial processes regarding rape utilize a male viewpoint. Consider, for instance, that until the late 1970s, most states did not treat spousal rape as a crime. This conclusion was based, at least in part, on the notion that a woman could not be raped by her husband because sexual consent was taken as implied in the marital contract.

Some researchers argue that the legal culture takes rape less seriously than other crimes of violence (Taslitz, 1999). Legal scholar Stephen J. Schulhofer (2000) has written that the law

> punishes takings by force (robbery), by coercive threats (extortion), by stealth (larceny), by breach of trust (embezzlement), and by deception (fraud and false pretenses). . . . Yet sexual autonomy, almost alone among our important personal rights, is not fully protected. The law of rape, as if it were only a law against the "robbery" of sex, remains focused almost exclusively on preventing interference by force. (pp. 100–101)

Schulhofer notes that this problem is linked to a culture that treats male sexual aggression as "natural." Taslitz (1999) asserts that the cultural stories brought

Rape culture: A social culture that provides an environment conducive to rape.

The 2016 film *X Men: Apocalypse* was widely marketed with an image of actress Jennifer Lawrence's character Mystique being choked by the powerful Apocalypse. The advertisement provoked critique for its casual depiction of violence. ■

into courtrooms render proceedings around rape problematic by situating them in myths, such as the idea that a female victim was "asking for it."

Some research in the fields of sociology and communications suggests that popular culture promotes rape culture by *normalizing violence.* This is not to argue that culture is a direct cause of sexual violence but rather to suggest that popular culture renders violence part of the social scenery by making its appearance so common in films, video games, and music videos that it evolves from being shocking to being utterly ordinary (Katz & Jhally, 2000a, 2000b). How does this process occur?

Some scholars argue that popular media embrace *violent masculinity,* a form of masculinity that associates "being a man" with being aggressive and merciless. As well, the messages of popular culture may serve to normalize violence against women. Hip-hop has long been associated with the use of misogynistic lyrics, although it is hardly alone in its objectification of women (Morgan, 1999; Pough, 2004; Weitzer & Kubrin, 2009). Many commercial films and music videos also feature rough—even violent—treatment of women, offered as entertainment. The most gratuitous violence in films such as *Hush* (2016), *The Cutting Room* (2015), *The Girl With the Dragon Tattoo* (2011), and *The Killer Inside Me* (2010) is reserved for female victims. In early 2010, citizens in Japan and around the world expressed dismay and disgust when reports emerged about the popular dissemination of the video game *RapeLay,* in which a player stalks a young woman, her mother, and her sister on a train. In the game, the player uses the mouse to grope—and eventually rape—his victims.

Popular culture's most predictable normalization of violence against women occurs in pornography, a multibillion-dollar-a-year industry in the United States. Fictionalized portrayals of sexual activity range from coercion of a compliant and always willing female to violent rape simulations in which consent is clearly refused.

Although researchers do not propose that lyrics or images disseminated by mass media cause sexual violence *directly,* some suggest that popular culture's persistent use of sex-starved, compliant, and easily victimized female characters sends messages that forced sex is no big deal, that women really want to be raped, and that some invite rape by their appearance. In a study of 400 male and female high school students, Cassidy and Hurrell (1995, cited in Workman & Freeburg, 1999) determined that respondents who heard a vignette about a rape scenario and then viewed a picture of the "victim" (in reality a model for the research) dressed in provocative clothing were more likely than those who saw her dressed in conservative clothing, or who saw no picture at all, to judge her responsible for her assailant's behavior, and to say his behavior was justified and not really rape. More recent studies have reproduced findings that rape myths are widely used to explain and even justify sexual violence (Hammond, Berry, & Rodriguez, 2011).

A 2003 study found that victims' attire is not a significant factor in sexual assault. Instead, rapists look for signs of passivity and submissiveness (Beiner, 2007). Why, with evidence to the contrary, do such rape myths, common but rarely true beliefs about rapists and rape victims, exist? Studies link regular exposure to popular print, television, film, and Internet media with acceptance of rape myths among college-age men and women (Kahlor & Morrison, 2007; Katz, 2006, cited in Lonsway et al., 2009; Reinders, 2006), although female undergraduates in a comparative study were less likely to believe rape myths and more likely to believe victims than their male peers (Stephens et al., 2016). Do research data suggest the existence of a rape culture? Is culture, particularly culture that includes music and movies that normalize violence against women, a sociological antecedent of real violence? What do you think?

CULTURE, CLASS, AND INEQUALITY

In their studies of culture and class, sociologists consider whether the musical and artistic tastes of different socioeconomic classes vary and, if so, why. Although the answer may be interesting in itself, researchers are also likely to go a step farther and examine the links among culture, power, and class inequality. Particularly when using a social conflict lens, sociologists have long sought to show how elites use culture to gain or maintain power over other groups.

Sociologist Pierre Bourdieu has used culture to help explain the phenomenon of **social class reproduction**, *the way in which class status is reproduced from generation to generation.* Bourdieu (1984) discusses the concept of **cultural capital**, *wealth in the form of knowledge, ideas, verbal skills, and ways of thinking and behaving.* Karl Marx argued that the key to power in a capitalist system is *economic capital,* particularly possession of the means of production. Bourdieu extends this idea by suggesting that cultural capital can also be a source of power. Children from privileged backgrounds have access to markedly different stores of cultural capital than do children from working-class backgrounds.

Children of the upper and middle classes come into the education system—the key path to success in modern industrial societies—with a set of language and academic skills, beliefs, and models of success and failure that fit into and are validated by mainstream schools. Children from less privileged backgrounds enter with a smaller amount of validated cultural capital; their skills, knowledge base, and styles of speaking are not those that schools conventionally recognize and reward. For example, while a child from a working-class immigrant family may know how to care for her younger siblings, prepare a good meal, and translate for non-English-fluent parents, her parents (like many first-generation immigrants) may have worked multiple jobs and may not have had the skills to read to her or the time or money to expose her to enriching activities. By contrast, her middle-class peers are more likely to have grown up with parents who regularly read to them, took them to shows and museums, and quizzed them on multiplication problems. Although both children come to school with *knowledge and skills,* the cultural capital of the middle-class child can be more readily "traded" for academic success—and eventual economic gains.

In short, schools serve as locations where the cultural capital of the better-off classes is exchanged for educational success and credentials. This difference in scholastic achievement then translates into economic capital as high achievers assume prestigious, well-paid positions in the workplace. Those who do not have the cultural capital to trade for academic success are often tracked into jobs in society's lower tiers. Class is reproduced as cultural capital begets academic achievement, which begets economic capital, which again begets cultural capital for the next generation.

Clearly, however, the structure of institutional opportunities, while unequal, cannot alone account for broad reproduction of social class across generations. Individuals, after all, make choices about education, occupations, and the like. They have free will—or, as sociologists put it, *agency,* which is understood as the capacity of individuals to make choices and to act independently. Bourdieu (1977) argues that agency must be understood in the context of structure. To this end, he introduces the concept of **habitus**, *the internalization of objective probabilities and the expression of those probabilities as choice.* Put another way, people come to want that which their own experiences and those of the people who surround them suggest they can realistically have—and they act accordingly.

Consider the following hypothetical example of habitus in action. In a poor rural community where few people go to college, fewer can afford it, and the payoff of higher education is not obvious because there are no immediate role models with such experience, Bourdieu would argue that an individual's "choice" not to prioritize getting into college reflects both agency *and* structure. That is, she makes the choice not to prepare herself for college or to apply to college, but going to college would likely not have been possible for her anyway as a result of her economic circumstances and perhaps as a result of an inadequate education in an underfunded school. By contrast, the habitus of a young upper-middle-class person makes the choice of going to college almost unquestionable. Nearly everyone

Social class reproduction: The way in which class status is reproduced from generation to generation, with parents "passing on" a class position to their offspring.

Cultural capital: Wealth in the form of knowledge, ideas, verbal skills, and ways of thinking and acting.

Habitus: The internalization of objective probabilities and subsequent expression of those probabilities as choice.

around her has gone or is going to college, the benefits of a college education are broadly discussed, and she is socialized from her early years to understand that college will follow high school—alternatives are rarely considered. Furthermore, a college education is accessible—she is prepared for college work in a well-funded public school or a private school, and family income, loans, or scholarships will contribute to making higher education a reality. Bourdieu thus suggests that social class reproduction appears on its face to be grounded in individual choices and merit, but fundamental structural inequalities that underlie class reproduction often go unrecognized (or, as Bourdieu puts it, "misrecognized"), a fact that benefits the well-off.

CULTURE AND GLOBALIZATION

There is a pervasive sense around the world that globalization is creating a homogenized culture—a landscape dotted in every corner of the globe with the Golden Arches and the face of Colonel Sanders beckoning the masses to consume hamburgers and fried chicken. The familiar songs of Justin Bieber, Taylor Swift, and Beyoncé are broadcast on radio stations from Bangladesh to Bulgaria to Belize, while rebroadcasts of such popular U.S. soap operas as *The Bold and the Beautiful* provide a picture of ostensibly "average" U.S. lives on the world's television screens. In fact, about 70% of studio revenue in Hollywood is generated in overseas markets; that is, many films make far more money abroad than in the United States. Action-oriented films in particular garner large audiences in markets like China and Russia (Brook, 2014): For example, in its first weekend of release, *The Fate of the Furious* (2017), the eighth installment of the *Fast and Furious* series, earned over $532 million, just $100 million of which came from its U.S. debut (Peters, 2017).

We see the effects of globalization—and of Americanization in particular—in cultural representations like McDonald's restaurants, U.S. pop music and videos, and bottles of Coca-Cola spreading around the world. According to press reports, even in the Taliban era in Afghanistan, a time when a deeply conservative Islamist ideology was enforced throughout society, the

Global culture: A type of culture—some would say U.S. culture—that has spread across the world in the form of Hollywood films, fast-food restaurants, and popular music heard in virtually every country

Many U.S. films earn more money abroad than they do in the U.S. Action films like *The Fate of the Furious* (2017) are particularly popular with moviegoers around the globe. What makes these films appealing to a global audience?

culture of global Hollywood seeped in through the cracks of fundamentalism's wall. In January 2001, the Taliban rounded up dozens of barbers in the capital city of Kabul because they had been cutting men's hair in a style known locally as the "Titanic": "At the time, Kabul's cooler young men wanted that Leonardo DiCaprio look, the one he sported in the movie. It was an interesting moment because under the Taliban's moral regime, movies were illegal. . . . Yet thanks to enterprising video smugglers who dragged cassettes over mountain trails by mule, urban Afghans knew perfectly well who DiCaprio was and what he looked like" (Freund, 2002, p. 24).

How should a sociologist evaluate the spread of a globalized culture? Is globalization, on balance, positive or negative for countries, communities, and corporate entities? Is it just business, or does it also have political implications? The conflict and functionalist perspectives offer us different ways of seeing contemporary **global culture**, a culture that *draws heavily, though by no means exclusively, on U.S. trends and tastes.*

A functionalist examining the development and spread of a broad global culture might begin by asking, "What is its function?" He or she could deduce that globalization spreads not only material culture in the form of food and music but also nonmaterial culture in the form of values and norms. Globalized norms and values can strengthen social solidarity and consequently serve to reduce conflict between states and societies. Therefore, globalization serves the integrative function of creating some semblance of a common culture that can foster mutual understanding and a foundation for dialogue.

Recall from Chapter 1 that functionalism assumes the social world's many parts are interdependent. Indeed, globalization highlights both the cultural and the economic interdependence of countries and communities. The book *Global Hollywood* (Miller, Govil, McMurria, & Maxwell, 2002) describes what its authors call a *new international division of cultural labor,* a system of cultural production that crosses the globe, making the creation of culture an international rather than a national phenomenon (though profits still flow primarily into the core of the filmmaking industry in Hollywood).

The blockbuster film *Slumdog Millionaire* (2008) offers an example of the international division of cultural labor. The film, about a poor 18-year-old orphan who finds himself on the cusp of winning India's "Who Wants to Be A Millionaire?" quiz show, was directed by Englishman Danny Boyle and codirected by New Delhi native Loveleen Tandan from a screenplay by Boyle's countryman Simon Beaufoy that was based on the 2005 novel *Q & A* by Indian writer Vikas Swarup. In 2009, the film, distributed in the United States by Warner Independent Pictures but shown internationally, received nine Academy Awards, including Best Picture. The Indian cast of *Slumdog Millionaire* includes both established local actors and young Mumbai slum dwellers, some of whom were later found to have earned very little from their efforts. Boyle has argued, however, that the filmmakers worked to ensure future educational opportunities and shelter for the young actors. The film's global appeal was huge, and it generated almost $378 million in box office returns, leading the *Wall Street Journal* to label it "the film world's first globalized masterpiece" (Morgenstern, 2008).

From the social conflict perspective, we can view the globalization of culture as a force with the potential to perpetuate economic inequality—particularly because globalization is a product of the developed world.

SAJJAD HUSSAIN/AFP/Getty Images

Not all of the actors who were part of *Slumdog Millionaire*, a blockbuster film, benefited from its success. The local extras—as well as some of the central characters—took away little financial gain from the film.

©iStockphoto.com/paulprescott72

In its more than half-century of operation, McDonald's has become one of the most recognized icons of U.S. life and culture; Ronald McDonald is said to be the most recognized figure in the world after Santa Claus. McDonald's serves 68 million customers every day in over 36,000 restaurants in 120 countries around the globe.

Although a functionalist would highlight the creative global collaboration and productive interdependence of a film like *Slumdog Millionaire,* a conflict theorist would ask, "Who benefits from such a production?" Although Western film companies, producers, and directors walk away with huge profits, the slum dwellers used as actors or extras garner far less sustained global interest or financial gain.

A conflict theorist might also describe how the globalization of cheap fast food can cripple small independent eateries that serve indigenous (and arguably healthier) cuisine. An influx of global corporations inhibits some local people from owning their own means of production

DISCOVER & DEBATE

Culture and Mass Media

Motion: Exposure to violence in films, television programs, music, and video games is harmful to children. It has negative individual and societal effects.

Background

Media is an important part of everyone's life, particularly in the age of smartphones and other technologies that bring us near constant access to news, entertainment, and social interaction. Violent content is common in the media to which we are exposed: According to one study, about 90% of movies, 68% of video games, and 60% of TV shows include some depictions of violence (Wilson, 2008). Research shows that, on average, young people spend more than 7 hours a day engaged with media (Rideout, Foehr, & Roberts, 2010). More than 20 hours per week are spent playing video games, and some males are exposed to video games for 40 hours or more per week (Bailey, West, & Anderson, 2011). Popular examples of violence in media include movies like the *Avengers* and *X Men* series; television programs like *Game of Thrones*, *The Walking Dead*, and *Power Rangers*; and video games like *Call of Duty* and *Grand Theft Auto.* The question of whether children's exposure to violence is causally related to increased aggressive behavior, desensitization to violence, and fear of being harmed is one that evokes significant debate.

Affirmative Arguments

- Media is an important agent of socialization, so we would expect exposure to violence in media to affect children and young people. Exposure to violence in films, television programs, and video is associated in numerous research studies with greater propensity for aggressive behavior in children and adolescents.
- Violence in media often does not show negative effects. Especially in the gaming world and in action films, harming or killing someone is often rewarded. This sends confusing messages to children.
- Research shows that children, particularly very young children, cannot distinguish reality from fiction.

Opposition Arguments

- Correlation is not causation: A correlation between the presence of violence in media and violence in real life does not establish a direct causal relationship between the two.
- Violent crime rates in the United States have declined in recent years. The experience of some other countries also challenges this argument. For example, Japan has high levels of media violence in popular films and video games, but the incidence of serious crimes committed by young people is falling.
- It is challenging to isolate triggers for real-life violence: In addition to media, violent behavior may be linked to mental health issues, exposure to interpersonal threats or violence, economic deprivation, and access to weapons, among others.

Questions for Consideration

- If research shows a relationship between exposure to violence in media and real-life consequences like aggression and desensitization to violence, whose responsibility is it to respond? How should the government, parents, and the producers of cultural products respond?
- Is the inclusion of violence in films, television, and other media an issue of free speech? Can it be legally controlled? Should it be legally controlled?
- Should adult exposure to violent media be a concern for society?

Debate Tip

▶ It is important to have strong opening and concluding statements. Direct quotations, facts and figures, and thought-provoking questions help in making a strong opening for a debate. Finish with a statement that wraps up your argument and guides your audience to a conclusion.

and providing employment to others. The demise of local restaurants, cafés, and food stalls represents a loss of the cuisines and thus the unique cultures of indigenous peoples. It also forces working people to depend on large corporations for their livelihoods, depriving them of economic independence.

Although functionalism and conflict theory offer different interpretations of globalization, both offer valuable insights. Globalization may bring people together through common entertainment, eating experiences, and communication technologies, and, at the same time, it may represent a threat—real or perceived—to local cultures and economies as indigenous producers are marginalized and the sounds and styles of different cultures are replaced by a single mold set by Western entertainment marketers.

Journalist Thomas Friedman has suggested that although most countries cannot resist the forces of globalization, it is not inevitably homogenizing. In *The Lexus and the Olive Tree: Understanding Globalization,* Friedman (2000) writes that "the most important filter is the ability to 'glocalize.' I define healthy glocalization as the ability of a culture, when it encounters other strong cultures, to absorb influences that naturally fit into and can enrich that culture, to resist those things that are truly alien and to compartmentalize those things that, while different, can nevertheless be enjoyed and celebrated as different" (p. 295). The concept of *glocalization* highlights the idea of cultural hybrids born of a pastiche of both local and global influences.

In *The Globalization of Nothing*, sociologist George Ritzer (2007) proposes a view of globalization that integrates what he calls "grobalization," the product of "the imperialistic ambitions of nations, corporations, organizations, and the like and their desire ... to impose themselves on various geographic areas" (p. 15). Ritzer adds that the "main interest of the entities involved in grobalization is in seeing their power, influence, and in many cases profits grow (hence the term *grobalization*) throughout the world" (p. 16). The concept of *grobalization* draws from classical sociological theorists like Karl Marx and Max Weber. For instance, where Marx theorized capitalism's imperative of economic imperialism, Ritzer offers contemporary examples of grobalization's economic and cultural imperialism, exporting not only brand-name products but also the values of consumerism and the practical vehicles of mass consumption, such as credit cards.

How will the world's cultures shift in the decades to come? Will they globalize or remain localized? Will they glocalize or grobalize? Clearly, the material culture of the West, particularly of the United States, is powerful: It is pushed into other parts of the world by markets and merchants, but it is also pulled in by people eager to hitch their stars to the modern Western world. Local identities and cultures continue to shape people's views and actions, but there is little reason to believe that McDonald's, KFC, and Coca-Cola will drop out of the global marketplace. The dominance of U.S. films, music, and other cultural products is also likely to remain a feature of the world cultural stage.

WHY STUDY CULTURE AND MEDIA THROUGH A SOCIOLOGICAL LENS?

Culture is a vital component of a community's identity—through language, objects, and practices, culture embodies a community and its environment. Culture is powerful and complex. As we have seen in this chapter, cultural products, including those disseminated by the mass media, both reflect and shape our societal hopes and fears, norms and beliefs, and rituals and practices. From flesh-eating zombies and classical music to folk dances and folkways, culture is at the core of the human experience. We are all profoundly "cultured."

Culture can be a source of integration and harmony, as functionalists assert, or it can be a vehicle of manipulation and oppression, as conflict theorists often see it. There is compelling evidence for both perspectives, and context is critical for recognizing which perspective better captures the character of a given cultural scenario.

The study of culture is much more than just an intellectual exercise. In this chapter, you encountered several key cultural questions that are important objects of public discussion today. Do the mass media foster viewer engagement in public life, or do they distract and disengage us from the pressing problems of our times? Is violence in the media just entertainment, or does it contribute, even indirectly, to violence in relationships and society? Will the evolution of a more global culture play an integrative role between societies, or will smaller cultures resist homogenization and assert their own power, bringing about conflict rather than harmony? These are questions of profound importance in a media-saturated and multicultural world—a sociological perspective can help us to make sense of them.

WHAT CAN I DO WITH A SOCIOLOGY DEGREE?

Critical Thinking

Critical thinking entails the evaluation of claims about society, politics, the economy, culture, the environment, or any other area of knowledge with the application of reason and evidence. *Critical thinking skills* are very broad, but they have several key elements, including the ability to rigorously evaluate data, carefully and systematically analyze a problem or situation, and draw conclusions that recognize strengths and weaknesses of an argument or position. They also include the inclination and knowledge to be a critical consumer of information, thoughtfully questioning rather than simply accepting arguments or solutions at face value. Critical thinking in sociology is not about *criticizing* but about developing a nuanced understanding of phenomena, institutions, and practices. Every chapter in this book seeks to help you sharpen your critical thinking by enabling you to see more deeply into the social processes and structures that affect our lives and society, and to raise questions about social phenomena we may take for granted. As a sociologist in training, you will develop a more comprehensive understanding of your social world and will learn to ask critical questions about why things are as they are and to seek out and find evidence-based answers to those questions.

Aniqa Anwar, Senior Analyst at R/GA

Brown University, AB in Sociology (Honors)

I currently work as a senior analyst at an advertising agency. My role consists of analyzing data across several marketing channels, interpreting and evaluating the information, coming up with actionable solutions to improve campaign/brand performance and strategy, and distilling the information into easily digestible presentations for our clients. My day to day consists of working with varying data sets and gleaning meaningful information from them, and presenting insights and solutions effectively. The theoretical foundation for this was built through a lot of my sociology classes and the papers and studies I had to read for them, and the practical foundation was built through assisting on research studies as well as conducting and working through my own data-heavy senior thesis.

One of the best skills one can learn from studying sociology is the ability to think critically and find meaningful patterns in data and interpret them effectively. Sociology provided a framework to help me understand and process quantitative and qualitative information and present them in a way that is impactful and evidence based. Critical thinking, while key in any job, is especially valuable in data-heavy roles like mine, as companies will always want to hire analytical thinkers who are data savvy.

Career Data: Market Research Analyst

- 2016 Median Pay: $62,560 per year
- Typical Entry-Level Education: Bachelor's degree
- Projected Job Growth by 2024: 19% (Much faster than average)

SOURCE: Bureau of Labor Statistics, Occupational Outlook Handbook, 2016.

SUMMARY

- **Culture** consists of the beliefs, norms, behaviors, and products common to members of a particular social group. **Language** is an important component of cultures. The Sapir–Whorf hypothesis points to language's role in structuring perceptions and actions. Culture is a key topic of sociological study because as human beings we have the capacity to develop it through the creation of artifacts such as songs, foods, and values. Culture also influences our social development: We are products of our cultural beliefs, behaviors, and biases.

- Sociologists and others who study culture generally distinguish between material and nonmaterial culture. **Material culture** encompasses physical artifacts—the objects created, embraced, and consumed by a given society. **Nonmaterial culture** is generally abstract and includes culturally accepted ideas about living and behaving. The two are intertwined because nonmaterial culture often gives particular meanings to the objects of material culture.

- Norms are the common rules of a culture that govern people's actions. **Folkways** are fairly weak norms, the violation of which is tolerable. **Mores** are strongly held norms; violating them is subject to social or legal sanction. **Taboos** are the most closely held mores; violating them is socially unthinkable. **Laws** codify some, although not all, of society's norms.
- **Beliefs** are particular ideas that people accept as true, although they need not be objectively true. Beliefs can be based on faith, superstition, science, tradition, or experience.
- **Values** are the general, abstract standards of a society and define basic, often idealized principles. We identify national values, community values, institutional values, and individual values. Values may be sources of cohesion or of conflict.
- **Ideal culture** consists of the norms and values that the people of a society profess to embrace. **Real culture** consists of the real values, norms, and practices of people in a society.
- Ethnocentrism is the habit of judging other cultures by the standards of one's own.
- Sociologists entreat us to embrace **cultural relativism**, a perspective that allows us to understand the practices of other societies in terms of those societies' norms and values rather than our own.
- Multiple cultures may exist and thrive within any country or community. Some of these are **subcultures**, which exist together with the dominant culture but differ in some important respects from it.
- **High culture** is an exclusive culture often limited in its accessibility and audience. High culture is widely associated with the upper class, which both defines and embraces its content. **Popular culture** encompasses entertainment, culinary, and athletic tastes that are broadly shared. As "mass culture," popular culture is more fully associated with the middle and working classes.
- **Rape culture** is a social culture that provides an environment conducive to rape. Some sociologists argue that we can best understand the high number of rapes and attempted rapes in the United States by considering both individual circumstances and the larger social context, which contains messages that marginalize and normalize the problem of sexual assault.
- **Global culture**—some would say U.S. culture—has spread across the world in the form of Hollywood films, fast-food restaurants, and popular music heard in almost every country.

KEY TERMS

culture, 65
material culture, 66
nonmaterial culture, 66
beliefs, 66
folkways, 67
mores, 68
taboos, 68
laws, 68
values, 69
ideal culture, 70
real culture, 70
cultural inconsistency, 70
doxic, 74
etic perspective, 74
emic perspective, 74
cultural relativism, 74
subcultures, 75
language, 76
multiculturalism, 78
high culture, 79
popular culture, 79
mass media, 79
rape culture, 83
social class reproduction, 85
cultural capital, 85
habitus, 86
global culture, 86

DISCUSSION QUESTIONS

1. This chapter discusses tensions between ideal and real culture in attitudes and practices linked to conventional attractiveness and honesty. Can you think of other cases where ideal and real cultures collide?
2. Following the ideas of the critical theorists in sociology, this chapter suggests that mass media may play a paradoxical role in society, offering both the information needed to bring about an informed citizenry and disseminating mass entertainment that distracts and disengages individuals from debates of importance. Which of these functions do you think is more powerful?
3. What is cultural capital? What, according to Bourdieu, is its significance in society? How does one acquire valued cultural capital, and how is it linked to the reproduction of social class?
4. The chapter presents an argument on the relationships among culture, social and mass media, and sexual violence with a discussion of the concept of a rape culture. Describe the argument. Do you agree or disagree with the argument? Explain your position.
5. Sociologist George Ritzer sees within globalization two processes—"glocalization" and "grobalization." What is the difference between the two? Which is, in your opinion, the more powerful process, and why do you believe this? Support your point with evidence.

edge.sagepub.com/eglitis

Want a better grade?

Get the tools you need to sharpen your study skills. Access practice quizzes, eFlashcards, video and multimedia at **https://edge.sagepub.com/eglitis**.

SOCIALIZATION AND SOCIAL INTERACTION

4.1 Describe how sociologists theorize the birth of the social self

4.2 Explain the significance of agents of socialization in the development of the self

4.3 Discuss socialization across the life course

4.4 Define the concept of total institutions

4.5 Theorize processes of social interaction from a sociological perspective

©iStockphoto.com/hadynyah

WHAT DO YOU THINK?

1. Is the personality of an individual determined at birth?
2. Has social media become a key agent of contemporary socialization of children and teens? Does its influence outweigh that of the other agents of socialization like family and schools?
3. Do people adjust the presentation of their personalities in interactions to leave particular impressions? Might we say that we have different "social selves" that we present in different settings?

SELFIE AND SOCIETY

It will not surprise you to hear that most Americans today are users of social media. According to the Pew Research Center, "Age is strongly correlated with social media usage: Those ages 18 to 29 have always been the most likely users of social media by a considerable margin. Today, 90% of young adults use social media, compared with 12% in 2005, a 78-percentage point increase. At the same time, there has been a 69-point bump among those ages 30–49, from 8% in 2005 to 77% today" (Perrin, 2015, "Social Media Usage by Age: Ubiquitous Among Youngest Adults, Notable Among Older Adults," para. 1). Although adults across the age spectrum use social media, they do not all use it the same way. Consider that while Facebook has grown in popularity with older adults, a recent study suggests that young people favor visually oriented social media like Snapchat and Instagram over more text-based media like Twitter and Facebook (PiperJaffray, 2016). A key component of contemporary young adult communication on social media—and a centerpiece of platforms like Snapchat and Instagram—is the "selfie," a term that made its debut in the Merriam-Webster dictionary in 2014 (Webster, 2014).

A recent *U.S. News & World Report* article suggests that "selfies contribute to the online personas teens create for themselves. From pictures to statuses, each component builds their online identity. And although this might seem overly self-interested to some adults, [media psychologist Pamela] Rutledge says teens today are no more concerned about their appearances than teens of the past. It's the same culture, just presented in a new format" (Webster, 2014, "What is the Selfie's Purpose?", para. 4). Indeed, sociologists have long pointed out that a significant component of our social self draws on the ways that others respond to us—or on the ways in which we believe others perceive us. Although in the past young adults in the process of constructing social selves may have been uncertain about how others perceived them, our contemporary social media culture, built on a platform of pursuing "likes," gives young people constant feedback on how others view them.

Sociologist Ori Schwarz (2010) suggests that selfies, which according to Pew Research over 90% of teens indicate they have shared on social media, also function as a form of social capital (Grimes, 2014). That is, Schwarz argues that certain types of selfies (for instance, a selfie with a "sexualized, ad-like pose") are traded in the online peer group for capital in the form of positive reinforcement—likes or complimentary comments. Grimes (2014) notes that "this social bartering process is one of the few forms of capital teens control" (para. 3)

This culture and the practices of online construction, revision, and dissemination of the self have become part of social life in contemporary culture. Social media are an evolving and expanding part of the socialization and social lives of the young. Sociologists are only beginning to address important questions about this phenomenon. As you read the chapter, consider research questions or projects that might emerge from an interest in the manifestations, costs, and benefits of our modern embrace of social media. ■

An Indian family observes the holiday of Diwali, the five-day festival of lights celebrated by Hindus, Sikhs, and Jains. Many components of one's culture are passed down through family practices and social rituals. ■

In this chapter, we examine the process of socialization and the array of agents that help shape our social selves and our behavioral choices. We begin by looking into the "nature versus nurture" debate and what sociology says about that debate. We then discuss key agents of socialization, as well as the ways in which socialization may differ in total institutions and across the life course. We then examine theoretical perspectives on socialization. Finally, we look at social interaction and ways in which sociologists conceptualize our presentation of self and our group interactions.

THE BIRTH OF THE SOCIAL SELF

Socialization is *the process by which people learn the culture of their society.* It is a lifelong and active process in which individuals construct their sense of who they are, how to think, and how to act as members of their culture. Socialization is our primary way of reproducing culture, including norms and values and the belief that our culture represents "normal" social practices and perceptions.

The principal agents of socialization—including parents, teachers, religious institutions, peers, television, and social media—exert enormous influence on us. Socialization takes place every day, usually without our thinking about it: when we speak, when others react to us, when we observe others' behavior—whether in person or on a screen—and in almost every other human interaction.

Socialization: The process by which people learn the culture of their society.

Debate has raged in the social sciences over the relative influence of genetic inheritance ("nature") and cultural and social experiences ("nurture") in shaping people's lives (Coleman & Hong, 2008; Ridgeway & Correll, 2004). If inborn biological predispositions explain differences in behaviors and interests between, say, sixth-grade boys and girls, or between a professional thief and the police officer who apprehends him, then understanding socialization will do little to help us understand those differences. On the other hand, if biology cannot adequately explain differences in attitudes, characters, and behaviors, then it becomes imperative that we examine the effects of socialization.

Almost no one today argues that behavior is entirely determined by either socialization or biology. There is doubtless an interaction between the two. What social scientists disagree about, however, is which is more important in shaping a person's personality, philosophy of life, and social actions. In this text, we lean toward socialization because we believe the evidence points in that direction.

Social scientists have found little support for the idea that personalities and behaviors are rooted exclusively in "human nature." Indeed, little human behavior is purely "natural." For example, humans have a biological capacity for language, but language is learned and develops only through interaction. The weight of socialization in the development of language, reasoning, and social skills is dramatically illustrated in cases of children raised in isolation. If a biologically inherited mechanism alone triggered language, it would do so even in people who grow up deprived of contact with other human beings. If socialization plays a key role, however, then such people would not only have difficulty learning to use language, but they would also lack a capacity to play the social roles to which most of us are accustomed.

Nina Leen/Contributor/Getty Images

Given the choice in an experiment between a wire mother surrogate and a surrogate covered with cloth, the infant monkey almost invariably chose the cloth figure. How are human responses to stimuli similar to and different from those we find in the animal kingdom?

One of the most extensively documented cases of social isolation occurred more than 200 years ago. In 1800, a "wild boy," later named Victor, was seen by hunters in the forests of Aveyron, a rural area of France (Shattuck, 1980). Victor had been living alone in the woods for most of his 12 or so years and could not speak, and although he stood erect, he ran using both arms and legs like an animal. Victor was taken into the home of Jean-Marc-Gaspard Itard, a young medical doctor who, for the next 10 years, tried to teach him the social and intellectual skills expected of a child his age. According to Itard's careful records, Victor managed to learn a few words, but he never spoke in complete sentences. Although he eventually learned to use the toilet, he continued to evidence "wild" behavior, including public masturbation. Despite the efforts of Itard and others, Victor was incapable of learning more than rudimentary social and intellectual skills; he died in Paris in 1828.

Other studies of the effects of isolation have centered on children raised by their parents, but in nearly total isolation. For 12 years, from the time she was one and a half years old, "Genie" (a pseudonym) saw only her father, mother, and brother, and only when one of them came to feed her. Genie's father did not allow his wife or Genie to leave the house or have any visitors. Genie was either strapped to a child's potty-chair or placed in a sleeping bag that limited her movements. Genie rarely heard any conversation. If she made noises, her father beat her (Curtiss, 1977; Rymer, 1993).

When Genie was 13, her mother took her and fled the house. Genie was unable to cry, control her bowels, eat solid food, or talk. Because of her tight confinement, she had not even learned to focus her eyes beyond 12 feet. She was constantly salivating and spitting, and she had little controlled use of her arms or legs (Rymer, 1993). Gradually Genie learned some of the social behavior expected of a child. For example, she learned to wear clothing and use the toilet. Nevertheless, although intelligence tests did not indicate reasoning disability, even after 5 years of concentrated effort on the part of a foster mother, social workers, and medical doctors, Genie never learned to speak beyond the level of a 4-year-old, and she did not interact with others. Although she responded positively to those who treated her with sympathy, Genie's social behavior remained severely underdeveloped for the rest of her life (Rymer, 1993).

Genie's and Victor's experiences underscore the significance of socialization, especially during childhood. Their cases show that even biologically rooted capacities do not develop into recognizable human ways of acting and thinking unless the individual interacts with other humans in a social environment. Children raised in isolation fail to develop complex language, abstract thinking, notions of cooperation and sharing, or even a sense of themselves as social beings. In other words, they do not develop the hallmarks of what we know as humanity (Ridley, 1998).

Sociologists and other social scientists have developed theories to explain the role of socialization in the development of social selves. What these theories recognize is that whatever the contribution of biology, ultimately people as social beings are made, not born. Below, we explore four approaches to understanding socialization: behaviorism, symbolic interactionism, developmental stage theories, and psychoanalytic theories.

BEHAVIORISM AND SOCIAL LEARNING THEORY

Behaviorism is *a psychological perspective that emphasizes the effect of rewards and punishments on human behavior.* It arose during the late 19th century to challenge the then-popular belief that human behavior results primarily from biological instincts and drives (Baldwin & Baldwin, 1986, 1988; Dishion, McCord, & Poulin, 1999). Early behaviorist researchers, such as Ivan Pavlov (1849–1936) and John Watson (1878–1958), and later B. F. Skinner (1904–1990), demonstrated that even behavior thought to be purely instinctual (such as a dog salivating when it sees food) may be produced or extinguished through the application of rewards and punishments. Thus, a pigeon will learn to press a bar if that triggers the release of food (Skinner, 1938, 1953; Watson, 1924). Behaviorists concluded that both animal and human behavior can be learned, and neither is purely instinctive.

When they turned to human beings, behaviorists focused on **social learning**, *the way people adapt their behavior in response to social rewards and punishments* (Baldwin & Baldwin, 1986; Bandura, 1977; Bandura & Walters, 1963). Of particular interest was the satisfaction people get from imitating others. Social learning theory thus combines the reward-and-punishment effects identified by behaviorists with the idea that we model the behavior of others; that is, we observe the way people respond to others' behavior.

Social learning theory would predict, for example, that if a boy gets high fives from his friends for talking back to his teacher—a form of encouragement rather than of punishment—he is likely to repeat this behavior. What's more, other boys may imitate it. Social learning researchers have developed formulas for predicting how rewards and punishments affect behavior. For instance, rewards given repeatedly may become less effective when the individual becomes satiated: If you have just eaten a huge piece of cake, you are less likely to feel rewarded by the prospect of another.

Social behaviorism is not widely embraced today as a rigorous perspective on human behavior. One reason is that only in carefully controlled laboratory environments is it easy to demonstrate the power of rewards and punishments. In real social situations, the theory is of limited value as a predictor. For example, whether a girl who is teased ("punished") for engaging in a "masculine" pursuit like football or wrestling will lose interest in the sport depends on many other variables, such as the support of family and friends and her own enjoyment of the activity. The simple application of rewards and punishments is hardly sufficient to explain why people repeat some behaviors and not others.

In addition, behaviorist theories violate Popper's principle of falsification (discussed in Chapter 2). Since what was previously rewarding may lose effectiveness if the person is satiated, if a reward does not work, we can always attribute its failure to satiation. Therefore, no matter the

Behaviorism: A psychological perspective that emphasizes the effect of rewards and punishments on human behavior.

Social learning: The way people adapt their behavior in response to social rewards and punishments.

outcome of the experiment, the theory has to be true; it cannot be proved false. For these reasons, sociologists find behaviorism an inadequate theory of socialization. To explain how people become socialized, they highlight theories that emphasize *symbolic interaction.*

SOCIALIZATION AS SYMBOLIC INTERACTION

Recall from the introductory chapter that *symbolic interactionism* views the self and society as resulting from social interaction based on language and other symbols. Symbolic interactionism has been especially fruitful in explaining how individuals develop a social identity and a capacity for social interaction (Blumer, 1969, 1970; Hutcheon, 1999; Mead, 1934, 1938).

An early contribution to symbolic interactionism was Charles Horton Cooley's (1864–1929) concept of the **looking-glass self**, the *self-image that results from our interpretation of other people's views of us.* For example, children who are frequently told they are capable and bright will tend to see themselves as such and act accordingly. On the other hand, children who are repeatedly told they lack intelligence or are "slow" will lose pride in themselves and act the part. According to Cooley (1902/1964), we are constantly forming ideas about how others perceive and judge us, and the resulting self-image—the way we view ourselves—is in turn the basis of our social interaction with others.

Cooley recognized that not everyone we encounter is equally important in shaping our self-image. **Primary groups** are small groups characterized by intense emotional ties, face-to-face interaction, intimacy, and a strong, enduring sense of commitment. Families, close friends, and lovers are all examples of primary groups likely to shape our self-image. **Secondary groups**, on the other hand, come together for reasons that are functional or fleeting rather than emotional or enduring. These groups may be based on interests or economic exchange: They could include a workplace, a running club, or even a military field exercise. Today, they may even include the "friends" that one acquires on social media platforms like Facebook: According to the Pew Research Center (2014c), the average number of such friends for millennials is 250, while for generation X, it averages 200. Younger baby boomers average 98 friends. Secondary groups typically have less influence in forming our self-image than do primary groups, although, arguably, social media has unleashed the modern power of "likes" that can have a profound effect on one's self-image. Both kinds of groups act on us throughout our lives; the self-image is not set at some early stage but continues to develop throughout adulthood (Barber, 1992; Berns, 1989).

Both primary and secondary groups also serve as **reference groups**, or as *groups that provide standards*

ColorBlind Images/The Image Bank/Getty Images

Society has unwritten but widely understood "rules" for standing with strangers in an elevator. We learn these conventional practices from interactions and observations. Can you identify these unwritten rules? What constitutes a violation, and how are these "rules" enforced?

Looking-glass self: The concept developed by Charles Horton Cooley that our self-image results from how we interpret other people's views of us.

Primary groups: Small groups characterized by intense emotional ties, face-to-face interaction, intimacy, and a strong, enduring sense of commitment.

Secondary groups: Groups that are impersonal and characterized by functional or fleeting relationships.

for judging our attitudes or behaviors. When you consider your friends' reactions to your dress or hairstyle or new smartphone, you are using your peers as a reference in shaping your decisions.

George Herbert Mead (1863–1931), widely regarded as the founder of symbolic interactionism, explored the ways in which self and society shape one another. Mead proposed that the self comprises two parts: the "I" and the "me." The **I** is *the impulse to act; it is creative, innovative, unthinking, and largely unpredictable.* The **me** is *the part of the self through which we see ourselves as others see us.* (Note the similarity between Mead's "me" and Cooley's "looking-glass self.") The I represents innovation and the me, social convention and conformity. In the tension between them, the me is often capable of controlling the I. When the I initiates a spontaneous act, the me raises society's response: *How will others regard me if I act this way?*

Mead further argued that people develop a sense of self through **role-taking**, *the ability to take the roles of others in interaction.* For example, a young girl playing soccer may pretend to be a coach; in the process, she learns to see herself (as well as other players) from a coach's perspective. Mead proposed that childhood socialization relies on an expanding ability to take on such roles, moving from the extreme self-centeredness of the infant to an adult ability to take the standpoint of society as a whole. He outlined four principal stages in socialization that reflect this progression: the preparatory, play, game, and adult stages. The attainment of each stage results in an increasingly mature social self.

1. During the *preparatory stage,* children younger than 3 years old relate to the world as though they are the center of the universe. They do not engage in true role-taking but respond primarily to things in their immediate environments, such as their mothers' breasts, the colors of toys, or the sounds of voices.
2. Children 3 or 4 years of age enter the *play stage,* during which they learn to take the attitudes and roles of the people with whom they interact. **Significant others** are *specific people important in children's lives whose views have the greatest impact on the children's self-evaluations.* By role-playing at being mothers or fathers, for example, children come to see themselves as their parents see them. Nevertheless, according to Mead, they have not yet acquired the complex sense of self that lets them see themselves through the eyes of *many* different people—or society.
3. The *game* stage begins when children are about 5 and learn to take the roles of multiple others. The game is an effective analogy for this stage. For example, to be an effective basketball player, an individual must have the ability to see him- or herself from the perspective of teammates, the other team, and the coach, and must play accordingly. He or she must know the rules of the game. Successful negotiation of the social world also requires that people gain the ability to see themselves as others see them, to understand societal "rules," and to act accordingly. This stage signals the development of a self that is aware of societal positions and perspectives.
4. Game playing takes the child to the final, *adult stage.* At this stage, young people begin to internalize the **generalized other**, *the sense of society's norms and values by which people evaluate themselves.* They act on a set of socially normative principles that may or may not serve their self-interest—for example, voluntarily joining the military to fight in a war that might injure or kill them because patriotic young people are expected to defend their country or choosing to return a wallet full of cash to its owner because taking something that belongs to someone else is wrong. By the adult stage, a person is capable of understanding abstract and complex cultural symbols, such as love and hate, success and failure, friendship, patriotism, and morality.

Reference groups: Groups that provide standards for judging our attitudes or behaviors.

I: According to George Herbert Mead, the part of the self that is the impulse to act; it is creative, innovative, unthinking, and largely unpredictable.

Me: According to George Herbert Mead, the part of the self through which we see ourselves as others see us.

Role-taking: The ability to take the roles of others in interaction.

Significant others: According to George Herbert Mead, the specific people who are important in children's lives and whose views have the greatest impact on the children's self-evaluations.

Generalized other: The abstract sense of society's norms and values by which people evaluate themselves.

Jim West/Alamy Stock Photo

Game playing is an activity found in some form in every culture. Some games, including basketball and soccer, require teamwork, while others, including checkers and mancala, are played by one person against another. Team games provide many socialization benefits as children learn how to interact with one another and develop their motor skills. ■

Mead also had a vision that in the future people would be able to assimilate a multitude of generalized others, adapting their behavior in terms of their own but also other people's cultures. Mead's "dream of a highly multicultural world" may someday be a reality as globalization makes ever more people aware of the value of other cultures.

STAGES OF DEVELOPMENT: PIAGET AND KOHLBERG

Like Mead and Cooley, the Swiss social psychologist Jean Piaget (1896–1980) believed humans are socialized in stages. Piaget devoted a lifetime to researching how young children develop the ability to think abstractly and make moral judgments (Piaget, 1926, 1928, 1930, 1932). His theory of **cognitive development**, based largely on studies of Swiss children at play (including his own), argues that *an individual's ability to make logical decisions increases as the person grows older.* Piaget noted that infants are highly **egocentric**, *experiencing the world as if it were centered entirely on them.* In stages over time, socialization lets children learn to use language and symbols, to think abstractly and logically, and to see things from different perspectives.

Piaget also developed a theory of moral development, which holds that as they grow, people learn to act according to abstract ideas about justice or fairness. This theory parallels his idea of cognitive development since both describe overcoming egocentrism and acquiring the ability to take other points of view. Eventually children come to develop abstract notions of fairness, learning that rules should be judged relative to the circumstances. For example, even if the rules say "three strikes and you're out," an exception might be made for a child who has never played the game or who is physically challenged.

Lawrence Kohlberg (1927–1987) extended Piaget's ideas about moral development. In his best-known study, subjects were told the story of the fictitious "Heinz," who was unable to afford a drug that might prevent his wife from dying of cancer. As the story unfolds, Heinz breaks into the druggist's shop and steals the medication. Kohlberg asked his subjects what they would have done, emphasizing that there is no "right" or "wrong" answer. Using experiments such as this, Kohlberg (1969, 1983, 1984) proposed three principal stages (and several substages) of moral development:

1. The *preconventional stage,* during which people seek simply to achieve personal gain or avoid punishment. A person might support Heinz's decision to steal on the grounds that it would be too difficult to get the medicine by other means, or oppose it on the grounds that Heinz might get caught and go to jail. Children are typically socialized into this rudimentary form of morality between ages 7 and 10.

2. The *conventional stage,* during which the individual is socialized into society's norms and values and would feel shame or guilt about violating them. The person might support Heinz's decision to steal on the grounds that society would judge him callous if he let his wife die, or oppose it because people would call Heinz a thief if he were caught. Children are socialized into this more developed form of morality at about age 10, and most people remain in this stage throughout their adult lives.

Cognitive development: The theory, developed by Jean Piaget, that an individual's ability to make logical decisions increases as the person grows older.

Egocentric: Experiencing the world as if it were centered entirely on oneself.

3. The *postconventional stage,* during which the individual invokes general, abstract notions of right and wrong. Even though Heinz has broken the law, his transgression has to be weighed against the moral cost of sacrificing his wife's life. People at the highest levels of postconventional morality will go beyond social convention entirely, appealing to a higher set of abstract principles.

Some scholars have argued that Kohlberg's theory reflects a strong male bias because it derives from male rather than from female experience. Foremost among Kohlberg's critics is Carol Gilligan (1982; Gilligan, Ward, & Taylor, 1989), who argues that men may be socialized to base moral judgment on abstract principles of fairness and justice, but women are socialized to base theirs on compassion and caring. She showed that women scored lower on Kohlberg's measure of moral development because they valued how other family members were affected by Heinz's decision more than abstract considerations of justice. Because it assumes that abstract thinking represents a "higher stage" of development, Gilligan suggests, Kohlberg's measure is biased in favor of male socialization.

Research testing Gilligan's ideas has found that men and women alike adhere to *both* care-based and justice-based forms of moral reasoning (Gump, Baker, & Roll, 2000; Jaffee & Hyde, 2000). Differences between the sexes in these kinds of reasoning are in fact small or nonexistent. Studies of federal employees (Peek, 1999), a sample of men and women using the Internet (Anderson, 2000), and a sample of Mexican American and Anglo-American students (Gump et al., 2000) have all found no significant difference between men and women in the degree to which they employ care-based and justice-based styles of moral reasoning. Might there be cases where men and women as groups exercise moral reasoning differently? Does gender affect moral reasoning? What do you think?

BIOLOGICAL NEEDS VERSUS SOCIAL CONSTRAINTS: FREUD

Sigmund Freud (1856–1939), an Austrian psychiatrist, had a major impact on the study of socialization as well as on the disciplines of psychology and psychiatry. Freud (1905, 1929, 1933) founded the field of **psychoanalysis**, *a psychological perspective that emphasizes the complex reasoning processes of the conscious and unconscious mind.* He stressed the role of the unconscious mind in shaping human behavior and theorized that early childhood socialization is essential in molding the adult personality by age 5 or 6. In addition, Freud sought to demonstrate that to thrive, a society must socialize its members to curb their instinctive needs and desires.

FIGURE 4.1 The Id, Ego, and Superego, as Conceived by Freud

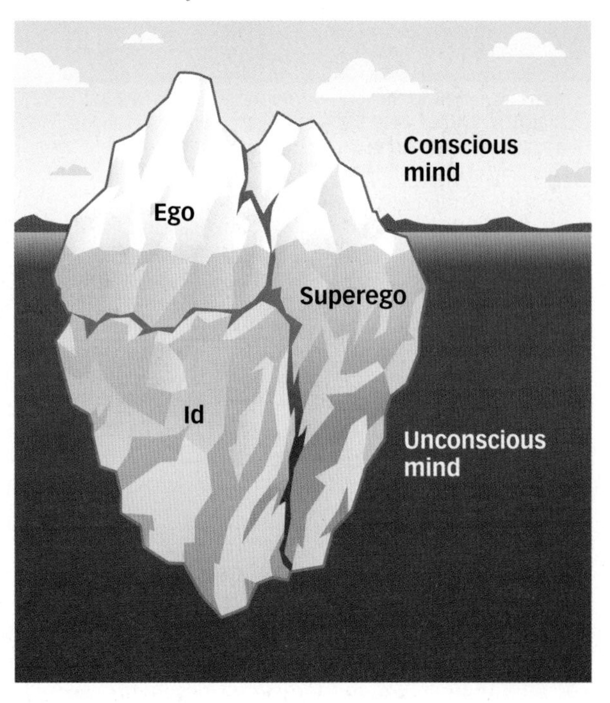

According to Freud, the human mind has three components: the id, the ego, and the superego (Figure 4.1). The **id** is *the repository of basic biological drives and needs,* which Freud believed to be primarily bound up in sexual energy. (*Id* is Latin for "it," reflecting Freud's belief that this aspect of the human personality is not even truly human.) The **ego** (Latin for "I") is *the "self," the core of what we regard as a person's unique personality.*

Psychoanalysis: A psychological perspective that emphasizes the complex reasoning processes of the conscious and unconscious mind.

Id: According to Sigmund Freud, the part of the mind that is the repository of basic biological drives and needs.

Ego: According to Sigmund Freud, the part of the mind that is the "self," the core of what is regarded as a person's unique personality.

TABLE 4.1 Comparison of Mead's and Freud's Theories of Socialization

Mead's Stages	Freud's Psychoanalytic Theory
Preparatory: Highly limited role-taking in which the individual views the world through his or her own eyes.	Id: The repository of basic biological drives and needs, which seeks instant gratification.
Play: The individual takes on the roles of significant others, one at a time.	Ego: The "self" that, once developed, balances the forces of the id and superego. The ego is necessary in the socialization process for the individual to become a well-adjusted adult.
Game: The individual is able to view the world through the eyes of multiple others, simultaneously.	Superego: The values and norms of society. May conflict with the id.
Maturity: The individual is able to take the attitude of the generalized other and can view the world through the eyes of society as a whole.	

SOURCE: Adapted from Mead, G. H. (1934). *Mind, self, and society.* Chicago: University of Chicago Press.

The **superego** consists of *the values and norms of society, insofar as they are internalized, or taken in, by the individual.* The concept of the superego is similar to the notion of a conscience.

Freud believed that babies are all id. Left to their own devices, they will seek instant gratification of their biological needs for food, physical contact, and nurturing. Therefore, according to Freud, to be socialized, they must eventually learn to suppress such gratification. The child's superego, consisting of cultural "shoulds" and "should nots," struggles constantly with the biological impulses of the id. Serving as mediator between id and superego is the child's emerging ego. In Freud's view, the child will grow up to be a well-socialized adult to the extent that the ego succeeds in bending the biological desires of the id to meet the social demands of the superego.

Since Freud claimed that personality is set early in life, he viewed change as difficult for adults, especially if psychological troubles originate in experiences too painful to face or remember. Individuals must become fully aware of their repressed or unconscious memories and unacceptable impulses if they ever hope to change (Freud, 1933). Freud's psychoanalytic therapy focused on accessing deeply buried feelings to help patients alter current behaviors and feelings. Whereas Mead saw socialization as a lifelong process relying on many socialization agents, for Freud it stopped at a young age. Table 4.1 compares Mead's and Freud's views point by point.

Superego: According to Sigmund Freud, the part of the mind that consists of the values and norms of society, insofar as they are internalized, or taken in, by the individual.

AGENTS OF SOCIALIZATION

Among primary groups, the family is for most people the most critical agent of socialization. Other significant agents are school, peer groups, work, religion, and technology and mass media, including the Internet and social media (Figure 4.2).

Child-rearing practices within families can vary along many dimensions—ethnic background, religious affiliation, even social class. Because U.S. culture is ethnically diverse, it is difficult to describe a "typical" American family (Glazer, 1997; Stokes & Chevan, 1996). Among Latinos, for example, the family often includes grandparents, aunts, uncles, cousins, and in-laws, who share child-rearing responsibilities. Among Latino youth, scholars have identified the family, especially mothers, as a central force that informs the ethnic identity development process (Knight et al., 2011; Supple, Ghazarian, Frabutt, Plunkett, & Sands, 2006).

THE FAMILY

The family is a primary group in which children, especially during the earliest years of their lives, are physically and emotionally dependent on adult members. It plays a key role in transmitting norms, values, and culture across generations, and as a result, it is the first and usually the foremost source of socialization in all societies.

Children usually first encounter their society in the family, learning socially defined roles like father, mother, sister, brother, uncle, aunt, and grandparent, and the expected behaviors attached to them. Parents often hold stereotypical notions of how boys and girls should be, and they reinforce gender behaviors in countless subtle and not-so-subtle ways. A father may be responsible for grilling and yard work, while a mother cooks dinner and cleans the house. On the other hand, some families embrace egalitarian or nonconventional gender roles. Although same-sex couple families are more likely than families headed by opposite-sex couples to challenge gender-normative roles and behaviors, they sometimes still enforce or support more traditional gender roles for their children (Ackbar, 2011; Bos & Sandfort, 2010).

The way parents relate to their child affects almost every aspect of the child's behavior, including the ability to resolve

FIGURE 4.2 Agents of Socialization

SOURCE: Supple et al., 2006; Umaña-Taylor et al., 2011.

conflicts through the use of reason instead of violence and the propensity for emotional stability or distress. The likelihood that young people will be victims of homicide, commit suicide, engage in acts of aggression against other people, use drugs, complete their secondary education, or have an unwanted pregnancy also is greatly influenced by childhood experiences in the family (Campbell & Muncer, 1998; McLoyd & Smith, 2002; Muncer & Campbell, 2000). For example, children who are regularly spanked or otherwise physically punished internalize the idea that violence is an acceptable means of achieving goals and are more likely than peers who are not spanked to engage in aggressive delinquent behavior. They are also more likely to have low self-esteem, suffer depression, and do poorly in school (Straus, Sugarman, & Giles-Sims, 1997). (See the *Private Lives, Public Issues* box on pages 106–107).

Among African Americans as well, child rearing may be shared among a broader range of family members than in White families (Lubeck, 1985). Extended family patterns also occur among Afro-Caribbean immigrants and the Amish religious community of Pennsylvania (Forsythe-Brown, 2007; Ho, 1993; Stokes & Chevan, 1996).

Child-rearing practices may vary by social class as well. Parents whose jobs require them to be subservient to authority and to follow orders without raising questions typically stress obedience and respect for authority at home, while parents whose work gives them freedom to make their own decisions and be creative are likely to socialize their children into norms of creativity and spontaneity. Since many working-class jobs demand conformity while middle- and upper-middle-class jobs are more likely to offer independence, social class may be a key factor in explaining differences in child rearing (Kohn, 1989; Lareau, 2002).

Family patterns are changing rapidly in the United States partly because of declining marriage rates and high rates of divorce. Such changes can affect socialization. For example, children raised by a single parent may not be actively exposed to a male or a female role model in the home or may experience economic hardship that in turn determines where they go to school or with whom they socialize. Children raised in blended families (the result of remarriage) may have stepparents and stepsiblings whose norms, values, and behavior are unfamiliar. Same-sex couple families may both challenge and, as noted earlier, reinforce conventional modes of socialization, particularly with respect to gender socialization. Although families are changing, their influence as agents of socialization remains powerful.

TEACHERS AND SCHOOL

Children in the United States often begin "schooling" when they enter day care or preschool as infants or toddlers, and they spend more hours each day and more days each year in school than was the case a hundred years ago (although they spend less time in school than their peers in Europe and Asia). Indeed, education has taken on a large role in helping

Child-Rearing and Punishment in U.S. Families

Although many people still believe in the adage "Spare the rod and spoil the child," the use of physical punishment in the United States has declined over time, although studies on the issue produce mixed results depending on whether respondents are queried about attitudes or practices. On the one hand, a large Child Trends study found high levels of support for the statement that children sometimes need a "good, hard spanking," although the response differed somewhat by gender: About 76% of men and 65% of women agreed with the assertion (Child Trends, 2014). On the other hand, a survey conducted by the Pew Research Center (2015b) reports that 53% of respondents "never spank" their child or children. By contrast, 17% answered that they spank "often" or "sometimes," and 28% said they spank "rarely." Interestingly, the study found that proportions of parents indicating that they spank varied by race and education. Even though, overall, the use of corporal punishment is low, just 8% of parents with graduate-level education reported that they spanked often or sometimes, compared with 22% for those with a high school education or less. There were also differences by race, with Hispanic parents most likely to indicate they "never spank" (58%) and Black parents more likely to say they spank sometimes or often (32%).

FIGURE 4.3 Use of Spanking by Racial and Educational Groups

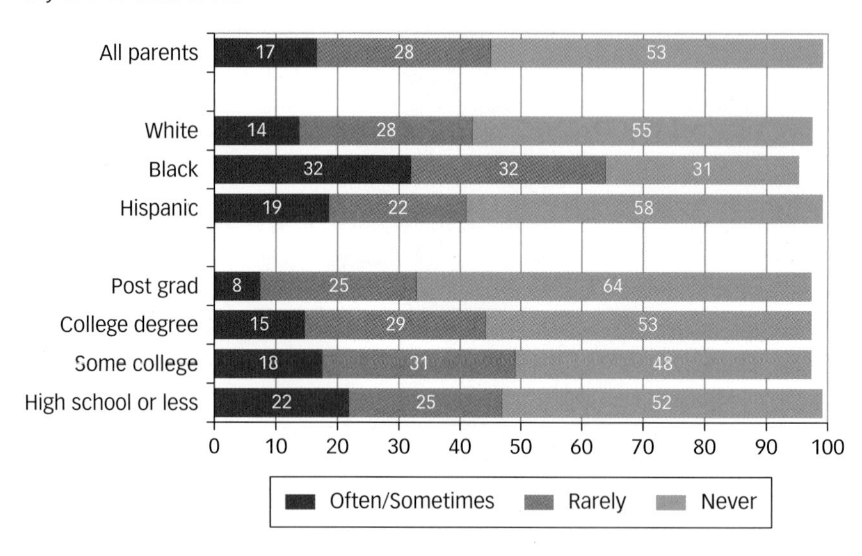

NOTE: Voluntary responses of "Child is too young/old" and "Don't know/Refused" not shown. Whites and Blacks include only those who are not Hispanic. Hispanics are of any race.

SOURCE: "Parenting in America," Pew Research Center, Washington, DC (December 2015b). http://www.pewsocialtrends.org/2015/12/17/parenting-in-america/

Spanking is of interest to sociologists because it highlights the nexus between private lives and public issues. On the one hand, it is a personal decision made by parents in the home; on the other hand, research suggests that it may have social consequences that are borne more widely. For example, a study on young children found that when boys and girls 6 to 9 years old were spanked, they became more antisocial—more likely to cheat, tell lies, act cruelly to others, break things deliberately, and get into trouble at school (Straus et al., 1997). Another study concluded that corporal punishment, and even some lesser forms of parental punishment, could have a strong effect on a child's ability to cope later in life (Welsh, 1998). More recently, a meta-analysis of spanking that covered 5 decades of research and included studies of over 160,000 children concluded that children who were spanked were more likely to have mental health problems and to be antisocial than their peers who were not spanked. In addition, being spanked also correlated with higher risks of depression, anxiety, and paranoia—and even a lower tested IQ (Gershoff & Grogan-Kaylor, 2016).

There has been research that suggests less malign effects. For example, research by psychologist Marjorie Lindner Gunnoe (1997), which tracked more than 1,100 children over a 5-year period, found that although some 8- to 11-year-old boys, but not girls, who had been spanked regularly got into more fights at school, children of both sexes ages 4 to 7 who had been spanked regularly got into fewer fights than children who were not spanked. As well, children who were spanked were found in some studies to be more compliant, though the effects were limited to the short term—in the long term, many children were more defiant. Significantly, there is also the question of whether correlation adds up to causation, and some researchers caution that it is possible that some children with a predisposition to aggressive behavior may elicit harsher punishments, thus throwing into question whether more aggressive behavior is a cause or consequence of spanking (Gershoff & Grogan-Kaylor, 2016).

Although the research findings on the effects of physical punishment differ somewhat, a significant proportion of the evidence suggests that spanking may result in detrimental outcomes for children and even society—suggesting that this private trouble can indeed be a public issue.

THINK IT THROUGH

- Using the knowledge you have gained through the study of socialization, and knowing the results of research on the effects of physical punishment on children's behavior, could you design a social policy or program to reduce the use of physical punishment in the home?

Follow us on Twitter to keep up with current sociological stories and research! We're at @DiscoverSoc1.
Share your own ideas at #DiscoverSociology.

young people prepare for adult society. In addition to reading, writing, math, and other academic subjects, schools are expected to teach values and norms like patriotism, competitiveness, morality, and respect for authority, as well as basic social skills. Some sociologists call this the **hidden curriculum**, that is, *the unspoken classroom socialization into the norms, values, and roles of a society that schools provide along with the "official" curriculum.* The hidden curriculum may include "lessons" in gender roles taught through teachers' differing expectations of boys and girls, with, for instance, boys pushed to pursue higher math while girls are encouraged to embrace language and literature (Sadker, Zittleman, & Sadker, 2003). It may entail "lessons" that reinforce class status, with middle- and upper-class children having access to classes and schools with advanced subjects, advanced technology, and outstanding teachers, and poor children provided a smaller selection of less academically challenging or vocational classes and limited access to advanced teaching technologies and highly trained educators (Bowles & Gintis, 1976; Kozol, 2005, 2013). At the same time, the hidden curriculum may also include what is not taught: For example, if an English class typically relies on reading material with White main characters, this may teach students of color that their cultures are not appreciated or people of their ethnic group cannot be heroes.

PEERS

Peers are people of the same age and, often, of the same social standing. Peer socialization begins when a child starts to play with other children outside the family, usually during the first year of life, and grows more intense in school. Conformity to the norms and values of friends is

Hidden curriculum: The unspoken classroom socialization into the norms, values, and roles of a society that schools provide along with the "official" curriculum.

especially compelling during adolescence and continues into adulthood (Harris, 2009; Ponton, 2000; Sebald, 2000). In U.S. society, most adolescents spend more time with their peers than with their families as a result of school, athletic activities, and other social and academic commitments. Sociological theories thus often focus on young people's peer groups to account for a wide variety of adult behavioral patterns, including the development of self-esteem and self-image, career choices, ambition, and deviant behavior (Cohen, 1955; Hine, 2000; Sebald, 2000).

Ronnie Kaufman/Larry Hirshowitz/Blend Images/Getty Images

Schools are an important agent of socialization. Students learn academic skills and knowledge, but they also gain social skills, acquire dominant values of citizenship, and practice obedience to authority.

Judith Rich Harris (2009) argues that after the first few years of life, a child's friends' opinions outweigh the opinions of parents. To manage these predominant peer group influences, she suggests, parents must try to ensure that their children have the "right" friends. But this is an increasingly complex problem when "friends" may be Internet acquaintances who are difficult to monitor and of whom parents may be unaware.

The adolescent subculture plays an extremely important part in the socialization of adolescents in the modern world. Researchers have described the following characteristics of this subculture (Hine, 2000; Sebald, 2000):

1. A set of norms not shared with the adult or childhood cultures and governing interaction, statuses, and roles.
2. An *argot* (the special vocabulary of a particular group) that is not shared with nonadolescents and is often frowned upon by adults and school officials. Think about the jargon used by young people who text—many adults can read it only with difficulty!
3. Various underground media and preferred media programs, music, and Internet sites.
4. Unique fads and fashions in dress and hairstyles that often lead to conflict with parents and other adult authorities over their "appropriateness."
5. A set of "heroes, villains, and fools." Sometimes adults are the "villains and fools," while the adults' "villains and fools" are heroes in the adolescent subculture.
6. A more open attitude than that found in the general culture toward experimentation with drugs and at times violence (fighting, for example).

Anticipatory socialization: Adoption of the behaviors or standards of a group one emulates or hopes to join.

Teenagers differ in the degree to which they are caught up in, and therefore socialized by, the adolescent subculture. Harris's (2009) claim that parents are largely irrelevant is no doubt an overstatement, yet in Western cultures, peer socialization does play a crucial part in shaping many of the ideas, self-images, and attitudes that will persist throughout individuals' lives.

Sociologists use the term **anticipatory socialization** to describe the process of *adopting the behaviors or standards of a group one emulates or hopes to join.* For example, teens who seek membership into a tough, streetwise gang will abandon mainstream norms for the dress and talk of the tougher youth they seek to emulate. Similarly, young people who aspire to be part of a respected group of athletes may adopt forms of dress and training practices that may lead to acceptance by the group. Anticipatory socialization looks to future expectations rather than to just present experience.

ORGANIZED SPORTS

Organized sports are a fundamental part of the lives of millions of children in the United States: By one estimate, 21.5 million children and teens ages 6 to 17 participate in at least one organized sport (Kelley & Carchia, 2013). About 40% of kids between 6 and 12 are involved in a team sport (Rosenwald, 2016). If it is the case, as psychologist Erik Erikson (1950) posited, that in middle childhood children develop a sense of "industry or inferiority," then it is surely the case that in a sports-obsessed country like the United States, one avenue for generating this sense of self is through participation in sports.

Being part of a sports team and mastering skills associated with sports are activities that are widely recognized in U.S. society as valuable; they are presumed to "build character" and to contribute to hard work, competitiveness, and the ability to perform in stressful situations and under the gaze of others (Friedman, 2013), all of which are positively evaluated. In fact, research suggests that there are particular benefits of sports for girls, including lower rates of teen sexual activity and pregnancy (Sabo, Miller, Farrell, Melnick, & Barnes, 1999) and higher rates of college attendance, labor force participation, and entry into male-dominated occupations (Stevenson, 2010). Some studies have also found improved academic performance relative to nonparticipants for all athletes, although they have shown some variation in this effect by race and gender (Eccles & Barber, 1999; Miller, Melnick, Barnes, Farrell, & Sabo, 2005).

At the same time, sports participation has been associated in some research literature with socialization into negative attitudes, including homophobia. In a study of more than 1,400 teenagers, Osborne and Wagner (2007) found that boys who participated in "core" sports (football, basketball, baseball, and/or soccer) were three times more likely than their nonparticipant peers to express homophobic attitudes. In a country in which sports and sports figures are widely venerated and participation, particularly for boys, is labeled as "masculine," there may also be negative effects for boys who are not athletic or who do not enjoy sports.

Source: Author

Since the passage of Title IX in 1972, millions of girls have had the opportunity to participate in organized sports. Do social messages conveyed by male-dominated sports differ from those in female-dominated sports?

RELIGION

Religion is a central part of the lives of many people around the world. Although the United States has a notable proportion of inhabitants who identify as atheists, about 76% of U.S. adults indicate they are members of a religion, and nearly 40% attend religious services once a week. Even among the one fifth of the population who declare themselves unaffiliated with any particular religion, 68% believe in God and more than 20% say that they pray every day (Pew Forum on Religion and Public Life, 2015). Beginning with Émile Durkheim, sociologists have noted the role of religion in fostering social solidarity. Talcott Parsons (1970) pointed out that religion also acts as an agent of socialization, teaching fundamental values and beliefs that contribute to a shared normative culture.

Different religions function in similar ways, giving their followers a sense of what is right and wrong, how to conduct themselves in society, and how to organize their lives. Some socialize their followers with abstract teachings about morality, service, or self-discipline, directing believers to, for example, serve their fellow human beings or to avoid the sin of vanity. Others contain abstract teachings but specific rules about dress and hairstyles. The Amish faith entreats young men to remain clean-shaven prior to marriage, but married men must grow beards. Sikh men of India wear turbans that cover their hair, which they do not cut.

Like other agents of socialization and social control, religion directs its followers to choose certain paths and behaviors and not others. This is not to say that we are compelled to behave a certain way but rather that socialization often leads us to control our own behavior because we fear social ostracism or other negative consequences.

MASS MEDIA AND SOCIAL MEDIA

Among the most influential agents of socialization in modern societies are technology and the mass media. Newspapers, magazines, movies, radio, and television are all forms of mass media. Television has long been an influential agent of socialization: According to Nielsen ratings, the typical American spends 5 hours and 4 minutes in front of a TV screen per day. The overall numbers are down from previous years; however, it is important to note that Nielsen only tracks live TV viewing. When we add time spent watching streaming content from Netflix, HBO, or other services—as well as time spent on social media—it's clear that overall screen time is rising in the United States (Kalogeropoulos, 2015). Americans now own four digital devices on average, and the typical U.S. consumer spends 60 hours a week consuming content across devices (Nielsen, 2014).

Child psychologists, sociologists, and parents' groups pay special attention to the impact of TV and other media violence on children and young adults. Media studies during the past 20 years have largely come to a common conclusion: Media violence has the clear potential to socialize children, teenagers, and even adults into a greater acceptance of real-life violence. This is true for males and females, Whites and non-Whites. Much media violence is directed against women, and a large body of research supports the conclusion that media violence promotes tolerance among men for sexual violence, including rape (Anderson et al., 2003; Greene & Krcmar, 2005). The argument is not that viewing violent shows is a direct cause of violence; rather, viewers may become immunized to the sight of violence. Still, given that most people who are exposed to violence in the media do not become violent, the part played by the media as an agent of socialization is probably less important than the contribution made by other agents, such as family and peers.

The media play a role in socialization by creating fads and fashions for how people should look, what they should wear, and what kinds of friendships they should have. These influences, and accompanying gender stereotypes, are particularly strong during adolescence. Children's cartoons, prime-time television, TV advertisements, and popular networks like MTV, TLC, and VH-1 often depict males and females, as well as people of particular races and ethnicities, in stereotyped ways. Teenage girls, for example, are likely to be depicted as boy-crazy and obsessed with their looks; teenage boys are shown as active, independent, and sexually and physically aggressive (Kahlenberg & Hein, 2010; Maher, Herbst, Childs, & Finn, 2008). Females' roles also portray mostly familial or romantic ideals, whereas males fulfill work-related roles (Lauzen, Dozier, & Horan, 2008). These stereotypes have been found to influence children's gender perceptions (Aubrey & Harrison, 2004; Gerding & Signorielli, 2014). Additionally, gender stereotypes influence beliefs across the spectrum of sexual orientation, with gay teens embracing stereotypes in ways comparable to their heterosexual peers (Bishop, Kiss, Morrison, Rushe, & Specht, 2014).

Social media, which is widely used across generations, affects socialization by, among other things, changing social interaction. To name just one effect that was impossible 20 years ago, large groups of semianonymous individuals, often separated by great distances, can interact with one another in virtual communities, even forming close ties and friendships.

On the positive side, especially when online interactions are mixed with off-line face-to-face interactions, Internet use can foster new personal relationships and build stronger communities (Valentine, 2006; Wellman & Hampton, 1999), as shown in Figure 4.4. The types of friendships adolescents create and maintain through social media reflect the friendships they have off-line (Mazur & Richards, 2011). Since online interaction is often anonymous and occurs from the safety of familiar places, people with characteristics society tends to stigmatize, such as obesity or a stutter, can enter virtual communities where differences are not perceived or punished (McKenna & Bargh, 1998) and interests such as chess or movies can be shared. Finally, the moderate use of e-mail and the Internet can help children and teens maintain and strengthen interpersonal relationships (Subrahmanyam & Lin, 2007).

The Internet can have negative social consequences, too. As we discuss elsewhere in the text, researchers have linked high levels of use with declines in communication within households, shrinking social circles, and increased depression and loneliness (Dokoupil, 2012a, 2012b; Kraut et al., 1998; Yen, Yen, & Ko, 2010). Extreme cases can develop into Internet addiction, a relatively recent phenomenon characterized by a search for social stimulation and escape from real-life problems (Armstrong, Phillips, & Saling, 2000; Block, 2008). Although the Internet can be a valuable learning tool for children, it can also damage their development by decreasing the time they spend in face-to-face

Silver Screen Collection/Getty Images; HBO/Getty Images; ABC Family via Getty Images

Television offers a variety of female images ranging from independent working women to "fashionistas." From the *Mary Tyler Moore Show* (1970–1977) to *Sex and the City* (1998–2004) to *Pretty Little Liars* (2010–2017), images can both reflect and construct ideas about femininity.

interactions and exposing them to inappropriate information and images (Bremer & Rauch, 1998; Lewin, 2011b; Livingstone & Brake, 2010).

Another form of negative socialization is *cyberbullying*—taunting, teasing, or verbal attacks through e-mail, text, or social networking sites with the intent to hurt the victim (Van DeBosch & Van Cleemput, 2008). Cyberbullying is a growing problem of acute concern to social workers, child psychologists, and school administrators (Slovak & Singer, 2011). Children and adolescents who are bullied in real life are sometimes both cyberbullies and victims of cyberbullying (Dilmac, 2009; Smith et al., 2008; Tyman, Saylor, Taylor, & Comeaux, 2010). Victims take to the Internet to get revenge, often through anonymous attacks, but this perpetuates the bullying cycle online and in real life. One study found that hurtful cyberteasing between adolescents in romantic relationships can escalate into real-life shouting, throwing of objects, or hitting (Madlock & Westerman, 2011).

Modern technology may foster positive socialization, but it also has the potential to be detrimental on both the micro level of individual and small-group interactions and the macro level of communities and countries. Consider the role played today by social media in turning interest groups, and even ethnic groups, against one another.

FIGURE 4.4 Percentage of Teens Who Have Made Friends Online

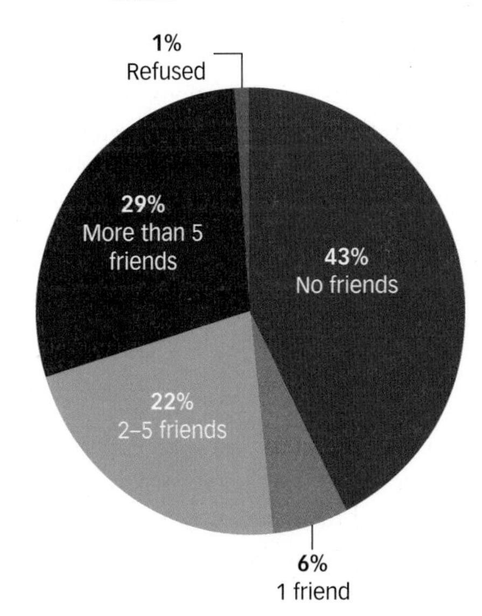

SOURCE: "Teens, Technology and Friendships," by Pew Research Center, Washington, DC (August 2015). http://www.pewinternet.org/2015/08/06/teens-technology-and-friendships/

WORK

For most adults in the United States, post-adolescent socialization begins with entry into the workforce. Although workplace norms calling for conformity or individuality are frequently taught by parents in the home, expectations at work can differ from those we experience in primary groups such as the family and peer groups.

FIGURE 4.5 Average Number of Hours per Week of Screen Time

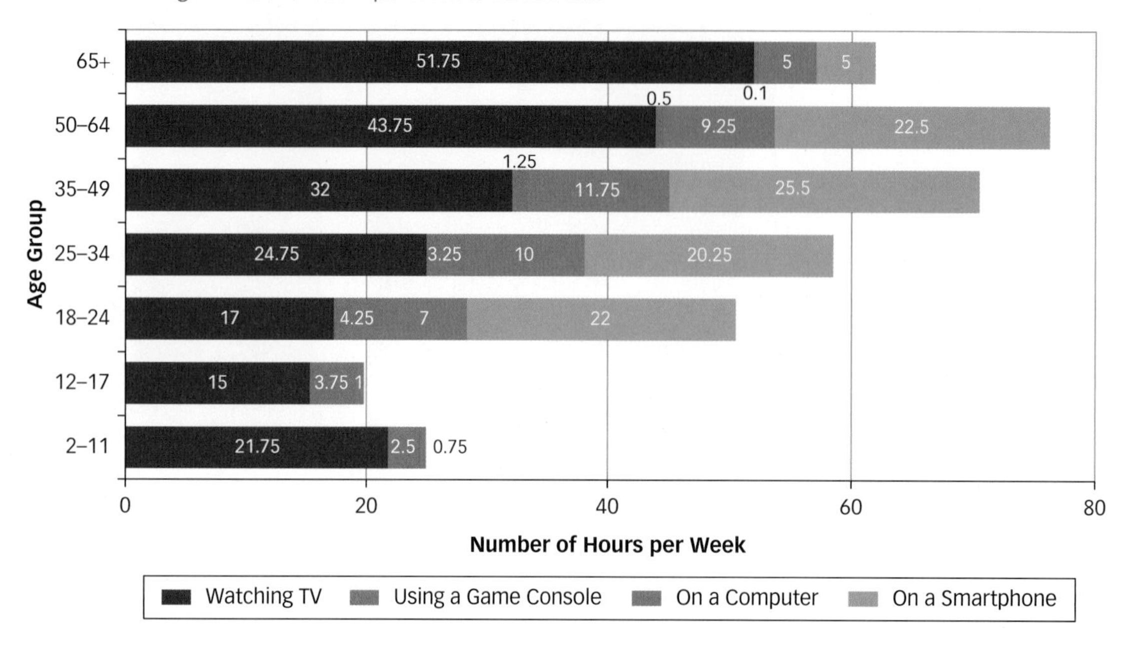

SOURCE: "The Nielsen Total Audience Report Q4 2016." Nielsen.com.

NOTE: Data not available for smartphone usage for 2- to 17-year-olds, but some studies have estimated that children 2 to 11 may spend as much as 14 hours a week on smartphones, and teens 12 to 17 nearly 27 hours per week (Houghton et al., 2015).

Arguably, workplace socialization has had a particular influence on women, dramatically changing gender roles in many countries, including the United States. Beginning in the 1960s, paid work afforded women increased financial independence, allowing them to marry later—or not at all—and bringing them new opportunities for social interaction and new social roles.

Maarten de Boer/Contour by Getty Images

Meyrowitz (1985) writes that "old people are respected [in media portrayals] to the extent that they can behave like young people" (p. 153). Betty White is a highly recognized actress, whose roles are often humorous and appealing to younger crowds. Think about portrayals of older persons you have seen recently in movies or on television. Do you agree with this assessment?

Employment also often socializes us into both the job role and our broader role as a "member" of a collective sharing the same employer. Becoming a teacher, chef, factory worker, lawyer, or retail salesperson, for instance, requires learning specific skills and the norms, values, and practices associated with that position. In that role, the employee may also internalize the values and norms of the employer and may even come to identify with the employer: Notice that employees who are speaking about their workplaces will often refer to them rather intimately, saying, for instance, not that "Company X is hiring a new sales manager" but rather that "*we* are hiring a new sales manager."

Even "occupations" outside the bounds of legality are governed by rules and roles learned through socialization. Harry King, a professional thief studied by one of the authors, learned not only how to break into buildings and open safes but also how to conform to the culture of the professional thief. A professional thief never "rats" on a partner, for example, or steals from mom-and-pop stores. In addition, King acquired a unique language that enabled him to talk to other thieves while in the company of nonthieves ("Square Johns"), police officers, and prison guards (King & Chambliss, 1984).

When Is Dinner?

In the past, late dinner times were the exclusive privilege of the upper classes, who could afford candles to illuminate their meals. The poorer classes were forced by circumstances to take their last meal of the day during the daylight hours.

As young people growing up, many evenings may have brought forth a pair of burning questions: What's for dinner? No less important: *When* is dinner? The memory of these exchanges with a parent, grandparent, or sibling may seem very personal, but we can also take a sociological perspective on these questions. That is, although we are socialized to see a particular time of day as the "normal" time to have a certain meal (and variations on this can elicit discomfort or unhappiness), this "normality" is a product of both cultural norms and structural forces. Historian Sharrie McMillan (2001) writes that "everyone in medieval England knew that you ate breakfast first thing in the morning, dinner in the middle of the day, and supper not long before you went to bed, around sundown. The modern confusion arose from changing social customs and classes, political and economic developments, and even from technological innovations" (para. 2)

Consider the issue of social class. How might social class affect mealtimes? In medieval England, dinner, eaten in the middle of the day, was the biggest and most important meal of the day. Royalty and esteemed members of the court might eat around noon, indulging in a massive and lavish meal that could last for hours and required the attendance of dozens of servers and chefs. The nascent middle class, largely composed of merchants, took their meal later in the afternoon, structuring their schedules not by tradition but guided by the demands of work and customers. Few people ate a large meal at the end of the day. Exceptions included the most privileged members of society, who could have their final meals of the day by candlelight. If one could not, however, afford the luxury of candles, then sundown brought the last light of day during which to settle in for supper (McMillan, 2001).

Economic developments also had a transformative effect on mealtimes in England. With the advent of capitalism and the development of a mass urban industrial workforce in the late 1700s and the 1800s, "people began to work further from home, and the midday meal had to become something light, just whatever they could carry to work. The main meal, still usually called dinner, was pushed to the evening hours after work, when they could get home for a full meal" (McMillan, 2001, para. 26). The privileged classes also ate late, but their mealtimes were driven more by desire than necessity.

The sociological roots of meals and mealtimes—suggesting their patterning is as much social and individual—can also be seen in the more recent advent of brunch. Brunch, of course, is a hybrid of breakfast and lunch, often associated with weekends and the luxury of a late-morning meal. Some evidence suggests that brunch has its roots in 19th-century British "hunt meals," which were lavish, multicourse meals for the upper class. Brunch as a weekend practice made its way to the United States, but according to some sources, it became more widespread and popular after World War II, as the number of churchgoers declined, opening Sunday mornings to a new indulgence (Winterman, 2012).

Today in the United States, our meals and mealtimes continue to be structured by a variety of sociological factors that include, but are not limited to, educational and economic imperatives like school and work. Consider the social weight that is put on the "family dinner," which is not seen as having only the manifest function of distributing a good meal to an intimate group. Rather, based on research showing the importance of family meals for, potentially, averting delinquency and substance abuse and boosting adolescent mental health (Musick & Meier, 2012), the family dinner has taken on the social function of being a prime forum for communication between adults and children.

Whether eaten by daylight, candlelight, or light bulb; whether eaten early or late; whether eaten with work colleagues, friends, or family, dinner—no less than breakfast, brunch, lunch, or any other meal—can be viewed through a sociological lens.

THINK IT THROUGH

- Describe a "typical" evening mealtime in your home. Consider it from a sociological perspective: What factors, both micro and macro level, have an impact on the timing of the meal, who participates, and how it wraps up? If you live away from home now, have you been "resocialized" in your new environment to different mealtime rituals?

SOCIALIZATION AND AGING

Most theories of socialization focus on infancy, childhood, and adolescence, but people do not stop changing once they become adults. Work, social relationships, and the media, for example, shape socialization over the life course.

Some processes of life course socialization remain steady into older age. For example, today, as younger adults enter the workforce later, older adults are staying in the workforce longer. According to Pew Research, nearly 27% of U.S. adults ages 65 to 74 are in the workforce, a figure that is projected to rise to 32% by 2022 (Drake, 2014). This upward trend is driven by a variety of factors that include economic pressures to continue working for pay, the larger number of women in the workforce who are choosing to stay longer, and improving health in the senior population.

Other processes of life course socialization shift as adults get older. As people approach retirement, for instance, anticipatory socialization kicks in to help them envision their futures. Seniors may pay more attention to how friends react to retirement, whether they are treated differently as they age, and how older people are portrayed in the media. Notably, in U.S. media programming and advertisements, seniors are seriously underrepresented relative to their numbers in the nation's population. When they are presented, older characters are often shown positively, although they are also likely to be gender stereotyped and wealthier than in the real world (Kessler, Racoczy, & Staudinger, 2004; Lee, Carpenter, & Meyers, 2007). As well, there has been a pattern in Hollywood films of ignoring or mocking seniors' sexuality: An article in *The Atlantic* on this topic pointed out that

> aging male actors are often relegated to "dirty old men" roles—but compared to older actresses, they have more opportunities to play people with active sex lives. It's just that they're usually having sex with younger women. The options for aging actresses are largely roles that in no way recognize their sexuality except as something that has faded, or those that depict them as deluded, wannabe sex kittens, fooling themselves about the extent

of their sexual attractiveness. (Kelly, 2012, para 6)

This observation underscores an earlier point that portrayals of seniors are often saturated with gender stereotypes but, as well, that stereotypes about age—and youth bias—permeate mass media images of older adults.

There is a perception that seniors are more likely than younger adults to disengage from society, moving away from relationships, activities, and institutions that previously played key roles in their lives. Although this is the case for some seniors, research suggests that most remain active as long as they are healthy (Rubin, 2006). In fact, the notion that seniors are disengaged is belied by the fact that many adults become more politically active in their older years. Consider the fact that Americans 65 and older are more likely than any other age group to vote (Figure 4.6; Taylor & Lopez, 2013).

■ **FIGURE 4.6** Reported Voting Rates, 1988–2016

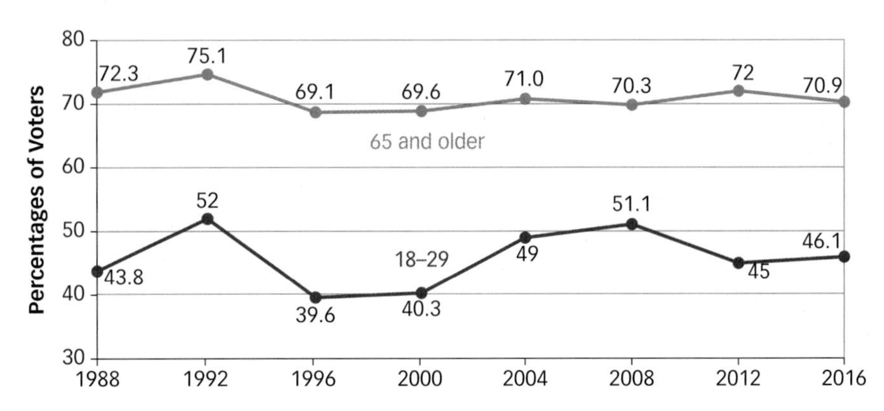

SOURCE: File, Thom. "Voting in America: A Look at the 2016 Presidential Election." *United States Census Bureau*. N.p., 10 May 2017. Web. 22 May 2017. https://www.census.gov/newsroom/blogs/random-samplings/2017/05/voting_in_america.html.

Older adults are also increasingly likely to be engaged in the digital world. Recent research shows that about 56% of adults 65 and older who go online use Facebook, a figure that represents nearly a third of seniors (Duggan, Ellison, Lampe, Lenhart, & Madden, 2015). Technology offers seniors a spectrum of ways to stay connected to family and friends and, as well, to meet new friends: Some research suggests that adults older than 60 are the fastest-growing segment of the online dating market. Accordingly, the Internet offers a variety of dating sites targeted specifically to older Americans who, according to researchers Wendy K. Watson and Claude Stelle,

> appear to market themselves differently on online dating sites than younger adults. Gone is the focus on appearance and status . . . the senior population appears to be more interested in honest self-representation and being compatible rather than discussing areas such as sexual prowess and nightlife. (Bowling Green State University, 2012, para. 4)

Interestingly, age is not the only factor that influences technology use: Although younger seniors are more likely to use technology, use is also significantly affected by income and education. For instance, while 87% of seniors with college degrees go online, just 40% of those without college do so (Pew Research Center, 2014d).

As people age, health and dying also become increasingly important and influential in structuring their perceptions and interactions. Married couples face the prospect of losing a spouse, and all seniors may begin to lose close friends. The question of what it might be like to live alone is more urgent for women than for men since men, on average, die several years younger than women do. Very old people in particular are likely to spend time in the hospital or in a nursing home, which requires being socialized into a total institution (discussed below). Growing older is thus influenced by socialization as significant and challenging as in earlier life stages.

Clearly, socialization is a lifelong process. Our early primary socialization lays a foundation for our social selves, which continue to develop through processes of secondary socialization, including our interactions with technology, media, education, and work. But can we be "resocialized"? That is, can our social selves be torn down and reconstituted in new forms that conform to the norms, roles, and rules of entirely different social settings? We explore this question in the following section.

TOTAL INSTITUTIONS AND RESOCIALIZATION

Although individuals typically play an active role in their own socialization, in one setting—the total institution—they

Scott Olson/Getty Images

These marines are part of a total institution in which they are subject to regimentation and control of their daily activities by an authoritative body. They are expected to exhibit obedience to authority and to elevate the collective over the individual good.

experience little choice. **Total institutions** are *institutions that isolate individuals from the rest of society to achieve administrative control over most aspects of their lives.* Examples include prisons, the military, hospitals—especially mental hospitals—and live-in drug and alcohol treatment centers. Administrative control is achieved through rules that govern all aspects of daily life, from dress to schedules to interpersonal interactions. The residents of total institutions are subject to inflexible routines rigidly enforced by staff supervision (Goffman, 1961; Malacrida, 2005).

A major purpose of total institutions is **resocialization**, *the process of altering an individual's behavior through total control of his or her environment.* Goffman (1961) referred to this as the "mortification of self," or the process of degrading and, over time, transforming the self of the individual subject to the discipline of the total institution. The first step is to break down the sense of self. In a total institution, every aspect of life is managed and monitored. The individual is stripped of identification with the outside world. Institutional haircuts, uniforms, round-the-clock inspections, and abuse, such as the harassment of new recruits to a military school, contribute to breaking down the individual's sense of self. In extreme situations, such as in concentration camps, psychological and even physical torture may also be used.

Once the institutionalized person is "broken," the institution begins rebuilding the personality. Desirable behaviors are rewarded with small privileges, such as choice of work duty in prisons. Undesirable behaviors are severely punished, such as by the assignment of humiliating or painful work chores. Since the goal of the total institution is to change attitudes as well as behaviors, even a hint that the resident continues to harbor undesirable ideas may provoke disciplinary action.

How effective are total institutions in resocializing individuals? The answer depends partly on the methods used, partly on the individual, and partly on peer pressure. In the most extreme total institutions imaginable, Nazi concentration camps, some inmates came to identify with their guards and torturers, even helping them keep other prisoners under control. Most, however, resisted resocialization until their death or release (Bettelheim, 1979).

Prisons often fail at resocialization because inmates identify more with their fellow prisoners than with the administration's agenda. Inmates in U.S. prisons may well be resocialized, but it is not likely to be to the norms of prison officials or the wider society. Rather, prisoners learn the norms of other prisoners, and as a result, many come out of prison more hardened in their criminal behavior than before.

Even when an institution is initially successful at resocialization, individuals who return to their original social environments often revert to earlier behavior. This reversal confirms that socialization is an ongoing process, continuing throughout a person's lifetime as a result of changing patterns of social interaction.

Total institutions: Institutions that isolate individuals from the rest of society to achieve administrative control over most aspects of their lives.

Resocialization: The process of altering an individual's behavior through control of his or her environment, for example, within a total institution.

SOCIAL INTERACTION

Socialization at every stage of life occurs primarily through *social interaction*—interaction guided by the ordinary,

DISCOVER & DEBATE

Socialization and Social Interaction

Motion: Students in grades K–12 have too much homework. Homework should be banned.

Background: Since the beginning of formal mass schooling in the United States, the practice of homework has been alternately embraced and frowned on by educators and parents, as well as by students. In the mid-1950s, the launch of the Sputnik satellite by the Soviet Union raised concerns about American educational standards, spurring reforms for greater academic rigor inside and outside the classroom. On the other hand, the late 1960s brought rising parental concern that homework was crowding out children's outdoor recreation and creative activities. In the 1980s, the National Commission on Excellence in Education's report, *A Nation at Risk* (1983), led to a new educational excellence movement and a new view of homework. Throughout the 1980s and 1990s, there was a push for more homework. By the end of the century, there was again a backlash against excessive homework. The debate over homework and how much is too much continues to invite discussion and disagreement.

Affirmative Arguments

- Students spend about 7 hours a day at school during the school year. Many students also participate in after-school activities like sports, clubs, or jobs and want to spend time with their families. Homework adds to young people's stress and time burdens.
- In the younger grades, homework often requires parental supervision and support, creating a burden for parents, who may be busy with work or other obligations.
- Homework can dull rather than encourage student enthusiasm for learning, particularly if tasks are rote rather than creative.

Opposition Arguments

- Students learn through practice and repetition. Homework is an opportunity to review materials and to improve retention of materials.
- Homework is needed beginning in the early grades to establish good study and time management habits that students will need in higher grades and in college.
- Homework gives parents an opportunity to play a role in a child's education and helps them to evaluate a child's progress.

Questions for consideration:

- Is technology like term paper writing services affecting the effectiveness of homework assignments?
- Does homework create opportunities for cooperative interaction when students ask for help or advice from friends, siblings, or parents? Or does it isolate busy students from family and social activities?
- How does the U.S. experience compare with that of other countries? What are standard homework practices in other countries, and how

does student academic performance in those countries compare to that in the United States?

Debate tip:

- It is important to know your argument but be flexible with it. Be a good listener, and take note of the arguments presented by the other team that you did not consider. Flexibility enhances the ability to respond to new ideas being brought up during the debate while linking them to your original argument.

taken-for-granted rules that enable people to live, work, and socialize together (Ridgeway & Smith-Lovin, 1999). Spoken words, gestures, body language, and other symbols and cues come together in complex ways to enable human communication. The sociologist must look behind the everyday aspects of social interaction to identify how it unfolds and how social norms and language make it possible.

Social interaction usually requires conformity to social conventions. According to Scheff (1966), violation of the norms of interaction is generally interpreted as a sign that the person is "abnormal," perhaps even dangerous. A person in a crowded elevator who persists in engaging strangers in loud conversations, for example, and disheveled homeless people who shuffle down the street muttering to themselves evoke anxiety if not repugnance.

Norms govern a wide range of interactive behaviors. For example, making eye contact when speaking to someone is valued in mainstream U.S. culture; people who don't make eye contact are considered dishonest and shifty. By contrast, among the Navajo and the Australian Aborigines, as well as in many East Asian cultures, direct eye contact is considered disrespectful, especially with a person of greater authority. Norms also govern how close we stand to friends and strangers in making conversation. In North American and Northern European cultures, people avoid standing closer than a couple of feet from one another unless they are on intimate terms (Hall, 1973). Men in the United States are socialized to avoid displays of intimacy with other men, such as walking arm in arm. In Nigeria, however, men who are close friends or relatives hold hands when walking together, while in Italy, Spain, Greece, and some Middle Eastern countries, men commonly throw their arms around each other's shoulders, hug, and even kiss.

Two different approaches to studying social interaction are Erving Goffman's metaphor of interaction as theater and conversation analysts' efforts to study the way people manage routine talk. We discuss these approaches later, but first we look briefly at some sociologists' studies of social interaction.

STUDIES OF SOCIAL INTERACTION

Studies of social interaction have frequently drawn on the symbolic interactionist perspective. They illuminate nearly every form and aspect of social interaction. For example, research on battered women shows how victims of domestic violence redefine their situations to come to grips with abusive relationships (Hattery, 2001). One strategy is to deny the partner's violent behavior altogether, whereas another is to minimize the partner's responsibility, attributing it to external factors like unemployment, alcoholism, or mental illness. Or the victim will define her own role as caretaker and assume responsibility for "saving" the abusive partner. A woman who eventually decides to leave an abusive relationship must, some research suggests, redefine her situation so as to change her self-image. She must come to see herself as a victim of abuse who is capable of ending the abusive relationship, rather than as someone responsible for "solving" her mate's "problem" (Johnson & Ferraro, 1984).

Recent studies of social interaction have covered many topics, including the following:

- The way online gamers coordinate their individual actions with one another and through the user interface to succeed at games such as *World of Warcraft* (Williams & Kirschner, 2012)

- The strategies homeless youth use to manage and alleviate stigma, including creating friendships or attempting to pass as nonhomeless, as well as acting aggressive and fighting back (Roschelle & Kaufman, 2004)
- The ways in which a sense of "corporate social responsibility" is promoted and learned by corporate executives in the work environment (Shamir, 2011)

THE DRAMATURGICAL APPROACH: ERVING GOFFMAN

Erving Goffman (1959, 1961, 1963a, 1967, 1972), a major figure in the study of social interaction, developed a set of theoretical ideas that make it possible to observe and describe social interaction. Goffman used what he termed the **dramaturgical approach**, *the study of social interaction as if it were governed by the practices of theatrical performance.*

According to Goffman, people in their everyday lives are concerned, much like actors on a stage, with the **presentation of self**, that is, *the creation of impressions in the minds of others to define and control social situations.* For instance, to serve many customers simultaneously, a waiter must take charge with a "presentation of self" that is polite but firm and does not allow customers to usurp control by taking too much time ordering. After only a short time, the waiter asserts control by saying, "I'll give you a few minutes to decide what you want" and walks away.

As people interact, they monitor themselves and each other, looking for clues that reveal the impressions they are making on others. This ongoing effort at *impression management* results in a continual realignment of the individuals' "performances" as the "actors" refit their roles using dress, objects, voice, and gestures in a joint enterprise.

Continuing the metaphor of a theatrical performance, Goffman divides spheres of interaction into two stages. In the *front stage,* we are social actors engaged in a process of impression management through the use of props, costumes, gestures, and language. A professor lecturing to her class, a young couple on their first date, and a job applicant in an interview all are governed by existing social norms, so the professor will not arrive in her nightgown, nor will the prospective employee greet his interviewer with a high-five rather than with a handshake. Just as actors in a play must stick to their scripts, so too, suggests Goffman, do we as social actors risk consequences (like failed interactions) if we diverge from the normative script.

Goffman offers insights into the techniques we as social actors have in our repertoire. Among them are the following:

- *Dramatic realization* is the actor's effort to mobilize his or her behavior to draw attention to a particular characteristic of the role he or she is assuming. What impression does a baseball umpire strive to leave on his audience (the teams and fans)? Arguably, he would like to embody authority, so he makes his calls loudly and with bold gestures.
- *Idealization* is an actor's effort to embody in his or her behaviors the officially accredited norms and values of a community or society. Those with fewer economic resources might purchase faux designer bags or watches to conform to perceived societal expectations of material wealth.
- *Misrepresentation* is part of every actor's repertoire, ranging from kind deception (telling a friend she looks great when she doesn't) to self-interested untruth (telling a professor a paper was lost in a computer crash when it was never written) to bald-faced prevarication (lying to conceal an affair). The actor wants to maintain a desired impression in the eyes of the audience: The friend would like to be perceived as kind and supportive, the student as conscientious and hardworking, and the spouse as loyal and loving.
- *Mystification* is largely reserved for those with status and power and serves to maintain distance from the audience to keep people in

Dramaturgical approach: Developed by Erving Goffman, the study of social interaction as if it were governed by the practices of theatrical performance.

Presentation of self: The creation of impressions in the minds of others to define and control social situations.

awe. Corporate leaders keep their offices on a separate floor and don't mix with employees, while celebrities may avoid interviews and allow their on-screen roles to define them as savvy and smart.

We may also engage in impression management as a team. A team consists of two or more actors cooperating to create a definition of the situation favorable to them. For example, members of a sports team work together, although some may be more skilled than others, to convey a definition of themselves as a highly competent and competitive group. Or the members of a family may work together to convey to their dinner guests that they are content and happy by acting cooperatively and smiling at one another during the group interaction.

The example of the family gives us an opportunity to explore Goffman's concept of the *back stage,* where actors let down their masks and relax or even practice their impression management. Before the dinner party, the home is a back stage. One parent is angry at the other for getting cheap rather than expensive wine, one sibling refuses to speak to the parent who grounded her, and the other won't stop texting long enough to set the table. Then the doorbell rings. Like magic, the home becomes the front stage as the adults smilingly welcome their guests and the kids begin to carry out trays of snacks and drinks. The guests may or may not sense some tension in the home, but they play along with the scenario so as not to create discomfort. When the party ends, the home reverts to the back stage, and each actor can relax his or her performance.

Goffman's work, like Mead's and the work of other sociologists focusing on socialization, sees the social self as an outcome of society and social interactions. Goffman, however, characterizes the social self not as a *possession*—a dynamic but still essentially real self—but rather as a *product* of a given social interaction, which can change as we seek to manage impressions for different audiences. Would you say that Mead or Goffman offers a better characterization of us as social actors?

ETHNOMETHODOLOGY AND CONVERSATION ANALYSIS

Routine, day-to-day social interactions are the building blocks of social institutions and ultimately of society itself. **Ethnomethodology** is used to study *the body of commonsense knowledge and procedures by which ordinary members of a society make sense of their social circumstances and interactions. Ethno* refers to "folk" or ordinary people; *methodology* refers to the methods they use to govern interaction—which are as distinct as the methods used by sociologists to study them. Ethnomethodology was created through Harold Garfinkel's work in the early 1960s. Garfinkel (1963, 1985) sought to understand exactly what goes on in social interactions after observing that our interpretation of social interaction depends on the context. For example, if a child on a playground grabs another child's ball and runs with it, the teacher may see this as a sign of the child's aggressiveness, while fellow students see it as a display of courage. Social interaction and communication are not

The film *The Wizard of Oz* offers a good example of mystification. Although the wizard is really, in his own words, "just a man," he maintains his status in Oz by hiding behind a curtain and using a booming voice and fiery mask to convey the impression of awesome power. ■

INEQUALITY MATTERS

Men and Women Talk

Do you think that men and women communicate differently? How would you articulate differences you observe? Would you attribute them to nature or nurture? ■

Men often claim they "cannot get a word in edgewise" when talking to women. Nevertheless, conversation analysis research challenges this claim: In hundreds of recorded conversations between men and women, researchers found that men more frequently interrupted women than women interrupted men and that men used the interruptions to dominate the conversation. Men tended to speak more loudly and to be less polite than women, using loudness and rudeness (such as sarcastic remarks about what a woman had said) to control the conversation (Campbell et al., 1992; Fishman, 1978; West, 1979; West & Zimmerman, 1977, 1983; Zimmerman & West, 1975, 1980). Although men set the agenda and otherwise dominated the conversation, women often did the "work" of maintaining conversations by nodding their heads, saying "a-hah," and asking questions (DeFrancisco, 1991; Fishman, 1978; Leaper & Robnett, 2011; Tannen, 2001; West & Zimmerman, 1977, 1983).

In contemporary times, a new word, "mansplaining," has evolved to describe the dynamic of conversations between men and women. This informal verb is an early 21st-century blend of the word "man" and "explain," defined by the *Oxford English Dictionary* in 2014 as "to explain something to someone, typically a man to woman, in a manner regarded as condescending or patronizing." An example is, "I'm listening to a guy mansplain his toolbox to his wife" (see also Steinmetz, 2014).

Research shows that the rules and conventions governing ordinary talk are grounded in the larger society—society's gender roles, in which men generally assume a dominant position in interaction with women without even realizing it. In fact, not only do men not realize they are dominating the conversation, but they also think women dominate and "talk too much."

The apparently private conversations between men and women thus reflect a fundamental issue in contemporary society: inequality between the sexes, including how inequality gets reproduced in subtle ways. The cultural stereotype of women as talkative and emotional and men as quiet and rational affects women even though its basis in reality is weak. No matter that men talk more and dominate conversations—women are made to feel unequal by the reproduction of the stereotype, and inequality between the sexes is reinforced. The private lives of people in conversations thus cannot be divorced from the way the larger social norms and stereotypes shape relationships between men and women.

THINK IT THROUGH

- The above discussion demonstrates how sociological research can shed light on "commonsense" assumptions—such as the assumption that women dominate conversations more than do men—by empirically testing them. Can you identify other stereotypical ideas about social interactions between different groups or individuals? How could you go about testing these ideas empirically?

possible unless most people have learned to assign similar meanings to the same interactions. By studying the specific contexts of concrete social interactions, Garfinkel sought to understand how people come to share the same interpretations of social interactions.

Garfinkel also believed that in all cultures people expect others to talk in a way that is coherent and understandable and become anxious and upset when this does not happen. Making sense of one another's conversations is even more fundamental to social life than cultural norms, Garfinkel argued, since without ways of arriving at meaningful understandings, communication, and hence culture, is not possible. Because the procedures that determine how we make sense of conversations are so important to social interaction, another field developed from ethnomethodology that focuses on talk itself: conversation analysis.

Conversation analysis investigates *the way participants in social interaction recognize and produce coherent conversation* (Schegloff, 1990, 1991). In this context, *conversation* includes just about any form of verbal communication, from routine small talk to emergency phone calls to congressional hearings and court proceedings (Heritage & Greatbatch, 1991; Hopper, 1991, Whalen & Zimmerman, 1987, 1990; Zimmerman, 1984, 1992).

Conversation analysis research suggests that social interaction is not simply a random succession of events. Rather, people construct conversations through a reciprocal process that makes the interaction coherent. One way in which we sequentially organize conversations is *turn taking,* a strategy that allows us to understand an utterance as a response to an earlier one and a cue to take our turn in the conversation. A person's turn ends once the other conversants indicate they have understood the message. For example, by answering "Fine" to the question "How are you?" you show that you have understood the question and are ready to move ahead.

On the other hand, answering "What do you mean?" or "Green" to the question "How are you?" is likely to lead to conversational breakdown. Conversational analysts have identified several techniques commonly used to repair such breakdowns. For example, if you begin speaking but realize midsentence that the other person is already speaking, you can "repair" this awkward situation by pausing until the original speaker finishes his or her turn and then restarting your turn.

Later research emphasized the impact of the larger social structure on conversations (Wilson, 1991). Sociologists looked at the use of power in conversations, including the power of the dispatcher over the caller in emergency phone calls (Whalen, Zimmerman, & Whalen, 1990; Zimmerman, 1984, 1992), of the questioner over the testifier in governmental hearings (Molotch & Boden, 1985), and of men over women in male–female interactions (Campbell, Klein, & Olson, 1992; Fishman, 1978; West, 1979; West & Zimmerman, 1977, 1983; Zimmerman & West, 1975, 1980). The last instance, in particular, illustrates how the larger social structure—in this case, gender structure—affects conversation. Even at the most basic and personal level—a private conversation between two people—social structures exercise a potentially powerful influence.

Ethnomethodology: A sociological method used to study the body of commonsense knowledge and procedures by which ordinary members of a society make sense of their social circumstances and interaction.

Conversation analysis: The study of how participants in social interaction recognize and produce coherent conversation.

WHY STUDY SOCIALIZATION AND SOCIAL INTERACTION?

Have you ever wondered why you and some of your classmates or neighbors differ in worldviews, coping strategies for stress, or values concerning right and wrong? Understanding socialization and social interaction sheds light on such differences and what they mean to us in everyday life. For example, if you travel abroad, you will have a sense of how cultural differences come to be and appreciate that no culture is more "normal" than another—each has its own norms, values, and roles taught from earliest childhood.

By studying socialization, you also come to understand the critical socializing roles that peers, schools, and work environments play in the lives of children, adolescents, and young adults. The growing influence of the mass media, including the Internet and other technological innovations in communication, means we must pay close attention to these sources of socialization and social interaction as well. As people spend more time on the Internet talking to friends and strangers, experimenting with new identities, and seeking new forms of and forums for social interaction, sociologists may need to rethink some of their ideas about the influence of agents like parents and schools; perhaps these may recede in importance—or grow. Sociologists also ask how our presentation of self is transformed when we create social selves in the anonymous space of social media. What kinds of research could you imagine conducting to learn more about the digital world as an agent of socialization and a site of modern social interaction?

WHAT CAN I DO WITH A SOCIOLOGY DEGREE?

Qualitative Research Skills

Sociologists use *qualitative research skills* to gather rigorous, in-depth information on social behavior, phenomena, and institutions. Qualitative research highlights data that cannot be quantified (that is, cannot be converted into numbers). It relies on the gathering of data through methods such as focus groups, participant and nonparticipant observation, interviews, and archival research. Generally, population samples are small in qualitative research because the aim of the research is to gain deep understanding.

Throughout this book, you will encounter qualitative research studies and you will see how they contribute to our knowledge of the social world. As you advance in your sociological studies, you will have the opportunity to learn how to do qualitative sociology. For example, you may learn to prepare interview questions that allow you to accurately assess respondents' attitudes toward a particular social trend, or you may learn to take detailed field notes on observations you make of a practice or population you seek to study.

Knowledge of qualitative research methods is a beneficial skill in today's job market. Learning to collect data through observation, interviews, and focus groups, for instance, prepares you to do a wide variety of job tasks, including survey development, questionnaire design, data collection and reporting, and market research. Furthermore, qualitative research experience fosters communication competencies through the processes of small-group management and rapport building, as well as through negotiation with study participants.

Elizabeth Bogumil, Professional Expert at Mt. San Antonio, California State University, Northridge, MA in Sociology

I work in the Research and Institutional Effectiveness Office of a community college. My office supports the mission of the college by collecting, analyzing, and summarizing accurate, timely, and reliable data. We work with various departments, centers, and projects across the college campus to determine and document the effectiveness of programs and services. Our office focuses on both qualitative and quantitative research, and stresses the collaborative nature of every stage of the research process. One does not often hear about institutional research in higher education; however, every university and community college has institutional researchers providing insight, data, and support to the administrative services, the instructional services, the student services, human resources, and the office of the college or university president.

Although our office uses both quantitative and qualitative research, my project focus is on qualitative research. When studying sociology, one of the most important skills I learned was how to perform systematic and rigorous qualitative research rooted in theory. I am typically provided a research question and a set of parameters (often student demographics) from which I have to conceive an appropriate form of qualitative inquiry (typically interviews, focus groups, or open-ended question surveys) to explore or answer the research question. After collecting the data, during the analysis process, it is important to make sure that the themes or conclusions being derived from the data make sense within the project's theory. Finally, as qualitative research yields large amounts of descriptive data, it is important to clearly and concisely refine the resulting key themes in a report that are accessible and useful to the department, center, or individual coordinating the project and who helped formulate the original research question. It is because of my sociology training that I have the ability to effectively engage in qualitative research, in a timely manner, and the knowledge of how to distill the pertinent results into a clear and understandable report.

Career Data: Operations Research Analyst

- 2016 Median Pay: $79,200 per year
- Typical Entry-Level Education: Bachelor's degree
- Projected Job Growth by 2024: 30% (Much faster than average)

Source: Bureau of Labor Statistics, Occupational Outlook Handbook, 2016.

SUMMARY

- **Socialization** is a lifelong, active process by which people learn the cultures of their societies and construct a sense of who they are.
- What we often think of as "human nature" is in fact learned through socialization. Sociologists argue that human behavior is not determined biologically, although biology plays some role; rather, human behavior develops primarily through social interaction.
- Although some theories emphasize the early years, sociologists generally argue that socialization takes place throughout the life course. The theories of Sigmund Freud and Jean Piaget emphasize the early years, while those of George Herbert Mead (although his **role-taking** theory focuses on the earlier stages of the life course), Lawrence Kohlberg, and Judith Harris give more consideration to the whole life course. According to Mead, children acquire a sense of self through symbolic interaction, including the role-taking that eventually enables the adult to take the standpoint of society as a whole.
- Kohlberg built on Piaget's ideas to argue that a person's sense of morality develops through different stages, from that in which people strictly seek personal gain or seek to avoid punishment to the stage in which they base moral decisions on abstract principles.
- The immediate family provides the earliest and typically foremost source of socialization, but school, work, peers, religion, sports, and mass media, including the Internet, all play a significant role.
- Socialization may differ by social class. Middle-class families place a somewhat greater emphasis on creativity and independence, while working-class families often stress obedience to authority. These differences, in turn, reflect the corresponding workplace differences associated with social class.
- In **total institutions**, such as prisons, the military, and hospitals, individuals are isolated so that society can achieve administrative control over their lives. By enforcing rules that govern all aspects of daily life, from dress to schedules to interpersonal interactions,

total institutions can open the way to **resocialization**, which is the breaking down of the person's sense of self and the rebuilding of the personality.

- According to Erving Goffman's **dramaturgical approach**, we are all actors concerned with the **presentation of self** in social interaction. People perform their social roles on the "front stage" and are able to avoid performing on the "back stage."
- **Ethnomethodology** is a method of analysis that examines the body of commonsense knowledge and procedures by which ordinary members of a society make sense of their social circumstances and interaction.
- **Conversation analysis**, which builds on ethnomethodology, is the study of the way participants in social interaction recognize and produce coherent conversation.

KEY TERMS

socialization, 97
behaviorism, 99
social learning, 99
looking-glass self, 100
primary groups, 100
secondary groups, 100
reference groups, 100
I, 101
me, 101
role-taking, 101
significant others, 101
generalized other, 101
cognitive development, 102
egocentric, 102
psychoanalysis, 103
id, 103
ego, 103
superego, 104
hidden curriculum, 107
anticipatory socialization, 108
total institutions, 116
resocialization, 116
dramaturgical approach, 119
presentation of self, 119
ethnomethodology, 120
conversation analysis, 122

DISCUSSION QUESTIONS

1. What are agents of socialization? What agents of socialization do sociologists identify as particularly important? Which of these would you say have the most profound effects on the construction of our social selves? Make a case to support your choices.
2. The United States is a country where sports are an important part of many people's lives—many Americans enjoy playing sports, while others follow their favorite sports teams closely in the media. How are sports an agent of socialization? What roles, norms, or values are conveyed through this agent of socialization?
3. What role does the way people react to you play in the development of your personality and your self-image? How can the reactions of others influence whether or not you develop skills as an athlete or a student or a musician, for example?
4. Recall Goffman's ideas about social interaction and the presentation of self. How have social media sites such as Facebook, Twitter, and Instagram affected the presentation of self? Have there been changes to what Goffman saw as our front and back stages?
5. What are the characteristics of total institutions such as prisons and mental institutions? How does socialization in a total institution differ from "ordinary" socialization?

GROUPS, ORGANIZATIONS, AND BUREAUCRACIES

LEARNING OBJECTIVES

5.1 Describe primary and secondary groups and their effects

5.2 Discuss the power of groups in terms of their composition, leadership, and conformity

5.3 Explain the sociological concepts of economic, cultural, and social capital

5.4 Describe three different types of formal organizations

5.5 Apply a sociological lens to analyze modern bureaucracies

David Ramos/Stringer/Getty Images

WHAT DO YOU THINK?

1. Do most people conform to the expectations of the groups to which they belong? What explains conformity? What explains dissent?
2. Why do many people think of bureaucracies as inefficient and annoying? What would be the alternative?
3. Could a group of college students working together on an issue like child hunger, opioid addiction, or veteran homelessness in their community bring about significant social change?

Reisig and Taylor/ABC via Getty Images

MAROONED: GROUP DYNAMICS ON A DESERTED ISLAND

In the fall of 2004, the American Broadcasting Corporation (ABC) premiered a program that would go on to become one of the most highly rated shows of the decade. *Lost* earned an average of 16 million viewers per episode in its first season and continued to enjoy high ratings through its sixth and final season on ABC. The dramatic series follows a group who survives the crash of a passenger jet traveling from Sydney, Australia, to Los Angeles. Passing over an island in the South Pacific, their jet breaks into two parts, marooning several dozen survivors on a stretch of tropical land inhabited by mysterious forces and an unfriendly group of "others." Jack, a California physician, emerges as the leader of the initial group of survivors, who largely follow his decisions, erecting shelters, collecting food from the surrounding jungle, and devising ways to protect themselves from the "others." The group's survival depends on cooperation, but shifting alliances, contests for power, and individual interests challenge the pursuit of a collective good, leaving behind a trail of lost hopes and lives (and six compelling seasons).

In 1954, fully 50 years earlier, British author William Golding published the novel *Lord of the Flies*, the story of 30 boys marooned on a Pacific island as the world around them erupts into war. The group of boys is initially led by Jack (perhaps coincidentally) and Ralph, and the survivors cooperate to construct shelters, gather and hunt food, and maintain a smoking fire to draw the attention of passing ships. Over time, however, the pursuit of the collective good frays as many of the boys shirk their tasks and develop a fear of a supernatural force, "the beast," on the island. A struggle for leadership emerges, impulses and forces for civility dissolve, and the group descends into deadly savagery, leaving two of the key characters dead before the group is finally rescued.

Secondary groups may evolve into primary groups for some members. For example, when students taking the same course begin to socialize outside of class, they may create bonds of friendship that come to constitute a primary group.

Although fictional and separated by half a century, *Lost* and *Lord of the Flies* are interesting (if somewhat hyperbolic) microcosms of the challenges of groups. Even where surviving or thriving depends on participation from all parties, a shared interest does not ensure cooperation. Competition over power and resources, individual interests that may conflict with the group interest, and interpersonal tensions can undermine a group's achievement of a goal.

Consider some real-life issues where group cooperation (although on a massive scale) would help to ensure that global society can survive and thrive: the challenges of climate change and its threat to island and shoreline communities; the danger of antibiotic overuse in both medicine and industrial agriculture, which is leading to the development of dangerous "superbugs" that cannot be treated with existing medicines; or the danger to all of humankind of nuclear weapons. To some degree, in each of these cases, the inhabitants of our planet have worked or are working together toward positive collective outcomes. At the same time, many problems remain unresolved, and efforts to work together may be undermined by struggles over power, leadership, ideology, and profit. Groups are a complex and fascinating phenomenon—and an important object of interest for sociologists.

We begin this chapter with an overview of the nature of social groups, looking at primary and secondary groups and their effects on our lives. We also examine the power of groups in fostering integration and enforcing conformity, among other key functions. We then turn to a discussion of the importance of capital in social group formation and action, followed by an exploration of the place of organizations in society. Next, we address a topic about which sociologist Max Weber wrote extensively and with which we all have some experience—bureaucracies. We end the chapter with a consideration of the modern roles of governmental and nongovernmental organizations in the pursuit of social change.

THE NATURE OF GROUPS

The male elephant is a solitary creature, spending much of its life wandering alone, interacting with other elephants only when it is time to mate or if another male intrudes on its territory. Female elephants, by contrast, live their lives in groups. Both male and female human beings are like the female elephant: We are social animals who live our entire lives in the company of others. Our lives are social, and we can better understand them by looking at the types of groups with which we are associated. Each of us is born into an emotionally and biologically connected group we know as "the family." As we mature, we become increasingly interconnected with other people, some our own age and others not, at school, on sports teams, and through various other social interactions and increasingly via the Internet and social media. We consolidate and accumulate friends, teammates, and classmates—different groups with whom we interact on

TABLE 5.1 The Characteristics of Primary and Secondary Groups

Characteristic	Primary Group	Secondary Group
Social distance of relationships	Low: face-to-face	High: indirect, remote
Intimacy	High: "fusion of personalities"	Low: relatively impersonal
Importance in forming the "social self"	Fundamental: earliest complete experience of social unity	Secondary: occurs later in life, no all-embracing experience of social unity
Degree of mutual identification with others	High: "we"	Low: "they"
Degree of permanence	High: change but slowly over time	Low: likely to change over time
Examples	Family; children's playgroups; neighborhood and community groups; clubs, fraternities, and sororities	Secondary schools, colleges, and universities; businesses and other workplaces; government agencies; bureaucracies of all sorts

a regular basis. Eventually we get jobs and engage with coworkers and other people we encounter in the course of our work. Along the way we may form and maintain friendship groups, either in person or virtually, that share our interests in particular activities or lifestyles, such as poker, model airplanes, or music. Sometimes we are part of groups that gather for special events, like watching a college football game or attending a presidential inauguration or political demonstration.

A moment's reflection on these types of groups reveals that they differ in many important ways, particularly in the degree of intimacy and social support their members experience. Sociologists distinguish between *primary* and *secondary* groups. Primary groups are characterized by *intense emotional ties, intimacy, and identification with membership in the group*. Secondary groups are *large, impersonal groups with minimal emotional and intimate ties* (Cooley, 1909). Interestingly, the Internet is increasingly blurring the boundary distinctions between primary and secondary groups—very large, ostensibly impersonal groups can take on an intimate feeling thanks to the power of virtual communication and information sharing.

Primary groups are of significance because they exert a long-lasting influence on the development of our social selves (Cooley, 1902/1964). Charles Horton Cooley (1864–1929), who first introduced the distinction between primary and secondary groups, argued that people belong to primary groups mainly because these groups satisfy personal needs of belonging and fulfillment. People become part of secondary groups such as business organizations, schools, work groups, athletic clubs, and governmental bodies to achieve specific goals: to earn a living, to get a college degree, to compete in sports, and so on. In a sense, the marooned survivors of our opening story are a secondary group that, over time, fosters the formation of smaller primary groups. (For a summary of the characteristics of primary and secondary groups, see Table 5.1.)

THE POWER OF GROUPS

As you learned in Chapter 4, we often judge ourselves by how we think we appear to others, which Cooley termed the "looking-glass self." Groups as well as individuals provide the standards by which we make these self-evaluations. Robert K. Merton (1968), following Herbert Hyman (1942), elaborated on the concept of the reference group as a measure by which we evaluate ourselves. Importantly, a reference group provides a standard for judging our own attitudes or behaviors.

For most of us, the family is the reference group with the greatest impact in shaping our early view of ourselves. As we mature, and particularly during adolescence, peers replace or at least compete with the family as the reference group through which we define ourselves. Today, thanks to the growth of social media, many people establish "virtual" reference groups and intimate primary groups with people they have never seen face-to-face.

Reference groups may be primary, such as the family, or secondary, such as a group of soldiers in the same branch of service in the military. They may even be fictional. One of the chief functions of advertising, for example, is to create sets of imaginary reference groups that will influence consumers' buying habits. We are invited to purchase a particular vehicle or fragrance, for instance, to join an ostensibly exclusive group of sophisticated, sexy consumers of that item. Reference groups can have powerful effects on our purchasing, as well as on our other social actions.

THE EFFECTS OF SIZE

Another significant way in which groups differ has to do with their size. The German sociologist Georg Simmel (1858–1918) was one of the first to call attention to the influence of group size on people's behavior. Since Simmel's time, small-group researchers have conducted several laboratory experiments to discover how group size affects both the quality of interaction in the group and the group's effectiveness in accomplishing certain tasks (Levine & Crowther, 2008; Lucas & Lovaglia, 1998).

The Washington Post/Contributor/Getty Images

College fraternities and sororities are groups that provide members a sense of belonging. To some degree, they are exclusive, limited to members selected by the group. At the same time, they must be somewhat inclusive to survive as they have to recruit new members every year.

The simplest group, which Simmel (1955) called a **dyad**, *consists of two persons*. Simmel reasoned that dyads, which offer both intimacy and conflict, are likely to be simultaneously intense and unstable. To survive, they require the full attention and cooperation of both parties. Dyads are typically the sources of our most elementary social bonds, often constituting the groups in which we are most likely to share our deepest secrets. The commitment two people make through marriage is one way to form a dyadic group. But dyads can also be very fragile. If one person withdraws from the dyad, it vanishes. That is why, as Simmel believed, a variety of cultural and legal norms arise to support dyadic groups, including marriage, in societies where such groups are regarded as an important source of social stability.

Adding one other person to a dyad changes the group relationship considerably, making what Simmel termed a **triad**. Triads are apt to be more stable than dyads since the presence of a third person relieves some of the pressure on the other two members to always get along and maintain the energy of the relationship. One person can temporarily withdraw his or her attention from the relationship without necessarily threatening it. In addition, if two members have a disagreement, the third can play the role of mediator, such as when you try to patch up a falling-out between two friends or coworkers (see Figure 5.1).

On the other hand, however, an **alliance (or coalition)** may form between two members of a triad, enabling them to "gang up" on the third member, thereby destabilizing the group. Alliances are most likely to form when no member is clearly dominant and all three are competing for the same

FIGURE 5.1 A Dyad and a Triad

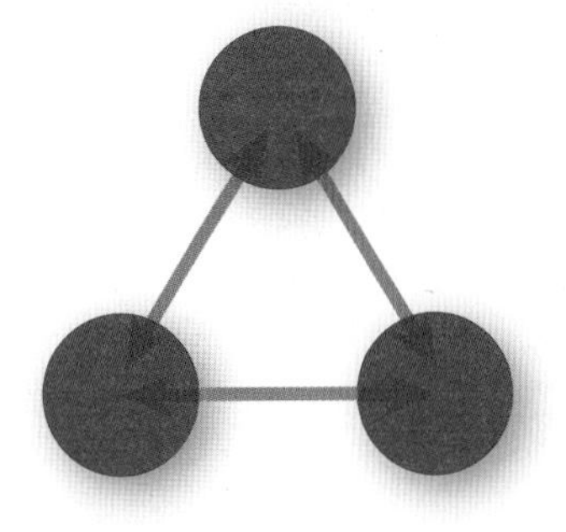

Dyad: A group consisting of two persons.

Triad: A group consisting of three persons.

PRIVATE LIVES, PUBLIC ISSUES

Individuals, Groups, and Academic Achievement

How did you do on your last exam or assignment in school? Certainly, all of us want to perform well and earn good grades. If your grade was outstanding, you probably credited the time you devoted to studying and preparing for class. If your grade was mediocre or poor, perhaps you attributed that to a lack of adequate time or effort on your part. Clearly, our own educational decisions and actions are of consequence in explaining our academic performance. Some research suggests, however, that *academic ability grouping*—that is, inclusion in a stronger, intermediate, or weaker group of learners—has a discernible effect on academic achievement. Consider the study described below, which was performed at the U.S. Air Force Academy (Carrell, Sacerdote, & West, 2011).

RJ Sangosti/Contributor/Getty Images

Members of the U.S. Air Force Academy's Class of 2015 head into Falcon Stadium in Colorado Springs for their graduation ceremony, May 28, 2015. Around 840 cadets graduated during the ceremony. ■

In an effort to improve academic performance and address the problem of dropouts, U.S. Air Force Academy leaders made a conscious effort to group cadets with weaker records together with those who had grade point averages above the mean. Their hypothesis was that the more academically able cadets would exercise a positive influence on their weaker peers, who were at greater risk of dropping out of the challenging program. In some instances, however, only stronger and weaker students were grouped, while in other experimental squadrons, stronger and weaker students were also mixed with those whose work was categorized as being in the middle. How would you hypothesize the effect of the conscious integration of academically weaker cadets with stronger students?

Perhaps predictably, the study found that weaker students did perform better in squadrons with stronger peers. Other research has also documented a positive effect for weaker learners in an environment with stronger students (Schofield, 2010). Nevertheless, in the Air Force Academy study, that effect was present only when the weaker students were grouped with high performers *and* middle-level students. When the middle-level students were removed, leaving the strongest and weakest students in a group, the low-performing students did *worse* than their prior results would have predicted. Why would this be the case?

The researchers suggest that when only the strongest and weakest students were grouped together, they splintered into academically homogeneous groups—that is, the stronger students hung together and the weaker students hung together, muting the effect of mixing the cadets. When middle-level students were also part of a group, they functioned as a "glue," binding the group together, hindering the splitting of the ability groups, and thus bringing up the performance of the weakest students.

Notably, the researchers also found that the middle-level performers did best when they had their own group. The presence of the stronger and weaker students appeared, then, to lead to lower test scores than the middle-level students achieved when working in a homogeneous group.

Clearly, groups matter: Academic achievement is the outcome of individual effort and, as the research suggests, is subject to group effects. The findings of this research present a challenge that may not be easy for academic leaders to resolve: What can they do when some students benefit from being in groups with mixed levels of ability while others see greater results in single-level groups? What do you think?

THINK IT THROUGH

- What are we to conclude from this research? Who benefits and who loses from academic ability grouping? If the better performance of one group comes at a cost to the performance of another group, how should school leaders proceed in grouping by ability?

thing—for example, when three friends are given a pair of tickets to a concert and have to decide which two will go. Larger groups share some of the characteristics of triads. For instance, on *Lost* or in *Lord of the Flies,* alliances form within the group of survivors as individuals forge special relationships with one another to get access to greater power or resources for survival.

Theoretically, in forming an alliance, a triad member is most likely to choose the weaker of the two other members, if there is one. But why would this be the case if picking a stronger member would strengthen the alliance? Choosing a weaker member enables the member seeking to form the alliance to exercise more power and control within the alliance. Nevertheless, in some "revolutionary" coalitions, the two weaker members form an alliance to overthrow the stronger one (Goldstone, 2001; Grusky, Bonacich, & Webster, 1995).

Going from a dyad to a triad illustrates an important sociological principle first identified by Simmel: *As group size increases, the intensity of relationships within the group decreases while overall group stability increases.* There are exceptions to every principle, however. Intensity of interaction among individuals within a group decreases as the size of the group increases because, for instance, more outlets or alternative arenas for interaction exist for individuals who are not getting along (Figure 5.2). In a dyad, only a single relationship is possible; in a triad, however, three different two-person relationships can occur. Adding a fourth person leads to six possible two-person relationships, not counting subgroups that may form. In a 10-person group, the number of possible two-person relationships increases to 45! When one relationship doesn't work out to your liking, you can easily move on to another, as you sometimes may do at large parties.

FIGURE 5.2 A Complex Network of Relationships

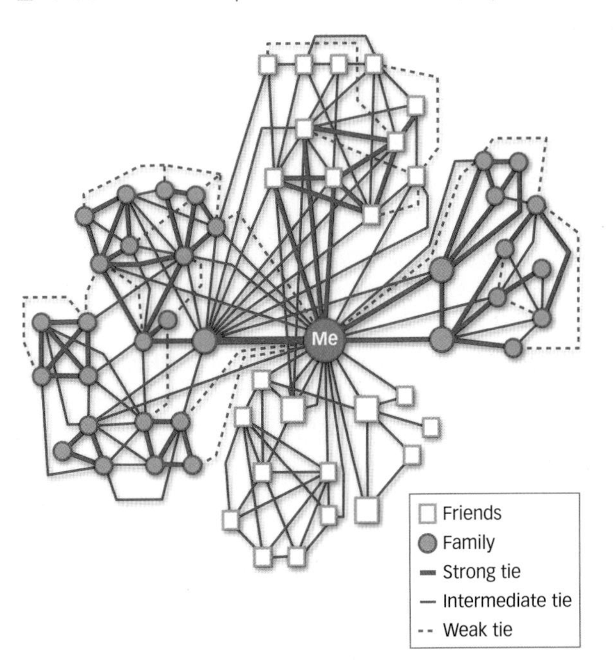

Alliance (or coalition): A subgroup that forms between group members, enabling them to dominate the group in their own interest.

Larger groups tend to be more stable than smaller ones because the withdrawal of some members does not threaten the survival of the entire group. For example, sports teams do not cease to exist simply because of the loss of one player, even though that player might have been important to the team's overall success. Beyond a certain size, perhaps a dozen people, groups may also develop a formal structure. Formal leadership roles may arise, such as president or secretary, and official rules may develop to govern what the group does. We discuss formal organizations later in this chapter.

Larger groups can sometimes be exclusive since it is easier for their members to limit their social relationships to the group itself, avoiding relationships with nonmembers. This sense of being part of an in-group or clique is often what unites the members of fraternities, sororities, and other campus organizations. Cliquishness is especially likely to occur when a group consists of members who are similar to one another in such social characteristics as age, gender, class, race, or ethnicity. Members of rich families, for example, may sometimes be reluctant to fraternize with people from the working class, men may prefer to play basketball only with other men, and students who belong to a particular ethnic group may seek out each other's company in the dormitory or cafeteria. The concept of **social closure**, originally developed by Max Weber, is especially relevant here insofar as it speaks to the *ability of a group to strategically and consciously exclude outsiders or those deemed "undesirable" from participating in the group or enjoying the group's resources* (Murphy, 1988; Parkin, 1979).

Groups don't always exclude outsiders, however (Blau, 1977; Stolle, 1998). For example, if your social group or club is made up of members from different social classes or ethnic groups, you are more likely to appreciate diversity thanks to your firsthand experience. This experience with difference may perhaps lead you to be more inclusive of others not like yourself in other aspects of your life, for example, in bringing together a group to work on a project. This, of course, is an optimistic outlook and one that we embrace and hope holds true in practice.

At the same time, researchers have found that exposure to differences of race, ethnicity, religion, social class, and other characteristics may in fact lead to negative consequences and exclusion—thus highlighting that there are two sides to every coin. The idea here is that exposure to "different" people or things may heighten the "threat" level that people feel and associate with differences, causing them to want to exclude those people or things from their lives (Blalock, 1967; Markert, 2010).

TYPES OF GROUP LEADERSHIP

A leader is a person able to influence the behavior of other members of a group. All groups tend to have leaders, even if the leaders do not have formal titles. Leaders come in a variety of forms: autocratic, charismatic, democratic, laissez-faire, bureaucratic, and so on. Some leaders are especially effective in motivating members of their groups or organizations, inspiring them to achievements they might not ordinarily accomplish. Such a **transformational leader** goes beyond the merely routine, *instilling in group members a sense of mission or higher purpose and thereby changing (transforming) the nature of the group itself* (Burns, 1978; Kanter, 1983; Mehra, Dixon, Brass, & Robertson, 2006).

Transformational leaders leave their marks on their organizations and can also be vital inspirations for social change in the world. Nelson Mandela, the first Black African president of postapartheid South Africa, had spent 27 years in prison, having been convicted of treason against the White-dominated government. Nonetheless, his moral and political position was so strong that upon his release he immediately assumed leadership of the African National Congress (ANC), leading that political group to the pinnacle of power in South Africa and then assuming the office of president of the country.

Most leaders are not as visionary as Mandela, however. A leader who simply "gets the job done" is a **transactional leader**, *concerned primarily with accomplishing the group's tasks, getting group members to do their jobs, and making certain the group achieves its goals*. Transactional leadership is routine leadership. For example, the teacher who effectively gets through the lesson plan each day but does not necessarily transform the classroom into a place

Social closure: The ability of a group to strategically and consciously exclude outsiders or those deemed "undesirable" from participating in the group or enjoying the group's resources.

Transformational leader: A leader who is able to instill in the members of a group a sense of mission or higher purpose, thereby changing the nature of the group itself.

Transactional leader: A leader who is primarily concerned with accomplishing the group's tasks, getting group members to do their jobs, and making certain that the group achieves its goals.

other human beings. Many ordinary Germans who participated in the mass execution of Jews in Nazi concentration camps allegedly did so on the ground that they were "just following orders." Milgram's research, although ethically questionable, produced sobering findings for those who believe that only "other people" would bow to authority.

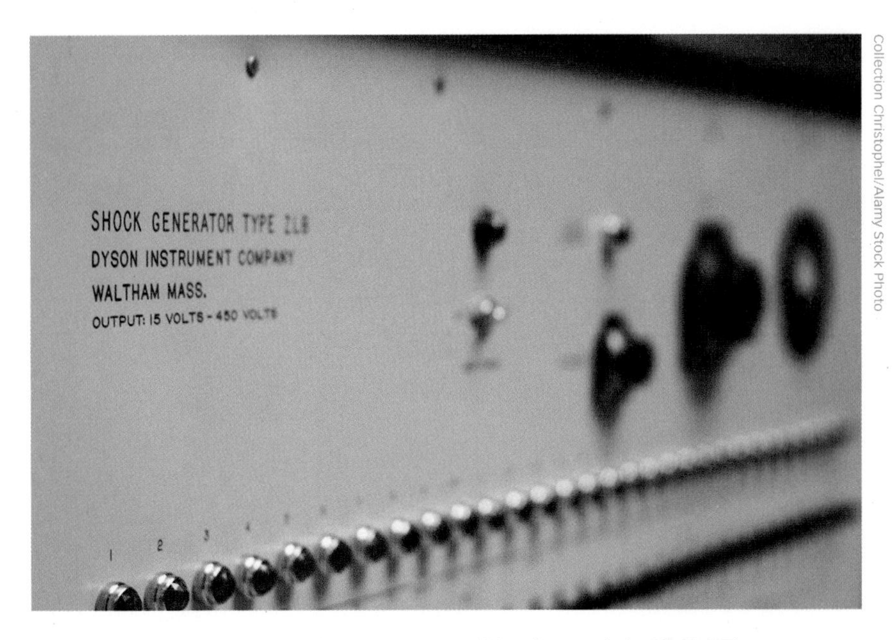

Most people would say that they are not capable of committing horrendous acts, yet Stanley Milgram's famous experiment illustrated how obedience to authority can lead people to commit actions that result in harm to others. ■

The 2012 film *Compliance,* which is based on real-life incidents, depicts the events that unfold when a prank phone caller, an unidentified male, calls a fast-food establishment and, pretending to be a police officer, enlists the aid of the store manager to help him crack an ostensibly important case. Once the manager agrees to help the "officer," the prankster tells the manager to perform increasingly invasive acts against a female employee. Obeying a figure believed to be a legitimate (although unseen) authority, in several of the incidents on which the movie is based, restaurant managers actually strip-searched female employees (Kavner, 2012; Wolfson, 2005).

Another example of obedience to authority even in the face of dangerous consequences took place at the Edgewood Arsenal in Maryland, the site of top-secret military experiments involving more than 7,000 U.S. soldiers from the 1950s through the 1970s. Many soldiers volunteered for duty at Edgewood unaware of, or even deceived about, exactly what would be asked of them. Once at Edgewood, they were informed that if they refused to participate in any "required" duties, they could face jail time for insubordination or receive an unsatisfactory review in their personnel files, and during the Vietnam era, some were reportedly threatened with being sent to war. The soldiers were experimented on repeatedly, often exposed to a variety of dangerous chemical and biological toxins, including sarin gas, VX gas, LSD, tranquilizers, and barbiturates, some of which produced extended and untreated hallucinations (Martin, 2012; Young & Martin, 2012). The Edgewood Arsenal experiments highlight the point that individuals are likely to comply with any demands made by persons in positions of authority out of fear of the repercussions associated with failure to comply, even if what they are asked to do seems dangerous or even potentially lethal to others—or to themselves.

GROUPTHINK Common wisdom may suggest that we "put our heads together" to solve a problem, but pressures to go along with the crowd sometimes result in poor decisions rather than in creative new solutions to problems. You have probably had the experience of feeling uneasy about voicing your opinion while in a group struggling with a difficult decision. Irving L. Janis (1972, 1989; Janis & Mann, 1977) coined the term **groupthink** to describe *what happens when members of a group ignore information that goes against the group consensus.* Not only does groupthink frequently embarrass potential dissenters into conforming, but it can also produce a shift in perceptions so that group members rule out alternative possibilities without seriously considering them. Groupthink may facilitate a group's reaching a quick consensus, but the consensus may also be ill chosen.

Janis undertook historical research to see whether groupthink had characterized U.S. foreign policy decisions, including the infamous Bay of Pigs invasion of

Groupthink: A process by which the members of a group ignore ways of thinking and plans of action that go against the group consensus.

Paul Schutzer/The LIFE Picture Collection/Getty Images

We often hear the phrase "It's not what you know; it's who you know." Indeed, history shows that social networks are important. The Kennedy family is one group that has had a disproportionate impact on American political life. Members of the Kennedy family have been elected to the presidency and Congress and have held other prestigious appointments in the federal government and private sector. ■

Cuba in 1961. Newly elected president John F. Kennedy inherited from the preceding administration a plan to provide U.S. supplies and air cover while an invasion force of exiled Cubans parachuted into Cuba's Bay of Pigs to liberate the country from Fidel Castro's communist government. Several of Kennedy's top advisers were certain the plan was fatally flawed but refrained from countering the emerging consensus. As it happened, the invasion was a disaster. The ill-prepared exiles were immediately defeated, Kennedy suffered public embarrassment, and the Cold War standoff between the Soviet Union and the United States deepened.

How could Kennedy's advisers, people of strong will and independent judgment educated at elite universities, have failed to voice their concerns adequately? Janis identified several possible reasons. For one, they were hesitant to disagree with the president lest they lose his favor. Nor did they want to diminish group harmony in a crisis situation where teamwork was important. The cohesion of the group was of key concern. In addition, there was little time for them to consult outside experts who might have offered radically different perspectives. All these circumstances contributed to a single-minded pursuit of the president's initial ideas rather than to an effort to generate effective alternatives.

Think about your own experiences working with groups, whether at work, on a class project, or in a campus organization. Have you ever "gone along to get along" or felt pressured to choose a particular path of action in spite of your own reservations? Or, conversely, have you ever chosen to refuse to conform in spite of the pressure? What factors affected your decision in either case?

Structuralism: The idea that an overarching structure exists within which culture and other aspects of society must be understood.

Economic capital: Money and material that can be used to access valued goods and services.

ECONOMIC, CULTURAL, AND SOCIAL CAPITAL

One of the most important additions to the sociological study of groups is the contribution of the French school of thought known as **structuralism**, or *the idea that an overarching structure exists within which culture and other aspects of society must be understood.* A leading proponent, the French sociologist Pierre Bourdieu, provides an analytical framework that extends our understanding of the way group relationships and membership shape our lives. Bourdieu argues that several forms of *capital*—that is, social currency—stem from our association with different groups. These forms of capital are of importance in the reproduction of socioeconomic status in society.

Economic capital, the most basic form, consists of *money and material that can be used to access valued goods and services.* Depending on the social class you are born into and the progress of your education and career, you will have more or less access to economic capital and ability to take advantage of this form of capital. Another form is *cultural capital,* or your interpersonal skills, habits, manners, linguistic styles, tastes, and lifestyles. For instance, in some social circles, having refined table manners and speaking with a distinctive accent place a person in a social class that enhances his or her access to jobs, social activities, and friendship groups.

Friendship groups and other social contacts also provide **social capital**, *the personal connections and networks that enable people to accomplish their goals and extend their influence* (Bourdieu, 1984; Coleman, 1990; Putnam, 2000). College students who join fraternities and sororities expect that their "brothers" or "sisters" will help them get through the often challenging social and academic experiences of college. Other political, cultural, or social groups on campus offer comparable connections and opportunities. Many new—as well as more seasoned—employees (and prospective employees) join LinkedIn, a social media site that offers possibilities for people to expand their professional social networks, a key part of nurturing social capital.

Although social capital is strongly influenced by socioeconomic class status, it may also be related to gender, to race, and intersectionally, to both gender and race (McDonald & Day, 2010; McDonald, Lin, & Ao, 2009). In a study of social networks and their relationship to people's information about job leads, sociologists Matt Huffman and Lisa Torres (2002) found that women benefited from being part of networks that included more men than women; those who had more women in their social networks had a diminished probability of hearing about good job leads. Interestingly, the predominance of men or women in a man's social network made no discernible difference. The researchers suggested that perhaps the women were less likely to learn about job leads, and notably, when they knew of leads, they were more likely to pass them along to men than to other women. Similarly, McDonald and Mair (2010) and Trimble and Kmec (2011) explored issues of networking in relation to women's career opportunities over their lifetimes and also the extent to which networks aid women in attaining jobs. Both teams of researchers found that social capital in the form of networks of relations has very distinct and important effects for women. The advent of professional networking sites online offers sociologists the opportunity to expand this research to see if and how gender affects social networks and their professional benefits, as research from the field of psychology suggests that job networking sites, including LinkedIn, play an important role in the job acquisition process (Bohnert & Ross, 2010).

Economic, cultural, and social capital confer benefits on individuals at least in part through membership in particular social groups. Characteristics such as class, race, ethnicity, and gender, among others, can have effects on the capital one has. Membership in organizations such as fraternities, exclusive golf clubs, or college alumni associations can offer important network access. These are some examples of the kinds of organizations that shape our lives and society, sometimes to our benefit, sometimes to our disadvantage. Below we look at organizations and their societal functions through the sociological lens.

ORGANIZATIONS

People frequently band together to pursue activities they could not readily accomplish by themselves. A principal means for accomplishing such cooperative actions is the **organization**, *a group with an identifiable membership that engages in concerted collective actions to achieve a common purpose* (Aldrich & Marsden, 1988). An organization can be a small primary group, but it is more likely to be a larger, secondary one: Universities, churches, armies, and business corporations are all examples of organizations. Organizations are a central feature of all societies, and their study is a core concern of sociology today.

Organizations tend to be highly formal in modern industrial and postindustrial societies. A **formal organization** is *rationally designed to achieve particular objectives, often by means of explicit rules, regulations, and procedures.* Examples include a state or county's department of motor vehicles or the federal Internal Revenue Service. As Max Weber (1919/1946) first recognized almost 100 years ago, modern societies are increasingly dependent on formal organizations. One reason is that formality is often a requirement for legal standing. For a college or university to be legally accredited, for example, it must satisfy explicit written standards governing everything from faculty hiring to fire safety. Today, formal organizations are the dominant form of organization across the globe.

TYPES OF FORMAL ORGANIZATIONS

Thousands of different kinds of formal organizations serve every imaginable purpose. Sociology seeks to simplify this diversity by identifying the principal types. Amitai Etzioni

Social capital: The social knowledge and connections that enable people to accomplish their goals and extend their influence.

Organization: A group with an identifiable membership that engages in concerted collective actions to achieve a common purpose.

Formal organization: An organization that is rationally designed to achieve its objectives, often by means of explicit rules, regulations, and procedures.

SOCIAL LIFE, SOCIAL MEDIA

Charity Organizations and Social Media

A recent National Public Radio story (Gharib, 2015) on small charity organizations' use of social media begins with the following observation:

> You hit the mall on #BlackFriday. You patronize local businesses on #SmallBizSaturday. You surf the web for deals on #CyberMonday. And if you're feeling a little guilty for how much cash you've dropped — along comes #GivingTuesday.

Social media has expanded the reach of modern charities—whether they are tiny nonprofits operating on a shoestring budget or massive, highly organized, and longstanding charitable organizations, social media has become one of the great equalizers of the modern age. Anyone with access to the Internet can join the social media fray and reach a potential audience of thousands or even millions of viewers and givers.

The idea for #GivingTuesday was born in 2012, the brainchild of 92Y in New York City and the U.N. Foundation. The goal of #GivingTuesday that year was to entice 50 nonprofit organizations to participate, and the template was simple: Charities would use #GivingTuesday in their online donation appeals on that day. The final count of participating charities in 2012 reached about 2,500. By 2014, that figure had grown to 35,000 and included appeals coming from charities but also from celebrities and private companies inviting fans or employees to donate (Gharib, 2015). In 2016, the day saw nearly $168 million in donations, which was an increase of 44% over the previous year (Jones, 2016). #GivingTuesday now occupies a spectrum of platforms with its own website (givingtuesday.org), Instagram account, and Facebook page (Reuters, 2015).

As a day that follows the massive spending of Black Friday and Cyber Monday, both of which come just on the heels of Thanksgiving, #GivingTuesday is meant to give people a chance to share as well as consume. It is, in some respects, an utterly modern phenomenon in the sense that, to this point at least, it belongs to no one: The hashtag can be freely used, and even though #GivingTuesday occupies space on social media, it is not run for profit and does not have an active governing body. As we saw in our discussion of social organizations, many are run hierarchically, divided into offices and activities and employees. Social media has begun to transform social action, moving it into a new realm in which the model of participation is not one of central or top-down management but of open participation. What are the strengths of such a model? What might be its weaknesses? What do you think?

THINK IT THROUGH

- How would you develop a social media campaign for a charity? Are social media appeals for charitable donations more effective or less effective than in-person, televised, or mailed appeals?

Follow us on Twitter to keep up with current sociological stories and research! We're at @DiscoverSoc1.
Share your own ideas at #DiscoverSociology.

(1975) grouped organizations into three main types based on the reasons people join them: utilitarian, coercive, and normative. In practice, of course, many organizations, especially utilitarian and normative organizations, include elements of more than one type.

Utilitarian organizations are *those that people join primarily because of some material benefit they expect to receive in return for membership.* For example, you probably enrolled in college not only because you want to expand your knowledge and skills but also because you know that a college degree will help you get a better job and earn more money later in life. In exchange, you have paid tuition and fees, devoted countless hours to studying, and agreed to submit to the rules that govern your school, your major, and your courses. Many of the organizations people join are utilitarian, particularly those in which they earn a living, such as corporations, factories, and banks.

Coercive organizations are *those in which members are forced to give unquestioned obedience to authority.* People are often forced to join coercive organizations because they have been either sentenced to punishment (prisons) or remanded for mandatory treatment (mental hospitals or drug treatment centers). Coercive organizations may use force or the threat of force, and sometimes confinement, to ensure compliance with rules and regulations. Guards, locked doors, barred windows, and monitoring are all features of jails, prisons, and mental hospitals. Sometimes people join coercive organizations voluntarily, but once they are members, they may not have the option of leaving as they desire. An example of such an organization is the military: Although enlisting is voluntary in the United States, once a person joins he or she is subject to close discipline and the demand for submission to authority in a rigidly hierarchical structure. Coercive organizations are examples of *total institutions,* which you read about in Chapter 4. By encompassing all aspects of people's lives, total institutions can radically alter people's thinking and behavior.

Normative organizations, or voluntary associations, are those that people join of their own will to pursue morally worthwhile goals without expectation of material reward. Belonging to such organizations may offer social prestige or moral or personal satisfaction. (Of course, such organizations may also serve utilitarian purposes, such as a charitable group you join partly to hand out your business card and boost your chances for monetary gain.)

The United States is a nation of normative organization joiners. Individuals affiliate with volunteer faith-related groups such as the YMCA, Hillel, and the Women's Missionary Society of the African Methodist Episcopal Church; charitable organizations such as the Red Cross; social clubs and professional organizations; politically oriented groups such as the National Association for the Advancement of Colored People (NAACP); and self-help groups such as Alcoholics Anonymous and Overeaters Anonymous. According to the National Center for Charitable Statistics (2013), there are more than a million public charities, 105,000+ private foundations, and 368,000+ other types of nonprofit organizations, such as fraternal organizations and civic leagues. Many of these organizations provide their members with a sense of connectedness while enabling them to accomplish personal and moral goals.

Normative organizations may also erect barriers based on social class, race, ethnicity, and gender. Those traditionally excluded from such organizations, including women, Latinos, Native Americans, African Americans, and other people of color, have, in response, formed their own voluntary associations. Although it may seem that these, too, are exclusionary, such groups have a different basis for their creation—the effort to remedy social inequality. Social justice, as a result, is often their primary concern.

Below we shift our gaze from voluntary and coercive organizations to a phenomenon that is familiar to most of us—the bureaucracy. Even though we have some control over our membership in many organizations, we are all—as U.S. residents, taxpayers, students, or recipients of mortgage or college loans, among others—subject to the reach of modern bureaucracy.

BUREAUCRACIES

The authority structure of most large organizations today is bureaucratic. In this section, we will look at the modern bureaucracy—the way it operates and some of its shortcomings. We will also see how bureaucratic structures have been modified or reformed to offer an alternative type of organization.

Max Weber (1919/1946) was the first sociologist to examine the characteristics of bureaucracy in detail. As noted in Chapter 1, Weber defined a bureaucracy as *a type of formal organization based on written procedural rules, arranged into a clear hierarchy of authority, and staffed by full-time paid officials.* Although Weber showed that bureaucracies could be found in many different societies throughout history, he argued that they became a dominant form of social organization only in modern society, where they came to touch key aspects of our daily lives.

Utilitarian organizations: Organizations that people join primarily because of some material benefit they expect to receive in return for membership.

Coercive organizations: Organizations in which people are forced to give unquestioned obedience to authority.

Normative organizations: Organizations that people join of their own will to pursue morally worthwhile goals without expectation of material reward; sometimes called voluntary associations.

AP Photo/Andy Manis

Today, a great deal of paperwork, like renewing a driver's license, is done online. Many tasks, however, still require us to seek assistance at an office. Have you encountered the ideal typical characteristics of bureaucracy described by Weber in your own experiences? ■

In particular, Weber suggested that bureaucracies are a highly rational form of organization because they were devised to achieve organizational goals with the greatest degree of efficiency—that is, to optimize the achievement of a task.

Note that when Weber characterized bureaucracies as rational he did not assume that they would always be *reasonable*. By *rational,* he meant that they were organized *based on knowable rules and regulations that laid out a particular path to a goal rather than on general or abstract principles or ideologies*. As we know from our own contacts with bureaucratic structures—whether they involve long waits on the phone to speak to a human being rather than a computer or the confusing pursuit of the correct person to whom one must turn in a critical student loan application—they are not, in fact, always reasonable.

To better understand the modern bureaucracy, Weber (1919/1946) identified what he referred to as the *ideal type* of this form of organization, describing the characteristics that would be found if the quintessential bureaucracy existed (Figure 5.4). Although Weber recognized that no actual bureaucracy necessarily possesses all of the characteristics he identifies, he argued that, by clearly articulating them, he was describing a standard against which actual bureaucracies could be judged and understood.

WRITTEN RULES AND REGULATIONS

The routine operation of the bureaucracy is governed by written rules and regulations, the purpose of which is to ensure that universal standards govern all aspects of bureaucratic behavior. Typically, rules govern everything from the hiring of employees to the reporting of an absence due to illness. They are usually spelled out in an organizational manual or handbook, now often available to employees on a human resources website, that describes in detail the requirements of each organizational position. Although these rules and regulations can be lengthy and complex, they are, in theory, knowable, and the expectation is that those who work in and seek the services of a given organization will adhere to them—sometimes even if they don't seem to make sense!

- **Specialized offices:** Positions in a bureaucracy are organized into "offices" that create a division of labor within the organization. The duties of each office, such as bookkeeping or paying invoices, are described in the organizational manual. Each office specializes in one particular bureaucratic function to the exclusion of all others. Such specialization is one of the reasons that bureaucratic organization is said to be efficient; bureaucratic officials are supposed to become experts at their particular tasks, efficient cogs in a vast machine. The efficiency is, ideally, beneficial for the organization and its clients. If you are seeking to clear up a problem with your tuition bill, you will not visit the admissions office because you know the expert advice you seek is to be found in the student accounts office.
- **Hierarchy:** A bureaucracy is organized according to the vertical principle of hierarchy, so that each office has authority over one or more lower level offices, and each in turn is responsible to a higher level office. At the top, the leader of the

organization stands alone; in the well-known words of then U.S. president Harry S. Truman, "The buck stops here." The organizational chart of a bureaucracy therefore generally looks like a pyramid. Again, efficiency is achieved through the knowable hierarchy of power that governs the organization.

- **Impersonality in record keeping:** Within a bureaucracy, communications are likely to be formal and impersonal. Written forms—"paperwork" or the electronic equivalent—substitute for more personalized human contact because bureaucracies must maintain written records or databases of all important actions. Modern computer technology has vastly increased the ability of organizations to maintain and access records. In some ways, this is an advantage—for example, when it allows you to register for classes via smartphone instead of standing in line for hours waiting to fill out forms. On the other hand, you may regret the loss of human contact and the inflexibility of the process, however efficient it may be. This "impersonality" also, ideally, has the effect of ensuring that all clients are treated equally and efficiently rather than capriciously; in reality, however, people with substantial economic, social, or cultural capital often have the easiest time navigating bureaucracies.
- **Technically competent administrative staff:** A bureaucracy generally seeks to employ a qualified professional staff. Anyone who by training and expertise is able to perform the duties of a particular position in an office of the organization is deemed eligible to fill the position. Work in the bureaucracy is a full-time job, ideally providing a career path for the bureaucrat, who must demonstrate the training and expertise necessary to fill each successive position. In its "ideal" form, the system is a meritocracy—that is, positions are filled on the basis of merit or qualifications, typically demonstrated by performance on competitive exams, rather than on applicants' knowing the "right" people. In practice, however—as is true of the other characteristics listed above—an actual bureaucracy is unlikely to meet this standard fully. In fact, getting hired into the organization and advancing in it are likely to be influenced not strictly by objective criteria such as education and experience but also by such social variables as age, gender, race, and social connections.

FIGURE 5.4 The Ideal Typical Bureaucracy

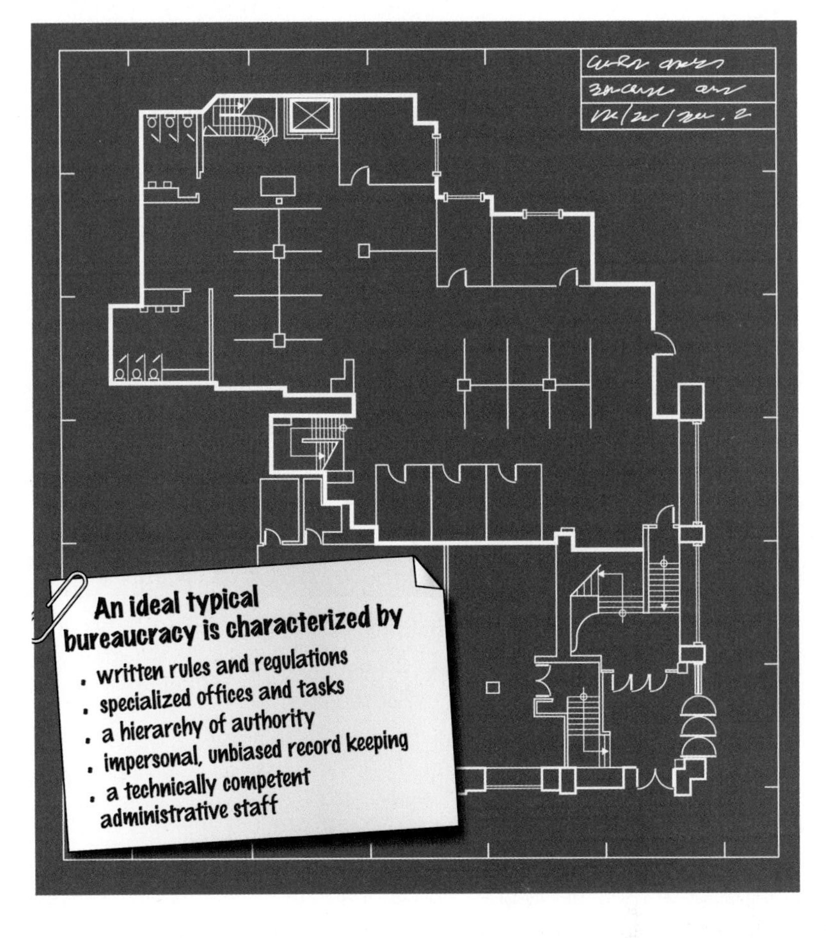

BUREAUCRACIES: A CRITICAL EVALUATION

Bureaucracies popularly evoke images of "paper pushers" and annoying red tape. In their studies of bureaucracy, sociologists, too, have had much to say about this form

DISCOVER & DEBATE

Groups, Organizations, and Bureaucracies

Motion: Schools should regulate and punish cyberbullying committed by their students against other students.

Background

Bullying in schools is not a new phenomenon. The story of a young victim and an aggressive classroom bully has been part of the educational landscape and even popular culture for decades. Cyberbullying, however, is a relatively new development as the problem of threats, shaming, and ostracism have moved from the school yard to cyberspace. Policy makers, school administrators, teachers, and parents are confronting a problem that occupies a legal gray area and demands a balance between free speech rights, privacy protections, institutional authority, and student safety.

Affirmative Arguments

- Schools should actively police bullying, including by checking students' social media accounts for evidence when bullying is suspected or reported. This contributes to the safety and psychological and physical well-being of all students.
- Most schools have an enumerated code of student conduct. The school's code of conduct should be applicable to students both at school and outside of school.
- The First Amendment free speech rights of a student are not limitless. The goal of protecting a student from bullying may trump the right to free speech.

Opposition Arguments

- Schools should strive to make the school environment safe, but they should not seek to regulate student behavior outside of school, including on social media. Schools should endeavor to educate students about the civil use of social media, but they should not be responsible for policing their use of social media outside of school.
- The regulation of student speech on social media, even if it is offensive, may constitute a violation of free speech rights guaranteed by the First Amendment.
- Parents, rather than schools, should be the primary regulators of young people's social media conduct. The problem of cyberbullying is one that parents should manage.

Questions for Consideration

- Who should have a say in determining what behaviors constitute cyberbullying?
- Do the characteristics of a school matter in this debate? Should one differentiate between private and public schools? Should students at colleges and universities be treated differently than students in elementary, junior high school, and high school when it comes to cyberbullying?
- If students create negative posts about teachers on social media, is this cyberbullying? Should this be treated the same as cyberbullying of other students?

Debate Tip

▶ Practice gathering data from academic sources like peer-reviewed journals. When seeking academic sources in a library database, try various combinations of key words to find the most effective and applicable search items.

of organization, with mixed conclusions. Max Weber recognized that bureaucracies can, indeed, provide organizational efficiency in getting the job done. In contrast to earlier organizational forms, many of which filled positions through nepotism, bribes, or other non–merit-based forms of promotion and were founded to serve the needs of their leaders or small elite groups, modern bureaucracies have many redeeming qualities in spite of the frustrations they cause.

At the same time, Weber argued that a bureaucracy may create what he termed an *iron cage*—a prison of rules and regulations from which there is little escape (DiMaggio & Powell, 1983; Weber, 1904–1905/2002). The iron cage, which Weber memorably described as having the potential to be a "polar night of icy darkness," is a metaphor. We become "caged" in bureaucratic structures when we build them to serve us (as rules and regulations would ideally do), but they ultimately come to trap us by denying our humanity, creativity, and autonomy.

As you think about this metaphor of the iron cage, consider encounters with bureaucratic structures that you have had: If you've ever had the feeling that solving a personal or family problem with something like tuition, taxes, or immigration would require speaking to a human being with the power to make a decision or to see that your case is an exception in some way—but no such human was available!—then you can see what Weber meant. We make rules and regulations to keep order and to have a set of knowable guidelines for action and decisions, but what happens when the rules and regulations and their enforcement become the *ends* of an organization rather than *a means to an end*? Then we are in the iron cage.

Sociologists have identified several specific problems that plague bureaucracies, many of which may be familiar and could be thought of as representing *irrationalities of rationality*:

- **Waste and incompetence:** As long as administrators appear to be doing their jobs—filing forms, keeping records, responding to memos, and otherwise keeping busy—nobody really wants to question whether the organization as a whole is performing effectively or efficiently. Secure in their positions, bureaucrats may become inefficient, incompetent, and often indifferent to the clients they are supposed to serve.
- **Trained incapacity:** We have all seen bureaucrats who "go by the book" even when a situation clearly calls for fresh thinking. Thorstein Veblen (1899), a U.S. sociologist and contemporary of Weber's, termed this tendency *trained incapacity,* a learned inability to exercise independent thought. However intelligent they may otherwise be, such bureaucrats make poor judgments when it comes to decisions not covered by the rule book. They become so obsessed with following the rules and regulations that they lose the ability and flexibility to respond to new situations.
- **Goal displacement:** Bureaucracies may lose sight of the original goals they were created to accomplish. Large corporations such as General Motors and Hewlett-Packard and government organizations such as the Department of Homeland Security employ thousands of middle-level employees whose job it is to handle the paperwork required in manufacturing automobiles or computers, or in protecting the country. Perhaps understandably, such people may over time become preoccupied with getting their own jobs done and, driven by the need to ensure the continuation of particular practices or programs linked to their positions, eventually lose touch with the larger goals of the

organization. This shift in focus adds to costs, lowers efficiency, and may prove detrimental to corporations that compete in a global economy and governments seeking to accomplish goals and stay within tight budgets.

Although Weber presented a sometimes chilling picture of bureaucracies operating as vast, inhuman machines, we all recognize that, in practice, there is often a human face behind the counter. In fact, much important work done in bureaucratic organizations is achieved through informal channels and personal ties and connections rather than through official channels, as sociologist Peter Blau showed in his research (Blau & Meyer, 1987). For example, a student who wishes to register late for a class may avoid having to get half a dozen signatures if he or she knows the professor or a staff person in the registrar's office. Because of the shortcomings of bureaucratic forms of organization, however, some theorists have argued for the development of alternative organizational forms. We discuss some of these after looking at the relationship between bureaucracy and democracy.

BUREAUCRACY AND DEMOCRACY

Max Weber argued that bureaucracies were an inevitable outgrowth of modern society, with its large-scale organizations, complex institutional structure, and concern with rationality and efficiency. Yet many observers have viewed bureaucracy as a stifling, irrational force that dominates our lives and threatens representative government. In *Les Employés* (1841/1985), French novelist Honoré de Balzac, who popularized the term *bureaucracy,* called it "the giant power wielded by pigmies" and a "fussy and meddlesome" government. Do bureaucracies inevitably lead to a loss of freedom and erosion of democracy? Are there more humanistic alternatives to bureaucracies that allow freer, more fulfilling participation in the organization? Let's look briefly at the views of sociologist Robert Michels on the incompatibility between democracy and bureaucracy, then see what some people have done to try to reform this organizational structure.

Michels (1876–1936), another contemporary of Weber's, argued that bureaucracy and democracy are fundamentally at odds. He observed that the Socialist Party in Germany, originally created to democratically represent the interests of workers, had become an oligarchy, a form of organization in which a small number of people exert great power. For him this was an example of what he termed the **iron law of oligarchy,** *an inevitable tendency for a large-scale bureaucratic organization to become ruled undemocratically by a handful of people.* (*Oligarchy* means the rule of a small group over many people.)

Iron law of oligarchy: Robert Michels's theory that there is an inevitable tendency for a large-scale bureaucratic organization to become ruled undemocratically by a handful of people.

Following Weber, Michels argued that in a large-scale bureaucratic organization, the closer you are to the top, the greater the concentration of power. People typically get to the top because they are ambitious, hard-driving, and effective in managing the people below, or because they have economic and social capital to trade for proximity to power. Once there, leaders increase their social capital through specialized access to information, resources, and influential people, access that reinforces their power. They also often appoint subordinates who are loyal supporters and thus further enhance their position. Such leaders may come to regard the bureaucracy as a means to meet their own needs or those of their social group. The democratic purposes of an organization may become subordinate to the needs of the dominating group.

Since all modern societies require large-scale organizations to survive, Michels believed that democracies—or, in some cases, organizations—may sow the seeds of their own destruction by breeding bureaucracies that eventually grow into undemocratic oligarchies. Although there are few signs that, for instance, the United States, which has many large-scale bureaucracies, is drifting from democracy, one could make a case that institutions like the U.S. Congress show some tendencies to act in the interests of political parties or powerful members rather than the interests of constituents. For example, a bill on disaster relief or unemployment insurance may be held up when a party leader feels that stalling the bill might confer political advantage on his or her party.

In response to what they feel is the stifling effect of bureaucratic organizations, some people have sought alternative forms of organizations designed to allow greater freedom and more fulfilling participation. For example, as part of the sweeping countercultural spirit of the late 1960s and early 1970s, many youthful activists joined collectives, small organizations that operate by cooperation and consensus. Food cooperatives, employee-run newspapers and health clinics, and "free schools" sprang up as organizations that sought to operate by consensus rather than by bureaucracy. Members of these organizations shunned hierarchy, avoided a division of labor based on expertise, and happily sacrificed efficiency in favor of more humanistic relationships.

The founders of these organizations believed they were reviving more personal organizational arrangements that could better enable society to reach certain goals. Although these organizations initially met with some success and left a legacy, they also confronted a larger society in which more conventional forms of organization effectively shut them out.

Members of such organizations as the food cooperatives and employee-run newspapers and health clinics of the 1960s and 1970s favored the values of cooperation and service over the more competitive and materialistic values of the larger society. In the exuberance of that period, members of collectives believed they were forging a radically new kind of antibureaucratic organization.

In her examination of early collectives, sociologist Joyce Rothschild-Whitt (1979) studied several that self-consciously rejected bureaucracy in favor of more cooperative forms. In one health clinic, for example, all jobs were shared (to the extent legally possible) by all members: Doctors would periodically answer telephones and clean the facility, while nurses and paramedical staff would conduct examinations and interview patients. Although the doctors were paid somewhat more than the other staff members, the differences were not large and were the subject of negotiation by everyone who worked at the clinic.

As long as the collectives remained small, they were able to maintain their founders' values. On the other hand, vastly reduced pay differentials between professional and nonprofessional staff, job sharing, and collective decision-making often made it difficult for the collectives to compete for employees with organizations that shared none of these values (Rothschild-Whitt, 1979). Doctors, for example, could make much more money in conventional medical practice without being expected to answer telephones or sweep the floor. Over time, the original cooperative values tended to erode, and many of the new organizations came to resemble conventional organizations in the larger society. Still, more than three decades after Rothschild-Whitt studied them, several these original groups still exist. Although they may have lost some of their collective zeal, they still operate more cooperatively than most traditional organizations.

A more recent foray away from hierarchically and bureaucratically organized entities has been made by the online retailer Zappos. In early 2014, the company announced that it planned to introduce a "holacracy," replacing traditional management structures with "self-governing 'circles.'" The goal of holacracy, according to a media account of the practice, is to "organize a company around the work that needs to be done instead of around the people who do it." Hence, a holacracy is devoid of job titles; instead, employees are integrated into multiple circles of cooperative workers. A few other companies are experimenting with holacracy as well (McGregor, 2014). Do workers perform well in contexts of dispersed or ambiguous authority? Results at Zappos, according to *Fortune* magazine, have been mixed, and after 3 years of the new management style, the company fell off the 100 Best Companies to Work For list, where it had occupied a place for the past 8 years. The change has been described as fostering both chaos and new ideas and is slated to continue (Reingold, 2016).

THE GLOBAL ORGANIZATION

Organizations from multinational corporations to charitable foundations span the globe and increasingly contribute to what some sociologists believe is a "homogenization" of the world's countries (McNeely, 1995; Neyazi, 2010; Scott & Meyer, 1994; Thomas, Meyer, Ramirez, & Boli, 1987). You can listen to the same music, employ the same Internet search engine, see the same films, and eat the same meals (if you wish) in Bangalore and Baku as you do in Berlin and Boston.

Global organizations are not new. The Hanseatic League, a business alliance between German merchants and cities, dominated trade in the North and Baltic Seas from the mid-12th to the mid-18th centuries. The British East India Company basically owned India and controlled the vast bulk of trade throughout the Far East for several centuries. In 1919, following World War I, the League of Nations was formed, uniting the most economically and militarily powerful nations of the world in an effort to ensure peace and put an end to war. When Germany withdrew and began expanding its borders throughout Europe, however, the League dissolved.

After World War II, a new effort at international governance was made in the form of the United Nations, begun in 1945. The United Nations is still important and active today: Its power is limited, but its influence has grown. It not only mediates disputes between nations, but it is also ever present in international activities ranging from fighting hunger and HIV/AIDS to mobilizing peacekeeping troops and intervening to address conflicts and their consequences.

International organizations exist in two major forms: those established by national governments and those established by private organizations. We consider each separately below.

INTERNATIONAL GOVERNMENTAL ORGANIZATIONS

The first type of global organization is the **international governmental organization (IGO)** established by treaties between governments. Most IGOs exist *to facilitate and*

International governmental organization (IGO): An international organization established by treaties between governments for purposes of commerce, security, promotion of social welfare and human rights, or environmental protection.

GLOBAL ISSUES

International Organizations, Disaster, and Development: Rebuilding Haiti After the 2010 Earthquake

Niko Guido/E+/Getty Images

On January 12, 2010, just before 5:00 p.m., the ground outside of Haiti's capital, Port Au Prince, began to tremble. The 7.0 magnitude earthquake that hit the island was the largest to strike Haiti since the 18th century, and it had a devastating effect on an already poor country. The earthquake killed about 200,000 Haitians and injured another 300,000. Even those fortunate enough to survive without injuries did not escape misfortune as the disaster left behind vast piles of rubble where homes, businesses, hospitals, and other critical infrastructure had stood. An estimated 1.5 million people were living in temporary tent cities after the earthquake.

In the wake of the disaster, there was a global outpouring of support and millions in goods and supplies were donated to help Haiti recover and rebuild. According to a recent National Public Radio story (Knox, 2015) recognizing the 5-year anniversary of the quake, "The catastrophe . . . unleashed an unprecedented flood of humanitarian aid—$13.5 billion in donations and pledges, about three-quarters from donor nations and a quarter from private charity" (para. 2).

But today Haiti is a long way from realizing the bullish goal of "building back better."

An estimated 80,000 people are still living in tent cities or other temporary structures, and the struggles made more acute by the earthquake have not abated for many Haitians (Voice of America News, 2015).

Why does the country continue to struggle to recover and rebuild—and to make progress—5 years and billions of dollars after the 2010 earthquake? There is a spectrum of political, social, and health challenges in Haiti, but among the obstacles to recovery have been the decision of governmental and nongovernmental agencies outside of Haiti to undertake recovery efforts with little inclusion of Haitians. One result of this: billions in donated funds and a relatively modest number of homes constructed and repaired. According to a report, in the fall of 2013, only about 7,500 homes had been built and another 27,000 repaired in Haiti (Johnston, 2014). Haiti's Prime Minister in 2015, Evans Paul, lamented:

> It's like if you came to my house and identified my needs and then you decide to address these needs without regard for my dignity. . . . You want to give me food, but you don't allow me the right to decide what I want to eat. (Quoted in Voice of America News, 2015, "Aid to Haiti," para. 2)

Consider, for instance, the path traveled by relief funds that come from the U.S. Recovery money from outside sources like the U.S. government or money donated to international nongovernmental organizations like the

Red Cross does not typically make a direct journey to the country in need. The movement of monies through layers of agencies peels away funds that might have been used for assistance. For example, according to the Center for Economic Policy and Research, USAID, a government agency that provides assistance abroad, has spent about $1.5 billion since the earthquake, but less than a penny of each dollar goes to a Haitian organization directly (Johnston, 2014). Rather, it is filtered through international contractors and subcontractors, dramatically inflating the cost of assistance and rendering it less economically efficient. For instance, while USAID spent about $33,000 to build a single housing unit through one agency program, a local Haitian organization could complete a housing unit for a displaced family for one fifth of that price using local labor (Knox, 2015).

There has also been critique of the work of nongovernmental agencies working in Haiti. A 2015 report (Elliott & Sullivan, 2015) questioned how the nearly half billion dollars raised by the American Red Cross was spent and pointed to the high costs of hiring non-Haitian contractors to work on the recovery effort.

Lacking the expertise to mount its own projects, the Red Cross ended up giving much of the money to other groups to do the work. Those groups took out a piece of every dollar to cover overhead and management. Even on the projects done by others, the Red Cross had its own significant expenses—in one case, adding up to a third of the project's budget.

According to the report, few Haitians were in significant decision-making positions in relief projects. Although the Red Cross brought in food and assisted with temporary shelter, its lasting contributions have been mixed: According to the 2015 *Pro Publica* report, only six permanent homes were constructed with the organization's funds (Elliott & Sullivan, 2015).

THINK IT THROUGH

- The goal of many INGOs like the Red Cross is to "do good." At the same time, their efforts may be driven by goals and practices that originate outside of the countries and communities they seek to help. How can INGOs support assistance efforts while recognizing the autonomy and dignity of local populations?

regulate trade between the member countries, promote national security (both the League of Nations and the United Nations were created after highly destructive world wars), *protect social welfare or human rights, or increasingly, ensure environmental protection.*

Some of the most powerful IGOs today were created to unify national economies into large trading blocs. One of the most complex IGOs is the European Union, whose rules now govern 28 countries in Europe; 5 additional countries have applied for EU entry. The European Union was formed to create a single European economy in which businesses could operate freely across borders in search of markets and labor and workers could move freely in search of jobs without having to go through customs or show passports at border crossings. EU member states have common economic policies, and 18 of them share a single currency (the euro). Not all Europeans welcome economic unity, however, since it means their countries must surrender some of their economic power to the EU as a whole. Being economically united by a single currency also means the economic problems felt by one country are distributed among all the other countries to some degree. Thus, when economic crisis hit Europe in 2008, the severe economic woes of Greece, Portugal, and Spain, among others, caused serious problems for stronger EU economies, like that of Germany.

IGOs can also wield considerable military power, provided their member countries are willing to do so. The North Atlantic Treaty Organization (NATO) and the United Nations, for example, have sent troops from some of their participating nations into war zones in Iraq and Afghanistan in recent years. Yet because nations ultimately control the use of their own military forces, there are limits to the

REUTERS/Reuters Staff

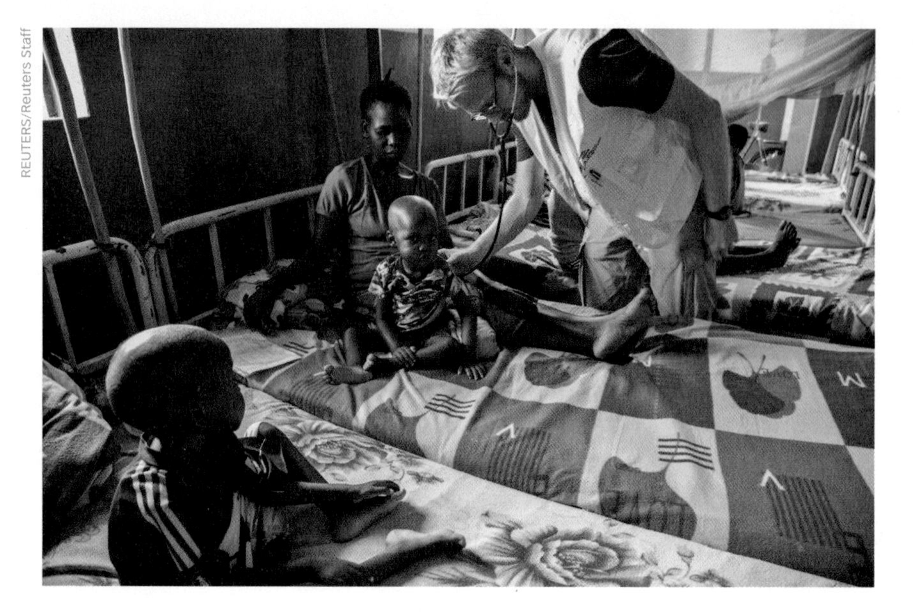

Médecins sans Frontières (MSF or Doctors Without Borders) works around the world to serve underserved or conflict-torn countries and communities. In this photo, a doctor from MSF examines children suffering from malnutrition in a hospital in Bambari, Central African Republic.

authority of even the most powerful military IGOs, whose strength derives from the voluntary participation of their member nations.

IGOs often reflect inequalities in power among their members. For example, the UN Security Council is responsible for maintaining international peace and security and is therefore the most powerful organization within the United Nations. Its five permanent members include the United Kingdom, the United States, China, France, and Russia, which gives these countries significant clout over the Security Council's actions. The remaining 10 Security Council member countries are elected by the UN General Assembly for 2-year terms and therefore have less lasting power than the permanent members.

At the beginning of the 20th century, there were only about three dozen IGOs in the world, although data for that time are incomplete. By 1981, when consistent reporting criteria were adopted, there were 1,039; by 2011, the most recent year for which data are available, there were 7,608 (Union of International Associations, 2011).

INTERNATIONAL NONGOVERNMENTAL ORGANIZATIONS

The second type of global organization is the **international nongovernmental organization (INGO)**, *established by agreements between the individuals or private organizations making up the membership and existing to fulfill an explicit mission.* Examples include Doctors Without Borders (*Médecins sans Frontières),* the International Sociological Association, the World Wildlife Federation, and the International Red Cross. Global business organizations (GBOs) represent a subtype within the broader category of INGOs. The concept of the GBO captures the fluid and highly interconnected nature of our modern, globalized labor market in which employees often interact and communicate with people from other nations and cultures, facilitated by technology and online networks. Like the number of IGOs, the number of INGOs, including GBOs, has increased exponentially in recent years—from fewer than 200 near the beginning of the 20th century to more than 20,000 by 1985 and up to 56,834 in 2011 (Union of International Associations, 2011).

INGOs are primarily concerned with promoting the global interests of their members, largely through influencing the United Nations, other IGOs, or individual governments. They also engage in research, education, and the spread of information by means of international conferences, meetings, and journals. INGOs have succeeded in shaping the policies of powerful nations. One prominent INGO is Islamic Relief Worldwide (IRW). The organization, founded in the United Kingdom, conducts projects in over 30 countries. IRW has affiliated partners in countries such as Chechnya, India, Kenya, and Pakistan. One of its most prominent branches, Islamic Relief USA (IRUSA), is based in Alexandria, Virginia. IRUSA has many domestic programs, such as the annual Day of Dignity ("Faiths unite," 2015) when volunteers distribute food, medical care, hygiene kits, blankets, clothing, and more to homeless and needy persons. IRUSA has also been active during natural disasters such as Hurricane Katrina and Hurricane Sandy. Staying true to the mission of IRW, IRUSA also works in 37 countries, such as Bosnia, Ghana, Ecuador, Jordan, and the Philippines. In

International nongovernmental organization (INGO): An international organization established by agreements between the individuals or private organizations making up its membership and existing to fulfill an explicit mission.

2015, IRUSA was named a Top-Rated Nonprofit by Great Nonprofits (Great Nonprofits, 2016). In 2016, IRUSA was awarded four out of four stars by Charity Navigator (Charity Navigator, 2016). Although they are far more numerous than IGOs and have achieved some successes, INGOs have less power over state actions and policies since legal power (including enforcement) ultimately lies with governmental organizations and treaties. At the same time, their influence in individual countries can be considerable, sometimes with very positive effects, and at other times, with more problematic outcomes, as our *Global Issues* box (above) shows.

WHY STUDY GROUPS AND ORGANIZATIONS?

You now have a good idea of how the groups and organizations to which you belong exert influence over your life. They help to determine who you know and, in many ways, who you are. The primary groups of your earliest years were crucial in shaping your sense of self—a sense that will change only very slowly over the rest of your life. Throughout your life, groups are the wellspring of the norms and values that enable and enrich your social life. At the same time, they are the source of nonconforming behavior; the rebel is shaped by group membership as much as the more mainstream and conventional citizen.

Although groups remain central in our lives, group affiliation in the United States is rapidly changing. To some degree, long-standing conventional groups appear to be losing ground. For example, today's typical college students are less likely to join civic groups and organizations—or even to vote—than were their parents. At the same time, many are active "netizens," joining and creating groups for both amusement and civic or political causes through such vehicles as Facebook and Twitter.

The global economy and information technology are also redefining group life in ways we can already perceive. For instance, workers in earlier generations spent much of their careers in a relatively small number of long-lasting, bureaucratic organizations; younger workers today are much more likely to be part of a succession of networked, "flexible," and even virtual organizations.

How will these trends affect the quality of our social relationships? Will the blurring between primary and secondary groups continue and expand? Will our growing reliance on social media as a key forum for interaction foster integration or alienation? In our changing social environment, these questions pose important frontiers for sociological analysis.

WHAT CAN I DO WITH A SOCIOLOGY DEGREE?

Leadership Skills and Teamwork

Sociology students not only examine theories and research about groups and organizations, they often have multiple opportunities both in and out of class to develop *leadership and teamwork skills* that are essential in the workplace. In fact, many of the skills discussed in other "Skills and Careers" sections in this book are essential to effective leadership and teamwork, including critical thinking (Chapter 2), ethical decision-making (Chapter 9), and problem solving (Chapter 10).

Good leaders must be able to harness organizational and community resources as well as human capital to meet goals. They must be able to identify and address challenging group dynamics to ensure people work together effectively. Leadership of a team requires the ability to work with team members and stakeholders of diverse backgrounds. Sociology students gain a critical understanding of issues of power and inequality and intergroup relationships, especially the ways in which social identities of race, class, gender, sexual orientation, and so forth, influence interaction and participation. Sociology students learn to ask critical questions about who is participating, who has the power to make decisions, and how people are affected by decisions. Sociology students are increasingly exposed to experiential learning opportunities that encourage the development of these skills firsthand through student leadership programs, internships, and service learning in various organizations.

Jillian Hubbard, Principal and Founder of Jillian Hubbard Consulting

The George Washington University, BA in Multicultural Studies

As a principal and founder of my own firm, I provide consulting services to organizations and individuals in the areas of organizational development, talent development, and diversity and inclusion to help organizations best achieve their identified steps for improvement. In my career, I've led and supported a variety of projects to assist individuals and organizations in initiatives such as volunteer recruitment, values development and implementation, staff management support, and workshop development and facilitation. Most recently, as a consultant with the American Conference on Diversity, I led the organization in the assessment of its Program Department and developed detailed plans to strengthen its intern, volunteer, and student alumni programs.

My long-standing passion for developing people, teams, and organizations stems from a series of formative educational and professional experiences, including my courses in sociology, that demonstrated to me how strong communication, shared understanding, team-oriented leadership, and thoughtful strategy can create lasting personal and professional transformation. Leadership and teamwork skills are important for all levels of organization leaders and supporters in a variety of environments, including corporate, government, education, and nonprofit.

Career Data: Training and Development Specialist

- 2016 Median Pay: $59,020 per year
- Typical Entry-Level Education: Bachelor's degree
- Projected Job Growth by 2024: 7% (As fast as average)

SOURCE: Bureau of Labor Statistics, Occupational Outlook Handbook, 2016.

SUMMARY

- The importance of social groups in our lives is one of the salient features of the modern world. Social groups are collections of people who share a sense of common identity and regularly interact with one another based on shared expectations. There are many conceptual ways to distinguish social groups sociologically to better understand them.
- Among the most important characteristics of a group is whether or not it serves as a reference

group—that is, a group that provides standards by which we judge ourselves in terms of how we think we appear to others, what sociologist Charles Horton Cooley termed the "looking-glass self."

- Group size is another variable that is an important factor in group dynamics. Although their intensity may diminish, larger groups tend to be more stable than smaller groups of two (**dyads**) or three (**triads**) people. Although even small groups can develop a formal group structure, larger groups develop a formal structure.

- Formal structures include some people in leadership roles—that is, those group members who are able to influence the behavior of the other members. The most common form of leadership is **transactional**—that is, routine leadership concerned with getting the job done. Less common is **transformational leadership**, which is concerned with changing the very nature of the group itself.

- Leadership roles imply that the role occupant is accorded some power, the ability to mobilize resources and get things done despite resistance. Power derives from two principal sources: the personality of the leader (**personal power**) and the position that the leader occupies (**positional power**). Max Weber highlighted the importance of charisma as a source of leadership as well as leadership deriving from traditional authority (a queen inherits a throne, for example).

- In general people are highly susceptible to group pressure. Many people will conform to group norms or obey orders from an authority figure, even when there are potentially negative consequences for others or even for themselves.

- Important aspects of groups are the networks that are formed between groups and among the people in them. Networks constitute broad sources of relationships, direct and indirect, including connections that may be extremely important in business and politics. Women, people of color, and lower-income people typically have less access to the most influential economic and political networks than do upper-class White males in U.S. society.

- As a consequence of unequal access to powerful social networks, there is an unequal division of social capital in society. **Social capital** is the knowledge and connections that enable people to cooperate with one another for mutual benefit and to extend their influence. Some social scientists have argued that social capital has declined in the United States during the last quarter century—a process they worry indicates a decline in Americans' commitment to civic engagement.

- **Formal organizations** are organizations that are rationally designed to achieve their objectives by means of rules, regulations, and procedures. They may be **utilitarian**, **coercive**, or **normative**, depending on the reasons for joining. One of the most common types of formal organizations in modern society is the bureaucracy. Bureaucracies are characterized by written rules and regulations, specialized offices, a hierarchical structure, impersonality in record keeping, and professional administrative staff.

- The **iron law of oligarchy** holds that large-scale organizations tend to concentrate power in the hands of a few people. As a result, even supposedly democratic organizations tend to become undemocratic when they become large.

- Several organizational alternatives to bureaucracies exist. These include collectives, which emphasize cooperation, consensus, and humanistic relations. Networked organizations, which increase flexibility by reducing hierarchy, are like collectives in their organization.

- Two important forms of global organizations are **international governmental organizations (IGOs)** and **international nongovernmental organizations (INGOs)**. Both kinds of organizations play increasingly important roles in the world today, and IGOs—particularly the United Nations—may become key organizational actors as the pace of globalization increases.

KEY TERMS

dyad, 131
triad, 131
alliance (or coalition), 131
social closure, 134
transformational leader, 134
transactional leader, 134
legitimate authority, 135
positional power, 135
personal power, 135
groupthink, 137
structuralism, 138
economic capital, 138
social capital, 139
organization, 139
formal organization, 139
utilitarian organizations, 140
coercive organizations, 141
normative organizations, 141
iron law of oligarchy, 146
international governmental organization (IGO), 147
international nongovernmental organization (INGO), 150

DISCUSSION QUESTIONS

1. Can you think of a time when a group to which you belonged was making a decision you thought was wrong—ethically, legally, or otherwise—but you went along anyway? How do your experiences confirm or refute Janis's characterization of groupthink and its effects?
2. List the primary and secondary groups of which you are a member, then make another list of the primary and secondary groups to which you belonged 5 years ago. Which groups in these two periods were most important for shaping (a) your view of yourself, (b) your political beliefs, (c) your goals in life, and (d) your friendships?
3. Think of a time when you chose to "go along to get along" with a group decision even when you were inclined to think or behave differently. Think of a time when you opted to dissent, choosing a path different from that pursued by your group or organization. How would you account for the different decisions? How might sociologists explain them?
4. What did Stanley Milgram seek to test in his human experiments at Yale University? What did he find? Do you think that a similar study today would find the same results? Why or why not?
5. Max Weber suggested that bureaucracy, while intended to maximize efficiency in tasks and organizations, could also be highly irrational. He coined the term *the iron cage* to talk about the web of rules and regulations he feared would ensnare modern societies and individuals. On one hand, societies create organizations that impose rules and regulations to maintain social order and foster the smooth working of institutions such as the state and the economy. On the other hand, members of society may often feel trapped and dehumanized by these organizations. Explain this paradox using an example of your own encounters with the "iron cage" of bureaucracy.

edge.sagepub.com/eglitis

Want a better grade?

Get the tools you need to sharpen your study skills. Access practice quizzes, eFlashcards, video and multimedia at **https://edge.sagepub.com/eglitis**.

PRACTICE AND APPLY WHAT YOU'VE LEARNED

► edge.sagepub.com/eglitis

SAGE edge™

CHECK YOUR COMPREHENSION ON THE STUDY SITE WITH:

- **Practice quizzes** that allow you to assess how much you've learned
- **eFlashcards** that strengthen your understanding of key terms and concepts.
- **Multimedia resources** that bring concepts to life through open-source videos and podcasts.

DEVIANCE AND SOCIAL CONTROL

6.1 Define deviance from a sociological perspective

6.2 Describe key theories used in sociology to explain deviance

6.3 Identify types of deviance studied by sociologists

6.4 Discuss how deviance is controlled and punished in the United States today

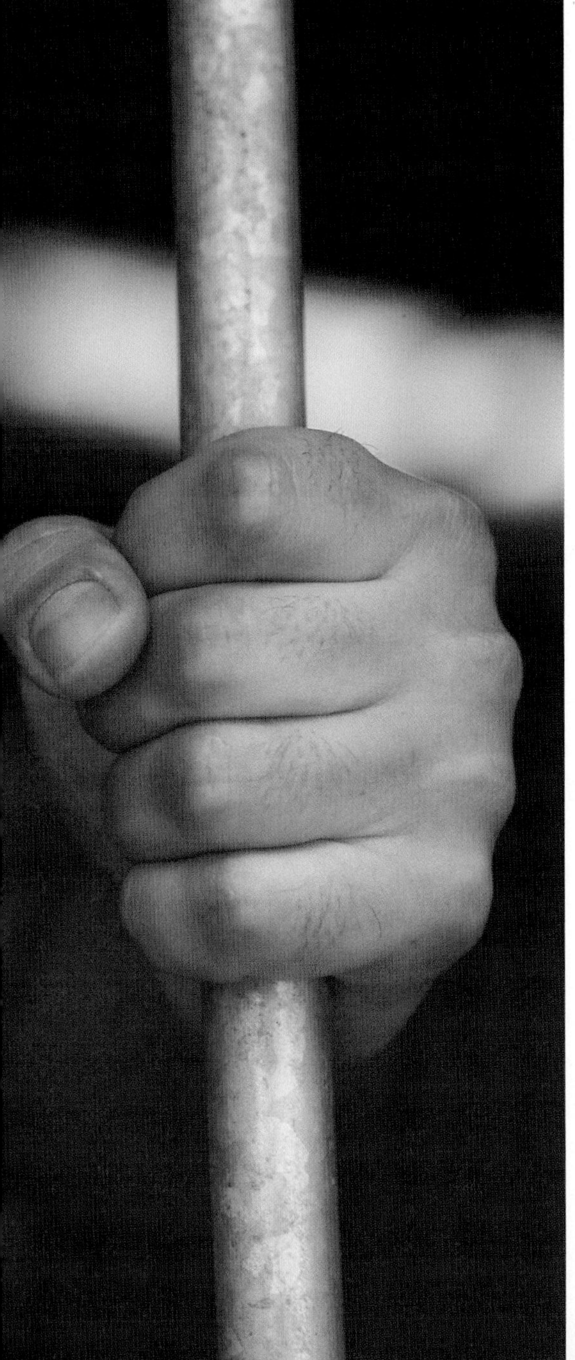

Ken Kaminesky/Getty Images

WHAT DO YOU THINK?

1. Is everyone deviant at least some of the time? Does this make deviance normal?
2. Why did the rate of imprisonment rise dramatically in the United States beginning in the 1980s?
3. What methods of controlling deviance are available to countries and communities? What methods do you believe are more or less effective for controlling deviance?

AP Photo/Files

THE DEATH OF LEN BIAS

In 1986, Len Bias was a University of Maryland basketball phenomenon, known to fans of the game across the country. Just 2 days after being drafted by the Boston Celtics, a team coming off of yet another National Basketball Championship victory, Bias died of a cocaine overdose that sent him into cardiac arrest (Weinberg, 2004). Although Bias had been using powdered cocaine, the press largely blamed crack for Bias's death, a rumor that exacerbated the widespread social panic over crack's dire impact on communities and the country (Schuppe, 2016). Reflecting on the roots of modern mass imprisonment in the United States, journalist Jon Schuppe (2016) writes:

> In life, Len Bias was basketball's next great hope, contender for a crown that went instead to Michael Jordan. In death, he became a trigger for the war on drugs. Bias' 1986 cocaine overdose helped sparked a panic, stoked by false rumors and a high-stakes political campaign, that culminated in a law that swept thousands of low-level drug offenders—most of them young and black—into prison. Thirty years later, America is still reeling from the impact. (para. 1)

The death of Len Bias coincided with a hotly contested midterm Congressional election campaign in which both parties were seeking an advantage. Eric Sterling, then a Congressional aide, points out that House Speaker Thomas O'Neill, a Democrat from Boston, "realized that the national concern about this could be the basis for a comprehensive anti-drug, anti-crime bill," shifting some advantage to his party (quoted in National Public Radio [NPR], 2011). When

Congressional Republicans reviewed the proposal, they were not satisfied with sentencing provisions for some offenders. An NPR (2011) report on the events of that year notes that "in the final days before adjournment—without any hearings—a mandatory sentencing provision was added" (para. 6).

The mandatory minimum sentences that arose from that bill had several important consequences, which continue to reverberate in communities today. First, they had a disproportionate impact on minority offenders, who were more likely to end up in prison for crimes, including possession of drugs, that previously would have earned a far lesser sentence. The penalties for crack cocaine, widely associated with users and sellers in poor Black neighborhoods, were particularly harsh: Laws "were weighted heavily against crack, requiring only 5 grams to trigger a five-year prison sentence, compared to 500 grams for powder cocaine. The sentences rose to 10 years with 50 grams of crack and 5,000 grams of powder" (Schuppe, 2016, "'Dark chapter,'" para. 1). Penalties for powdered cocaine, more costly and seen as more likely to be the drug of choice for better-off White users, were dramatically lower.

FIGURE 6.1 U.S. State and Federal Prison Population, 1925–2015

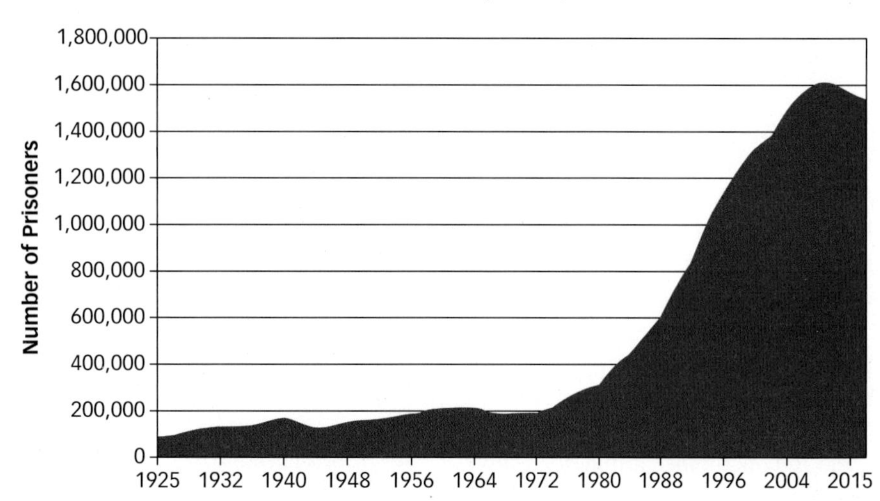

SOURCE: Reprinted with permission from The Sentencing Project.

Second, the laws had a deep impact on some impoverished minority neighborhoods. Because males were most likely to be arrested, convicted, and imprisoned, many families were suddenly without sons, brothers, and fathers for extended periods of time. As a recent article on the effects of mass incarceration on families notes, "By 2000, more than 1 million black children had a father in jail or prison—and roughly half of those fathers were living in the same household as their kids when they were locked up. Paternal incarceration is associated with behavior problems and delinquency, especially among boys" (Coates, 2015, Part II, para. 8). The costs to families accrue even after release as ex-offenders may be excluded from public housing and have a difficult time finding employment.

Third, mandatory minimum sentences contributed to the dramatic rise of the prison population in the United States (Figure 6.1). In 2007, the rate of imprisonment in the United States peaked at 767 people per 100,000 (Coates, 2015). More recently, it has dropped to 612 per 100,000, although this continues to be far more than other modern democratic states around the globe (Carson, 2015).

The use of drugs and their possession is broadly understood as deviant, but responses to deviance can vary dramatically. The political reaction to Len Bias's death was to criminally punish a range of actions associated with drugs. As this chapter shows, however, deviance is an expansive concept, encompassing an array of attitudes, behaviors, and conditions, of which only a small part fall under the category of "crime." We begin this chapter by looking at how deviance is defined. This is followed by an examination of different perspectives that sociologists employ to understand and explain deviant behavior. We then consider the spectrum of ways in which U.S. society exercises social control over groups and behaviors defined as deviant.

WHAT IS DEVIANT BEHAVIOR?

Sociologists suggest that what is labeled *deviant* depends on cultural norms and changes over time and place. Tattoos, once limited to a few subcultures, are widely accepted in U.S. society, although individuals who change their appearance very dramatically may still be subject to this label.

Deviance *is any attitude, behavior, or condition that violates cultural norms or societal laws and results in disapproval, hostility, or sanction if it becomes known*. By contrast, a **crime** *is an act, usually considered deviant, that is punishable by fines, imprisonment, or both*.

Several important aspects of our definition of deviance deserve greater elaboration. First, *deviance* is a broad term that may encompass crimes but often refers to noncriminal attitudes, practices, and conditions. Second, deviance is not restricted to specific groups, genders, or generations. Third, what is considered deviant can include things that are not consciously chosen, such as medical conditions, mental or physical illnesses, and physical defects and abnormalities. Fourth, deviance is a relative, subjective concept. Definitions of deviance vary from place to place, across time, and among groups within society. Finally, our definition of deviance suggests that it is primarily a reaction against something. Therefore, deviance is best seen as a label applied to the attitudes, practices, or conditions of other people or groups. As such, moral, social, and legal judgments play a role in decisions regarding what is or is not deviant.

Is all deviance criminal? In fact, most of the attitudes, practices, and conditions considered "deviant" by society at any given time are not criminal. For example, while having extensive tattoos or piercings may be considered deviant, it is not criminal. The follow-up question—Are all criminal acts deviant?—has a more complicated answer. Although the label *crime* applies to acts that are widely agreed to be deviant in nature (for example, murder, robbery, rape, the sexual exploitation of children, and arson), such consensus is lacking regarding other kinds of crimes. Use of illicit drugs, some types of gambling, vagrancy, and adult prostitution are just a few examples of crimes that lack societal consensus about their deviance. Once an act is labeled *criminal*, formal sanctions can be applied to control it and the people who engage in it. One should be cautious not to make the assumption that every act labeled a crime is considered deviant by all of society's members, or that every form of deviance is, or should be, criminalized.

The diversity of opinion surrounding deviance and criminality stems from the fact that most societies in the modern world are pluralistic. **Pluralistic societies** are *made up of many different groups with different norms and values,* which may or may not change over time. In a pluralistic society, what is deviant for one social group may be acceptable or normal in another, and even long-held beliefs and practices are sometimes subject to transformation over time. For example, in the 1800s, members of the Church of Jesus Christ of Latter-day Saints (Mormons) practiced polygamy—specifically, men could have multiple wives—but by the end of the 19th century the church officially condemned that practice. Similarly, in 2005, after centuries of supporting the execution of juveniles for **capital offenses**, which are crimes punishable by death, the U.S. Supreme Court ruled that it is unconstitutional to execute anyone for a crime he or she committed before the age of 18. Prior to this ruling, 22 individuals had

Deviance: Any attitude, behavior, or condition that violates cultural norms or societal laws and results in disapproval, hostility, or sanction if it becomes known.

Crime: Any act defined in the law as punishable by fines, imprisonment, or both.

Pluralistic societies: Societies made up of many diverse groups with different norms and values.

Capital offenses: Crimes considered so heinous they are punishable by death.

been executed for crimes they committed while younger than age 18 (Death Penalty Information Center, n.d.). The shifting legal status of marijuana, which is now legal to purchase and consume for medical purposes in several states and is legal for recreational use in Colorado, Washington State, Oregon, Alaska, and Washington, DC (Drug Policy Alliance, n.d.), is also illustrative of dynamic definitions of deviance. In each case, norms pertaining to practices or punishment shifted over time, creating a "new normal."

HOW DO SOCIOLOGISTS EXPLAIN DEVIANCE?

What explains deviance? Below we look at a spectrum of theoretical perspectives that seek to explain why people engage in deviance. We divide these theories broadly into explanatory and interactionist categories. Theories that try to explain *why* deviance does (or does not) occur, including biological, functionalist, and conflict perspectives, differ from interactionist theories, which seek to understand *how* deviance is defined, constructed, and enacted through social processes like labeling.

BIOLOGICAL PERSPECTIVES

Early social scientists were convinced that deviant behavior—from alcoholism to theft to murder—was caused by biological or anatomical abnormalities (Hooton, 1939). For example, some early researchers claimed that *skull configurations of deviant individuals differed from those of nondeviants,* a theory known as **phrenology**. Other theorists claimed that deviants were **atavisms**, or *throwbacks to primitive early humans* (Lombroso, 1896), and that they also had body types that differed from those of noncriminals (Sheldon, 1949). These early biological theories have been disproved, but the search for biological causes of deviance continues, with some interesting findings in individual cases (Wright, Tibbetts, & Daigle, 2008). Advances in medical technology, especially increased use of magnetic resonance imaging (MRI and fMRI, or functional MRI), have enabled researchers to uncover patterns of brain function, physiology, and response unique to some deviant or criminal individuals (Giedd, 2004). Nevertheless, most modern biological theories do not attribute deviance to biology alone. Instead, they argue that some deviance may be the product of an interaction between biological and environmental factors (Denno, 1990; Kanazawa & Still, 2000; Mednick, Moffitt, & Stack, 1987).

One method for testing biological theories is to compare children with their parents to see whether children of parents with deviant lifestyles are more likely to recreate those lifestyles than are children whose parents are not deviant. Research has found that people who suffer from alcoholism and some forms of mental illness (particularly schizophrenia, chronic depression, and bipolar personality disorder) are indeed more likely to have parents with similar problems than are people who do not have these conditions (Dunner, Gershon, & Barrett, 1988; Scheff, 1988).

Nevertheless, studies comparing the frequency of deviance between generations do not always control for the possibility that children of alcoholic, schizophrenic, depressed, or bipolar parents may have learned coping strategies that show up as symptoms of these problems, rather than having inherited a biological predisposition. Children of farmers are more likely to be farmers than are children of urban office workers, but we would not argue that farming is a biologically determined trait. Furthermore, many children of parents who are deviant are not deviant themselves, and many people with deviant lifestyles come from mainstream families (Chambliss & Hass, 2011; Katz & Chambliss, 1995; Scheff, 1988).

Studies that have found similarities in patterns of deviant behavior between twins are often cited as evidence in support of biological theories of deviance. The Danish sociologist Karl Christiansen (1977) examined the life histories of 7,172 twins. Among these, 926 had been convicted of a crime. Christiansen found that 35% of the identical male twins who had been convicted of a crime had twin brothers who had also been convicted of a crime. Among male fraternal twins, 21% who had committed a crime had brothers who also had committed a crime (Christiansen, 1977). Biological theorists interpret these findings as support for the theory that biological factors contribute to deviant and criminal behavior (Mednick, Gabrielli, & Hutchings, 1987).

Interestingly, critics of biological theories see this evidence as *disproving* the influence of biology. Among both men and women, in most cases where one twin has committed a crime, the other twin has not. Moreover, if criminal behavior were genetically determined, we should expect that nearly all twin brothers or sisters of identical twins who are criminals should also be criminals (Katz & Chambliss, 1995). To the extent that

Phrenology: A theory that the skull shapes of deviant individuals differ from those of nondeviants.

Atavisms: Throwbacks to primitive early humans.

identical twins do show similar patterns of deviance as adults, we can attribute these patterns to their common socialization: Identical twins are more likely than other siblings to be treated the same, dressed alike, and sometimes even confused with one another.

A more nuanced approach to biological explanations of deviance attempts to incorporate *both* sets of factors. The nature *versus* nurture paradigm is essentially converted to nature *and* nurture. Criminologist Kevin Beaver and a team of researchers took a more critical approach to this question by examining a general theory of crime posited by Gottfredson and Hirschi. A major tenet of this theory is that low self-control is largely a result of parental management influences and not of biogenetic factors. Beaver's study, which analyzed twin data drawn from the National Longitudinal Study of Adolescent Health, estimated that genetic factors accounted for 52% to 64% of the variance in low self-control, with twins' nonshared environments accounting for the remaining variance (Beaver, Wright, DeLisi, & Vaughn, 2008). As expansive genetic and biological data become increasingly accessible, a school of thought within criminology is pursuing the question of how biological factors may play a part in crime and deviance.

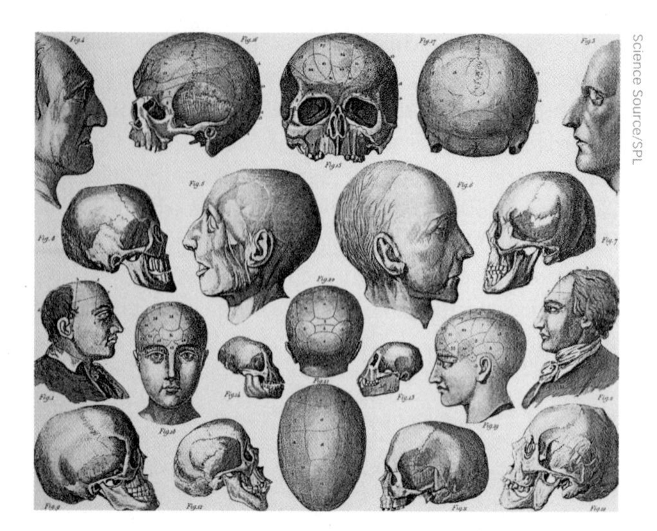
Science Source/SPL

Cesare Lombroso, an early criminologist, theorized that criminals were throwbacks to primitive humans. Although his theory has been disproved by research, the search for biological causes of criminality continues.

FUNCTIONALIST PERSPECTIVES

Functionalist theories suggest that we must examine culture, especially shared norms and values, to understand why people behave the way they do. Recall that functionalist theory assumes society is characterized by a high degree of consensus on norms and values. It regards deviance as an abnormality that society seeks to eliminate, much as an organism seeks to rid itself of a parasite. At the same time, functionalist theory sees a certain amount of deviant behavior as useful—or functional—for society. It suggests that deviance—or the labeling of some behaviors as deviant—contributes to social solidarity by enhancing members' sense of the boundary between right and wrong (Durkheim, 1893/1997).

DEVIANCE AND SOCIAL SOLIDARITY Émile Durkheim (1858–1917), the father of functionalist theories of deviance, hypothesized that deviant behavior serves a positive function in society by drawing "moral boundaries," delineating what behavior is acceptable and what is not within a community. Durkheim argued that we can describe a society lacking consensus on what is right and wrong as being in a state of *anomie,* a condition of confusion that occurs when people lose sight of the shared rules and values that give order and meaning to their lives. In one of his most famous studies, Durkheim sought to show that anomie is a principal cause of suicide, itself a deviant act.

Durkheim (1897/1951) gathered extensive data on suicide in France and Italy and found that these data supported the theory that societies characterized by high levels of anomie also have high levels of suicide. Moreover, he argued that his research demonstrated that suicide rates vary depending on the level of *social solidarity,* or the social bonds that unite members of a group. Durkheim discovered, for example, that single men had higher rates of suicide than married men, Protestants a higher rate than Catholics, and men higher rates than women. Durkheim suggested that the higher rates were correlated with lower levels of social solidarity in the groups to which people were attached.

Durkheim's research methods—the statistics as well as the sampling procedures—were primitive compared with modern-day methods. Since he first published his research, however, hundreds of studies have looked at suicide differences between men and women, between industrialized and developing countries, and even among the homeless. Most of these empirical studies have found considerable support for Durkheim's anomie theory (Cutright & Fernquist, 2000; Diaz, 1999; Kubrin, 2005; Lester, 2000; Simpson & Conklin, 1989; Wasserman, 1999). Durkheim's theory has spawned some of the most influential contemporary theories of deviance, including those of Robert K. Merton, Richard Cloward, and Lloyd Ohlin, which we discuss below.

STRUCTURAL STRAIN THEORY In the 1930s, American sociologist Robert K. Merton (1968) adapted Durkheim's concept of anomie into a general theory of deviance. According to Merton's theory, **structural strain** is *a form of anomie that occurs when a gap exists between the culturally defined goals of a society and the means available in society to achieve those goals.*

Merton argued that most people in a society share a common understanding of the goals they should pursue as well as the legitimate means for achieving those goals. For example, success, as measured in terms of wealth, consumption, and prestige, is widely regarded as an important goal in U.S. society. Moreover, there appears to be widespread consensus on the legitimate means for achieving success—education, an enterprising spirit, and hard work, among others.

Most people pursue the goal of "success" by following established social norms. Merton referred to such behavior as *conformity*. Nevertheless, success is not always attainable through conventional means, or conformity. When this occurs, Merton argued, the resulting contradiction between societal goals and the means of achieving them creates *strain*, which may result in four different types of deviant behavior. His **strain theory** suggests that *when there is a discrepancy between the cultural goals for success and the means available to achieve those goals, rates of deviance will be high.* Reactions to the discrepancy will lead to the types of deviance depicted in the first column in Table 6.1. Since Merton's original formulation of strain theory, other researchers have expanded on his work. For example, Kaufman (2009) explored the relation between general strains and gender, finding that serious strains may affect men and women differently and influence their inclination to engage in deviance. Women, Kaufman found, are especially likely to engage in deviance in response to depression.

TABLE 6.1 Merton's Typology of Deviance

Type of Response	Cultural Goals	Legitimacy of Means
Conformity	Accept	Accept
Innovation	Accept	Reject
Ritualism	Reject	Accept
Retreatism	Reject	Reject
Rebellion	Reject/substitute	Reject/substitute

SOURCE: Data from Merton, Robert K. (1968, orig. 1938). *Social theory and social structure.* NY: Free Press, pp. 230–246.

OPPORTUNITY THEORY Although Merton's theory helps us understand the structural conditions leading to high rates of deviance, it neglects the fact that not everyone has the same access to deviant solutions. This is the point made by Richard Cloward and Lloyd Ohlin (1960), who developed **opportunity theory** as an extension of Merton's strain theory. According to Cloward and Ohlin, *people differ not only in their motivations to engage in deviant acts but also in their opportunities to do so.* For instance, only the presence of a demand for illicit drugs, plus access to supplies of those drugs through producers, offers opportunities for individuals to become drug dealers. Similarly, unless you have access to funds you can secretly convert to your own use, you are unlikely to consider embezzlement as an option, much less carry it out. Deviance, then, is more likely in a community when the opportunities for it exist.

CONTROL THEORY Agreeing with the functionalist claim that a society's norms and values are the starting point for understanding deviance, Gottfredson and Hirschi's (1990/2004) **control theory** *explains that the probability of delinquency or deviance* among children and teenagers *is rooted in social control.* Gottfredson and Hirschi differ from Durkheim and Merton, however, regarding the importance of a general state of anomie in creating deviance, arguing instead that a person's acceptance or rejection of societal norms depends on that individual's life experiences.

Structural strain: In Merton's reformulation of Durkheim's functionalist theory, a form of anomie that occurs when a gap exists between society's culturally defined goals and the means society makes available to achieve those goals.

Strain theory: The theory that when there is a discrepancy between the cultural goals for success and the means available to achieve those goals, rates of deviance will be high.

Opportunity theory: The theory that people differ not only in their motivations to engage in deviant acts but also in their opportunities to do so.

Control theory: The theory that the cause of deviance is rooted in social control and, specifically, the life experiences and relationships that people form.

GLOBAL ISSUES

Globalization and Criminal Opportunities

Globalization has increased the potential for crime networks to gain wealth and political power (Block & Weaver, 2004; Naylor, 2002). At the top of the list of crimes facilitated by processes linked to globalization are money laundering and the smuggling and illicit selling of drugs, weapons, and human beings, among others. Digital networks have multiplied these opportunities, opening new doors to global criminality.

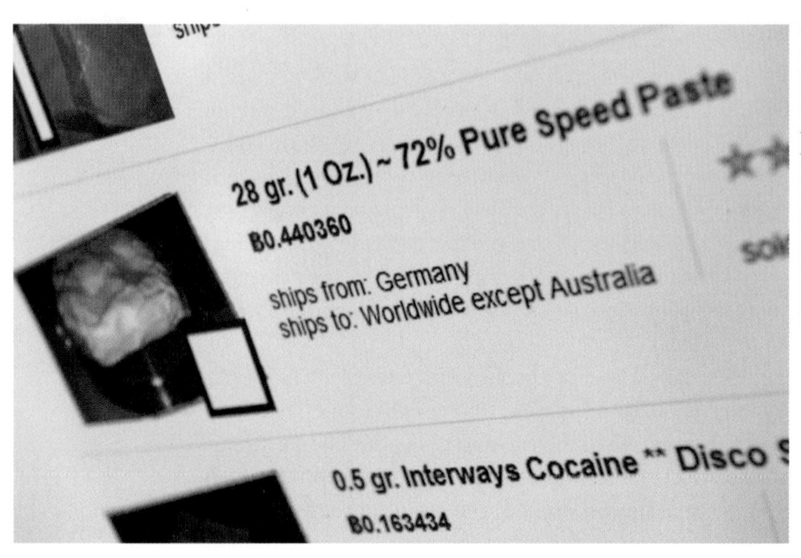

Boris Roessler/dpa/picture-alliance/Newscom

Some of the criminal behavior takes place within legitimate institutions. For example, nearly every major bank in Europe and the United States has been found guilty of laundering money or other significant fraud at some point. In December 2012, the British bank HSBC was fined $1.9 billion for laundering billions of dollars in drug profits and for allowing terrorist groups to launder money through its Mexican affiliate (Douglas, 2013). In 2011 and 2014, the Swiss bank UBS, the British bank Barclays, and the Royal Bank of Scotland were found guilty of international rigging of interest rates by fraudulently setting the rates established through the London Interbank Offered Rate, a benchmark for interest rates covering everything from home mortgages to student loans (BBC, 2014a; Douglas, 2013). There are no reliable data on how many of these crimes occur annually in part because of the complexity of the transactions and the lack of transparency in many aspects of global banking.

Much global criminality, however, takes place in the shadowy corners of the global marketplace. One key site for the international trade in drugs, weapons, and other illicit goods is the "dark web," an encrypted network that is not easily accessed by users of the Internet. For example, the Silk Road, a site on the dark web, was estimated at its peak to be a $1.2 billion market; it traded in illegal drugs and guns, among others. Its operator, Ross Ulbricht, was sentenced to life in prison without parole in 2015 after being caught in an Federal Bureau of Investigation (FBI) sting and prosecuted. A year later, the FBI shut down a copycat site, Silk Road 2.0. Interestingly, one of the reasons the prosecution asked for such a harsh sentence was that they hoped it would send a message to other would-be dealers on the dark web. Alas, detection and prosecution of transactions on the dark web is challenging. A recent article in *Wired* notes that an independent researcher

> has documented in an ongoing survey of more than 70 Dark Web drug markets created after Ulbricht founded the Silk Road, [that] only five of those sites' administrators have been arrested. For many of the others, the security model Ulbricht pioneered—using Tor and bitcoin to protect administrators, buyers and sellers—has successfully kept law enforcement fumbling in the shadows. (Greenberg, 2015, para. 2)

Trafficking in exotic and endangered plants and animals is yet another lucrative business. In recent years, smuggling of these products has increased in part due to the emergence of consumer markets for plant and animal products in rising economies like China and Vietnam (Bremer, 2012). Goods ranging from traditional Asian medicines to carved ivory to high-priced furs to exotic pets are smuggled from their places of origin and sold clandestinely. By one estimate, the trade in illegal wildlife alone is a $19 billion a year global business. According to a recent article, "The black market in wildlife parts and products is the fourth-largest illegal industry worldwide, behind narcotics, counterfeiting and human trafficking, and it may well outstrip other illicit enterprises in terms of the variety of crimes and the complexities they pose for law enforcement" (Rosen, 2014, para. 11).

The smuggling of people has also become a major international criminal enterprise. People pay large sums of money to be smuggled from poorer countries into wealthier ones where they imagine an opportunity for a better life. Women and girls are smuggled across borders for prostitution, sometimes under false pretenses, such as promises of jobs as waitresses or nannies. The extent of trafficking in women and girls for prostitution can only be estimated, but law enforcement and international task forces point to an alarming increase in the smuggling of human beings (Polaris Project, n.d.).

Globalization has brought benefits to countries and communities, but it has also, as we have seen, contributed to the expansion of criminal enterprises.

THINK IT THROUGH

- Who is responsible for addressing the problem of globalized crime in the contemporary world? What sociological factors make the prevention and prosecution of globalized crime particularly challenging?

Gottfredson and Hirschi (1990/2004; also Hirschi, 2004) assert that deviance arises from **social bonds**, or *individuals' connections to others,* especially institutions, rather than from anomie. Forming strong social bonds with people and institutions that disapprove of deviance, they argue, keeps people from engaging in deviant behaviors. Conversely, people who do not form strong social bonds will engage in deviant acts because they have nothing to lose by acting on their impulses and do not fear the consequences of their actions.

Furthermore, control theorists argue that most deviant acts are spontaneous. For example, a group of teenagers see a drunken homeless man sleeping on a bench and decide to take his backpack, or a man learns of a house whose owners are on vacation and decides to burglarize it. Some people will succumb to such temptations. Those who do not, according to Gottfredson and Hirschi, have a greater willingness to conform. This willingness, in turn, comes from associating with people who are committed to conventional roles and morality.

Social bonds: Individuals' connections to others (see also control theory).

Some evidence supports control theory. For example, delinquency is somewhat less common among youth who have strong family attachments, perform well in school, and feel they have something to lose by appearing deviant in the eyes of others (Gottfredson & Hirschi, 1990/2004; Hirschi, 1969). On the other hand, we could scarcely argue that white-collar criminals such as Bernie Madoff, who pleaded guilty to massive financial fraud in 2009, do not have strong social bonds to society. The success of many white-collar criminals in business suggests that they have spent their lives conforming to societal norms, yet they also commit criminal acts that cost U.S. taxpayers, investors, and pension holders billions of dollars (McLean & Elkind, 2003). Thus, although control theory explanations of deviance may prove useful in certain instances, they have limitations.

CONFLICT PERSPECTIVES

Recall that the conflict perspective makes the assumption that groups in society have different interests and differential access to resources with which to realize those interests. In contrast to the functionalist perspective, the conflict perspective does not assume shared norms and

Roy Morsch/Corbis/Getty Images

Cloward and Ohlin (1960) argue that people are more likely to engage in deviance when the social context presents opportunities for it to occur. For instance, unless you have access to a significant amount of money at your workplace, you are unlikely to engage in embezzlement of funds. ■

values. Rather, it presumes that groups with power will use that power to maintain control in society and keep other groups at a disadvantage. As we will see below, conflict theory can be fruitfully used in the study of deviance.

SUBCULTURES AND DEVIANCE More than three quarters of a century ago, Thorsten Sellin (1938) pointed out that the cultural diversity of modern societies results in conflicts between social groups over what kinds of behavior are right and wrong. Sellin argued that deviance is best explained through **subcultural theories**, which *identify the conflicting interests of different segments of the population,* whether it be over culture (as in Sellin's case) or, more generally, over particular rituals or behaviors. For example, immigrants to the United States bring norms and values with them from their original cultures and, to the extent that these conflict with the norms and values of the adopted country, they may be perceived—and sometimes punished—as deviant by the dominant culture.

Some practices of migrant communities might breach U.S. conventions: For instance, some Southeast Asian families (among others) still choose to follow traditional customs of arranged marriages for adult children. Although this is clearly not the norm in the United States, it is not illegal. Other customary practices, however, violate U.S. criminal laws. For instance, the practice of female genital circumcision by some immigrants from North Africa and the Middle East is a violation of U.S. law. As well, even though physical violence against a woman is understood in some communities as a husband's prerogative in marriage, immigrants to the United States who practice domestic violence are subject to arrest and prosecution.

It is not only cultural differences between immigrants and the host country that create subcultures of perceived or real deviance. Sociologists also analyze juvenile gangs, professional thieves, White racist groups, and a host of other groups as subcultures in which deviance is the norm (Chambliss & King, 1984; Cohen, 1955; Etter, 1998; Hamm, 2002).

CLASS-DOMINANT THEORY **Class-dominant theories** propose that what is labeled deviant or criminal—and therefore who gets punished—is determined by the interests of the dominant class (Quinney, 1970). For example, since labor is central to the functioning of capitalism, those who do not work will be labeled as deviant in capitalist societies (Spitzer, 1975). In a similar vein, since private property is a key foundation of capitalism, those who engage in acts against property, such as stealing or vandalism, will be labeled as criminal. And because profits are realized through buying and selling things in the capitalist marketplace, unregulated market activities (like selling drugs on the street or making alcohol without a license, or even operating a catering service out of one's home without proper licensing) will also be defined as deviant and criminal.

Critics of class-dominant theory point out that laws against the interests of the ruling class do get passed. Laws prohibiting insider trading on the stock market, governing the labor practices of corporations, and giving workers the right to strike and form trade unions were all signed over the strident opposition of big business interests (Chambliss, 2001). To incorporate these facts, criminologist William

Subcultural theories: Theories that explain deviance in terms of the conflicting interests of more and less powerful segments of a population.

Class-dominant theories: Theories that propose that what is labeled deviant or criminal—and therefore who gets punished—is determined by the interests of the dominant class in a particular culture or society.

J. Chambliss (1988a) proposed a structural contradiction theory that takes into account the limitations, as well as the power, of capitalists in a capitalist society.

STRUCTURAL CONTRADICTION THEORY Rather than seeing the ruling class as all-powerful in determining what is deviant or criminal, **structural contradiction theory** argues that *conflicts generated by fundamental contradictions in the structure of society produce laws defining certain acts as deviant or criminal* (Chambliss, 1988a; Chambliss & Hass, 2011; Chambliss & Zatz, 1994). For instance, there is a fundamental structural contradiction in capitalist economies between the need to maximize profits (which keeps wages down) and the need to maximize consumption (which requires high wages). Consider a U.S. business that, to maximize profits, keeps wages and salaries down, perhaps by moving its factories to a part of the world where wages are low. As jobs move overseas, the availability of jobs to unskilled and semiskilled workers in the United States declines. The loss of jobs produces downward pressure on wages and a loss of purchasing power. Yet capitalism depends on people buying the things that are produced—corporations cannot profit unless they sell their products.

Trapped in the contradiction between norms valuing consumerism and an economic system that can make consumption of desired material goods and services difficult or even impossible for many, some, but not all, people will resolve the conflict by resorting to deviant and criminal acts such as cheating on income taxes, writing bad checks, or profiting from illegal markets, by, for instance, selling drugs or committing theft. Of course, it is not just lower income people who deviate to increase their consumption of material goods. Everyone who wants to enjoy a higher standard of living is a candidate for deviant or criminal behavior, according to structural contradiction theory. The head of a giant corporation may be as tempted to violate criminal laws to increase company profits (and personal income) as is the 13-year-old from a poor family who snatches a pair of sunglasses from the drugstore.

Structural contradiction theory holds that societies with the greatest gaps between what people earn and what they are normatively enticed to consume will have the highest levels of deviance. Since industrial societies differ substantially in this regard, we can compare them to test this theory. Societies such as Finland, Denmark, Sweden, and Norway, for instance, provide a "social safety net" that guarantees all citizens a basic standard of living. Therefore, poorer residents in Scandinavian countries are able to come much closer to what their societies have established as a "normal" standard of living. The fact that rates of assault, robbery, and homicide are anywhere from 3 to 35 times higher in the United States than in these countries (depending on which country is compared) is what structural contradiction theory would predict (Archer & Gartner, 1984).

Globalization is another example of the way structural contradictions lead to changes in deviant behavior. The ability to trade worldwide increases the wealth of populations and nations that are able to take advantage of global markets. Nevertheless, it also increases opportunities for criminal activities such as money laundering, stealing patents and copyrights, and trafficking in people, arms, and drugs.

FEMINIST THEORY The sociological study of deviance—like most areas of academic study—has for centuries been dominated by men. As a result, most theories and research have reflected a male point of view. Recent years, however, have witnessed a sea change in the sociological perspective as women have become better represented in sociology and criminology.

In the 1980s, a **feminist perspective on deviance** emerged within the sociological tradition (Campbell, 1984; Chesney-Lind, 1989, 2004; Messerschmidt, 1986). The starting point of feminist explanations of deviance is the observation that *studies of deviance have been biased because almost all the research has been done by, and about, males, largely ignoring female perspectives on deviant behavior as well as analyses of differences in the types and causes of female deviance* (Messerschmidt, 1993). By ignoring the female population, deviance theory has avoided one of the most challenging issues in the field: Why do rates of deviance—and especially criminal deviance—vary by gender?

Early feminist theory argued that gender-specific cultural norms partly account for the different rates of deviance between men and women (Adler, 1975; Steffensmeier & Allen, 1998). For example, women traditionally have been socialized into the roles of wife and mother, where behavior is more tightly prescribed than it is for men. Moreover,

Structural contradiction theory: The theory that conflicts generated by fundamental contradictions in the structure of society produce laws defining certain acts as deviant or criminal.

Feminist perspective on deviance: A perspective that suggests that studies of deviance have been subject to gender bias and that both gender-specific cultural norms and the particular ways in which women are victimized by virtue of their gender help to account for deviance among women.

Marvin Recinos, Stringer/AFP/Getty Images

Girls sometimes form gangs in neighborhoods where male street gangs are prevalent. These girl gangs are often "auxiliaries" of male gangs engaged in selling drugs and committing petty crimes. Joining a gang may require an initiation ritual that includes violence, including rape.

women's deviant behavior is more likely to be subject to **stigmatization**—that is, to be *branded as highly disgraceful*—than is comparable male behavior. For example, a woman who has multiple sexual partners may be socially shamed as a "slut," while a sexually promiscuous man is not disdained and might even be praised and admired by peers.

Feminists have argued that an adequate theory of deviance must take into account the particular ways in which women are victimized by virtue of their gender (Chesney-Lind, 2004; Mann & Zatz, 1998; Sokoloff & Raffel, 1995). For example, studies show that before becoming involved in the juvenile justice system, many girls labeled delinquent were runaways escaping sexual and physical abuse. In a 2014 study, 31% of girls reported a personal experience of sexual violence in the home, 41% reported being physically abused, and 84% reported experiencing family violence. Girls reported having been sexually abused at a rate 4.4 times higher than boys (Levintova, 2015). This research supports the hypothesis that many girls labeled delinquent have been driven out of their homes by abusive parents or relatives.

Women also continue to be disproportionately represented in cases of inmate sexual assault and victimization. Although women constitute under 7% of the total inmate population in the United States, they make up one third of all prisoner sexual victimization cases (Guerino & Beck, 2011).

Stigmatization: The branding of behavior as highly disgraceful (see also labeling theory).

Labeling theory: A symbolic interactionist approach holding that deviance is a product of the labels people attach to certain types of behavior.

Primary deviance: A term developed by Edwin Lemert; the first step in the labeling of deviance, it occurs at the moment an activity is labeled deviant (see also secondary deviance).

Secondary deviance: A term developed by Edwin Lemert; the second step in the labeling of deviance, it occurs when a person labeled deviant accepts the label as part of his or her identity and, as a result, begins to act in conformity with the label (see also primary deviance).

INTERACTIONIST PERSPECTIVES

Interactionist perspectives provide a language and framework for looking at how deviance is constructed, including how individuals are connected to the social structure. Interactionist approaches also explain why some people are labeled deviant and behave in deviant ways while others do not. A central tenet of many interactionist approaches is that we see ourselves through the eyes of others, and our resulting sense of ourselves conditions how we behave. This idea has been applied to the study of deviant behavior in the development of both labeling theory and differential association theory.

LABELING THEORY **Labeling theory** holds that *deviant behavior is a product of the labels people attach to certain types of behavior* (Asencio & Burke, 2011; Lemert, 1951; Tannenbaum, 1938). From this perspective, deviance is seen as socially constructed. That is, labeling theory holds that deviance is the product of interactions wherein the response of some people to certain types of behaviors produces a label of *deviant* or *not deviant*. In turn, these labels, which also end up being applied to people engaging in certain types of behavior, can influence how people conduct themselves. Thus, labeling theory is sometimes referred to as *societal reaction theory*.

One of the founders of labeling theory, Edwin Lemert (1951), argued that the labeling process has two steps: primary deviance and secondary deviance. **Primary deviance** occurs *at the moment an activity is labeled as deviant by others*. **Secondary deviance** occurs *when a person labeled deviant accepts the label as part of his or her identity and, as a result, begins to act in conformity with the label*. To illustrate his theory, Lemert reported on a group of people in the U.S. Northwest with an unusually high incidence of stuttering. Observing the interactions among people in this group, he concluded that stuttering was common in the group partly because the members were stigmatized and labeled as "stutterers" (primary deviance). These "stutterers" then began to view themselves through this label and increasingly acted in accordance with it—which included a greater amount of stuttering than otherwise would have been the case (secondary deviance).

Chambliss's (2001) observations of the Saints and the Roughnecks also support labeling theory. In spite of engaging in similar kinds of crime and mischief, the working-class teens (the "Roughnecks") he studied in one community were labeled deviant while the middle-class boys (the "Saints") he observed were not. Chambliss sought to understand this difference. He noted that, first, the actions of the Roughnecks were far more visible than those of the Saints. With their access to automobiles, the Saints were able to remove themselves from the sight of the community, but the Roughnecks congregated in a public area where they could be seen by teachers or the police. Second, the demeanors of the gang members differed. Although the Saints showed remorse and respect, the Roughnecks offered a barely veiled contempt for authority. This resulted in different responses to their misdeeds. Third, adults in the community showed bias toward the Saints, who were presumed to be "good boys sowing wild oats" rather than "bad boys." Chambliss concluded that labels matter. Those who were labeled as "bad" largely lived up (or down) to expectations. Those whose youthful transgressions were not transformed into labels lived up to more positive expectations and became successful adults. These self-fulfilling prophecies suggest that the ways in which we opt to label individuals and groups can have important effects on outcomes.

DIFFERENTIAL ASSOCIATION THEORY Another interactionist approach to the study of deviance looks at how deviance is transmitted culturally and argues that we learn deviant behaviors through our social interactions. **Differential association theory** holds that *deviant and criminal behavior results from regular exposure to attitudes favorable to acting in ways that are deviant or criminal* (Burgess & Akers, 1966; Church, Jaggers, & Taylor, 2012; Sutherland, 1929). For example, the corporate executive who embezzles company funds may have learned the norms and values appropriate to this type of criminal activity by associating with others already engaged in it. Similarly, kids and teenagers living in areas where selling and using drugs are common practices will be more likely than their peers not exposed to that subculture to develop attitudes

FAYEZ NURELDINE/Staff/Getty Images

Sutherland's differential association theory suggests that the more we associate with people whose behavior is deviant, the greater the likelihood that our behavior will also be deviant. Does membership in virtual groups on the Internet that embrace deviant beliefs or behavior also raise the likelihood of deviance?

favorable toward using and selling drugs. Conversely, populations with different subcultures or attitudes toward particular forms of deviance (such as illicit drug usage) may not experience the same rates of crime.

According to Sutherland's (1929) differential association theory, the more we associate with people whose behavior is deviant, the greater the likelihood that our behavior will also be deviant. Sutherland, therefore, linked deviance with such factors as the frequency and intensity of our associations with other people, how long they last, and how early in our lives they occur. Much has changed since Sutherland developed his theory, and today many of our interactions take place through technologies such as the Internet and smartphones. A modern adaptation of Sutherland's theory would certainly have to take into account the importance of the unique methods of interacting today in promoting both deviant and conforming behavior.

Symbolic interactionist theories, like functionalist and conflict theories, provide us with considerable insight into the social processes that lead to deviance and crime in society. We might come to the conclusion that each of the competing theories "makes sense" and has some empirical support yet also fails to explain all the behaviors we classify as deviant or criminal. This debate and interaction

Differential association theory: The theory that deviant and criminal behavior results from regular exposure to attitudes favorable to acting in ways that are deviant or criminal.

DISCOVER & DEBATE

Deviance and Social Control

Motion: Mandatory minimum sentences for drug crimes are good policy for deterring and punishing drug use and trafficking.

Background

Mandatory minimum sentencing practices have a long history in U.S. criminal justice. According to the U.S. Sentencing Commission, Congress put into place the first mandatory minimum sentences in the late 18th century. Mandatory minimum penalties have long been associated with the most serious criminal offenses, including murder and treason. The broad application of mandatory minimums to drug crimes is more recent: The Anti-Drug Abuse Act of 1986 set out many of the sentencing guidelines that are currently used or were recently used for drug crimes.

Affirmative Arguments

- Mandatory minimum sentencing ensures that a standard of justice is uniformly applied.
- Mandatory minimum sentencing deters criminal behavior because consequences for that behavior are predictable and unambiguous.
- Mandatory minimum sentencing encourages cooperation by lower level defendants seeking to avoid harsh punishments and may thus help catch higher level offenders.

Opposition Arguments

- Mandatory minimum sentencing does not ensure the uniform application of a standard of justice because bias may be introduced at other levels of the criminal justice system. For example, prosecutors choose what charges to file and police determine whom to surveille and arrest.
- The lack of discretion in sentencing can lead to sentences that are disproportionate to the seriousness of the crime (for instance, possession of a small quantity of a drug for personal use) or the circumstances of the crimes (for instance, a perpetrator may also be a victim of coercion).
- Mandatory minimum sentencing practices have contributed to mass incarceration in the United States, which imprisons more Americans per capita than any other developed, democratic country.

Questions for Consideration

- Under what circumstances should judges be granted discretion in handing down a sentence for a drug crime?
- Are there crimes for which mandatory minimum sentences are always appropriate?
- Is mass incarceration an inevitable outcome of mandatory minimum sentencing practices?

Debate Tip

▶ Conduct a mock debate with your team members. This will help you to practice your speech and present your arguments in a more articulate and composed manner.

between theories is essential to the development of scientific knowledge (Popper, 1959). Thus, even though there are many unique ways to examine the same topic without necessarily reaching one perfect answer with any of them, we should be reassured that each theoretical orientation presented in this chapter can be useful in explaining certain facets of deviance and crime. It is up to the researcher to decide which theory to use and why, and for others to determine whether the use of the theory was a success or failure.

TYPES OF DEVIANCE

As noted in the opening to this chapter, deviance comes in many varieties, from the relatively benign to the extremely harmful. In this section, we explore some of the ways in which deviance can manifest in society.

EVERYDAY DEVIANCE

A broad spectrum of acts could fall under the label of "everyday deviance," from plagiarism among high school or college students, to shoplifting, underage alcohol consumption, using pornography, smoking, eating meat, or calling in sick to work or school when you actually feel fine. All of these are considered deviant behaviors, actions, or conditions by some individuals and/or groups, although they are also actions in which many people engage at some point—or regularly.

In the discussion of everyday deviance, we recognize the pluralistic nature of U.S. society. Taking a subcultural perspective, we may find that smoking is more acceptable among some societal subgroups (for instance, truck drivers) than it is among others (such as fitness instructors). So too with eating meat: The owner of a barbecue restaurant and a vegan are likely to hold starkly different views regarding the deviance of eating meat or subsisting on a vegan diet. In turn, these views are representative of the broader societal subcultures and groups to which these individuals belong.

Everyday deviance can be explained in a variety of ways. For instance, we might use labeling theory. Pornography represents an example in which both the behavior (using pornography) and the physical object (the pornographic movie or magazine) have been labeled as deviant. We could therefore make the argument that pornography is deviant simply because people have chosen to label it as such. Yet this explanation, as you might have sensed, is pretty basic.

We could strengthen our understanding of what makes pornography deviant by including a conflict perspective. Thus, we could look at who in society has the power to define pornography as deviant and what goals such a definition might serve for that particular group. The point is that deviance in its various forms has many potential explanations, which can be strengthened through the combination of different theoretical perspectives.

SEXUAL DEVIANCE

Sex, sexual orientations, and sexual practices are diverse, as are the responses to them. We are currently witnessing a process of redefinition of what deviance means within the context of intimate relationships. Look no further than the popular novel *Fifty Shades of Grey,* and the book sequels and films that followed, which made headlines for the depiction of kinky sex and for being on the nightstands of many "ordinary" men and women. *The New York Times* recently published an article titled, "Is An Open Marriage A Happier Marriage" (Dominus, 2017), a piece that spent several days atop the newspaper's "most popular" list online. As public interest in these cultural products grows, we might argue that some *traditional* notions regarding sex, sexual orientation, and sexual activities are themselves increasingly becoming deviant because they simply do not reflect the realities of modern intimate life.

Definitions of sexual deviance can include many things—from the choices we make in terms of those with whom we begin intimate relationships to how and where those relationships are carried out. Although we could use many explanations to examine sexual deviance, looking at the continuing controversy over same-sex marriage from a conflict perspective, we see an ongoing struggle between those groups that have long determined what passes for acceptable sexual behavior (for instance, religious groups) and those that seek to redefine normal and acceptable sexual behavior to include things other than heterosexual sex and marriage.

DEVIANCE OF THE POWERFUL

The crimes of the famous and powerful are ubiquitous and wide ranging, from the fraudulent reporting of corporate profits to the misleading of investors to bribery, corruption, misuse of public trust, and violence. The most powerful people in public life engage in many of the same types of deviance as ordinary men and women (McLean & Elkind,

2003; McLean & Nocera, 2010; Reiman & Leighton, 2012). Sociologically, what must be taken into account is that deviance knows no class bounds.

There is normally quite a bit of public and press interest in deviance committed by athletes, celebrities, and political figures. According to *Sports Illustrated*, between January 2012 and September 2014, 33 National Football League players were arrested on charges of domestic violence, battery, assault, and murder; nearly half of the charges involved violence against women (*Sports Illustrated*, 2014). Major League Baseball player Alex Rodriguez of the New York Yankees was suspended for the 2014 season for using banned substances and lying about it. Actor and comedian Bill Cosby, accused by more than 50 women of drugging and sexual assault, was charged in late 2015 with aggravated indecent assault, and rapper Vanilla Ice was arrested for burglary and grand theft for stealing bicycles and a couch, among other items, from a foreclosed house (Seemayer & Chestang, 2015).

The response of the public to the deviance of political leaders is often particularly pointed given the trust, responsibility, and power vested in those individuals. In 2016, former Speaker of the U.S. House of Representatives, Dennis Hastert, pled guilty for illegal actions linked to a $3.5 million payment to silence allegations of sexual misconduct with a student when he was a high school teacher and coach decades ago. Prosecutors say he molested at least four high-school-age boys (Davey & Smith, 2016). In Crystal City, Texas, five of the small city's key officials, including the mayor, city manager, and a city council member, were arrested in February 2016 for taking tens of thousands of dollars in bribes linked to an illegal gambling operation. Another member of the city council was arrested earlier on human smuggling charges. Interestingly, the U.S. Attorney in the region cannot remove the officials from office; it will be incumbent on the voters to do that (Kaplan, 2016).

On the one hand, empirical data show that the powerful are more likely than those without power to escape punishment for deviance. On the other hand, public figures who are caught in acts of deviance are often subject to acute media attention and broad disdain. Should public figures

In 2016, Dennis Hastert, former Speaker of the House of Representatives (1999–2007), was sentenced to serve prison time for sexually abusing young athletes he coached several decades earlier.

receive particular scrutiny for their behavior, or should they be treated like everyone else?

CRIME

Our discussion thus far has been concerned primarily with deviance in a general sense—those attitudes, behaviors, and conditions that are widespread but generally not condemned by all or seen as especially serious. In this section, we discuss crime—acts that are sometimes considered deviant and are defined under the law as punishable by fines, imprisonment, or both. Law enforcement agencies across the United States take rigorous steps to record formally how much crime occurs, to prosecute criminal offenders, and to control and prevent crime.

VIOLENT AND PROPERTY CRIMES A great deal of effort is expended on the measurement of crime in U.S. society. This is accomplished through official, limited records like the FBI's Uniform Crime Reports (UCR) and the collection of survey data from individuals and households across the country via the National Crime Victimization Survey (NCVS). These measures of crime, especially the UCR, focus predominantly on violent and property crimes, serious forms of deviance that nearly every person in society agrees should be made illegal (see the *Behind the Numbers* box in this chapter).

According to the FBI UCR Program, **violent crimes** are composed of four offenses: murder and negligent manslaughter, rape, robbery, and aggravated assault. They are "those offenses that involve force or threat of force" (FBI, 2015d, para. 1). **Property crimes** in

Violent crimes: Crimes that involve force or threat of force, including robbery, murder, assault, and rape.

Property crimes: Crimes that involve the violation of individuals' ownership rights, including burglary, larceny/theft, arson, and motor vehicle theft.

the UCR include the offenses of burglary, larceny-theft, motor vehicle theft, and arson. According to the FBI, "The object of the theft-type offenses is the taking of money or property, but there is no force or threat of force against the victims" (FBI, 2015c, para. 1). Property crimes are much more common in the United States than violent crimes, although their number, like the number of violent crimes (Figure 6.2), has been steadily declining (Figure 6.3). Recent data show that in the 5-year period between 2010 and 2015, violent crimes and property crimes declined by 14.6% (Pew Charitable Trusts, 2016). Variations of serious deviance, including violent and property crimes, can be analyzed from a variety of perspectives. For instance, violent crimes might be viewed from an opportunity theory perspective and property crimes in terms of societal strain. How might such analyses look?

FIGURE 6.2 Violent Crime Rate in the United States

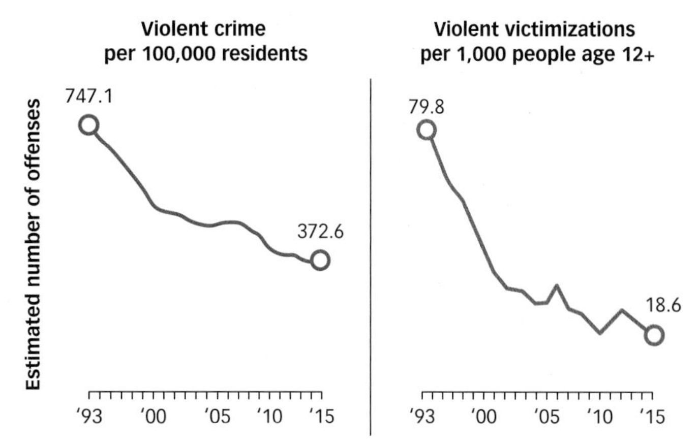

SOURCE: Pew Research and Bureau of Justice Statistics and FBI.

NOTE: FBI figures include reported crimes only. BJS figures include unreported and reported crimes. 2006 BJS estimates are not comparable with other years due to methodological changes.

FIGURE 6.3 Property Crime Rate in the United States

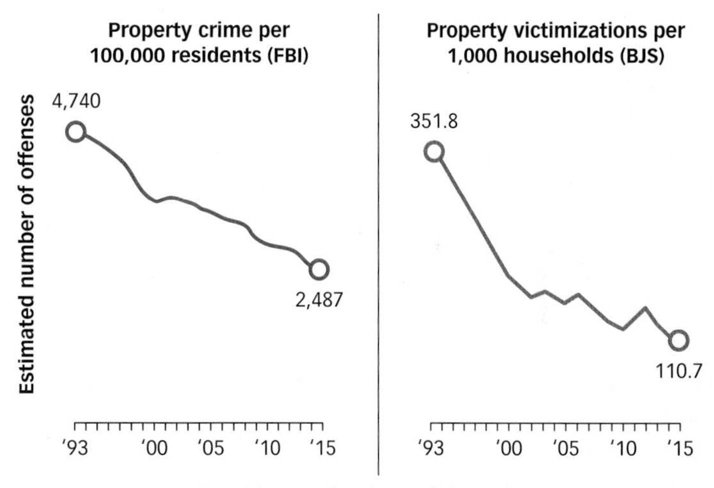

SOURCES: Pew Research and Bureau of Justice Statistics and FBI.

ORGANIZED CRIME Sociologists define **organized crime** as *crime committed by criminal groups that provide illegal goods and services.* Gambling, prostitution, selling and trafficking in illegal drugs, black marketeering, loan sharking, and money laundering are some of the most prominent activities of organized crime (Block & Chambliss, 1981; Glenny, 2009; McCoy, 1991; Paoli, 2003).

WHITE-COLLAR CRIME To meet the demand for illegal goods and services, criminal organizations have flourished in U.S. urban areas since the 1800s (Woodiwiss, 2000). Over the years, they have recruited members and leadership from more impoverished groups in society, such as new immigrants in big cities, who may have great aspirations but limited means of achieving them (Block & Weaver, 2004). Consequently, organized crime has been dominated by the most recent arrivals to urban areas: Irish, Jewish, and Italian "mobs" in the past, and Asian, African, South American, and Russian "mobs" today (Albanese, 1989; Finckenauer & Waring, 1996; Hess, 1973).

Depictions of organized crime in movies and television shows such as *The Sopranos, The Godfather, Scarface,* and *Goodfellas* have popularized the erroneous impression that there is an international organization of criminals (the "Mafia") dominated by Italian Americans. The reality is that organized crime consists of thousands of different groups throughout the United States and the world. No single ethnic group or organization has control over most or even a major share of these activities, which include human trafficking and weapons and drug smuggling (Block & Weaver, 2004; Chambliss, 1988a).

Organized crime: Crime committed by criminal groups that provide illegal goods and services.

BEHIND THE NUMBERS

Counting Crime in the United States

Measuring the incidence of crime is challenging. Consider what factors might stand in the way of achieving a rigorously accurate accounting of crimes that occur in the United States in any given year. Many crimes are never reported to the police: If you forget your textbook at the library and it's gone when you return, you may choose to report the theft to the authorities or you may just decide it's too much of a bother since you probably won't get the book back. In some communities, there is a high level of distrust in law enforcement officials, so even more serious crimes like aggravated assault may go unreported. Violent crimes are more likely than property crimes to be reported to the police, although some property crimes, like auto theft, will be reported in high numbers since insurance companies normally require a police report before compensating the victim. Notably, the percentage of crimes reported to police has risen steadily in the last 20 years (M. Schwartz, personal communication, June 28, 2016).

What we know quantitatively about crime in the United States is built on the foundations of two programs. First, many statistical reports on crime are based on the FBI's *Uniform Crime Reporting (UCR) Program*. The UCR counts as crime that which has been brought to the attention of the police through reports or arrests. It gathers information for a limited set of crimes: murder and nonnegligent manslaughter, forcible rape, robbery, aggravated assault, burglary, larceny-theft, motor vehicle theft, and arson. (Data on other crimes are also collected but based on arrest data only.) According to the FBI, "The UCR Program is a voluntary city, university and college, county, state, tribal, and federal law enforcement program that provides a nationwide view of crime based on the submission of statistics by law enforcement agencies throughout the country" (FBI, n.d., para. 1). Note that UCR is dependent on the "submission of statistics," so crimes that occur but are not reported do not appear in the data.

Second, data on the incidence of crime are also gathered through the National Crime Victimization Survey (NCVS). The NCVS, unlike the UCR, does not rely on police report or arrest data. Rather, it relies on a sample of the U.S. population: Every year, about 90,000 households composed of about 160,000 people are surveyed to learn about the "frequency, characteristics, and consequences of criminal victimization in the United States." Every household is interviewed twice during the year and asked about a spectrum of crimes: rape or sexual assault, robbery, aggravated and simple assault, theft, household burglary, and motor vehicle theft. Murder is not included in the victimization survey because it cannot be a self-reported crime. The NCVS also sorts the information to learn about the victimization of particular demographic groups like racial minorities, the elderly, the young, urban residents, and so forth (U.S. Bureau of Justice Statistics, Office of Justice Programs, n.d.). Because the NCVS is based on a sample rather than on reported numbers like the UCR, the resulting figures are extrapolated to the larger U.S. population.

Because each of these reports uses a different methodology, the results can be quite different. For example, consider the following case: You have gone out to a restaurant with a friend. You hang your leather jacket on a rack by the door rather than taking it to your table. As you prepare to leave after the meal, you realize that your jacket is gone. Do you report it to the restaurant management? Probably. Do you report it to the police? If you choose to report it, it is likely to become a part of the UCR, where it will be recorded as a larceny, whether or not the perpetrator is caught or you get your jacket back. If you choose not to report it, deciding that the likelihood of recovering it is low and the hassle of reporting it high, it will not appear in the UCR. If you happen to be a part of the national sample of the NCVS, it will be recorded as a theft in those figures. If you are not part of the sample, your loss will not be recognized directly in the figures.

How do larceny and theft figures compare in the UCR and NCVS? In 2013, the UCR reported that there were 1,899 larcenies per 100,000 people in the United States. In the same year, the NCVS reported that there were 100.5 thefts per 1,000 people 12 years of age and older. If we multiply the NCVS figure by 100 to get comparable figures, we see that the NCVS figure of 10,050 per 100,000 population is about 5.3 times higher than the UCR figure of 1,899 per 100,000 population. Although the comparison is imperfect, it suggests that there is a significant gap between the incidence of crimes and their reporting to police. Both the UCR and the NCVS provide valuable information about crime in the United States, but fully conclusive figures cannot be determined from either report.

THINK IT THROUGH

- If you were to create a program with the goal of rigorously measuring crime on your campus, how would you structure the program? What lessons would you draw from the UCR and NCVS approaches?

When most people think of crime, they think of the violent and property crimes discussed above—and they think of crimes committed by those in lower socioeconomic groups. But the forms of crime perpetrated by individuals and groups who possess great power, authority, and influence are also often deeply harmful to society.

White-collar crime is *crime committed by people of high social status in connection with their work* (Sutherland, 1949/1983). There are two principal types: crimes committed for the benefit of the individual who commits them, and crimes committed for the benefit of the organization for which the individual works.

Among the many white-collar crimes that benefit the individual are the theft of money by accountants who alter their employers' or clients' books and the overcharging of clients by lawyers. More costly types of white-collar crime occur when corporations and their employees engage in criminal conduct either through *commission,* that is, by doing something criminal, or *omission,* by failing to prevent something criminal or harmful from occurring.

White-collar crimes of all sorts receive considerable media attention. The following constitute just a sample of white-collar criminal cases publicized over the past few years:

- In 2008, at the height of the U.S. recession, Bernard "Bernie" Madoff, a former Wall Street executive, was arrested and charged with managing an intricate criminal scheme that stole at least $50 billion from corporate and individual investors. Madoff pled guilty to 11 criminal counts in Manhattan's federal district courthouse and was sentenced to 150 years in prison (Rosoff, Pontell, & Tillman, 2010).
- In 2010, financial giant JPMorgan Chase was fined $48.6 million by British financial regulators for "failing to keep clients' funds separate from those of the firm." The error went undetected for more than 7 years and placed billions of dollars of client funds at risk of being lost (Werdigier, 2010).
- General Motors Corporation, which received close to $50 billion in "bailout" funds from American taxpayers to stay financially solvent, was implicated in a scandal in early 2014 for failing to fix a defective ignition switch in its Chevrolet Cobalt

White-collar crime: Crime committed by people of high social status in connection with their work.

MANDEL NGAN/AFP/Getty Images

Volkswagen Group of America President and CEO Mike Horn was called in front of the U.S. Congress in 2015 to respond to questions about why his company used illegal software in diesel-powered VW cars to circumvent emissions regulations. ■

line of vehicles (Isidore, 2012; Wald, 2014). The company allegedly chose not to make the fix, which caused vehicles to lose power while running and may have resulted in more than a dozen deaths, because doing so would have added to the cost of each car (Lienert & Thompson, 2014). The National Highway Transportation Safety Administration, which is charged with regulating and investigating complaints about motor vehicle safety, knew of the deaths linked to the vehicles with defective switches as early as 2007 but did not act (Wald, 2014).

- In 2014, JPMorgan was fined again, this time more than $461 million, by the Financial Crimes Enforcement Network (FinCEN) of the U.S. Department of the Treasury for violating the Bank Secrecy Act by failing to report the suspicious activities of Bernie Madoff (Financial Crimes Enforcement Network, 2014).
- In 2015, the Consumer Financial Protection Bureau (2015) fined Citibank $700 million for the deceptive marketing of credit card add-on products.
- In 2017, the car manufacturer Volkswagen AG (VW) agreed to plead guilty to 3 criminal felony counts and to pay a penalty of $2.8 billion for selling 590,000 diesel fuel vehicles in the United States that employed a "defeat device" to cheat on mandated emissions tests and then seeking to cover up the crime (U.S. Department of Justice Office of Public Affairs, 2017).

POLICE CORRUPTION AND POLICE BRUTALITY Policing is a job vested with trust, responsibility, and authority. Police officers are the frontline enforcers of laws that are expected to limit the amount of crime that occurs in society. When violent or property crimes are committed, we rely on the police for protection and investigation. Members of the law enforcement community, however, are not immune to deviance, including corruption. In 2016, for example, three New York Police Department commanders were arrested for taking extensive gifts, including hotel rooms, jewelry, and basketball tickets from businessmen seeking "illicit favors from the police" (Rashbaum & Goldstein, 2016).

Police brutality is another form of deviance that has a long history in the United States. The responses of southern police officers and sheriffs, such as Bull Connor in Birmingham, Alabama, to the 1960s civil rights marches provide well-documented examples. Police brutality continues to occur, although it often escapes detection and sanction. The videotaped beating of Rodney King in the 1990s by four White members of the Los Angeles Police Department served as a vivid example of the treatment many minority city residents suffered at the hands, and batons, of the police. Violence committed by police officers has been in the headlines with much greater frequency in recent years perhaps because it is more likely today that incidents of violence will be caught by someone's mobile phone camera or a police body camera. Public attention has been particularly focused on the killing of unarmed Black men by police: Of 963 police shootings documented in 2016, about 5% were cases in which unarmed civilians were shot. According to a *Washington Post* analysis of the data, "unarmed black men were seven times as likely as unarmed whites to die from police gunfire" (Somashekhar, Lowery, Alexander, Kindy, & Tate, 2015, para. 8). In one case, a University of Cincinnati police officer pulled a Black driver over for having no front license plate. The incident ended with the officer shooting Samuel Du Bose in the head. Because the killing was captured on a body camera, the officer was arrested and charged with murder (Blow, 2015). Policing is a dangerous profession, and officers need to protect themselves and their colleagues, but violence against civilians, even if it is committed only by a few, is a high-profile problem that cannot be ignored.

Both corruption and brutality represent important forms of criminal deviance committed by official representatives of state authority. But how can we make sense of these forms of deviance?

In the case of both police corruption and the use of excessive force by law enforcement officers, Sutherland's differential association theory may provide insights. Some studies and first-person accounts demonstrate that police officers are often exposed to various forms of deviance once they become members of the force (Kappeler, Sluder, & Alpert, 1998; Maas, 1997). Exposure to attitudes favorable to the commission of deviance and crime, especially in light of the intensity and duration of the relationships police officers form with one another, may lead some to engage in those same types of deviant or criminal behaviors. We can also view the police as having a distinct culture and, thus, see police brutality and corruption in terms of the subcultural expectations that accompany police work. Some members of the police subculture may see certain behaviors, actions, and perspectives, especially regarding the use of force, as a necessary part of accomplishing the demands of police work.

STATE CRIMES Finally, we turn to perhaps the most harmful form of crime among the powerful: state crime.

AP Photo/Chuck Burton

Protesters in many U.S. cities have sought to draw attention to the problem of police brutality. In this photo, marchers demonstrate after the shooting of Keith Lamont Scott in Charlotte, North Carolina, in September 2016.

Although police brutality and corruption are especially egregious examples of crimes occurring among those with power, state crimes rank above even them in terms of the seriousness and potential harm that may result from their commission.

State crimes consist of criminal or other harmful acts of commission or omission perpetrated by state officials in the pursuit of their jobs as representatives of the government. Needless to say, governments do not normally keep statistics on their own criminal behavior. Nonetheless, we do know from various contemporary and historical examples that such crimes are not uncommon (Chambliss, Michalowski, & Kramer, 2010; Green & Ward, 2004; Moloney & Chambliss, 2014; Rothe, 2009). Contemporary examples of state crime cover a spectrum of deviance and take place across the globe. Some examples include the routine torture of detainees at the U.S. military prison in Guantánamo Bay, Cuba; the secret transportation and torture of battlefield detainees in foreign prisons; and even the violation of international laws leading up to the 2004 invasion of Iraq (Grey, 2006; Kramer & Michalowksi, 2005; Paglen & Thompson, 2006; Ratner & Ray, 2004). In one study, the Chinese government was found to have taken a role in the trafficking of human body parts. The study's author found that the organs of executed prisoners were harvested by government-approved doctors and were sold to corporations and other entities for use in organ transplantation and cosmetic surgery, often at substantial profits, without the consent of the prisoners' families (Lenning, 2007). More recently, some members of Russia's Olympic Team and the entire Paralympic Team were barred from the 2016 Rio Olympic Games due to a far-reaching doping conspiracy.

State crimes: Criminal or other harmful acts committed by state officials in the pursuit of their jobs as representatives of the government.

Social control: The attempts by certain people or groups in society to control the behaviors of other individuals and groups to increase the likelihood that they will conform to established norms or laws.

Social power: The ability to exercise social control.

Informal social control: The unofficial mechanism through which deviance and deviant behaviors are discouraged in society; most often occurs among ordinary people during the course of their interactions.

Formal social control: Official attempts to discourage certain behaviors and visibly punish others; most often exercised by the state.

SOCIAL CONTROL OF DEVIANCE

The persistence of deviant behavior in society leads inevitably to a variety of measures designed to control it. **Social control** is defined as the *attempts by certain people or groups in society to control the behaviors of other individuals and groups to increase the likelihood that they will conform to established norms or laws.* Thus, deviance, the definition of which tends to require some sort of moral judgment, also attracts attempts at social control, usually exercised by those people or groups who possess **social power**, or *the ability to exercise social control.*

Informal social control is *the unofficial means through which deviance is discouraged in everyday interactions.* It ranges from frowning at someone's sexist assertion to threatening to take away a child's cell phone to coerce conformity to the parent's wishes. Informal social control mechanisms explain why people don't spit on the floor in a restaurant, do choose to pay back a friend who lent them $5, or say "thank you" in response to a favor. These behaviors and responses are governed not by formal laws but by informal expectations of which we are all aware and that lead us to make certain choices. Much of the time these informal social controls lead us into conformity with societal or group norms and away from deviance. Informal controls are thus responsible for keeping most forms of noncriminal deviance in check.

Socialization, which we have discussed in earlier chapters, thus, plays a significant role in the success of informal social control. When parents seek to get their children to conform to the values and norms of their society, they teach them to do one thing and not another. Peer groups of workers, students, and friends also implement informal social control through means, such as embarrassment and criticism, that work to control behavior and thus deviance. Bonds to institutions and people enact various informal social controls on our behavior. Such bonds have been shown to be crucial in explaining why some people engage in deviance and others do not (Laub & Sampson, 2003; Sampson & Laub, 1990).

Formal social control is defined as *official attempts to discourage certain behaviors and visibly punish others.* In the modern world, formal social control is most often exercised by societal institutions associated with the state, including the police, prosecutors, courts, and prisons. The goal of all these institutions is to suppress, reduce, and punish those individuals or groups who engage in criminal forms of deviance. Theft, assault, vandalism, cheating on income taxes, fraudulent reporting of corporate earnings, and insider trading on the stock market—all have been deemed crimes and represent forms of criminal deviance. As such, they are subject to formal social control.

For an act to be criminal, several elements must be present. First, a specific law must prohibit the act, and a punishment of either prison or a fine, or both, must be specified for violation of the law. Most important, the act must be *intended, and the person committing the act must be capable of having the necessary intent.* Someone judged to be mentally ill, which U.S. criminal law defines as the person "not knowing right from wrong" at the time of the act, cannot have the required legal intent and therefore cannot be held criminally liable for committing an illegal act. Nevertheless, the insanity defense is not accepted in all states: Idaho, Montana, Kansas, and Utah do not recognize insanity as a defense. In other state courts and federal courts, the burden of proof regarding a defendant's mental state is on the defendant. The U.S. Supreme Court refused to hear a case from Idaho in which a defendant claimed he had a constitutional right to claim insanity as a defense (Barnes, 2012).

Suspension and expulsion significantly reduce the chance that young people will finish high school. Importantly, those without a high school degree are at greater risk of imprisonment. More than two thirds of males in state and federal prison do not have a high school diploma.

In the sections that follow, we discuss some key issues associated with formal social control in U.S. society, including discipline in schools, the phenomenon of mass imprisonment, and the death penalty.

SCHOOLS AND DISCIPLINE: IS THERE A SCHOOL TO PRISON PIPELINE?

As many U.S. public schools have tightened discipline in recent years, some observers suggest that children are diverging onto two roads: Some are tracked to careers and college, while others, to prison. The **school to prison pipeline** refers to *the policies and practices that push schoolchildren, especially the most at-risk children, out of classrooms and into the juvenile and criminal justice systems* (American Civil Liberties Union, n.d.). Schools have made an attempt to ameliorate disciplinary problems and to promote safety in schools, but what effect has this had on children? This tightened discipline has not only affected high school students but has trickled down to preschools, increasing the probability of student infractions being harshly punished. What can a preschooler do to merit suspension? Suspensions in preschool have resulted from such behaviors as the child kicking off his or her shoes, and crying. Where this is categorized as a disturbance to the classroom, the child may be subject to disciplinary action.

What factors can help us understand the school to prison pipeline? First, following the 1999 Columbine shooting, when two high school students killed 13 and injured 24 students in a shooting rampage and then shot themselves, some schools enacted **zero tolerance policies**, *school or district policy which sets predetermined punishments for certain misbehaviors, and punishes the same way no matter the severity or the context of the behavior.* This potentially helpful measure has also caused problems. The policy punishes children for a variety of infractions, including minor ones: Punishable offenses may range from carrying aspirin, which is considered a drug, to skipping class, to threatening a teacher, to concealing a weapon. Zero tolerance policies have led to a rise in detentions, suspensions, and expulsions (U.S. Department of Education Office for Civil Rights, 2014).

Second, school officials have increased police presence in the schools with the intention of protecting students. This, however, has resulted in more student arrests for infractions that would have previously been handled by the school. Together with zero tolerance policies, this has

School to prison pipeline: The policies and practices that push students, particularly at-risk youth, out of schools and into the criminal justice system.

Zero tolerance policies: School or district policy that sets predetermined punishments for certain misbehaviors, and punishes the same way no matter the severity or the context of the behavior.

resulted in more severe punishment and more student contact with the justice system (American Civil Liberties Union, n.d.). Students as young as 10 have been treated like criminals for minor offenses such as talking back or cutting class. In a case in Queens, New York, a 12-year-old girl was taken away in handcuffs after doodling on her desk with an erasable marker (Herbert, 2010). In-school police presence increases the risk of students being pushed into the juvenile justice system, which in turn puts them at higher risk for dropping out as well as for future encounters with the criminal justice system.

Netflix/Photofest

The television series *Orange Is the New Black,* which began its fifth season in June 2017, tells the story of Piper Chapman, a young woman imprisoned for a decade-old drug crime. The popular program is based on Piper Kerman's best-selling book of the same name and shows both the extraordinary and banal experiences of life in a women's prison. ■

Third, some observers have suggested that the increased emphasis on standardized testing results as a measure of school success may be introducing a perverse incentive to push out students who are less likely than their peers to perform well on these tests (Advancement Project, 2010). For example, a National Bureau of Economic Research paper used four years of data from Florida at the time that the state introduced a high-stakes testing regime. The author found that, "While schools always tend to assign harsher punishments to low-performing students than high-performing students . . . this gap grows substantially throughout the testing window. Moreover, this testing window-related gap is only observed for students in testing grades" (Figlio, 2005, pp. 4–5).

Some policies that underpin the school to prison pipeline appear to be easing; for instance, the New York City Council, seeking greater transparency in the discipline process, now calls for detailed police reports on which students are arrested and why ("Criminalizing children at school," 2013). Nevertheless, the disproportionately high suspension and expulsion rate for students of color continues to be a key concern. Black students are three times more likely than White students to be both suspended and expelled. The police presence in schools has exacerbated the racial divide: Although Black students only represent 16% of student enrollment, they represent 31% of school-related arrests (U.S. Department of Education Office for Civil Rights, 2014). The divide has called into question the equality of the school system and the justice system. How can schools balance the need to ensure student safety while providing support for the success of all their students? What do you think?

IMPRISONMENT IN THE UNITED STATES

Controlling serious, criminal forms of deviance typically includes the arrest and prosecution of individuals who have committed violent crimes or property crimes and, to a lesser extent, individuals engaged in police brutality or corruption, white-collar crime, organized crime, or state crime. Common sense would seem to indicate that most of the people subject to various formal social controls would be those implicated in some type of violent criminal deviance, such as murder, rape, or assault. Interestingly, however, of the roughly 11 million arrests in the United States in 2015, the highest number of arrests were for drug abuse violations (estimated at 1,488,707 arrests), larceny-theft (estimated at 1,160,390), and driving under the influence (estimated at 1,089,171) (FBI, 2015b).

Another indication of the importance of formal social control in the modern world is the very high number of people imprisoned (Figure 6.1). The 2015 imprisonment rate in the United States was 458 per 100,000 residents (Carson & Anderson, 2016). Indeed, even though the U.S. prison population has declined slightly in recent years, the United States still imprisons a vastly higher percentage of its population than does any other industrial society. In total, 6,741,400 or about 1 in 37 U.S. adults today is under some form of correctional system supervision, in either prison or jail, on probation, or on parole (Kaeble & Glaze,

2016). In the opening story of this chapter, we talked about the death of college basketball star Len Bias and some of the echo effects of his tragic death. Below we revisit some of these issues to examine the phenomenon of mass imprisonment in the United States today.

The large and sudden increase in the number of people in prison or under some form of correctional supervision that began around the 1980s (see Figure 6.1) is intriguing to sociologists since it occurred during a period when both violent and property crime rates had been declining. What accounts for the unprecedented rise in imprisonment in the United States? Among the key reasons, researchers cite the following:

1. **Mandatory minimum sentences**: Federal and state legislators in the 1980s passed legislation stipulating that a person found guilty of a particular crime had to be sentenced to a minimum number of years in prison. This reduced judges' ability to use their discretion in sentencing and led to a substantial increase in the average prison term.
2. **"Three strikes" laws**: Some states and the federal government can sentence anyone to life in prison who has been found guilty of committing three felonies, or serious crimes punishable by a minimum of one year in prison. Three strikes laws became popular after several high profile murders were committed by ex-felons, raising concerns that their release was leading to more crimes in the community. *The New York Times* reported in 2013 that 9,000 offenders were serving life in prison in California, comprising many whose "third strike" was a nonserious, nonviolent offense. In 2011, U.S. Supreme Court ordered the state to reduce its prison population by 137.5 percent of capacity (The New York Times, 2013).
3. **The "war on drugs"**: As we saw in the opening story, mandatory minimums are intertwined with the "war on drugs," which was born in the 1980s. To some degree, panic over the dangers of crack cocaine fueled efforts to punish drug possession, use, and trafficking more harshly. This led to a significant increase in the number of people in prison. For example, in 2015, there were about 11 million arrests in the United States, of which roughly 1.5 million were for minor drug law violations—not for serious trafficking or distribution offenses (FBI, 2015b). In late 2015, nearly half of the federal prisoners incarcerated were serving time for drug offenses (Carson & Anderson, 2016).

FIGURE 6.4 Incarceration Rates by Race and Gender in the United States, 2014

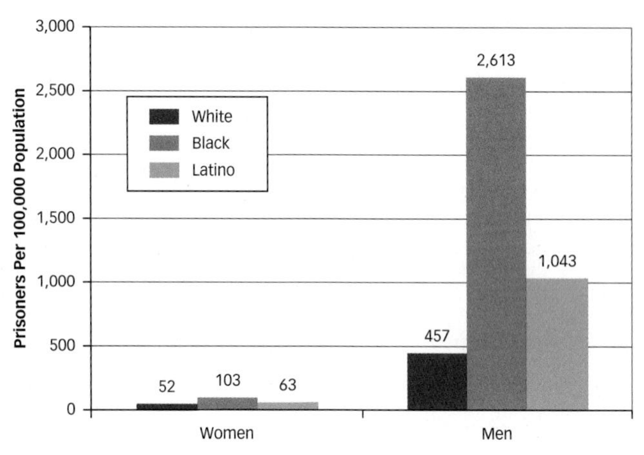

SOURCE: Reprinted with permission from The Sentencing Project.

Over the past several decades, changes in criminal laws and criminal sentencing have resulted in much stricter forms of social control in relationship to certain types of crime. In turn, this led to a huge increase in the U.S. prison population, although the imprisonment rate has turned downward in recent years: At year's end in 2014, the United States imprisoned 458 persons per 100,000 residents of all ages and 593 persons per 100,000 residents age 18 or older. Both statistics represent the lowest rate of imprisonment in more than a decade and continue decreases that began in 2007 and 2008 (Carson & Anderson, 2016).

Formal mechanisms of social control administered through the criminal justice system have not been applied equally, or proportionally, to all groups in society. Those most likely to be imprisoned and punished for engaging in criminal deviance are disproportionately people of color. Blacks and Hispanics are arrested and imprisoned at much higher rates than Whites, despite the fact that Whites make up a much larger proportion of the total U.S. population (Glaze & Herberman, 2013). Statistics show that Black men have a 32% chance of serving time in prison at some point during

Mandatory minimum sentences: Legal requirements that persons found guilty of particular crimes must be sentenced to set minimum numbers of years in prison.

"Three Strikes" Laws: State and federal laws that sentence an individual to life in prison who has been found guilty of committing three felonies, or serious crimes punishable by a minimum of a year in prison.

"War on drugs": Actions taken by U.S. state and federal governments that are intended to curb the illegal drug trade and reduce drug use.

INEQUALITY MATTERS

The Stigma of Imprisonment

©iStockphoto.com/lezsnow

We often refer to those leaving prison as people who have "done their time" or "paid their debt to society." Arguably, however, an array of laws and policies essentially ensure that ex-offenders continue to be punished by limiting their access to political voice, housing, and employment. This is significant because we live in what some writers have referred to as a "mass-imprisonment society" (Alexander, 2010). As we have discussed in this chapter, the United States has one of the highest rates of incarceration in the world. Most prisoners are serving time for nonviolent crimes, and the vast majority will eventually be released. According to the U.S. Department of Justice (n.d.), about 650,000 ex-offenders are released from prison every year. Notably, an estimated two thirds will reoffend within three years. A careful consideration of the roadblocks faced by former prisoners when they are released may, arguably, help society to both understand and reduce the problem of recidivism.

First, ex-offenders who have served time for a felony are denied a political voice in many states in this country. Although a poll released by YouGov showed that about 54% of Americans believe that ex-felons should have their right to vote restored once they have completed their sentences (Moore, 2016), only two states (Maine and Vermont) have laws that allow persons with felony convictions to never lose their right to vote and only 14 states have automatic restoration after release (National Conference of State Legislatures, 2016).

Second, many ex-offenders face significant barriers to housing after release. Many people who are released from incarceration do not know where they are going to live. Approximately one third expect to go to homeless shelters upon release. Ex-offenders have been, in many areas, banned from public housing, although studies show that stable housing can reduce recidivism. Notably as well, in some instances, entire families have been evicted from their homes in public housing after taking in a family member returning from prison. In response, several cities have started to rethink their housing policies: Accordingly, "local public housing authorities can no longer use arrest records as 'the sole basis for denying admission, terminating assistance or evicting tenants'" (Carpenter, 2015, para. 3). In 2016, the U.S. Department of Housing and Urban Development released new guidelines that also make it more difficult for landlords and home sellers to discriminate against those with criminal backgrounds (Abdullah, 2016).

Third, ex-offenders face the often daunting challenge of finding a job. Data from the New York State Division of Parole show that only 36% of able-bodied parolees who had been out of prison for 30 days or more were employed in 2014. As a recent article on the problem notes, "Former inmates often face enormous challenges finding work after they've been released: not only have many of them been out of the workforce for years, but often their criminal record prevents them from even getting their foot in the door in the first place" (Vega, 2015, para. 4). A national "ban the box" movement has arisen in some areas with the goal of eliminating the "box" that job applicants are sometimes required to check if they have been convicted of a crime, most often a felony. Recently, 14 states and several dozen cities passed laws requiring employers to postpone background checks until the later stages of the hiring process to reduce discrimination against ex-offenders (Appelbaum, 2015). Ensuring access to job opportunities in the legal economy remains a key way to reintegrate former prisoners into society.

The U.S. justice system releases several hundred thousand men and women from prisons and back into society every year. Although they have, in theory, "served their time," the costs of having been behind bars are not alleviated with release. There are two paths that an ex-offender can follow: the road back to the criminal justice system or the road to reintegration. Arguably, laws and policies that erect obstacles to stable housing and employment, as well as participation in society through access to the ballot, play a role in determining the probability an ex-prisoner will follow one or the other path.

THINK IT THROUGH

- Should ex-offenders who have completed their sentences be required to disclose their status to potential landlords and employers? Should this depend on the crime committed, or should the same rules apply to everyone?

Follow us on Twitter to keep up with current sociological stories and research! We're at @Discoversoc1.
Share your own ideas at #DiscoverSociology.

their lives; for Latino men, the chance is 17% and for White men, 6% (Sentencing Project, 2017). Black men are incarcerated at a rate of about 1,824 per 100,000; for Hispanic men the rate is more than 820 per 100,000. White men, by contrast, have an incarceration rate of 312 per 100,000 (Carson & Anderson, 2016). If current trends continue, Black males between the ages of 19 and 34 will experience an even greater overrepresentation in the prison population (Figure 6.4). Incarceration rates for women, although lower overall than those for men, exhibit a similar disproportionate racial trend, with Black women twice as likely as Hispanic women and three times more likely than White women to end up in jail or prison (Carson & Golinelli, 2013; Sipes, 2012).

People of color are more likely than Whites to be arrested and imprisoned for several reasons, all of which relate to the extension of formal social control over criminal deviance (Mann & Zatz, 1998). First, impoverished inner-city residents are disproportionately non-White, and the inner city is where the "war on drugs" has been most avidly waged (Anderson, 1999; Chambliss, 2001). As a consequence, drug-related arrests disproportionately affect people of color, who, despite constituting only 13% of the total U.S. population, represent more than 30% of people arrested for drug violations.

Second, the work of policing generally focuses on poor neighborhoods, where crowded living conditions force many activities onto the streets. Illegal activities are therefore much more likely to attract police attention in poor neighborhoods than in dispersed suburban neighborhoods.

Finally, racism in practices of prosecution and sentencing may also account for greater arrest and imprisonment rates of people of color. Even though many more Whites than non-Whites are arrested for crimes, people of color are more likely to be imprisoned for their offenses (Austin, Dimas, & Steinhart, 1992).

THE DEATH PENALTY IN THE UNITED STATES

A **capital crime**, sometimes called a capital offense, is a *crime, such as murder, which is severe enough to merit the death*

Capital crime: Crimes, such as murder, which are severe enough to merit the death penalty.

FIGURE 6.5 Death Penalty in the United States

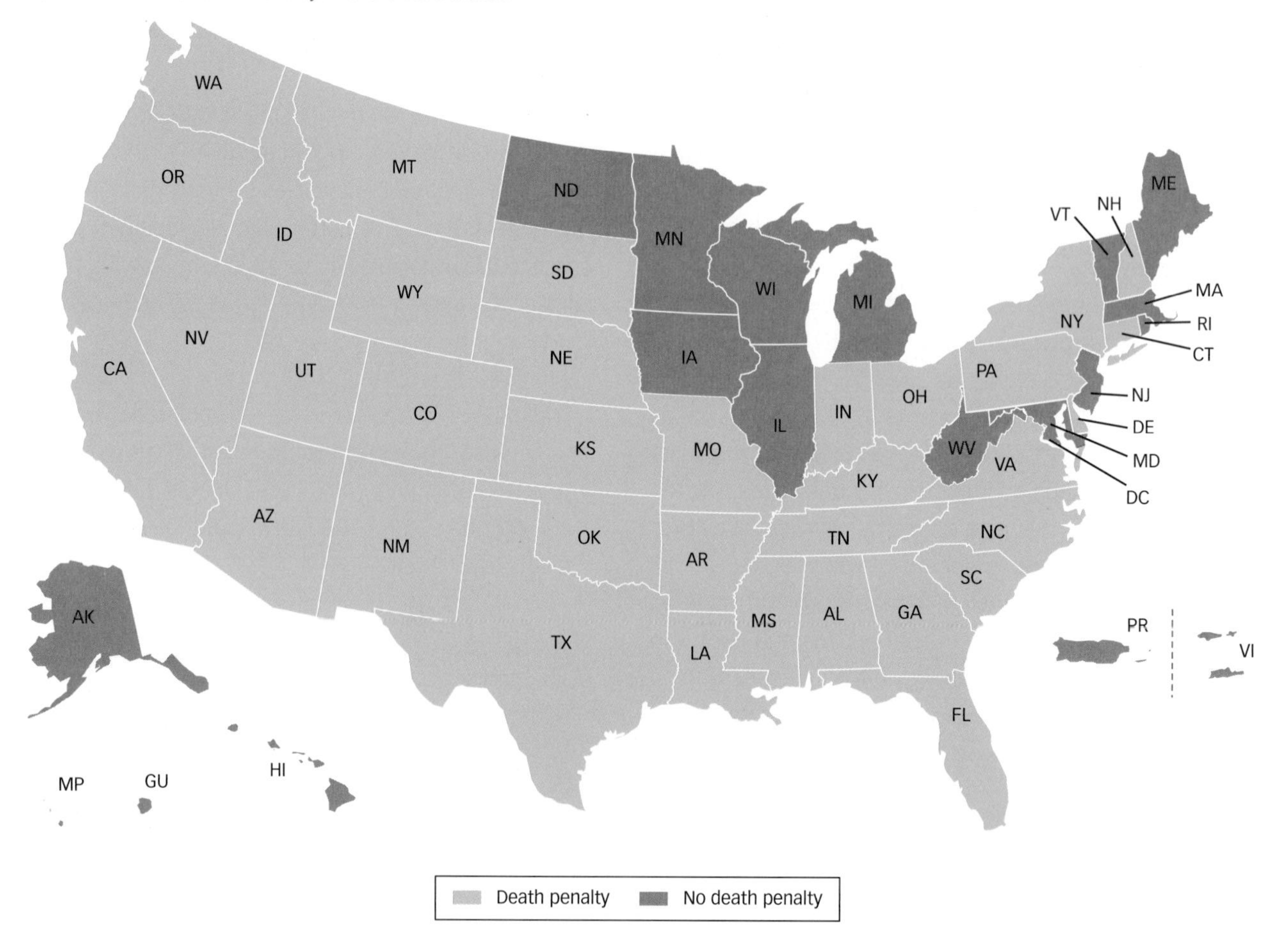

penalty (capital punishment). There are 41 offenses listed by the federal government as being punishable by death. Crimes that fall under this category include espionage, treason, and aircraft hijacking, as well as murder in particular circumstances.

In the United States, some states have and use the death penalty; others do not impose a death penalty, and still others have the death penalty but operate under a governor-imposed moratorium on the practice. Eighteen states use capital punishment; the most prominent are Texas and Georgia, although California has the most inmates on death row—741 at the end of 2016. In 2016, 20 people were executed in six states: 7 of these were in Texas, and 9 in Georgia. Nineteen states and the District of Columbia have abolished the death penalty. Four states have a governor-imposed moratorium; that is, the governor has the discretion to halt the use of the death penalty while in office (Figure 6.5; Death Penalty Information Center, 2016a).

The death penalty is a controversial practice in the United States. Few modern democratic states use it. Countries that practice it most frequently include China, Iran, North Korea, and Yemen. The United States is the fifth member of that group (Amnesty International, 2012). Those in favor of the death penalty argue that it is an appropriate punishment that may deter future crime and uphold a safe society by eliminating threats to the public. Beyond the argument of deterrence, they suggest that it is a form of retributive justice and provides closure for the families of the victims. Opponents of the death penalty challenge the idea that the death penalty is an effective deterrent: Consider that the South, which accounts for 80% of executions, has a higher murder rate than the Northeast, which accounts for just 1% of executions. They argue that erroneous punishments are irreversible: Indeed, since 1973, 150 people have been released from death row after it was found that they had been wrongfully convicted (Death Penalty Information Center, 2016b). Furthermore, the cost of a death penalty case is usually greater than the cost of life in prison in part because the appeals process can stretch for years. Finally, although more White prisoners were executed in the past year, the imposition of the death penalty has historically been biased against Black defendants, who are disproportionately found on death row (Figure 6.6). For example, a 2007 Yale University study found that African American defendants received the death penalty at three times the rate of White defendants when the victim was White (cited in Amnesty International, 2012).

In 2014, Maryland became the latest state to abolish the death penalty. Governor Martin O'Malley signed the ban into law and took the unusual step of emptying out death row, commuting the sentences of the four remaining prisoners (Berman, 2014). Efforts are underway in many other states to follow Maryland's lead, although the public and politicians continue to be divided on this controversial means of punishment.

FIGURE 6.6 Death Row Inmates by Race, 2016

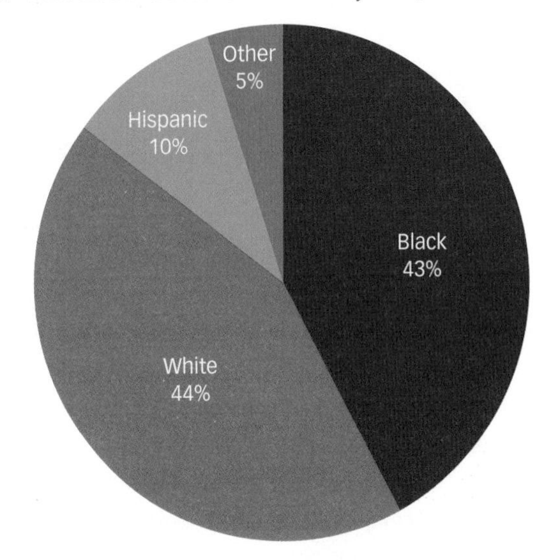

NOTE: Percentages may not equal 100% due to rounding.

SOURCE: NAACP Legal Defense Fund, "Death Row U.S.A.," January 1, 2016.

WHY STUDY DEVIANCE?

The sociological perspective focuses the lens through which we view deviant behavior. It highlights the fact that the line between "deviant" and "normal" behavior is often arbitrary: What is deviant to one group is normal and even expected behavior to another.

Mainstream media and "official" depictions of deviance often overlook or ignore some of the more serious manifestations of deviance in the culture. So too do local communities. For example, in his research on "the Saints" and "the Roughnecks," Chambliss (2001) found that middle-class boys were much more likely to have their deviant behavior written off as simply "sowing their wild oats," even though the behavior was dangerous and costly to society. On the other hand, the community was quick to judge, and apply deviant labels to, a lower income group of boys. Such findings suggest a need for sociologists to delve more deeply into stereotypes of "gangs" and "delinquency" as phenomena associated almost exclusively with poor urban youth.

Similarly, sociological research and theory remind us that focusing on the deviance of the poor and minorities blinds us to an understanding of deviance among the rich and powerful. Criminal deviance, as discussed earlier in this chapter, is widespread throughout modern societies. Some of the most dangerous and costly patterns of deviant behavior are systematically practiced by corporate executives, politicians, and government officials. The sociological perspective demands that in such cases we ask questions about power and who has the power to define deviance and to enforce their definitions.

The findings of sociologists who study deviant behavior generally and criminal deviance in particular suggest that social control policies such as imprisonment have limited effects. Instead, these findings point to the need to change the social conditions that lead to criminality in the first place. The implications of most sociological studies of deviance are that street crime and gang activity in poor urban neighborhoods can best be controlled through the creation of jobs and other opportunities for those who otherwise cannot hope to succeed. In the case of white-collar, political, and governmental crimes, the organizational structures that make it rewarding to violate laws and social norms will have to change for there to be any hope of reducing deviance among the elite.

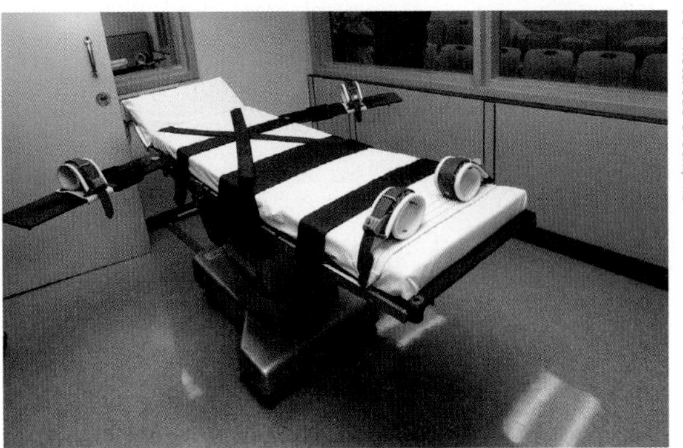

AP Photo/Sue Orocki,File

Since 1977, most executions in the United States have been done by lethal injection, a method that replaced the electric chair in many states. About 80% of executions are by lethal injection.

WHAT CAN I DO WITH A SOCIOLOGY DEGREE?

Written Communication Skills

Written communication is an essential skill for a broad spectrum of 21st-century careers. Sociology students have many opportunities to practice and sharpen written communication skills. Among others, sociologists learn to write *theoretically,* applying classical and contemporary theories to construct an analysis of social issues and phenomena, and to write *empirically,* preparing and communicating evidence-based arguments about the social world. Sociology majors write papers in a variety of forms and for a variety of audiences; these may include reaction papers, book reviews, theoretical analyses, research papers, quantitative analysis reports, field note write-ups, letters to decision makers or newspaper editors, and reflections on sociological activities or experiences. Excellent written communication is fundamental in many occupational fields, including politics, business and entrepreneurship, communications and marketing, law and criminal justice, community organizing and advocacy, journalism, higher education, law, and public relations.

Laura Kiehl, Presentence Investigator

Boise State University, BA in Sociology, minor in English

The goal of the presentence investigator is to provide the court with a depiction of a criminal defendant once he or she has been found guilty of a felony offense. My goal is to not only document the defendant's version of the crime they committed, but also to provide the court with an outline of who that person is as an individual. This information comes from a one-on-one interview with the defendant as well as from collateral contacts made with friends, family, employers, educators, and medical professionals. With this information, I prepare a PSI for the sentencing judge that contains information pertaining to the instant offense, criminal history, family/social history, educational background, employment history, and medical and substance abuse history, and document the defendant's goals for the future. I also provide the court with a recommendation for sentencing. The recommendation includes my perception of the criminal defendant based on my interactions with him or her, as well as my contacts with collateral sources. There are three main options for recommendations: probation, rider (Retained Jurisdiction—meaning that the offender will spend a short time, typically 90 days, in prison followed by probation), and prison. Within the three recommendations, I add specific treatment/programming guidelines that might benefit the defendant. The recommendations I make are based on the defendant's risk factors and criminal history, combined with any additional concerning or protective factors I have determined through the investigative process.

One of the most important traits for someone to have as a presentence investigator is a desire to get to know people. The saying "You catch more flies with honey than with vinegar" goes a long way in this line of work. The defendant has already been convicted, and therefore, it is not the job of the presentence investigator to interrogate. I find that my best interviews, which have gained the most information valuable to the court, were interviews where I made the defendant feel comfortable and feel that they could trust me to tell their story in a fair and honest manner. An investigative mind is also beneficial, as learning to "dig" for information is part of what makes this job fun and interesting on a day-to-day basis.

If you want to be a presentence investigator, hone your writing skills. Ultimately, while this job is investigative in nature, the report should be the main focus and needs to be well written and detailed. Reports can take between 10 and 12 hours (or more) to complete. Also, you cannot be afraid to ask questions. I have heard some of the craziest stories from criminal defendants, some of which were extremely uncomfortable to hear. Defendants willing to open up and provide details about their lives need an investigator who is not afraid to keep asking questions. Be ready to be surprised on a daily basis! This job is never boring and is different and challenging every day, with every different case.

Career Data: Private Detectives and Investigators

- 2016 Median Pay: $48,190 per year
- Typical Entry-Level Education: High school diploma or equivalent
- Projected Job Growth by 2024: 5% (As fast as average)

SOURCE: Bureau of Labor Statistics, Occupational Outlook Handbook, 2016.

SUMMARY

- Notions of what constitutes **deviance** vary considerably and are relative to the norms and values of particular cultures as well as the labels applied by certain groups or individuals to specific behaviors, actions, practices, and conditions. Even **crimes**, which are particular forms of especially serious deviance, are defined differently from place to place and over time, and they depend on social and political processes.
- In **pluralistic societies** such as the United States, it is difficult to establish universally accepted notions of deviance.
- Most sociologists do not believe there is a direct causal link between biology and deviance. Whatever the role of biology, deviant behaviors are culturally defined and socially learned.
- Functionalist theorists explain deviance in terms of the functions it performs for society. Émile Durkheim argued that some degree of deviance serves to reaffirm society's normative boundaries. Robert K. Merton argued that deviance reflects structural strain between the culturally defined goals of a society and the means society provides for achieving those goals. **Opportunity theory** emphasizes access to deviance as a major source of deviance. **Control theory** focuses on the presence of interpersonal bonds as a means of keeping deviance in check.
- Conflict theories explain deviance in terms of the conflicts between different groups, classes, or subcultures in society. **Class-dominant theories** of deviance emphasize how wealthy and powerful groups are able to define as deviant any behavior that runs counter to their interests. **Structural contradiction theory** argues that conflicts are inherent in social structure; it sees the sorts of structural strains identified by Merton as being built into society itself. The **feminist perspective on deviance** reminds us that, until relatively recently, research on deviance was conducted almost exclusively on males. Recent feminist theories argue that many women labeled as deviant are themselves victims of deviant behavior, such as "delinquent" girls who are, in fact, runaways escaping sexual and physical abuse.
- Symbolic interactionist theorists argue that deviance, like all forms of human behavior, results from the ways in which we come to see ourselves through the eyes of others. One version of symbolic

interactionism is **labeling theory**, which argues that deviance results mainly from the labels others attach to our behavior.

- **Violent crimes** are the most heavily publicized, but the most common are **property crimes** and victimless crimes. Although there is a public perception in the United States that crime is increasing, both of those crime rates have decreased.
- Although crime is often depicted as concentrated among poor racial minorities, crimes are committed by people from all walks of life. **White-collar crime** and **state crime** are two examples of crime committed by people in positions of wealth and power. They exact enormous financial and personal costs from society.
- Deviance and **criminal deviance** are both controlled socially through mechanisms of **informal social control**, such as socialization, and **formal social control**, such as arrests and imprisonment.
- Means of formal social control include the growth of **zero-tolerance policies** and policing in schools, mandatory minimum sentences for certain crimes and mass incarceration, and the use of the death penalty.
- A disproportionate number of people of color are arrested and incarcerated in the United States. This phenomenon is linked to a variety of factors that include the concentration of the "war on drugs" on poor, minority neighborhoods and racism in arrest, prosecution, and sentencing of those who engage in deviant behavior.

KEY TERMS

deviance, 160
crime, 160
pluralistic societies, 160
capital offenses, 160
phrenology, 161
atavisms, 161
structural strain, 163
strain theory, 163
opportunity theory, 163
control theory, 163
social bonds, 165
subcultural theories, 166
class-dominant theories, 166
structural contradiction theory, 167
feminist perspective on deviance, 167
stigmatization, 168
labeling theory, 168
primary deviance, 168
secondary deviance, 168
differential association theory, 169
violent crimes, 172
property crimes, 172
organized crime, 173
white-collar crime, 175
state crimes, 178
social control, 178
social power, 178
informal social control, 178
formal social control, 178
school to prison pipeline, 179
zero tolerance policies, 179
mandatory minimum sentences, 181
"three strikes" laws, 181
"war on drugs", 181
capital crime, 183

DISCUSSION QUESTIONS

1. As we saw in the *Behind the Numbers* box, measuring crime, including property crimes and violent crimes, can be challenging. Often, a single source is not enough to provide a comprehensive picture. What kinds of factors affect the accuracy of statistics on the incidence of crime? How can a researcher overcome such problems to gain an accurate picture?
2. Labeling theories in the area of criminology suggest that labeling particular groups as deviant can set in motion a self-fulfilling prophecy. That is, people may become that which is expected of them—including becoming deviant or even criminally deviant. Can you think of other social settings where labeling theory might be applied?

3. Think about some theoretical explanations for why people commit crime—differential association, social control, labeling, and so on. You might conclude that they all make sense on an intuitive level. Yet there is contradictory evidence for each of these theories; that is, some data support each theory, and some data contradict it. What is the difference between seeing intuitive sense in a theory and testing it empirically?

4. Why, according to the chapter, did the rate of imprisonment rise in the United States in the 1980s? Why are a disproportionate number of prison inmates people of color?

5. Why, according to sociologists, are the "crimes of the powerful" (politicians, businesspeople, and other elites) less likely to be severely punished than those of the poor, even when those crimes have mortal consequences?

Want a better grade?

Get the tools you need to sharpen your study skills. Access practice quizzes, eFlashcards, video and multimedia at **https://edge.sagepub.com/eglitis**.

SOCIAL CLASS AND INEQUALITY

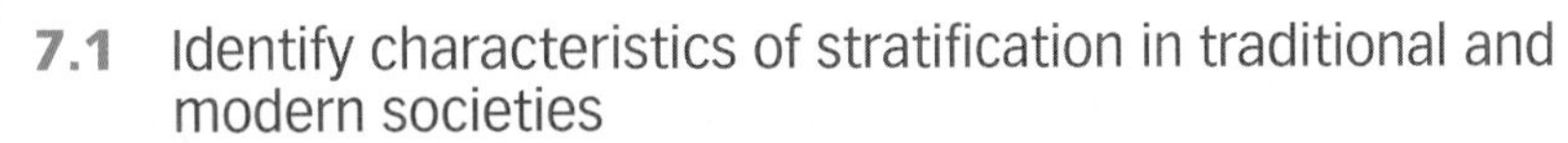

LEARNING OBJECTIVES

7.1 Identify characteristics of stratification in traditional and modern societies

7.2 Describe components of social class, including income, wealth, occupation, status, and political voice

7.3 Describe dimensions of socioeconomic inequality in the United States

7.4 Discuss the problem of neighborhood poverty

7.5 Analyze the existence and persistence of stratification and poverty from sociological perspectives

7.6 Describe quantitative and qualitative dimensions of global poverty and inequality

7.7 Apply theoretical perspectives to analyze the existence and persistence of global inequality

Yong Kim/The Philadelphia Inquirer via AP

WHAT DO YOU THINK?

1. What factors explain rising income inequality in the U.S. in recent decades?
2. What explains the existence and persistence of widespread poverty in the United States?
3. Why are some countries tremendously prosperous while others are desperately poor?

POVERTY AND PROSPERITY IN THE UNITED STATES TODAY

According to the U.S. Census, about 6% of the U.S. population—more than 20 million people—reside in trailer parks. The high demand for affordable housing, which grew when hundreds of thousands of Americans lost their homes in the foreclosure crisis that began after the economic downturn in late 2007, has made the parks an attractive investment opportunity. Among those earning significant returns on this demand are high-profile investors like Sam Zell, whose controlling interest in about 140,000 parks earned him $777 million in revenue in 2014, and Warren Buffet, the second richest man in the United States, who owns both the country's largest mobile home manufacturer and two biggest mobile home lenders. In the words of one investor, "'Sell to the masses, eat with the classes.' There's a lot more poor people than there are rich people and they're not making any more trailer parks" (Neate, 2015, "'There's more poor people every day,'" para. 7).

In 2014, an article in *Bloomberg Markets* profiled an investor:

> When Dan Weissman worked at Goldman Sachs Group Inc. and, later, at a hedge fund, he didn't have to worry about methamphetamine addicts chasing his employees with metal pipes. Or SWAT teams barging into his workplace looking for arsonists.
>
> Both things have happened since he left Wall Street and bought five mobile home parks: four in Texas and one in Indiana. Yet he says he's never been so relaxed in his life. . . .

[He] attributes his newfound calm to the supply-demand equation in the trailer park industry. With more of the U.S. middle class sliding into poverty and many towns banning new trailer parks, enterprising owners are getting rich renting the concrete pads and surrounding dirt on which residents park their homes.

"The greatest part of the business is that we go to sleep at night not ever worrying about demand for our product. . . . It's the best decision I've ever made" (Effinger & Burton, 2014, para. 4).

For those interested in investment, millionaire Frank Rolfe offers Mobile Home University, a 3-day, $200 "boot camp" to prepare them. Among the lessons for would-be landlords: "[The rents] do not go down, that's one thing that's a safe bet in the trailer park world" (Neate, 2015, "'The rents do not go down,'" para. 4).

The decline of the U.S. middle class has wrought substantial consequences for millions of families. It has also, as the story above suggests, opened new economic opportunities for others, including members of the upper class. The economic security of the middle class, particularly its less educated fraction, has been declining since the 1970s, a process accelerated by the recession of 2007–2010, the effects of which are still felt in many families and communities. At the top of the economic ladder, however, incomes have risen and fortunes have expanded. These important changes in the U.S. class structure are of great interest to sociologists. Helping you to understand them is a key goal of this chapter. ■

We begin this chapter with an examination of forms of stratification in traditional and modern societies, followed by a discussion of the characteristics of caste, social class, and stratification. Next, we look at important quantitative and qualitative dimensions of inequality and both household and neighborhood poverty in the United States. We then turn to a discussion of theoretical perspectives on class and inequality. Next we shift our gaze to key dimensions of global inequality and ask why these deep global disparities exist and persist.

STRATIFICATION IN TRADITIONAL AND MODERN SOCIETIES

In the United States today, there is substantial **social inequality**—a *high degree of disparity in income, wealth, power, prestige, and other resources.* Sociologists capture the disparities between social groups conceptually with an image from geology: They suggest that society, like the earth's surface, is made up of different layers. **Social stratification** is thus *the systematic ranking of different groups of people in a hierarchy of inequality.* Sociologists seek to outline the quantitative dimensions and the qualitative manifestations of social stratification in the United States and around the globe, but—even more important—they endeavor to identify the social roots of stratification.

Stratification systems are considered "closed" or "open," depending on how much mobility between layers is available to groups and individuals within a society. Caste societies (closed) and class societies (open) represent two important examples of systems of stratification.

CASTE SOCIETIES

In a **caste society** *the social levels are closed, so that all individuals remain at the social level of their birth throughout life.* Social status is based on personal characteristics—such as race or ethnicity, parental religion, or parental caste—that are present at birth, and social mobility is virtually impossible. Social status, then, is the outcome of ascribed rather than of achieved characteristics.

Historically, castes have been present in some agricultural societies, such as rural India and South Africa prior to the end of White rule in 1992. In the United States before the end of the Civil War in 1865, slavery imposed a racial caste system because enslavement was usually a permanent condition (except for those slaves who escaped or were freed by their owners). In the eyes of the law, the slave was a form of property without personal rights. Some argue that institutionalized racial inequality and limits on

Social inequality: A high degree of disparity in income, wealth, power, prestige, and other resources.

Social stratification: The systematic ranking of different groups of people in a hierarchy of inequality.

Caste society: A system in which the social levels are closed, so that all individuals remain at the social level of their birth throughout life.

A key characteristic of an ideal-typical class system is the existence of social mobility. Can you identify particular opportunities for and obstacles to mobility in the U.S. class system?

social mobility for African Americans remained fixtures of the U.S. landscape even after the end of slavery (Alexander, 2010; Dollard, 1957; Immerwahr, 2007). Indeed, enforced separation of Blacks and Whites was supported by federal, state, and local laws on education, family formation, public spaces, and housing as late as the 1960s.

Caste systems are far less common in countries and communities today than they were in centuries past. For example, India is now home to a rising middle class, but it has long been described as a caste-based society because of its historical categorization of the population into four basic castes (or *varnas*): priests, warriors, traders, and workmen. These categories, which can be further divided, are based on the country's majority religion, Hinduism. At the bottom of this caste hierarchy one finds the *Dalits* or "untouchables," the lowest caste.

Since the 1950s, India has passed laws to integrate the lowest caste members into positions of greater economic and political power. Some norms have also changed, permitting members of different castes to intermarry. Although members of the lowest castes still lag in educational attainment compared with higher caste groups, India today is moving closer to a class system.

CLASS SOCIETIES

In a **class society** *social mobility allows an individual to change his or her socioeconomic position.* Class societies exist in modern economic systems and are defined by several characteristics. First, they are *economically based,* at least in theory—that is, the hierarchy of social positions is determined largely by economic status (whether earned or inherited) rather than by religion or tradition. Second, class systems are *relatively fluid*: Boundaries between classes are violable and can be crossed. In fact, in contrast to caste systems, in class systems, social mobility is looked at favorably. It has long been an American aspiration for parents to hope that their children will live better than they do. Finally, class status is understood to be *achieved rather than ascribed*: Status is, ideally, not related to a person's position at birth or religion or race or other inherited categories, but to the individual's merit and achievements in education, entrepreneurship, and work.

As we will see in this chapter, these ideal-typical characteristics of class societies do not necessarily correspond to historical or contemporary reality, and class status can be profoundly affected by factors like race, gender, and class of birth.

SOCIOLOGICAL BUILDING BLOCKS OF SOCIAL CLASS

Nearly all socially stratified systems share three characteristics. First, rankings apply to **social categories** of people—that is, to *people who share common characteristics without necessarily interacting or identifying with one another.* In many societies, women may be ranked differently than men, wealthy people differently than the poor, and highly educated people differently than those with little schooling. Individuals may be able to change their rank (through education, for instance), but the categories themselves continue to exist as part of the social hierarchy.

Second, people's opportunities and experiences are shaped by how their social categories are ranked. Ranking

Class society: A system in which social mobility allows an individual to change his or her socioeconomic position.

Social categories: Categories of people sharing common characteristics without necessarily interacting or identifying with one another.

may be linked to **achieved status**, which is *social position linked to a person's acquisition of socially valued credentials or skills,* or **ascribed status**, which is *social position linked to characteristics that are socially significant but cannot generally be altered (such as race or gender).* Although anyone can exercise individual agency, membership in a social category may influence whether an individual's path forward (and upward) is characterized by obstacles or opportunities.

The third characteristic of a socially stratified system is that the hierarchical positioning of social categories tends to change slowly over time. Members of groups that enjoy prestigious and preferential rankings in the social order tend to remain at the top, although the expansion of opportunities may change the composition of groups over time.

REUTERS/Larry Downing

Across the United States, increases in rent have dramatically outpaced increases in wages, contributing to high rates of eviction in many poor neighborhoods. By one estimate, about a fifth of Black women renters have faced eviction, often more than once (Desmond, 2016a, b).

Societal stratification has evolved through different historical stages. The earliest human societies, based on hunting and gathering, had little social stratification; there were few resources to divide, so differences within communities were not very pronounced, at least materially. Advances in agriculture produced considerably more wealth and a consequent rise in social stratification. The hierarchy in agricultural societies increasingly came to resemble a pyramid, with a large number of poor people at the bottom and successively smaller numbers in the upper tiers of better-off members.

Modern capitalist societies are, predictably, even more complex: Some sociologists suggest that the shape of class stratification resembles a teardrop (Figure 7.1), with a large number of people in the middle ranks, a slightly smaller number of people at the bottom, and very few people at the top.

Before we continue, let's look at what sociologists mean when they use the term *class.* **Class** refers to *a person's economic position in society, which is associated with income, wealth, and occupation.* Class position at birth strongly influences a person's **life chances**, *the opportunities and obstacles the person encounters in education, social life, work, and other areas critical to social mobility.* **Social mobility** is *the upward or downward status movement of individuals or groups over time.* Many middle-class Americans have experienced downward mobility in recent decades. Upward social mobility may be experienced by those who earn educational credentials or have social networks they can tap. A college degree is one important step toward upward mobility for many people.

The class system in the United States is complex, as class is composed of multiple variables. We may, however, identify some general descriptive categories. Our descriptions follow the class categories used by Gilbert and Kahl, as shown in Figure 7.1 (Gilbert, 2011). At the bottom of the economic ladder, one finds what economist Gunnar Myrdal (1963), writing in the 1960s, called the *underclass*: "a class

Achieved status: Social position linked to an individual's acquisition of socially valued credentials or skills.

Ascribed status: Social position linked to characteristics that are socially significant but cannot generally be altered (such as race or gender).

Class: A person's economic position in society, usually associated with income, wealth, and occupation, and sometimes associated with political voice.

Life chances: The opportunities and obstacles a person encounters in education, social life, work, and other areas critical to social mobility.

Social mobility: The upward or downward status movement of individuals or groups over time.

■ **FIGURE 7.1** Class in the United States (Gilbert-Kahl Model)

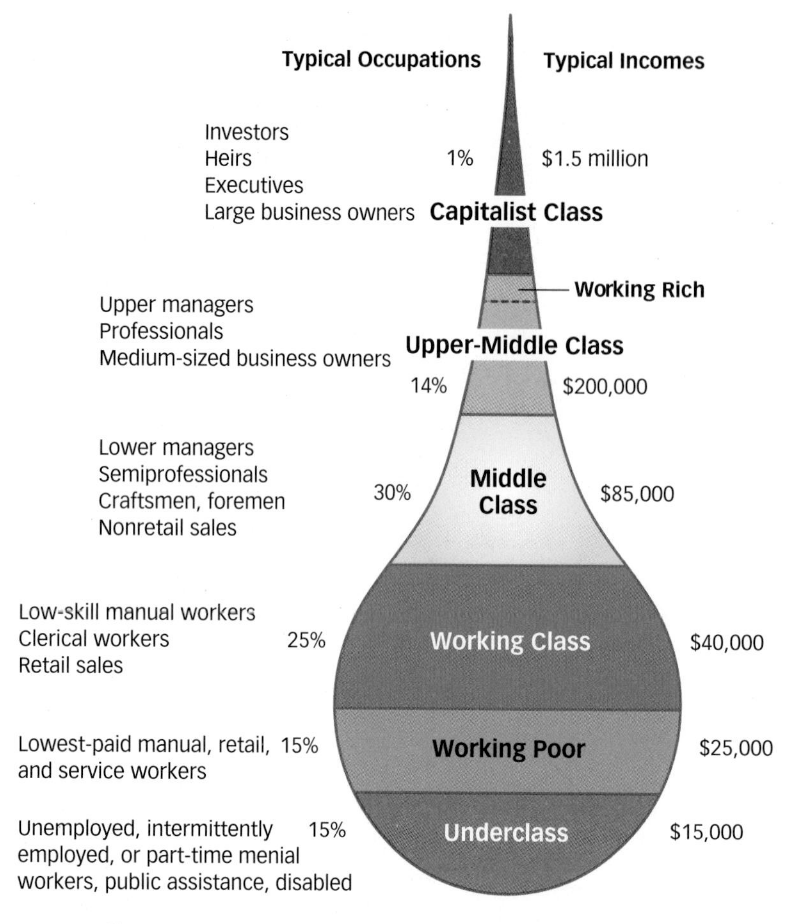

SOURCE: Gilbert, D. L. (2011). *The American class structure in an age of growing inequality.* Thousand Oaks, CA: Pine Forge Press.

of unemployed, unemployables, and underemployed who are more and more hopelessly set apart from the nation at large" (p. 10). The term has been used by sociologists like Erik Olin Wright (1994) and William Julius Wilson (1978), whose work on the "black underclass" described that group as "a massive population at the very bottom of the social ladder plagued by poor education and low-paying, unstable jobs" (p. 1).

People who perform manual labor or work in low-wage sectors like food service and retail jobs are generally understood to be working class, although some sociologists distinguish those in the *working class* from the *working poor.* Households in both categories cluster below the median household income in the United States and are characterized by breadwinners whose education beyond high school is limited or nonexistent. People in both categories depend largely on hourly wages, even though the working poor have lower incomes and little or no wealth; although they are employed, their wages fail to lift them above the poverty line, and many struggle to meet even basic needs. Author David Shipler (2005) suggests that they are "invisible," as U.S. mainstream culture does not equate work with poverty.

Those who provide skilled services of some kind (whether legal advice, electrical wiring, nursing, or accounting services) and work for someone else are considered—and usually consider themselves—middle class. Lawyers, teachers, social workers, plumbers, auto sales representatives, and store managers are all widely considered to be middle class, although there may be significant income, wealth, and educational differences among them, leading some observers to distinguish between the (middle) *middle class* and the *upper middle class.* As most Americans describe themselves in surveys as "middle class," establishing quantitative categories is challenging. In fact, in 2010, the White House Task Force on the Middle Class, led by Vice President Joe Biden, opted for a descriptive rather than a statistical definition of the middle class, suggesting that its members are "defined by their aspirations more than their income. [It is assumed that] middle class families aspire to homeownership, a car, college education for their children, health and retirement security and occasional family vacations" (U.S. Department of Commerce, Economics and Statistics Administration, 2010).

Those who own or exercise substantial financial control over large businesses, financial institutions, or factories are generally considered to be part of the upper class, a category Gilbert and Kahl term the *capitalist class* (Gilbert, 2011). This is the smallest of the categories and consists of those whose wealth and income, whether gained through work, investment, or inheritance, are dramatically greater than those of the rest of the population.

Below we look more closely at some key components of social class position: *income, wealth, occupation, status,* and *political voice.*

INCOME

FIGURE 7.2 U.S. Real Median Household Income by Racial and Ethnic Group, 1967–2016

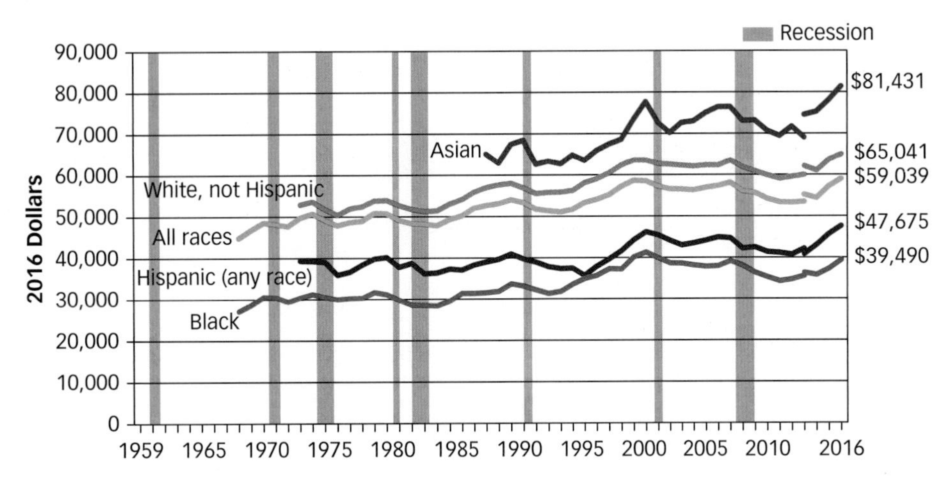

SOURCE: Table A-1. Semenga, Fontent, & Kollar. 2017. Income and poverty in the United States. https://www.census.gov/content/dam/Census/library/publications/2017/demo/P60-259.pdf

Income is *the amount of money a person or household earns in a given period of time.* Income is earned most commonly at a job and less commonly through investments. Household income also includes government transfers such as Social Security payments, veterans' benefits, or disability checks. Income typically goes to pay for food, clothing, shelter, health care, and other costs of daily living. It has a fluid quality in that it flows into a household in the form of pay-period checks and then flows out again as the mortgage or rent is paid, groceries are purchased, and other daily expenses are met.

U.S. household incomes have largely stagnated over the past decades, a topic we cover in detail later in the chapter. Effects of the recent economic crisis have not been felt evenly, but they have been experienced by all U.S. ethnic and racial groups (Figure 7.2). Income gains in the United States, however, have been disproportionately concentrated among top earners. According to a recent study by Glassdoor Economic Research, average CEO pay in S&P 500 companies is around $13.8 million per year; average median worker pay in those companies is about $77,800. Thus, the average ratio of CEO pay to median worker pay is 204 (meaning that CEOs earn 204 times more than their employees earn; Glassdoor, 2015). Starting in 2017, public companies will be required to share the ratio of CEO to worker salaries, providing even more transparency for inequalities in some of the world's biggest companies (U.S. Securities and Exchange Commission, 2015).

WEALTH

Wealth (or net worth) differs from income in that it is *the value of everything a person owns minus the value of everything he or she owes.* Wealth becomes a more important source of status as people rise on the income ladder.

For most people in the United States who possess any measurable wealth, the key source of wealth is home equity, which is essentially the difference between the market value of a home and what is owed on the mortgage. This form of wealth is *illiquid* (as opposed to *liquid*); illiquid assets are those that are logistically difficult to transform into cash because the process is lengthy and complicated. So a family needing money to finance car repairs, meet educational expenses, or even ride out a period of unemployment cannot readily transform its illiquid wealth into cash.

Economists and sociologists treat **net financial assets** as *a measure of wealth that excludes illiquid personal assets such as home and car.* Examples of net financial assets are stocks, bonds, cash, and other forms of investment assets. These are the principal sources of wealth used by the rich to secure their position in the economic hierarchy and, through reinvestment and other financial vehicles, to accumulate still more wealth.

Wealth, unlike income, is built up over a lifetime and may be passed down to the next generation. It is used to create new opportunities rather than merely to cover routine expenditures. Income buys shoes, coffee, and car repairs; wealth buys a high-quality education, business ventures, and access to travel and leisure that are out of

Income: The amount of money a person or household earns in a given period of time.

Wealth (or net worth): The value of everything a person owns minus the value of everything he or she owes.

Net financial assets: A measure of wealth that excludes illiquid personal assets such as home and car.

How would you define the U.S. middle class? Is the definition used by the White House Task Force on the Middle Class too broad or not broad enough? Should aspirations or achievements be the foundation of a definition of a socioeconomic class?

reach of most, as well as financial security and the creation of new wealth. Those who possess wealth have a decided edge at getting ahead in the stratification system. In the United States, wealth is largely concentrated at the very top of the economic ladder.

OCCUPATION

An **occupation** is *a person's main vocation.* In the modern world, this generally refers to *paid employment.* Occupation is an important determinant of social class because it is the main source of income in modern societies. The U.S. Bureau of Labor Statistics tracks 840 detailed occupational categories in the United States. Sociologists have used various classifications to reduce these to a far smaller number of categories. For example, jobs are described as *blue collar* if they are based primarily on manual labor (factory workers, agricultural laborers, truck drivers, and miners) and *white collar* if they require mainly analytical skills or formal education (doctors, lawyers, and business managers). The term *pink collar* is sometimes used to describe semiskilled, low-paid service jobs that are primarily held by women (waitresses, salesclerks, and receptionists).

In the 1990s, some writers adopted the term *gold collar* to categorize the jobs of young professionals who commanded huge salaries and high occupational positions very early in their professional careers thanks to the technology bubble and economic boom of the 1990s (Wonacott, 2002). After the bubble burst, gold-collar workers were more often found in the financial sector, earning very substantial salaries and benefits. The economic recession that commenced in 2007 put a damper on growth in salaries and benefits of gold-collar workers, but they have risen again in recent years.

STATUS

Status refers to *the prestige associated with social position.* It varies based on factors such as family background and occupation. A considerable amount of social science research has gone into classifying occupations according to the degrees of status or prestige they hold in public opinion.

We might expect white-collar jobs to rank more highly in prestige than blue-collar jobs, but do they? Doctors and scientists are indeed at the top of the prestige scale—but so are less highly paid professionals such as nurses and firefighters (who top the poll results discussed in this section, with 76% of respondents indicating that firefighters have "very great prestige"). Also in the top ranks are teachers and military officers (both with 69% conferring "very great prestige" on them). At the bottom are actors, stockbrokers, accountants, and real estate agents (just 27% of respondents indicated "very great prestige" for real estate agents). It seems occupations that require working with ideas (scientist, engineer) or providing professional services that contribute to the public welfare (teacher, doctor, firefighter) have the highest prestige, and perhaps surprisingly, the U.S. public does not always relate prestige to income (Harris Poll, 2014).

Prestige rankings of specific occupations have been relatively stable over time, although changes do occur. For instance, since 1977, both scientists and lawyers have lost ground, falling 9 points to 57% and 10 points to 26%, respectively. What factors might explain these drops? Have societal changes taken place that might contribute to our understanding of why occupations like these rise and fall on the prestige scale?

Occupation: A person's main vocation or paid employment.

Status: The prestige associated with a social position.

POLITICAL VOICE

Political power is *the ability to exercise influence on political institutions and/or actors to realize personal or group interests.* It involves the mobilization of resources (such as money or technology or political support of a desired constituency) and the successful achievement of political goals (such as the passage of legislation favorable to a particular group).

Sociological analyses of power have revealed a pyramid-shaped stratification system in the United States—as well as in most advanced industrial societies, including those of Western Europe. At the top are a handful of political figures, businesspeople, and other leaders with substantial power over political decision-making and the national economy. Moving down the pyramid, we encounter more people—and less power (Domhoff, 2009).

Sociologist C. Wright Mills began to write as early as the 1950s about the existence of a "power elite," which he defined as a group comprising elites from the executive branch of government, the military, and the corporate community who share social ties, a common "worldview" born of socialization in prestigious schools and clubs, and professional links that create revolving doors between positions in these three areas (Mills, 1956/2000a).

In contrast to the *pluralist perspective* on U.S. democracy, which suggests that political power is fluid and passes, over time, among a spectrum of groups and interests who compete in the political arena, Mills offered a critical perspective. He described a concentration of political power in the hands of a small elite. According to Mills, even though some power over local issues remains in the hands of elected legislatures and interest groups, decision-making power over issues of war and peace, global economic interests, and other matters of international and national consequence remain with the power elite. The power of the masses is little more than an illusion in Mills's view; the masses are composed of "entirely private" individuals wrapped up in personal concerns and largely disconnected from the political process.

Today, the middle class is at the center of political discourse, but are decision makers addressing the fundamental economic concerns, including stagnating wages, of the middle class? Or do the interests of the wealthy guide policy making? Are the voices of the poor present in politics? What do you think? In the following we look more closely at trends in inequality in the United States.

CLASS AND INEQUALITY IN THE UNITED STATES: DIMENSIONS AND TRENDS

The United States prides itself on being a nation of equals. Indeed, except for the period of the Great Depression of the 1930s, inequality declined throughout much of the 20th century, reaching its lowest levels during the 1960s and early 1970s. But during the past three decades, inequality has been on the rise again. The rich have gotten much richer, middle-class incomes have stagnated, and a growing number of poor are struggling to make ends meet.

INCOME INEQUALITY

Sociologist Richard Sennett (1998) writes that "Europeans from [Alexis de] Tocqueville on have tended to take the face value for reality; some have deduced we Americans are indeed a classless society, at least in our manners and beliefs—a democracy of consumers; others, like Simone de Beauvoir, have maintained we are hopelessly confused about our real differences" (p. 64). Was Tocqueville right, or Beauvoir? Are we classless or confused? What are the dimensions of our differences? Let us look at what statistics tell us.

Every year the U.S. Census Bureau calculates how income is distributed across the population of earners. All households are ranked by annual income and then categorized into *quintiles,* or fifths. The Census Bureau calculates how much of the *aggregate income,* or total income, generated in the United States each quintile gets. In other words, imagine all legally earned and reported income thrown into a big pot—that is the aggregate income. The Census Bureau wants to know (and we do too!) how much of this income goes to each quintile of earners. In a society with equal distribution across quintiles, each fifth of earners would get about one-fifth of the income in the pot. Conversely, in a society with complete inequality across quintiles, the top would get everything, and the bottom quintiles would be left empty-handed. The United States, like all other countries, falls between these two hypothetical extremes.

In Figure 7.3, we see how aggregate income in the United States is divided among quintiles of earners. When

Political power: The ability to exercise influence on political institutions and/or actors to realize personal or group interests.

FIGURE 7.3 Shares of Aggregate U.S. Income by Quintile, 2016

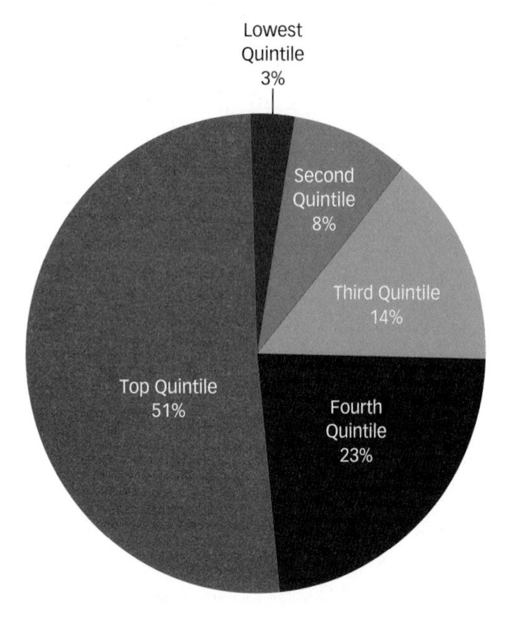

NOTE: Values add up to 99%.

SOURCE: Table A-2. Semenga, Fontent, & Kollar. 2017. Income and poverty in the United States. https://www.census.gov/content/dam/Census/library/publications/2017/demo/P60-259.pdf

FIGURE 7.4 Changes in Income Inequality in the United States, 1967–2015

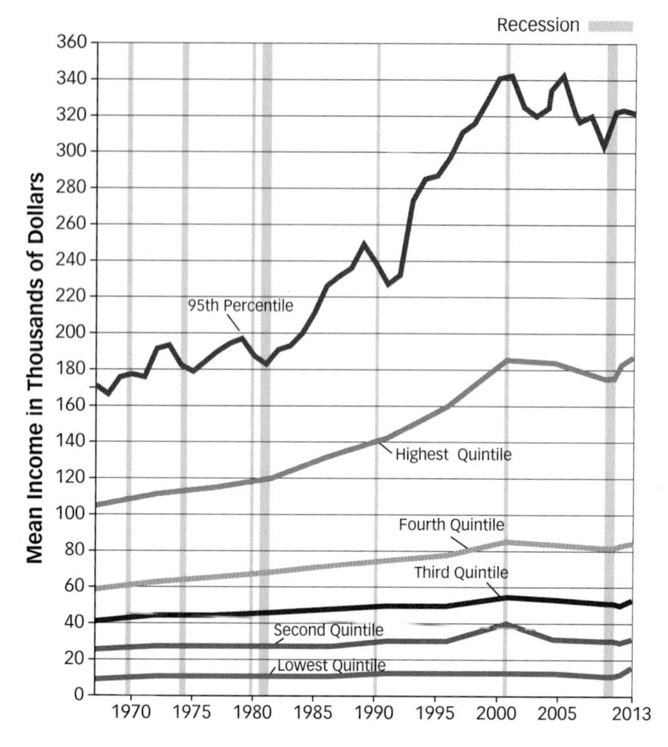

SOURCE: Table A-2. Semenga, Fontent, & Kollar. 2017. Income and poverty in the United States. https://www.census.gov/content/dam/Census/library/publications/2017/demo/P60-259.pdf

we look at the pie, we see that income earners at different levels take in disparate proportions of the income total. Those in the bottom quintile take in just over 3% of the aggregate income, while those in the top quintile get more than half; that means the top 20% of earners bring in as much as all in the bottom 80% combined. No less significant is the fact that the top 5% take in more than 22% of the total income—more than the bottom 40% combined (DeNavas-Walt & Proctor, 2014).

Data compiled by economists Emmanuel Saez and Thomas Piketty, with a formula that uses pretax income (as do the census figures) but includes capital gains, suggest an even more stratified picture. According to Saez and Piketty's calculations, about 50% of pretax income goes to the top 10% of earners: Notably, the income is not composed primarily of wages, but of capital income such as capital gains and dividends (Tankersley, 2016). Within this well-off decile (or tenth) of earners, there is a still more dramatic division of income, because the top *1%* of earners takes about a fifth of the aggregate income (Saez, 2010). Clearly, gains have been concentrated at the top of the income ladder. As economist Joseph Stiglitz (2012) points out, the fraction of the aggregate income taken by the upper 1% has doubled since 1980, while the fraction that goes to the upper 0.1% has nearly tripled over that period.

When we study issues like income inequality, we benefit from understanding the data we gather in their historical context. Figure 7.3 presents a snapshot of one moment in time, but what about decades past? The economic prosperity of the middle to late 1990s brought some benefit to most American workers: The median U.S. income rose faster at the end of the 1990s than it had since the period from the late 1940s to the middle 1950s. Saez (2010) calculates that the real annual growth of income among the bottom 99% of earners grew 2.7% in the period he terms the "Clinton Expansion" (1993–2000), but it dropped during the 2000–2002 recession (by 3.3%) and again during the 2007–2008 period (by 6.9%). On the whole, the period from 1993 to 2008 saw a real annual growth of just 0.75% for the incomes of the bottom 99%. Over the same period, the top 1% of earners experienced a real annual growth of almost 4% (although this group also experienced significant losses in the recessionary periods).

From about World War II until the middle 1970s, the top 10% earned less than a third of the national income pool (Pearlstein, 2010). In the years since, however, the incomes of people at or near the top have risen far faster than those of earners at the bottom or middle of the income scale (Figure 7.4). The stagnation of wages is well illustrated by the poor growth of average wages of young high school and college graduates (Figure 7.5). The economic position of college graduates is significantly better than that of high school graduates, but wage growth has been slow for both groups. For those with no college degree, who comprise over two thirds of young workers, lagging wage growth has contributed to economic struggles in recent decades (Kroeger & Gould, 2017).

WEALTH INEQUALITY

We see the growth of inequality in the distribution of income, but what about the wealth gap? What are its dimensions? Is it growing or shrinking? Recall that even though income has a fluid quality—flowing into the household with a weekly or monthly check and flowing out again as bills are paid and other goods of daily life are purchased—wealth has a more solid quality. Wealth represents possessions that do not flow into and out of the household regularly but instead provide a set of assets that can buy security, educational opportunity, and comfortable retirement years. The distribution of wealth gives us another important gauge of how U.S. families are doing relative to one another in terms of security, opportunity, and prospects.

Today more Americans than ever have money invested in the stock market—many through 401(k) and other retirement accounts. Does that mean wealth is more evenly spread across the population than before? No, it does not—in fact, the distribution of wealth is even more unequal than the distribution of income. If we exclude the ownership of cars and homes—which, as we noted, are not normally sources of wealth that people can use to pay regular bills or get richer—the difference in wealth between high-income families and everyone else is particularly pronounced. Figure 7.7 shows the growing concentration of wealth at the very top of the U.S. economic ladder (Saez & Zucman, 2014). Data suggest that in the last 30 years, the share of household wealth held by the top 0.1% has risen to about 22%; significantly, this share is nearly equal to that held by the bottom 90% of households, whose worth has been eroded by declining wages, a fall in home values, and an increase in debt (Monaghan, 2014).

Minority groups hold far fewer net financial assets than Whites. The wealth held by minority households has historically lagged; for instance, in 1990, Black households

FIGURE 7.5 Average Hourly Wages of U.S. College and High School Graduates Ages 21–24, 1989–2017

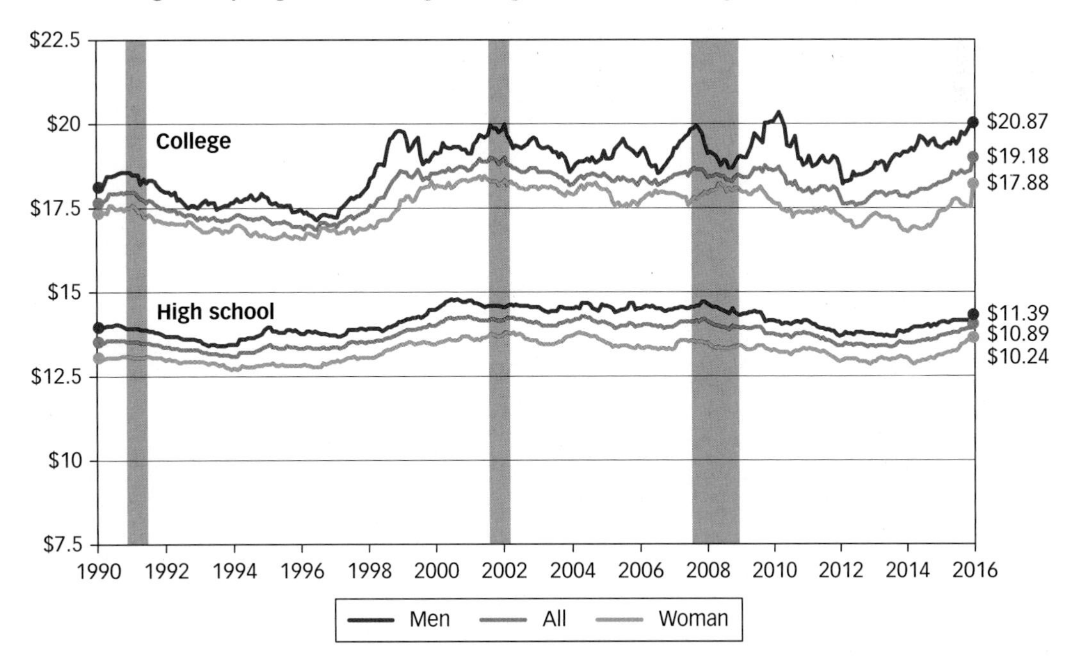

Source: "The Class of 2017," by Teresa Kroeger and Elise Gould, May 4, 2017. Economic Policy Institute. Retrieved from http://www.epi.org/publication/the-class-of-2017/

■ **FIGURE 7.6** Wealth Gap by Race/Ethnicity 1983–2013

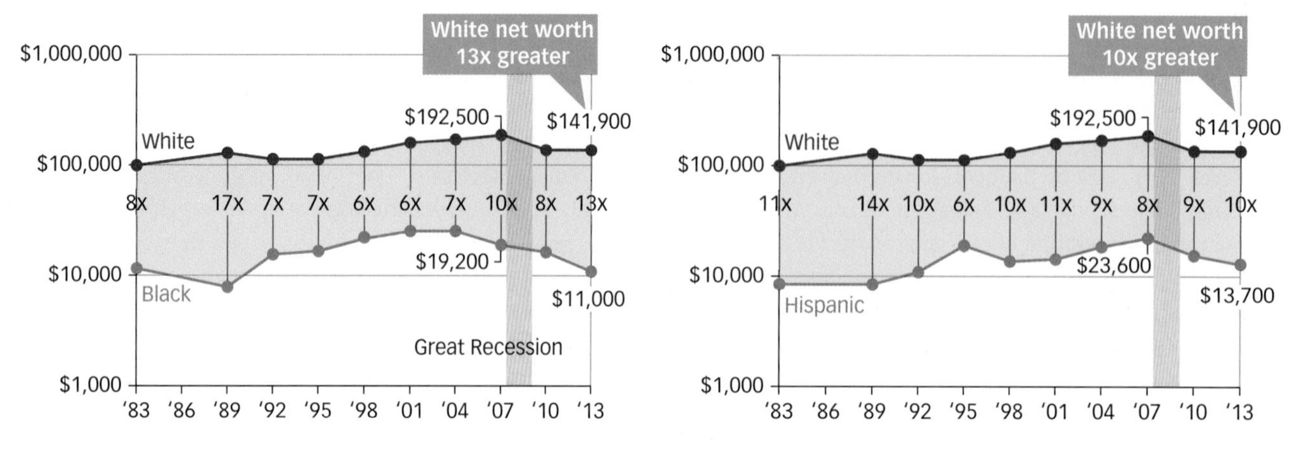

NOTES: Blacks and Whites include only non-Hispanics. Hispanics are of any race. Chart scale is logarithmic; each gridline is ten times greater than the gridline below it. Great Recession began Dec.'07 and ended June'09.

SOURCE: "Wealth inequality has widened along racial, ethnic lines since end of Great Recession." Pew Research Center, Washington, DC (December, 2014). http://www.pewresearch.org/fact-tank/2014/12/12/racial-wealth-gaps-great-recession/

held about 1% of total U.S. wealth (Conley, 1999). This percentage rose markedly in the economic boom years of the 1990s and continued to expand into the 2000s. Black household wealth reached an average of just over $12,000 in 2005. This climb, however, was reversed by the housing crisis and the Great Recession, which saw a fall in household wealth among minorities. In 2013, the U.S. median net worth of a household was just over $81,400 and differences by race and ethnicity were stark: Although White median net worth was $141,900, Black household wealth was just $11,000 and Hispanic household wealth was $13,700 (Figure 7.6; Kochhar & Fry, 2014; Kochhar, Fry, & Taylor, 2011).

Many U.S. families have zero or negative net worth, a condition worsened by the recent recession. Consider a Pew Research Center finding that in 2009, nearly one third of Hispanic households had zero or negative net worth, a figure that put them between White households (15% had zero or negative net worth) and Black households (35% had zero or negative net worth; Kochhar et al., 2011). Using a different measurement, a more recent report estimated that up to half of U.S. households have zero wealth—that is, debts are roughly equal to assets (Saez & Zucman, 2014).

■ **FIGURE 7.7** Share of U.S. Wealth, 1913–2012

SOURCE: Copyright Guardian News & Media Ltd. 2016.

OTHER GAPS: INEQUALITIES IN HEALTH CARE, HEALTH, AND ACCESS TO CONSUMER GOODS

Along with the gap in income and wealth, there is a critical gap in employer benefits, including health insurance. From the 1980s to the 1990s, health care coverage for workers in the bottom quintile of earners fell more dramatically than for any other segment of workers: From a rate of 41% coverage it dropped to just 32% in the late 1990s (Reich, 2001). In 2011, about 25% of those living in households earning less than $25,000 a year were uninsured, along with more than 21% of those in households earning $25,000–$49,999 (U.S. Census Bureau, 2012a). Altogether, more than 15% (48.6 million) of the U.S. population was without health insurance, including 7 million children younger than 18 years of age (U.S. Census Bureau, 2012a).

Many city neighborhoods lack access to large, well-stocked supermarkets with competitive prices. Residents must often choose between overpriced and often poor-quality goods, and a long trip to a suburban market. The low rates of private vehicle ownership among the urban poor can make shopping for healthy food a burden. ■

Many of the jobs created in the 1980s and 1990s were positions in the service sector, which includes retail sales and food service. Although the *quantity* of jobs created in this period helped push down the unemployment rate, the *quality* of jobs created for those with less education was not on par with the quality of many of the jobs lost as U.S. manufacturing became automated or moved overseas. Many service sector jobs pay wages at or just above minimum wage and have been increasingly unlikely to offer employer benefits.

One goal of President Obama's Patient Protection and Affordable Care Act (known simply as the Affordable Care Act or ACA), signed into law in 2010, was to expand insurance coverage for the working poor. In the first year the law was in effect, more than 8 million people signed up for health insurance plans under the Affordable Care Act, and 57% of those people had been uninsured before enrolling in ACA-compliant plans. Moreover, those who enrolled in ACA-compliant plans reported slightly worse health than nonenrollers, and most said that they would not have sought insurance if the law had not taken effect (Hamel et al., 2014). The rolls of ensured Americans have also grown with expanded access through Medicaid, a government health insurance program that primarily serves the poor, many of whom do not have employer-provided insurance and cannot afford to purchase insurance. Although some states, like Michigan, Alaska, and Louisiana, have recently joined many other states in offering greater coverage for poor residents, others, like Florida, have resisted expansion of access (ObamaCare Facts, 2016). The Republican-dominated Congress elected in November 2017 has indicated an intention to repeal the ACA and to replace it with an alternative plan. The degree to which political and policy changes will affect access to care and coverage is as yet uncertain.

Perhaps predictably, data show a powerful relationship between health and class status. Empirical data show that those with greater income and education are less likely than their less well-off peers to have and die of heart disease, diabetes, and many types of cancer. Just as income is distributed unevenly in the population, so is good health. Notably, modern medical advances have disproportionately provided benefits for those at the top of the income spectrum (Scott, 2005).

Children in disadvantaged families are more likely than their better-off peers to have poor physical and mental health. According to the Kaiser Family Foundation (2008), the rate of hospitalization for asthma for Black children is four to five times higher than that for White children. The problem is not only the lack of health insurance in families—although this factor is important—but also the lack of physical activity that may result when children don't have safe places to play and exercise, and when their families are unable to provide healthy foods because both money and access to such foods are limited.

The problem of poor health related to a lack of good food is linked to another disadvantage experienced by those on the lower economic rungs: lack of access to

SOCIAL LIFE, SOCIAL MEDIA

New Research on Food Deserts in the United States

As we saw in the main text, food deserts are "urban neighborhoods or rural towns characterized by poor access to healthy and affordable food" (DeChoudhury et al., 2016), and they are a topic of interest to sociologists who study health and inequality (Schafft, Jensen, & Hinrichs, 2009; Whelan, Wrigley, Warm, & Cannings, 2002). One of the ways in which sociologists identify food deserts is by examining the distance residents of a neighborhood have to travel to get to a well-stocked, affordable grocery store. The alternative is often a convenience store with a worse selection of fresh foods and less competitive prices. Nevertheless, as a recent news article points out, "What's harder to measure is what the residents of these areas are actually eating day to day" (Beck, 2016, para. 1).

A key reason that food deserts are of concern to researchers and policy makers is that access to healthy and fresh food is an important component of good health. Research has linked living in a food desert to higher rates of heart disease, overweight and obesity, and diabetes. Notably as well, "Food deserts may contribute to social disparities, whereby area-level deprivation compounds individual disadvantage" (p. 1): By one U.S. government estimate, about 23.5 million people live in food deserts (DeChoudhury et al., 2016).

Recently, scientists from Georgia Tech and Microsoft Research experimented with a new way to study food deserts in the United States—examining what people around the country are eating using Instagram. This popular social media platform is used by many diners to share with friends and the world what they are eating. The researchers, who define what they are doing as "social computing," used a computer program to mine 3 million publicly available Instagram posts that were tagged with food-related words and geotagged by location. Using U.S. government data, they categorized areas as food deserts and nonfood deserts and compared each desert to a nondesert in the same region with comparable demographics. Among others, the researchers "observed that posts from food deserts depict consumption of food higher in fat, sugar and cholesterol by 5–17% over the same measured in posts from 'matching' . . . non-food desert areas" (DeChoudhury et al., 2016, p. 2). Posts were also less likely to depict fresh fruits and vegetables as part of a meal. About 80% of the time, the scientists were able to use a computer model to predict whether an Instagram post originated in a food desert (DeChoudhury et al., 2016).

©iStockphoto.com/ansonmiao

©iStockphoto.com/LauriPatterson

There are, of course, important limitations to this data. Although it can help to show what people in different geographic locations are eating, it cannot tell researchers how much they are eating or how often they eat the photographed food. As well, it cannot determine whether certain types of food happen to be photographed more often in particular locations. At the same time, the researchers suggest that their social computing can improve the detection of food deserts, noting that "Instagram may lend valuable empirical insights into food and nutritional choices in areas challenged by healthy food access" (DeChoudhury et al., 2016, p. 13).

THINK IT THROUGH

- This box explores the use of the social media platform Instagram to examine the phenomenon of food deserts in the United States. Can you think of other sociological research questions that could be studied using social media platforms like Instagram, Twitter, or Facebook, among others?

Follow us on Twitter to keep up with current sociological stories and research! We're at @DiscoverSoc1.
Share your own ideas at #DiscoverSociology.

high-quality goods at competitive prices. Most middle-class shoppers purchase food at large chain grocery stores that stock items like fresh fruit and vegetables and meat at competitive prices. In contrast, inhabitants of poor neighborhoods are likely to shop at small stores that have less stock and higher prices because large grocery chains choose not to locate in poor areas. If they want to shop at big grocery stores, poor residents may need to travel great distances, a substantial challenge for those who do not own cars and a costlier proposition for those who do. As one study noted, "lower-income shoppers must travel further and/or have fewer shopping options than do higher-income shoppers" (Hatzenbuehler, Gillespie, & O'Neil, 2012, p. 54).

Some researchers refer to *areas, often urban neighborhoods or rural towns characterized by poor access to healthy and affordable food,* as **food deserts** (DeChoudhury, Sharma, & Kiciman, 2016). A *USA Today* article describes the situation, for instance, of Louisville retiree Jessie Caldwell, who regularly makes an hour-long bus trip to get fresh vegetables or meat: "For her and many others, it's often tempting to go to a more convenient mini-market or grab some fast food. 'The corner stores just sell a lot of potato chips, pop and ice cream,' she said. 'But people are going to eat what's available'" (Kenning & Halladay, 2008, para. 8).

Although we do not always think of access to stores with competitive prices and fresh goods as an issue of class inequality, lack of such access affects people's quality of life, conferring advantage on the already advantaged and disadvantage on those who struggle to make ends meet. Writer Barbara Ehrenreich (2001) highlights this point:

> There are no secret economies that nourish the poor; on the contrary, there are a host of special costs. If you can't put up the two months' rent you need to secure an apartment, you end up paying through the nose for a room by the week. If you have only a room, with a hot plate at best, you can't save by cooking up huge lentil stews that can be frozen for the week ahead. You eat fast food and hot dogs and Styrofoam cups of soup that can be microwaved in a convenience store. (p. 27)

WHY HAS INEQUALITY GROWN?

There is a significant split between the fortunes of those who are well educated and those who do not or cannot attend college. The demand for labor over the past several decades has been differentiated on the basis of education and skills—workers with more education are more highly valued, while those with little education are becoming less valuable. These effects are among the results of the transition to a postindustrial economy in the United States.

The nation's earlier industrial economy was founded heavily on manufacturing. U.S. factories produced a substantial proportion of the goods Americans used—cars,

Food deserts: Areas characterized by poor access to healthy and affordable food.

washing machines, textiles, and the like—and a big part of the economy depended on this production for its prosperity. This is no longer the case. In the postindustrial economy of today, the United States manufactures a smaller proportion of the goods Americans consume and fewer goods overall. Many manufacturing jobs have either been automated or gone abroad, drawn to the low-cost labor in developing countries. New manufacturing jobs created in the United States offer lower wages overall than did their predecessors in the unionized factories of the industrial Midwest (we discuss this issue in greater detail in Chapter 11). The modern U.S. economy has produced larger numbers of jobs in the production of knowledge and information and the provision of services.

One group that has grown is made up of professionals who engage in what former secretary of labor Robert Reich (1991) has called "symbolic analysis," or "problem-solving, problem-identifying, and strategic-brokering activities" (p. 111). These occupational categories—law, engineering, business, technology, and the like—typically pay well and offer some job security, but they also require a high level of skill and at least a college education. Even well-educated middle-class workers, however, have been touched by automation and outsourcing. As well, a rising proportion of middle-level jobs have converted from relatively stable and secure long-term positions to contractual work.

The fastest-growing sector of the postindustrial economy beginning in the 1980s was the service sector, which includes jobs in food service, retail sales, health care (for instance, home health aides and nurse's aides), janitorial and housecleaning services, and security. These jobs do not require advanced education or technical skills, but they typically pay poorly and offer weak job security and few benefits.

In the period following the official end of the Great Recession, the bulk of new jobs created by the economy were low-wage positions, many of them service sector positions in areas like hospitality, tourism, and retail. Notably, by 2015, unemployment numbers were down significantly and more jobs were being created across sectors. At the same time, "job losses and gains are unevenly distributed across industries" and new jobs in higher wage sectors have not yet replaced those lost in the recession (Figure 7.8). According to one report, "today, there are nearly two million fewer jobs in mid- and higher-wage industries than there were before the recession took hold" (National Employment Law Project [NELP], 2014, p. 2).

By providing jobs to those with less education, the service sector has, in a sense, moved into the void left by the manufacturing sector of the industrial economy over the past few decades. The service sector, which offers lower pay scales and fewer benefits, does not typically provide the kinds of jobs that offer a solid road to the middle class. Another difference is that manufacturing, especially in the automaking and steel industries, was overwhelmingly a male bastion, while service jobs favor women. The "advantage" enjoyed by less educated women over their male counterparts does not, however, translate into substantial economic gains for women or their families. Wage gains for women overall have been more fully driven by gains made by college-educated women.

The stratification of the U.S. labor force into a low-wage service sector and a better-paid knowledge and technology sector appears to be continuing unabated. The narrative of a "disappearing middle class" has become a common theme in both social science and mainstream political discourse. Do

FIGURE 7.8 Job Losses and Gains in the U.S. Economy, 2008–2014

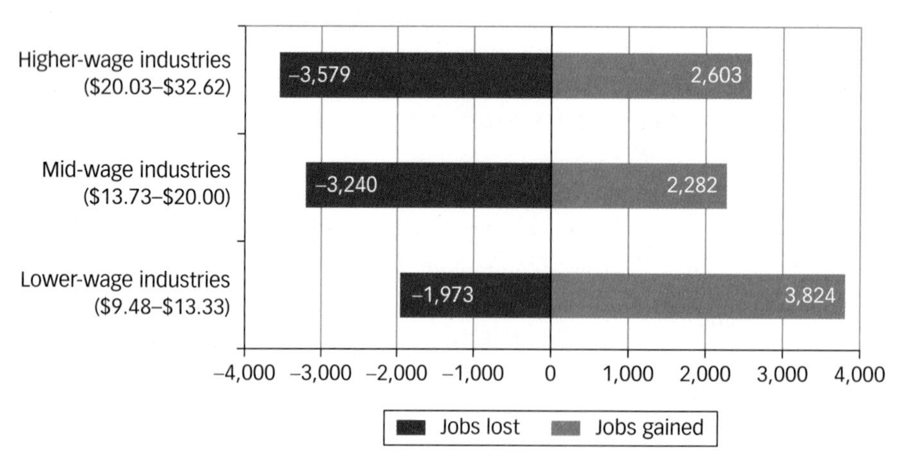

NOTE: Wage ranges are updated from earlier reports to adjust for inflation and are in 2013 dollars. At the time of publication, employment data for disaggregated industries was only available through February 2014.

SOURCE: Adapted from National Employment Law Project, "The Low-Wage Recovery and Growing Inequality." Data Brief, April 2014, p. 2.

you see such a trend in your own community? How does this narrative coexist with Americans' long-existing tendency to self-identify as middle-class, almost regardless of income?

AT THE BOTTOM OF THE LADDER: POVERTY IN THE UNITED STATES

> There is a familiar America. It is celebrated in speeches and advertised on television and in the magazines. It has the highest mass standard of living the world has ever known.
>
> In the 1950s this America worried about itself, yet even its anxieties were products of abundance. . . . There was introspection about Madison Avenue and tail fins; there was discussion of the emotional suffering taking place in the suburbs. In all this, there was an implicit assumption that the basic grinding economic problems had been solved in the United States. . . .
>
> While this discussion was being carried on, there existed another America. In it dwelt between 40,000,000 and 50,000,000 citizens of this land. They were poor. They still are.
>
> To be sure, the other America is not impoverished in the same sense as those poor nations where millions cling to hunger as a defense against starvation. This country has escaped such extremes. That does not change the fact that tens of millions of Americans are, at this very moment, maimed in body and spirit, existing at levels beneath those necessary for human decency. If these people are not starving, they are hungry, and sometimes fat with hunger, for that is what cheap foods do. They are without adequate housing and education and medical care. (Harrington, 1963, pp. 1–2)

TABLE 7.1 Poverty Rates of Selected U.S. Subgroups, 2016

Category	Percentage
All people	12.7%
Whites	11.0%
Blacks	22.0%
Hispanics	19.4%
Asians	10.1%
18 years of age and younger	18.0%
65 years of age and older	9.3%

SOURCE: Semenga, Fontent, & Kollar. 2017. Income and poverty in the United States. https://www.census.gov/content/dam/Census/library/publications/2017/demo/P60-259.pdf

These words, first published in 1963, helped to open the eyes of many to the plight of the U.S. poor, who were virtually invisible to a postwar middle class comfortably ensconced in suburbia. Michael Harrington's classic book *The Other America: Poverty in the United States* also caught the interest of President John F. Kennedy's administration and later the Johnson administration, which inaugurated the War on Poverty in 1964.

When President Lyndon B. Johnson began his War on Poverty, around 36 million U.S. citizens lived in poverty. Within a decade, the number had dropped sharply, to around 23 million. But then, beginning in the early 1970s, poverty again began to climb, reaching a high of 39 million people in 1993 before receding. Poverty climbed again in the period of economic crisis, but it has begun to decline slowly in its aftermath (Figure 7.9).

FIGURE 7.9 Poverty Levels in the United States, 1959–2016

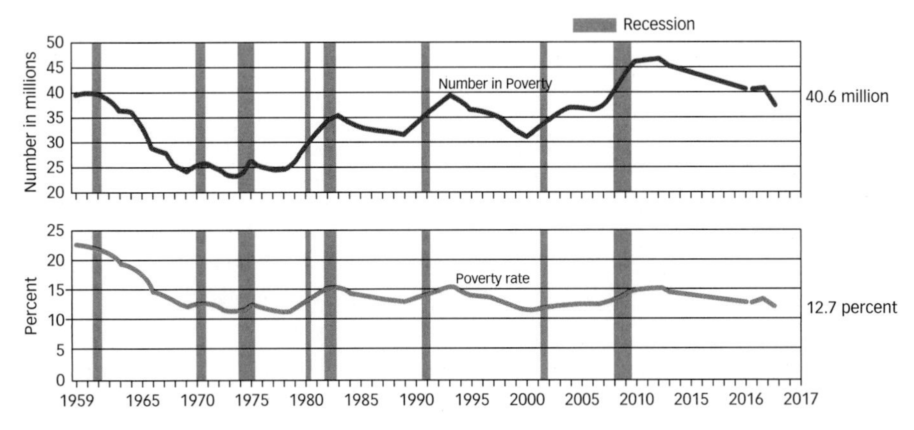

SOURCE: Semenga, Fontent, & Kollar. (2017). Income and poverty in the United States. https://www.census.gov/content/dam/Census/library/publications/2017/demo/P60-259.pdf

We pause on the topic of "official poverty" because it is important for us to be critical consumers of information. We are surrounded

FIGURE 7.10 Neighborhood Poverty Maps

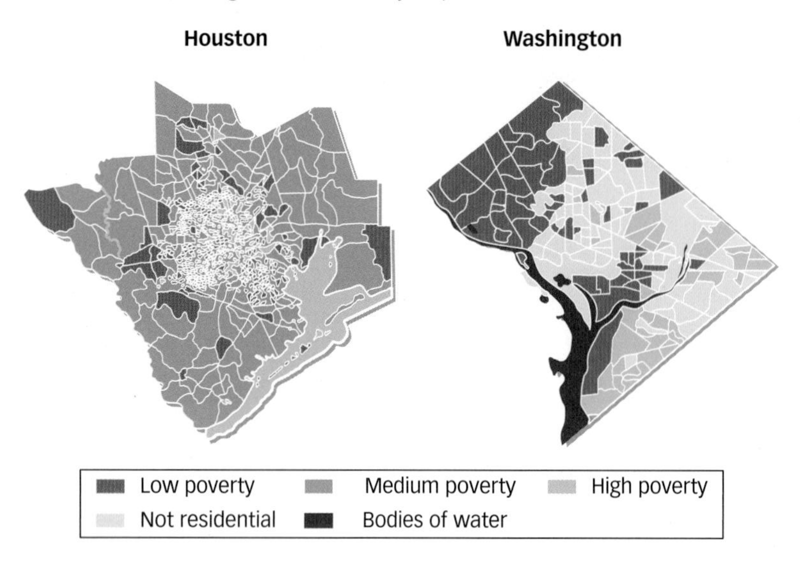

SOURCE: "Neighborhood Poverty and Household Financial Security," The PEW Charitable Trusts, January 28, 2016 (www.pewtrusts.org/en/research-and-analysis/issue-briefs/2016/01/neighborhood-poverty-and-household-financial-security).

by statistics, subject to a barrage of information about the proportion of the population who support the president or reject the health care initiatives of a political party, about the numbers of teen pregnancies and births, about the percentages who are unemployed or in poverty. These statistics illuminate the social world around us and offer us a sense of what we as a nation are thinking or earning or debating. On the other hand, statistics—including social indicators like the poverty numbers (Table 7.1)—may also obscure some important issues. To use indicators such as the poverty numbers wisely, we should know where they come from and what their limitations are.

What is poverty from the perspective of the U.S. government? How were these numbers generated? The **official poverty line** is *the dollar amount set by the government as the minimum necessary to meet the basic needs of a family.* In 2016, the U.S. government used the following thresholds:

- One person, younger than age 65: $12,486
- One person, 65 or older: $11,511
- Three persons (one adult, two children): $19,337
- Four persons (two adults, two children): $24,339
- Five persons (two adults, three children): $28,643

Official poverty line: The dollar amount set by the government as the minimum necessary to meet the basic needs of a family.

From the federal government's perspective, those whose pretax income falls beneath the threshold are officially poor; those whose pretax income is above the line (whether by $10 or $10 million) are "nonpoor." How are these thresholds generated? The *Behind the Numbers* box on page 209 explains.

Notably, official poverty numbers and the data we see in Table 7.1 offer us a picture of what the Census Bureau calls the annual poverty rate. This figure captures the number of households whose total income over the 12 months of the year fell below the poverty threshold, but it does not illuminate how many families may have dropped into or climbed out of poverty and how many dwell there over a longer period. A recent Census Bureau report points out that even though the official poverty figure is around 12.7% in the period 2009 to 2011, about one third of U.S. households fell below the poverty threshold for at least 2 months. At the same time, just 3.5% remained poor for the full 3-year period under study (Edwards, 2014). Although few households languish at the very bottom of the economic ladder for years, it is significant that nearly 10 times more households experienced periods of poverty.

Inequality and poverty in the United States are serious issues that demand both analysis and attention. Even though inequality is part of any modern capitalist state, the steep rise of inequality in recent decades presents a challenge to societal mobility and perhaps, ultimately, stability.

THE PROBLEM OF NEIGHBORHOOD POVERTY

In this section, we discuss the issue of concentrated poverty, looking specifically at measures, causes, and consequences of high levels of neighborhood (or area) poverty. We thus distinguish between *household poverty*, which an individual or family may experience while living in a mixed-income neighborhood, and *neighborhood-level poverty*. Notably, research suggests that being poor in a poor neighborhood has more negative social, economic, and educational effects than household poverty in a more economically heterogeneous context (Wilson, 2010).

BEHIND THE NUMBERS

Calculating U.S. Poverty

How does the U.S. government measure poverty? In the early 1960s, an economist at the Social Security Administration, Mollie Orshansky, used a 1955 U.S. Department of Agriculture study to establish a poverty line. She learned from the study that about one third of household income went to food, so she calculated the cost of a "thrifty food basket" and tripled it to take into account other family needs such as transportation and housing. Then she adjusted the figure again to take into account the size and composition of the family and the age of the head of household. The result was the poverty threshold, which is illustrated in Figure 7.11.

FIGURE 7.11 The Poverty Threshold Calculation

SOURCE: U.S. Census Bureau. (2010). Poverty: 2008 and 2009. American community survey briefs. Washington, DC: A. Bishaw & S. Macartney.

Orshansky's formula represented the first systematic federal attempt to count the poor, and it has been in use for more than half a century. But its age makes it a problematic indicator for the 21st century. Some critics argue that it may underestimate the number of those struggling with material deprivation. Consider the following points:

- The multiplier of three was used because food was estimated to constitute one third of a family budget in the 1960s. Food is a smaller part of budgets today (about one fifth), and housing and transport are much bigger ones. Using a higher multiplier would raise the official poverty line and, consequently, increase the number of households classified as poor.
- The formula makes no adjustment for where people live, even though costs of living vary tremendously by region. Although a family of three may be able to make ends meet on a pretax income of about $19,000 in South Dakota or Nebraska, it is doubtful that the housing costs of such areas as Boston, San Francisco, New York City, and Washington, D.C., would permit our hypothetical family to survive in basic decency.

On the other hand, some critics have suggested that the poverty rate overestimates the problem because it does not account for noncash benefits that some poor families receive, including food stamps and public housing vouchers. Adding the value of those (although they cannot be converted into cash) would increase the income of some families, possibly raising them above the poverty line.

We might thus conclude that even though the official poverty statistics give us some sense of the problem of poverty and poverty trends over time, they must be read with a critical eye.

THINK IT THROUGH

▶ Taking into consideration forms of inequality and issues of poverty discussed in this chapter, how would you create an instrument to measure poverty in the United States? The current measurement focuses on a "crisis food basket." What variables would you include?

Bloomberg/Bloomberg/Getty Images

Living in an impoverished neighborhood has significant consequences for both poor and nonpoor households. Diminished opportunities for work, education, consumption, and recreation affect entire neighborhoods.

Neighborhood poverty affects those households that are poor, but it also affects those in the neighborhood who are not officially poor.

A Census Bureau report shows that a growing proportion of Americans reside in "poverty areas," defined in the report as census tracts featuring 20% or more households in poverty (Bishaw, 2014). (Census tracts are areas with between 1,200 and 8,000 residents; most tracts fall in the 4,000 range.) In 2000, just over 18% of U.S. inhabitants lived in poverty areas; by 2010, nearly a quarter did. Poverty areas can be rural, suburban, or urban: Just over half are in central cities, another 28% are in the suburbs, and about 20% are outside metropolitan areas. Female-headed households are more likely than other family types to live in poverty areas: In 2010, more than 38% of female-headed households resided in areas with more than 20% poverty. Recent data also show a rise in residents living in "high-poverty neighborhoods," defined as census tracts where 40% or more households fall below the poverty line. According to a 2015 report, "more than one in four of the black poor and nearly one in six of the Hispanic poor lives in a neighborhood of extreme poverty, compared to one in thirteen of the white poor" (Jargowsky, 2015, para. 3).

Sociologists study the development of poverty areas, particularly in urban neighborhoods (Wilson, 1996, 2010). The rise of the suburbs in the post–World War II period fostered the out-migration of many city residents, particularly members of the White middle class, and was accompanied by a shift of public resources to new neighborhoods outside cities. Public housing built in U.S. cities around the same period was intended to offer affordable domiciles for the poor, but it also contributed to the development of concentrated poverty, as policies foresaw income limitations that foreclosed the possibility of maintaining mixed-income neighborhoods. Racially discriminatory policies and practices, including limitations on Black access to mortgages or to homes in White neighborhoods, made Blacks far more vulnerable than their White counterparts to becoming trapped in poor neighborhoods. Even today, Black and Hispanic households are more likely to reside in poverty areas (Bishaw, 2014).

As many families moved to the suburbs in the 1950s and 1960s, jobs eventually followed, contributing to a "spatial mismatch" between jobs in the suburbs and potential workers in urban areas (Wilson, 2010). The decline of manufacturing in the 1970s and the decades following also had a profound effect on some urban areas, such as Chicago and Detroit, which were deeply reliant on heavy industry for employment.

As noted earlier, area poverty compounds the negative effects of household poverty and presents challenges to all residents of economically disadvantaged neighborhoods. Research has shown, for instance, that nonpoor Black children are more likely than their White counterparts to reside in poor neighborhoods and to experience limitations to social mobility; no less importantly, children are more likely than adults to be living in high poverty areas (Jargowsky, 2015). Poor areas are more likely than better-off or even mixed-income neighborhoods to experience high levels of crime, to have low-quality housing and education, and to offer few job opportunities to residents (Federal Reserve System & Brookings Institution, 2008; Jargowsky, 2015). Among the challenges to poor neighborhoods is that individual households that have enough resources to leave may choose to do so, contributing to even less circulating capital and an increasing withdrawal of businesses, fewer employed residents, weaker social and economic networks, and more empty buildings (Wilson, 1996). Cities like Detroit and Cleveland have, in fact, lost thousands of residents in recent decades.

The revival of economically devastated neighborhoods is an important public policy challenge. How can the fortunes of poor—particularly very poor—neighborhoods be reversed? How does such a process begin and what does it entail? What do you think?

In the following section, we examine the issues of stratification and poverty from the functionalist and conflict perspectives. As you read, consider how these perspectives can be used as lenses for understanding phenomena like income and wealth inequality, household and neighborhood poverty, and other issues discussed above.

WHY DO STRATIFICATION AND POVERTY EXIST AND PERSIST IN CLASS SOCIETIES?

We find stratification in virtually all societies, a fact that the functionalist and social conflict perspectives seek to explain. The functionalist perspective highlights the ways in which stratification is functional for society as a whole. Social conflict theorists, in contrast, argue that inequality weakens society as a whole and exists because it benefits those in the upper economic, social, and political spheres. We take a closer look at each of these theoretical perspectives next.

THE FUNCTIONALIST EXPLANATION

Functionalism is rooted in part in the writings of sociologist Émile Durkheim (1893/1997), who suggested that we can best understand economic positions as performing interdependent functions for society as a whole. Using this perspective, we can think of social classes as equivalent to the different organs in the human body: Just as the heart, lungs, and kidneys serve different yet indispensable functions for human survival, so do the different positions in the class hierarchy.

In the middle of the 20th century, Kingsley Davis and Wilbert Moore (1945) built on these foundations to offer a detailed functionalist analysis of social stratification. They argued that in all societies some positions—the most "functionally important" positions—require more skill, talent, and training than others. These positions are thus difficult to fill—that is, they may suffer a "scarcity of personnel." To ensure they get filled, societies may offer valued rewards like money, prestige, and leisure to induce the best and brightest to make "sacrifices," such as getting a higher education, and to do these important jobs conscientiously and competently. According to Davis and Moore, social inequality is an "unconsciously evolved device by which societies ensure that the most important positions are conscientiously filled by the most qualified persons" (p. 243).

An implication of this perspective is that U.S. society is a **meritocracy**, *a society in which personal success is based on talent and individual effort.* That means your position in the system of stratification depends primarily on your talents and efforts: Each person gets more or less what he or she deserves or has earned, and society benefits because the most functionally important positions are occupied by the most qualified individuals. Stratification is then ultimately functional for society because the differential distribution of rewards ensures that highly valued positions are filled by well-prepared and motivated people. After all, Davis and Moore might say, we all benefit when we get economic information from good economists, drive across bridges designed by well-trained engineers, and cure our ills with pharmaceuticals developed by capable medical scientists.

Clearly the idea that the promise of higher pay and prestige motivates people to work hard has some truth. Yet it is difficult to argue that the actual differences in rewards across positions are necessarily suitable ways of measuring the positions' relative worth to society (Tumin, 1953, 1963, 1985; Wrong, 1959). Is an NBA point guard really worth more than a teacher or a nurse, for instance? Is a hedge fund manager that much more important than a scientist (particularly given that both positions require extensive education)?

Moreover, when people acquire socially important, higher status positions by virtue of their skills and efforts, they are then often able to pass along their economic privilege, and the educational opportunities and social connections that go with it, to their children, even if their children are not particularly bright, motivated, or qualified. As Melvin Tumin (1953) points out in his critique of Davis and Moore, stratification may *limit* the discovery of talent in society rather than *ensure* it, by creating a situation in which those who are born to privilege are given fuller opportunities and avenues to realize occupational success while others are limited by poor schooling, little money, and lack of networks upon which to call. Such a result would surely be dysfunctional for society rather than positively functional.

Meritocracy: A society in which personal success is based on talent and individual effort.

How would functionalism account for the fact that people are often discriminated against because of their skin color, sex, and other characteristics determined at birth that have nothing to do with their talents or motivations, resulting in an enormous waste of society's human skills and talents? Can you see other strengths or weaknesses to Davis and Moore's perspective on stratification?

In a twist on the functionalist perspective, sociologist Herbert Gans (1972) poses this provocative question: How is poverty positively functional in U.S. society? Gans begins with a bit of functionalist logic, namely, that if a social phenomenon exists and persists, it must serve a function or else it would evolve out of existence. But he does not assume that poverty is functional for everyone. So *for whom* is it functional? Gans suggests that eliminating poverty would be costly to the better-off. Thus, poverty is functional for the nonpoor but not functional for the poor—or even for society as a whole.

Among the "benefits" to the nonpoor of the existence of a stratum of poor people, Gans includes the following:

- Poverty ensures there will be low-wage laborers prepared—or driven by circumstances—to do society's "dirty work." These are the jobs no one else wants because they are demeaning, dirty, and sometimes dangerous. A large pool of laborers desperate for jobs also pushes down wages, a benefit to employers.
- Poverty creates a spectrum of jobs for people who help the poor (social welfare workers), protect society from those poor people who transgress the boundaries of the law (prison guards), or profit from the poor (owners of welfare motels and cheap grocery shops). Even esteemed sociologist Herbert Gans has built an academic career on analyzing poverty.
- Poverty provides a market for goods and services that would otherwise go unused. Day-old bread, wilting fruits and vegetables, and old automobiles are not generally purchased by the better-off. The services of second-rate doctors and lawyers, among others, are also peddled to the poor when no one else wants them.
- Beyond economics, the poor also serve cultural functions. They provide scapegoats for society's problems and help guarantee some status for those who are not poor. They also give the upper crust of society a socially valued reason for holding and attending lavish charity events.

Gans's (1972) point is stark. He notes that the "functions" served by the poor have *functional alternatives*—that is, they could be fulfilled by means other than poverty. Nevertheless, he suggests, those who are better-off in society are not motivated to fight poverty comprehensively because its existence is demonstrably functional for them. Although he is not arguing that anyone is in favor of poverty (which is difficult to imagine), he is suggesting that "phenomena like poverty can be eliminated only when they become dysfunctional for the affluent or powerful, or when the powerless can obtain enough power to change society" (p. 288). Do you agree with his argument? Why or why not?

THE SOCIAL CONFLICT EXPLANATION

Social conflict theory draws heavily from the work of Karl Marx. As we saw in the opening chapter, Marx divided society into two broad classes: workers and capitalists, or *proletarians* and *bourgeoisie*. The workers do not own the factories and machinery needed to produce wealth in capitalist societies—they possess nothing of real value except their labor power. The capitalists own the necessary equipment—the *means of production*—but require the labor power of the workers to run it.

These economic classes are unequal in their access to resources and power, and their interests are opposed. Capitalists seek to keep labor costs as low as possible to produce goods cheaply and make a profit. Workers seek to be paid adequate wages and to secure safe, decent working conditions and hours. At the same time, the two groups are interdependent: The capitalists need the labor of the workers, and the workers depend on the wages they earn (regardless of how meager) to survive.

Although more than a century has passed since Marx formulated his theory, a struggle between workers and owners (or, in our time, between workers and owners, managers, and even stockholders, who all depend on a company's profits) still exists. Conflict is often based on the irreconcilability of these competing interests. A study found that collective action lawsuits alleging wage and hour violations have skyrocketed, increasing 400% in the past 11 years. Among companies such as Bank of America, Walmart, and Starbucks, Taco Bell has been one of the latest to be sued for allegedly forcing employees to work overtime without pay (Eichler, 2012).

The source of inequality, then, lies in the fact that the bourgeoisie own the means of production and can use their assets to make more money and secure their position in society. Most workers do not own substantial economic assets aside from their own labor power, which they use to earn a living. Although successful lawsuits for lost wages show that workers have avenues for asserting their rights against employers, the conflict perspective contrasts these small victories with the far more significant power and control exercised by large economic actors in modern society.

In short, the conflict perspective suggests that significant and persistent stratification exists because those who have power use it to create economic, political, and social conditions that favor them and their children, even if these conditions are detrimental to the lower classes. Inequality thus is not functional, as Davis and Moore argued. Rather, it is dysfunctional, because it keeps power concentrated in the hands of the few rather than creating conditions of meritocracy that would give equal opportunity to all.

Sarah Leen/National Geographic Creative

Herbert Gans suggests that poverty ensures a pool of workers "unable to be unwilling" to do difficult and dirty jobs for low pay. Such jobs could also be filled in the absence of poverty—through better pay and benefits. But, says Gans, this would be costly and, thus, dysfunctional to the nonpoor. ■

Like the functionalist perspective, the conflict perspective has analytical weaknesses. It overlooks cooperative aspects of modern capitalist businesses, some of which have begun to take a more democratic approach to management, offering workers the opportunity to participate in decision-making processes in the workplace. Modern workplaces in the technology sector, for instance, thrive when decision-making and the production of ideas come from various levels rather than just from the top down.

DIMENSIONS OF GLOBAL INEQUALITY AND POVERTY

Many of the world's people are poor. According to a Pew Research Report, about 15% of the globe's inhabitants live on the equivalent of less than $2 a day; another 56% subsist on between $2 and $10 a day (Kochhar, 2015). Nearly all of these economically marginal people live in the developing world. At the same time, according to a 2016 report issued by Oxfam, just 62 people (all of them billionaires) own as much wealth as the bottom half of the world's population (Hardoon, Fuentes-Nieva, & Ayele, 2016).

We can look at inequality in terms of individuals or households, but we can also compare the economic positions of countries, recognizing a global class system with prosperous states, poor states, and a wide swath of countries in between. In this chapter, we look at some of the dimensions of **global inequality**, which can be defined as the *systematic disparities in income, wealth, health, education, access to technology, opportunity, and power among countries, communities, and households around the world.* Although the focus is largely on differences among countries, we will see that these are only one part of a broader picture of global inequality.

We follow the World Bank in categorizing countries using four economic categories: high income, upper-middle income, lower-middle income, and low income (Figure 7.12; World Bank, 2017). In 2017, the World Bank defined these classifications quantitatively using the following gross national income (GNI) per capita limits:

- Low-income economies: $1,025 or less
- Lower middle-income economies: $1,026 to $4,035
- Upper middle-income economies: $4,036 to $12,475
- High-income economies: $12,476 or more

Global inequality: The systematic disparities in income, wealth, health, education, access to technology, opportunity, and power among countries, communities, and households around the world.

FIGURE 7.12 The World by Income, Based on Gross National Income Per Capita, 2015

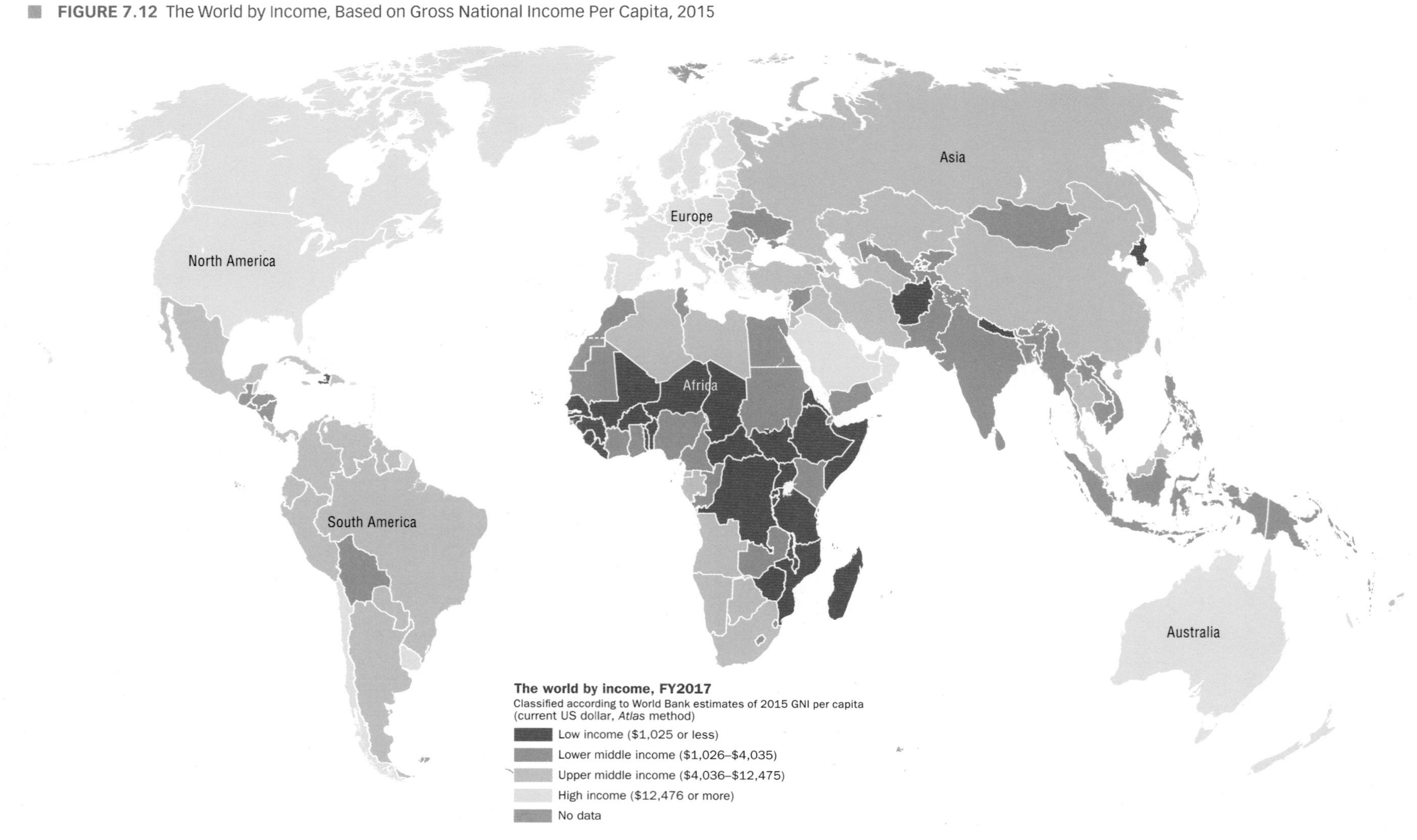

SOURCE: "WDI 2017 Maps: The World by Income, 2017," The World Bank (http://data.worldbank.org/products/wdi-maps). Reprinted with permission from The World Bank.

Qualitatively, we can describe the *high-income countries* as those that are highly industrialized, characterized by the presence of mass education, and both urbanized and technologically advanced. Among the high-income countries we find nations such as the United States, Canada, Japan, Germany, Norway, Estonia, and Australia. High-income countries are home to about 15% of the global population.

More than 70% of the world's population lives in *middle-income countries* (the lower and upper middle categories combined), which include a wide variety of nations, among them former Soviet states like Armenia and Belarus; South and Central American states like Brazil and Belize; Middle Eastern countries like Lebanon and Iran; Asian states such as Indonesia, India, and China; and African countries like Morocco and Senegal. Many of these countries are on a path to economic diversification and development, although most also started down the road to urbanization and industrialization much later than the high-income countries and still lag in instituting mass education. Some middle-income countries, like those in the Middle East and Africa, are home to vast natural resources, even though the conversion of those resources to shared prosperity has, for reasons that theorists and observers debate, not been widespread.

Like high-income countries, *low-income countries* constitute a relatively small proportion of the global total. Many are agricultural states with rapidly growing populations. Although urbanization is a growing phenomenon, cities in these countries often lack the jobs and services that rural migrants seek, and both rural and urban dwellers struggle with hunger and malnutrition, economic and educational deprivation, and preventable diseases. Low-income countries may have small and wealthy groups of elites, but they lack stable middle-class populations. Low-income countries include South Asian states like Bangladesh and Cambodia, as well as Africa's poorest countries, like Somalia and the Central African Republic.

In the remainder of this section, we describe some ways in which inequalities are manifested around the globe. Later in the chapter, we consider the key question of *why* this inequality exists and persists and examine various theoretical perspectives on the issue.

We begin with a look at **gross national income–purchasing power parity per capita (GNI-PPP)**, a comparative economic measure that uses international dollars to indicate the amount of goods and services someone could buy in the United States with a given amount of money. At one end of the class spectrum, we find countries with very high GNI-PPP, such as the United States ($56,430), Canada ($43,970), Norway ($64,590), Germany ($48,260), and Japan ($38,870). In the middle are countries ranging from Botswana ($15,600) and Estonia ($27,510) to Turkey ($19,360) and Brazil ($15,020). At the bottom are countries whose GNI-PPP can be as low as that of Nicaragua ($4,670), Senegal ($2,390) or Gambia ($1,580; Population Reference Bureau, 2016). Although GNI-PPP cannot tell us a great deal about the resources of individual families in the given countries, it gives us some insight into the economic resources available to the state and society from a macro perspective, and it offers a comparative measure for looking at stratification in the global system.

HUNGER, MORTALITY, AND FERTILITY IN POOR COUNTRIES

As we saw in our discussion of social stratification in the United States, one important indicator of inequality is health. One key aspect of good health is adequate food, in terms of both sufficient calories and basic nutrition. Although the world has the capacity to produce enough food for all its inhabitants, the United Nations (2015) estimates that 795,000 million people are chronically undernourished, and over 90 million children under age 5 are "dangerously underweight." At the turn of the millennium, the United Nations set as a goal the substantial reduction of hunger around the globe. In fact, data suggest that there have been marked improvements in access to adequate food supplies in many of the world's regions, most notably in those that have experienced rapid economic growth, including parts of Southeast Asia and Central and South America. At the same time, hunger has increased in other areas, including sub-Saharan Africa.

An important cause of hunger at the household level is poverty; many of those who lack sufficient food do not have the economic resources to acquire it. Subsistence farmers in developing countries, many of whom survive from season to season on their own small-scale crop yields, are vulnerable to weather events and natural disasters that can push their families into destitution and starvation. Hunger at a community level is more complex. Although entire communities may suffer poverty and malnutrition,

Gross national income–purchasing power parity per capita (GNI-PPP): A comparative economic measure that uses international dollars to indicate the amount of goods and services someone could buy in the United States with a given amount of money.

large-scale hunger is often the outcome of political decisions or armed conflicts. In 2016, for example, the government of Bashar al-Assad in Syria continued to impede the delivery of food supplies to civilians in areas held by his opponents in the Syrian civil war that has raged since 2011: By one estimate, over 270,000 have been killed in the war (Al Jazeera, 2016). Millions more have been displaced, fleeing Syria for safer shores. Many of those left behind are the victims of hunger, which some, including the Secretary General of the United Nations, Ban Ki-moon, claim are being used by al-Assad as a weapon of war (Melvin, Walsh, & Hume, 2016). Regardless of the causes of hunger, the costs of undernourishment are serious and often lasting: By one estimate, fully 25% of all children younger than age 5 are stunted—that is, their growth progression is impaired—by lack of access to adequate nutrition (United Nations International Children's Emergency Fund [UNICEF], 2013).

Infant mortality rate: The number of deaths of infants younger than age 1 per 1,000 live births per year.

In evaluating global health, we can also compare across countries the **infant mortality rate**—that is, *the number of deaths of infants younger than age 1 per 1,000 live births per year.* This figure gives some insight into the health status of populations, and of women and children in particular, because infant mortality rates are lowest in states that offer access to safe pre- and antenatal care and sanitary childbirth facilities, as well as good nutrition during pregnancy. Consider the vast differences in the infant mortality rates among categories of countries: In 2014, the most developed countries had an infant mortality rate of just 5 per 1,000 live births. By contrast, the less developed countries had a rate of 44 per 1,000 live births and the least developed countries posted a rate of 62 per 1,000 live births. Across specific countries, rates vary from lows in countries such as Sweden (2.2) and Austria (3.0) to highs such as those in Haiti (42), Pakistan (69), and Angola (95; Population Reference Bureau, 2015).

Global health indicators like infant and child mortality rates are linked not only to income differences *between countries* but also to income stratification *within countries.* Data suggest that those countries with highly

TABLE 7.2 Global Inequality Indicators, 2016

	GNI-PPP	Total Fertility Rate	Infant Mortality Rate per 1,000 Live Births	Percentage Undernourished
World	$15,415	2.5	36	11%
By Level of Development				
More Developed	$39,963	1.7	5	<5.0%
Less Developed	$10,214	2.6	39	12.9%
Least Developed	$2,424	4.3	59	26.7%
By Specific Country				
United States	$56,430	1.8	5.8	<5.0%
France	$40,470	1.9	3.5	<5.0%
Mexico	$17,150	2.2	13	<5.0%
China	$14,160	1.6	11	9.3%
Jordan	$10,740	3.5	16	<5.0%
Yemen	$3,660	4.2	43	26.1%
Niger	$950	7.6	56	9.5%

SOURCE: Population Reference Bureau. (2017). *2017 World Population Data Sheet.* Source on undernourishment: Food and Agriculture Organization of the United Nations.

unequal distribution of income also experience highly variable health outcomes. For instance, in Cambodia, which is deeply stratified by income, among the top fifth of income earners the infant mortality rate is 23 per 1,000 live births, while for those in the bottom fifth, the rate is 77 per 1,000 live births (Population Reference Bureau, 2013).

Our discussion of health may also be linked to the issue of fertility. Demographers measure **total fertility rate (TFR)**, which is *the average number of children a woman in a given country will have in her lifetime if age-specific fertility rates hold throughout her childbearing years* (ages 15–49). We can use this measure to look at childbearing over space and time. It is notable that many of the world's poorest countries have the highest fertility rates. For example, although the TFR is 1.7 in Norway, 1.5 in Germany, 1.5 in Japan, and 1.8 in the United States, rates in the least developed countries remain high. In 2016, some of the world's highest TFRs were found in Chad (6.4), Mozambique (5.9), Nigeria (5.5), and Afghanistan (5.3; Population Reference Bureau, 2017).

What sociological factors help explain differences in fertility? One factor is the link between infant and child mortality and fertility: In regions or countries where early child survival is threatened by disease, poverty, or other risks, families may choose to have more children to ensure that some survive into adulthood to contribute to the household and care for elderly parents, particularly in countries without social welfare supports for retirees. Second, it has been said that children are a poor man's riches—indeed, in many agricultural economies, many hands are needed to do work, and children are active contributors to a family's economic well-being. Economic modernization correlates historically with drops in fertility (see Chapter 17 for a fuller discussion of this topic). As well, where a lack of access to maternal and child health care is common, there may also be little access to safe, effective contraceptives that would enable women to control their fertility. In Nigeria, for instance, which has a TFR of 6.0, less than 10% of women use modern contraceptive methods (Population Reference Bureau, 2013).

EDUCATION MATTERS

In most developed countries, nearly all young people complete primary school, and most move on to high school. In less developed states, access to education is more limited, and the opportunity to go to school may be affected by a spectrum of factors. In some countries and communities, girls are discouraged or even prevented from attending school by economic or cultural factors. In others, school fees present obstacles to poor families who cannot afford to enroll their children. Sometimes schools and teachers are themselves not available because of the presence of armed conflict or the absence of communities that could sustain them.

A study by UNESCO (2015a) found that in 2013, about 124 million adolescents and children worldwide were out of school. Although many children do not attend school because of armed conflicts in their countries or regions, many of those not in school are, according to UNESCO, unlikely to ever attend school. For instance, an estimated 80% of West and South African girls who are out of school now will never attend. The figure for boys is considerably lower: 16%. Even where schools are available in poor countries, the quality of education is lacking: UNESCO (2014b) reports that about 250 million children are without basic literacy and numeracy skills, although about half of them have completed at least 4 years of school. Inadequate teacher preparation may combine with overcrowding—the African state of Malawi reported an average of 130 children in a grade 1 classroom—and lack of textbooks to render efforts to educate children ineffective.

Uneducated or poorly educated children pass into adulthood without basic skills. Literacy and numeracy skills not achieved in the years of primary school are rarely achievable in adulthood in developing countries, which have not established a tradition of adult education. UNESCO (2015b) estimates that in 2013 there were 757 million fully illiterate adults worldwide, about two thirds of whom were women, although data show steady improvement across regions.

Education improves the lives of communities and families in a multitude of ways. UNESCO (2014b) estimates that, on the global level, a year of school can equal a 10% boost in income. Education benefits both those who work for wages, by improving skills, and those who farm, by increasing access to knowledge about effective, efficient farming methods. Education also helps workers to avoid exploitation and better advocate for their interests. Apart from opening up broader avenues for economic advancement, better education is also linked to positive health outcomes. This relationship is particularly strong for women's education and child health outcomes. Research

Total fertility rate (TFR): The average number of children a woman in a given country will have in her lifetime if age-specific fertility rates hold throughout her childbearing years.

Wealth and Poverty on the Road

REUTERS/Finbarr O'Reilly (CHAD)

How did you get to your sociology class today? Perhaps you walked from your dormitory, or maybe you took a bus or the subway to the campus. You may have driven a car or ridden your bicycle from home or work. How did you reach your last vacation destination? Did you fly, drive, or maybe take the train? Did you go by ship? There are many ways in which we reach the places we need or want to go—school, a job, the doctor's office, the mall, an amusement park, a friend's home. The means people choose—or are compelled by circumstances to use—to get where they are going can tell us something about their economic conditions as well. Consider the following two stories.

According to an article in the *New York Times*: "If you wish and are a person of means, you can fly first-class round trip in luxury between Los Angeles and Dubai on an Emirates Airline A380 superjumbo jet. You will enjoy superb food and drink and be cosseted in a private compartment with a sliding door, a lie-flat seat with mattress, a vanity, a personal minibar and flat-screen television set, and a luxury bathroom down the aisle where you can take a shower. The fare: $32,840" (Sharkey, 2014, para. 4). The article points out that in the middle of the 20th century, flying was often luxurious, but it was largely limited to the very few passengers who could afford air travel in its early days. By the 1970s, more Americans had economic access to air travel as fares fell, but the level of airborne comfort became increasingly stratified in the decades that followed. The article notes that "technology, including elaborate premium cabin and in-flight entertainment innovations, began more sharply delineating first and business class from coach when British Airways and Virgin Atlantic introduced lie-flat beds in luxurious new international business-class cabins in the mid-'90s" (para. 8). Today, "premium passengers" account for just over 8% of the share of fliers; the rest share the increasingly cramped quarters of economy class high in the sky.

On the ground, 30,000 feet below the jets crisscrossing the world's oceans and continents, many communities are unable to meet even the most basic transportation needs. According to a report by World Bank researchers, women in particular struggle across much of the developing world with finding safe, reliable, and affordable transportation: "Women in most developing countries have very limited access to transport services and technology. This imposes severe constraints on their access to health, education and other social facilities and services, making them and their children more vulnerable to serious injury or death as a result of childbirth or another medical emergency" (Riverson, Kunieda, Roberts, Lewi, & Walker, 2006, p. 2). Among the problems encountered by women are lack of access even to donkeys, mules, or wheelbarrows to carry water or firewood: "Consequently the women experienced not only the physical burden of transportation by back loading and head loading but also the time burden as a result of the lack of transport" (p. 4). Amnesty International (2014) has focused a campaign on rural South African women whose lack of access to transportation puts them at greater risk of illness or injury, as it limits their ability to reach health providers or shelter from gender-based violence.

THINK IT THROUGH

▶ What is the relationship between access—or lack of access—to transport services and poverty in developing countries? Can you think of ways in which expanded global access to technology like mobile phones might contribute to addressing this problem?

has documented a positive correlation between maternal education (even at the primary level) and decreased risk of child mortality (Glewwe, 1999; LeVine, LeVine, Schnell-Anzola, Rowe, & Dexter, 2012). For instance, a study on Nigeria found that better reading skills among mothers were linked to lower rates of child mortality (Smith-Greenaway, 2013). Other work has suggested that greater maternal education translates into a greater probability that a woman's children will be educated (UNESCO, 2014b).

Significant strides have been made in many countries and regions in recent decades in educating young people, and women in particular, but much remains to be done. Even today, an estimated 115 million young people around the globe ages 15 to 24 are unable to read or write a sentence (UNESCO, 2015b).

What explains global inequality? Sociologists and other social scientists have addressed this question and we discuss their perspectives below.

THEORETICAL PERSPECTIVES ON GLOBAL INEQUALITY

In this section we analyze global inequality from several theoretical perspectives, raising the questions of what explains global inequality and why it exists and persists. Later, we take a critical look at the theories.

Modernization theory is *a market-oriented development theory* associated with the work of Walt Rostow (1961) and others. In contrast to many perspectives on stratification, the modernization perspective asks not why some countries are poor but why some countries are rich. In asking this question, it makes the assumption that the historical norm in states has been poverty; that is, the populations of most countries at most times have subsisted rather than prospered. The answer it proposes is that affluent states have "modern" institutions, markets, and worldviews; by "modern," Rostow meant those that emulate the democratic and capitalist states of the West. He argued that economically underdeveloped states can progress if they adopt Western institutions, markets, and worldviews. Rostow used the analogy of an airplane taking flight to illustrate his key ideas about the stages of development:

- **The traditional stage:** In this "pre-Newtonian" (that is, prescientific) stage, societies are present and past time oriented, looking back into history for models of economic and political behavior rather than looking forward and seeking new models. They embrace tradition over innovation. Economic development is limited by low rates of savings and investment, and by a work orientation that elevates subsistence over ambition and prosperity. The airplane is grounded and has not yet begun its journey to affluence. Today, few such countries exist. One might look at individual communities within developing countries to find these traditional orientations.

Modernization theory: A market-oriented development theory that envisions development as evolutionary and guided by "modern" institutions, practices, and cultures.

In some developing countries, however, traditional beliefs about women's roles hinder their educational attainment and access to the labor market. Arguably, this is a cultural norm that also stifles national development, as it keeps a segment of the population that could potentially constitute half the workforce (women) from contributing its talents and skills.

- **The takeoff stage:** In this stage, societies are moving away from traditional cultural norms, practices, and institutions and are embracing economic development with a sense of purpose and increasing practices of savings and investment. The plane rises as the weight of tradition is cast overboard in favor of modernity.

Rostow, an originator of modernization theory, was an adviser to President Kennedy, whose administration was responsible for the development of the Peace Corps. The Peace Corps, which has for decades sent young U.S. workers abroad to spread innovations in agriculture and technology, to teach English, and to train leaders in developing countries in methods of modern governance, could be seen as a vehicle for moving countries from the traditional to the takeoff stage. Today, some African countries with modernity-oriented leadership, such as Liberia, might be categorized as members of the "takeoff" group.

- **In flight with technological progress and cultural modernity:** In this next stage, as the plane moves forward, technology is spreading to areas like agriculture and industry, innovation is increasing, and resistance to change is declining. Many people are adopting "modern" cultural values, and governance increasingly reflects the rule of law. Advanced countries facilitate these processes by offering advice and money.

Progress may take the form of industrialization, which drives greater urbanization as rural dwellers leave poor agricultural areas to seek their fortunes in cities. It may also be accompanied by lower fertility, driven by the increased use of contraception as opportunities for women grow in education and the labor market. India might be considered a modern example of this stage, as it has a growing educated middle class, rising urbanization and industrialization, and (for better or worse) soaring consumer ambitions.

- **The stage of high mass consumption and high living standards:** In this stage, there is a greater emphasis on the satisfaction of consumer desires, as new affluence expands the ranks of those with disposable income. This is the stage that advanced countries like those of Western and Northern Europe, the United States, Israel, and Japan have reached.

As these stages suggest, modernization theory assumes we can understand a given state's level of development by looking at its political, economic, and social institutions and its cultural orientation. That is, the theory uses a country's *internal variables* as key measuring sticks. In contrast, two later theories take a conflict perspective, focusing on countries' conflicting interests, unequal resources, and exploitative relationships, although they emphasize different aspects of inequality.

Just as Marx posited a fundamentally exploitative relationship between the bourgeoisie and the proletariat, so too does **dependency theory** (Emmanuel, 1972; Frank, 1966, 1979; Ghosh, 2001), which argues that *the poverty of some countries is a consequence of their exploitation by wealthy states, which control the global capitalist system.* Although exploitation originated in colonial relationships, when powerful Western states such as Britain, the Netherlands, and Belgium dominated countries such as the Congo, South Africa, and India, it continues through the modern vehicle of multinational corporations that reap great profits from the cheap labor and raw materials of poor countries while local populations draw only bare subsistence from their human and natural resources.

Dependency theory draws its name from the idea that prices on the global market for human and natural resources held by poor states are intentionally kept low to benefit high-income states, so low-income states cannot fully develop industrially, technologically, or economically. Thus, these states remain in a *dependency relationship* with the well-off states that buy and exploit their labor and raw materials. Whereas modernization theory implies that high-income states want to encourage the full development of low-income countries, dependency theory suggests there is a direct relationship between the affluence of one and the poverty of the other.

Dependency theory: The theory that the poverty of some countries is a consequence of their exploitation by wealthy states, which control the global capitalist system.

World systems theory shares some of these basic ideas. Immanuel Wallerstein (1974, 1974/2011a, 1980/2011b, 1989/2011c, 2011d), one of the pioneers of the theory, argues that *the global capitalist economic system has long been shaped by a few powerful economic actors, who have constructed it in a way that favors their class interests.* He suggests that the world economy is populated by three key categories of countries:

- **Core countries:** The core countries are economically advanced, technologically sophisticated, and home to well-educated, skilled populations. They control the vast majority of the world's wealth and reap the greatest benefits from the world economic order, including trade and production practices. They include the United States, Canada, the states of Western and Northern Europe, and Japan, among others.
- **Peripheral countries:** The peripheral states have low national incomes and low levels of technological and industrial development; many still depend on agriculture. They have been exploited by the core states for their cheap labor (and, historically, slave labor) and for cheap raw materials that are exported to advanced countries and made into finished goods that bring far greater profit to core companies and consumers. Peripheral countries include parts of Central and Latin America, Asia, and many of sub-Saharan Africa's states. Some of those in Africa provide the critical mineral components of modern electronics for which consumers pay top dollar, such as smartphones and iPads, but they still suffer dire poverty.
- **Semiperipheral states:** The semiperiphery shares some characteristics with both the core and peripheral states, occupying an intermediate and sometimes stabilizing position between them. Semiperipheral states such as China, India, and Brazil may be exploited by core states, but they may in turn have the capacity to exploit the resources of peripheral states. For example, China, which has advanced industrial capacity and a growing middle class of consumers, has begun to foster economic relationships with African countries that can offer oil resources for the populous and economically growing state.

World systems theory sees the world as dynamic rather than as static, with peripheral and semiperipheral states seeking to rise in the ranks and core countries attempting to hold fast to global power. The key unit of analysis in world systems theory is less individual countries (as it is in modernization theory) than it is relationships between countries and regions of the world. Like dependency theory, world systems theory sees relationships between states, such as those between core and periphery states, as fundamentally exploitative; that is, some countries benefit to the detriment of others.

Below we use these perspectives to examine the case of Nigeria, a developing African country. Application of the perspectives will help us to assess their utility as analytical tools for understanding development and global inequality.

APPLYING THE THEORIES: THE CASE OF NIGERIAN OIL WEALTH

A *National Geographic* story on the Niger Delta begins like this:

> Oil fouls everything in southern Nigeria. It spills from the pipelines, poisoning soil and water. It stains the hands of politicians and generals, who siphon off its profits. It taints the ambitions of the young, who will try anything to scoop up a share of the liquid riches—fire a gun, sabotage a pipeline, kidnap a foreigner.
>
> Nigeria had all the makings of an uplifting tale: poor African nation blessed with enormous sudden wealth. . . . By the mid-1970s, Nigeria had joined OPEC (Organization of Petroleum Exporting Countries), and the government's budget bulged with petrodollars. (O'Neill, 2007, para. 1–2)

Using the case of Nigeria and its vast oil reserves in the southern Niger Delta, we can evaluate the theories we have just described and compare how well they illuminate the case of Nigeria, a country with a per capita GNI-PPP of just $5,800 (Population Reference Bureau, 2017).

Recall that the modernization perspective highlights internal variables such as the lack of modern state, economic, and legal institutions and inadequately modern cultures to explain why some countries have lagged in

World systems theory: The theory that the global capitalist economic system has long been shaped by a few powerful economic actors, who have ordered it in a way that favors their interests.

development. A modernization theorist would thus point to the rampant culture of corruption and lack of rule of law that have characterized countries like Somalia and North Korea, which Transparency International (2011), a corruption watchdog agency, has ranked as the most corrupt countries in the world. Nigeria is also near the top of the agency's list. Clearly, there are links between state corruption, the lack of an effective legal and civic structure, and the dire poverty in and around Port Harcourt. Although it is the capital of Nigeria's oil-rich River State, Port Harcourt has "no electricity, no clean water, no medicine, no schools" (O'Neill, 2007, para. 5). But does the modernization perspective miss some key aspects of the problem of global poverty?

Critics argue that in attending almost exclusively to internal variables, the modernization perspective fails to recognize external obstacles to development and the ways in which well-off states benefit from the inferior economic position of poor states. According to *National Geographic,* in the wake of independence from colonial Britain, few observers expected that Nigeria would become a global oil source. In the decades that followed, however, five multinational oil companies—Royal Dutch Shell, Total, Italy's Agip, ExxonMobil, and Chevron—transformed the Rivers state. "The imprint: 4,500 miles . . . of pipelines, 159 oil fields, and 275 flow stations" (O'Neill, 2007, para. 5). This massive oil infrastructure continues to leave a significant environmental footprint in the area. According to Amnesty International (2015),

> Royal Dutch Shell and the Italian multinational oil giant ENI have admitted to more than 550 oil spills in the Niger Delta last year, according to an Amnesty International analysis of the companies' latest figures. By contrast, on average, there were only 10 spills a year across the whole of Europe between 1971 and 2011. (para. 1)

The United Nations Development Programme and the International Crisis Group point to decades of problematic economic strategies employed by oil companies, which have taken advantage of weak environmental controls, offered little compensation for land and few employment opportunities to local communities, engaged in corrupt deals for oil, and used private security forces to commit violence against those who resisted their efforts to control the oil fields of the Niger Delta (Brock & Cocks, 2012; O'Neill, 2007).

From the dependency and world systems perspectives, a relationship of fundamental exploitation exists between Nigeria and high-income countries, including the United States and Britain, for which Nigeria provides a critically important resource. If the United States is a core state, Nigeria appears from this perspective a peripheral state supplying oil, the basic raw building block of modern economies, without seeing the benefit of its own natural wealth. Semiperipheral states aggressively seeking to develop their own economies and wealth are also part of the picture: "China, India, and South Korea, all energy-hungry, have begun buying stakes in Nigeria's offshore [oil] blocks" (O'Neill, 2007, para. 10). The dependency theory perspective suggests that developed and rapidly developing states benefit from lax government oversight of environmental pollution, low-wage pools of local labor, and corruptible officials willing to bend rules to accommodate corporate wishes.

REUTERS/Akintunde Akinleye

Friedrich Stark/Alamy

Port Harcourt, located in Nigeria's River State, is a key exporter of crude oil. Despite the region's valuable natural resources, many citizens in the region still face extreme hardship, including poverty, and environmental threats.

Class and Inequality

Motion: Gentrification is reviving urban neighborhoods in the United States that have suffered from poverty and crime.

Background

Gentrification is a term used to describe a process of commercial and residential rehabilitation of an economically distressed urban neighborhood. Gentrification is characterized by the movement of wealthier residents and new shops and restaurants into a neighborhood, often leading to changes in the cost and value of housing, as well as the neighborhood culture. Gentrification in some cities, including Washington, D.C., and New York City, has also changed the racial composition of neighborhoods, with White residents moving in while some Black and Hispanic residents leave. Gentrification in U.S. cities has both avid supporters and detractors.

Affirmative Arguments

- Gentrification leads to rehabilitation of old housing stock and new housing development. The infrastructure in poor neighborhoods is further improved with new shops, restaurants, and other businesses moving in.
- Gentrification is associated with a reduction in violent crimes in a neighborhood.
- Gentrification improves the tax base of a city, as it contributes to rising property values in an economically developing neighborhood.

Opposition Arguments

- Gentrification leads to an increase in rents and home prices. This may lead to the displacement of low-income families. Existing rental units may be replaced by luxury housing that long-time residents cannot afford.
- Gentrification hurts local businesses that do not cater to the desires of new residents.
- Gentrification changes the character of neighborhoods, as long-term residents and their historical and cultural knowledge and institutions are overtaken by new inhabitants and their practices and preferences.

Questions for Consideration

- Can the benefits of gentrification be realized while minimizing its consequences? If so, how?
- Should local and/or state governments subsidize the gentrification of poor neighborhoods through tax credits or other policies? Should subsidies be contingent upon conditions like the maintenance or production of low-income housing in the neighborhood?
- Can gentrification contribute to economically and racially integrated neighborhoods that have positive benefits for residents and cities?

Debate Tip

▶ Listen carefully to the arguments made by your teammates. Build on them, but don't repeat them.

Like modernization theory, the dependency and world systems theoretical perspectives illuminate some aspects of the case while obscuring others. Variables like the exploitative power of Western oil companies are a key part of understanding the failure of Nigeria to develop in a way that benefits the broader population, but conflict-oriented perspectives pay little attention to the agency of poor states and, in particular, their governing bodies in setting a solid foundation for development.

WHY STUDY INEQUALITY IN THE UNITED STATES AND AROUND THE WORLD?

Many people today struggle to make ends meet on wages that have stagnated in recent decades. As we saw in this chapter's opening story, the downward mobility of many in the U.S. middle class is spawning new investor interest in market sectors like low-cost trailer parks. We looked at the dimensions of both class and inequality in the United States and asked why inequality exists and persists.

The questions raised by the theoretical perspectives we have studied are not just academic: They are critical to our understanding of the world in which we live and in which (if we so choose) we will raise our children. Is it the case, as functionalists Davis and Moore asserted, that inequality is positively functional for society, and that we collectively benefit from it because it ensures that the best and brightest take the most important jobs? Or, as Tumin argued, does inequality ensure just the opposite, limiting the discovery of the full range of talent in society? How much should we worry about inequality and its growth? The answer may depend on whether we subscribe to the functionalist or the conflict view of socioeconomic stratification.

What about poverty? Poverty in individual cases may be the result of bad luck or poor choices, but the sheer magnitude of the problem of poverty suggests that it has structural roots as well, and a full explanation cannot be found at the individual level. Neighborhood poverty, as we have seen, is also a key public issue, although it is certainly experienced as a personal trouble, even by residents of poor neighborhoods who are not poor. Why does poverty exist and persist in a country that is arguably the wealthiest in the world? This is a question that asks us to fire up our sociological imaginations.

As we have learned in this chapter, global poverty also exists across different areas; it is rarely only a disparity of income that characterizes poverty. Economic disadvantage is a product but also a root of other disadvantages in areas like health and education. At the global level, we find countries arranged in a stratified hierarchy of positions, with some exercising economic, political, and cultural dominance and others lagging behind, unable to convert valued human and natural resources into national prosperity. What accounts for these differences? Sociology offers us some insights—it's up to us to study different cases and to test a variety of explanations.

Global inequality matters because in an ever more densely populated, interconnected, and interdependent world, the misfortunes and good fortunes of different countries and classes will not remain isolated in their effects.

WHAT CAN I DO WITH A SOCIOLOGY DEGREE?

Community Resource And Service Skills

Community resource competencies link knowledge of nonprofit, government, and private community resources with the skills to access appropriate services

LEARNING OBJECTIVES

8.1 Describe how sociologists understand race and ethnicity

8.2 Describe different types of minority and dominant group relations in history and today

8.3 Discuss theoretical approaches to the concepts of ethnicity, racism, and minority status

8.4 Distinguish between prejudice, stereotyping, and discrimination

8.5 Identify major racial and ethnic groups in the United States

8.6 Define genocide and its relationship to national, ethnic, racial, or religious group membership

Robert Alexander/Contributor/Getty Images

WHAT DO YOU THINK?

1. What makes a group a "minority"? Does this term have both qualitative and quantitative dimensions?
2. Why does racial residential segregation exist and persist in major U.S. cities? What are the consequences of racial residential segregation?
3. How is the ethnic and racial composition of the United States changing?

Rolls Press/Popperfoto/Getty Images

AP Photo/John Bazemore, File

ATHLETES STAND FOR RACIAL EQUALITY

The United States is a country that loves sports and idolizes its greatest athletes. Some of those talented athletes are among those who have used their status and visibility to draw attention to racial inequality.

Jackie Robinson was the first African American baseball player in the major leagues, joining the Brooklyn Dodgers at first base in 1947. Robinson was a player of exceptional talent, which helped him gain acceptance in the ranks of White-dominated Major League Baseball, although he was still subject to racism. Robinson was a tireless advocate for racial equality. When Robinson retired and took a senior position at the Chock Full O'Nuts company, he used his power to advocate for fair wages for Black workers in the company. At his final public appearance in 1972, Robinson declared in an award acceptance speech at the World Series that he would be even more proud of Major League Baseball if he looked over toward third base and saw an African American coach: The first Black MLB manager, Frank Robinson, took that position in 1975. Although Jackie Robinson was one of the first prominent Black athletes to use his status to take a stand against racial inequality, he was not by any means alone.

After medaling in the 200 meter race at the 1968 Olympic Games in Mexico City, U.S. team members Tommie Smith and John Carlos famously raised their fists in a Black power salute to protest the treatment of African Americans (Cosgrove, 2014). They stood on the podium as the U.S. national anthem played with their fists raised and shoeless, wearing black socks to symbolize the struggle of Black poverty. In response to what was construed as a political action, the International Olympic Committee expelled Smith and Carlos from the games. Smith later reflected on the moment, saying that "if I win, I am American, not a black American. But if I did something bad, then they would say 'a Negro.' We are black and we are proud of being black. Black America will understand what we did tonight" (BBC, 2005).

Contemporary athletes have also used their visibility to bring attention to Black community issues. In December 2014, Cleveland Cavaliers basketball players LeBron James and Kyrie Irving entered the team warm-up against the Brooklyn Nets wearing t-shirts emblazoned with the words "I can't breathe." Four players from the opposing team wore them as well. The words were the last ones uttered by Eric Garner, a Staten Island man who died in July of that year in a confrontation with a New York City police officer. Eric Garner was the fourth unarmed African American man to die in a confrontation with police in August 2014 (Harkinson, 2014). James told reporters that "as a society we have to do better. We have to be better for one another no matter what race you are" (Strauss & Scott, 2014, para. 14).

During the 2016–2017 National Football League season, San Francisco 49ers quarterback Colin Kaepernick made the decision to kneel rather than stand when the national anthem was played at the start of a game. Kaepernick chose to take a knee, he said, to protest police brutality against minorities. He noted that, "To me, this is bigger than football and it would be selfish on my part to look the other way" (Barr, 2017, para. 8). Inspired by Kaepernick, several other NFL players did the same. Some observers suggest that Kaepernick's refusal to stand for the anthem and the criticism that evoked from some fans and commentators is the reason he remained unsigned to a team at the start of the 2017–2018 season (Barr 2017).

From the time Jackie Robinson integrated the MLB to the time NBA and NFL players launched their recent protest actions, there has been important progress, including better access to education, stronger political and social voice, and expanded legal protections for minorities. At the same time, race—and racism—continues to shape opportunities and obstacles in the United States. Black athletes are among those who continue to take a stand for equality. ■

Race and ethnicity are key issues in sociology. We begin this chapter with a discussion of the sociological definitions of race and ethnicity. We then consider some of the forms that minority–majority group relations have taken in history and today. Next we look at theoretical perspectives on ethnicity, racism, and minority group status. This leads to a discussion of prejudice, discrimination, and stereotypes and various manifestations and consequences of these social phenomena. We then examine the experiences of different racial and ethnic groups in the United States and how group membership may shape people's political, economic, and social status. Finally, we talk about genocide as a race-based atrocity that continues to claim new victims in the 21st century.

THE SOCIAL CONSTRUCTION OF RACE AND ETHNICITY

Sociologists W. I. Thomas and Dorothy Thomas (1928) observed that "if [people] define situations as real, they are real in their consequences" (pp. 571–572). The wisdom of the Thomases' observation is powerfully demonstrated by the way societies construct definitions of race and ethnicity and then respond as though the definitions represent objective realities.

RACE

One of the most dynamic areas of scientific research in recent years has been the Human Genome Project. Among its compelling findings is the discovery that genetically all human beings are nearly identical. Less than 0.01% of the total gene pool contributes to racial differences (as manifested in physical characteristics), whereas thousands of genes contribute to traits that include intelligence, artistic and athletic talent, and social skills (Angier, 2000; Cavalli-Sforza, Menozzi, & Piazza, 1994). Based on this research, many scientists agree that "race is a *social concept,* not a *scientific* one . . . we all evolved in the last 100,000 years from the same small number of tribes that migrated out of Africa and colonized the world" (Angier, 2000, para. 6).

Sociologists define a **race** as *a group of people who share a set of characteristics (usually physical characteristics) deemed by society to be socially significant*. Notice that this definition suggests that physical characteristics are not the only—or even necessarily the most important—way of defining "races." For many years, Catholics and Protestants in Ireland defined one another as separate races, and the United States long considered Jews a separate racial category from Europeans, even though distinctive physical characteristics between these groups are in the eye of the beholder rather than objectively verifiable (Schaefer, 2009).

Although sociologists do not treat race as scientifically significant, it is, as we will see in this chapter, *socially significant*. Following the observation of the Thomases, we can conclude that because race is defined as real, it is real in its consequences. Racial differentiation has historically been linked to power: Racial categories have facilitated the treatment (or maltreatment) of others based on membership in given racial groups.

Notably, race is also social scientifically significant. Statistical data on phenomena ranging from obesity and poverty to crime and educational attainment are gathered and sorted by race. This book features such data throughout its pages. Even though sociologists generally agree that races cannot be objectively, biologically differentiated, it is a fact that they also use race to sort statistics and establish social facts about groups in society. This implicitly acknowledges that this "social concept" is profoundly real as a differentiating mechanism with historical and contemporary consequences.

ETHNICITY

Although race may be a particularly significant social category in terms of consequences for people's lives, other socially defined categorizations are also important. **Ethnicity** refers to *characteristics of groups associated with national origins, languages, and cultural and religious practices*. Although ethnicity can be based on cultural self-identification (that is, one may choose to embrace one's Irish or Brazilian roots and traditions), an acknowledgment or degree of acceptance by a larger group is often necessary. For example, a third-generation Italian American may choose to self-identify as Italian. If she cannot speak Italian, however, others who identify as Italian may not see her as "authentically" Italian. The sociological significance of belonging to a particular racial or ethnic group is that society may treat group members differently, judging them or giving them favorable or unfavorable treatment based on membership and perceived affiliation.

MINORITIES

Any racial, ethnic, religious, or other group can constitute a "minority" in a society. **Minorities** are less powerful groups who are dominated politically and economically by a more powerful group and, often, who experience discrimination on the basis of characteristics deemed by the majority to be socially significant. Minorities are usually distinguished by physical and cultural attributes that make them recognizable to the dominant group. Minorities often are fewer in number than the dominant population. In the United States, African Americans, Latinos, and Asians are less numerous than the White majority, although the higher number of births among non-Whites, combined with immigration, will begin to change this fact in coming decades.

Although both the common understanding of the term and the implied numerical difference of the term itself suggest that minorities are fewer in number than the majority, an important aspect of minority group status is that the group has relatively less access to power and resources valued by society. Thus, sociologically, women in the United States, and in most cultures worldwide, may be considered a minority despite the fact that they typically outnumber men. In South Africa before the end of apartheid rule in the early 1990s, a small number of Whites dominated the much larger minority of what were termed Black, colored, and mixed races.

MINORITY AND DOMINANT GROUP RELATIONS

Modern societies are characterized by racial and ethnic heterogeneity, as well as divisions between dominant and

Race: A group of people who share a set of characteristics (usually physical characteristics) deemed by society to be socially significant.

Ethnicity: Characteristics of groups associated with national origins, languages, and cultural and religious practices.

Minorities: Less powerful groups who are dominated by a more powerful group and, often, discriminated against on the basis of characteristics deemed by the majority to be socially significant.

FIGURE 8.1 American Indian Reservations in the Continental United States

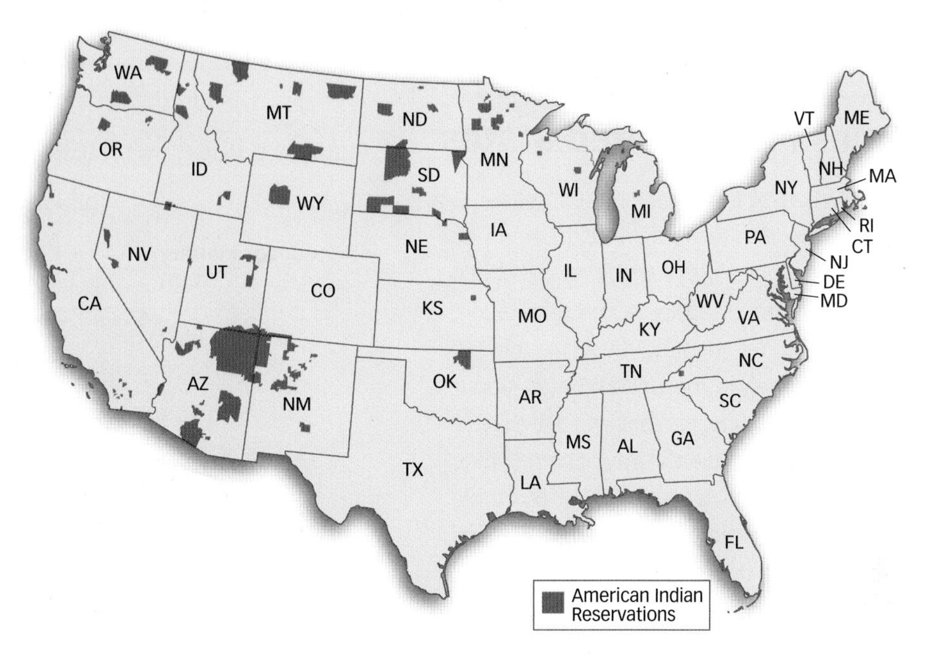

SOURCE: U.S. Parks Service.

minority groups. The coexistence of racial and ethnic groups can be a source of social conflict. Among minorities' most frequently used methods of resolving such conflict are social movements designed to challenge and change existing social relations. In extreme cases, resolution may be sought through revolution or rebellion. Dominant populations respond to such social movements with a variety of social and political policies, ranging from expulsion and segregation to assimilation of minorities and the acceptance of cultural pluralism. We discuss this spectrum of relationships between majority and minority groups below.

EXPULSION

Conflicts between White settlers and Native Americans over land and resources in the United States in the 1800s often ended with the removal of Native Americans to isolated reservations. Sociologically, *the process of forcibly removing people from one part of the country* is referred to as **expulsion**. Native Americans populated broad swaths of North America when the first European settlers arrived. As U.S. settlement expanded westward, Native Americans were driven under military arms to march, sometimes thousands of miles, to areas designated by the government as Native American reservations. These reservations continue to be socially and economically marginal areas (Figure 8.1).

Today, across the globe, people are being forced from their homes due to civil wars and ethnic and sectarian conflicts. According to recent figures from the United Nations High Commissioner for Refugees, in 2014 there were almost 60 million refugees and internally displaced people around the globe. In a global context, that means that one person in every 122 has been displaced from their home, most of those forcibly (Gaynor, 2015).

SEGREGATION

Segregation is *the practice of separating people spatially or socially on the basis of race or ethnicity.* In South Africa, apartheid was state policy until the beginning of the 1990s. The release from prison of antiapartheid activist Nelson Mandela in 1990 and the end of a ban on previously forbidden political groups began the

Expulsion: The process of forcibly removing a population from a particular area.

Segregation: The practice of separating people spatially or socially on the basis of race or ethnicity.

BEHIND THE NUMBERS

Counting—and Not Counting—Hate Crimes in the United States

The U.S. Federal Bureau of Investigation (FBI) defines a hate crime as a "criminal offense against a person or property motivated in whole or in part by an offender's bias against a race, religion, disability, sexual orientation, ethnicity, gender, or gender identity." In 2014, the FBI reported 6,418 hate crimes in the United States, about two thirds of which were against persons and one third of which were against property. The majority of hate crimes in the report were motivated by racial (47%) or ethnic (11.9%) animosity. Most of the crimes against persons were cases of intimidation or simple assault, while most property crimes were vandalism and destruction or damage of property (Federal Bureau of Investigation, 2015a).

FIGURE 8.3 Hate Crime Breakdown

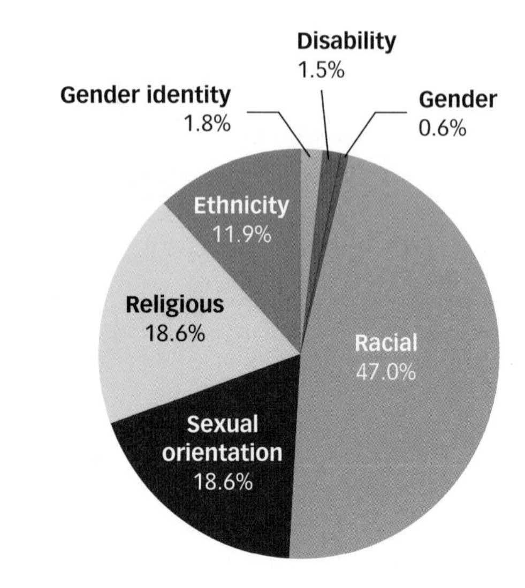

SOURCE: Federal Bureau of Investigation, 2015a.

According to a recent Associated Press report on FBI hate crimes data,

> Under FBI guidelines, an incident should be reported as a suspected hate crime if a "reasonable and prudent" person would conclude a crime was motivated by bias. Among the criteria for evaluation is whether an incident coincided with a significant holiday or date, specifically citing the King holiday. A suspect need not be identified to meet the threshold for reporting. (Cassidy, 2016, para. 12)

The filing of hate crime reports to federal authorities is voluntary, although guidelines ask that reports be submitted by local policing agencies even if the count is zero.

FBI hate crimes reports are an important source of information for policymakers, police, and the public. They offer a means for tracking trends in hate crimes. For example, even though hate crimes against African Americans, Latinos, Jews, and the LGBT community fell in the 2015 report, a growing number of hate crimes have been documented against American Muslims (Potok, 2015).

At the same time, some research suggests that FBI statistics fail to capture the full picture of hate crimes in the United States: "[Bureau of Justice Statistics] studies have found that while the FBI has reported over the last 20 years between about 6,000 and about 11,500 total hate crimes in America each year, the real annual totals in recent years have been nearly 260,000" (Potok, 2015, para. 5). Why is there a gap between FBI figures and what the Southern Poverty Law Center report calls the "real annual totals" (Potok, 2015) of hate crimes? Several factors may explain the gap.

First, the U.S. Bureau of Justice Statistics (Masucci and Langton, 2017) suggests that about half of hate crimes go unreported because victims "believed the police could not or would not help" (Langton, Planty, & Sandholtz, 2013). Second, victims may be frightened of a backlash from the community if they report hate crimes. For example,

> In recent years, members of the Sikh community have been targeted by attackers who, in some cases, confused them with Muslims because of their turbans or other head coverings. But S. Gulbarg Singh Basi, chairman of the American Sikh Council, said that some in his community

fear that reporting those incidents might invite even more hate crimes. (Cassidy, 2016, Section 3, para. 3)

Third, because reporting is voluntary, a significant number of incidents may go unreported. A recent Associated Press report points out that "more than 2,700 city police and county sheriff's departments across the country . . . have not submitted a single hate crime report for the FBI's annual crime tally during the past six years—about 17 percent of all city and county law enforcement agencies nationwide" (Cassidy, 2016, para. 4). The report highlights the case of Barbara Hicks Collins, an African American woman and daughter of a prominent civil rights leader in Louisiana who was closely involved with legal efforts to desegregate area schools. When Ms. Hicks Collins's car and home were set alight on Martin Luther King Jr. Day in 2012, she reported the case to local authorities, but the incident was never counted in the federal report of hate crimes. As the Associated Press notes, "Neither the police department nor the local sheriff has filed a hate crime report with the FBI since at least 2009" (Cassidy, 2016, para. 3). Finally, a component of labeling a hate crime is determining the existence of bias: Investigators must not only look at *what* happened but also *why* it happened, and motivation may not always be easy to discern.

Accurate documentation of hate crimes is important. Effective enforcement and policymaking depend on reliable figures. As well, full reporting of hate crimes recognizes the victims and their experiences as important. As the Associated Press story on Ms. Hicks Collins, whose home and car were burned, notes, "For Hicks Collins, the failure to count the 2012 attack as a hate crime is a painful reminder of the continuing struggle for racial progress" (Cassidy, 2016, para. 13).

THINK IT THROUGH

- This essay described several factors that may stand in the way of the collection of hate crimes statistics. How might these obstacles be addressed to foster more accurate reporting?

process of desegregation in that country, which has slowly evolved in the wake of the establishment of democracy in 1994. Apartheid was an extreme form of segregation that included not only prohibitions on where members of different racial and ethnic groups could live, but where they could travel and at what hours of the day they could be in different parts of particular cities. Although apartheid is no longer policy, the legacy of segregation lives on in many South African communities, where the White, Black, and colored populations still live separately and unequally.

Before the 1960s, segregation on the basis of race was common practice and legally upheld in many parts of the United States In some places it was a crime for Whites to rent apartments or sell homes to non-Whites (Molotch, 1972). In the South, Blacks could not sit in the same restaurants as Whites. When they rode the same buses, Blacks were required by law to sit at the back. In other parts of the country, restaurants and hotels could refuse to serve dark-skinned customers.

The civil rights movement of the 1960s succeeded in securing the passage of federal laws that outlawed segregation. Despite this success, high levels of racial segregation remain a reality in U.S. cities. Why is this the case in the post–civil rights era? First, it is legal and commonplace for housing markets to be segregated by income. Since racial minorities as a group have lower household incomes than Whites as a group, some cannot afford to live in predominantly White neighborhoods, where residents may be wealthier and housing costs higher. Second, laws outlawing the consideration of race in home rental and sale practices are not always followed by real estate agents, landlords, and lenders, who may steer minorities away from predominantly White neighborhoods

David Trnley/Corbis Historical/Getty Images.

South Africa's apartheid was a system of privilege based on race. With racial identity determining social status and access to resources in society, Whites sat atop a hierarchy of power, while Black South Africans were at the bottom.

Bettmann/Bettmann/Getty Images

In 1968, Black Memphis sanitation workers went on strike carrying placards stating "I Am a Man" in bold red letters. This phrase became an embodiment of the civil rights movement, as it showed that workers were not just fighting for better wages or working conditions, but for the recognition of their humanity.

(Squires, 2003; Squires, Friedman, & Saidat, 2002). Third, White residents sometimes move out of neighborhoods when increasing numbers of minority residents move in (Woldoff, 2011).

Notably, many cities that appear to be racially and ethnically diverse, are, in fact, highly segregated. Consider Chicago: The city's population is about 33% Black, 32% White, and 29% Hispanic (Silver, 2015). At the neighborhood level, however, segregation by race and ethnicity is dramatic (Figure 8.2). For example, Chicago's south side is largely Black: Neighborhoods like Washington Park are about 97% African American. By contrast, in the city's north, Lincoln Park neighborhoods are typically at least 80% White. To the west, the Cicero area is about 90% Hispanic (Block, Cox, & Giratiknon, 2015). Racial residential segregation remains a significant phenomenon, particularly in the larger, older cities of the Northeast and Midwest that are home to older housing stock and relatively large populations of poor minorities. Where integration has taken place, it has been limited mostly to areas with "relatively affluent and well-educated minority populations, low levels of anti-Black and anti-Latino sentiment, low rates of immigration, and permissive regimes of density zoning" (Rugh & Massey, 2014, p. 221).

Segregation has negative consequences for minority groups. Apart from denying them residential choice, it may compel them to live in poorer neighborhoods that offer less access to high-quality schools, jobs, and medical facilities (Kozol, 1995; Massey & Denton, 1993). Some of the effects of segregated neighborhoods can be seen in the significant racial and ethnic wealth gap: In 2013, White median household net worth was just under $142,000; by contrast, Black median household wealth was $11,000 and Hispanic net worth was $13,700 (Kochhar & Fry, 2014). As we noted in Chapter 7, the primary source of wealth for most working- and middle-class Americans is home equity. Lower average property values in minority neighborhoods translate to lower wealth in the community.

Poor and segregated neighborhoods and regions are also more likely to be home to hazardous waste facilities and other sources of pollution, a problem that plagues minority communities from urban Los Angeles to rural Louisiana. As an article on segregation and pollutant exposure notes,

> Studies dating back to the 1970s have pointed to a consistent pattern in who lives near the kinds of hazards—toxic waste sites, landfills, congested highways—that few of us would willingly choose as neighbors. The invariable answer: poor people and communities of color. (Badger, 2014, p. 1)

In sum, racial residential segregation contributes to the concentration of economic disadvantage. Pursuing greater opportunities, members of minority groups may seek to move to more diverse neighborhoods. Unfortunately, historically and today, powerful

FIGURE 8.2 Concentration of Whites, Blacks, and Hispanics in Chicago, 2010

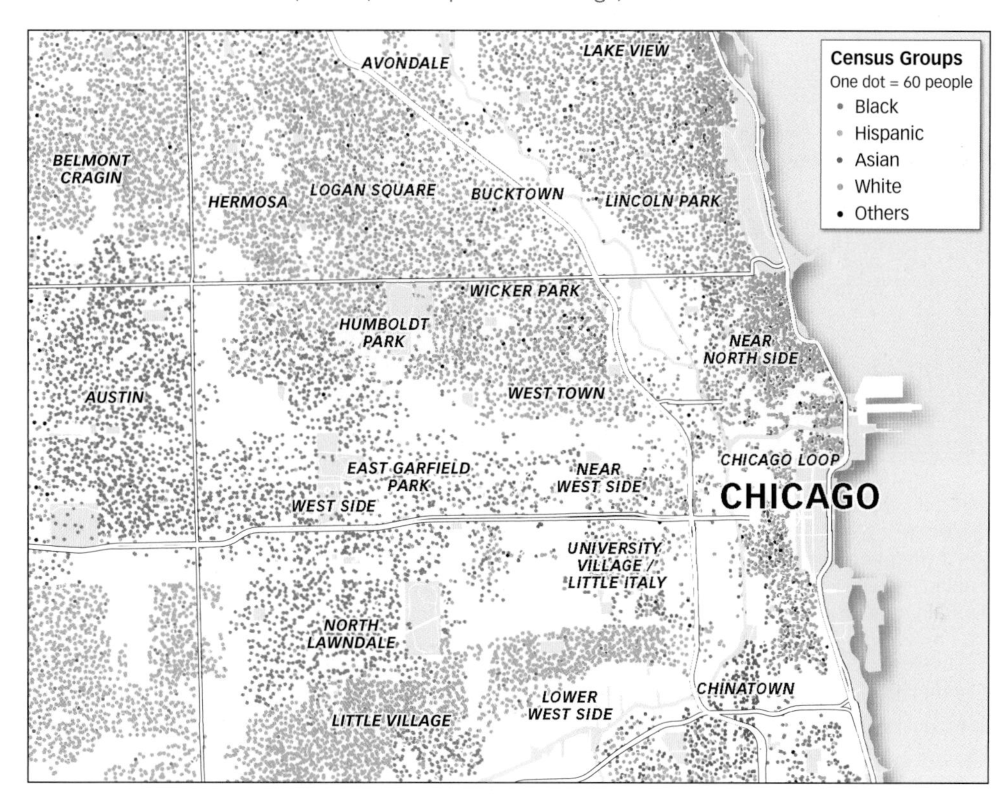

SOURCE: From "Mapping Segregation," *The New York Times,* July 8, 2015.

social forces of poverty and discrimination have kept and continue to keep many from achieving this goal.

ASSIMILATION AND CULTURAL PLURALISM

Throughout much of the 20th century, sociologists who studied minorities, race, and ethnicity assumed that the ultimate destiny of most minority groups was **assimilation**, or *absorption into the dominant culture.* U.S. citizens have long prided themselves on being part of a vast "melting pot" in which significant differences between groups gradually disappear and the population is boiled into a single cultural soup. This view was strengthened by the experience of many immigrant groups, particularly from Northern European countries, who adopted the norms, values, and folkways of the dominant culture to increase their social acceptance as well as their economic success.

Although migrant groups have historically sought to assimilate into the dominant majority group, many also want to retain their unique identities. Some American Indian nations, for example, have long sought to keep alive their own traditions and beliefs. In **cultural pluralism**, *the coexistence of different racial and ethnic groups is characterized by acceptance of one another's differences.* Such a society resembles a *salad bowl* rather than a *melting pot.* Cultural differences are respected for their contribution to the richness of society as a whole. Even though cultural pluralists criticize the forced segregation that results from prejudice and discrimination, they argue that people's continuing connections to their own ethnic communities help them to preserve their cultural heritages and, at the same time, provide networks of mutual social and economic support.

Assimilation: The absorption of a minority group into the dominant culture.

Cultural pluralism: The coexistence of different racial and ethnic groups, characterized by acceptance of one another's differences.

AP Photo/LM Otero

Families living in this West Port Arthur, Texas, public housing project are routinely exposed to the pollution generated by surrounding oil refineries. One in five households has a member with a respiratory illness (Stephenson, 2014). Those with the least political voice in society are most likely to find themselves in highly polluted residential areas.

The relative merits of assimilation and cultural pluralism remain controversial, but sociologists generally agree that the debates over these issues will continue to be a fundamental part of changing racial and ethnic relations in the modern world.

THEORETICAL APPROACHES TO ETHNICITY, RACISM, AND MINORITY STATUS

Throughout this text, we seek to highlight the ways in which key theoretical perspectives in sociology can illuminate social phenomena, including socioeconomic stratification, poverty, and deviance. In this section, we look at ethnicity, racism, and minority group status using the functionalist, conflict, and symbolic interactionist lenses.

THE FUNCTIONALIST PERSPECTIVE

One of functionalism's key assumptions is that a social phenomenon exists and persists because it serves a positive function in a community or society, contributing to order and harmony. Beginning with classical sociologists Auguste Comte and Émile Durkheim and extending to contemporary functionalist theorizing, the basic functionalist assumption is that solidarity characterizes social groupings. Durkheim believed that social groups held together by *mechanical solidarity* and based on homogeneity in, among other things, language and culture are more culturally durable than are those based on *organic solidarity,* which involves interdependence (for instance, economic interdependence). This may help us understand the cohesion of many ethnic groups in the United States. Whether they are Armenian Americans, Egyptian Americans, Cuban Americans, or some other group, people gravitate toward those who are like them, a process rooted in shared pasts and practices.

Racism: The idea that one racial group is inherently superior to another; often results in institutionalized relationships between dominant and minority groups that create a structure of economic, social, and political inequality based on socially constructed racial or ethnic categories.

It is far more challenging to apply the functionalist perspective to *racism* as a phenomenon. Racism cannot be positively functional for a community or society because, by definition, it marginalizes some members of the group. It can, however, be positively functional for some groups while being detrimental for others. Asking "How is this functional for some groups?" takes us close to the key conflict question: "Who benefits from this phenomenon or institution—and who loses?" In the next section, we examine *who benefits* from racism.

THE CONFLICT PERSPECTIVE

Consider that **racism**, *the idea that one racial or ethnic group is inherently superior to another,* offers a justification for racial inequality and associated forms of stratification such as socioeconomic inequality. If a powerful group defines itself as "better" than another group, then the unequal treatment and distribution of resources can be rationalized as acceptable—or even "natural."

Slavery in the United States was a fundamentally racist phenomenon. It was possible for Whites in the South (and many in the North) to justify the maltreatment of Blacks because they did not see Blacks as fully human.

Senator John Calhoun, who represented South Carolina and died just over a decade before the Civil War, wrote in a letter that "the African is incapable of self-care and sinks into lunacy under the burden of freedom. It is a mercy to him to give him the guardianship and protection from mental death" (quoted in Silva, 2001, p. 71). In legal terms, racism was clear in the Three-Fifths Compromise, which emerged at the Constitutional Convention in Philadelphia in 1787. Delegates from the North and South agreed that for purposes of taxation and political representation, each slave would be counted as three fifths of a person. The compromise was needed because abolitionists wanted to count only free people. Slaveholders and their supporters wanted to count slaves, whose presence would add to their states' population counts and thus their representation in Congress. Those who held slaves but did not permit them to be free or to vote still gained politically from their presence. In economic terms, slavery was of benefit to plantation owners and their families, who could reap the financial benefits of a population of workers who could be bought and sold, who could be exploited and abused, and who performed difficult and demanding work without pay.

It can be argued that capitalism and economic development in the early United States would not have been so robust without the country's reliance on an enslaved labor force, which contributed most fully to the development of a growing agricultural economy in the South. The North, too, was home to numerous beneficiaries and proponents of slavery.

After the end of slavery, racism continued to manifest in new forms, including Jim Crow laws, which followed in the decade after slavery and lasted until the middle of the 20th century. These laws legally mandated segregation of public facilities in the South and fundamentally limited Blacks' ability to exercise their rights. The schools, accommodations, and opportunities afforded to Blacks were invariably inferior to those offered to Whites. Local and state governments could therefore expend fewer funds on their Black populations, and White populations benefited from reduced competition in higher education and the labor market. Racism made Jim Crow laws both possible and widely acceptable, because it offered a justification for their existence and persistence.

Although racism is clearly of no benefit to its victims and has negative effects on society as a whole, the conflict perspective entreats us to recognize the ways in which it has been functional for more powerful groups in society.

The cognitive dissonance of espousing values of freedom, equality, and justice for all, while simultaneously maintaining an inhumane system of slave labor, required some kind of rationalization. The cruel treatment of Blacks in the era of slavery suggests that many White Americans at the time did not view them as fully human. ■

These benefits help explain the existence and persistence of racism over time.

THE SYMBOLIC INTERACTIONIST PERSPECTIVE

Sociologist Louis Wirth (1945) has noted that minority groups share particular traits. First, membership in a minority group is essentially involuntary—that is, someone is socially classified as a member of a group that is discriminated against and is not, in most instances, free to opt out. Second, as we discussed above, minority status is a question not of numbers ("minorities" may outnumber the dominant group) but rather of control of valued resources. Third, minorities do not share the full privileges of mobility or opportunity enjoyed by the dominant group. Finally,

AP Photo/David Longstreath

Many popular sports teams proudly use Native Americans as their mascots, a practice that has generated controversy. Opponents argue that the images are demeaning and promote negative stereotypes. Where do you stand on the use of Native Americans as sports mascots?

membership in the minority group conditions the treatment of group members by others in society. Specifically, Wirth states, societal minorities are "treated as members of a category, irrespective of their individual merits" (p. 349).

Wirth's definition recalls symbolic interactionist Erving Goffman's concept of a **stigma**, an attribute that is deeply discrediting to an individual or a group because it overshadows other attributes and merits the individual or group may possess. Goffman (1963b) presented the unlikely scenario of a young woman born without a nose: Although the young woman has a spectrum of interesting and engaging characteristics—she is a bright student and a good dancer—she is defined by her stigma, and her treatment by others is ever defined and determined by her "difference."

Goffman examined what he called **mixed contacts**—that is, *interactions between those who are stigmatized and those who are "normal"* (by *normal,* he meant only those who are members of the dominant, nonstigmatized group—the term was not intended to denote normality as contrasting with deviance). Goffman concluded that mixed contacts are shaped by the presence of the stigma, which influences the way each social interaction unfolds. Although the stigmatized identity may not be the point of the interaction, it is inevitably a part of it. Think about your own social interactions: Have you experienced what Goffman describes? How would you expand or modify his sociological description based on those experiences?

In the next section, we turn to issues of prejudice and discrimination, considering how our judgments about someone's race or ethnicity—or about the racial or ethnic identity of an entire group—are manifested in practice.

Stigma: An attribute that is deeply discrediting to an individual or a group because it overshadows other attributes and merits the individual or group may possess.

Mixed contacts: Interactions between those who are stigmatized and those who are "normal."

Prejudice: A belief about an individual or a group that is not subject to change on the basis of evidence.

Stereotyping: The generalization of a set of characteristics to all members of a group.

PREJUDICE, STEREOTYPING, AND DISCRIMINATION

Prejudice is *a belief about an individual or a group that is not subject to change on the basis of evidence.* Prejudices are thus inflexible attitudes toward others. Sociologist Zygmunt Bauman (2001), writing about the Holocaust, eloquently captures this idea: "Man *is* before he *acts*; nothing he does may change what he is. That is, roughly, the philosophical essence of racism" (p. 60). Recall Wirth's point about the characteristics of a social minority: Membership in the disadvantaged group matters more than individual merit.

When prejudices are strongly held, no amount of evidence is likely to change the belief. Among neo-Nazis, for example, prejudice against Jews runs deep. Some neo-Nazis even deny the occurrence of the Holocaust, despite clearly authentic firsthand accounts, films, and photographs of Nazi Germany's concentration camps, where millions of Jews, Roma, Soviet prisoners of war, and other victims were killed during World War II. Why do prejudicial beliefs trump evidence in cases such as Holocaust denial? Why is prejudice difficult to overcome, even with facts? We may gain some insight into these issues by looking at another social phenomenon linked to prejudice—stereotyping.

Stereotyping is *the generalization of a set of characteristics to all members of a group.* Ethnic and racial stereotypes are often produced and reproduced in popular films: Think about images in U.S. action movies of scheming Italian mafiosi, tough African American street gangs, and violent Asian gangsters or martial artists. Or consider the ways that we may attribute characteristics—intelligence, entrepreneurship, sloth, or slyness—to entire groups based on experiences with or information from others about just a few members of that group. Stereotyping offers a way for human beings to organize and categorize the social world—but the attributions we make may be deeply flawed.

David Carson/St. Louis Post-Dispatch via AP

In September 2017, protesters in St. Louis, Missouri, staged a sit-in to protest police brutality and the acquittal of a police officer charged in the shooting death of a Black man, Anthony Lamar Smith. These practices, as we saw earlier, have had a powerful effect on the wealth gap between Whites and African Americans. Because most wealth held by the U.S. middle class exists in the form of home equity, the opportunity to own a home in a neighborhood with good property values is a key way to accrue wealth. ■

From a sociological perspective, we may argue that even though stereotypes are often flawed, they are also functional for some groups—although dysfunctional for others. Consider that one of the social forces contributing to racism is the desire of one group to exploit another. Research on early contacts between Europeans and Africans suggests that negative stereotypes of Africans developed *after* Europeans discovered the economic value of exploiting African labor and the natural resources of the African continent. That is, White Europeans stereotyped Black Africans as inferior when such images suited the Europeans' need to justify enslavement and economic exploitation of this population.

Discrimination is *the unequal treatment of individuals on the basis of their membership in a group.* Discrimination is often targeted and intentional, but it may also be unintentional—in either case, it denies groups and individuals equal opportunities and blocks access to valued resources.

Sociologists distinguish between individual and institutional discrimination. **Individual discrimination** is *overt and intentional unequal treatment, often based on prejudicial beliefs.* If the manager of an apartment complex refuses to rent a place to someone on the basis of his or her skin color or an employer chooses not to hire a qualified applicant because he or she is foreign-born, that is individual discrimination. **Institutionalized discrimination** is *discrimination enshrined in law, public policy, or common practice—it is unequal treatment that has become part of the routine operation of major social institutions like businesses, schools, hospitals, and the government.* Institutionalized discrimination is particularly pernicious because, although it may be clearly targeted and intentional, it may also be the outcome of customary practices and bureaucratic decisions that result in discriminatory outcomes.

Discrimination against African Americans and women was initially institutionalized in the Constitution of the United States, which excluded members of both groups from voting and holding public office. In 1866, Congress passed the first civil rights act, giving Black men the right to vote, hold public office, use public accommodations, and serve on juries. In 1883, however, the U.S. Supreme Court declared the 1866 law unconstitutional, and states

Discrimination: The unequal treatment of individuals on the basis of their membership in a group.

Individual discrimination: Overt and intentional unequal treatment, often based on prejudicial beliefs.

Institutionalized discrimination: Unequal treatment that has become a part of the routine operation of such major social institutions as businesses, schools, hospitals, and the government.

PRIVATE LIVES, PUBLIC ISSUES

Locked Out: Poor Black Women and the Struggle of Eviction

A *New York Times* article on eviction describes a scene on a cold morning in Wisconsin:

> Shantana Smith, a single mother who had not paid rent for three months, watched on a recent morning as men from Eagle Moving carried her tattered furniture to the sidewalk.
>
> Bystanders knew too well what was happening.
>
> "When you see the Eagle movers truck, you know it's time to get going," a neighbor said.
>
> On Milwaukee's impoverished North Side, the mover's name is nearly as familiar as McDonald's, because Eagle often accompanies sheriffs on evictions. They haul tenants' belongings into storage or, as Ms. Smith preferred, leave them outside for tenants to truck away. (Eckholm, 2010, para. 1–4)

For women like Ms. Smith, eviction is a personal trouble—but it is also a public issue. After years of studying the problem, sociologist Matthew Desmond observed that "if incarceration had come to define the lives of men from impoverished black neighborhoods, eviction was shaping the lives of women. Poor black men were locked up. Poor black women were locked out" (quoted in Ehrenreich, 2016, para. 7). In Milwaukee, home to Shantana Smith, about one fifth of Black women have

■ **FIGURE 8.4** Rental Assistance Programs Reach Only a Fraction of Needy Renters

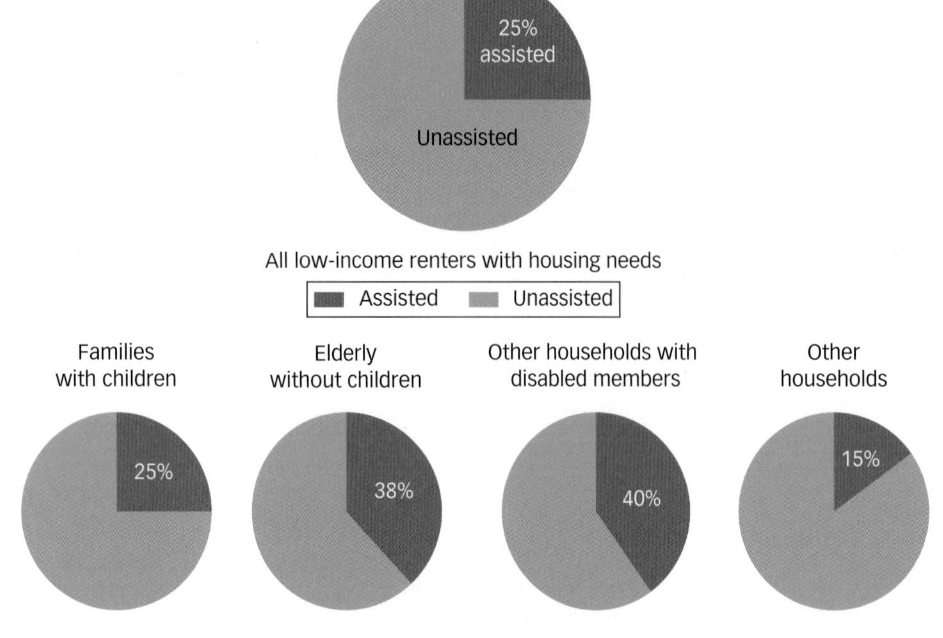

SOURCE: Reprinted with permission from Center on Budget and Policy Priorities.

NOTE: Share of households with rental assistance among those at or below 80 percent of the area median income who either: 1) receive rental assistance; or 2) are unassisted and face housing cost burdens above 30 percent of income or live in overcrowded or physically inadequate housing.

experienced eviction. A significant number have been evicted more than once (Desmond, 2016b).

Put in the simplest terms, eviction happens when there is a gap between income and rental cost: The bigger the gap, the greater the risk of eviction. It is significant that among all low-income renters with housing needs, only 25% receive rental assistance (Fischer & Sard, 2016, p.10). Although many families qualify for assistance, housing assistance budgets have not kept pace, and only a fraction can claim a place in public housing or get a housing voucher to subsidize the cost of a private rental. For the three quarters of poor renters without financial support, meeting the rent can be a significant struggle: Desmond estimates that over half of low-income renters spend more than 50% of their income on housing, and a quarter must spend over 70% of the income (Desmond, 2016a). For poor renters, every payment can be uncertain.

Importantly, argues Desmond, poverty is not just a cause of eviction—eviction is also a cause of poverty, and African American women are among the most vulnerable to this cycle. Among the ways in which eviction functions as a cause of poverty include the following. First, many landlords reject prospective tenants with eviction records. As one writer notes, "Like incarceration, eviction can brand a person for life, making her an undesirable tenant and condemning her to ever more filthy, decrepit housing" (Ehrenreich, 2016, para. 10). Second, housing instability makes it more difficult for adults to get or keep a job or to apply for benefits: among others, letters and phone calls may be missed and the stress of eviction and its threat may be debilitating (Desmond, 2016a). Third, as Desmond notes, "Some people make a lot of money off low-income families and directly contribute to their poverty" (quoted in Schuessler, 2016, para 27). In the book *Evicted: Poverty and Profit in the American City* (2016a), he recognizes that the significant incomes of many of the landlords he encounters in trailer parks, houses, and apartments are enabled by the dire poverty of tenants who fear complaining about conditions or costs because they don't want to be put out of their homes and who rarely have legal recourse for violations of their rights (90% of people in housing court have no expert or legal representation; Desmond, 2016b).

Eviction is an outcome of a personal shortage of resources. It is a source of individual struggle and stress. It is not, however, only a personal trouble. It is a public issue that asks us to consider why so many poor minority women are facing the reality or threat of being left without safe shelter.

THINK IT THROUGH

▶ Desmond proposes that housing should be a right in the United States. This suggests that if residents cannot afford a home, they should be entitled to state or federal support. Do you agree with this? Why or why not?

passed laws restricting where minorities could live, go to school, receive accommodations, and such. These laws were upheld by the U.S. Supreme Court in the case of *Plessy v. Ferguson* in 1896. It took more than 75 years for the court to reverse itself.

In the 1960s, the Supreme Court held that laws institutionalizing discrimination were unconstitutional. Open forms of discrimination, such as signs and advertisements that said "Whites only" or "Jews need not apply," were deemed illegal. Research and experience suggest, however, that discrimination often continues in more subtle and complex forms. Consider, once again, the case of housing and discrimination. Institutionalized discrimination affects opportunities for housing and, by extension, opportunities for building individual and community wealth through home ownership. We noted earlier in the chapter that

African Americans often still live in segregated neighborhoods. Discrimination is part of the reason; for example, Blacks have been historically less likely to secure mortgages. Paired testing studies in which researchers have sent Black and White applicants with nearly identical financial profiles to apply for mortgages have determined that Whites as a group continue to be advantaged in their treatment by lending institutions (Silverman, 2005). Among other benefits, Whites enjoy higher rates of approval and better loan conditions (Turner, Popkin, & Rawlings, 2009).

The turn of the millennium, however, ushered in a shift in mortgage lending. Banks had plenty of money to lend for home purchases, and among those targeted by banks eager to make mortgage loans were minorities, even those with low incomes and poor credit. The lending bonanza was no boon for these groups, however, because many of the loans made were subprime (subprime loans carry a higher risk that the borrower will default, and the terms are more stringent to compensate for this risk). Subprime loans were five times more common in predominantly Black neighborhoods than in White ones (Pettit & Reuben, 2010), and many borrowers did not fully understand the terms of their loans, such as "balloon" interest rates that rose dramatically over the life of a loan. One consequence was a massive wave of foreclosures beginning in 2008. Although minority and poor communities were not the only ones affected by the subprime loan fiasco, they were disproportionately harmed and have been slow to regain economic ground. According to a recent investigation,

> Nationwide, home values in predominantly African American neighborhoods have been the least likely to recover. . . . Across the 300 largest U.S. metropolitan areas, homes in 4 out of 10 Zip codes where blacks are the largest population group are worth less than they were in 2004. That's twice the rate for mostly white Zip codes across the country. (Badger, 2016, para. 6)

In the sections that follow, we discuss other contemporary manifestations and consequences of individual and institutionalized discrimination in the United States, highlighting the criminal justice system, women's and children's health, and the Internet housing market.

PRISON, POLITICS, AND POWER

One of the key rights of U.S. citizenship is the right to vote—that is, the right to have a voice in the country's political process. Some citizens, however, are denied this right. Many of those who cannot vote have been legally disenfranchised because of state laws that prohibit ex-felons who have served their prison sentences from voting. Statistically speaking, this translates into over 5.3 million disenfranchised individuals, including roughly 1.4 million Black men. A staggering 13% of the Black population cannot legally vote as a direct result of these laws (Sentencing Project, 2011).

In the mid-20th century, more than 70% of those incarcerated in the United States were White; by the end of the 20th century those numbers had reversed, and most prisoners were non-White (Wacquant, 2002; Western & Pettit, 2010). This shift has had a profound effect on African Americans's political voice: 48 states prohibit inmates from voting while they are incarcerated; 14 states and the District of Columbia restore voting rights after incarceration; four states restore it after incarceration and parole; and 20 states restore it after incarceration, parole, and probation have been completed. Alabama, Arizona, Delaware, Florida, Iowa, Kentucky, Mississippi, Nevada, Tennessee, and Wyoming foresee the possibility of a lifetime voting ban on anyone who has been convicted of a felony (ProCon, 2017).

Among those disenfranchised African Americans is Jarvious Cotton. Law professor Michelle Alexander writes about Cotton in *The New Jim Crow: Mass Incarceration in the Age of Colorblindness* (2010):

> Like his father, grandfather, great-grandfather, and great-great-grandfather, [Jarvious Cotton] has been denied the right to participate in our electoral democracy. . . . Cotton's great-great-grandfather could not vote as a slave. His great-grandfather was beaten to death by the Ku Klux Klan for attempting to vote. His grandfather was prevented from voting by Klan intimidation. His father was barred from voting by poll taxes and literacy tests. Today, Jarvious Cotton cannot vote because he, like many black men in the United States, has been labeled a felon and is currently on parole. . . .
>
> . . . Once you're labeled a felon, the old forms of discrimination—employment discrimination, housing discrimination, denial of the right to vote, denial of educational opportunity, denial of food stamps and other public benefits, and exclusion from jury service—are suddenly legal. . . . We have not ended racial caste in America; we have merely redesigned it. (pp. 1–2)

FIGURE 8.5 Racial Disparities in Birth Outcomes in the United States, 2012

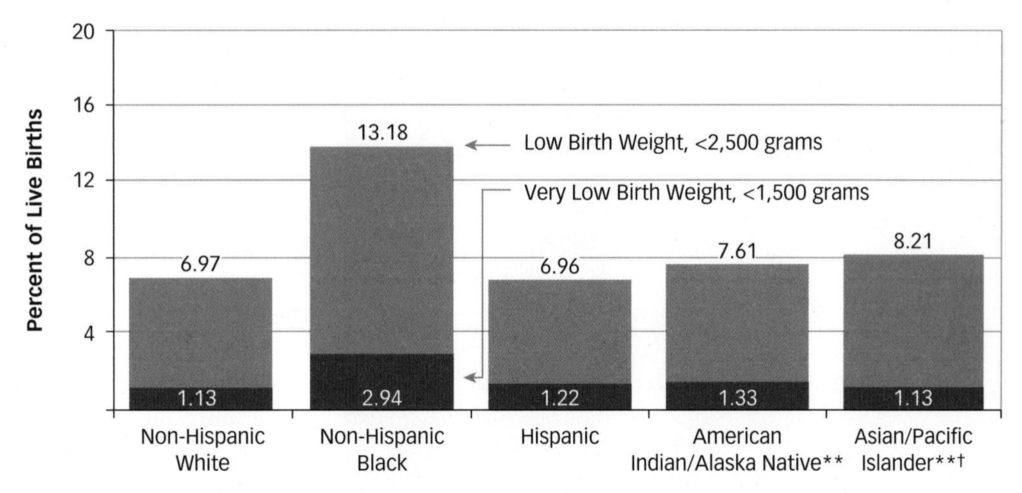

**Data for 2012. **Includes Hispanics. †Separate data for Asians and Native Hawaiians and other Pacific Islanders not available.*

SOURCE: *Racial Disparities in Birth Outcomes and Racial Discrimination as an Independent Risk Factor Affecting Maternal, Infant, and Child Health: An Executive Summary of Existing Research*, by Shandanette Molnar, JD, MPH.

Alexander (2010) argues that the U.S. criminal justice system effectively functions as a modern incarnation of the Jim Crow laws. Today, she suggests, the expansion of the prison population to include nonviolent offenders, particularly people of color (a topic discussed in Chapter 6 of this book), has contributed to the development of a population denied opportunities to have a political voice as well as education, work, and housing.

CONSEQUENCES OF PREJUDICE AND DISCRIMINATION: RACE AND HEALTH

Sociologists studying discrimination take an interest in the health of minority populations. For example, some researchers argue that racism and other disadvantages suffered by Black women in the United States contribute to the much higher level of negative birth outcomes, including low birth weight and infant mortality (Colen, Geronimus, Bound, & James, 2006). Consider the following statistics: Black women are 60% more likely than White women to experience premature births, and Black babies are about 230% more likely than White babies to die before the age of 1 (Norris, 2011). Black women are also more than twice as likely to give birth to very low-weight infants than their White or Latina sisters (Ventura, Curtin, Abma, & Henshaw, 2012).

These data suggest that race trumps other identified predictors of health, including age, income, and educational attainment (Norris, 2011). Although health outcomes are predictably favorable among White women as they gain economic status and give birth in their 20s and early 30s (rather than their teens), Black women's birth outcomes do not appear to follow this pattern (Colen et al., 2006).

Why is race such a powerful predictor of birth outcomes? Answers to this question are varied and complex. Access to prenatal care may be one factor: Data show that nearly 10% of Black women receive late or no prenatal care. By comparison, about 4% of White women and 8% of Latina women get late or no prenatal care (ChildTrends, 2015). Notably, however, public health researcher Arline Geronimus (1992) argues that the racial disparity in birth outcomes—and its stubborn resistance to improvement even as Black women make educational and economic gains—can be attributed to a phenomenon she terms *weathering*. Geronimus describes weathering as an amalgamation of racism and stressors ranging from environmental pollutants to crime to poor health care. These lead, she argues, to a demonstrable deterioration of health, including poor birth outcomes, advanced aging, and even early death.

Geronimus's argument was met with skepticism when she proposed it two decades ago, but it has increasingly gained acceptance. Even in their 20s and 30s,

Theo Wargo/Getty Images Entertainment/Getty Images

In 2016, the hip-hop musical *Hamilton*, written and scored by Lin-Manuel Miranda (front), won 11 awards at the Tony Awards, including Best Musical. The unique take on U.S. history, populated by a talented and multicultural cast, has been wildly popular on Broadway. ■

Geronimus says, African American women are "suffering from hypertension at two or three times the rate of whites their own age. African Americans at age 35 have the rates of disability of white Americans who are 55, and we haven't seen much traction over 20 to 30 years of trying to reduce and eliminate these disparities" (quoted in Norris, 2011, "'Enormous Stressors' Take A Toll On Black Women," para. 13). To see such medical statistics through the prism of social science is a goal of **social epidemiology**, which is *the study of communities and their social statuses, practices, and problems with the aim of understanding patterns of health and disease.*

It is challenging to draw a direct connection between race-related social stressors and negative health outcomes; critics have questioned the link, and more work remains to be done. Nevertheless, the work of Geronimus demonstrates how sociology can highlight connections between private troubles—such as the birth of a low-weight or preterm infant—and public issues, including lack of access to care and the wearing effects of racism (Figure 8.5).

TECHNOLOGIES OF DISCRIMINATION

Today, most people who are seeking housing go to the Internet first. According to a joint study from the National Association of Realtors and Google, 90% of homebuyers searched online during their home buying process (National Association of Realtors, 2012). Sites like Craigslist cater to those seeking temporary or long-term rentals. Enforcement of the Fair Housing Act, the primary purpose of which is to keep discriminatory practices in check, has not kept pace with the explosive growth of the online home buying and rental markets. From blatant "Whites only" statements to more veiled implications that people of color will not be accepted, the Internet is rife with the potential for housing discrimination.

Recent research shows that some housing providers and sellers are selecting interested parties who have "White"-sounding names over those whose names sound "ethnic." For example, one study used Craigslist to analyze responses of potential housing providers to home seekers giving their names as Neil, Tyrone, and Jorge (Friedman, Squires, & Galvan, 2010). The researchers found that respondents with "White-sounding" names (for example, Neil) were most likely to get multiple responses, be put in touch with the housing provider, be offered the opportunity to look at the house, and be told the property is available. Although racial and ethnic discrimination are not legal in modern America, new forms of digitally enabled discrimination are challenging integration efforts and reinforcing long-existing patterns of segregation in U.S. communities.

We conclude this section on prejudice, discrimination, and stereotypes with a look at the underrepresentation of minority actors and actresses in Hollywood—and a discussion of some promising new paths to diversifying popular culture both on the stage and the big screen.

RACE AND ETHNICITY IN HOLLYWOOD—AND ON BROADWAY

Who are the actors and actresses most likely to be recognized for their cultural achievements in the United States? It is notable that out of more than 2,900 Oscars awarded since the founding of the Academy Awards, which recognize achievements in film, just 38 have gone to African Americans (Sangweni, 2017). Up to this time (2017), there has not been an Asian, Hispanic, or Native American Best Actor winner, and only one African American—Halle Berry in 2001—has won Best Actress (Sender, 2015). In 2017, actress Viola Davis won the Best Supporting Actress award.

Social epidemiology: The study of communities and their social statuses, practices, and problems with the aim of understanding patterns of health and disease.

Actor George Clooney has suggested that the problem is not primarily who the Academy is choosing to nominate but rather, "How many options are available to minorities in film, particularly in quality films" (Setoodeh, 2016, para. 2). Indeed, we often see African Americans in stereotypical roles like gangsters, single parents, singers, dancers, maids, or slaves. Their characters are more likely than others to be violent, hypersexualized, or poor; fewer are presented as leaders, intellectuals, or professionals. This lack of diversity in available roles extends as well to Asian American, Native American, and Hispanic actors, who are frequently slotted into stereotypical film roles. No less notably, minority characters are less likely to be prominent in films: A study done at the Annenberg School for Communication and Journalism at the University of Southern California found that in 600 popular films from 2007 to 2013, White actors populated about 75% of speaking roles. Nearly a fifth of films had no Black speaking characters at all (Smith, Choueiti, & Pieper, 2014).

FIGURE 8.6 U.S. Population by Race and Hispanic Origin, 2012 and 2060 (projected)

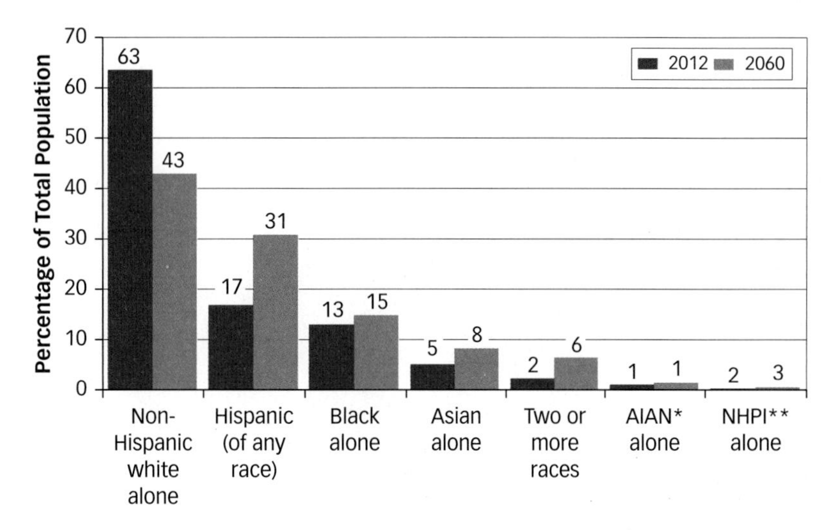

SOURCE: U.S. Census Bureau. (2012f). USA QuickFacts.

*AIAN: American Indian and Alaska Native

**NHPI: Native Hawaiian and Other Pacific Islander

In response to the marginalization of Black actors and actresses in Hollywood, some celebrities like Will Smith and Jada Pinkett Smith boycotted the 2016 Oscars. The Academy released a statement recognizing that a problem exists and committing to increase diversity by doubling the number of women and people of color in its membership by 2020 (Wagner, 2016). Indeed, as the *Los Angeles Times* reported in July of 2016,

> The motion picture academy, responding to the outcry over an absence of minorities in its ranks—and consequently its nominees—invited nearly 700 film professionals to become members. It's by far the academy's biggest new class, with more than 40% of the invitees people of color. (Zeitchik, 2016, para. 2)

Hollywood appears to be taking steps to embrace greater diversity. Meanwhile, a wildly popular Broadway musical has brought drama and diversity to thousands of theatergoers. The musical hit *Hamilton*, based on a biography of Alexander Hamilton by Ron Chernow and written and scored by Lin-Manuel Miranda, who was also part of the original cast, has taken New York City by storm. *Hamilton* is a historical tale rendered through hip-hop lyrics; its key historical figures, including Hamilton, George Washington, Thomas Jefferson, and Aaron Burr, are played by Black or Hispanic actors. At the 2016 Tony Awards, which recognize achievements in musicals, the show won 11 awards, including Best Musical, Best Actor, Best Supporting Actor and Actress, and Best Choreography (Marks, 2016).

Hollywood has been slow in embracing diversity, in spite of an increasingly diverse audience of filmgoers. Will big screen films follow the example of *Hamilton*, offering unexpected but celebrated new roles to minority actors and actresses? Why are visibility and diverse roles in popular culture important? What do you think?

In the next section, we look at some of the major groups that make up the U.S. population and see how their numbers are contributing to the changing composition of the country.

RACIAL AND ETHNIC GROUPS IN THE UNITED STATES

The area now called the United States was once occupied by hundreds of Native American nations. Later came Europeans, most of whom were English, although early settlers also included the French, Dutch, and Spanish, among others. Beginning in 1619, Africans were brought as slaves and added a substantial minority to the European population. Hundreds of thousands of Europeans continued to arrive from Norway, Sweden, Germany, and Russia to start farms and work in the factories of early industrial America. In the mid-1800s, Chinese

■ **FIGURE 8.7** Diversity of the U.S. Population, 2016

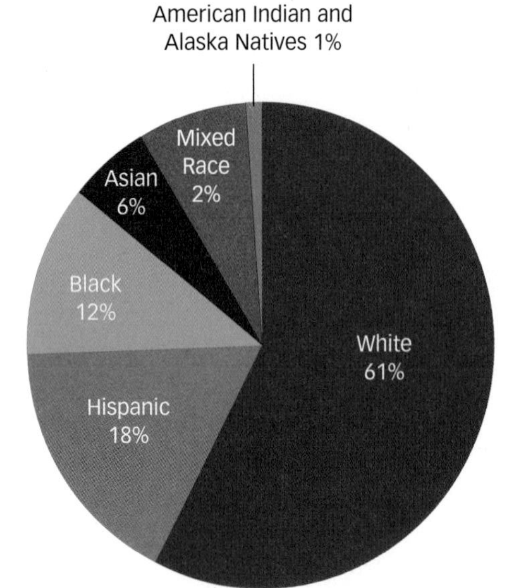

SOURCE: Kaiser Family Foundation, 2017.

immigrants were brought in to provide the heavy labor for building railroads and mining gold and silver. Between 1890 and 1930, nearly 28 million people immigrated to the United States. After the 1950s, immigrants came mostly from Latin America and Asia.

The U.S. population is growing increasingly diverse (see Figure 8.7). According to one recent source, in 2014, Whites comprised about 61% of the population; Blacks about 12%; Hispanics nearly 18%; Asians 6%; American Indians and Alaska Natives just 1%; and people self-identifying as mixed race about 2% (Kaiser Family Foundation, 2017).

If current trends hold, non-Whites will constitute a numeric majority nationwide by about 2040.

The rapid growth of minority populations reflects growth from both new births and migration. Migration is the primary engine of population growth in the United States. In fact, demographers estimate that by the middle of the 21st century, fully one fifth of the U.S. population will be immigrants. In a population estimated to reach more than 438 million by 2050, 67 million will be immigrants, and about 50 million will be the children and grandchildren of immigrants (Pew Research Center, 2008). Overall, the trend toward a more racially and ethnically diverse country is clear: At the time of the 2010 census, the majority of children under 2 years old were non-White.

In the following sections we look in more depth at the racial and ethnic groups that have come together to constitute U.S. culture and society today.

AMERICAN INDIANS

There is no agreement on how many people were living in North America when the Europeans arrived around the beginning of the 16th century, but anthropologists' best guess is about 20 million. Thousands of thriving societies existed throughout North and South America in this period. Encounter between European explorers and Native Americans soon became conquest, and despite major resistance, the indigenous populations were eventually defeated and their lands confiscated by European settlers. It is believed that between 1500 and 1800 the North American Indian population was reduced from more than 20 million to fewer than 600,000 (Haggerty, 1991). American Indians, like conquered and oppressed peoples everywhere, did not passively accept the European invasion. The "Indian Wars" are among the bloodiest in U.S. history, but resistance was not enough. First, White settlers had access to superior weaponry that Native Americans could not effectively counter. Second, Whites' control of political, economic, and environmental policies gave them a powerful advantage. Consider, for instance, the U.S. government's decision to permit the unregulated slaughter of bison (buffalo) in the post–Civil War era. From about 1866, when millions of bison roamed the American West and the Great Plains, to the 1890s, this key Native American resource was decimated until just a few thousand remained (Moloney, 2012; Smits, 1994).

Since the 1960s, some Native Americans have focused on efforts to force the U.S. government to honor treaties and improve their living conditions, particularly on reservations. In 1969, the group Indians of All Tribes (IAT), citing the Treaty of Fort Laramie (1868), which states that all unused or abandoned federal land must be returned to the Indians, seized the abandoned island of Alcatraz, a former prison island in the San Francisco Bay, and issued a proclamation that contained the following (deliberately ironic) declarations: "We, the native Americans, re-claim the land known as Alcatraz Island in the name of all American Indians by right of discovery. . . . We feel that this so-called Alcatraz Island is more than suitable for an Indian Reservation, as determined by the white man's own standards." The IAT went on to note the island's "suitability" by pointing out that, among other things, it had no fresh running water, no industries to provide employment, no health care facilities, and no oil or mineral rights for inhabitants. This comparison was intended to point to the devastating conditions on most reservations.

The IAT occupied Alcatraz for more than 18 months. The occupation ended when some IAT members left due to poor living conditions, as the federal government shut off all power and water to the island, and others were removed when the government took control of the island in June 1971.

Despite centuries of struggle, more than 60% of the 4.9 million American Indians in the United States today live in urban areas and are among the poorest people in the nation: More than half of all Native American children are born into poverty, three times the rate for White children. About 1.9 million Native Americans live on reservations, where unemployment rates run as high as 50%. With limited economic opportunities, Native Americans also have relatively low educational attainment: Just 13% have earned bachelor's degrees (Ogunwole, Drewery, & Rios-Vargas, 2012).

AARON HUEY/National Geographic Creative

American Indians lived in the territorial United States long before the political state was established. They suffered the loss of territory and population as a result of U.S. government policies. Even today, American Indian communities face unique challenges.

The *Inequality Matters* box on page 250 raises another issue pertinent to the status of Native Americans in the United States: Who has the power to name this population?

AFRICAN AMERICANS

In 1903, W.E.B. Du Bois penned the following words: "The problem of the Twentieth Century is the problem of the color line" (1903/2008, p. 9). By that he meant that grappling with the legacy of 250 years of slavery would be one of the great problems of the 20th century. Indeed, as this chapter shows, Du Bois was right, although he did not foresee that the "color line" would incorporate not just African Americans but Hispanics, Asians, American Indians, and other minorities as well.

Slavery forcibly brought more than 9 million people, mostly from West Africa, to North and South America. Although the stereotype of slaves gratefully serving their White masters dominated U.S. culture for many years, the fact is that slave revolts were frequent throughout the South. More than 250 Black uprisings against slavery were recorded from 1700 to 1865, and many others were not recorded (Greenberg, 1996; Williams-Meyers, 1996).

Immediately following the end of slavery, during the Reconstruction period, African Americans sought to establish political and economic equality. Former slaves gained the right to vote, and in some jurisdictions they constituted the majority of registered voters. Black legislators were elected in every southern state. Between 1870 and 1901, 22 Blacks served in the U.S. Congress, while hundreds of others served in state legislatures, on city councils, and as elected and appointed officials throughout the South (Holt, 1977). Their success was short-lived. White southern legislators, still a majority, passed Jim Crow laws excluding Blacks from voting and using public transportation. In time, every aspect of life was constrained for Blacks, including access to hospitals, schools, restaurants, churches, jobs, recreation sites, and cemeteries. By 1901, because literacy was required to vote and most Blacks had been effectively denied even a basic education, the registration of Black voters had dwindled to a mere handful (Morrison, 1987).

The North's higher degree of industrialization offered a promise of economic opportunity, even though social and political discrimination existed there as well. Between 1940 and 1970, more than 5 million African Americans left the rural South for what they hoped would be a better life in the North (Lemann, 1991). Whether they stayed in the South or moved to the North, however, many Blacks were still being denied fundamental rights nearly 100 years after slavery was abolished.

By the 1950s, the social landscape was changing—consider the fact that having fought against a racist regime in Nazi Germany in the 1940s, the United States found it far more difficult to justify continued discrimination against its own minority populations. Legal mandates for equality, however, did not easily translate to actual practices, and the 1960s saw a wave of protest from African Americans eager to claim greater rights and opportunities. The civil rights movement was committed to nonviolent forms of

INEQUALITY MATTERS

Who Has the Power to Name?

"A language is a dialect that has an army and a navy," said sociolinguist Max Weinreich. Before White Europeans came to North America, one of the largest Indian nations was the Dineh, a name that means "the People of the Earth." No one knows exactly why, but the Spaniards renamed them "Navajo," the designation by which Americans have referred to them ever since. Although Native Americans were being outgunned and oppressed by the wave of White European settlers, their language was also subject to marginalization, as was their power to name themselves.

Sociologist Pierre Bourdieu (1991) has pointed out that language is a medium of power, a vehicle that may confer status or function as a means of devaluation and exclusion. Historically, minority groups have been denied opportunities to name themselves. What is the appropriate name for the people who lived for thousands of years in what today is known as North and South America? They are commonly referred to in the United States as *Indians, Native Americans, indigenous peoples,* or simply *Natives.* These are not the only terms used to label this group. U.S. sports teams from the professional to the high school level use a variety of monikers: in football, we find the Washington *Redskins* and Kansas City *Chiefs*; in baseball, the Atlanta *Braves;* at the high school level, there are a variety of *Warriors, Big Reds, Redmen, Scouts*, and *Savages*. Particularly at the professional level, these names have evoked controversy, with some American Indian groups arguing that they are demeaning.

Two prominent organizations—the National Congress of American Indians and the American Indian Movement—use *American Indian* to describe themselves. Yet others object to the term because, like the word *Navajo,* it was given to them by European settlers and their descendants. Those who object to *American Indian* feel the alternative, *Native American,* captures the fact that they alone among ethnic groups are truly native to this continent, but this name also was given by European settlers. Others argue that nothing short of the correct name for each nation (such as Sioux, Pawnee, Cheyenne, Dineh, or Cherokee) is acceptable. Nevertheless, referring to each separate nation is problematic when one speaks of the collective. After years of controversy, their leaders agreed to accept *American Indian* to refer to themselves collectively (Scott, Tehranian, & Mathias, 2002).

The name for a particular racial or ethnic group may be highly contested, since it carries with it information about the group's social history. The effort by many groups to "name themselves" reflects their belief that to passively accept the name given by society's dominant group is to potentially accept being silenced. American Indian activists Laura Waterman Wittstock and Elaine J. Salinas (1998) suggest in their history of the American Indian Movement that "in the 30 years of its formal history, the American Indian Movement (AIM) has given witness to a great many changes. We say formal history, because the movement existed for 500 years without a name. The leaders and members of today's AIM never fail to remember all of those who have traveled on before, having given their talent and their lives for the survival of the people."

THINK IT THROUGH

- Bourdieu highlights the "power to name" as one that is more likely to be held and exercised by dominant groups in society. Can you name another situation in which the power to name gives an advantage to one group and disadvantage to another?

Follow us on Twitter to keep up with current sociological stories and research! We're at @DiscoverSoc1.
Share your own ideas at #DiscoverSociology.

protest. Participants in the movement used strikes, boycotts, voter registration drives, sit-ins, and freedom rides in their efforts to achieve racial equality. In 1964, following what was at the time the largest civil rights demonstration in the nation's history, a march on Washington, D.C., the federal government passed the first in a series of civil rights laws that made it illegal to discriminate on the basis of race, sex, religion, physical disability, or ethnic origin.

All African Americans have not benefited from legislation aimed at abolishing discrimination (Wilson, 2010). In particular, the poorest Blacks—those living in disadvantaged urban and rural areas—lack the opportunities that could make a difference in their lives. Many poor Black Americans suffer from having little cultural and social capital; inadequate schools, lack of skills and training, and poor local job opportunities raise the risk of persistent poverty. Today, nearly half of African American workers are employed in unskilled or semiskilled service jobs—as health care aides, janitors, and food service workers, for example—compared with only a quarter of Whites. Few of these occupations offer the opportunity to earn a living wage.

Over time, many African Americans have been broadly successful in improving their economic circumstances, particularly as they have gained access to education. The economic gains of African Americans, however, have been more tenuous than those of most other groups. As we saw earlier in the chapter, the Great Recession that began in 2007 substantially eroded Black wealth and income in America, and many communities are still struggling to recover.

Although African Americans have had mixed success in gaining economic power, as a group they have seen important gains in political power. In the early 1960s, there were only 103 African Americans holding public office in the United States. By 1970, about 715 Blacks held elected office at the city and county levels. By the 1990s, however, the figure had surpassed 5,000, and in recent decades major cities—including New York, Los Angeles, Chicago, and Washington—have elected Black mayors, and Black representation on city and town councils and state bodies has grown dramatically. At the federal level there have been fewer gains, although, clearly, President Obama's election in November 2008 and reelection in 2012 represented a profound political breakthrough for Blacks. Following the congressional elections of November 2012, the House of Representatives had 42 Black members, but only a single African American was serving in the Senate.

LATINOS/LATINAS

The category of Latino/a (or Hispanic, the term used by the U.S. Census Bureau) includes people whose heritages lie in the many different cultures of Latin America. According to a recent Pew Research Center estimate, about 57 million Hispanics reside in the U.S., making them the largest minority group. Latinos are increasing in numbers more rapidly than any other minority group, because of both high immigration rates and high birthrates.

FIGURE 8.8 Foreign-Born Hispanics in the United States

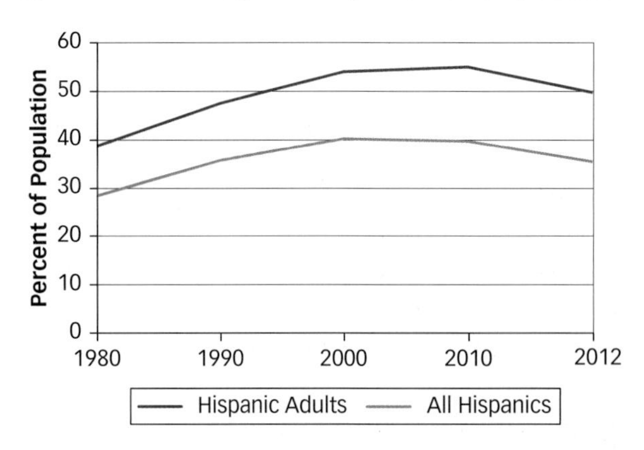

SOURCE: Krogstad, J.M. and M.H. Lopez. 2014. "Hispanic Nativity Shift," Pew Research Center, April 29 (www.pewhispanic.org/2014/04/29/hispanic-nativity-shift/).

Many Latinos trace their ancestry to a time when the southwestern states were part of Mexico. During the mid-19th century, the United States sought to purchase from Mexico what are now Texas and California. Mexico refused to sell, leading to the 1846–1848 U.S.–Mexican War. Following its victory, the U.S. government forced Mexico to sell two fifths of its territory, enabling the United States to acquire all the land that now makes up the southwestern states, including California, Texas, New Mexico, and Arizona. Along with this vast territory came the people who inhabited it, including tens of thousands of Mexicans who were forced by White settlers to forfeit their property and who suffered discrimination at the hands of the Whites (Valenzuela, 1992).

Latinos have experienced some of the same obstacles of prejudice and discrimination in the United States as have African Americans. They continue to be discriminated against and live below the standards of the dominant population. At the same time, the very category of *Latino* is problematic for sociologists because it encompasses several different ethnic groups with very different experiences of immigration. Latinos are often referred to in a way that implies uniformity across members of this group, when in reality Latinos constitute a diverse ethnic population with roots in a range of countries in Central America, South America, and the Caribbean. Today, about half of Hispanic adults were born in the U.S. and about half are foreign-born (Figure 8.8). We discuss two of the most prominent Latino groups below.

Beginning in 1942, the U.S. government relocated an estimated 110,000 Japanese Americans living on the West Coast to internment camps. The government feared disloyalty after the Japanese attack on Pearl Harbor, in spite of the fact that more than 60% of those interned were U.S. citizens. ■

MEXICAN AMERICANS Mexicans are the largest group of Latinos in the United States. A large proportion of the Mexican American population lives in California, New Mexico, Texas, and Arizona, although migration to the American South has grown substantially. The immigration of Mexican Americans has long reflected the immediate labor needs of the U.S. economy (Barrera, 1979; Muller & Espenshade, 1985). During the 1930s, state and local governments forcibly sent hundreds of thousands of Mexican immigrants back to Mexico, but when the United States experienced a labor shortage during World War II, immigration was again encouraged. After the war, the *bracero* (manual laborer) program enabled 4 million Mexicans to work as temporary farm laborers in the United States, often under exploitative conditions. The program was ended in 1964, but by the 1980s, immigration was on the upsurge, with millions of people fleeing poverty and political turmoil in Latin America by illegally entering the United States.

The debate over how to deal with illegal immigrants seeking U.S. jobs has been a subject of heated debate in American politics, although the numbers of such immigrants appear to be falling. In fact, data suggest that a host of factors—including the dangers of crossing the U.S.–Mexico border due to drug violence on the Mexican side, harsher immigration laws in states from Georgia to Arizona, and the dearth of employment in the wake of the recession—have pushed illegal immigration down (Massey, 2011).

Most ethnic Mexicans in the United States are legal residents, and the number of those rising into the middle class has grown considerably, although the number living in poverty rose after the economy crisis that began in 2008.

CUBAN AMERICANS When Fidel Castro came to power in Cuba in 1959, Cubans who opposed his communist regime sought to emigrate to the United States. These included some of Castro's political opponents, but most were middle-class Cubans whose standard of living was declining under Castro's economic policies and the U.S. economic embargo of Cuba. About half a million entered the United States, mostly through Florida, which is just 90 miles away from Cuba.

The Cuban community has enjoyed both economic and, perhaps as a result, political success in Florida (Ferment, 1989; Stepick & Grenier, 1993). In contrast to many immigrants, who tend to come from the poorer strata of their native countries, Cuban immigrants were often highly educated professionals and businesspeople before they fled to the United States. They brought with them a considerable reserve of training, skill, and sometimes wealth.

The anticommunist stance of the new migrants was also a good fit with U.S. foreign policy and the effort to crush communist politics in the Western Hemisphere. The U.S. government provided financial assistance such as small business loans to Cuban immigrants. It also offered a spectrum of language classes, job training programs, and recertification classes for physicians, architects, nurses, teachers, and lawyers who sought to reestablish their professional credentials in the United States. About three-quarters of all Cubans arriving before 1974 received some form of government benefits, the highest rate of any minority community.

Although Cuban migrants have tended to have higher levels of education than Mexican immigrants do, their status in the United States has also been strongly influenced by the political and economic (that is, the structural) needs of the U.S. government. U.S. economic needs have determined whether the government encouraged or discouraged the migration of manual labor power from Mexico, while political considerations have fostered a support network for migrants endorsing the U.S. government's effort to end the communist Castro regime in Cuba.

ASIAN AMERICANS

Asian immigrants were instrumental in the development of industrialization in the United States. In the mid-1800s, construction began on the transcontinental railroad that would link California with the industrializing East. At the same time, gold and silver were discovered in the American West. Labor was desperately needed to mine these natural resources and to work on building the railroad. At the

FIGURE 8.9 Countries of Origin of the Asian Population in the United States, 2010

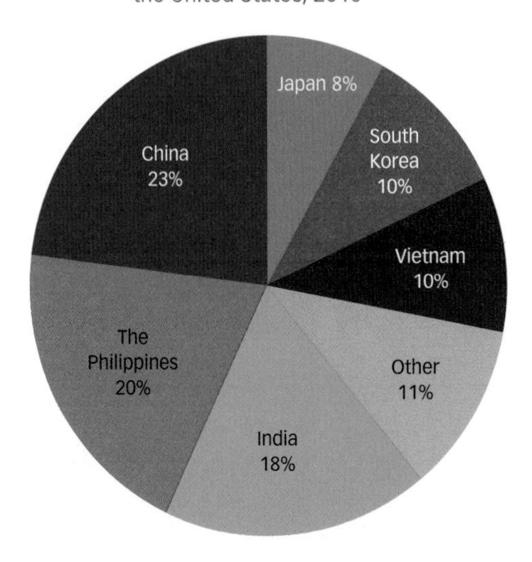

SOURCE: Data from Pew Research Center. 2012. *The rise of Asian Americans*. Pew Social & Demographic Trends.

time, China was suffering a severe drought. U.S. entrepreneurs seeking labor quickly saw the potential fit of supply and demand, and hundreds of thousands of Chinese were brought to the United States as inexpensive manual labor. Most came voluntarily, but some were kidnapped by U.S. ship captains and brought to the West Coast.

About 4% of Americans today trace their origins to Asian countries such as India, China, Japan, Korea, and Vietnam. The number of Asian Americans is growing, primarily because of immigration (Asian American birthrates, following the pattern in Asian countries, are low). Like Latinos, Asian Americans constitute a population of great ethnic diversity; the wide-ranging characteristics of this population cannot be fully captured by the term *Asian American* (Figure 8.9).

Asian Americans, like members of other minority groups, have experienced prejudice and discrimination. For example, during World War II, many Japanese Americans were forcibly placed in internment camps, and their property was confiscated (Daniels, 2002; Harth, 2001). The U.S. government feared their allegiances were with Japan—an enemy in World War II—rather than the United States. Although the teaching of German was banned in some schools, drastic measures were not taken against German or Italian Americans, although Germany and Italy were allied with Japan during the war.

In spite of obstacles, the Asian American population has been successful in making economic gains. Asian Americans as a whole have the highest median household income of any minority group, as well as the lowest rates of divorce, teenage pregnancy, and unemployment. Their economic success reflects the fact that, like Cuban Americans, recent Asian immigrants have come from higher socioeconomic backgrounds, bringing greater financial resources and more human capital (Zhou, 2009). Family networks and kinship obligations also play an important role. In many Asian American communities, informal community-based lending organizations provide capital for businesses, families and friends support one another as customers and employees, and profits are reinvested in the community (Ferment, 1989; Gilbertson & Gurak, 1993; Kasarda, 1993).

At the same time, there are substantial differences within the Asian American population. Nearly half of all Asian Indian Americans, for example, are professionals, compared with less than a quarter of Korean Americans, who are much more likely to run small businesses and factories. Poverty and hardship are more prevalent among those from Southeast Asia, particularly immigrants from Cambodia and Laos, which are deeply impoverished countries with less educated populations.

ARAB AMERICANS

Immigrants from Arab countries began coming to the United States in the 1880s. The last major wave of Arab migration occurred in the decade following World War II (PBS, 2011). Contrary to popular perceptions, most members of today's Arab American population were born in the United States. The majority trace their roots back to Lebanon, Syria, Palestine, Egypt, and Iraq (Arab American Institute, 2012).

Arab Americans face a unique set of challenges and obstacles. Immediately following the September 11, 2001, terrorist attacks, Arab Americans as a group suffered stigma, and acts of discrimination against them increased sharply. The terror attacks provided an avenue for legitimating the views of racists and xenophobes (Salaita, 2005), but institutionalized prejudice was also obvious in the increase in "random" screenings and searches that targeted Arab Americans.

At the same time, Arab Americans represent a "model minority"—a racial or ethnic group with higher levels of achievement than the general population in areas such as education and income. Like Asian Americans, Arab Americans as a demographic group have been notably successful in these two fields; 45% have at least a bachelor's degree or higher (compared to 28% for the general population), and in 2008 their mean individual income was 27% higher than the national average (Arab American Institute Foundation, 2011).

■ **FIGURE 8.10** Legal Migration to the United States by Region of Origin, 1820–2015

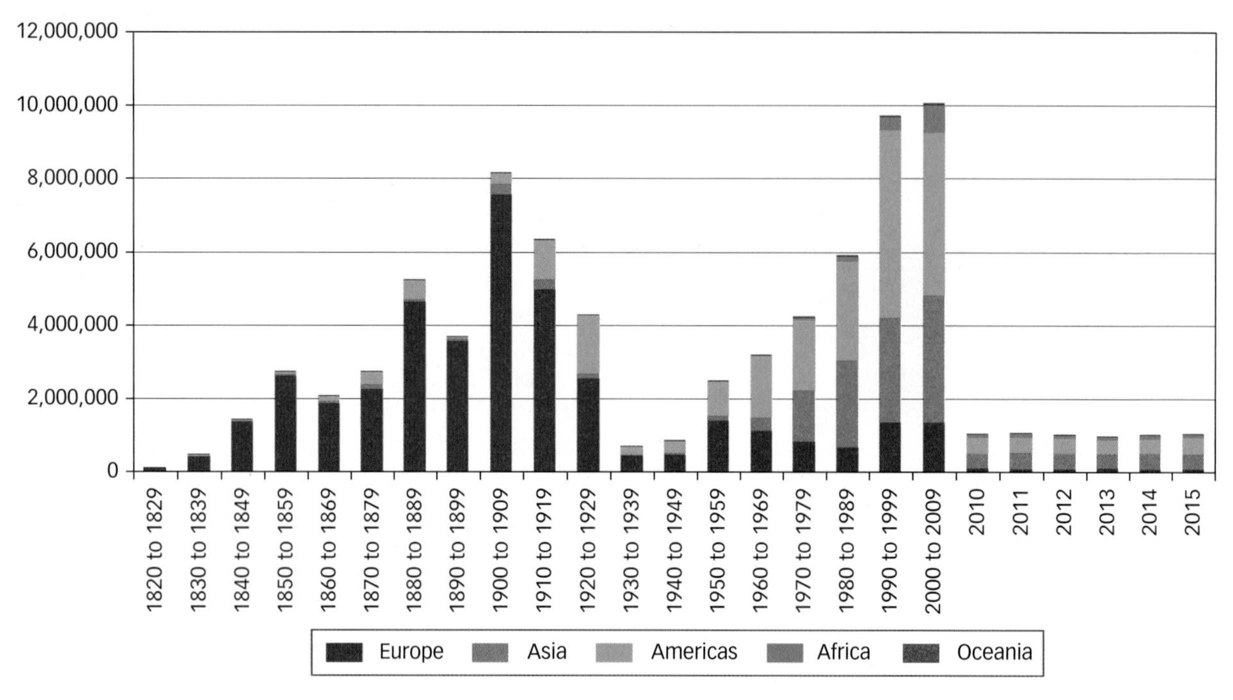

SOURCE: Data from Table 2, Persons Obtaining Legal Permanent Resident Status by Region and Selected Country of Last Residence: Fiscal Years 1820 to 2015. *Yearbook of Immigration Statistics: 2015 Legal Permanent Residents*. U.S. Department of Homeland Security.

WHITE ETHNIC AMERICANS

White people have always made up a high percentage of the foreign-born population in the United States. The stereotype of minorities as people of color leaves out significant pockets of White ethnic minorities. In the early days of mass migration to the United States, the dominant group was White Protestants from Europe. Whites from Europe who were not Protestant—particularly Catholics and Jews—were defined as ethnic minorities, and their status was clearly marginal in U.S. society.

In mid-19th-century Boston, for example, Irish Catholics made up a large portion of the city's poor and were stereotyped as drunken, criminal, and generally immoral (Handlin, 1991). The term *paddy wagon,* used to describe a police van that picks up the drunk and disorderly, came from the notion that the Irish were such vans' most common occupants. (*Paddy* was a derogatory term for an Irishman.) Over time, however, White ethnic groups assimilated with relative ease because, for the most part, they looked much like the dominant population (Prell, 1999). To further their assimilation, some families changed their names and encouraged their children to speak English only. Today, most of these White ethnic groups—Irish, Italians, Russians, and others—have integrated fully into U.S. society (Figure 8.10). They are, on the whole, born wealthier, have more social capital, and encounter fewer barriers to mobility than other racial and ethnic groups.

If dark skin has historically been an obstacle in U.S. society, light skin has been an advantage. That advantage, however, may go unrecognized. As Peggy McIntosh writes in her thought-provoking article "White Privilege: Unpacking the Invisible Knapsack" (1990), "as a white person, I realized I had been taught about racism as something that puts others at a disadvantage, but had been taught not to see one of its corollary aspects, white privilege, which puts me at an advantage. . . . I have come to see white privilege as an invisible package of unearned assets that I can count on cashing in each day, but about which I was 'meant' to remain oblivious" (p. 31).

McIntosh goes on to outline these "assets," including the following: When Whites are told about their national heritage, or the origins of "civilization," they are shown that White people shaped it. Posters, picture books, greeting cards, toys, and dolls all overwhelmingly feature White images. As a White person, she need not worry that her coworkers at an affirmative action employer will suspect she got her job only because of her race. If she needed any medical or legal help, her race alone would not be considered a risk factor or hindrance in obtaining such services. These are

Questions for consideration:

- Should refugees' state of origin affect whether they are accepted for resettlement?
- Should individual states in the United States have a say in determining whether refugees are welcomed there, or should the decision be taken exclusively by the federal government?
- How have recent waves of refugees who settled in the United States done educationally and economically? What do their experiences suggest about resettlement policies for refugees in the United States?

Debate tip:

▶ Do not limit your research to one city, state, or country. Collect and compare statistics about a topic from different places around the world to develop a better understanding of the situation.

an obligation to intervene is loose and open to interpretation, as history has shown. Humanitarian organizations such as Genocide Watch and institutions such as the U.S. Holocaust Memorial Museum have sounded the alarm on recent atrocities, often labeling them genocide even while many governments have resisted using the term.

Genocides in the second half of the 20th century include slaughters carried out by the Khmer Rouge in Cambodia in the 1970s, Saddam Hussein's 1987–1988 campaign against ethnic Kurds in Iraq, and Serb atrocities in the former Yugoslav states of Bosnia-Herzegovina and Kosovo in the late 1990s (Figure 8.12). The 21st century has already seen the genocidal destruction of Black Africans, including the Darfuris, Abyei, and Nuba, by Arab militias linked to the government in Sudan.

One of the most discussed cases of genocide in the late 20th century took place in Rwanda, where in 1994 no fewer than 800,000 ethnic Tutsis were killed by ethnic Hutus in the space of just 100 days. Many killings were done by machete, and women and girls were targeted for sexual violence. By most accounts, Tutsis and Hutus are not so different from one another; they are members of the same ethnic group, live in the same areas, and share a common language. One cultural difference of considerable importance, however, is that for the Tutsis the cow is sacred and cannot be killed or used for food. The Hutus, who have a long tradition of farming, were forced to leave large areas of land open for cattle grazing, thus limiting the fertile ground available for farming. As the cattle herds multiplied, so did tensions and conflict. Notably, for many years the Tutsis, while fewer in number (representing approximately 14% of the population), dominated the Hutus politically and economically (Kapuscinski, 2001).

Rwanda was long a colony of Belgium, but in the 1950s, Tutsis began to demand independence, as did many other colonized peoples in Africa. The Belgians incited the Hutus to rebel against the Tutsi ruling class. The rebellion was unsuccessful, but the seeds for genocide were planted in fertile soil, and sporadic ethnic violence erupted in the decades that followed. Belgium finally relinquished power and granted Rwanda independence in 1962. From the early 1970s, the government was headed by a moderate Hutu leader, Major General Juvénal Habyarimana (BBC, 2008). In the early 1990s, General Habyarimana agreed to a power-sharing arrangement with Tutsis in Rwanda, angering some nationalist Hutus, who did not want to see a division of power. In 1994, the general was assassinated (his private jet was shot down), and radical Hutus took the opportunity to turn on both Tutsi countrymen and moderate Hutus, murdering at least 800,000 people in just a few short months.

In the section below, we consider the question of how genocide—such as the mass killing of Rwanda's Tutsi population in 1994—looks through a sociological lens.

WHAT EXPLAINS GENOCIDE?

Taking a sociological perspective, we might ask, "Who benefits from genocide?" Why do countries or leaders make a choice to pursue or allow genocidal actions? Genocide is the product of conscious decisions made by those who stand to benefit from it and who anticipate minimal costs for their actions.

Joe McNally/Hulton Archive/Getty Images

In the 1994 genocide in Rwanda, nearly a million ethnic Tutsis were systematically killed by ethnic Hutus in fewer than 100 days.

Chalk and Jonassohn (1990) suggest that those who pursue genocide do so to eliminate a real or perceived threat, to spread fear among enemies, to eliminate a real or potential threat to another group, to gain wealth or power for a dominant group, and/or to realize an ideological goal. Shaw (2010) has noted that "genocide is a crime of social classification, in which power-holders target particular populations for social and often physical destruction" (p. 142).

Anton Weiss-Wendt (2010) points out that to the degree that genocide "requires premeditation" (p. 81), governments are generally implicated in the crime. Among the necessary parts is also the creation of a "genocidal mentality," not only among the leadership but also among a sufficient number of individuals to ensure the participation, or at least the support or indifference, of a large proportion of the population (Goldhagen, 1997; Markusen, 2002). Part of creating a genocidal mentality is dehumanizing the victims. By emphasizing their "otherness," or the idea that the group to be victimized is less than fully human, agents of genocide stamp out sympathy for their targets, replacing it with a sense of threat or disgust. Modern media have made the process of disseminating the propaganda of dehumanization increasingly easy. Radio broadcasts to a Hutu audience in Rwanda in the time leading up to the genocide implored Hutus to "kill [Tutsi] cockroaches" (Gourevitch, 1999).

Another mechanism is the "establishment of genocidal institutions and organizations," which construct propaganda to justify and institutions or other means to carry out the genocide. Finally, the recruitment and training of perpetrators is important, as is the establishment of methods of group destruction (Markusen, 2002). In Rwanda, it is notable that some Hutu Power groups had already in the early 1990s begun to arm civilians with hand weapons like machetes, ostensibly as self-defense against Tutsi rebels. Many of these were later used in the genocide. As Hutus and Tutsis lived side by side in many cities and rural areas, identification of victims was rapid and easy.

Choosing genocide as a policy incurs costs as well as benefits. Clearly, outside forces can impose costs on a genocidal regime; we have seen that signatories to the 1948 U.N. convention are theoretically obligated to intervene. But historically, intervention has often been too little and too late. Why, in the face of overwhelming evidence of genocide (as in Rwanda or Bosnia-Herzegovina or Sudan), does the international community not step in? One answer that these states also make choices based on perceived costs and benefits. Intervention in the affairs of another state can be costly, and many leaders avoid it. In a historical overview of U.S. responses to genocide, for instance, Samantha Power (2002) argues: that "American leaders did not act because they did not want to. They believed that genocide was wrong, but they were not prepared to invest the military, financial, diplomatic, or domestic political capital needed to stop it" (p. 508).

Genocide is an extreme and brutal manifestation of majority–minority relations. It is the effort to destroy indiscriminately an entire racial or ethnic group. Does genocide continue to be a viable option for states or regimes wishing to destroy groups labeled by powerful leaders as inferior or dangerous? How should outside states—and concerned individuals—respond when conflict and intolerance evolve into genocide? What do you think?

WHY STUDY RACE AND ETHNICITY FROM A SOCIOLOGICAL PERSPECTIVE?

Living in the United States, we are surrounded by serious and casual discussions and comments about race, ethnic jokes, and anecdotes, stories, and studies about race and ethnicity. Rarely do we stop to ask ourselves what racial and ethnic categories really mean and why they are significant. Who decided they should be significant, and why? What institutions in society reinforce this belief? What institutions challenge it? As a society we have simply accepted such categories as "Black" and "White" as real. Sociologists, however, argue that they are "socially constructed"—what is real is not race but rather the consequences of racism, with its accompanying prejudice and discrimination.

Sociologically defined concepts such as "race"—as well as prejudice, discrimination, assimilation, and the like—help us see domestic and international conflicts in a different light. We may begin to understand that socially constructed categories marginalize and even dehumanize certain groups, and that we must recognize these symbolic acts, as well as the violent acts—from hate crimes to genocides—that may accompany them.

We benefit in our personal lives too from recognizing the socially constructed nature of categories such as race. We ought to pause and ask ourselves: Why is treatment of individuals often conditioned on skin color? Why has our society opted to define this marker as significant? What must we do culturally, socially, politically, educationally, and economically to pull down the artificial barriers imposed by socially constructed categories?

WHAT CAN I DO WITH A SOCIOLOGY DEGREE?

Making an Evidence-Based Argument

Making an Evidence-Based Argument

We live in a sound bite society where news and information are circulated in tweets and texts, and memes go viral in the blink of an eye. We regularly hear people make claims about their lives, communities, or government based on their personal experiences or things they've heard or read in passing. Have you ever forwarded a story over email or social media without checking its validity, only to realize later that it was not true or only partially true? In a fast-moving social world, we may feel we lack the time or inclination or even the skills to determine whether information we accept and share is fully reliable. Sociology invites us to become critical consumers of information, a skill that is of vital importance in both civic life and the job market.

In Chapters 1 and 2, you learned how sociology entreats us to go beyond "common wisdom" about social issues such as homelessness and the wage gap and to study society scientifically. Unlike conversations where someone makes an argument based on anecdotal evidence or a small and unrepresentative sample, sociology highlights the necessity of *evidence-based arguments*. Sociology students learn how to collect and analyze quantitative and qualitative data and to evaluate that data for scientific rigor. In this book, you will find *Behind the Numbers* boxes that contribute to that understanding. Being able to make an evidence-based argument is an important skill in any occupation. Budget reports, employee evaluations, scientific and social scientific research, grant proposals, program and policy evaluations, and arguing a case in court all require evidence-based arguments. The ability to communicate effectively is a requirement of most jobs and necessitates showing or proving your points, not just stating your thoughts or opinions. Sociology students learn not only how to make evidence-based arguments but also how to evaluate the claims of others.

Jenny Xia, Data Analyst at the Institute for Women's Policy Research

University of Pennsylvania, BA in Sociology

My interest in gender equity as a sociology major led me to my current position as a data analyst at the Institute for Women's Policy Research (IWPR). At IWPR, I analyze data and compile research reports on topic areas related to women's well-being, including workplace equity and work-family policies. As IWPR's research is cited in media outlets and used to inform lawmakers, building strong evidence-based arguments is essential to my work. Before a report can be publicly disseminated, it is evaluated for the strength of its rationale and supporting evidence. For example, we must address the limitations of our research findings and ensure that the data we use in a report have sample sizes that are large enough to contribute to meaningful analysis.

As a student of sociology, you are trained to think critically about the information you consume as well as put forth concerning the world around you. The ability to identify and craft strong evidence-based arguments was one of the most important skills I honed as a sociology major, as it helped me develop a critical thinking mindset, something that is highly valuable to any occupation.

Career Data: Social Science Research Assistant

- 2016 Median Pay: $46,820 per year

SOURCE: Bureau of Labor Statistics, Occupational Outlook Handbook, 2016.

SUMMARY

- **Race** is not a biological category but a social construct. Its societal significance derives from the fact that people in a particular culture believe, falsely, that there are biologically distinguishable races and then act on the basis of this belief. The perceived differences among "races" are often distorted and lead to **prejudice** and **discrimination**.
- Many societies include different ethnic groups with varied histories, cultures, and practices.
- **Minorities**, typically because of their race or **ethnicity**, may experience prejudice and discrimination. Different types of minority–dominant group relations include **expulsion**, **assimilation**, **segregation**, and **cultural pluralism**.
- Prejudice usually relies on **stereotyping** and **scapegoating**. During difficult economic times prejudice may increase, as people seek someone to blame for their predicament.
- The civil rights struggles that began in the United States more than 60 years ago led to passage of civil rights and affirmative action legislation that has reduced, but not eliminated, the effects of prejudice and discrimination against minorities.
- Although discrimination is against the law in the United States, it is still widely practiced. **Institutionalized discrimination** in particular results in the unequal treatment of minorities in employment, housing, education, and other areas.
- The United States is a multiethnic, multiracial society. Minority groups—including American Indians, African Americans, Latinos, and Asian Americans—make up close to 40% of the population. This figure

out in disproportionate numbers; and female enrollment skews higher among older students, low-income students, and Black and Hispanic students. (Williams, 2010, para. 1–4)

Data show the dimensions of the shift toward greater college enrollment among women than men, a trend that holds true, albeit to different degrees, across all major demographic groups: For instance, in 1975, 29% of males and about 24% of females ages 18 to 24 were enrolled in a degree-granting post-secondary institution. Among Whites, the gap in enrollment favored men by about 6 points. Among Black students, it favored women by 1 point and among Hispanics, it favored men by 2 points. In 2015, more women were enrolled (43%) than men (38%). Among White students, there was a 5-point gap; among Black students, a 1-point gap; and among Hispanic students, an 8-point gap, in enrollment between females and males (National Center for Education Statistics, 2016a).

Our opening story suggests that women are moving ahead in academic achievement—and men are falling behind. What explains this trend? What are its causes? What are its consequences? The growing gap in attainment of higher education between women and men is a significant social phenomenon that we explore in this chapter.

This trend, however, is only part of a story that still finds women earning less than their male counterparts in the workforce and reaching fewer positions at the top of the corporate ladder and in politics. Women across the globe remain deeply vulnerable to violence and exploitation. Deep-seated prejudices hamper both men and women who do not behave as their societies expect: Gays, lesbians, transgendered individuals, and others who "do gender" differently are subject to ostracism, discrimination, and abuse. In this chapter, we look at the social category of gender and its continuing significance in modern society, examining its effects on individuals, groups, and societies. ■

We begin with a discussion of key concepts of sex and gender and how those are used in sociological study. We then address the construction of gendered selves, looking at agents of socialization—including the family, media, and schools—and examining the idea that gender is as much a process as an identity. This leads us to a wide-ranging discussion of gender and society. We focus on gender and family life, higher education, the wage gap, and sexual harassment to understand how gender norms, roles, and expectations shape the experiences of men and women in key societal institutions. Next we turn to both the classical canon and contemporary feminist thinking about gender, ending with a section on women's global concerns, including maternal mortality, sex trafficking, and rape in war. We examine the marginality of women and the steps being taken to empower them to change their own lives and communities.

CONCEPTS OF SEX, GENDER, AND SEXUALITY

Sociologists acknowledge that complex interactions between biology and culture shape behavioral differences associated with gender. They seek to take both forces into account, though most believe culture and society play more important roles in structuring gender and **gender roles**, *the attitudes and behaviors considered appropriately "masculine" or "feminine" in a particular culture.* Sociologists thus argue that gender-specific behaviors are not reducible to biological differences; rather, biology, culture, and social learning all interact to shape human behaviors.

To highlight the distinction between biological and social factors, sociologists use the term *sex* to refer to biological identity and the term *gender* to refer to the "masculine" or "feminine" roles associated with sex. **Sex** encompasses the *anatomical and other biological differences between males and females that originate in human genes.* Many of these biologically based sex differences, such as differences in genitalia, are usually present at birth. Others, triggered by male or female hormones, develop later—for example, female menstruation and differences in muscle mass, facial hair, height, and vocal characteristics.

Gender roles: The attitudes and behaviors that are considered appropriately "masculine" or "feminine" in a particular culture.

Sex: The anatomical and other biological characteristics that differ between males and females and that originate in human genes.

Gender encompasses the norms, roles, and behavioral characteristics associated in a given society with being male or female. Gender is less about being biologically male or female than about conforming to mainstream notions of masculinity and femininity, though the characteristics we associate with gender vary across time and space. Biologically based sex differences are not unimportant in shaping social norms of gender. The fact that only biological women can bear and nurse children, for example, has enormous implications for women's roles in all societies (Huber, 2006), but this does not mean that, as Sigmund Freud asserted, biology is destiny.

REUTERS/Andres Stapff

The U.S. military continues to be numerically dominated by men, but women are joining in greater numbers today. In 2013, the U.S. military lifted the ban on women in combat, opening new roles for women in fields like artillery and infantry.

Sexuality is a term used in a variety of ways. Sociologically, we can think of it as *encompassing sexual identity, attraction, and relationships*. Sexuality may or may not align conventionally with one's sex and gender. Sociologists use the term *heteronormative* to designate the beliefs and practices that align with heterosexuality; that is, in modern Western societies, social institutions and norms embrace and elevate heterosexual relationships between biological males and females. This has often led to the marginalization of other sexualities, including homosexuality, bisexuality, and asexuality.

Sociologists generally consider sex and gender to be dynamic concepts. Although it is clear that *gender,* which is associated with norms, roles, and behaviors that shift over time, is socially constructed and thus subject to transformations, a growing number of researchers have suggested that *sex* is also socially constructed rather than solely biological (Preves, 2003). They cite cases of infants born with ambiguous sex characteristics and/or an abnormal chromosomal makeup. Doctors, parents, or society rarely tolerate uncertainties in sex categorization. As a result, these children are usually subjected to surgeries and medications intended to render them "categorizable" in societally normative terms.

Transgender is an umbrella term used to describe those whose gender identity, expression, or behavior differs from their assigned sex at birth or is outside the two gender categories. A person who was female assigned at birth (FAAB) but identifies as a man (FTM) may be described as transgender (or trans), as may a person who was male assigned at birth (MAAB) but identifies as a woman (MTF). Transgender also includes, but is not limited to, other categories and identities, such as transsexual, cross-dresser, androgynous, genderqueer, bigender, third gender, and gender nonconforming. **Transsexual** usually refers to people who use surgery and hormones to change their sex to match their preferred gender. Transgender people may have heterosexual, lesbian, gay, or bisexual sexual orientation.

The issue of the transgender community and its visibility and rights have garnered attention in the media recently. In a revolutionary interview with Diane Sawyer (ABC News, 2015) and iconic *Vanity Fair* photo spread in the spring

Gender: Behavioral characteristics that differ between males and females based on culturally enforced and socially learned norms and roles.

Sexuality: The ways in which people construct their sexual desires and relationships, including the norms governing sexual behavior.

Transgender: An umbrella term used to describe those whose gender identity or expression differs from their assigned sex or is outside the gender binary.

Transsexual: A term used to refer to people who use surgery and hormones to change their sex to match their preferred gender.

A transgender man and his partner await the birth of their child. Caitlyn Jenner (right) drew enormous interest as she made her transition from Olympic athlete and television celebrity Bruce Jenner to a feminine appearance and identity. ■

of 2015, U.S. Olympic gold medalist and television celebrity Bruce Jenner introduced the world to Caitlyn, sharing her decision to embrace a feminine identity after years of uncertainty about who she was or how her decision would be received. "For all intents and purposes, I'm a woman," Jenner explained to journalist Diane Sawyer. She told the interviewer that she has not and will not undergo surgery to remove her male genitalia (ABC News, 2015), though she underwent "facial feminization surgery" (Bissinger, 2015). In terms of sexuality, Caitlyn Jenner labels herself as heterosexual. She also identifies as a woman, and her gender display is clearly feminine.

The size of the transgender community in the United States is difficult to ascertain, as many people still live under the radar. A study from the Williams Institute at the University of California, Los Angeles, suggests a figure of 700,000 (Gates, 2011). In 2016, a fight continued in several U.S. states, including North Carolina, over bills to require people to use the restroom of the "sex they were assigned at birth," regardless of their gender identity or outward presentation of self. North Carolina's "bathroom bill" spurred some notable backlash: The National Basketball Association (NBA) pulled the 2017 league's all-star game out of Charlotte, citing "the issue of legal protections for the LGBT [lesbian, gay, bisexual, and transsexual] community" (Helin, 2016). Some institutions have reacted to this issue by embracing nongendered restrooms: The Cooper Union, a college in New York, announced that it is removing gender identification from restrooms on campus and opening single-occupancy toilets for anyone's use. "We have always been ahead of our time and we must continue being leaders on issues of social justice," Bill Mea, acting president, wrote in an e-mail to the campus (Sutter, 2016). Other significant societal institutions have also taken steps against discrimination: In July of 2016, the U.S. military reversed a ban on transgender service members, allowing transgender members of the military forces to serve openly.

Is sex at birth an immutable category? Should individuals have the freedom to define themselves, pushing boundaries of sex, gender, and sexuality to find the space in which they feel at home? How should institutions respond? What do you think?

CONSTRUCTING GENDERED SELVES

Across the diverse cultures of our world, males are generally expected to behave in culturally defined "masculine" ways and females in "feminine" ways. Few people fully conform to these stereotypes—most exhibit a blend of characteristics. Still, in many cultures people believe male and female stereotypes represent fundamental and real sex differences, and although some "blending" is acceptable, there are social consequences for diverging too far from the social scripts of gender.

What is considered "masculine" and "feminine" differs across cultures, and gender displays can vary dramatically. Among the Canela of Brazil, for example, large, colorful disks called *kui* are inserted into holes pierced into a boy's ears. Repeated piercings and insertions stretch the holes to a large size in order to enable the ears to eventually accommodate disks that are several inches across. This painful process is performed to enable the boy to better hear the wisdom of his elders, as well as to make him attractive to women (Crocker, 1986, 1990, 1994). This practice would not be considered masculine in U.S. culture, although earrings, once considered a mark of femininity, are now commonplace symbols of masculinity in some U.S. subcultures.

The Surma people of the Omo Valley in Ethiopia use body adornments as part of members' gender display. Ear labrets are worn by women as well as men, though lip plates, which stretch the lower lip away from the mouth, are only worn by women. ■

Pressures to conform to conventional gender roles exist in all cultures. At the same time, norms and characteristics are dynamic: men and women both shape and are shaped by these expectations. We can think of gender roles as being continuously learned and relearned through social interaction (Fenstermaker & West, 2002). That is, they are neither biologically determined nor passively acquired from others. Rather, each of us plays an active role in learning what it means to be a boy or a girl and a man or a woman in a particular culture. In becoming accomplished actors in our roles, we often forget we are playing parts and become closely identified with the roles themselves. Yet, because we are constantly renegotiating our gender roles in social interaction, we can change and challenge "rules" regarding gender that we find to be limiting.

Critical early influences on gender roles include family, peer groups, the mass media, and schools. These are among the important *agents of gender socialization* that contribute to the creation of our gendered selves.

THE ROOTS OF GENDER: THE FAMILY

Children learn a great deal about socially normative gender roles from their families, particularly their parents. The power of the family in the production and reproduction of gender has led some sociologists to call the home a "factory of gendered personalities" (Fenstermaker Berk, 1985; Goldscheider & Waite, 1991).

Parents often have particular beliefs about how their infant daughters and sons are supposed to behave, and they communicate these attitudes in countless subtle and not-so-subtle ways. A girl may play with a toy truck with few social consequences, while a boy may be teased for enjoying a baby doll. This difference appears to favor girls, but we can also argue that it highlights the stigmatization of practices and objects associated with femininity.

Some studies have shown that parents' ideas about gender affect their behaviors toward children, even before birth (Eliot, 2009; Marini, 1990). One study found that mothers spoke differently to their babies in utero depending on if they knew the babies were boys or girls (K. Smith, 2005). Hilary Lips (2008) has written that parents give their daughters "roots" and their sons "wings"—that is, they nurture closer and more dependent ties with girls than they do with boys. Some research also suggests that boys are more likely to be taught to complete tasks on their own, while girls are instructed to ask for help or have tasks completed for them (Lindsey &

Mize, 2001), a difference that has also been documented in the early-education classroom (Sadker & Zittleman, 2009). A recent study points to an interesting difference in the influence of a male and female parent: that is, "For sons but not daughters, mothers' more traditional attitudes toward women's roles predicted attaining more gender-typed occupations." At the same time, "spending more time with fathers in childhood predicted daughters attaining *less* and sons acquiring *more* gender-typed occupations in young adulthood" (Lawson, Crouter, & McHale, 2015, p. 26).

Toys and books also function as staples of early childhood socialization in the family. Consider a recent study that examined 300 children's picture books published from 1902 to 2000 (DeWitt, Cready, & Seward, 2013). The researchers studied portrayals in the books of mothers and fathers as, variously, companions, disciplinarians, caregivers, nurturers, and providers. Perhaps surprisingly, they found that, in spite of dramatic societal changes over the period examined, the traditional model of the nurturing, homemaking mother and the breadwinning father still prevailed in books published late in the 20th century. Underscoring the significance of the finding, the authors note that books do not just "entertain"; they also "socialize."

Although parental practices may reinforce gender stereotypes, parents can play an equally important part in countering gender stereotyping by being role models and socializing their children into norms and values reflecting greater gender equality. For example, daughters encouraged to excel in traditionally "male" areas like science and mathematics are more likely to grow up to pursue science- or math-related careers (Bhanot & Jovanovic, 2005; Tenenbaum & Leaper, 2003). Just a few decades ago, women were a clear minority in most institutions of higher education. Legal measures such as Title IX legislation, which was enacted in 1972, prohibited discrimination in educational institutions receiving federal funding and opened more educational opportunities to women. By the 1960s and 1970s, young women had greater social and economic support at home as well. Both society and families have been part of the revolution in women's higher education, which we discuss in greater detail further along in the chapter.

GENDER AMONG FRIENDS: PEER INFLUENCES

The actions and judgments of our peers affect the ways we enact our gender roles. Beginning at an early age, girls and boys learn stereotypical gender roles in peer groups (Martin & Fabes, 2001). Aina and Cameron (2011) suggest that friendship patterns and peer pressure reflect and affirm stereotypes. This is particularly acute among boys, who "police" peers, stigmatizing perceived feminine traits. Playing in same-sex peer groups, interestingly enough, may have a different effect from playing more often in mixed groups. Martin and Fabes (2001) point to a "social dosage effect," such that play among young girls who stay with all-girl groups tends to reflect norms of encouragement and support, while young boys in same-gender groups develop a tendency toward more aggressive and competitive play.

Research on elementary school playgroups has found that girls often gather in smaller groups, playing games that include imitation and the taking of turns. Boys, on the other hand, play in larger groups at rule-governed games that occur over larger physical distances than girls occupy (Richards, 2012; Thorne, 1993). Long before they become teenagers, young people learn that gender matters and that the roles, norms, and expectations of boys and girls are often different.

During late childhood and adolescence, children are especially concerned about what their friends think of them—far more than about what their parents think. In her ethnography of a racially diverse working-class high school, C. J. Pascoe (2007) uncovered how teenage boys reinforced norms of masculinity and heterosexuality by disciplining behavior deemed inappropriate, feminine, or otherwise "unmanly," using slurs like "fag" and "faggot." Homophobia can be acute during adolescence (Wyss, 2007).

Pressures for peer conformity remain strong into college, where sororities, fraternities, athletic teams, and other social groups may reproduce stereotypical gender behavior (K. Edwards, 2007). Significantly, however, attitudes toward and practices of gendered behavior and sexuality are changing in the millennial generation. For example, a recent study (Pew Research Center, 2017a) found acceptance for same-sex marriage to be significantly higher (71%) among millennials (defined as young adults born in 1981 or later) than among generation X (born 1965 through 1980) respondents (56%) or baby boomers (born 1946 through 1964; 46%). As well, a report from the Public Religion Research Institute, based on a survey of adults ages 18 to 35, found that "[7%] of millennials identify either as lesbian, gay, bisexual, or transgender" (Jones & Cox, 2015). By contrast, an estimate by the Williams Institute of the size of the

LGBT population in the United States as a whole pegged the figure of lesbian, gay, and bisexual adults at about 3.5% and the transgender population at about 0.3% (Gates, 2011).

MEDIA POWER: REFLECTING AND REINFORCING GENDER

Scholars have written extensively on the role television plays in reinforcing gender identities in society (Barner, 1999; Condry, 1989; Gauntlett, 2008). According to the American Academy of Child and Adolescent Psychiatry (2011), the average child in the United States spends 3 to 4 hours per day in front of the TV, more if the child has a television in his or her bedroom. The advent of smartphones, which find their way even into the hands of elementary schoolers, has further increased the "screen time" of many children.

We might predict that the gendered messages conveyed by everything from characters to themes to advertisements will affect the perceptions, norms, and identities of young people. Although much has changed in U.S. society in terms of gender roles, media images often appear frozen in time, persistently peddling domestic or highly sexualized images of women—or cattiness and personal deceit, traits that appear frequently on "reality" TV programs like the various *Real Housewives* shows and *Dance Moms,* as well as fictional shows like *Pretty Little Liars*. Television images of men are rarely diverse: they are still likely to be portrayed as more aggressive and analytical than women; they also disproportionately occupy fictional positions of leadership, whether in business, politics, or the media (think of programs like *Mad Men* and *House of Cards*).

Cartoons also convey gendered images. One study found that male cartoon characters outnumber female characters four to one—the same ratio as 25 years before. Moreover, male cartoon characters tend to be powerful, dominant, smart, and aggressive; female characters are more likely to lack personalities altogether (Spicher & Hudak, 1997; Thompson & Scantlin, 2007). Other research has found that male cartoon characters use more physical aggression, while females are more likely to display behaviors that are fearful, polite and supportive, or romantic (Gokcearslan, 2010; Leaper, Breed, Hoffman, & Perlman, 2002). Researchers draw attention not only to how characters look and what they do, but also what they say. A recent linguistic analysis of several decades of Disney "princess" films uncovered a striking finding: In Disney's older "classic" princess films, female characters were more likely to speak than female characters in newer Disney films. For example, in *Cinderella* (1950), women spoke about 60% of lines. In *The Little Mermaid* (1989), female characters spoke just 32% of the time, and in *Mulan* (1998), 23% of the time. In the hit film *Frozen* (2013), two young princesses take center stage, but female characters have 41% of spoken lines (Guo, 2016).

Are gender differences between little girls and little boys more natural or learned? Think about evidence you would use to support both arguments. Which seems more persuasive? Why?

In another interesting study, researchers examined accounts of heterosexuality in media for children by analyzing G-rated films grossing $100 million dollars or more between 1990 and 2005. The study found that, first, heterosexuality is constructed through heteroromantic love relationships as exceptional, magical, and transformative. Second, heterosexuality outside of relationships is constructed through portrayals of men gazing desirously at women's bodies. Male characters are usually clothed, while the female characters are shown with deep cleavage, visible stomachs, and lean bodies (Martin & Kazyak, 2009). Nevertheless, newer Disney movies may be challenging how female characters are portrayed on screen: *Moana* (2016) did not involve a love interest but a journey of a young girl trying to save her island.

Data suggest that the popular music industry traffics in gender stereotypes. Wallis (2011) and Turner (2011) found that popular music videos tend to portray women as sex objects who are submissive in relation to men. Indeed, as Aubrey and Frisby (2011) state, "although sexual objectification is commonplace in media culture, music videos provide the most potent examples of it" (p. 475). Caputi (2014) notes the sexism inherent in the way that young female pop stars are "branded," with the media hypersexualizing them and subjecting their romantic relationships to intense scrutiny. Although research finds the objectification of women in the music industry to be strongest in hip-hop and pop music, it can be observed across genres (Aubrey & Frisby, 2011). Moreover, because music videos today are often viewed online and on mobile devices in addition to the more traditional outlets of television channels such as MTV, these gendered images reach a wider audience than they might have even a decade ago.

In the Disney film *Moana* (2016), a young girl trying to save her island is the leading character. Can you think of other recent films in which female characters take on roles that differ from conventional film portrayals? ■

Video games offer an area for expanding research on media and socialization. By some estimates, fully 91% of children ages 2 to 17 play video games. The majority of gamers are male, though the proportion of girls has been growing, and the percentage of players among the very young has also risen, particularly as more gaming has moved to mobile devices (NPD Group, 2011). This is significant because content studies suggest that popular video games consistently convey stereotypical gender images. Downs and Smith (2010), in an analysis of 60 video games with a total of 489 characters, determined that women were likely to be presented in hypersexualized ways that included being partially nude or wearing revealing attire. Reflecting common findings that men are "action" figures while women are largely passive, Haninger and Thompson (2004) discovered that in the 81 teen-rated games they sampled, fully 72 had playable male characters, while just 42 had playable female characters. Interestingly, among adults who play video games, the perception of gender representation is mixed: a recent study found that 26% of all players and 35% of frequent players (those who labeled themselves "gamers") do not think women are portrayed poorly in most games. Another 16% of players and 24% of "gamers" agreed that women are portrayed poorly in most games (Duggan, 2015).

In an age of growing media influence, when stories and images and ideas reach us not only through television, films, and games but also through computers, phones, and other devices, it is important to consider what kinds of gender images are conveyed. Do new media sources offer more diverse images? Are old stereotypes still pervasive? What do you think?

GENDER IN THE CLASSROOM: SCHOOLS AND SOCIALIZATION

According to some researchers, in addition to providing instruction in basic subjects, schools are an important site of a "hidden curriculum," or the unspoken socialization to norms, values, and roles—including gender roles (Basow, 2004; Margolis, 2001). For example, there is evidence that from an early age shyness is discouraged in boys at school because it is viewed as violating the masculine norm of assertiveness (Doey, Coplan, & Kingsbury, 2013). The roles of teachers, administrators, and other adults in the school provide some early lessons to students about their future career prospects. Pre-K and elementary teaching is still largely female dominated, and in many elementary schools the only men are administrators, physical education teachers or coaches, and janitors (Figure 9.1).

Classroom materials reflect gender power and position too. Books on history, for instance, are still heavily populated by male characters, the great heroes and villains of the global and local past. Until very recently, when books began to present a more diverse cast of historical characters,

> women were not viewed as an integral part of the historical record. The vast majority remained silent and invisible, their history subsumed under general descriptions of men's lives. . . . Extraordinary figures like the queens of sixteenth-century Europe

FIGURE 9.1 Percentage of Female Teachers in Educational Occupations, 2015

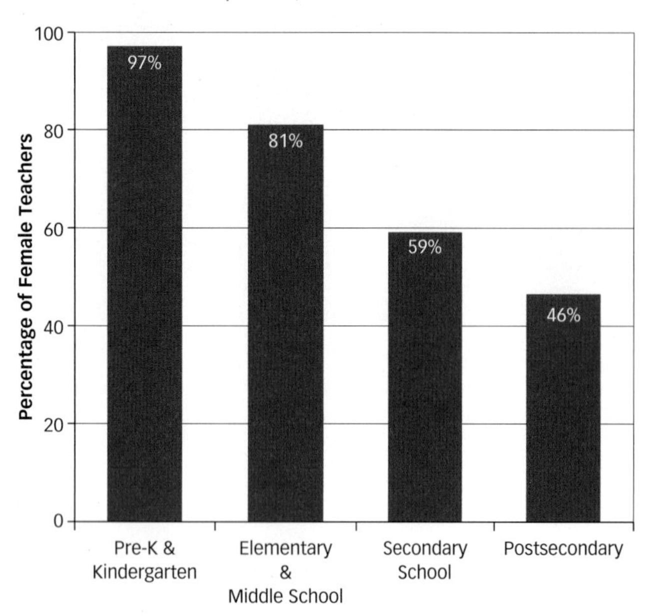

SOURCE: U.S. Bureau of Labor Statistics.

> or the nineteenth-century reformers in the United States, active agents in their own right, fared no better. Though [they were] sometimes praised for having successfully assumed male roles, traditional, patronizing phrases and denigrating stereotypes abstracted and diminished even their exceptional personalities and experiences. (Zinsser, 1993, p. 3)

Even today, where women and, often, racial and ethnic minorities, appear in history textbooks, they are often shown in special features outside the main text that are more likely to be overlooked. In their book *Failing at Fairness* (1997), David Sadker and Myra Sadker argue that in most history texts students see few women. Their study of one 819-page text yielded less than a full page of references devoted to women. Another book contained four pictures of men for every one of women, and just about 3% of the text was allotted to telling about women.

The authors write about challenging high school seniors to name 20 famous U.S. women, past or present (not including sports or entertainment figures). In the allotted 5 minutes, most students were able to come up with just a handful, but they had little trouble naming famous men (Sadker & Sadker, 1997). Important changes have taken place in the teaching of history since Sadker and Sadker's work. For instance, the advanced placement U.S. history curriculum devotes considerable space to women's rights movements. Have changes like this altered the gender landscape in U.S. history teaching and learning? How would you perform in a quiz like that administered by the Sadkers to students in 1997, and what sociological factors would you cite to explain your performance?

DOING GENDER

Sociologists commonly define gender as a product of agents of socialization, the combined influences of which create gendered selves. The implication is that gender is an internalized identity, not natural, but still a fundamental aspect of the social self. Another sociological perspective, described below, suggests that gender is less an identity than an activity.

As we saw in Chapter 4, sociologist Erving Goffman (1959) argued that the social self is the *product* of a social interaction. Thus, the individual engages in "impression management" to tailor his or her presentation of self in a way most favorable to the given situation. Goffman argued that the individual (or a group) is concerned with defining the situation and ensuring a believable performance.

Goffman's work does not have gender at its center, though some of his examples of impression management are telling. For instance, he illustrated *idealization,* in which we present ourselves in ways that exemplify the values and norms of society, with a young woman choosing not to appear smarter than her male date. Although her decision to "play dumb" may have gone the way of the 1950s (when Goffman's book was written), it demonstrates how individuals seek to perform gender in accordance with societal expectations.

Building on some of Goffman's ideas, Candace West and Don Zimmerman's (1987) article "Doing Gender" suggests that gender is an activity we *do* rather than a fixed identity. West and Zimmerman posit that *sex* is a set of biological categories for classifying people as male or female; a person's **sex category** is the *socially required identification display that confirms*

Sex category: The socially required identification display that confirms someone's membership in a given category.

his or her membership in a given category, including displaying and enacting gender as social norms and expectations determine. Thus, *gender* is an activity that creates differences between men and women that, although not biological, appear natural because they are so consistently enacted. Membership in a sex category also brings differential access to power and resources, affecting interpersonal relationships and social status.

Bill O'Leary/The Washington Post via Getty Images

How do you see the future division of labor in your family? If you are already a spouse or parent, think about your level of satisfaction with how household work is divided in your family. What might you want to change and why?

GENDER AND SOCIETY

Anthropological studies have found that inequalities in almost all known societies, past and present, favor men over women (Huber, 2006). Women are occasionally equal to men economically, politically, or socially, but in no known society do they have greater control over economic and political resources, exercise greater power and authority, or enjoy more prestige than men (Chafetz, 1984). Many sociologists explain this inequality by noting that women alone can give birth to and (particularly important before modern bottle-feeding) nurse infants, two activities essential to a society's continuation but usually lacking in social status. Given that a major source of power, wealth, and status is the ability to earn money or acquire other material goods of value, any limitations on women's ability to pursue these rewards affects their social position.

In hunting and gathering and early horticultural societies, women produced nearly as much food as men and were more equal in power and prestige, though wealth differences were minimal in such subsistence economies (Huber, 1990, 1993; Mukhopadhyay & Higgins, 1988). With the emergence of agricultural societies and the development of metallurgy, trade and warfare became much more central features of social organization. Because women spent large portions of their active years pregnant or nursing infants, they were less likely to become merchants or warriors. Strong states emerged to manage warfare and trade, and these were controlled by men. Research suggests that women's status suffered accordingly (Friedl, 1975; Grant, 1991).

In modern industrial societies, the requirements of physical survival, reproduction, and economic organization no longer exert the same sorts of constraints. The advent of reliable birth control, along with the invention of bottle-feeding around 1910, freed women from long periods of pregnancy and nursing. Mass education, established in most industrial nations by the end of the 19th century, encouraged women to seek knowledge and eventually careers outside the home.

Today, gender stratification persists, but in a rapidly changing and dynamic social environment. Two areas in which we can explore both stasis and change are the family and education.

GENDER AND FAMILY LIFE

Domestic tasks—child care, cooking, cleaning, and shopping for necessities of living—can entail long hours of work. In the United States, women still do the disproportionate share of housework and child care. Men are more likely to engage in nonroutine domestic tasks, such as making home repairs, preparing a barbeque, or taking the children on outings.

Attitudes and practices change, although slowly. Just over a generation ago, a study found that fewer than 5% of husbands did as much housework as their wives (Coltrane & Ishii-Kuntz, 1992). In a 15-year study that tracked thousands of men and women born after World

War II, Goldscheider and Waite (1991) found that, in two-parent families with teenage boys and girls, girls were assigned five times as many household chores as their brothers.

A 2007 *Time* magazine survey found that 84% of respondents (men and women) agreed that husbands and wives "negotiate the rules, relationships and responsibilities more than those earlier generations did" (Gibbs, 2009). A study by the University of Michigan found that the total amount of housework done by women has fallen since 1976 from an average of 26 hours per week to about 17, while the amount done by men has grown from 6 hours to 13 hours (Achen & Stafford, 2005; Reaney & Goldsmith, 2008). Clearly, there has been some convergence. Labor-saving devices (like the microwave oven) have contributed to changes, as has the ability of more dual-earner households to pass the burden of domestic work to housekeepers, gardeners, and the like. At the same time, women are still primarily responsible for domestic work in most two-parent heterosexual households (Davis, Greenstein, & Marks, 2007), a phenomenon Arlie Hochschild (2012) calls the **second shift**—*the unpaid housework women typically do after they come home from their paid employment.* Interestingly, recent research suggests that place of residence—in this case the state where couples live—has an influence on the household division of labor. Ruppanner and Maume (2016) found that in states where women have more labor market power (measured by, among others, the number of women who are in the paid labor force, are college educated, work in management), married men are spending more time on domestic tasks. Mothers in these states, whether or not they work, are spending less time on housework. Conversely, in states with lower female labor market power and greater cultural traditionalism (measured by, for instance, higher church attendance and higher marriage and fertility rates), married men spent less time on housework and mothers devoted more hours to home chores.

Second shift: The unpaid housework that women typically do after they come home from their paid employment.

Some data show that unmarried women who live with men spend less time on housework than do married women—even when numbers of children and hours of paid work are taken into account (Davis et al., 2007). The division of household labor is also more likely to be equal among lesbian and gay couples (Kurdek, 2007). What might explain these differences? One study with about 17,000 respondents in 28 countries suggests that marriage has a "traditionalizing" effect on couples, even those who describe themselves and their practices in egalitarian terms (Davis et al., 2007).

FIGURE 9.2 Average SAT Mathematics Scores for Males and Females, 1972–2015

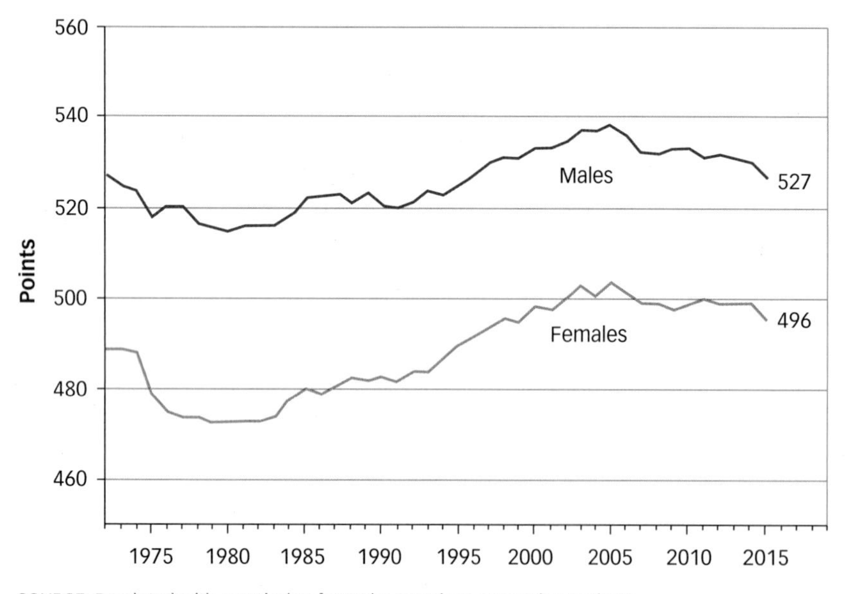

SOURCE: Reprinted with permission from The American Enterprise Institute.

GENDER IN HIGH SCHOOL: WHY DO BOYS OUTSCORE GIRLS ON THE SAT?

Girls outperform boys on many academic measures: earning high grades, enrolling in many of the Advanced Placement (AP) courses, achieving academic honors, finishing in the top 10% of their class, and graduating, to name a few. One measure where boys have consistently outpaced their female peers, however, is the SAT (originally the Scholastic Aptitude Test, later renamed the Scholastic Assessment Test, and now officially known by the initials SAT). In 2015, the average score for boys on the mathematics section of the SAT was 527 out of 800; girls scored an average of 496. Although both boys' and girls' scores have risen over time (though there has been a decline in recent years), the gap has remained steady (Figure 9.2). Even though boys' advantage on the verbal section of the SAT is smaller, it too has persisted, though girls tend to earn markedly better average grades in courses such as English.

AP Photo/Rui Vieira

Think back to our discussion of agents of gender socialization. Are there any clues in these materials about why boys outscore girls on standardized math tests such as the SAT?

What explains the difference? Some researchers suggest the gap points to a gender bias in the test (Sadker & Sadker, 1997; Sadker & Zittleman, 2009). Why, they ask, do boys continue to outscore girls if girls do better in school and continue doing better in college? After all, the SAT is intended to measure college readiness. In a study published in 1989, Rosser argued that girls did better than boys on questions focused on relationships, aesthetics, and the humanities, while boys performed better when questions involved sports, the natural sciences, or business. Rosser's study followed an earlier report by Carol Dwyer of the Educational Testing Service (ETS). Dwyer (1976) concluded that gender differences could be altered through selective use of test items. In an effort to "balance" the test, she reported, ETS added more test items highlighting politics, sports, and business, areas on which boys did better. Questions about whether the test favors boys continue to be raised 40 years later (Sadker & Zittleman, 2009).

Some researchers argue that girls may underperform on math tests because they have been socialized to believe that boys are better at math. This is an example of what researchers call **stereotype threat**, *a situation in which an individual is at risk of confirming a negative stereotype about his or her social group* (Steele & Aronson, 1995). This concept highlights the assertion that a person's performance on a task may be negatively affected by anxiety related to perceived low expectations of the individual's group—such as the expectation that "girls are not good at math." One experimental study showed that informing female test takers of stereotype threat before a test improved their performance (Johns, Schmader, & Martens, 2005).

On the other hand, some observers suggest that boys' higher scores on the math section of the SAT are a result of a different phenomenon. Christina Hoff Sommers (2000) argues that more girls—and girls representing more varying levels of achievement and ability—take the test, explaining their lower average score. Boys' higher average score, suggests Hoff, is the product of a limited pool of test takers representing the best-prepared young men.

Is the SAT gender biased because it shows boys outperforming girls, even though girls end up earning better grades and dropping out of college less frequently? Or is it evidence of girls' advantages, because girls are more likely to take college entrance exams and go to college? What other factors may be at play here?

GENDER AND HIGHER EDUCATION

We began this chapter by noting that more women than men are studying in U.S. institutions of higher education. In 2014, more women in U.S. society also held a bachelor's degree. The difference in the population as a whole is

Stereotype threat: A situation in which an individual is at risk of confirming a negative stereotype about his or her social group.

small: 29.9% of men and 30.2% of women have completed a bachelor's degree. The gap in younger age groups, however, is more substantial—and growing. Among young adults ages 24 to 34, over 37% of women hold bachelor's degrees compared to just under 30% of men (Figure 9.3; Bauman & Ryan, 2015).

In decades and centuries past, women were actively discouraged from pursuing higher education. In the late 19th century, powerful social barriers stood in the way, such as beliefs about women's capacity to succeed at *both* education and reproduction. Some believed that the "ovaries—not the brain—were the most important organ in a woman's body" (Brumberg, 1997). Author Joan Brumberg (1997) writes,

> The most persuasive spokesperson for this point of view was Dr. Edward Clarke, a highly regarded professor at Harvard Medical School, whose popular book *Sex in Education; Or, A Fair Chance for the Girls* (1873) was a powerful statement of the ideology of "ovarian determinism." In a series of case studies drawn from his clinical practice, Clarke described adolescent women whose menstrual cycles, reproductive capacity, and general health were all ruined, in his opinion, by inattention to their special monthly demands [menstruation]. . . . Clarke argued against higher education because he believed women's bodies were more complicated than men's; this difference meant that young girls needed time and ease to develop, free from the drain of intellectual activity. (p. 8)

Although the idea of a "brain–womb conflict" faded as the United States entered the 20th century, other beliefs persisted. Ordinary families with resources to support college study were more likely to invest them in their sons, who were expected to be their future families' primary breadwinners. Families that did seek education for their daughters ran into structural barriers. For example, until the passage of Title IX in 1972, some U.S. colleges and universities, particularly at the graduate and professional school level, limited or prohibited female enrollment. Title IX is often associated with increasing equity in women's access to collegiate athletic opportunities. It is, however, a much broader mandate, as it foresees gender equity for men and women in every educational program receiving federal funding.

FIGURE 9.3 Percentage of the Population 25 and Older With a Bachelor's Degree or Higher by Sex and Age Group, 2014

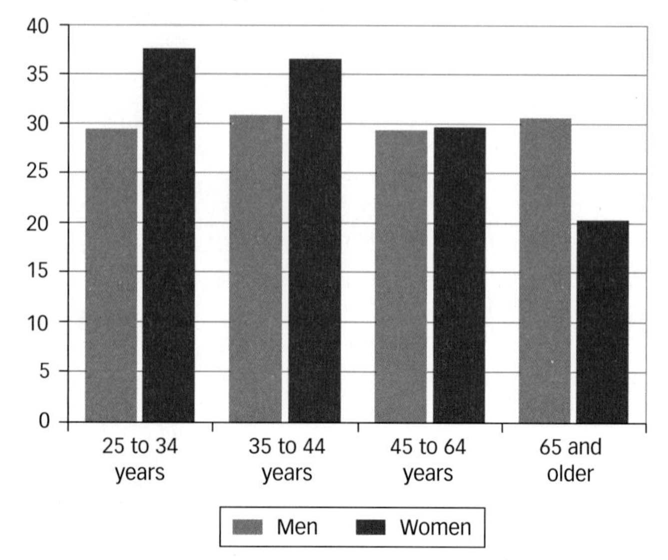

SOURCE: Bauman, K. & C. Ryan. (2015).

Women's representation among bachelor's graduates has soared in recent decades. It has risen considerably as well in professional degrees (Figure 9.4). In 1972, women earned just 7% of law degrees and 9% of medical degrees in the United States (National Organization for Women, n.d.). According to the American Bar Association (2014), in 2013, women earned 47% of law degrees conferred. In 2015, women were 48% of medical school graduates in the United States (Kaiser Family Foundation, 2015).

The *proportion* of women enrolled in college has been greater than the proportion of men since 1991, though the actual *numbers* of women have been greater since the early 1980s, since women make up a larger share of the population. Women's climb to equality in educational opportunity has been long, but their gains in higher education since Title IX have been dramatic. At the same time, men's higher education gains have slowed.

Researchers suggest several reasons for the growing college enrollment gap. First, a high school degree is a prerequisite to college, and significantly more men than women leave high school without diplomas. High school, as well as college, struggles have been attributed in some instances not to differences in "cognitive abilities," which are comparable in boys and girls, but rather to differences in "'non-cognitive skills' among boys, including the inability to pay attention in class, to work with others, to organize and keep track of homework or class materials and to seek help from others" (Jacob, 2002, p. 4). Boys are also more likely than girls to have behavioral or disciplinary problems that lead to dropping out before completion of high school (Stearns & Glennie, 2006).

Second, and related in some respects to the "noncognitive" factors noted above, young women as a group have higher grades than young men, a factor that is predictive of college matriculation and success: A large-scale study found that the mean high school grade point average for female students was 3.1 of a possible 4.0, while for male students it was 2.9 (National Center for Education Statistics, 2009).

Third, women perceive college as bringing greater returns. A Pew Research Center survey found that women are more likely than men to say college was "very useful" in increasing their knowledge and helping them grow intellectually (81% compared to 67%), as well as helping them grow and mature as a person (73% compared to 64%). Perceptions about the necessity of a college education for "getting ahead in life" were also split by gender: 77% of respondents indicated this was true for women, while 68% felt it was true for men (Wang & Parker, 2011).

Indeed, the benefits of a college education have grown for women (Goldin, Katz, & Kuziemko, 2006) and they may be more motivated to use college as a stepping-stone to a desired job. A recent study (Olivieri, 2014) makes this argument based on the observation that in the last half century, women have made significant inroads into historically male-dominated occupations: According to the author's calculations, of all White women who were either staying home or employed in 1960, just 8% were in male-dominated occupations. In 2010, fully 29% worked in these occupations, which include physicians, lawyers, managers, and scientists. By contrast, the proportion of men in female-dominated occupations like teaching and nursing has remained low. Olivieri concludes that sexism is at the foundation of this phenomenon: that is, even though women are occupying a greater share of historically "male" jobs that require a college education, sexist notions about masculinity and "women's" jobs are keeping men from pursuing other occupations—including in growing fields like nursing—that need a college credential. Rather, men may be choosing other historically "masculine" fields like construction and manufacturing, even though those sectors have seen declines in recent decades.

Finally, men are more likely than women to leave college without finishing a degree. A recent study points to the pivotal role of student debt in this process. For most American college students, the ability to secure loans has become a prerequisite to entering college. For some, mounting debt

FIGURE 9.4 Percentage of the Population Aged 25 to 28 With a Bachelor's or Higher Degree, by Sex: 1967 to 2015

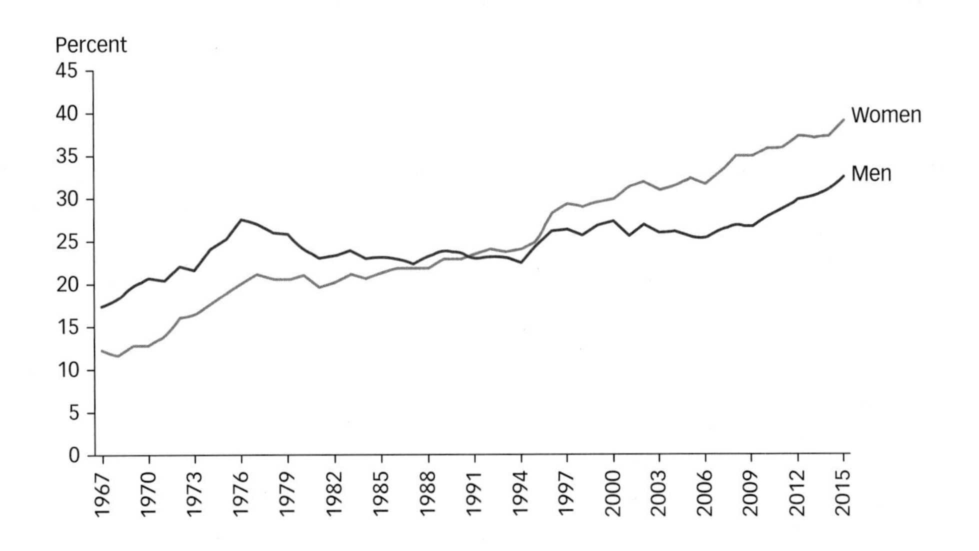

SOURCE: Ryan, Camille L., and Kurt Bauman. (2016). "Educational Attainment in the United States: 2015." Figure 7, United States Census Bureau, March (www.census.gov/content/dam/Census/library/publications/2016/demo/p20-578.pdf).

■ **FIGURE 9.5** U.S. College Degree Gap in Favor of Women, 2016

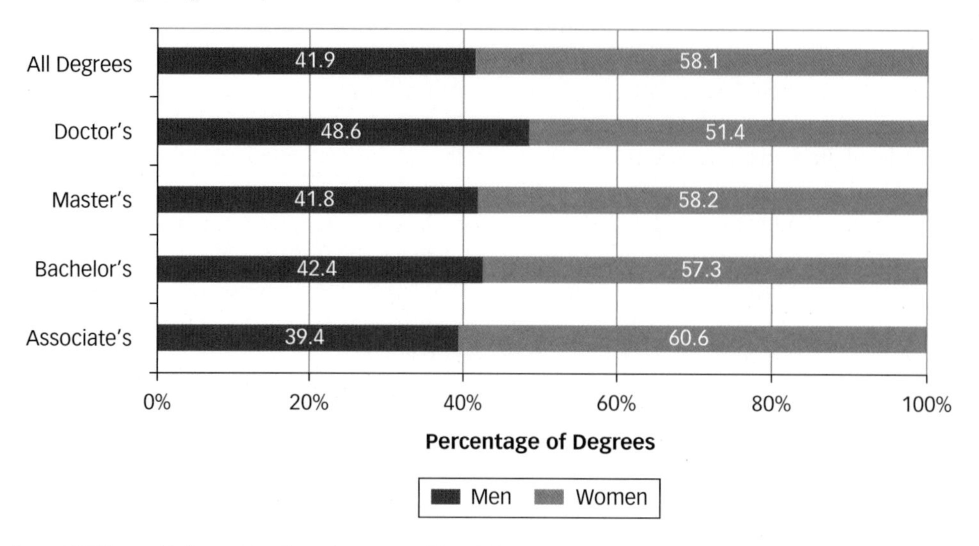

Women in the class of 2016 earned about 139 college degrees at all levels for every 100 earned by men. This translates to a 610,000 college degree gap in favor of women for 2016 college graduates (2.195 million total degrees for women vs. 1.585 million total degrees for men).

SOURCE: National Center for Education Statistics, U.S. Department of Education (https://nces.ed.gov/programs/digest/d14/tables/dt14_318.10.asp).

■ **FIGURE 9.6** Median Annual Earnings, by Race/Ethnicity and Gender, 2015

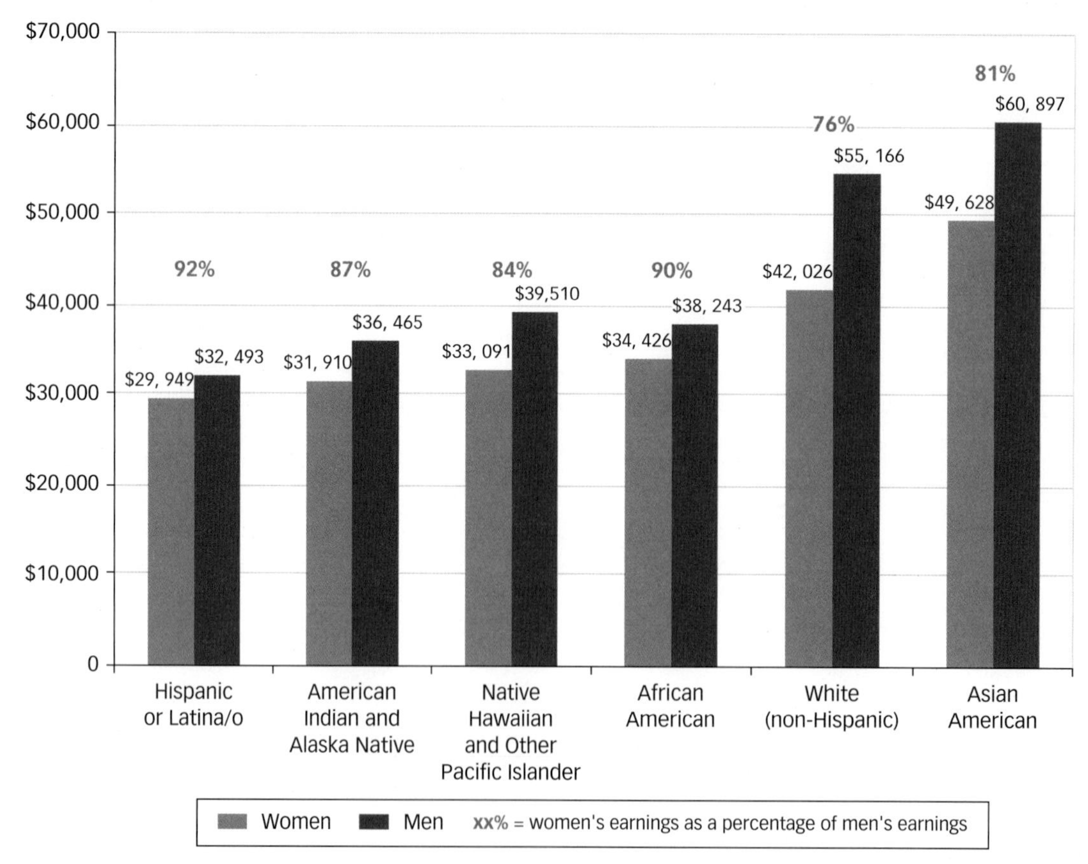

SOURCE: Reprinted with permission from The American Association of University Women. http://www.aauw.org/research/the-simple-truth-about-the-gender-pay-gap/.

during their undergraduate years leads to a rethinking of the benefit of the degree versus dropping out to enter the workforce. Data suggest that men may be more averse than women to accruing debt: Men drop out with lower levels of debt than women do, but they are also more likely to leave before graduating (Dwyer, Hodson, & McCloud, 2013).

As we have noted above, there are identifiable factors that help us understand the growing gap between men and women in college attendance and completion. Notably, however, the picture becomes more complex when we look not only at gender but also sexuality. Recent research suggests that the probability of college completion is reversed when we look at gay men and lesbian women: Gay men are more likely to finish college than their heterosexual male and female peers, and lesbian women are less likely to complete their higher education than either gay men or heterosexual men and women. One study found that homosexual men had a 44% probability of completing a college degree by age 30, while heterosexual men had a 28% probability of doing the same. Among women, however, heterosexual women had a 34% probability of completion by age 30, while homosexual women's probability was only 24% (Fine, 2012). How might sociologists study these differences? How might they go about explaining them?

Cherry Blossom/Alamy

Recent U.S. Department of Education data show that women have a lower probability of acceptance to many private elite colleges than their male peers. Because private institutions are exempt from Title IX prohibitions against discrimination on the basis of gender, some schools may choose to "balance" their admitted classes between men and women even when more qualified women apply.

GENDER AND ECONOMICS: MEN, WOMEN, AND THE GENDER WAGE GAP

Given their rising achievements in education, are women enjoying earnings that equal or surpass those of men? Women have made tremendous gains in the workplace, but in the United States and across the globe, they continue to lag behind men in earnings in most occupational categories. The **gender wage gap** is *the difference between the earnings of women who work full-time year-round as a group and those of men who work full-time year-round as a group.* It exists across all men as a group and all women as a group, and as well, within racial and ethnic groups. Why does it persist?

At the end of the 19th century, only one in five women age 16 or older was paid for her work; most paid female employees were young, unmarried, or poor (often all three) and held very low-wage jobs. By 1950, 5 years after the end of World War II, the proportion of American women working outside the home for pay rose to one third. The enormous economic expansion that continued through the 1970s drew even more women into the paid workforce, attracted by higher pay and supported by the passage of laws such as the Equal Pay Act of 1963, which made unequal pay for doing the same job illegal. Women's educational gains also opened up more professional and well-paid positions to them. By 1980, more than half of U.S. women were in the paid workforce.

At the beginning of the 20th century, median earnings for women working in full-time, year-round jobs were only half as much as those for men. In 1963 they were still only about three fifths as much, but by 1999 the gap had

Gender wage gap: The difference between the earnings of women who work full-time year-round as a group and those of men who work full-time year-round as a group.

FIGURE 9.7 Median Usual Weekly Earnings of Women and Men Who Are Full-Time Wage and Salary Workers, by Age, 2015 Annual Averages

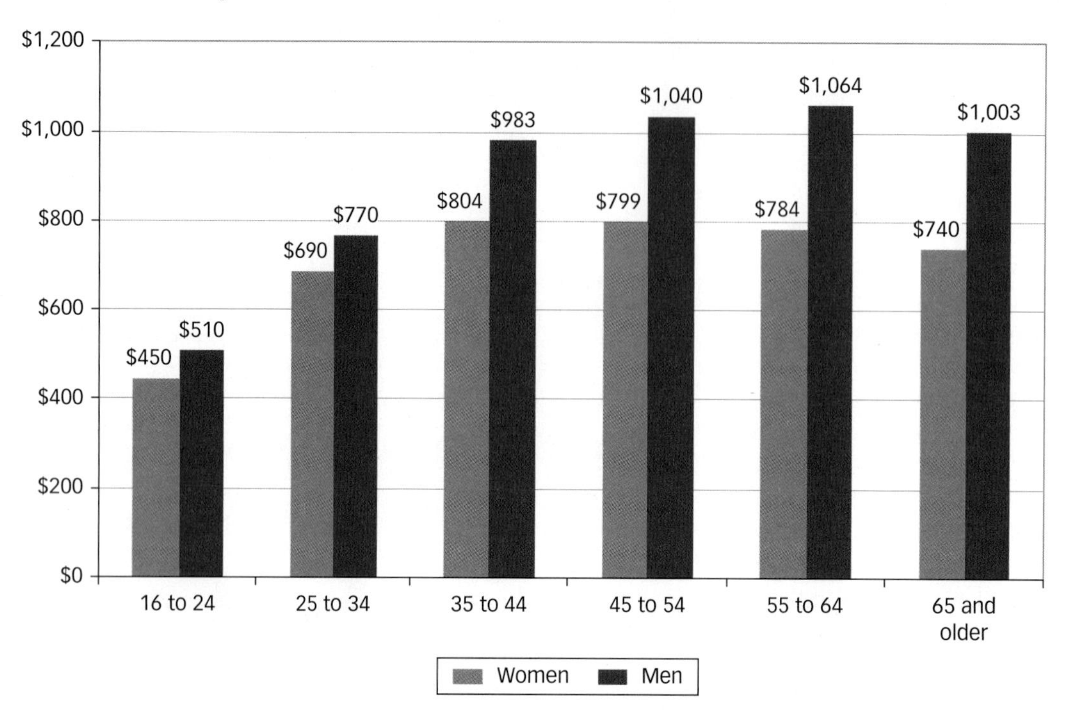

SOURCE: Bureau of Labor Statistics. https://www.bls.gov/opub/reports/womens-earnings/2015/home.htm.

narrowed, and women earned just over 72% of the median male wage. These gains were partly the result of postwar "baby boom" women, many of them educated and skilled, entering the workforce and moving into higher-paying jobs as they gained experience.

U.S. Bureau of Labor Statistics figures from 2014 show that women working full-time and year-round earned about 83% of what their male counterparts earned, with variations by age (see Figure 9.7). This translates to average weekly earnings of $719 for women and $871 for men (U.S. Bureau of Labor Statistics, 2016a).

An important aspect of the gender wage gap is the fact that *men and women are still*, and more than we might think, *concentrated in different occupations*. Researchers label this phenomenon **occupational segregation by gender**. When we identify the 20 most common occupations for women and for men, only three appear on both lists: "first-line supervisors of retail sales workers; managers, all other; and retail salespersons" (Institute for Women's Policy Research, 2015). Nearly 40% of women are employed in "traditionally female" occupations, and about 44% of men work in "traditionally male" occupations (Hegewisch & Liepmann, 2012).

Why does gender occupational segregation exist and persist? To answer this question, we borrow some terms from economics. For the purposes of our analysis, **labor supply factors** *highlight reasons that women or men may "prefer" particular occupations*, preparing for, pursuing, and accepting these positions in the labor force. **Labor demand factors** highlight *the needs and preferences of the employer.*

Labor supply factors draw our attention to the agency we exercise in choosing a career path and the decisions we make about how and when to be a part of the paid labor force. Several decades ago, many high school- or college-educated working women were likely to work in one of three occupational categories: secretarial work, nursing, and teaching (below the college level). Why were women opting for these occupations? One factor was socialization;

Occupational segregation by gender: The concentration of men and women in different occupations.

Labor supply factors: Factors that highlight reasons that women or men may "prefer" particular occupations.

Labor demand factors: Factors that highlight the needs and preferences of the employer.

women were encouraged to choose "feminine" occupations, and many did. Another factor was choices women made based on their families' needs: For instance, a schoolteacher's daytime hours and summers off were a good fit with her children's schedules. Today, women are far less limited by either imagination or structural obstacles, as we have seen in the educational and occupational statistics. At the same time, the top 10 jobs most commonly occupied by women today still include several heavily and traditionally "feminine" jobs done by women since they entered the workforce in large numbers starting in the 1960s and 1970s (see Table 9.1).

We can also use labor supply factors to talk about men's "preferences" in the workforce. Men are more broadly spread throughout the U.S. Census Bureau's occupational categories than are women, though in many categories, such as engineer and pilot, they make up a substantial share of all workers. Imagine a young man interested in health and medicine. Would he be encouraged to pursue a career as a nurse? There is still a powerful sense in our society that nursing is a "female" occupation. A study of five popular U.S. medical television shows, including *Grey's Anatomy, Nurse Jackie,* and *Mercy*, found that "common stereotypes that the shows reinforced include the nurse who is mistaken for a doctor and the gay or emasculated male nurse. Male nurses and midwives in the shows tend to suffer condescension from their colleagues and patients and are the object of comedy" (Goodier, 2013). We even use the term *male nurse* when referring to men in the nursing profession because our default understanding of "nurse" is a woman. Perhaps it is not surprising, then, that men still make up just a small fraction of nurses, though the occupation is growing and offers a wide variety of professional opportunities and specialties.

Labor demand factors highlight what employers need and prefer—employees with **human capital**, or *the skills, knowledge, and credentials valuable in the particular workplace.* A landscaper seeking a partner will want to hire someone with skills in landscaping; an office manager will seek an administrative assistant who is tech savvy and organized; an accounting firm will want a well-trained certified accountant and a legal firm a well-trained lawyer who has passed the bar. These preferences are not gendered but instead focus on skills, knowledge, and credentials. It is, however, notable that a pay gap exists at every educational level; in a sense, women cannot educate themselves out of the gap (Figure 9.8).

FIGURE 9.8 Average Hourly Wages, by Gender and Education, 2015

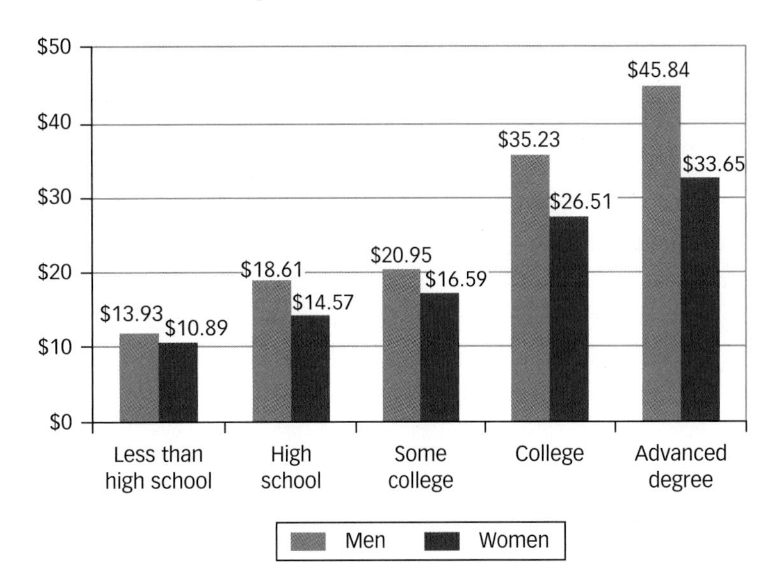

SOURCE: "Women's work" and the gender pay gap: How discrimination, societal norms, and other forces affect women's occupational choices—and their pay," by Jessica Schieder and Elise Gould, July 20, 2016. Figure A. Washington, DC: Economic Policy Institute. Reprinted with permission.

Nevertheless, other labor supply factors may introduce gender more explicitly into employer preferences. For example, some employers believe they will incur higher *indirect labor costs* by hiring females. **Indirect labor costs** include *the time, training, or money spent when an employee takes time off to care for sick family members, opts for parental leave, arrives at work late, or leaves after receiving employer-provided training.* Because women are still associated with the roles of wife and mother, employers may assume they are more likely than men to be costly employees.

Stereotypes may also condition employers' views, especially when jobs are perceived as "feminine" or "masculine." Just as a preschool or child-care center might be wary of hiring a man to work with small children or infants (because women are perceived to be more nurturing), a construction firm might hesitate to hire a woman to head

Human capital: The skills, knowledge, and credentials a person possesses that make him or her valuable in a particular workplace.

Indirect labor costs: Costs in time, training, or money incurred when an employee takes time off to care for sick family members, opts for parental leave, arrives at work late, or leaves a position after receiving employer-provided training.

Technology Takes on the Wage Gap

Some new smartphone apps are geared to help female employees address the persisting gender wage gap in the United States. The apps focus on a variety of tasks, including helping women to negotiate higher salaries and to learn more about pay disparities in their occupational field. The apps are part of an effort on the part of the U.S. Department of Commerce, together with the White House Council on Women and Girls, to bring attention to the issue of the pay gap, to disseminate usable information on disparities in pay, and to provide some tools to address it. They were introduced at an event at the White House in July 2016, which was the culmination of a 2-month "United State of Women Hackathon" (https://paygap.pif.gov) inviting tech firms and entrepreneurs to #hackthepaygap by creating tools to address the gap.

The collection of apps includes a negotiation simulator intended to help users develop negotiation skills and build "soft skills" for interviews. The program is immersive, simulating a variety of scenarios for the user as she prepares for real-world negotiation (Morath, 2016). Some research has shown that women are less comfortable with salary negotiation—and less likely to be successful at it. In a study conducted by the career-building website Levo.com, millennial women were queried about negotiation. It found that among respondents, 63% were uncomfortable negotiating, 58% feared losing their job or offer in negotiation, 56% were uncertain what to ask for, and just over half did not know they should negotiate (Harris, 2016). Although the results of the opt-in survey cannot be generalized, they are consistent with academic findings on women's greater discomfort with negotiation, though the discomfort may be conditional: According to a National Bureau of Economic Advisors working paper, "when there is no explicit statement that [starting] wages are negotiable, men are more likely to negotiate than women. Nevertheless, when [researchers] explicitly mention the possibility that wages are negotiable, this difference disappears, and even tends to reverse" (Leibbrandt & List, 2012).

Importantly, although negotiation skills are valuable, apps are less likely to be able to address the gendered work environment in which they occur: A recent article in the *Harvard Business Review* points out that

> in repeated studies, the social cost of negotiating for higher pay has been found to be greater for women than it is for men. Men can certainly overplay their hand and alienate negotiating counterparts. However, in most published studies, the social cost of negotiating for pay is not significant for men, while it *is* significant for women. (Bowles, 2014, para. 3)

The new technologies also feature an app that uses U.S. Department of Commerce data to calculate an employee's "personal gender pay gap" based on demographic characteristics that include race, age, occupation, and field. The app's data, which is based on the American Community Survey, opens a trove of salary information that has been difficult for ordinary users to access. Most firms and organizations do not publish salaries, and many employees are uncomfortable asking colleagues about salaries, situations that can lead to uneven pay scales. Negotiation can then be based on information rather than assumption. Indeed, examination of government data turns up a variety of notable points. For example, data assembled by the Commerce Data Service at the Department of Commerce shows that the pay gap rises among the top 80% and 90% of earners. Indeed, the gap within the 1% of earners is particularly stark: women earn 46 cents to men's dollar at the top of earnings scale. Several high-profile examples have served to underscore the disparity:

> Robin Wright, who plays Claire Underwood on the Netflix series *House of Cards*, recently had to

> negotiate for the same pay as her costar Kevin Spacey. Yahoo's CEO Marissa Mayer was paid less than the man who held the job before her. And General Motors CEO Mary Barra received a first-year compensation package that was less than half of what her male predecessor was offered. (Hunter, 2016, para. 3)

There is also an app under development that seeks to ensure gender equity in the growing "gig" or contract labor market, in which the stable, long-term employment of decades past is being replaced by a fluid labor market characterized by a growing number of shorter-duration positions occupied by "freelancing" professionals. As workers' job titles and occupational identities become more fluid as well, such an app may help women to ensure fair pay (#hackthepaygap, 2016).

Technology is not, on its own, an infallible solution to social problems, including longstanding issues like discrimination or devaluation. At the same time, it offers new and compelling tools for recognizing and addressing the gender wage gap.

THINK IT THROUGH

- Think about other social issues raised in this chapter. Is there an app for that? Identify an issue and imagine a creative technological means to address the problem or some aspect of the problem.

Follow us on Twitter to keep up with current sociological stories and research! We're at @Discoversoc1.
Share your own ideas at #DiscoverSociology.

a team of workers (because men are widely perceived to be more comfortable under male leadership).

Looking at labor supply and labor demand factors can help us to sort out how men and women have become concentrated in different occupations. Gender occupational segregation is significant because jobs dominated by men have historically paid more than jobs dominated by women. That is, those jobs have higher pay scales, which means that men's earnings tend to start higher and end higher than women's earnings.

Even *within* occupational categories, however, men commonly earn more than their female counterparts. Consider a recent study of earnings among doctors in academia, in this case, physicians who teach at U.S. public medical schools. Research on over 10,000 faculty members (65% male, 35% female) at 24 schools found a gender earnings gap: Without accounting for rank and other differences like specialty and years of residency, male doctors were found to average $257,000 annual salary, while women averaged $206,000. Importantly, even controlling for factors like rank, age, specialty, publications, years of residency, and research funding, the researchers found a gap of close to $20,000 (Anupam, Olenski, & Blumenthal, 2016). Differences exist across the occupational spectrum. Data show that, for example, in retail sales, a robust field of employment for both men and women, women earn about 70% of what men earn. Among managers, as well as waitstaff, women earn about 82% of men's earnings. Even in fields where women make up a significant share of all employees, men outearn their female peers: For instance, among registered nurses, women earn 90% of men's earnings (Institute for Women's Policy Research, 2015).

What explains these differences within occupations? First, although the Equal Pay Act of 1963 made it illegal to pay men and women different wages for the same work, differences have been documented in fields from journalism to construction to academia. For example, a recent study of several major media outlets, including the *Wall Street Journal* and *Barron's*, which are owned by Dow Jones, found that, "'male reporters' at the company typically make 11 percent more than female reporters. . . . [and] Male 'senior special writers,' a high-level distinction, also outearn their female counterparts by 11 percent" (Paquette, 2016, para. 15). As we note in the *Social Life, Social Media* box in this chapter, many employees do not know what their colleagues earn and are hesitant to ask, raising the risk that differences could persist unbeknownst to workers.

Second, in some occupations, men and women concentrate in different specialties, with men tending to occupy the most lucrative sectors. For instance, male physicians are more likely than females to specialize in cardiology, which pays better than areas where women tend to concentrate, such as pediatrics and obstetrics. Similarly, women real estate agents are more likely to sell residential properties, while men are more likely to sell commercial properties, which bring in higher profits and commissions. Even among restaurant servers, men tend to concentrate in high-end restaurants, while women dominate in diners and chain restaurants.

Third, recent work by economist Claudia Goldin (2014) suggests that a key factor in understanding the wage gap both within occupations and more broadly is *temporal flexibility*. She argues that the persistence of the wage gap lies in how jobs are structured and remunerated: Many women are economically disadvantaged by their need or desire for flexibility in work hours. Women may work a comparable number of hours to men, but they are less likely to work odd hours or be willing or able to be available at any hour. Some writers have described this as a "caregiving penalty" (Slaughter, 2015), as the lack of women workers' flexibility is usually linked to their obligations to children or aging parents. Goldin suggests that "the gender gap in pay would be considerably reduced and might vanish altogether if firms did not have an incentive to disproportionately reward individuals who labored long hours and worked particular hours" (Goldin, 2014, p. 1091)

Finally, sociologist Christine Williams's (1995) work points to ways in which men who work in traditional "women's" fields, such as librarianship, social work, nursing, and elementary school teaching, benefit from a **glass escalator**, a *nearly invisible promotional boost that men gain in female-dominated occupations*. Williams found that bosses often presumed that the men in her study wanted to move up—for example, a teacher was assumed to want an administrative position, or a nurse was assumed to want to be a head nurse. Many of the men were put on promotional tracks even when they were ambivalent about leaving positions in which they felt satisfied. Nevertheless, it should be noted that men experience the glass escalator effect differently based on their race. Wingfield (2008), for example, found that African American male nurses did not benefit from their gender in the same way that White male nurses did.

The concept of the glass escalator recalls one final concept that may illuminate gender disparities in the workplace: the glass ceiling. When it comes to the positions with the highest status and pay, data suggest that qualified women may still encounter a **glass ceiling**, *an artificial boundary that allows them to see the next occupational level even as structural obstacles keep them from reaching it.* A study of 1,200 executives in eight countries, including the United States, Austria, and Australia, found that a substantial proportion of women (70%) and a majority of men (57%) agreed that a glass ceiling prevents women from moving ahead in the business hierarchy (Clark, 2006). They may be correct; women occupied just 23 chief executive officer positions in the *Fortune* 500 companies in 2015 (Bellstrom, 2015).

In this section, we have reviewed some key aspects of the gender wage gap. Although it is a persistent problem in the United States, women have made tremendous strides toward closing the gap: Legal protection against discrimination and high rates of women's college completion are among the factors that have contributed to improvements in women's economic status. Notably, however, a part of the declining gap can also be attributed to men's worsening labor market position, a topic we will cover in greater detail in Chapter 15. Wages of men without a college education have been on the decline in recent decades, as well-paying jobs in sectors like manufacturing have been automated or moved to lower-wage areas abroad. A decreasing pay gap, then, is attributable to improvements for women—but also diminished economic prospects for some men.

Glass escalator: The nearly invisible promotional boost that men gain in female-dominated occupations.

Glass ceiling: An artificial boundary that allows women to see the next occupational or salary level even as structural obstacles keep them from reaching it.

CLASSICAL THEORIES, FEMINIST THOUGHT, AND THE SOCIOLOGY OF MASCULINITIES

Until the middle of the 20th century, most sociological theories assumed that existing sex roles and norms were natural, and by extension, positively functional for society. Contemporary scholarship, particularly by feminist sociologists, challenges this perspective, taking a critical look at both the genesis and consequences of rigid gender rules and roles.

CLASSICAL SOCIOLOGICAL APPROACHES TO GENDER

For the "founding fathers" of sociology, whom we met in Chapter 1, gender stratification was all but invisible.

■ **TABLE 9.1** Most Common Occupations for U.S. Women and Men (Full-Time), 2015

Rank	Most Common Occupations for Women	Most Common Occupations for Men
1	Secretaries and administrative assistants	Drivers/sales workers and truck drivers
2	Elementary and middle school teachers	Managers, all others
3	Registered nurses	First-line supervisors/managers of retail sales workers
4	Nursing, psychiatric, and home health aides	Construction laborers
5	First-line supervisors/managers of retail sales workers	Janitors or building cleaners
6	Customer service representatives	Laborers and freight, stock, and material movers
7	Managers, all other	Retail salespersons
8	Cashiers	Software developers, applications and systems software
9	Accountants and auditors	Sales representatives, wholesale and manufacturing
10	Receptionists and information clerks	Grounds maintenance workers

SOURCE: Hegewisch, A. and Matite, M. (2013). Gender wage gap by occupation. *IWPR #C350a,* Tables 1 and 2. Institute for Women's Policy Research, Washington, DC. Reprinted with permission.

Although Friedrich Engels addressed women's experience of inequalities, a common theme was that men and women were organically suited to the (unequal) gender roles in European society. Auguste Comte and Émile Durkheim drew on earlier philosophers, including Jean-Jacques Rousseau, to argue that women were best suited to "private" family roles such as nurturance and child rearing and were "naturally" subordinate to men. Men were seen as possessing inherent advantages in such spheres as science, industry, and government (Comte, 1975; Durkheim, 1895/1964).

To a significant degree, these perspectives were rooted in now-dated understandings of human physiology. In one popular theory, women were reported to have smaller brain capacity than men based on their relative skull sizes. (By this standard, elephants should be more intelligent than humans, because their skulls are larger.) Because of ostensible differences in brain size, men were assumed to be biologically more rational, with an advantage in pursuits that required reasoning and logic, such as business and governance. Women were seen as inherently more emotional and better at pursuits requiring emotional skills, such as nurturing.

Few women's voices were present in early sociology. Charlotte Perkins Gilman (1898/2006) was one of the first female and feminist sociologists. Gilman viewed heterosexual marriage between males and females as a *sexuoeconomic relation:* Women were expected to be financially dependent on men, and in turn, to serve as caregivers for their husbands and children. Women's gender socialization included significant pressure to find husbands, who in turn felt obligated to support their wives. Thus, the sexual relationship between men and women also became an economic one, with negative effects for the relationship, as well as women's autonomy.

Until the middle of the 20th century, some sociologists argued that sex-role differences—whether biological or social in origin—were positively functional for social harmony, order, and stability. For example, functionalist sociologist Talcott Parsons offered a theory of sex roles in the U.S. kinship system that sought to explain them in terms of their functionality for family and society (Parsons, 1954; Parsons & Bales, 1955). Parsons argued that in a modern capitalist society, women make their contribution by raising children and maintaining the family unit; men do so by earning the family income through outside labor. Parsons did not attribute this role specialization to biology; rather, he argued, women were socialized in the family to acquire "expressive" qualities, such as sympathy and emotionality, needed in the private sphere of the home. Men were socialized into "instrumental" qualities like rationality and competitiveness, which were needed for the capitalist workplace. Competition for standing in the family was avoided with a division of roles, and the family's status in society was clear because it derived from the man's position in the workforce. Sex roles, suggested Parsons, functioned positively on both the micro (family) and macro (society) levels.

Feminist theorists rejected Parsons's theory. Although he recognized sex roles as the product of socialization

INEQUALITY MATTERS

The Internet Haters: Movies, Journalism, Misogyny

AF archive/Alamy Stock Photo

Moviestore collection Ltd/Alamy Stock Photo

A remake of the popular film *Ghostbusters* (1984) came out in the summer of 2016 with an all-female cast of leads. The new version earned both praise and critique. Some of the criticism took on acutely sexist and misogynist tones. ■

One of 1984's blockbuster films was *Ghostbusters*, the story of four funny and somewhat awkward men, played by Bill Murray, Dan Akroyd, Harold Ramis, and Ernie Hudson, making an improbable living chasing down spirits across New York City. The theme song, sung by Ray Parker Jr., reached the top of the Billboard chart in August of that year, stayed there for 3 weeks, and can still be sung from memory by many of those who watched the film that summer. In 2015, the U.S. Library of Congress placed *Ghostbusters* in the National Film Registry, thus identifying the film as "culturally, historically, or aesthetically significant."

In July 2016, Columbia Pictures released a remake of the *Ghostbusters* film. This was the first film in the franchise in many years: *Ghostbusters II* premiered in 1989 with much of the original cast. The 2016 *Ghostbusters: Answer the Call* film attracted both interest and controversy because the spirit chasers in the film were played by women: Melissa McCarthy, Kristin Wiig, Leslie Jones, and Kate McKinnon. Even prior to the release of the movie, some users of the Internet expressed their negative evaluations of the new *Ghostbusters*. A *Washington Post* examination of the responses noted that, even prior to the release of the film, "on the trailer's YouTube page, more than 100,000 people . . . liked the video and nearly 200,000 . . . disliked it. That might be a record-breaking amount of hate for a trailer" (Merry, 2016, para. 4). Was this just a response to a poor trailer? Comments on the trailer's page suggest the backlash was spurred in large part by the casting of women in the iconic ghostbuster roles previously occupied by male actors:

> Aside from the vague proclamations that director Paul Feig has just destroyed a classic film and countless childhoods, many of the comments are variations on a theme. Some examples:
>
> - "Women are just incapable of being funny. What a terrible idea."
> - "Feminists ruin the world."
> - "Shouldn't they be in the kitchen?"

- "Did this just become a chick flick?"
- "I'll call the real Ghostbusters instead."
- "Congrats Sony, you've killed another beloved franchise. 'I know! We'll get a bunch of unfunny comedic nobodies and put them together in an even more childish and immature version of an already childish and immature comedy! We'll sell it to Social Justice Warriors and feminists, since they control SUCH A LARGE PORTION OF THE SERIES DEMOGRAPHIC. What could possibly go wrong?!'" (Merry, 2016, para. 7)

The entertainment newspaper *Variety* offered some responses from those involved with the film's remake, noting that Kristin Wiig, one of the film's lead actresses, was disappointed by the response: "The fact there was so much controversy because we were women was surprising to me.... Some people said some really not nice things about the fact that there were women. It didn't make me mad, it just really bummed me out. We're really honoring those movies." The film's director, Paul Feig, offered a scathing critique of the online responses, calling them, "some of the most vile, misogynistic s— I've ever seen in my life." Interestingly, he added,

> I figure it's some wacked-out teenager. . . . But almost constantly it's someone whose bio says "Proud father of two!" And has some high-end job. You're raising children and yet you're bashing me about putting women in my movie? (quoted in Stedman, 2015, para. 2–4)

As most readers know, the comments sections of many online articles and videos attract rude and crude anonymous feedback. A recent study (Gardiner et al., 2016) of its online comments section by the United Kingdom newspaper *The Guardian*, however, turned up some notable results:

> New research into our own comment threads provides the first quantitative evidence for what female journalists have long suspected: that articles written by women attract more abuse and dismissive trolling than those written by men, regardless of what the article is about.
>
> Although the majority of our regular opinion writers are white men, we found that those who experienced the highest levels of abuse and dismissive trolling were not. The 10 regular writers who got the most abuse were eight women (four white and four non-white) and two black men. Two of the women and one of the men were gay. And of the eight women in the "top 10," one was Muslim and one Jewish.
>
> And the 10 regular writers who got the least abuse? All men. (para. 4–6)

What accounts for the greater abuse, some attributable and some anonymous, heaped online on the *Ghostbusters* remake and its actresses and director? What about the writers at *The Guardian* newspaper? What do these two stories share in common and how would a sociologist examine and explain the phenomenon of online abuse directed toward women?

THINK IT THROUGH

- Should individuals, institutions, and societies respond to the profusion of hateful speech on the Internet? How should they do so?

rather than of nature, his perspective appeared to justify what many feminists saw as fundamentally unequal positions in society. In a capitalist society, power derives from the ability to earn independently, and the role Parsons foresaw for women was one of economic and social dependence.

CONTEMPORARY U.S. FEMINIST THINKING ON GENDER

> If you were a woman . . . 40 years ago, the odds were good that your husband provided the money to buy [this magazine]. That you voted the same way he did. That if you got breast cancer, he might be asked to sign the form authorizing a mastectomy. That your son was heading to college but not your daughter. That your boss, if you had a job, could explain that he was paying you less because, after all, you were probably working just for pocket money. (Gibbs, 2009, para. 1)

The fact that the world looks fundamentally different today is to a large degree thanks to the feminist movements of both the distant and the recent past.

Feminism is *the belief that social equality should exist between the sexes*; the term also refers to *social movements aimed at achieving that goal.* Feminism is directly tied to both analysis and action. It seeks to explain, expose, and eliminate **sexism**, *the belief that one sex is innately superior to the other and is therefore justified in having a dominant social position.* In the United States and most other societies, sexism takes the form of men's dominance over women. Feminists seek to analyze why it exists and how it can be eliminated.

Feminism emerged in the United States in connection with abolitionism, the campaign to end slavery in the 1830s; this movement gave birth to the struggle by women to achieve basic rights, including the right to vote and own land. The first wave of feminism began in 1848, when Elizabeth Cady Stanton and Lucretia Mott organized a convention in Seneca Falls, New York, to pursue women's expanded rights. Although their efforts were a landmark in women's history, the results they sought were achieved only much later (women did not gain the vote in the United States until 1920). Feminist activism was limited to a small group of women and their male supporters in an environment that saw sex differences as natural.

The 1963 publication of Betty Friedan's *The Feminine Mystique,* which argued that rigid stereotypes of femininity distorted women's real-life experiences and contributed to their unhappiness, helped initiate the second wave of the women's movement, with social theorizing and activism that was much broader in scope (Bernard, 1981, 1982; Friedan, 1963, 1981). Women's experiences in the civil rights and anti–Vietnam War social movements also helped shape a growing feminist consciousness.

The second wave, like the first, called for the equal treatment of women. Women and men were to be viewed not as fundamentally different but as similar; given equal opportunity, women would show themselves the equals of men in all respects. This revival of feminist thinking strongly appealed to the growing number of well-educated, professional women drawn to work and public life during the 1960s (Buechler, 1990), and an explosion of feminist thinking and activism followed.

Women in their 20s, 30s, and 40s today came of age after the feminist social movement had already made great strides and are less likely to have experienced the same degree of discrimination as their predecessors. At the same time, although only about a quarter of U.S. women describe themselves as "feminist," more than two thirds believe the women's movement has made their lives better—including 75% of women under age 35. Furthermore, 82% believe that the status of women has improved over the past 25 years, and about half of all younger women believe there is still a need for a strong women's movement (Alfano, 2009).

Several broad streams of feminist thinking agree on the importance of basic economic, social, and political equality for women—equal pay for equal work and the sharing of housework. They differ in their analyses of the causes of inequality, however, and in the solutions they propose. Below we provide a brief overview of feminism's varied manifestations.

Liberal feminism, reflected in the work of Betty Friedan and those who followed her lead, holds that

Feminism: The belief that social equality should exist between the sexes; also, the social movements aimed at achieving that goal.

Sexism: The belief that one sex is innately superior to the other and is therefore justified in having a dominant social position.

Liberal feminism: The belief that women's inequality is primarily the result of imperfect institutions, which can be corrected by reforms that do not fundamentally alter society itself.

women's inequality is primarily the result of imperfect institutions, which can be corrected by reforms that do not fundamentally alter society itself. To eliminate this inequality, liberal feminists have fought to elect women to the U.S. House and Senate, to enact legislation to ensure equal pay for equal work, and to protect women's rights to make choices about their fertility and their family lives.

As its name implies, **socialist feminism** is rooted in the socialist tradition. It is deeply critical of capitalist institutions and practices and regards *women's inequality as the result of the combination of capitalistic economic relations and male domination (patriarchy), arguing that both must be fundamentally transformed before women can achieve equality* (Chafetz, 1997). This viewpoint originated in the writings of Marx and Engels, who argued that inequality, including that of women, is an inevitable feature of capitalism. Engels (1884/1942), for example, sought to demonstrate that the family unit was historically based on the exploitation and male "ownership" of women (the practice of a father "giving away" his daughter in marriage is rooted in the symbolic "giving" of a young woman from one "keeper" to a new one). Socialist feminism in the United States emerged in the 1960s, when liberal feminists became frustrated by the pace of social reform and sought to address more fundamental sources of women's oppression (Hartmann, 1984; Jaggar, 1983; MacKinnon, 1982; Rowbotham, 1973).

Some feminists also grew frustrated with the civil rights and antiwar organizations of the 1960s and 1970s, which were headed by male leaders who often treated women as second-class citizens. Mindful that full equality for women has yet to be achieved in any existing political or economic system, **radical feminism** argues that *women's inequality underlies all other forms of inequality.* Radical feminists point to gender inequality in the economy, religion, and other institutions to argue that relations between the sexes must be radically transformed before women can hope to achieve true equality. Radical feminists thus focus their attention on the nature of **patriarchy**, *any set of social relationships in which men dominate women,* pointing to male dominance in economics and politics as chief examples.

Radical feminists argue that if patriarchal norms and values go unchallenged, many women will accept them as normal, even natural. Thus, although men should also work to end male domination, it is only by joining with other women that women can empower themselves. Radical feminists advocate all-women efforts to provide shelters for battered women, rape crisis intervention, and other issues that affect women directly (Barry, 1979; Dworkin, 1981, 1987, 1989; Faludi, 1991; Firestone, 1971; Griffin, 1978, 1979, 1981; Millett, 1970).

Multicultural feminism aims to understand and end inequality for all women, regardless of race, class, nationality, age, sexual orientation, physical ability, or other characteristics (B. Smith, 1990). Multicultural feminists seek to build coalitions among women, creating international and global organizations, networks, and programs to achieve women's equality. They acknowledge that much of the contemporary women's movement originated among heterosexual, White, and middle- or upper-class women in Europe and North America and that as a result its central ideas reflect these women's perspectives. These perspectives are being challenged and changed by feminists of color from Africa, Asia, and Latin America, as well as homosexual, bisexual, queer, and trans women, contributing to an enriched multicultural feminist understanding (Andersen & Collins, 1992; Anzaldúa, 1990; Chafetz, 1997; Narayan & Harding, 2000; Zinn, Weber, Higginbotham, & Dill, 1986).

Third-wave feminism emerged in the early 1990s as a response to some of the perceived shortcomings of second-wave feminism, but also as a product of changing societal norms and opportunities—and the Internet. Although third-wave feminists have paid significant attention to issues such as gendered violence and reproductive rights, they also argue that any issue a feminist finds important can and should be talked about. Choice is a central tenet; whether a woman wants to wear makeup, dress in feminine clothing, and be a stay-at-home mother or whether she wants to cut her hair short, wear gender-ambiguous clothing, and work in a male-dominated field—any choice is valid. A journalistic exploration of "new wave feminism" suggests that

Socialist feminism: The belief that women's inequality results from the combination of capitalistic economic relations and male domination; argues that both must be transformed fundamentally before women can achieve equality.

Radical feminism: The belief that women's inequality underlies all other forms of inequality, including economic inequality.

Patriarchy: Any set of social relationships in which men dominate women.

Multicultural feminism: The belief that inequality must be understood—and ended—for all women, regardless of race, class, nationality, age, sexual orientation, physical ability, or other characteristics.

■ **FIGURE 9.9** Percentage of People Who Identify as Feminist, 1995 and 2015

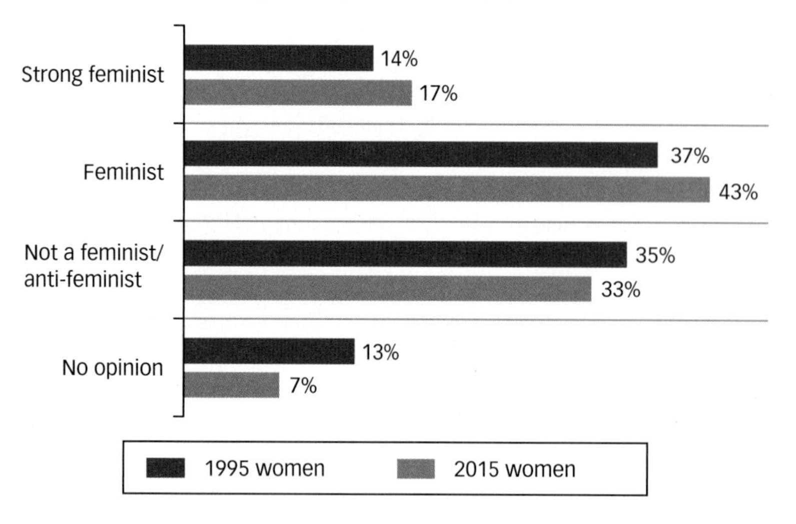

NOTE: 1995 results based on Feminist Majority Foundation poll. Percentages may not add up to 100% due to rounding.

SOURCE: Sheinin, D., K. Thompson, S.N. McDonald, & S. Clement. (2016). New Wave Feminism. *The Washington Post,* January 31: A1, A17.

> this feminism looks different, in many ways, than that of earlier generations. . . . [It] is shaped less by a shared struggle against oppression than by a collective embrace of individual freedoms, concerned less with targeting narrowly defined enemies than with broadening feminism's reach through inclusiveness, and held together not by a handful of national organizations and charismatic leaders but by the invisible bonds of the Internet and social media. (Sheinin, Thompson, McDonald, & Clement, 2016, p. A1)

Interestingly, a recent poll suggests that in the last 20 years, more women are calling themselves feminists, though nearly 40% do not identify as feminists at all or call themselves anti-feminists (Figure 9.9). Among millennial women, about 63% call themselves feminists, a figure higher than that of generation X women but just below the proportion of baby boomer women calling themselves feminists (68%; this generation of women is most likely to have been part of the second wave feminist movement).

Standpoint theory: A perspective that says the knowledge we create is conditioned by where we stand, or our subjective social position.

Standpoint epistemology: A philosophical perspective that argues that what we can know is affected by the position we occupy in society.

There is also an emphasis on *intersectionality* in the new wave, which recognizes the intersecting identities and oppressions of race, class, gender, sexuality, and so on. "Like much of American society, the feminist agenda has migrated to the Internet, making it at once less centered and communal, but more accessible and democratized" (Sheinin et al., 2016, p. A17).

Do you identify with any of the types of feminism mentioned above? What would you identify as important feminist issues today?

FEMINIST PERSPECTIVES ON DOING SOCIOLOGY

Sociologists Dorothy Smith and Patricia Hill Collins offer valuable perspectives on what it means to do sociology from a feminist perspective, explicitly recognizing women as both subjects and creators of new knowledge. Dorothy Smith (1987, 1990, 2005) is an important contributor to **standpoint theory**, which suggests that *the knowledge we create is conditioned by where we stand—that is, by our subjective social position.* Our sociological picture of the world has emerged from a variety of standpoints, but until recently they were largely the perspectives of educated and often economically privileged White males. Smith thus suggests that our base of knowledge is incomplete because much of what we know—or think we know—about the social world has come from a limited number of perspectives.

Standpoint theory offers a challenge to the sociological (and general scientific) idea that researchers can be, in Max Weber's words, "value-free." Smith argues that standpoint does matter, since we do not so much *discover* knowledge as we *create* it from data we gather and interpret from our own standpoint. Recall Victorian doctor Edward Clarke's influential book about the "brain–womb" conflict, positing that higher education could damage young women's reproductive capacity. Could such "knowledge" have emerged from the research of a female physician of that time? Would the theorizing of Karl Marx or Talcott Parsons look the same from a woman's perspective? What do you think?

Patricia Hill Collins (1990) has integrated elements of this idea into her articulation of "Black feminist thought." She offers **standpoint epistemology**, *a philosophical perspective that what we can know is affected by the*

Activists have long sought to bring attention to conditions of female oppression and male dominance. Although mid-20th-century activists including Bella Abzug highlighted problems such as limited roles for women outside of motherhood, 21st-century activists have come out against societal practices such as the shaming of women who violate conventional norms of dress or sexuality.

position we occupy in society. Epistemology is the study of how we know what we know and how we discern what we believe to be valid knowledge. Collins argues that Black women have long been denied status as "agents of knowledge"—that is, creators of knowledge about their own lives and experiences. Other groups have used their power to define Black women, creating a picture that is incomplete and disempowering. Collins calls for recognition of Black women as agents of knowledge and the use of Black feminist thought as a tool for resisting oppression.

Collins points to factors that fundamentally affect status and standpoint, including gender, race, class, and sexual orientation. The concept of a **matrix of domination**, *a system of social positions in which any individual may concurrently occupy a status (for example, gender, race, class, or sexual orientation) as a member of a dominated group and a status as a member of a dominating group,* highlights this point. Collins (1990) writes that "all groups possess varying amounts of penalty and privilege in one historically created system.... Depending on the context, an individual may be an oppressor, a member of an oppressed group, or simultaneously oppressor and oppressed" (p. 225).

Black women's experience of multiple oppressions makes them wary of dominant frames of knowledge, few of which have emerged from their own experience. Thus, Collins argues, comprehensive knowledge is born of a multitude of standpoints, and creation of knowledge is a form of power that should extend across social groups.

THE SOCIOLOGY OF MASCULINITIES

Integrating women's voices into contemporary sociology is an important goal and one that is being achieved. At the same time, as sociologist Michael Kimmel (1986) argues, because men still dominate sociology—as well as society—it is also necessary to develop a *sociology of masculinities.* Raewyn Connell (2010) notes that "masculinities" are not the same as men, adding that masculinities concern in particular the position of men in the gender order. Among men, status and power are not evenly distributed and may diverge along lines of class, race, and sexuality, among others. Hence, the focus is not on recognizing and analyzing *masculinity* (in the singular) so much as it is on examining the variety of cultural, social, and institutional influences that "make men."

At the same time, there may be a dominant strand of masculinity. Kimmel (1996) follows David and Brannon's (1976) idea that in U.S. culture there are four "basic rules of manhood":

- No "sissy stuff"—avoid any hint of femininity.
- Be a "big deal"—acquire wealth, power, and status.
- Be a "sturdy oak"—never show your emotions.
- "Give 'em hell"—exude a sense of daring and aggressiveness.

These "rules" reflect the concept of *hegemonic masculinity,* or the culturally normative idea of male behavior, which often emphasizes strength, control, and aggression

Matrix of domination: A system of social positions in which any individual may concurrently occupy a status (for example, gender, race, class, or sexual orientation) as a member of a dominated group and a status as a member of a dominating group.

(Connell & Messerschmidt, 2005). This is a variety of masculinity that we may recognize in men's sports like football. In a recent investigative book on brain injuries among football players and the reticence of the National Football League—as well as many players—to acknowledge the risks and injuries to athletes, the authors profile a player, Gary Plummer, who tells them that

> I had been playing football since I was eight years old, and there is nothing more revered in football than being a tough guy . . . The coaches have euphemisms. They'll say: "You know, that guy has to learn the difference between pain and injury.". . .What he's saying is the guy's a pussy and he needs to get tough or he's not going to be on the team." (quoted in Fainaru-Wada & Fainaru, 2014, pp. 79–80)

Kimmel (1996, 2013) argues that some notions of masculinity are so deeply ingrained in culture that when we discuss social problems like "teen violence," particularly shootings, in U.S. schools, we forget that we are talking almost entirely about the behavior of men. Consider the issue of mass shootings in the United States more generally: A *Washington Post* investigation of "mass shootings" (defined as shootings in which four or more people were killed by a lone shooter, though in three instances, there were two shooters) in the United States over the past 50 years found that of the 129 shooters, most were ages 20 to 49 and all but three were male (Berkowitz, Gamio, Lu, Uhrmacher, & Lindeman, 2016). As journalist James Hamblin (2016) wrote in the aftermath of the killing of 49 victims at a gay nightclub in Orlando, Florida, in June 2016, "That makes masculinity a more common feature than any of the elements that tend to dominate discourse—religion, race, nationality, political affiliation, or any history of mental illness" (para. 3). What explains this commonalty? Why are men more likely to be mass shooters—or to commit homicide (which is a crime committed by men over 90% of the time; D. Ford, 2015)? Educator Jackson Katz points to the rarity, and importance, of this question by offering a hypothetical scenario: "Imagine if 61 out of 62 mass killings were done by women? Would that be seen as merely incidental and relegated to the margins of discourse? . . . No. It would be the first thing people talked about" (quoted in Murphy, 2012, para. 18).

The National Football League long denied the dangers of repeated head trauma to players' long-term health. A "masculine" ethic of toughness in the face of injury helped to maintain this position among coaches and players.

Some writers suggest that "men's studies"—the study of masculinities—should become as much a part of the college curriculum as "women's studies." In many respects, men are already well integrated into the curriculum: As Kimmel writes, "Every course that isn't in 'women's studies' is de facto a course in men's studies. Except we call it history, political science, literature, chemistry" (Kimmel, 2000, pp. 5–6). At the same time, this fails to give scholars and students insight into ways in which masculinities shape boys, men, institutions, and societies. In a recent interview with the *New York Times*, Kimmel suggested that studying masculinity would entail a cross-disciplinary examination of

> What makes men men, and how are we teaching boys to fill those roles? It would look at the effects of race and sexuality on masculine identity and the influence of the media and pop culture. It would also allow scholars to take seemingly unrelated phenomena—male suicide and the fact that men are less likely to talk about their feelings, say, or the financial collapse and the male tendency for risk-taking—and try to connect the dots. (Bennett, 2015, para. 25)

Only by studying the social construction of masculinity can we understand that "men" are made and not born. And that, sociologists of masculinity believe, is an important step toward achieving gender equality in both attitudes and practices.

WOMEN'S LIVES IN A GLOBAL PERSPECTIVE

Being born a woman is a risk. If you are reading these words in the United States, you might feel that statement is an exaggeration. Certainly, women in the United States are at greater risk than their male counterparts of falling victim to crimes such as sexual assault or rape, of experiencing discrimination in the workplace, or of being subjected to sexual harassment on the street, at work, or in school. U.S. women are also more likely to be poor or uninsured than their female counterparts in other advanced states, including Denmark, France, and Canada. At the same time, as we have seen in this chapter, women have made dramatic gains in areas like education, which have brought them independence, earning power, and greater workplace opportunities. Women are assuming positions of power in politics, the economy, culture, and education.

In many places across the globe, if you are reading these words, you are likely a male because millions of women are denied education and cannot read. They are at greater risk of being denied medical care, trafficked into the sex trade, and refused the right to own or inherit property. They are less likely than their male counterparts to go to school, to earn wages equivalent to their work, and to eat or get medical care when family resources are scarce. In this section, we highlight issues of gender and equality from a global perspective.

MOTHERS AND CHILDREN: THE THREAT OF MATERNAL MORTALITY

In a small hospital in Yokadouma, Cameroon, 24-year-old Prudence died in childbirth. Here is a small piece of her story:

> Prudence had been living with her family in a village seventy-five miles away [from the hospital], and she had received no prenatal care. She went into labor at full term, assisted by a traditional birth attendant who had no training. But Prudence's cervix was blocked, and the baby couldn't come out. After three days of labor, the birth attendant sat on Prudence's stomach and jumped up and down. That ruptured Prudence's uterus. The family paid a man with a motorcycle to take Prudence to the hospital. The hospital's doctor . . . realized that she needed an emergency cesarean. But he wanted $100 for the surgery, and Prudence's husband and parents said that they could raise only $20. . . . If she had been a man, the family probably would have sold enough possessions to raise $100. (Kristof & WuDunn, 2009, pp. 109–110)

The dangers of childbirth have been nearly alleviated in industrialized countries, and maternal mortality is a rarity. In many developing countries, however, women have little control over their fertility and childbirth is a persistent risk (Table 9.2). Kristof and WuDunn (2009) write that Prudence died due to a massive infection, but her death can also be linked more broadly to problems like the lack of schooling, lack of rural health care capacity, and cultural disregard for women.

WOMEN AND EDUCATION Educated, literate women are healthier women; there is a strong correlation between education and health that manifests in a variety of ways. For instance, a global study found a conclusive link between greater education of mothers and lower child mortality, as more educated mothers are more likely to understand and practice good hygiene and health practices (Brown, 2010). Declining child mortality in a society further correlates with fewer pregnancies and smaller families; according to the *child survival hypothesis* (Taylor, Newman, & Kelly, 1976), if women feel confident their children will survive, they are less inclined to feel the need for "extra" children to ensure that some reach adulthood.

Education may foster healthier mothering and better care of mothers. A better-educated birth attendant can treat her patient more effectively; she is clearly less likely to sit on a patient's stomach and risk rupturing her uterus. A United Nations Population Fund report on midwifery (2014) suggests that "implementing quality midwifery services could prevent about two thirds of women's and infants' deaths globally," but those states most in need have the fewest trained midwives, nurses, and physicians.

LACK OF RURAL HEALTH SYSTEMS Kristof and WuDunn (2009) write that "if Cameroon had a better

GLOBAL ISSUES

Fighting Sextortion Around the World

The International Association of Women Judges (IAWJ) defines sextortion as follows:

> [W]hen people in positions of authority – whether government officials, judges, educators, law enforcement personnel, or employers – seek to extort sexual favors in exchange for something within their power to grant or withhold. In effect, sextortion is a form of corruption in which sex, rather than money, is the currency of the bribe. (IAWJ, n.d., para. 1)

Although nearly anyone could potentially fall victim to this practice, poor women around the world, according to the United Nations Development Project, are particularly vulnerable "because they may be more dependent on public officials for access to such services as health care, water, or education, and, with lower literacy levels, they may have less awareness of their entitlements to public programs, making them more susceptible to extortion" (as quoted in Bigio, 2016, para. 4). Although men may also fall victim to this practice, evidence suggests that women are the most likely targets.

Sextortion may take the form of an immigration official demanding sex in exchange for approval of a refugee application or a border crossing, or a United Nations peacekeeper trading relief supplies to desperate women or children in return for sexual favors (Bigio, 2016). A recent Reuters news article reported that the African country of Tanzania was undertaking efforts to combat sextortion after 9 out of 10 women working in the public sector reported sexual harassment, including superiors using positions of power to coerce women into sex (Makoye, 2015).

Sextortion, according to the IAWJ (n.d.), is fundamentally a form of corruption because officers, officials, or others with authority are using their power "for personal benefit rather than with integrity, fairness, and impartiality expected of their position." Notably, sextortion is a form of corruption that is widely recognized anecdotally but poorly tracked in official measures. As Jamille Bigio (2016, para 3) points out, "Regional and global instruments also don't capture sextortion: none of the most common tools used to measure corruption include sex-disaggregated data, and so do not track how men and women are affected differently by corruption."

What can be done about sextortion? How can the victimization of vulnerable populations be stopped? Bigio (2016) suggests the following: First, there is a need for strong data collection to systematically document the problem. Second, countries can pass stronger anti-corruption laws and policies. Third, the stigma of victimization should be addressed and victims should be encouraged to speak out.

THINK IT THROUGH

- How could sociologists take a role in combating sextortion? What skills do sociologists possess that would enable them to participate in addressing this problem?

health care structure, the hospital would have operated on Prudence as soon as she arrived. It would have had powerful antibiotics to treat her infection. It would have trained rural birth attendants in the area, equipped with cell phones to summon an ambulance. Any one of these factors might have saved Prudence" (p. 114).

"Brain drain" is also an obstacle to the development of rural health care systems: Nurses and physicians from developing states are welcomed by wealthier countries experiencing shortages of health care providers, further diminishing access in poorer countries and communities. Consider the dramatic differences in the ratio of physicians to population across the globe, with wealthy countries far more likely to have a significant number of doctors per 1,000 population than poor states (see Table 9.3).

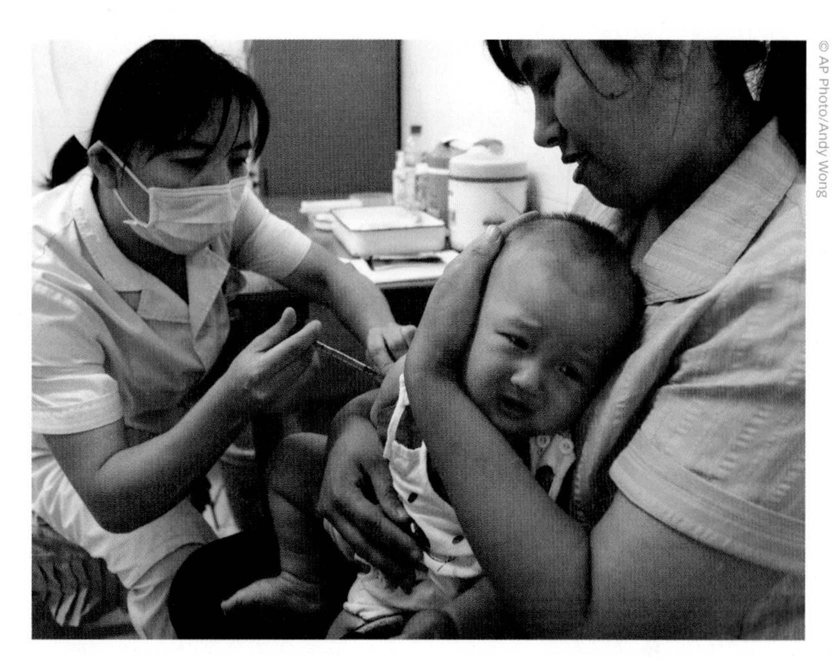

Hospitals in many industrialized countries have tried to cope with nursing shortages by enticing trained nurses from developing countries to migrate. Because modern hospitals offer good pay and clean, well-supplied working conditions, many nurses, by choice or necessity, leave their home countries to work abroad. ■

DISREGARD FOR WOMEN Countries where women are marginalized have higher rates of maternal mortality. Indeed, where women have little social, cultural, economic, or political voice, their lives have less significance than those of men, and scarce resources may be directed elsewhere (Hausmann, Tyson, & Zahidi, 2011). In 21st-century China, "39,000 girls die annually... because parents don't give them the same medical care and attention that boys receive—and that is just in the first year of life" (Kristof & WuDunn, 2009, p. xiv). The All-India National Family Health Survey recently found that, for instance, about 72% of boys were brought for treatment of acute respiratory infections versus 66% of girls and boys suffering from diarrhea were 7% more likely to be taken to a health facility than girls with the same problem. Oxfam India reports that the head of pediatrics at a government medical college confirmed this bias, noting, "More boys are vaccinated than girls, even though it is free. Because unlike the Pulse Polio programme, where a health worker goes from home to home to administer the drops, the children have to be brought to a medical facility for these shots. Parents are willing to make the effort for their sons, but not their daughters" (Trivedy, 2015, para. 14).

In spite of the power of some women on the global stage (among others, Democratic presidential nominee Hillary Clinton, recent U.S. secretaries of state Condoleezza Rice and Madeleine Albright, as well as German chancellor Angela Merkel and influential International Monetary Fund head Christine Lagarde of France), women's global voice is still limited. Inadequate funding of "women's concerns," including maternal health initiatives—and perhaps even their definition as "women's concerns" rather than family or national concerns—speak to the priority they hold.

THE PRICE OF (BEING) A GIRL

On the illicit global market, available goods include weapons, drugs, pirated software and films, and women and girls. Impoverished girls from the developing world are particularly vulnerable to sexual exploitation and trafficking. According to the annual *Trafficking in Persons Report* published by the U.S. Department of State (2012), it is difficult to pin down the extent of this "modern-day slavery." The International Labour Organization, however, estimates that almost 21 million people are victims of forced labor: about 11.4 million women and girls and 9.5 million men and boys (International Labour Organization, n.d.). Of those exploited by individuals or enterprises, 4.5 million are victims of forced sexual exploitation (International Labour Organization, n.d.).

In India, the sex trade and sex trafficking are pervasive (Kara, 2009). A British Broadcasting Corporation (Patel, 2013) examination of Indian brothels told the story of one woman:

> Guddi was only 11 years old when her family was persuaded by a neighbour to send her to the

TABLE 9.2 Maternal Mortality Rate for Selected Countries, 2015

Country	Maternal Deaths per 100,000 Live Births
Cameroon	596
Afghanistan	396
Bangladesh	176
India	174
Brazil	44
China	27
United States	14
Turkey	16
Canada	7
Denmark	6

SOURCE: World Health Organization. (2015). Maternal mortality country profiles. Global Health Observatory (GHO).

TABLE 9.3 Physician Density Rate in Selected Countries, 2011

Country	Physicians per 1,000 Population
Germany	3.50 (2008)
Denmark	3.40 (2007)
Austria	2.99 (2009)
Egypt	2.80 (2009)
United States	2.60 (2004)
Brazil	1.70 (2007)
India	0.59 (2005)
Cameroon	0.19 (2004)
Mali	0.04 (2008)
Afghanistan	0.02 (2009)

SOURCE: World Health Organization. (2011). Health workforce—Aggregated data, density per 1,000. *Data Repository: World Health Statistics.*

> city of Mumbai hundreds of miles away from her poverty-stricken village in the eastern state of West Bengal.
>
> They promised her a well-paid job as a housemaid to help feed her family.
>
> Instead, she ended up at one of Asia's largest red light districts to become a sex worker.
>
> Trafficked by her neighbour, she arrived at a brothel. She was raped by a customer and spent the next three months in hospital.
>
> Guddi's sad and harrowing story is similar to many of the estimated 20,000 sex workers in Kamathipura, established over 150 years ago during colonial rule as one of Mumbai's "comfort zones" for British soldiers. (para. 1–5)

Kristof and WuDunn (2009) estimate that there are 2 to 3 million prostitutes in India.

The size of the sex trade in some developing states is rooted in several factors. First, in conservative societies like India, Pakistan, and other regional states, societal norms dictate that young couples wait until marriage to consummate a relationship. "Respectable" middle-class girls are expected to save their virginity for their husbands. For young men, then, access to prostitutes offers a penalty-free way to gain sexual pleasure and experience before marriage. Second, the girls and young women in the brothels are usually poor, illiterate villagers with no power or voice and few advocates or protectors (Kara, 2009). Police are not only unlikely to help them but may participate in their exploitation as well.

The diminished status conferred by deep poverty and being female imposes a profound double burden on girls and women. It is no coincidence that in a global environment that so often marginalizes women and girls, the trade in their bodies and lives is vast, widespread, and often ignored by authorities.

WOMEN AND CONFLICT: RAPE IN WAR

The existence of rape in war has a long and grim history across the globe. Women, who are often perceived in society as property rather than autonomous individuals, have been taken by soldiers and officers as "spoils of war" for many centuries. During World War I, when Germany invaded Belgium and France, German soldiers terrorized villages by burning houses, raping women, and killing villagers. During World War II, rape was practiced by all sides, with Nazi German forces assaulting girls and women as they beat a path into the Soviet Union. Historians have also documented mass rapes by

Soviet soldiers, particularly at the end of the war, when brutal assaults were perpetrated against German women and even women liberated from the Nazi camps. In the Asian theater of conflict in World War II, it is estimated that between 100,000 and 200,000 Korean women were kidnapped by Japanese soldiers and transported to the front lines, where they were pressed into sexual slavery as "comfort women."

In the late 20th and early 21st centuries, wars in Rwanda, the Democratic Republic of Congo (DRC), and the former Yugoslavia have been scenes of mass sexual violence against women. In the DRC, for example, tens of thousands of women have been raped by armed combatants in the country's civil war. In recent years, scholars have begun to draw attention to the proposition that rape is not just a *product* of war but also a *policy* of war. That is, rape is a conscious instrument of war for combatants (Niarchos, 1995).

As in any rape, the victim in war is likely to see the assault and its consequences as a serious personal trouble, which it clearly is. Nevertheless, the scale of the phenomenon of rape in war suggests that it is not just a private trouble but also a public issue. We might begin with the question, "What is the role of rape in war?" To ask the question is not to justify rape in war (such a thing is morally impossible) but to analyze how it functions as a practice and policy in conflict. We propose several responses to this question.

First, rape has historically been a "normal" component of war and a "right" of the victors. Those who have conquered their enemies may make a claim on the spoils of war, which include female bodies perceived as another form of property to be appropriated or conferred as "rewards." Amnesty International, a nonprofit organization that lobbies for awareness and change in the area of human rights, reported that in Northern Uganda, the Lord's Resistance Army (LRA) was abducting young girls and women and handing them over as "wives" to LRA fighters as prizes for "good behavior," which included following orders to kill villagers and prisoners of war (Amnesty International, 2004; Lough & Denholm, 2005). Women suffer in a multitude of ways, as journalist Marc Ellison (2015) shows in a story on "The Girls of the Lord's Resistance Army":

> Rose [Achayo] is a three-time victim: torn away from her home by the LRA rebels; forced to be a "wife" in the bush, and now stigmatized by her community and even her family upon return.
>
> "My husband did not want me as a wife again when I came home," says Rose. "He would tell me the rebels had already slept with me so I was now a rebel wife."
>
> "He blamed me, saying that I was responsible for my abduction because I always made myself smart and wanted to look beautiful."
>
> The 42-year-old says she is now by herself. ("Rose Achayo: 'A Rebel Wife'," para. 1–4)

Second, rape targets women for political and strategic reasons, including territorial gain. In the former Yugoslavia, for instance, rape and its threat were used to drive women from their homes so that the territory could be occupied by the aggressors (Thomas & Ralph, 1999). Rape may also be a way of physically destroying a community or group, as the brutality of war rapes can leave women unable to bear children (Frederick & AWARE Committee on Rape, 2001). In some areas, raped women are also considered dishonorable and may be shunned by their families and the community, as has sometimes been the case in the DRC (Moore, 2010).

Third, it has been suggested that rape is a means of communication between male combatants on opposing sides. Where women are considered the "property" of their fathers, husbands, brothers, or the patriarchal social order itself, rape is a symbolic assault on the men who have failed to protect them. This "function" has powerful historical roots: "Even as a system of law [on war] developed, rape was defined as a property crime against the man who owned the raped woman" (Frederick & AWARE Committee on Rape, 2001, p. 12).

Rape in war is thus not just an incidental phenomenon but a strategic one as well. Women are targeted as representatives of a community and a gender. They are victimized by their rapists and often again by families and communities that feel shamed by the rapes. This private trouble has, as we see, many links to public issues.

CHANGE HAPPENS: WOMEN'S EMPOWERMENT

It is possible to empower women across the globe. The nonprofit organization Oxfam America (www.oxfamamerica.org), for example, features a program called Saving for Change, which emphasizes "savings-led microfinance." Participating groups of women save and pool their money, agree on guidelines for investing or lending

DISCOVER & DEBATE

Equal Gender Representation

Motion: Equal gender representation should be a priority in the U.S. president's cabinet appointments. One way to ensure fair gender representation is through a quota system.

Background

The cabinet, an important part of the U.S. government, acts as an advisory board to the president. It comprises the vice president, the heads of 15 executive departments, and several additional cabinet-level appointments. Cabinet members are nominated by the president and subject to approval by the U.S. Senate. Gender representation in the first-term cabinets of recent presidents has been mixed. President Donald Trump's cabinet includes 24 members: 4 women and 20 men. President Barack Obama had 7 female cabinet members out of 23 total members; President George W. Bush had 5 female members out of 22 members; and President Bill Clinton had 6 female members out of 22 members. Some counties where voluntary quotas have been adopted by political parties include the United Kingdom, France, the Czech Republic, Argentina, Australia, Canada, and Germany.

Affirmative Arguments

- The president's cabinet should be reflective of the general population. A male-dominated cabinet fails to represent the gender balance of the country, which in turn affects the inclusion of a spectrum of interests in policy making.
- Countries like Canada and Norway showcase gender equality in their executive cabinets. Having a quota, as these countries do, reduces structural obstacles that prevent women from breaking the glass ceiling.
- Having a significant proportion of women in the cabinet minimizes the pressure a female member assuming the role of the "token woman."

Opposition Arguments

- Cabinet members should be selected based on their knowledge and experience. Having a mandatory minimum gender representation threatens to undermine a merit-based selection process that ensures the most qualified candidates occupy cabinet jobs.
- Quotas do not advance the cause of gender equality because women may be perceived as only having a position on the basis of gender rather than of qualifications.
- There is a strong case for diversity in the U.S. cabinet, such as public perception of the cabinet by citizens as well as foreign nationals, and research data showing benefits of diversity. This provides an incentive to increase gender diversity even without a mandated quota.

Questions for Consideration

- If the government introduces a mandatory gender quota, is it also obligated to create quotas based on race, ethnicity, sexual orientation, religion, and other categories?
- What have been the experiences of democratic countries that have a gender-based

quota system? What can these experiences and public reaction to the quota system tell us about the necessity or desirability of a quota system?

- Are quotas in a free, open political system democratic or undemocratic?

Debate Tip

- Conduct the necessary research for the debate. Be open during the research process to find evidence not supporting your debate stance. Prepare in advance for possible arguments the other team may present.

in their communities, and organize their resources to serve local needs. The groups enhance not only the women's economic capital but also their social capital, building ties that support them in times of economic or other crises. Although Oxfam funds coaches who help the women get started, Saving for Change groups are not financed or managed from the outside; they are fully autonomous and run by the women themselves.

According to the Population Reference Bureau (2015), just 40 girls are in school for every hundred boys enrolled in secondary school. Mali has high rates of early marriage and few legal protections for women. But Mali, a site of where the Saving for Change program is in operation, also has a growing practice of savings-led microfinance empowering women to save, earn, lend, and invest. According to Oxfam, "households in villages [in Mali] with savings groups experienced an 8 percent increase in food security and saved 31 percent more on average" (Kramer, 2013). With coaching, women gain financial literacy and empowerment despite their lack of schooling. More mature savings groups are serving the global market for local commodities such as shea butter, a popular cosmetic ingredient. Other countries where women are participating in savings-led microfinance programs include Senegal, Cambodia, and El Salvador (Oxfam, 2015).

According to the nonprofit organization Oxfam, more than 700,000 women around the world had participated in Saving for Change by 2015. The women in the groups make small weekly deposits into a common fund and lend to one another from the fund at a 10% monthly interest rate. More women today are using cellphones to save and track money, which has led to greater saving.

Some fear that women's empowerment can foster backlash, manifested as violence or social repercussions. Some patriarchal, conservative societies may not be ready to see women take the initiative to address sexual exploitation, bring attention to crimes against women, or grow economically independent of men, and the victimization of women who step out of traditionally subjugated roles is a risk.

On the other hand, greater independence—social or economic—may allow women to leave violent relationships or challenge norms that marginalize them. The effects of women's economic empowerment can also go beyond their own lives, improving prospects for their children and communities. Studies suggest that when women earn and control economic resources, family money is more likely to go toward needs such as food, medicine, and housing (Kristof & WuDunn, 2009). Maternal and child mortality are reduced with women's empowerment, as are the poverty, marginality, and illiteracy that may lead desperate girls and women to the global sex trade. Mobilization of human and intellectual capital is a critical part of domestic development for a country. It is not a coincidence that countries offering opportunity and mobility to women prosper economically; where fully half the population is deprived of rights, education, and access to the labor market, the consequences are ultimately borne by the whole society and state.

WHY STUDY GENDER FROM A SOCIOLOGICAL PERSPECTIVE?

Gender matters. Whether we are talking about the toys a child may receive on a birthday, encouragement to study different academic subjects, or pay and promotions on the job, gender can make a difference in someone's experience. It can determine whether someone has the opportunity to visit a health clinic, attend school, or work in a paid job. Historically and often today it still gives men the power to choose whom women will marry, what they can own, and whether they can assert control over their own lives, fertility, economic independence, and physical safety.

When we study gender roles, we have the opportunity to recognize the power of sex and gender as categories that offer opportunities and construct obstacles. Girls and women have made tremendous strides in schools, families, and workplaces, and for many, equality seems achievable. For many others, marginality is still the hallmark of societal experiences. But women have agency, and even women in deprived circumstances can develop economic and political and social voice. Public interest and political will can open doors to better lives for millions of girls and women.

Boys and men are a key part of this picture too. Women's growing roles challenge men to reconsider long-held ideas about sex and gender and to imagine, along with women, a world in which gender equality improves not only individual lives but also families, communities, and countries.

WHAT CAN I DO WITH A SOCIOLOGY DEGREE?

Ethical Decision-Making

As you learned in Chapter 6 on deviance and social control, ideas of right and wrong are socially constructed. Ethical standards are socially, culturally, and even historically specific, and societies may struggle to adopt new ethical standards that keep pace with the speed of discovery and technological innovation. Although many occupations have written codes of ethics to guide employees, like the Hippocratic Oath that instructs medical professionals to "do no harm," most of us are on our own to make personal and professional decisions. Ethical decision-making requires understanding the impact of those outcomes on others, be they individuals, groups, communities, society, or even the world.

Sociology can help you develop the skills to make decisions that are effective and ethical. Sociology demands a complex understanding of social life and tries to get at the root of social issues; for example, by examining the links between housing discrimination and educational segregation or the limited effects of social control policies in the criminal justice system. Sociology also looks at the ways in which access and outcomes are affected by social categories of class, race, gender, sexual orientation, age, and religion. Sociology also asks us to think about our own theoretical perspectives and social locations. It illuminates how different assumptions about how society operates lead to very different explanations for the causes and therefore solutions to social problems. By understanding these differences, you can unmask your own and other's potential biases and better understand the impact of decisions. To make ethical decisions, you have to understand how different groups of people will be affected and you need to understand root causes. Both are at the core of sociology.

Leah Hubbard, Associate at Estolano LeSar Perez Advisors, Loyola Marymount University, BA in Sociology and Music, University of Southern California, MPA

ELP Advisors is a mission-driven consulting firm that exists to build better communities through strategic vision. We work with public agencies, foundations, businesses, nonprofits, and other stakeholders to provide innovative approaches to complex policy issues. When taking on a new project or providing strategic guidance to a client, we must understand and dissect the broad, complex issues of community and economic development, including markets, local and national policy, and social inequalities, as well as consider the impact of potential outcomes on various groups of stakeholders. This helps us effectively address client challenges with integrity and equity.

Sociology provides the perfect opportunity to get a first look at these complex social systems at work. My theoretical classes gave me the ability to think critically through policy and planning recommendations and to consider their unintended consequences. On the other hand, my quantitative courses gave me the skills to translate data into narratives that can be used to inform and generate solutions. Consulting requires that I be a problem solver who is not only a creative thinker but an ethical decision maker who understands the roots of inequality and biases.

Career Data: Urban and Regional Planner

- 2016 Median Pay: $70,020 per year
- Typical Entry-Level Education: Master's degree
- Projected Job Growth by 2024: 6% (As fast as average)

Source: Bureau of Labor Statistics, Occupational Outlook Handbook, 2016.

SUMMARY

- **Gender roles** are the attitudes and behaviors considered appropriately "masculine" or "feminine" in a particular culture. In understanding such roles, sociologists use the term **sex** to refer to biological differences between males and females, and **gender** to refer to differences between males and females that are socially learned.
- Children begin to learn culturally appropriate masculine and feminine gender identities as soon as

they are born, and these roles are reinforced and renegotiated throughout life.

- Gender roles are learned through social interaction with others. Early family influences, peer pressure, the mass media, and the hidden curriculum in schools are especially important sources of gender socialization.
- Gender stratification is found in virtually all known societies, largely because, until the advent of modern industrial production, the requirements of childbearing and nursing constrained women to roles less likely to provide major sources of food. In modern societies, technological changes have removed such barriers to full equality, although stratification continues to persist.
- Women do more housework than men in all industrial societies, even when they engage in full-time paid employment outside the home.
- Women typically work in lower-paying occupations than men and are paid less than men are for similar jobs. They have made gains but are still less likely to be promoted in most positions than are their male peers.
- **Liberal feminism** argues that women's inequality is primarily the result of imperfect institutions. **Socialist feminism** argues that women's inequality results from the combination of capitalistic economic relations and male domination. **Radical feminism** focuses on **patriarchy** as the source of domination. Finally, **multicultural feminism** emphasizes ending inequality for all women, regardless of race, class, nationality, age, sexual orientation, or other characteristics. Third-wave feminism is a nascent movement highlighting women's agency. A key vehicle of its dissemination is the Internet.
- Some sociologists advocate for the creation of a study of masculinities to understand more fully the sociological influences on the perceptions and practices of men and boys.
- Globally, being born female is still a risk. Women are disadvantaged in access to power, health care, and safety. At the same time, women are taking the initiative in many developing areas to improve their own lives and those of their communities and families.

KEY TERMS

gender roles, 267
sex, 267
gender, 268
sexuality, 268
transgender, 268
transsexual, 268
sex category, 274
second shift, 276
stereotype threat, 277
gender wage gap, 281
occupational segregation by gender, 282
labor supply factors, 282
labor demand factors, 282
human capital, 283
indirect labor costs, 283
glass escalator, 286
glass ceiling, 286
feminism, 290
sexism, 290
liberal feminism, 290
socialist feminism, 291
radical feminism, 291
patriarchy, 291
multicultural feminism, 291
standpoint theory, 292
standpoint epistemology, 292
matrix of domination, 293

DISCUSSION QUESTIONS

1. How does one "become" a boy/man or a girl/woman? Explain how an individual is socialized into the gender you identify with at the following life stages: early childhood, preteen years, adolescence, young adulthood, parenthood. Now consider the other gender. How is this socialization different?
2. Throughout the chapter, we learned about gender inequalities in institutions including the family, education, and the workplace. Think about another institution, such as religion, politics, or criminal justice. What kinds of research questions could we create to study gender inequality in those institutions?
3. There have been several waves of feminism, and women have gained a spectrum of legal rights and new opportunities. Is feminism as an ideology still needed in our society? What would be the key characteristics of a feminism that meets today's societal challenges?
4. In this chapter, we discussed the overwhelming proportion of men among those who commit both individual homicides and mass shootings in the United States. Can any aspects of gender norms, roles, expectations, or practices in this country help us to understand the overrepresentation of men among perpetrators?
5. Why is maternal mortality much higher in some developing countries than in more economically advanced countries? How might countries with high rates of maternal mortality address this problem effectively? How can the international community contribute to reducing the incidence of maternal mortality?

edge.sagepub.com/eglitis

Want a better grade?

Get the tools you need to sharpen your study skills. Access practice quizzes, eFlashcards, video and multimedia at **https://edge.sagepub.com/eglitis**.

FAMILIES AND SOCIETY

LEARNING OBJECTIVES

10.1 Explain key concepts sociologists use to study families

10.2 Apply theoretical perspectives, including functionalism and feminist theory, to the study of marriage and the family

10.3 Describe trends in U.S. family formation and family life, including marriage, divorce, child care arrangements, and domestic violence; describe family patterns in immigrant, Native American, and deaf families

10.4 Explain what sociological research suggests about ways in which social class may influence parenting practices, as well as family formation

10.5 Understand the relationship between globalization and family life, in particular for U.S. families and women from less-developed countries

Hill Street Studios/Getty Images

WHAT DO YOU THINK?

1. Why are U.S. young adults today less likely to marry than previous generations of young adults?
2. What is a family? Who should have the power to decide what constitutes a family?
3. Do styles and priorities of parenting differ across the socioeconomic class spectrum?

MILLENNIALS AND MARRIAGE

A May 2015 blog in the *Washington Post* begins as follows:

> Millennials are poised to become the nation's largest living generation this year. As they grow as a percentage of the population, more of them will reach the age at which Americans historically have gotten married. And many baby-boomer parents are probably eagerly anticipating the big day when their son or daughter walks down the aisle (and the grandkids that will follow).
>
> But, according to new research, millennials are not showing many signs of interest in getting hitched as they get older, and, as a result, the marriage rate is expected to fall by [2016] to its lowest level to date.
>
> . . . "Millennials are such a big generation, we're going to have more people of prime marriage age in the next five years than we've had at any time in U.S. history. For that alone, we'd expect an uptick in marriage rates," said Sam Sturgeon, president of Demographic Intelligence. "That's not happening."
>
> In the firm's new *U.S. Wedding Forecast,* compiled from demographic data, Google searches, and a variety of other sources, Sturgeon projects that by 2016, the marriage rate will fall to 6.7 per 1,000 people, a historic low. That includes

people getting married for the second and third time.

> In 1867, the first year for which national marriage statistics were recorded, the marriage rate was 9.6 per 1,000 Americans. It peaked in 1946 at 16.4 per 1,000 as men were returning from World War II, and it bounced around from 8.5 in 1960 to a high of 10.8 in the mid-1980s. Starting in the 1990s, it began a long and . . . precipitous drop. (Schulte, 2015, para. 1–4)

Marriage is just one way in which young people create families today. For example, according to a Pew Research Center analysis, about a quarter of never-married young adults (25–34) are living with a partner (Wang & Parker, 2014). Parenthood has also become increasingly separated from marriage, and a family today may well consist of a never-married mother (or, less commonly, a father) raising a child or children. Today, more than 44% of single mothers have never been married (the rest are divorced or widowed); by contrast, that figure in 1960 was 4% (Caumont, 2013).

At the same time, most young adults are not opposed to marriage. According to Pew, "only 4% of never-married adults ages 25 to 34 say they don't want to get married. A majority of them either want to marry (61%) or are not sure (34%)," although the collective attitude to marriage is far less traditional than that of older generations: only about a third of those in the 18 to 29 age group agreed that it was "very important" that a couple marries if they plan to spend their lives together, while about half of those 50 to 64 agreed, and fully 65% of those 65 and over agreed (Wang & Parker, 2014).

What factors are shaping young adults' opportunities for marriage and decisions about marriage? How have changes in norms, educational attainment, and the economy, among others, affected marriage trends in the United States? Further along, we examine these questions, look at practices of family formation, and explore modern challenges to family life.

In this chapter, we focus on the U.S. family in the past and today. We begin by introducing the key concepts used in the sociological study of families and discuss the idea of the family as an institution. Then we review functionalist and feminist perspectives on families and, in particular, on traditional sex roles in marital relationships. We devote a broad section of the chapter to an overview of modern U.S. families, looking at trends in marriage and divorce, as well as family life in a sampling of subcultures—immigrant, Native American, and deaf families. Sociologists take a strong interest in issues of social class and its roots and effects, so next we explore practices of child rearing and differences across class, the decline of marriage in the poor and working classes, and work and family life in the middle class. Finally, we explore the relationship between globalization and family in the United States and beyond.

HOW DO SOCIOLOGISTS STUDY THE FAMILY?

Families come in a broad spectrum of forms, but they share important qualities. A **family**, at the most basic level, is *two or more individuals who live together and have a legally or normatively recognized relationship* based on, among other things, marriage, birth, or adoption. The family is a key social institution. Although families and their structures vary, the family as an institution is an organized system of social relationships that both reflects societal norms and expectations and meets important societal needs. It plays a role in society as a site for the reproduction of community and citizenry, socialization and transmission of culture, and the care of the young and old. Families, as micro units in the social order, also serve as sites for the allocation of social roles, like "breadwinner" and "caregiver," and contribute to the economy as consumers.

Many families are formed through marriage. Sociologists define **marriage** as a culturally normative relationship, usually between two individuals, that provides

Family: Two or more individuals who identify themselves as being related to one another, usually by blood, marriage, or adoption, and who share intimate relationships and dependency.

Marriage: A culturally approved relationship, usually between two individuals, that provides a degree of economic cooperation, emotional intimacy, and sexual activity.

FIGURE 10.1 Historical Trends in Family Living Arrangements

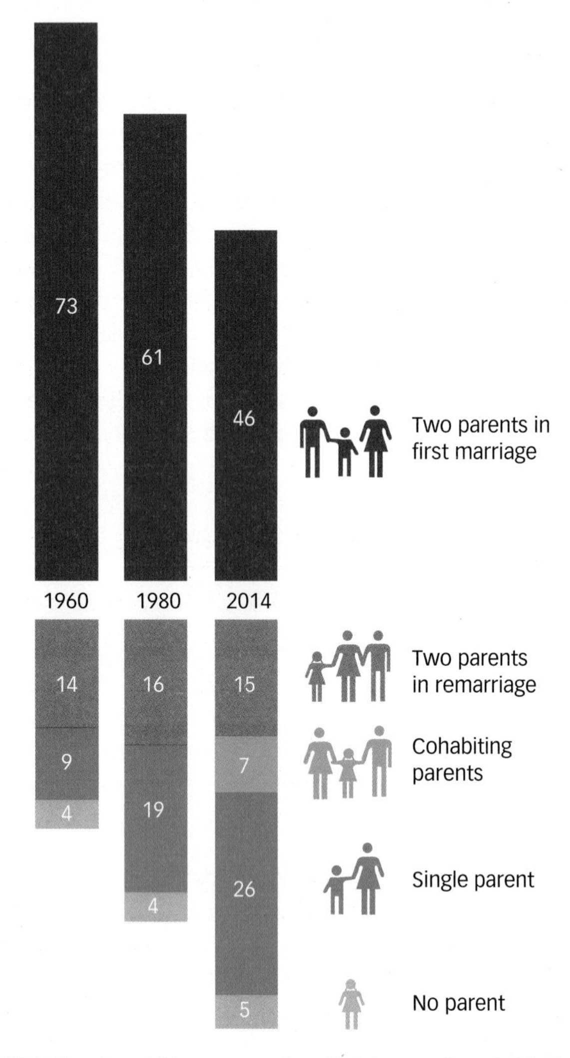

NOTE: Based on children younger than 18. Data regarding cohabitation are not available for 1960 and 1980; in those years, children with cohabiting parents are included in "one parent." For 2014, the total share of children living with two married parents is 62% after rounding. Figures do not add up to 100% due to rounding.

SOURCE: "The American family today," Pew Research Center, Washington, DC (December, 2015) http://www.pewsocialtrends.org/2015/12/17/1-the-american-family-today/.

a framework for economic cooperation, emotional intimacy, and sexual relations. Marriages may be legitimated by legal or religious authorities or, in some instances, by the norms of the prevailing culture. Although marriage has historically united partners of different sexes, same-sex marriages have become increasingly common in the United States and other modern countries, although their legal recognition is still incomplete.

Most societies have clear and widely accepted norms regarding the institution and practice of marriage that have varied across time and space. Two common patterns are **monogamy**, in which *a person may have only one spouse at a time,* and **polygamy**, in which *a person may have more than one marital partner at a time.* Within the latter category are **polygyny**, in which *a man may have multiple wives,* and **polyandry**, in which *a woman is permitted to have multiple husbands.* In feudal Europe and Asia monogamy prevailed, although in some parts of Asia, wealthy men supported concubines (similar to mistresses; Goody, 1983). George Peter Murdock's (1949) classic anthropological study of 862 preindustrial societies found that 16% had norms supportive of monogamy, 80% had norms that underpinned the practice of polygyny, and just 4% permitted polyandry.

The polygynist practice of a man taking multiple wives is unusual (and not legally recognized) in the United States, but according to researchers at Brigham Young University, an estimated 30,000 to 50,000 U.S. residents practice polygamy. Many are members of breakaway sects of the Mormon church.

Some sociologists have suggested that, because divorce and remarriage are so common in postindustrial countries such as the United States, our marriage pattern might be labeled **serial monogamy**, the *practice of having more than one wife or husband, but only one at a time.* Most modern societies are strongly committed to monogamy, and the selection of a lifelong mate—in principle, if not always in practice. Later in this chapter, we will explore a trend noted in our opener: More women and men in the U.S., as well as other countries across the globe, are foregoing marriage altogether, turning the tables on an institution that has long been considered normative in the life course—and the social order.

Monogamy: A form of marriage in which a person may have only one spouse at a time.

Polygamy: A form of marriage in which a person may have more than one spouse at a time.

Polygyny: A form of marriage in which a man may have multiple wives.

Polyandry: A form of marriage in which a woman may have multiple husbands.

Serial monogamy: The practice of having more than one wife or husband, but only one at a time.

In many societies, marriages tend to be **endogamous**—that is, *limited to partners who are members of the same social group or caste.* Sexual or marital partnerships outside the group may be cause for a range of sanctions, from family disapproval to social ostracism to legal consequences. Consider that in the United States, **antimiscegenation** laws—that is, *laws prohibiting interracial sexual relations and marriage*—were ruled unconstitutional only in 1967. Until then, some states defined miscegenation as a felony, prohibiting residents from marrying outside their racial groups. Today such laws are history. In fact, the Pew Research Center reports that in 2010 nearly 15% of new marriages were between spouses of different races or ethnicities, more than double the figure in 1980 (6.7%). The data show that among newlyweds in 2010, about 9% of Whites, 17% of Blacks, 26% of Hispanics, and 28% of Asians married outside their own race or ethnicity (Wang, 2012).

Although intermarriage has increased, most people who marry still do so within their own racial or ethnic group. Think about married couples you know: Would you say that most "match up" on the basis of characteristics such as race, ethnicity, religion, and educational attainment? How much of this matching might be attributable to chance or personal preferences? To exposure in "marriage markets" such as college or places of worship? To normative pressures? What do you think?

FAMILIES AND THE WORK OF RAISING CHILDREN

The role of *parent* or primary caregiver in the United States and much of Europe has traditionally been assumed by biological parents (occasionally stepparents), but this is one of many possible family formations in which adults have raised children in different times and places. Consider the Baganda tribe of Central Africa, in which the biological father's brother was traditionally responsible for raising the children (Queen, Habenstein, & Adams, 1961). The Nayars of southern India offer another variation, assigning responsibility to the mother's eldest brother (Renjini, 2000; Schneider & Gough, 1974). In Trinidad and other Caribbean communities, extended family members have often assumed the care of children whose parents have migrated north (to the United States in most instances) to seek work (Ho, 1993).

A substantial minority of children in the United States also live in **extended families**, social groups consisting of one or more parents, children, and other kin, often spanning several generations, living in the same household. An extended family may include grandparents, aunts and uncles, cousins, and other close relatives. In Northern and Western Europe, Canada, the United States, and Australia, most children live in **nuclear families**—that is, families characterized by parents living with their biological children and apart from other kin—while extended families are more common in Eastern and Southern Europe, Africa, Asia, and Central and Latin America. In the United States, the extended family form is most common among those with lower income, in rural areas, and among recent migrants and minorities.

For close and extended family members to function as caregivers is neither new nor unusual. In fact, a growing number of children in the United States live with one or a pair of grandparents, although the proportion who live with neither parent is still just 4%. In 2015, 69% of children lived with two parents, and just under 23% lived with only their mothers, while just under 4% resided with just their father and 2% with grandparents or a grandparent (U.S. Census Bureau, 2015a).

THEORETICAL PERSPECTIVES ON FAMILIES

When sociologists study families, their perspectives are shaped by their overall theoretical orientations toward society. Thus, as in the study of other institutions, it is helpful to distinguish between the functionalist and conflict perspectives, although, as we will see, there are some important variations and additions to these classic categories.

Endogamous: A characteristic of marriages in which partners are limited to members of the same social group or caste.

Antimiscegenation laws: Laws prohibiting interracial sexual relations and marriage.

Extended families: Social groups consisting of one or more parents, children, and other kin, often spanning several generations, living in the same household.

Nuclear families: Social groups consisting of one or two parents and their biological, dependent children, living in a household with no other kin.

THE FUNCTIONALIST PERSPECTIVE

Recall a key functionalist question: What positive functions does a given institution or phenomenon serve in society? Based on this question and the foundational assumption that if something exists and persists, it must serve a function, functionalist theory has highlighted in particular the economic, social, and cultural functions of the family. Arguably, the shift from an agricultural to industrial to postindustrial economy in the U.S. has made the family's economic purpose less central than its reproductive and socializing functions, although micro-level consumption decisions made by families continue to drive a national economy that is deeply dependent on consumer activity and acquisition.

In his work on sex roles in the U.S. kinship system, functionalist sociologist Talcott Parsons (1954) theorized that men and women play different but complementary roles in families. In the "factory of personalities"—in other words, the family—socialization produces males and females prepared to fulfill and to want different roles in the family and society. Parsons posited that women were socially prepared for the *expressive* role of mothers and wives, while men were prepared for *instrumental* roles in the public sphere, working and earning money to support the family. These complementary roles, he suggested, were positively functional, as they ensured cooperation rather than competition for status or position. Distinct sex roles also clarified the social status of the family, which was derived from the male's social position.

Aside from his belief that the family served the function of primary socialization—that is, the process of learning and internalizing social roles and norms (such as those relating to gender)—Parsons suggested that the nuclear family of his time functioned to support adult family members emotionally, a phenomenon he called *personality stabilization* (Parsons & Bales, 1955). In industrial societies, in which the nuclear family unit was often disconnected from the extended kin networks that characterized earlier eras, this stabilization function was particularly vital.

Writing in the 1950s, Parsons worried that disruption of the roles he observed in families could have dysfunctions for the family and society. Indeed, there is some correlation between women's assumption of autonomous roles outside the home and the rise of divorce. Correlation is, of course, not causation. Possible explanations for the link include the advent of no-fault divorce laws, decline in the normative stigma related to divorce, and women's greater economic independence, which has enabled them to leave unhappy marriages that might earlier have been sustained by their dependence on spouses' wages.

Critics see Parsons's work as reinforcing and legitimating traditional roles that have both positive functions and problematic dysfunctions. The functionalist perspective—and Parsons's expression of it—has been criticized for neglecting the power differentials inherent in a relationship where one party (the wife) is economically dependent on the other (the husband). In a capitalist system, power tends to accrue to those who hold economic resources. Functionalists also neglect family dysfunctions, including ways in which the nuclear family, central to modern society yet in many respects isolated from support systems such as kin networks, may perpetuate gender inequality and even violence.

THE FEMINIST APPROACH: A CONFLICT PERSPECTIVE . . . AND BEYOND

You can probably anticipate that in looking at the family, the conflict perspective will ask how it might produce and reproduce inequality. Feminist theorizing about the family has reflected a conflict orientation in its efforts to unpack and understand the family as a potential site of both positive support and unequal power. From the 1970s, a period following intense activity in the women's movement and an increase in the number of women taking jobs outside the home, feminist perspectives became central to sociological debates on the family.

Although early theorizing about the family highlighted its structure and roles, as well as its evolution from the agricultural to the industrial era, feminist theorizing in the late 20th century turned its attention to women's experiences of domestic life and their status in the family and social world. Feminists endeavored to critique the **sexual division of labor in modern societies**, *the phenomenon of dividing production functions by gender (men produce, women reproduce) and designating different spheres of activity: the "private" to women and the "public" to men.* Even though theorists including Parsons saw this division as fundamentally functional, feminists challenged a social order that gave males privileged access to the sphere offering capitalism's most prized rewards, including social status, opportunities for advancement, and economic independence.

Sexual division of labor in modern societies: The phenomenon of dividing production functions by gender and designating different spheres of activity, the "private" to women and the "public" to men.

HIS AND HER MARRIAGE An important sociological analysis that captures some of liberal feminism's key concerns is Jessie Bernard's *The Future of Marriage* (1982). (See Chapter 9 for a fuller discussion of varieties of modern feminism, including liberal feminism.) Bernard confronts the issue of equality in marriage, positing that a husband and wife experience different marriages. In her analysis of marriage as a cultural system comprising beliefs and ideals, an institutional arrangement of norms and roles, and a complicated individual-level interactional and intimate experience, Bernard identifies *his and her marriage experiences*:

- *His* marriage is one in which he may define himself as burdened and constrained (following societal norms that indicate this is what he *should* be experiencing) while at the same time experiencing authority, independence, and a right to the sexual, domestic, and emotional "services" of his wife.
- *Her* marriage is one in which she may seek to define herself as fulfilled through her achievement of marriage (following societal norms that indicate this is what she *should* be experiencing) while at the same time experiencing associated female dependence and subjugation.

Bernard understood these gender-differentiated experiences as rooted in the cultural and institutional foundations of marriage in the era she studied. Marriage functioned, from this perspective, to allocate social roles and expectations—but not to women's advantage. In a good example of the sociological imagination, Bernard saw a connection between the personal experiences of individual men and women and the norms, roles, and expectations that create the context in which their relationship is lived.

Bernard's analysis pointed to data showing that married women, ostensibly "fulfilled" by marriage and family life, and unmarried men, ostensibly privileged by "freedom," scored highest on stress indicators, while their unmarried female and married male counterparts scored lowest. Although this was true when Bernard was writing several decades ago, recent social indicators show a mix of patterns. Some are similar to those she identified. For instance, a 2010 article in the *Harvard Men's Health Watch Newsletter* reported:

> A major survey of 127,545 American adults found that married men are healthier than men who were never married or whose marriages ended in divorce or widowhood. Men who have marital partners also live longer than men without spouses; men who marry after age 25 get more protection than those who tie the knot at a younger age, and the longer a man stays married, the greater his survival advantage over his unmarried peers. (Harvard Medical School, 2010, "Men, marriage, and mortality," para. 1)

Other studies paint a different picture. For instance, an examination of a spectrum of marriage studies determined that married women were less likely to

Harold M. Lambert/Getty Images

FOX via Getty Images

According to the Census Bureau, about one fifth of U.S. households are composed of married couples with children. In 1950, about 43% of households fit this description. Some contemporary television shows like *Family Guy* (above right) both parody and reproduce traditional family images and gender roles.

Harold M. Lambert/Getty Images

The Granger Collection NYC – all rights reserved.

"White flight" to residential suburbs in the post–World War II period left many minority families behind in economically struggling neighborhoods. Suburban advantages in access to good education, housing, and recreation were in many cases a stark contrast to the disadvantages of poor urban areas.

experience depression than their unmarried counterparts. Researchers controlled for such factors as the possibility that less depressed people were more likely to get married (which would confound results) and found that self-selection was not an issue. That is, marriage did seem to have positive health effects for women (Wood, Goesling, & Avellar, 2007).

In fact, however, the issue is more complex than either Bernard's work or recent scientific studies can embrace in a single narrative. Consider some other variables at play here. For example, men do seem to have *more* health benefits than women from marriage, even if women have some. Yet marriage as an institution does not appear to confer health benefits; rather, it is the *quality* of marriage that matters. According to a recent study, people in happy marriages rate their health better as they age (Proulx & Snider-Rivas, 2013) Solid and low-conflict marriages are healthy, and unstable, high-conflict marriages are not. The never married are better off than those in high-conflict marriages (Parker-Pope, 2010).

Bernard's work gives us an opportunity to look at marriage as a *gendered institution*—that is, one in which gender fundamentally affects the experience on a large scale. Although her analysis, which is nearly 4 decades old, cannot fully capture the reality of today's U.S. marriages, her recognition that men and women may experience marriage in different ways remains an important insight.

The feminist perspective and other conflict-oriented perspectives offer a valuable addition to functionalist theorizing. Nevertheless, their focus on the divisive and unequal aspects of family forms and norms may overlook the valuable functions of caring, socializing, and organizing that families have long performed and continue to perform in society. Indeed, both these macro-level approaches may have difficulty capturing the complexities of any family's lived experiences, particularly as they evolve and change over the years. Nonetheless, they offer a useful way of thinking about families and family members, their place in the larger social world, and the way they influence and are influenced by societal institutions and cultures.

THE PSYCHODYNAMIC FEMINIST PERSPECTIVE

Sociologist Nancy Chodorow (1999) asks, "Why do women mother?" She suggests that to explain women's choice to "mother," a verb that describes a commitment to the care and nurturing of children, and men's choice to "not mother" (that is, to assume a more distant role from child rearing), we must look at personality development and relational psychology. Although mothering is rooted in biology, Chodorow argues that biology cannot fully explain mothering, because fathers or other kin can perform key mothering functions as well.

Drawing from Sigmund Freud's object relations perspective, Chodorow argues that an infant of either sex forms his or her initial bond with the mother, who satisfies all the infant's basic needs. Later, the mother pushes a son away emotionally, whereas she maintains the bond with a daughter. Through such early socialization, daughters come to identify more fully with their mothers than with their fathers; boys, on the other hand, develop "masculine" personalities, but those draw from societal models of masculinity (or, sometimes, hypermasculinity) rather than predominantly from their fathers, who take a far less prominent role in child rearing than do mothers. Chodorow suggests that "masculinity" in boys may thus develop in part as a negation and marginalization of qualities associated with femininity, which is rejected for both social and psychological reasons.

Women, reared by mothers who nurture close and critical bonds, are rendered "relational" through this process, seeking close bonds and defining themselves through relationships (Anna's mom, Joe's wife, and the like). Men, by contrast, define themselves more autonomously and have a harder time forming close bonds. Again, the roots of this difficulty are social (society defines men as autonomous and independent) and psychological (the pain of an early break in the mother–son bond results in fear or avoidance of these deep bonds). So why do women "mother" then? Because men in heterosexual relationships are not socially or psychologically well prepared for close relational bonding, women choose to mother to reproduce this intimate connection with a child.

Although these processes play out primarily on the micro level of the family and relationships, Chodorow also recognizes macro-level effects. She suggests that because of a lack of available male role models at home, the masculine personality develops in part as a negation of the feminine personality. Chodorow argues that the higher valuation of traits associated with masculinity in areas such as politics, business, and the labor market, which men still dominate, is, at least in part, linked to the *devaluation of the feminine* that men carry with them from their early childhood experiences.

Chodorow's work on sex roles and socialization in the family offers a unique marriage of Freud and feminism that is both challenging and compelling, asking us to consider the effects that psychological processes in early childhood have on social institutions from the family to politics and the economy.

U.S. FAMILIES YESTERDAY AND TODAY

The traditional nuclear family often appears in popular media and political debates as a nostalgic embodiment of values and practices to which U.S. families should return. Historian Stephanie Coontz (2000, 2005), who has written about the history of U.S. families, points out that the highly venerated traditional nuclear family model is, in fact, a fairly recent development.

Consider that in the preindustrial era, when the U.S. economy was primarily agricultural, families were central social and economic units. Households often included multiple generations, and sometimes boarders or farmworkers too. Families were typically large and children were valued for their contributions to a family's economic viability, participating along with the other members in productive activities. Marriages tended to endure; divorce was neither normative nor especially easy to secure. At the same time, average life expectancy was about 45 years (Rubin, 1996). As life spans increased, divorce also became more common, replacing death as the factor most likely to end a marriage.

The period of early industrialization shifted these patterns somewhat, not least because it was accompanied by urbanization, which brought workers and their families to cities for work. The family's economic function declined; some children worked in factories, but the passage of child labor laws and the rise of mass public schooling made this increasingly uncommon (although, according to one source, at the end of the 19th century a quarter of textile workers in the American South were children, whose cheap labor was a boon to employers; Wertheimer, 1977). Over time, children became more of an economic cost than a wage-earning benefit; in a related development, families became smaller and began to evolve toward the nuclear family model.

The basic nuclear family model, with a mother working in the private sphere of the home while focused on child rearing and a father working in the public sphere for pay, evolved among middle-class families in the late 19th century. It was far less common among the working class at this time; working-class women, in fact, often toiled in the homes of the burgeoning middle class, as housekeepers and nursemaids.

Coontz (2000) points out that, just as the popular imagination suggests, the mother-as-homemaker and father-as-breadwinner model of the nuclear family is most characteristic of the widely idealized era of the 1950s. The post–World War II era witnessed a range of interconnected social phenomena, including suburbanization, supported by federal government initiatives to build a network of highways and encourage home ownership; a boom in economic growth and wages that brought greater consumption power, along with technologies that made the home more comfortable and convenient; and a "baby boom," as a wave of pregnancies delayed by the years of war came to term.

Although prosperity and technology brought new opportunities to many, mass suburbanization largely left behind minorities, including Black Americans, who were not given access to the government's subsidized mortgages and were left in segregated, devalued neighborhoods.

As the jobs followed White workers to the suburbs, the economic condition of many Black families and their neighborhoods deteriorated.

Furthermore, it is not clear that all was well in the prosperous suburbs either. As we noted in the section on feminist theoretical perspectives, some sociological observers detected a streak of discontent that ran through the idealized nuclear family. Betty Friedan's book *The Feminine Mystique* (1963) highlighted "the problem that has no name," a broad discontent born of women's exclusion from or marginalization in the workplace and the disconnect between their low status and opportunities and society's expectation that marriage and children were the ultimate feminine fulfillment. Coontz (2000) points out that tranquilizers, one of many medical innovations of the era, were largely consumed by women, and in considerable quantities—at least 1.15 million pounds in 1959 alone.

FIGURE 10.2 Importance of Marriage and Parenthood for Millennials and Gen Xers

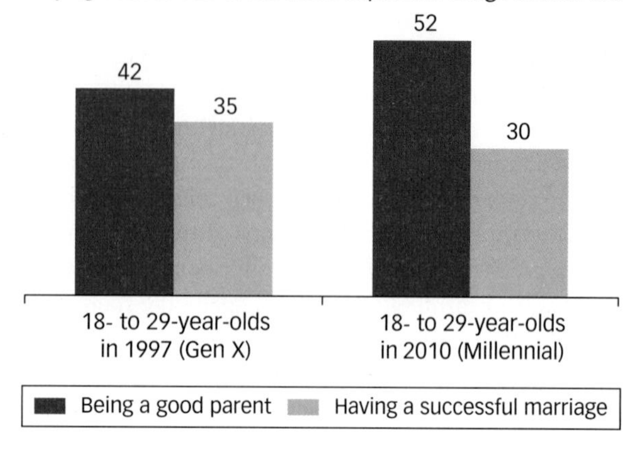

SOURCE: "For Millennials, Parenthood Trumps Marriage," Pew Research Center, Washington, DC (March 2011). http://www.pewsocialtrends.org/2011/03/09/for-millennials-parenthood-trumps-marriage/.

MARRIAGE AND DIVORCE IN THE MODERN UNITED STATES

The traditional nuclear family with the man as breadwinner and the woman as caregiver is still in existence, although it has changed in many respects since the 1950s and today represents only about 7% of U.S. households. At the same time, even though commentators often lament the "decline of the family," most children in the United States still live in two-parent households, and as we saw above, all but about 5% live with at least one parent (U.S. Census Bureau, 2013; see Figure 10.1). More children are living with single parents than in the past, but more adults are also living in nonfamily households, consisting of either a single householder or unrelated individuals. Today, about a quarter of adults live alone.

One reason for the growth of single-person households is the rising median age at first marriage, which is 30 for men and 27 for women (U.S. Census Bureau, 2017). This suggests that many people are not marrying until their 30s or even later. Most U.S. adults indicate a desire to marry, and most will at some point in their lives; more than 2.2 million married in 2015, and the U.S. marriage rate of 6.9 per 1,000 population exceeds that of many other economically advanced countries, including the states of Western and Northern Europe (Centers for Disease Control and Prevention, 2017).

Cohabitation: Living together as a couple without being legally married.

Common-law marriage: A type of relationship in which partners live as if married but without the formal legal framework of traditional marriage.

At the same time, rates of marriage in the U.S. have declined and far fewer adults today are married than in generations past (Figure 10.6). We opened this chapter with a story about decline of marriage in the millennial generation and asked what factors might be driving this drop. Here we examine several key issues.

First, there is a relationship between attitudes and practices. Data appear to show a declining sense that marriage is a necessary part of the adult life course. Consider data from a Pew Research Center study that shows a shift that has taken place across just one generation (Figure 10.2): In 1997, 42% of 18- to 29-year-olds (generation X) indicated that being a good parent was "one of the most important things" in their lives, and 35% said that having a successful marriage was "one of the most important things in their lives." In 2010, young adults in the same age group (millennials) were more likely to value parenthood but less likely to value marriage: Although 52% said that being a good parent was important to them, just 30% said the same about having a successful marriage. Even though most millennials said that they would like to get married, this traditional milestone is no longer perceived as the vital component of adulthood that it once was. Consider that just over a fifth of 18- to 29-year-olds today are married; by contrast, when members of earlier generations like those who today are 65 or older were young adults younger than 30, more than half were married (Pew Research Center, 2011).

Second, there are more viable and normatively acceptable alternatives to marriage available. **Cohabitation** and **common-law marriage**, *in which partners live as* *if married but without the formal legal framework of traditional marriage,* are options that have gained popularity in recent decades. An estimated quarter of never-married young adults (25–34) live with a partner (Wang & Parker, 2014). The decision to forego marriage in favor of short- or long-term cohabitation is not one limited to today's young adults: More older adults are choosing to build households without traditional marriage as well.

Third, economic circumstances, including the rising burden of student debt, are having an influence on decisions about family formation. Research shows some correlation between debt and the ability or willingness of young adults to start families (Smock, Manning, & Porter, 2005). Students graduating from higher education in the past decade are the first U.S. generation to finance so much of their education with interest-bearing loans. A 2002 survey from Nellie Mae, a nonprofit corporation and until recently the largest private source of student loans, offers some early insights into the relationship between debt and delayed family formation: In the survey, 14% of borrowers indicated that "loans delayed marriage," a rise from 9% in 1987, when the debt burden was smaller. More than one fifth responded that they had "delayed having children because of student loan debt," an increase from 12% in 1987. More recently, an IHS Global Insight report highlighted the fact that even though other types of debt have declined, student loan debt continues to rise—and it correlates with a discernible trend among young adults of delaying marriage and childbearing (Dwoskin, 2012). In fact, financial concerns more generally appear to have an effect on young adults' decisions about marriage: In a Pew Research Center (2014a) survey, a third of young adults indicated that economic reasons were a key obstacle to getting married (Figure 10.3).

Fourth, the marriage market has shifted. If it is the case that nearly a third of young adults indicate that they have not met someone they would like to marry yet, some of that can be explained with the application of the sociological imagination. That is, rather than looking at this on an individual level, we may want to ask what sociological factors may underpin difficulty in meeting a suitable partner. For instance, even though there are more unmarried young adult men than unmarried young adult women (implying a robust pool of partners), a closer look at the marital pool shows that there are fewer *employed* unmarried men than women.

Figure 10.4 shows the number of men per 100 women among never-married adults aged 25 to 34.

FIGURE 10.3 Reasons Adults in the United States Give for Not Being Married

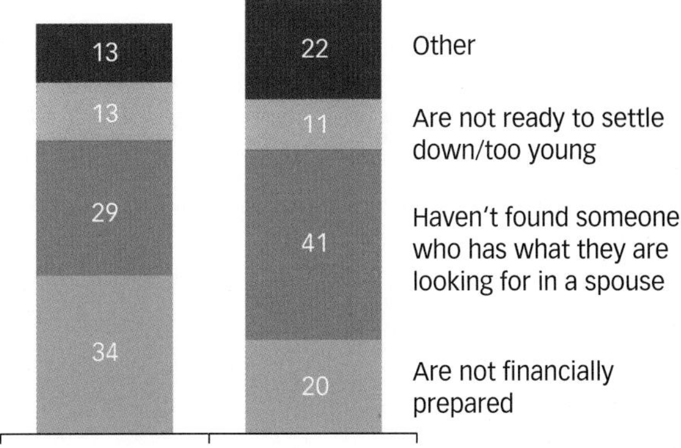

NOTE: Based on never-married adults ages 25 and older who want to marry or are not sure (n = 208). "In school" and "engaged to be married" not shown.

SOURCE: Record Share of Americans Have Never Been Married, September 24, 2014.

In the figure, we see that there are 126 never-married men aged 25 to 34 for every 100 never-married women aged 25 to 34. Notably, however, the number of *employed* never-married men aged 25 to 34 per 100 never-married women in the same age group is just 91. To the degree that being employed is a variable that makes a man "marriageable," the data suggest that the marriage market may be weaker than it appears (Pew Research Center, 2014b).

FIGURE 10.4 Male to Female Ratio (number of men per 100 women)

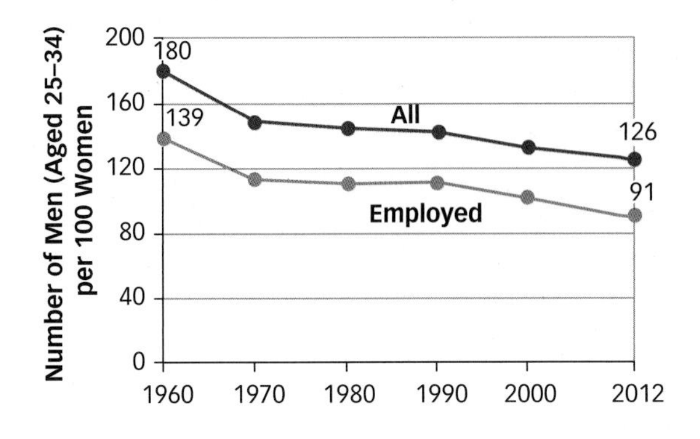

SOURCE: Pew Research Center analysis of the 1960–2000 decennial censuses and 2010–2012 American Community Survey, Integrated Public Use Microdata Series (IPUMS)

FIGURE 10.5 Median Age at First Marriage in the United States, 1950–2015

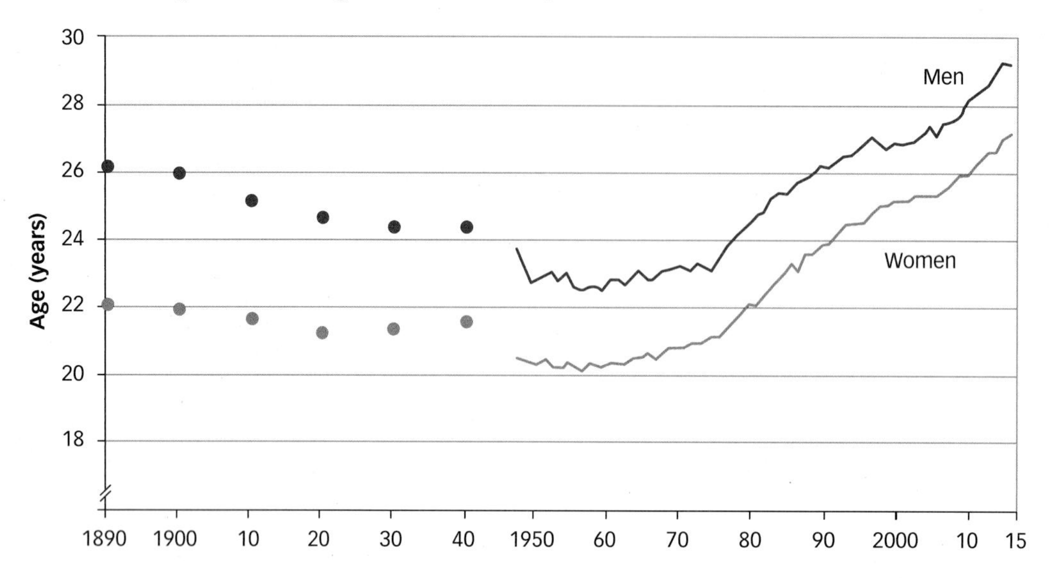

SOURCE: U.S. Census Bureau, Decennial Censuses, 1890 to 1940, and Current Population Survey, Annual Social and Economic Supplements, 1947 to 2015.

FIGURE 10.6 Marital Status in the United States, 1960–2015

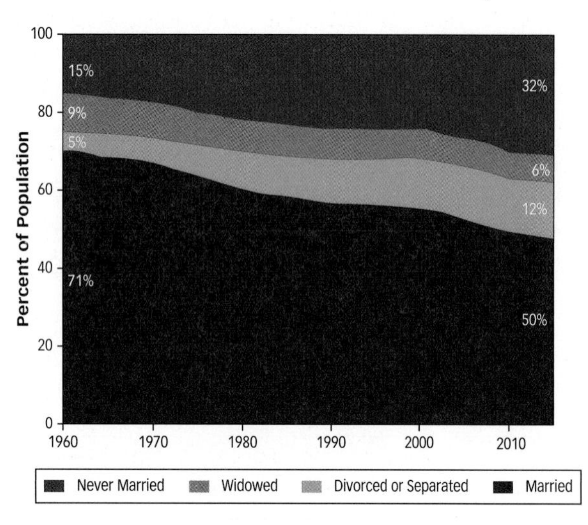

SOURCE: U.S. Census Bureau. (2015a). America's families and living arrangements: 2015: Adults (A table series): Table A1.

Interestingly, as younger generations of heterosexual adults have drifted away from marriage as a normative part of the life course, many of their gay and lesbian peers have been fighting for the opportunity to marry. Just a few years ago—2014—33 states prohibited same-sex marriage while just 17 states and the District of Columbia permitted it (Ahuja, Barnes, Chow, & Rivero, 2014). States that rejected same-sex marriage tended to cite the same language as the federal law prohibiting same-sex marriage, the Defense of Marriage Act (DOMA): "The word 'marriage' means only a legal union between one man and one woman as husband and wife." DOMA was signed into law by President Bill Clinton in 1996. It also included the provision that states were not obligated to recognize same-sex marriages conducted in states or cities that permit them.

A dramatic shift took place in June of 2015, when the U.S. Supreme Court held in *Obergefell v. Hodges* that states must allow same-sex couples to marry and that they must recognize same-sex marriages from other states. The 5 to 4 decision indicated that a fundamental right to marry is guaranteed to same-sex couples by the Due Process Clause and the Equal Protection Clause of the Fourteenth Amendment to the Constitution. According to a Gallup poll reported in the *Washington Post* just prior to the Obergefell decision, about 390,000 married same-sex couples resided in the United States. Another 1.2 million adults were living in same-sex domestic partnerships (Schwarz, 2015). Whether the newly gained right to marry will have any significant effect on the falling rate of marriage in the United States remains to be seen.

With the decline of marriage, the United States has also experienced a decline in divorce. After rising through the 1960s and 1970s, the rate of divorce has leveled off (Figure 10.7). There is a relationship between these two phenomena, since a smaller number of marriages reduces the pool of people who can divorce. The rate overall is still high, however, and the United States has one of the highest divorce rates in the world, with the rate for second and later marriages exceeding that for first marriages.

Why is the U.S. divorce rate, while declining, persistently high? Historian Stephanie Coontz (2005) argues that divorce is in part driven by our powerful attachment to the belief that marriage is the outcome of romantic love. Although historically many societies accepted marriage primarily as part of an economic or social contract, and some still do, modern U.S. adults are smitten with love. Yet the powerful early feelings and passion that characterize many relationships are destined to wane over time. In a social context that elevates romantic love and passion in films, music, and books, we may have less tolerance for the more measured emotions inherent in most long-term marriages. Could our strong focus on romantic love be a driver of both marriage *and* divorce? What do you think?

Families are surely in the process of changing—and not only in the United States. See the *Global Issues* box on page 323 for a look at family issues in Japan.

FIGURE 10.7 U.S. Divorce Rate, 1950–2014

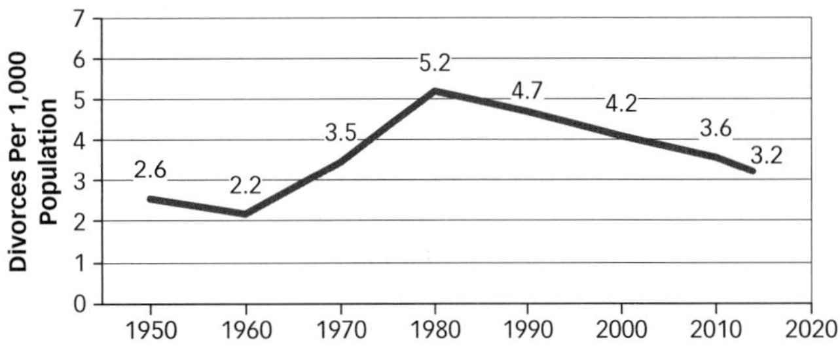

SOURCE: National Center for Health Statistics. (2015). *Aggregate data 1950–2014*. Atlanta, GA: Centers for Disease Control and Prevention.

WHO'S MINDING THE CHILDREN? CHILD CARE IN THE UNITED STATES TODAY

In a reversal of a longtime (nearly four-decade) trend in the United States, increasing numbers of mothers are staying home to care for children: In 2012, 29% of mothers reported that they did not work outside the home (Figure 10.8). About two thirds of today's stay-at-home mothers are part of "traditional" families; that is, they care for children in the home while their husbands work for pay. The rest include single and cohabiting women, as well as women whose husbands are unemployed. The shift toward fewer mothers working outside the home is driven by a variety of social, cultural, and economic factors. Among these are the growing percentage of immigrant women who are mothers and stagnating wages that have led some women to conclude that the costs of outside child care outweigh the benefits of working for pay (Cohn, Livingston, & Wang, 2014).

At the same time, in the slow growth of another trend, more fathers are assuming the primary child-care role in the home. According to one study, about 16% of stay-at-home parents today are fathers, up from 10% in 1989. Interestingly, this trend appears to be driven by labor market and health issues more than by changes in social or cultural norms that support more active fathering. Data show that even though about three quarters of mothers are motivated by a desire to care for the family, only one fifth of men offer the same explanation: Almost 60% of stay-at-home fathers indicate that they are at home because they are either ill or disabled or because they are unemployed (Livingston, 2014). Notably, public attitudes about men as primary caregivers are, in spite of myriad changes in family life, still only nominally supportive. Livingston (2014) reports on

iStock Photo/Jason_Lee_Hughes

Interracial marriages are on the rise in the United States. About 10% of marriages are interracial, and in 2015, fully 17% of newlyweds married a partner of a different race (Livingston, 2017).

■ **FIGURE 10.8** Percentage of Stay-at-Home Mothers in the United States

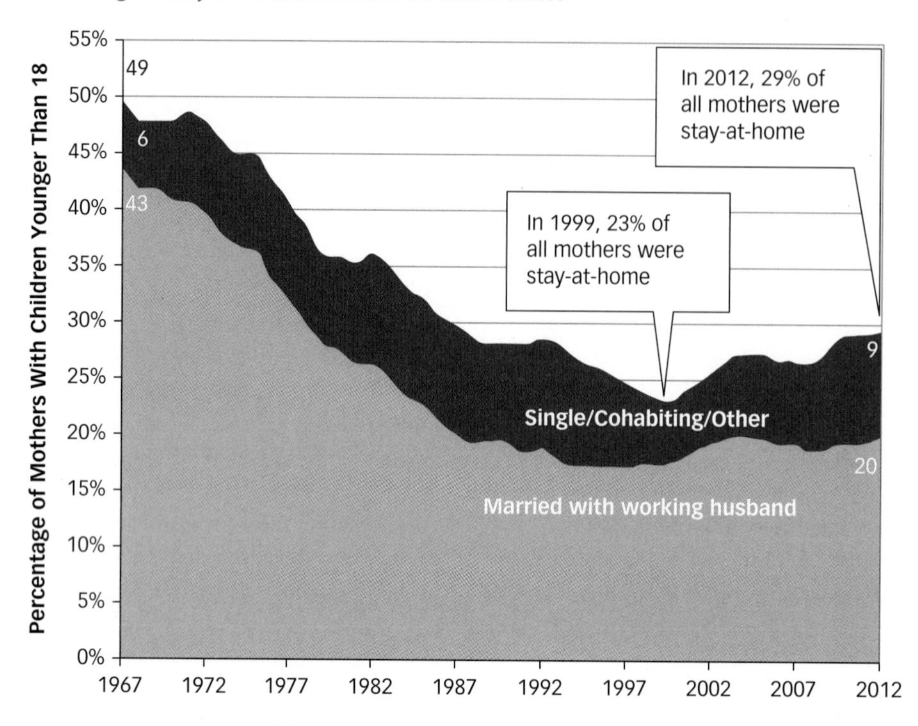

NOTE: Based on mothers ages 18–69 with own child(ren) younger than 18 in the household. Mothers are categorized based on employment status in the year prior to the survey. "Other" stay-at-home mothers are those who are married with a non-working or absent husband.

SOURCE: 7 Key Findings About Stay-at-Home Moms, D'Vera Cohn and Andrea Caumont, April 8, 2014.

a Pew Research Center poll in which about 76% of respondents said that they believed children are "just as well off" if their father works, but only 34% said that children are "just as well off" if their mother works, and 51% said that children are "better off" if the mother stays home; just 8% responded that the children are "better off" with the father at home (Figure 10.9).

Most mothers and fathers of young children are, in fact, in the labor force, although child care has remained largely in the domain of the family. Data show that about half of children age 4 and younger whose mothers work for pay are cared for by relatives. A quarter get their primary care in child-care centers or preschools, and around 13% are looked after in home-care arrangements or by a nanny or other nonrelative (ChildStats, 2013).

Although choosing who will care for a young child is a highly personal decision for a family, there are some discernible patterns in child-care arrangements by socioeconomic status. For example, poorer fathers are more likely to be stay-at-home parents than are their better-off male

■ **FIGURE 10.9** Public Opinion of the Importance of Stay-at-Home Moms and Stay-at-Home Dads 2014

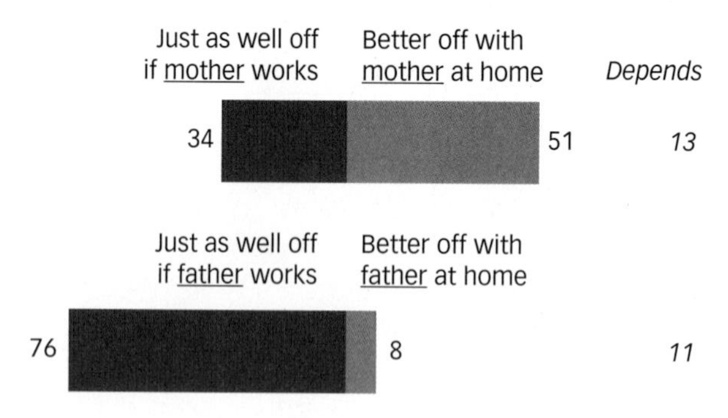

NOTE: The questions were asked separately for mothers and fathers. "Don't know/Refused" not shown.

SOURCE: "Public Differs on Importance of Stay-at-Home Moms and Stay-at-Home Dads," Pew Research Center, Washington, DC (June, 2014). http://www.pew socialtrends.org/2014/06/05/growing-number-of-dads-home-with-the-kids/st-2014-06-05-stay-at-home-dads-03/.

peers (Livingston, 2014). As well, working mothers who hold college degrees are most likely to use center-based child care, which is often very costly (ChildStats, 2013). How would you explain these patterns? What other patterns of child care could you hypothesize? Below we turn to an examination of family patterns in immigrant, Native American, and deaf families in the United States.

IMMIGRATION AND FAMILY PATTERNS

The United States has more foreign-born residents than any other country in the world. Given its low fertility rate, a substantial proportion—about a third—of the country's population growth is the result of immigration (Table 10.1 and Figure 10.10). With the proportion of foreign-born residents at about 13%, it is not surprising that immigrants and the cultures they carry with them have important effects on family patterns in the United States.

Predictably, more recent immigration correlates with a group's stronger ties to its homeland culture (Moore & Pinderhughes, 2001). Many scholars are now focusing on the *transnational* nature of immigrant families. Embodying transnationalism may mean living, working, worshipping, and being politically active in one nation while still maintaining strong political, social, religious, and/or cultural ties to other nations (Levitt, 2004). Family members may send money to relatives in their countries of origin, keep in nearly constant contact with those they left behind through modern communication technologies, and travel back and forth between countries frequently to maintain close emotional ties.

Many immigrant parents also prefer their children to marry within the group. According to research by the Center for Immigration Studies, in some devout Muslim communities parents' traditional values exist in a tense relationship with new norms embraced by their children:

> Just when Muslim girls traditionally would be separated from boys, taken out of school, and perhaps start wearing a head covering, their American counterparts begin to discover and experiment with their sexuality. To prevent such experimentation, Muslim parents seek to enforce the traditional rules . . . sometimes even cloistering their daughters. [Nevertheless,] . . . by law, girls must go to school until 16 or so; and at 18, they acquire additional rights . . . .
>
> To encourage the young to marry within the faith, American Muslims are developing several novel solutions, including summer camps, socials for singles, and marriage advertisements. But even these Muslim institutions have a difficult time keeping boys and girls apart. (Pipes & Durán, 2002, pp. 5–6)

REUTERS/Jim Young

In nearly half of two-parent household, both parents work full time. About 60% of mothers and 52% of fathers say it is difficult to find a balance between family and work demands (Pew Research Center, 2015a).

Interestingly, reflecting the influence of home cultures on migrants that we discussed in the opening of this section, first-generation migrants often have birthrates above those of the native-born U.S. population. One study found that among some groups, immigrant women in the United States were having more children on average (2.9) than women in their home countries (2.3; Camarota, 2005). In the second generation, however, the rate typically declines to the average U.S. rate—that is, approximately 2.1 children per woman (Hill & Johnson, 2002). Nevertheless, some studies have found that the trend toward decreasing fertility in first- and second-generation immigrant women may actually be reversed in the third generation for some groups (Parrado & Morgan, 2008). Historically, fertility rates have decreased for immigrant families the longer they reside in the United States. It is important, however, to note that factors such as country of origin, education, religion, and cultural attitudes add to the complexity of understanding these trends.

Below we narrow our focus to a pair of specific examples of family subcultures in the United States—those of Native Americans and deaf families.

■ **FIGURE 10.10** Top 10 Largest U.S. Immigration Groups, 2014

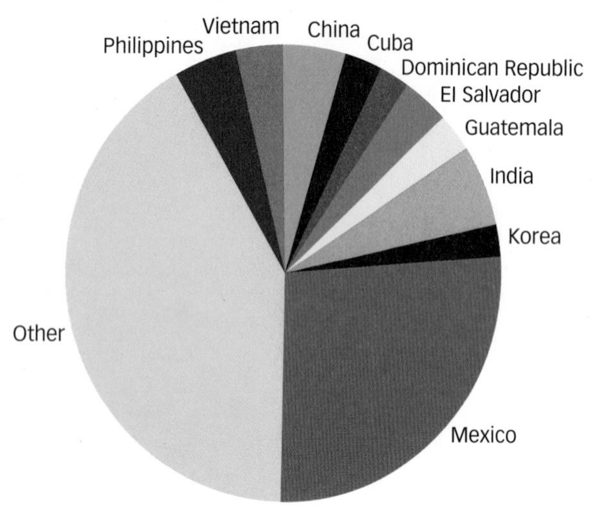

SOURCE: Migration Policy Institute. (2015). Largest U.S. Immigrant Groups over Time, 1960-Present. Retrieved from http://www.migrationpolicy.org/programs/data-hub/charts/largest-immigrant-groups-over-time.

AMERICA'S FIRST NATIONS: NATIVE AMERICAN FAMILIES

Family patterns among Native Americans are highly diverse. There are nearly 500 different nations, although more than half of all American Indians identify as coming from just 6 of these (U.S. Census Bureau, 2011). American Indians often live in extended family households that include uncles, aunts, cousins, and grandparents. According to Harriett Light and Ruth Martin (1986), writing in the *Journal of American Indian Education,* "The central unit of Indian society is the family. . . . Indian families do not have the rigid structure of relationships found in Western white culture. Instead, Indians relate to people outside the immediate family in supportive and caring ways (Levine & Laurie, 1974)."

An example of family involvement in child rearing outside the immediate parents is found in Sioux families. This involvement begins early in a child's life, when a second set of parents are selected for the newborn (Sandoz, 1961). Therefore, the "total" family involved in child rearing and support includes unrelated members of the Indian community (Ryan, 1981). This community support and protection can be viewed as responsibility for others' actions (Light & Martin, 1986).

More recent studies have shown that Native American family ties extend across generations. Native American grandparents have shown high levels of involvement in the care of their grandchildren (Mutchler, Baker, & Lee, 2007). Native Americans also report high levels of caregiving to their elderly relatives (McGuire, Okoro, Goins, & Anderson, 2008). Indeed, Native American culture and families traditionally emphasize sensitivity toward kin, tribe, and land and value the collective over the individual, in contrast to the mainstream U.S. emphasis on individual fulfillment and achievement (Light & Martin, 1986; Newcomb, 2008). Research on Native Americans of the Southwest suggests that many members of these groups see their children as belonging to the entire American Indian nation: to the land, the sky, the tribe, and its history, customs, and traditions (Nicholas, 2009).

Some controversies over family life taking place within Native American communities mirror those taking place in U.S. society more generally. For instance, beginning in 2008, some tribes began to permit same-sex marriage; in that year, the Coquille tribe of Oregon was the first to pass a law defining marriage or domestic partnership as a "formal and express civil contract entered into by two persons, regardless of their sex." The sovereign Navajo Nation, together with tribes like the Kickapoo and Chicksaw, has

■ **TABLE 10.1** Top 10 Feeder Countries for Migration to the United States, 2010

Country of Birth	Population	Percentage of U.S. Migrants by Country of Origin
Mexico	11,711,103	29
China	1,608,095	5
India	1,780,322	4
Philippines	1,777,588	4
Vietnam	1,240,542	3
El Salvador	1,214,049	3
Cuba	1,104,679	3
Korea	1,100,422	3
Dominican Republic	879,187	2
Guatemala	830,824	2

SOURCE: U.S. Census Bureau. (2010). *Place of birth for the foreign-born population.* Washington, DC: U.S. Government Printing Office.

GLOBAL ISSUES

Functional Alternatives to the Family in Modern Japan

People need and want families for a wide variety of reasons. Some are emotional: Families can provide warmth, comfort, and pleasurable interactions. Others are social and cultural: Families are expected to be in attendance at key cultural rituals in our lives, such as holidays, weddings, and religious ceremonies. Some needs are practical, as families also fulfill important caregiving functions. But what if family members are estranged or far away? Or if someone has no living relatives? In Japan, modernity has brought what Robert Merton termed "functional alternatives" to the family. Below we describe two of them.

YOSHIKAZU TSUNO/AFP/Getty Images

The high-tech robot "Pepper" greets some young and curious visitors. The website that markets Pepper humanizes the robot, suggesting that "Pepper wants to learn more about your tastes, your habits and quite simply who you are." ■

Japan is the first country to develop a nascent market in "rental families." In the early 1990s, Japan Efficiency Corporation was "doing a booming business renting families to the lonely," especially the elderly. Asked to comment on the small but significant phenomenon, a Japanese sociologist stated, "It's extremely strange to me that people would want to rent families, and even more surprising that they seem to be satisfied. . . . I suppose people nowadays really find the need for kinship. Compared to 50 years ago, the family system in Japan has really changed, and family-like relationships are gradually disappearing" (quoted in Watanabe, 1992).

Today the market for rental families has expanded further. Office Agents, a Tokyo firm, offers "friends" and "family members" for rent as event guests. "Many in Japan see weddings as a formal event that must be attended by as many family members, friends, and co-workers as possible. . . . But what if you've got no one to do that for you?" Office Agents has about 1,000 "fakes" available for occasions that may vary from weddings to funerals to training seminars. The company's head notes that sometimes even a marriage partner is unaware there are fake guests at his or her wedding (Kubota, 2009).

In 2014, global media reported on a technological breakthrough with implications for society—and the family in particular. In June, the Japanese company Softbank introduced Pepper, a robot with the capability of sensing and responding to emotions. According to a press report on Pepper, "with a rapidly ageing population, coupled with a falling birth rate, the demand for robots is expected to increase. . . . The growth is expected to come not only from businesses looking to offset labour shortages and rising wage costs, but also from households seeking an alternative to paying for care workers for elderly relatives" (BBC, 2014c). Pepper, who is described on its maker's webpage as "kindly, endearing, and surprising" (https://www.aldebaran.com/en/cool-robots/pepper), is already welcoming customers into Japanese businesses and is a resident in some Japanese homes.

THINK IT THROUGH

- What do the phenomena described above say about family and its functions? Are rented "relatives" a viable functional alternative for people who lack families? Are robots a viable alternative? Could you see these phenomena taking root in the United States? Why or why not?

Follow us on Twitter to keep up with current sociological stories and research! We're at @DiscoverSoc1.
Share your own ideas at #DiscoverSociology.

Science Source/Lawrence Migdale

The 2010 U.S. Census counted just over half a million (557,185) American Indian and Alaska Native families in the United States. About 57% were reported to be married-couple families. ■

resisted this step, even after the legalization of same-sex marriage by the U.S. Supreme Court in 2015: According to the Navajo nation's marriage law, "Marriage between persons of the same sex is void and prohibited." These sovereign tribes' laws are not affected by the Supreme Court ruling because the tribes were never parties to the U.S. Constitution (Drew, 2015). Interestingly, some research shows that gay partnerships were historically accepted in many tribal cultures, where the term *two spirits* was used to categorize gay, lesbian, bisexual, and transgender members (Kronk, 2013).

DEAF CULTURE AND FAMILY LIFE

Census Bureau data show that about one-fifth of the U.S. population has some kind of disability. How does disability affect family life? In this subsection, we examine the case of deaf people and the choices and challenges that family life brings for them. According to Gallaudet University (2012) figures, in 2012 approximately 13% of the U.S. population had hearing problems that may range from being fully deaf to being hard of hearing. Fewer than 1 in 1,000 were deaf before the age of 18; more than half became deaf at some point after childhood (Gallaudet Research Institute, 2005). Family life poses unique challenges for many deaf people, and, as a consequence, some prefer to practice endogamy, marrying others who are deaf and therefore share a common experience.

There has been a movement within the deaf community to redefine the meaning of deafness to denote not a form of disability but a positive culture. Some deaf people see themselves as similar to an ethnic group: sharing a common language (American Sign Language, or ASL), possessing a strong sense of cultural identity, and taking pride in their heritage. Identifying as an ethnic group rather than as a disability group, some deaf people believe that cochlear implant surgery, a procedure through which some deaf people can become hearing, is problematic, especially when it is performed on children who cannot consent. Often, deaf people who undergo this surgery are still unable to attain mastery of any oral language (Lane, 2005). The National Association of the Deaf (2000) takes a cautionary stance on cochlear implants, advising hearing parents of deaf children to conduct thorough research, create a support system, and, most important, communicate with their children before undertaking the transition. Julie Mitchiner takes pride in being deaf. She writes,

> Growing up with deaf parents and attending deaf schools, I have a strong sense of pride of being deaf and being part of the Deaf community. I do not look at myself as disabled. I often say if I were given a choice to hear or stay deaf, I'd choose to stay deaf. It is who I am. My family, my friends, and my community have taught me that being deaf is part of our culture and is a way of life. (Mitchiner & Sass-Lehrer, 2011, p. 3)

Many deaf people succeed in the hearing world, but they may confront daunting problems (Heppner, 1992). Often they are not able to speak in a way that hearing people fully understand, and most hearing people do not know ASL. It is not surprising that an estimated 85% of deaf people choose to marry others who share their own language and culture (Cichowski & Nance, 2004), or that many deaf parents are wary when their deaf children form relationships with hearing people. When a deaf couple has a hearing child, the family must make difficult choices as they negotiate not only the ordinary challenges of child rearing but also the raising of a child who may be "functionally hearing" but "culturally deaf" (Bishop & Hicks, 2009; Preston, 1994).

Families typically confer their own cultural status on their children, but this may not be true for 9 of 10 deaf children born to hearing parents. On one hand, hearing parents want the same sorts of things for their deaf children as any parents want for their children: happiness, fulfillment, and successful lives as adults. Many would like their children to mainstream into the hearing world as well as possible, in spite of challenges. On the other hand, some in the deaf community argue that the deaf children of hearing parents can never fully belong to the hearing world. Many in the deaf community believe hearing parents should send their deaf children to residential schools for the deaf, where they will be fully accepted, learn deaf culture, and be with people who share their experience of deafness (Dolnick, 1993; Lane, 1992; Sparrow, 2005).

Gallaudet University in Washington, D.C., is unique in serving specifically the deaf and hearing-impaired, offering bilingual instruction in English and ASL. The rising proportion of students who are hearing or come from mainstream schools and do not know ASL has led to debates over the centrality of deaf culture at the school.

The situations of deaf parents raising a hearing child and hearing parents raising a deaf child raise interesting and fundamental questions about what happens when family members are also members of different cultures and how the obstacles of difference within a micro unit such as the family are negotiated.

VIOLENCE AND THE FAMILY

Domestic (or family) violence is *physical or sexual abuse committed by one family member against another.* It may be perpetrated by adults toward their children, by one spouse against another, by one sibling toward another, or by adult children against their elderly parents. As little as three to four decades ago, domestic violence was rarely studied. Many people regarded violence in the home as a private matter, an attitude that was reflected in lawmaking as well, which provided few sanctions for violence that did not reach the level of severe injury or death. Today domestic violence is understood to be a serious public issue, as researchers have come to realize that it is sadly commonplace (Catalano, 2012).

Accurate data on family violence are difficult to obtain for a variety of reasons. Abused partners or children are reluctant to call attention to the fact that they are abused. Police do not want to mediate or make arrests in family conflicts, and even today the courts are hesitant to intervene in what are often perceived as family matters (Tolan, Gorman-Smith, & Henry, 2005). Some good estimates of the prevalence of this crime are available, however. According to the U.S. Bureau of Justice Statistics, between 2003 and 2013, domestic violence made up about a fifth of all violent crime in the United States. The most common form of domestic violence is intimate partner violence, that is, violence that involves current or former spouses or nonmarried partners (Truman & Morgan, 2014).

The National Intimate Partner and Sexual Violence Survey, an ongoing survey developed and administered by the Centers for Disease Control and Prevention, found in 2010 that one in three women and one in four men surveyed had been victims of *intimate partner violence* (IPV) in their lifetimes. As defined by the CDC, IPV includes physical violence, rape, and stalking by a former or current partner or spouse. About one in four women and one in seven men surveyed had experienced severe physical violence at the hands of their partners. Although these data are for experiences over the life course, even the data from a single year reveal a serious epidemic of intimate partner violence. According to the survey, more than 12 million people experienced IPV in 2010 (Centers for Disease Control and Prevention, 2010).

Domestic (or family) violence: Physical or sexual abuse committed by one family member against another.

Child abuse—sexual and/or physical assaults on children by adult members of their families—is also common in our society. According to the U.S. Department of Health and Human Services (2010), approximately 3.3 million child abuse reports and allegations were made in 2009 involving about 6 million children. On any given day, no fewer than five children die as the result of abuse (U.S. Government Accountability Office, 2011), although the main form of abuse is neglect (U.S. Department of Health and Human Services, 2010). Boys and girls are equally likely to be physically abused, but girls are more likely to be sexually abused as well. According to Childhelp (2010), an organization dedicated to the prevention of child abuse, the cycle of abuse is difficult to break; one study suggests that about 30% of abused and neglected children will later abuse their own children.

Elder abuse is the victimization of elderly persons by family members or other caregivers. In a National Institute of Justice study, 11% of elderly U.S. adults (those 65 or older) surveyed reported experiencing either emotional, physical, or sexual abuse or potential neglect (Acierno, Hernandez-Tejada, Muzzy, & Steve, 2009). Like child abuse, elder abuse is likely underreported, because victims are often in a subordinate position in the family and unable to access help outside the home. Elder abuse also shares with child abuse some of its forms, including neglect—the failure of caregivers to provide for basic needs like nutritious food and hygienic conditions—and physical abuse. Some aspects of elder abuse differ from abuse of other kinds of victims, however. For example, elder abuse may take the form of financial exploitation or outright theft of property. Those who care for elderly relatives may feel entitled to the resources the seniors possess—or they may just take advantage of the older persons' vulnerabilities.

As sociologists examining a problem that is both a private trouble and a public issue, we need to ask, "Why does domestic violence exist and persist in family life?" The acceptance of a husband's "right" to subject his wife to physical discipline has roots in Anglo-American culture. British common law permitted a man to strike his wife and children with a stick as a form of punishment, provided the stick was no thicker than his thumb; the phrase "rule of thumb" originates in this practice. Through the end of the 19th century in the United States, men could legally beat their wives (Renzetti & Curran, 1992). Research has found that domestic violence is most likely to be prevalent in societies in which family relationships are characterized by high emotional intensity and attachment, there is a pattern of male dominance and sexual inequality, a high value is placed on the privacy of family life, and violence is common in other institutional spheres, such as entertainment or popular culture (Straus & Gelles, 1990; Straus, Gelles, & Steinmetz, 1988).

People have become more aware of child and spouse abuse and its spectrum of consequences in recent years, largely because of efforts by the women's movement to bring them into the open. Shelters for battered women and children enable victims to be protected from violence. Although still limited in number, such refuges have enabled women to get counseling while terminating abusive relationships in relative safety (Haj-yahia & Cohen, 2009). Family violence is clearly a dysfunctional social phenomenon. It is both a personal trouble and a public issue. A fuller understanding of its roots and consequences can contribute to both a better-informed national conversation about the problem and more robust efforts to address it.

SOCIOECONOMIC CLASS AND FAMILY IN THE UNITED STATES

An array of family differences are linked to social class differences. In this section we consider research showing that social class may have an effect on child-rearing practices, as well as on family formation through marriage.

SOCIAL CLASS AND CHILD REARING

Parents are often caught in a dilemma: They must instill some degree of conformity in their children as they attempt to socialize them into the norms and values that will be socially appropriate for adult behavior, but at the same time they must foster a degree of independence—after all, children must eventually leave the nest and survive in the adult world. Given the tension between protecting children and instilling independence, it should not be surprising that in most families neither is fully achieved. Parents may understand that they need to help build their children's independence yet still be unwilling to trust their children's judgment, especially during adolescence. They may hang on to their children, prolonging dependence past the point where the children are ready to make decisions on their own. Growing up includes some degree of conflict no matter what approach parents use.

Some studies suggest that parental attitudes toward children's independence may differ by social class. In the United States, middle- and upper-class families tend to value self-direction and individual initiative in their children. Working-class parents, by contrast, have been

DISCOVER & DEBATE

Sociology of the Family

Motion: Marriage is a fundamental part of a healthy society and a healthy family. The state should adopt policies that encourage and support marriage.

Background

Traditional marriage has long been a part of the religious, cultural, and social fabric of the United States, but some important changes have taken place. According to the Pew Research Center, fewer Americans are married today than in the past: Although in 1960, 72% of adults were married, by 2000, the figure had fallen to 57%. Today, about half of adults are in a marital relationship. Marriage rates among young adults are far lower than they were in previous generations.

Affirmative Arguments

- Families are a fundamental cornerstone of society, and the government should encourage and support family formation with policies like tax benefits for married couples.
- There is evidence that marriage has positive psychological and health benefits for couples.
- Marriage has positive benefits for children, including a lower risk of poverty in married-couple families.

Opposition Arguments

- Financial incentives to marriage such as tax benefits unfairly penalize those who are unmarried.
- Marriage is a private decision, and the state should neither encourage nor discourage it. The government should accept and adopt policies that support a wide variety of family forms without prioritizing one over another.
- The psychological and health benefits of marriage are mixed and heavily dependent on the level of conflict in a relationship.

Questions for Consideration

- How does the debate over same-sex marriage, legalized by the U.S. Supreme Court in 2015, fit into the debate over the state's role in marriage?
- A recent study (Kalmijn, 2017) suggests that even though marriage has a small positive effect on life satisfaction, the negative effect of divorce on satisfaction is pronounced. What does this suggest about the desirability of policies that incentivize marriage?
- What should be the role of the government in related issues like childbearing, child care, and divorce?

Debate Tip

- Anecdotal evidence ("I know someone who . . .") is something upon which we rely in conversations about issues. In a debate, however, anecdotal evidence may be of limited value because the experience of one person or small group of people cannot be generalized. Look for strong empirical evidence to support your arguments.

Are middle-class parents "overparenting," raising risk-averse young people characterized by a sense of entitlement? Popular magazines have run articles with provocative titles such as "How to Land Your Kid in Therapy" (Gottlieb, 2011), expounding the virtues of less-involved parenting. How might this debate fit into Lareau's characterization of middle-class parenting styles? ■

observed by some researchers to value respect for authority, obedience, and a higher degree of conformity, and to rely on punishment when these norms are violated. Sociologist Melvin Kohn (1989), who spent many years studying class differences in child rearing, attributes these differences to the parents' work experiences: Middle- and upper-class jobs often require individual initiative and innovation, while working-class jobs tend to emphasize conformity.

Annette Lareau (2002) goes beyond Kohn's focus on work experiences to argue that social class, which we experience in a multitude of ways, has an impact on family life, in particular on the styles of child rearing in which parents engage. In reporting her study, in which 88 White and Black American families were interviewed and 12 were closely observed at home, Lareau writes,

> It is the interweaving of life experiences and resources, including parents' economic resources, occupational conditions, and educational backgrounds, that appears to be most important in leading middle-class parents to engage in concerted cultivation and working-class and poor parents to engage in the accomplishment of natural growth. (pp. 771–772)

These two concepts, concerted cultivation and accomplishment of natural growth, form a key foundation for Lareau's argument. She defines *concerted cultivation* as a style of parenting associated most fully with the middle class and characterized by an emphasis on negotiation, discussion, questioning of authority, and cultivation of talents and skills through, among other things, participation in organized activities. Lareau explains the *accomplishment of natural growth* as a parenting style associated with working-class and poor families. Directives rather than negotiation and explanation, a focus on obedience, and an inclination to care for children's basic needs characterize this style, in which parents leave children to play and grow in a largely unstructured environment. Notably, Lareau identifies a tension between obedience and trust in this style, suggesting it is characterized by something close to distrustful consent born of frustration with authority and dominant institutions but a sense of powerlessness in their presence. From this, she suggests, children take away an emerging sense of constraint. Consider the following observation by Kathryn Edin and Maria Kefalas (2005):

> While poor mothers see keeping a child housed, fed, clothed, and safe as noteworthy accomplishments, their middle-class counterparts often feel they must earn their parenting stripes by faithfully cheering at soccer league games, chaperoning boy scout camping trips and attending ballet recitals or martial arts competitions. (p. 141)

What are the effects of these differing styles of child rearing, which Lareau argues are associated with class status? Examining the outcomes for children in her study as they approached adulthood, Lareau (2002) concludes that the accomplishment of natural growth style not only tends to cultivate early independence but also leads young people toward jobs that require respect for authority and obedience to directives, like those associated with the working class. In contrast, the concerted cultivation approach to child raising tended to lead young people both to hold a sense of entitlement and to pursue careers that require a broad vocabulary and ease in negotiating with people in authority. Following up with the families she studied, Lareau found that all the middle-class children had completed high school and that most were attending college. Many of the children of low-income families had left high school and few were in college. "In sum," she writes, "differences in family life lie not only in the advantages parents obtain for their children, but also in the skills they transmit to children for negotiating their own life paths" (p. 749).

The studies discussed above strongly suggest that family life, and practices of child rearing in particular, contributes to the reproduction of class status. Although structural factors, including obstacles related to educational and economic resources, are an important part of the picture, Lareau suggests that the orientations and skills developed in childhood, which become part of a young adult's human capital as he or she negotiates the path through school and toward a job, are also relevant to understanding socioeconomic outcomes and the reproduction of class status.

ECONOMY, CULTURE, AND FAMILY FORMATION

Class status is linked with changing patterns of family life in another important way. Some sociologists believe that macro-level economic changes, in particular the rise of a postindustrial economy and associated labor market, have had a powerful effect on micro-level practices of family formation (Edin & Kefalas, 2005; Wilson, 1996, 2010). In this section we examine the sociological roots of the decline of marriage and the rise of nonmarital births in poor and working-class Black, White, and Latino communities.

In 1965, Daniel Patrick Moynihan, a former professor of sociology who was then assistant U.S. secretary of labor and would later become a U.S. senator from New York, published a controversial study of the African American family titled *The Negro Family: The Case for National Action,* which later came to be called the Moynihan Report. In it, Moynihan argued that lower-class Black family life was often dysfunctional, as reflected in high rates of family dissolution, single parenting, and the dominance of female-headed families.

Moynihan saw the breakdown of Black families, together with continued racial inequality, as leading to "a new crisis in race relations." He identified the legacy of slavery, which intentionally broke up Black families, as one of the roots of the problem. He also argued that many rural Blacks had failed to adapt adequately to urban environments. Moynihan concluded that these patterns in family life were at least in part responsible for the failure of many low-income Black Americans to make it into the economic mainstream in the United States. He saw Black poverty and inner-city violence, which exploded in the urban riots of the 1960s, as partly the result of Black family breakdown.

The Moynihan Report was widely criticized as racist and sexist, and Moynihan was accused of blaming the victims of racism and poverty (primarily Black female heads of household) for their disadvantages. Many critics ignored Moynihan's attention to *structural* as well as *cultural* factors in his analysis, however. Although he wrote that "at the center of the tangle of pathology is the weakness of the family structure," he also implicated social phenomena such as unemployment, poverty, and racial segregation in the decline of families and the rise of dysfunctions. Still, critics focused largely on his cultural analysis, and Moynihan's findings were disregarded while sociologists avoided examining the connections among race, family characteristics, and poverty for at least two decades.

In 1987, sociologist William Julius Wilson published *The Truly Disadvantaged: The Inner City, the Underclass, and Public Policy,* in which he revisited the issues Moynihan had raised in the 1965 report. In the two intervening decades, much had changed—and much had stayed the same. The family patterns that Moynihan had identified as problematic, including nonmarital births and high levels of family dissolution, had become more pronounced among poor and working-class Black Americans. At the same time, social problems such as joblessness in the inner city had grown more acute, as deindustrialization and the movement of jobs to the suburbs dramatically reduced the number of positions available for less educated and low-skilled workers. These changes, Wilson noted, had important consequences for family formation.

Almost 10 years later, Wilson (1996) argued that falling rates of marriage and rising numbers of nonmarital births were, at least in part, rooted in the declining numbers of "marriageable men" in inner-city neighborhoods. He posited that the ratio of unmarried Black women to single and "marriageable" Black men of similar age was skewed by male joblessness, high rates of incarceration, and high death rates for young Black men. The loss of jobs in the inner city had a powerfully negative effect on male employment opportunities. The consequences were felt not only in the economic fortunes of communities but also, and no less importantly, in families, where women were choosing motherhood but options for marriage were diminished by the uneven ratio of single women to marriageable men. Although rates of nonmarital births had previously been high in Black communities, where extended families have traditionally been available to support mothers and children (Gerstel & Gallagher, 1994), Wilson saw new urban circumstances as central to the rise of nonmarital births among Black Americans from one-quarter in 1965 (when Moynihan published his report) to about 70% by the middle 1990s, where it remains today (Figure 10.11). By then about half of Black American families were headed by a woman (Wilson, 2010).

When Wilson revisited this issue in 2010, he found that research on the relationship between male employment and rates of marriage and single parenthood offered mixed findings:

> Joblessness among black men is a significant factor in their delayed entry into marriage and in the decreasing rates of marriage after a child has been born, and this relationship has been exacerbated by sharp increases in incarceration that in turn lead to continued joblessness. Nevertheless, much of the decline in marriages in the inner city, including marriages that occur after a child has been born, remains unexplained when only structural factors are examined. (p. 108)

Wilson (2010) also cited cultural factors in the fragmentation of the poor Black family. Although sociologists have been reluctant to use culture as an explanation, not least due to fear of the backlash generated by the Moynihan Report, Wilson writes that structure and culture interact to create normative contexts for behavior. He points out, for instance, that "both inner-city black males and females believe that since most marriages will eventually break up and no longer represent meaningful relationships, it is better to avoid the entanglements of wedlock altogether. . . . Single mothers who perceive the fathers of their children as unreliable or as having limited financial means will often—rationally—choose single parenthood" (p. 125). In this social context, the stigma of unmarried parenthood is minimal, and behaviors rooted in structure become culturally normative.

FIGURE 10.11 Nonmarital Birthrate by Race/Ethnicity in the United States, 2015

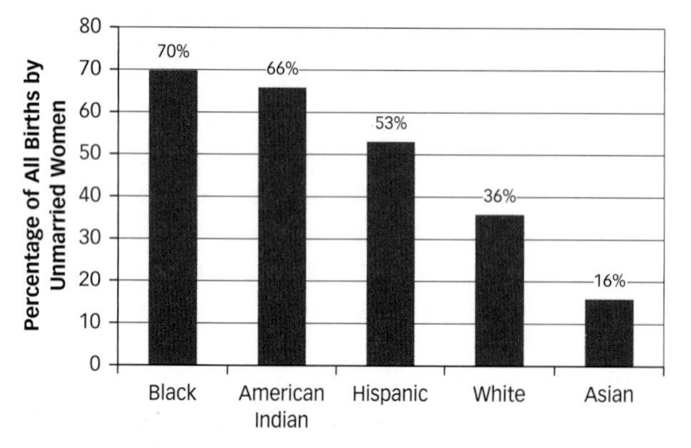

SOURCE: National Vital Statistics Report, Vol. 66, No. 1, Table 15, p. 46 (January 5, 2017).

Examining the phenomenon of low marriage rates and high nonmarital births in some communities, sociologists Kathryn Edin and Maria Kefalas (2005) looked at data on low-income White, Black, and Puerto Rican single mothers in Camden, New Jersey, and Philadelphia, Pennsylvania. Black communities have historically had higher nonmarital birthrates and lower rates of marriage than White and Latino communities, but in low-income White and Latino communities comparable trends have taken root.

Edin and Kefalas found that the women in their study placed a high value on both motherhood and marriage. They saw motherhood as a key role and central achievement in their lives, and few made serious efforts to delay motherhood. If anything, they saw early motherhood as something that had forced them to mature and kept them from getting into trouble. At the same time, they held a utopian view of marriage that may, ironically, have put it out of their reach. Many dreamed of achieving financial security and owning a home before marrying—but their poverty made this a challenge. More problematic, perhaps, was that they did not consider the men in their lives—often the fathers of their children—to be good partners, their marriageability undermined by low education, joblessness, poor economic prospects, criminal records, violence, drug and alcohol abuse, and infidelity.

Notably, then, even though they highly valued marriage, the women had few realistic opportunities to achieve stability and independence first, and little hope of finding stable partners. Motherhood, however, was an achievable dream, an opportunity to occupy an important social role and to achieve success as a parent, where other paths of opportunity were often blocked by poor structural circumstances.

Statistics show that children in single-mother homes are among those most likely to be born and to grow up impoverished. They are also more likely than their better-off peers to repeat the patterns of their parents and to remain in poverty. Here some interesting sociological questions emerge: Is single parenthood a cause (not the only one) of poverty, or is living in poverty a sociological root of single parenthood? Or perhaps both are true? What are the implications of the answers to these questions for the design of public policies that address poverty?

The relationships among class, poverty, and family patterns are complex, but Wilson and Edin and Kefalas offer sociological lenses for understanding some of the structural and cultural roots of low marriage rates and high nonmarital birthrates in many poor U.S. communities. As Wilson notes in his 2010 book *More Than Just Race: Being Black and Poor in the Inner City,* "How families are formed among America's poorest citizens is an area that cries out for further research" (p. 129). What other factors should sociologists examine? How would you conduct such a study? What kinds of questions would you ask?

FAMILY LIFE IN THE MIDDLE CLASS

Today, parents in the U.S. middle class, particularly its upper fraction, devote an unprecedented amount of resources to child rearing. Although some of the rising financial outlays are for basic needs and child care, parents are also committing time and money to "enrichment" activities intended to give their offspring advantages in competition, education, and the future labor market. According to a 2013 study, the growing U.S. income gap is reflected in a gap in spending on children that opened up in the period from the 1990s to the 2000s, with families in the top half of the income distribution spending more on their progeny while the bottom spend less (Kornrich & Furstenberg, 2013). More economically advantaged parents are actively engaged in building what Hilary Levey Friedman (2013) calls "competitive kid capital." Friedman's study of 95 families with elementary school–age children who were involved in competitive after-school activities such as chess, dance, and soccer found that many parents "saw their kids' participation in competitive afterschool activities as a way to develop certain values and skills: the importance of winning; the ability to bounce back from a loss to win in the future; to succeed in stressful situations; and to perform under the gaze of others" (p. 31). Interestingly, Friedman points out that parents of upper-middle-class girls are more likely to enroll their girls in soccer or chess than in dance, pursuing an "aggressive femininity" that they perceive to offer their daughters a future labor market advantage.

Middle-class family life is often characterized by a strong commitment to constructive and active child rearing (as we saw in Lareau's study and the research described above) and to the parents' pursuit of careers. These competing commitments often leave parents without the time to do everything, to do it well, and to feel satisfied instead of rushed and stressed.

Sociologist Arlie Russell Hochschild (2001b) has come to some interesting and perhaps surprising conclusions about this modern dilemma. Hochschild conducted a series of interviews with employees at a well-known *Fortune* 500 firm that had gone to some lengths to be family-friendly, offering flextime, the option of part-time work, parental leave, job sharing, and even a course titled "Work-Life Balance for Two-Career Couples." But she noticed that the family-friendly measures didn't make much of a difference. Most employees said they put "family first," but they also felt strained to the limit, and almost none cut back on work time. Few took advantage of parental leave or the option of part-time employment.

Why do people say they want to strike a better balance between work and the rest of their lives yet do nothing about it when they have the opportunity? Some reasons are practical; several employees in Hochschild's study feared that taking advantage of liberal work policies would count against them in their careers, while others simply needed the money—they couldn't afford to work less. Yet Hochschild identified a more surprising reason many people worked long hours: They liked being at work better than being at home. Previous research had shown that many men regard work as a haven, and Hochschild found that a notable number of working women now feel the same way. Despite the stress of long hours and guilt about being away from their families, they are reluctant to cut back on their commitment to paid work.

Hochschild found that both men and women often derive support, companionship, security, pride, and a sense of being valued when they are working. In the absence of family time and kin and community support at home, some parents sought and found—and sometimes preferred—a sense of competence and achievement in the workplace. In about a fifth of the families Hochschild studied, work rather than home was the site at which the parents derived the most satisfaction.

Many studies since have found that workplaces with more "family-friendly" policies have higher levels of workplace satisfaction and productivity, as well as lower levels of stress (Bilal, Zia-ur-Rehman, & Raza, 2010; Frye & Breaugh, 2004). Still, Hochschild's (2001b) research

Parenting in Poverty

Parents across the economic spectrum seek to raise healthy and happy children and to meet the many challenges of shepherding boys and girls from infancy to adulthood. But parenting in poverty presents a range of obstacles and fears that well-off families are far less likely to face.

For one thing, parenting in poverty is expensive. As a recent blog post in the *Washington Post* noted, for parenting families in the middle quintile of the household income spectrum, diapers consume just under 3% of their income; for those in the upper two quintiles, the figure is closer to 1 to 2%. By contrast, nearly 14% of the household income of the poorest quintile goes to diapers (Badger & Eilperin, 2016). What explains this dramatic difference? Consider the fact that today many middle- or upper-income families buy their disposable diapers in bulk from shopping clubs like Sam's Club or through the mail from Amazon, which offers free shipping for subscribed members. This can considerably reduce the cost and increase the convenience of buying a good that has become a basic necessity of modern life.

For low-income families, these avenues are often foreclosed. Poor parents may not be able to afford a costly membership to a shoppers club—or even a car to travel to a distant warehouse shop where they could be bought. They may not have space at home to store bulk purchases of diapers or other household goods. Those with little money may not be able to purchase the larger bags of diapers that offer a better value, instead being forced by economic circumstances to buy in small quantities. As the authors of the blog write,

> Cheap diapers are hard to come by for the families that have the least to spend on them. Mora, 27, scans coupons and travels for bargains. She tells her children "no" at the grocery store, when she has to choose between the kiwis they want and the diapers 2-year-old Nathan needs.

REUTERS/Shannon Stapleton

> Then, sometimes, when she finds a good deal, it comes in the wrong sizes. "Sometimes you have to decide between 'Okay, this box has 120 diapers, and this is the size that he doesn't use. But if I get the size that he's using, it's just 70 diapers, and I have 50 diapers more. So what should I do?'" she says, knowing that a too-small size might chafe her son's skin. "You just have to make things happen" (Badger & Eilperin, 2016, para. 3).

The challenges do not end at the doorstep of an individual household. Parenting in poverty often means raising children in economically disadvantaged neighborhoods, which present a further set of challenges. A recent Pew Research Center report titled "Parenting in America" reports that "higher-income parents are nearly twice as likely as lower-income parents to rate their neighborhood as an 'excellent' or 'very good' place to raise kids (78% to 42%)." Fully 38% of families with incomes under $30,000 described their neighborhood as only a "fair or poor" place to raise children. Among families with incomes over $75,000, the figure was just 7%. The differences do not stop there: Nearly half of the poorest families expressed a fear that their child could get shot, and over half worried that their child could get beat up or attacked. Although these concerns were also expressed by better-off families, 22% of whom worried about shooting and 38% of whom were concerned about other physical violence, the figures suggest a lower perceived degree of threat (Pew Research Center, 2015a).

There are, to be sure, commonalities that many parents share regardless of income. Comparable numbers of parents expressed fears of a son or daughter struggling with anxiety or depression or having problems with drugs or alcohol (Pew Research Center, 2015a). At the same time, families with greater economic means are likely to have fuller access to resources to address these problems, again highlighting some of the challenges to poor parents seeking, like their better-off peers, to make a good life for their children.

THINK IT THROUGH

- How does this essay on parenting in poverty highlight the intersection between "private troubles" and "public issues"? What are the private troubles and the public issues to which the essay draws our attention?

George Wilhelm/Los Angeles Times via Getty Images

The effects of economic globalization on families have been uneven, with negative consequences borne disproportionately by those with less education. Can you identify any current trends that suggest the circumstances of households headed by adults with a high school education or less will improve or worsen in coming decades?

suggests that many people derive satisfaction from being workaholics. As she concludes, "Working families are both prisoners and architects of the time bind in which they find themselves" (p. 249).

GLOBALIZATION AND FAMILIES

The impact of globalization on families depends to a substantial degree on social class and country or region of residence. In this section, we look at ways in which different families experience globalization and its myriad costs and benefits.

Consider the economic and labor market impact of globalization on U.S. families. On the one hand, globalization has contributed to an increase in many employers' demands for men and women with high degrees of skill and formal training, particularly in technical fields. On the other hand, low-skilled U.S. workers have been priced out of many sectors of the global job market by the fact that lower-wage labor is readily available elsewhere around the globe. Globalization can produce national economic gains even as it diminishes the prospects of some categories of workers.

About 70% of the individuals who make up the U.S. labor force do not hold 4-year college degrees. As we see elsewhere in this text, these are the workers who have been hit hardest by global economic change. Writing about domestic manufacturing industries, journalist Louis Uchitelle

(2007) observes: "As customers defected, sales plummeted and failed to bounce back. Nowhere was that more apparent than in the auto industry's struggle with [lower-cost] Japanese imports. But nearly every manufacturer was hit, and the steep recession in 1981 and 1982 compounded the damage. The old world has never returned" (p. 8).

Many working-class families have found themselves confronting flat or declining incomes as a result of competition with a global workforce. Household incomes at the bottom of the economic spectrum have declined most dramatically since the 1970s, when globalization began to transform the domestic economy. This decline has had a multitude of effects on U.S. families. Recall our discussion in this chapter of the diminished pool of "marriageable" males. Here we see some of the effects of declining job opportunities and wages in manufacturing, which used to offer gainful employment to less educated men.

The need for a family to have two incomes to make ends meet is one of the reasons for the dramatic increase in the number of women working outside the home. The movement of women into the paid workforce has, in turn, provided some women with a degree of economic independence and an opportunity to rethink the meaning of marriage. As women join the paid workforce, some postpone marriage until they are older. Couples choose cohabiting as an alternative to marriage, and when they do decide to have children, their families are likely to be smaller. Some may never marry; as we learned earlier, marriage is continuing to decline among young adults.

Globalization means greater mobility for families and more fluid ways of organizing work and life. The benefits of globalization enjoyed by some U.S. families, however, are accompanied by the losses suffered by others.

INTERNATIONAL FAMILIES AND THE GLOBAL WOMAN

Macro-level processes of globalization affect U.S. families in a variety of ways. In this section, we examine the dual phenomena of *international families* and the *global woman* to emphasize some of the micro-level effects of globalization on women, particularly women from the developing world.

Anthropologist Christine Ho (1993) has examined what she terms **international families**—that is, *families that result from globalization.* Focusing on mothers who emigrate from the Caribbean to the United States, Ho documents how they often rely on child minding, an arrangement in which extended family members and even friends cooperate in raising the women's children while they pursue work elsewhere, often thousands of miles away. This practice adds a global dimension to cooperative child-rearing practices that are a long-standing feature of Caribbean culture.

Ho suggests in her profiles of these female global citizens, most of whom work in lower-wage sectors of the economy, including clerical work and child care, that such global family arrangements enable Caribbean immigrants to avoid becoming fully Americanized: International families and child minding provide a strong sense of continuity with their Caribbean homeland culture. Ho predicts that Caribbean immigrants will retain their native culture by regularly receiving what she characterizes as "bicultural booster shots" through the shuttling of family members between the United States and the Caribbean. At the same time, Ho notes, this process contributes to the Americanization of the Caribbean region, which may eventually give rise to an ever more global culture.

Barbara Ehrenreich and Arlie Russell Hochschild (2002) have turned their attention to what they call the "global woman." Like Ho, they examine the female migrant leaving home and family to seek work in the wealthy "first world." Unlike Ho, however, they take a pointedly critical view of this phenomenon, suggesting that these female workers, many of them employed as nannies or housekeepers (or even prostitutes), are filling a "care deficit" in the wealthier countries, where many female professionals have pursued opportunities outside the home. In doing so the migrants create a new deficit at home, leaving their own children and communities behind: "Third World migrant women achieve their success only by assuming the cast-off domestic roles of middle- and high-income women in the First World—roles that have been previously rejected, of course, by men. And their 'commute' entails a cost we have yet to fully comprehend" (Ehrenreich & Hochschild, 2002, p. 3).

Ehrenreich and Hochschild (2002) argue that Western global power, previously manifested in the extraction of natural resources and agricultural goods, has evolved to embrace an "extraction" of women's labor and love, which is transferred to the well-off at a cost to poorer countries, communities, and—most acutely perhaps—families:

> The lifestyles of the First World are made possible by a global transfer of the services associated with a wife's traditional role—child care, homemaking, and sex—from poor countries to rich ones. To generalize and perhaps oversimplify: in an earlier phase

International families: Families that result from globalization.

of imperialism, northern countries extracted natural resources and agricultural products. . . from lands they conquered and colonized. Today, while still relying on Third World countries for agricultural and industrial labor, the wealthy countries also seek to extract something harder to measure and quantify, something that can look very much like love. (p. 4)

Arlie Hochschild defines the nanny chain thus: "An older daughter from a poor family in a third world country cares for her siblings, while her mother works as a nanny caring for the children of a nanny migrating to a first world country, who, in turn, cares for the child of a family in a rich country" (Hochschild, 2001a, para 3).

Although the women from the developing world are, for the most part, agents in their own choice to migrate to countries of the developed world in search of work (unless they are trafficked or tricked into migration), Ehrenreich and Hochschild point to powerful social forces that figure into this "choice." On one hand, many women encounter the "push" factor of poverty, the choice of facing destitution at home or leaving families behind to earn what are, for them, substantial wages abroad. On the other hand, there is the "pull" factor of opportunities abroad: Their services are welcomed and needed and they may gain human as well as economic capital. Even though these women make choices, their decisions may be driven by strong economic pressures and carry substantial noneconomic costs.

WHY STUDY FAMILY THROUGH A SOCIOLOGICAL LENS?

In the United States today, there are many possible ways of understanding what constitutes a family. They range from the narrower definitions embraced by the U.S. government and socially conservative communities to the broader options a growing number of groups are recognizing. A sociological perspective helps us to understand the roots of both stasis and change in family life and family formation. The decline of marriage, the rise of divorce beginning in the latter part of the 20th century, and the dramatic increase in nonmarital births are, as Émile Durkheim might have suggested, "social facts," and *social facts can be explained only by other social facts.* These are not changes that appear randomly; rather, they are the results of complex sociological phenomena with identifiable and interesting social, cultural, and economic antecedents.

Theoretical perspectives on the family and associated sex roles add another layer of analysis to the picture. Functionalist theory looks at the family's functions for societal stability, emphasizing reproduction, the nurturance and socialization of children, and the allocation of family members into complementary roles that ensure harmony and order. The more conflict-oriented feminist theory looks at the way the family reproduces gender inequality, ignoring the differential experiences and resources of men and women in relationships. The psychodynamic feminist perspective blends psychology and sociology to draw together the experiences of early childhood with relationship choices of adulthood and structural obstacles and opportunities. Although all these perspectives have strengths and weaknesses, they offer us a range of possible lenses through which we can consider why families and roles are constituted as they are. The field remains open for new theoretical perspectives, and the family remains a fruitful area of research for sociologists.

Sociologists are concerned with commonalities and differences across families and explanations for these. Class, race, immigration status, health status—all of these may influence the ways that family formation, roles, cultures, and practices are manifested. Macro-level societal changes also have powerful impacts on families; globalization, deindustrialization, and the massive growth of student debt in an era of rapidly rising college costs are all seemingly "nonfamily" phenomena that may, in fact, have important impacts on families across the globe. Sociology helps us to make these connections.

Son Preference and the Problem of Marriage in China and India

Millions of women are missing from our planet. According to a 2012 United Nations Population Fund (UNFPA) report, "If China had had a normal sex ratio at birth... it would have had 721m girls and women in 2010. In fact it had only 655m—a difference of 66m, or 10% of the female population" (Guilmoto, 2012). In India, "Had [the ratio] been normal, the country would have had 43m more women, or 7% more, than it actually did" ("Bare Branches, Redundant Males," 2015, para 6). What are the sociological roots of this dramatic loss?

AP Photo/Manish Swarup

The village of Sorkhi in the northern Indian state of Haryana is one of many places where sex-selective abortions have led to a skewed gender ratio. What are the consequences of skewed gender ratios for men and for women?

The missing girls and women are the result of systematic gender discrimination manifested as son preference. Globally, the natural ratio of male births to female births varies from 104:100 to 106:100. In some Asian countries, however, male births dramatically outpace female births. In China, between 2010 and 2015, the sex ratio at birth was 116 boys to 100 girls. In India over this period, the ratio was 111 boys to 100 girls. Although the skewed ratios have declined marginally in recent years, their effects promise to be felt for years to come ("Bare Branches, Redundant Males," 2015).

In China and India, among other regional states, there has been widespread use of prenatal sex selection: That is, parents learn the sex of their fetus prior to birth and are more likely to opt for an abortion if it is female, particularly if the family already has a girl child (Guilmoto, 2012). Even though sex-selective abortion is illegal, enforcement of the prohibition has been difficult and often lax.

Reasons for son preference are complex. In India, preference is driven by a widespread belief that boys have greater economic, social, and religious value for the family. Where a bride's parents are required to pay dowry to the groom's family, the costs to a poor (or even middle-class) family can be great; consequently, girls are often seen as economic liabilities (Mutharayappa, Choe, Arnold, & Roy, 1997; Seager, 2003). Even among families who can afford dowries for their daughters (and, paradoxically, dowry sizes have decreased as brides have become more scarce), boys are more highly valued because they pass on the family line, provide old-age security to parents, and are responsible for fulfilling religious traditions such as lighting the pyres at parents' funerals (International Development Research Centre, n.d.; Mutharayappa et al., 1997). Interestingly, sex selection is more prevalent among affluent urban dwellers in India than among their rural counterparts, although traditional norms are more likely to be associated with the latter. Urban residents have greater access to medical technologies such as prenatal sex screening. In addition, they typically want and have fewer children than do rural dwellers, so the perceived urgency of having a son in the first two or three births is more acute (Hvistendahl, 2011).

Personal decisions based on economic considerations as well as on societal and cultural norms are made in individual families, but they have macro-level consequences. Among other consequences, Guilmoto (2012) has hypothesized a "marriage squeeze" in

FIGURE 10.12 Effects of Son Preference in China and India

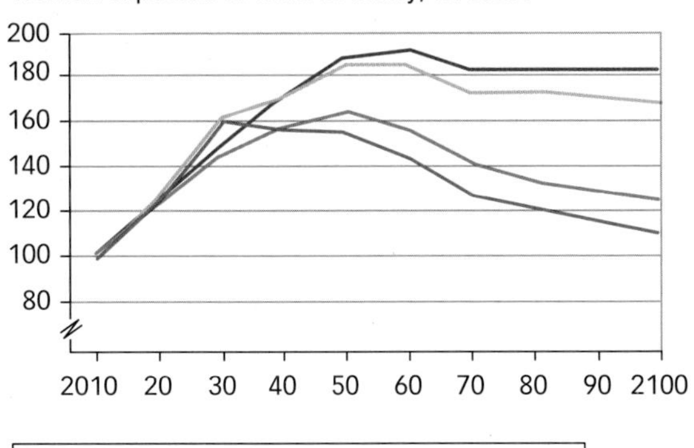

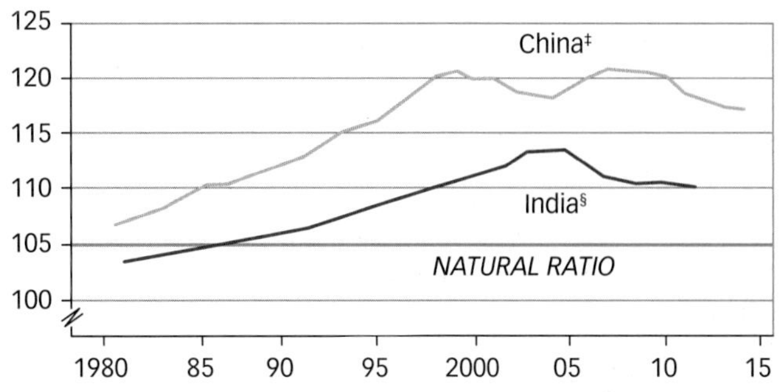

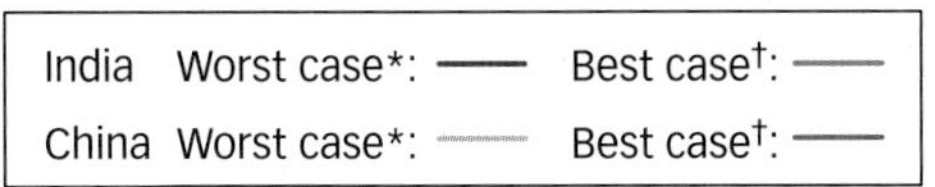

‡Five-year moving average
§Three-year moving average from 2001

Sex ratio at birth: *stays at 120 for China, 113 for India
†returns to 105 in 2020

SOURCE: Bare branches, redundant males. (2015, April 18). *The Economist*. http://www.economist.com/news/asia/21648715-distorted-sex-ratios-birth-generation-ago-are-changing-marriage-and-damaging-societies-asias

China and India. He estimates that between 2020 and 2055, unmarried men will outnumber unmarried women in China by as much as 60% and that in India, unmarried men will outnumber unmarried women by a similar proportion between 2040 and 2060. In addition, the fall in fertility rates in both countries (although China is experiencing a small uptick) has the potential to further diminish the pool of potential brides: "Fertility is important, because men tend to marry women a few years younger than themselves. In India the average age of marriage for men is 26; for women, it is 22. This means that when a country's fertility is falling, the cohort of women in their early 20s will be slightly smaller (or will be rising more slowly) than the cohort of men they are most likely to marry—those in their late 20s" ("Bare Branches, Redundant Males," 2015, "Missing girls, missing brides," para. 3).

China and India are the globe's biggest countries. They remain bastions of traditionalism in many respects, and marriage has long been an expected part of the life course. Demographic realities are already beginning to have an effect on family formation. How will this change societies and families?

WHAT DO YOU THINK?

- How should states and societies respond to the manifestations of son preference? Are solutions to the problem more likely to be a product of changes in norms and attitudes or a result of changes in policies? How are the two related?

WHAT CAN I DO WITH A SOCIOLOGY DEGREE?

Problem Solving

Problem solving is a fundamental skill in social scientific disciplines such as sociology—and in a wide variety of contemporary occupational fields. Managing and addressing complex problems by identifying their dimensions, researching their roots, and using the knowledge to craft well-reasoned responses is a skill set that is developed through careful study, training in research and analysis, and practice. Problem solving is, in many respects, comprised of other key skills we discuss in this feature, including data and information literacy, critical thinking, quantitative and qualitative research competency, and understanding of diversity. At the same time, it is a skill that has its own characteristics as a product of sociological training. Sociological research data, which form the foundation of what sociologists do and teach, cannot solve problems; rather, research data contribute to the informed understanding of the dimensions of a problem. Data are also used to hypothesize the roots of a problem. Once the roots of a problem are identified, they can be addressed through, for instance, policy or community interventions. Research can be used to follow up on whether and how solutions worked and to rework hypotheses based on new information.

Researching the roots of a problem can involve a spectrum of different approaches, and a sociologist often needs to try more than one to generate a comprehensive picture of the problem. Social life is complex, and most serious social problems are not amenable to simple solutions. At the same time, the probability of successfully addressing a problem is appreciably greater when one has used careful research to understand its causes.

The problems encountered in different occupational fields vary, but the need for people who are skilled in breaking down a problem, defining it, analyzing it, crafting solutions based on good data, and effectively communicating identified paths of action is common across many areas.

Skyler Larrimore, Executive Assistant for the Metropolitan Planning Council

Macalester College, BA in Sociology and Geography with a concentration in Urban Studies

As a professional community organizer, my job is to enable people to identify problems, envision solutions, and use tactics for neighborhood- and policy-level change. I've held many different roles in this capacity, from a resident connections coordinator at an affordable housing organization, to a community organizer in public schools, to an assistant at a public policy nonprofit. Sociological "research" in these roles looks like talking with people, like renters in their homes and parents outside of schools, to deeply examine the detriments to community well-being.

After grounded research on a social problem, much of my work involves communicating the need for change through tools like door knocking, community meetings, lobbying, rallies, policy research, blogs, and social media. My typical day entails coordinating meetings to brief civic leaders, identifying relevant news updates for our work, and writing grants to build the case for our efforts. Sociology provides you with the analytical skills necessary to advance policy change that will impact the most pressing social and environmental issues of our time.

Career Data: Social and Community Service Manager

- 2016 Median Pay: $64,680 per year
- Typical Entry-Level Education: Bachelor's degree
- Projected Job Growth by 2024: 10% (Faster than average)

Source: Bureau of Labor Statistics, Occupational Outlook Handbook, 2016.

SUMMARY

- The meaning of **family** is socially constructed within a particular culture, and in the United States, as in other modern societies, the meaning and practices of family life have been changing.
- **Marriage**, found in some form in all societies, can take several different forms, from the most common, **monogamy**, to many variations including **polygamy**, in which a person has multiple spouses simultaneously.
- The functionalist perspective highlights the family's functionality in terms of social stability and order, emphasizing such activities as sex-role allocation and child socialization.
- Feminist perspectives on the family are more conflict oriented, highlighting the **sexual division of labor** in society and its stratifying effects. Feminist perspectives also examine the different experiences of men and women in marriage and the way social expectations and roles affect those experiences. The psychodynamic feminist perspective takes a sociopsychological approach, emphasizing the impact of early mothering on the later assumption of gender roles.
- In U.S. society today the composition of families and the roles within families are shifting. The age at first marriage has risen across the board, and rates of marriage have declined, particularly among the less educated. Same-sex marriage was recognized as legal in the entire United States in 2015. Young adults are less likely than prior generations to marry, although most still value parenthood. Nonmarital births account for more than 40% of all births. Divorce has leveled off but remains at a high level.
- Socioeconomic class status affects child-rearing practices and family formation patterns. Lower rates of marriage and high rates of nonmarital births are present in the working class and among the poor. Middle-class family life is often structured around the needs of children.
- In the United States, the effects of globalization include changes in household income and employment opportunities. Women from developing countries often leave their homes and children to work for families in the developing world.

KEY TERMS

family, 309
marriage, 309
monogamy, 310
polygamy, 310
polygyny, 310
polyandry, 310
serial monogamy, 310
endogamous, 311
antimiscegenation laws, 311
extended families, 311
nuclear families, 311
sexual division of labor in modern societies, 312
cohabitation, 316
common-law marriage, 316
domestic (or family) violence, 325
international families, 334

DISCUSSION QUESTIONS

1. Why do people get married? Why do people *not* marry? Think about individual and sociological reasons. Link your answers to the discussion of marriage trends and the experience of marriage discussed in this chapter.
2. Recent data show some changes in the child-care practices of U.S. families. What do trends show? How do sociological factors help to explain the changes?
3. How does the case of deaf families with hearing children show the opportunities and challenges of family life characterized by different cultures? Can this case be compared to immigrant families with children? What similarities and differences can you identify?
4. Lareau's research suggests that middle- and working-class families have different child-rearing styles. How does she describe these styles? Why might the differences be sociologically significant? Does the essay on "parenting in poverty" help to shed light on differences?
5. Who is the "global woman"? What are the costs and benefits to women and families of a global labor market for care work?

edge.sagepub.com/eglitis

Want a better grade?

Get the tools you need to sharpen your study skills. Access practice quizzes, eFlashcards, video and multimedia at **https://edge.sagepub.com/eglitis**.

EDUCATION AND THE ECONOMY

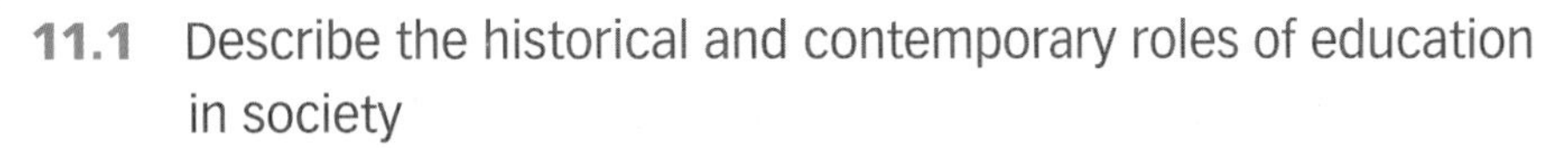

LEARNING OBJECTIVES

11.1 Describe the historical and contemporary roles of education in society

11.2 Apply conflict, functionalist, and symbolic interactionist theoretical perspectives to the institution of education

11.3 Explain how education may function to both reduce and reproduce social inequalities

11.4 Describe the three major economic revolutions that have shaped the contemporary world

11.5 Discuss current and potential effects of automation, robotics, and artificial intelligence on the labor market

iStock Photo/Kali9

WHAT DO YOU THINK?

1. What is the relationship between family socioeconomic status and educational attainment? What explains this relationship?
2. Why do significant numbers of students drop out of college before completing a degree?
3. What will be the role of robotics and artificial intelligence in the future economy? Will technology replace human workers? Will technology contribute to the creation of new jobs?

REUTERS/Sheng Li

ROBOTS AND THE FUTURE OF WORK

Here is what the former CEO of Carl's Jr. and Hardee's, two national fast-food chains, recently said about robot "employees": "They're always polite, they always upsell, they never take a vacation, they never show up late, there's never a slip-and-fall, or an age, sex, or race discrimination case" (Taylor, 2016, para 12). Neither of these restaurants has robot employees—yet—but some U.S. restaurants have begun to experiment with service designs that are almost "employee free." In San Francisco and Los Angeles, a new healthy food restaurant, Eatsa, was named one of the most influential brands in the restaurant industry by *Nation's Restaurant News* with an eatery that, although not without employees, is without any conventional interaction:

> When customers enter Eatsa, they order their food at an [Apple] iPad kiosk.
>
> Then they wait in front of a wall of glass cubbies, where their food will be appear when it's ready.
>
> Hidden behind the wall of cubbies, kitchen staff prepare the food.
>
> When an order is ready, an employee will place it in one of the cubbies. The door to that cubbie will then light up with the name of the customer who ordered the bowl.
>
> The entire process requires zero human interaction between customers and workers. (Peterson, 2016)

With few human employees, Eatsa claims it is able to sell its quinoa bowls for a competitively low price. Living employees, after all, are a significant cost to employers: About 30% of business costs in the industry are comprised by labor (DePillis, 2015).

The restaurant industry, however, is a vital part of the U.S. employment picture, providing jobs for about 2.4 million servers, almost 3 million cooks and food preparers, and a large proportion of the country's 3.3 million cashiers (DePillis, 2015). Technology may be changing that picture in the near future: Some well-known chains like Olive Garden and Wendy's are introducing tablet ordering that will reduce or eliminate the need for wait staff and cashiers.

The road to robotic restaurants does not promise to be a smooth one, and there is little imminent danger of a dramatic decline in this employment sector. Recent reports indicate that several restaurants in China that were attempting to use robots as servers had to "fire" them for a spectrum of customer service failures, including an inability to carry soup (Kraft, 2016). At the same time, automation, which has had a transformative effect on manufacturing in recent decades, promises to bring significant changes to the service sector, which includes restaurant and retail jobs, among others. But it will not stop there: Professional sectors from journalism to medicine to the law have the potential to be transformed by fast-moving technological innovations. ■

In this chapter, we discuss key issues of education and the economy. We begin the chapter with a discussion of the roots of mass public education in the United States and the development of the "credential society" that is driving rising enrollments in higher education today. We continue with a critical look at education, using the functionalist, conflict, and symbolic interactionist perspectives to think about the roles played by the education system in modern society. We then turn to the issue of education and inequality, examining education as a key to understanding how inequality is both reduced and reproduced in society. We also consider the relationship between higher education and income and the problem of college dropouts. Education has become a key path to economic success, and we continue the chapter with an examination of the evolving economy. To this end, we look at the characteristics and potential sociological implications of the growing high-technology economy, focusing, as we did in the opening story, on automation of jobs, artificial intelligence, and the future of work for those with and without higher and professional education.

EDUCATION, INDUSTRIALIZATION, AND THE "CREDENTIAL SOCIETY"

As societies change, so too does the role of **education**, *the transmission of society's norms, values, and knowledge base by means of direct instruction.* For much of human history, education occurred informally, within the family or the immediate community. Children often learned by doing—by working alongside their parents, siblings, and other relatives in the home, in the field, or on the hunt.

With the emergence of industrial society, **formal education**, *education that occurs within academic institutions such as schools,* became increasingly common. As schooling became important in industrial societies, it came to be seen as the birthright of all society members. **Mass education**, or *the extension of formal schooling to wide segments of the population,* is the norm today. Not only is mass education consistent with the democratic ideals held in most modern and economically advanced or advancing societies, but it is also the principal means by which people acquire the skills they need to participate effectively as workers and citizens in the midst of technological, cultural, and economic change of dramatic proportions.

Modern society requires its members to master a large number of complex skills. People must know how to read and write and do basic math, but that is rarely enough. Societies need people to organize production, invent new products, and program computers—others engage in creating art or literature, curing diseases, resolving human conflicts, and addressing scientific challenges like climate change.

Education: The transmission of society's norms, values, and knowledge base by means of direct instruction.

Formal education: Education that occurs within academic institutions such as schools.

Mass education: The extension of formal schooling to wide segments of the population.

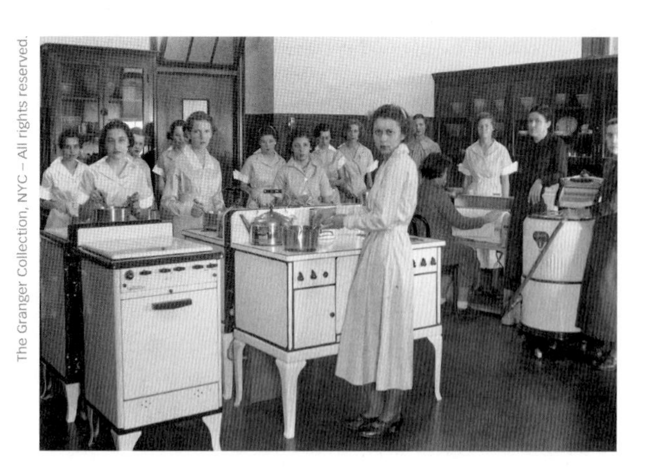

In the United States, girls and boys used to be educated separately and unequally in many public schools. Far fewer young women had the opportunity to go to college and their high school education was more likely to emphasize domestic skills like meal preparation.

Building an educated population requires more than the on-the-job training of apprentices or helpers. It requires the transmission of more knowledge than most families are willing or able to pass on from one generation to the next.

The first educational institutions in the United States were created in the 17th century by the religious leaders of the New England Puritan communities. Their original intent was to provide religious education; children were taught to read so that they could study Scripture (Monroe, 1940; Vinovskis, 1995). In 1647, the Massachusetts Bay Colony passed a law requiring every community of 50 or more people to establish a town school. The law, named Ye Old Deluder Satan Act, was intended to protect New England's youth from acquiescing to the temptations of the devil.

By the 18th century, the goal of education had shifted from religious training to cultivating practical and productive skills (Vinovskis, 1995). The emergence of industrial societies not only increased the need for people to be literate—**literacy** is defined as *the ability to read and write at a basic level*—but it also required that they learn skills, work habits, and discipline that would prepare them for jobs as industrial laborers, accountants, inventors, designers, merchandisers, lawyers, operators of complex machinery, and more (Bergen, 1996).

From the outset, schools in the United States were divided along social class lines. The sons of the middle and upper classes went to private schools that trained them for business and the professions. There were initially few public schools, and those that existed provided working- and lower-class children with the minimal education necessary for them to acquire the skills and obedience for factory work or farming (Bowles & Gintis, 1976; Wyman, 1997).

When workers began forming labor unions in the 19th century, one of their demands was for free **public education** for their children, *a universal education system provided by the government and funded by tax revenues rather than student fees* (fees served to exclude economically disadvantaged students from the classroom; Horan & Hargis, 1991). Political activists, philanthropic organizations, and newspapers joined the unions in their demand. By the late 19th century, public elementary schools had been established in most of the industrial centers of the United States, and mass public schooling soon spread throughout the country, though segregated by gender and race. In some places, no schooling was provided for girls or African Americans. In other places, girls and boys were educated separately and unequally, with girls receiving training in cooking and homemaking skills and boys studying academic subjects like literature and mathematics (Riordan, 1990; Tyack & Hansot, 1982). Schools for African Americans were segregated by law in the southern states until the U.S. Supreme Court ruled the practice unconstitutional in 1954; elsewhere in the country, Blacks and Whites attended different schools that offered unequal opportunities in education because they lived in different neighborhoods and schools were locally funded (Aviel, 1997; Bergen, 1996).

In some states, school attendance was compulsory for at least the first 6 years. The concept of public education

Literacy: The ability to read and write at a basic level.

Public education: A universal education system provided by the government and funded by tax revenues rather than student fees.

was soon expanded to include high schools, and by the end of the 19th century, the average U.S. student achieved 8 years of schooling, while 10% completed high school and 2% completed college or university (Bettelheim, 1982; Vinovskis, 1992; Walters & James, 1992).

With the creation of mass public education, the United States increasingly became a **credential society**, one in which *access to desirable jobs and social status depends on the possession of a certificate or diploma certifying the completion of formal education* (Collins, 1979; Vinovskis, 1995). A socially validated credential such as a bachelor's degree or professional degree thus serves as a filter, determining the kinds of jobs and promotions for which a person is eligible. People with only high school diplomas have a difficult time competing in the job market with those who have college degrees, even if they possess keen intellect and good skills. If a position announcement indicates that a college degree is required, the candidate with only a high school diploma is unlikely to be considered at all. Since a person's job is a major determinant of income and social class, educational credentials play a major role in shaping opportunities for social and economic mobility.

Next we look at some key theoretical perspectives on education and its functions in modern society.

THEORETICAL PERSPECTIVES ON EDUCATION

What is the role of the educational system in society? Although functionalist theorists highlight the ways in which the educational system is positively functional for society, conflict theorists point to its role in reinforcing and reproducing social stratification. Symbolic interactionist theories help to illuminate how relational processes in the classroom may contribute to educational success—or failure.

THE FUNCTIONALIST PERSPECTIVE

Émile Durkheim (1922/1956, 1922/1973b), whose work forms a foundation for functionalist theorizing in sociology, wrote about the importance of education in modern societies. According to Durkheim, modern societies are complex, with specialized yet interdependent institutions. This complexity creates a special problem for *social solidarity*—that is, the bonds that unite the members of a social group. Modern society is no longer characterized by communities with high degrees of cultural, religious, or social homogeneity, so social ties have weakened. One function of mass education is to address this problem by socializing members of a society into the norms and values necessary to produce and maintain social solidarity. Durkheim talked about this function in terms of *moral education,* meaning that educational institutions not only provide the knowledge and training necessary for members to fulfill their economic roles in modern society but also function to socialize individuals, building solidarity in the group.

Contemporary functionalist theories echo Durkheim's concerns about social solidarity, emphasizing the function of formal education in socializing people into the norms, values, and skills necessary for society to survive and thrive (Parsons & Mayhew, 1982). Functionalist theory also proposes that education has both manifest and latent functions (Bourdieu & Coleman, 1991; Merton, 1968). What are these functions?

The manifest, or intended, functions of education include the transmission of general knowledge and specific skills needed in society and the economy, such as literacy and numeracy. The latent, or unintended, functions include the propagation of societal norms and values that Durkheim argued should be explicit concerns of *moral education.* For example, beginning with kindergarten, children learn to organize their lives according to schedules, to sit at desks, to follow rules, and to show respect for authority. Sociologist Harry Gracey (1991) has argued that "the unique job of the kindergarten seems. . . to be teaching children the student role. The student role is the repertoire of behavior and attitudes regarded by educators as appropriate to children in school" (p. 448). Having "mastered" the student role, children internalize the external social norms and rules that govern the school day and their academic lives.

Consider other latent functions of the system of mass public education in the United States. For example, in keeping children occupied from about 8:00 a.m. until 3:00 p.m., schools serve as supervisors for a large population of children whose parents work to contribute to both the micro-level economies of their homes and the productivity of the macro-level economy. Schools are also sources of peer socialization, offering an environment in which conventional gender roles are enacted and enforced. Although some young people challenge expected roles through dress, for example, many conform to avoid conflict or ostracism.

Credential society: A society in which access to desirable work and social status depends on the possession of a certificate or diploma certifying the completion of formal education.

School is an important agent of socialization. Among the lessons young children learn in school are obedience to authority and conformity to schedules, imperatives that some sociologists say are rooted in early capitalism's need for compliant workers.

For example, Phelan and McLaughlin (1995) found that people with higher levels of education are more sympathetic to and less likely to blame homeless people for their condition than are people with lower levels of education.

Can you think of other latent functions of mass education that are social, cultural, economic, or political?

What are the weaknesses of the functionalist perspective in furthering our understanding of the system of education? Critics suggest that it ignores schools' contribution to reproducing social inequality. Functionalist theory assumes, for instance, that the educational system educates people in accordance with their abilities and potential, giving credentials to those who deserve them and who can contribute most to society while withholding credentials from those incapable of doing the most demanding work. Critics, however, say schools function to reproduce the existing class system, favoring those who are already the most advantaged and putting obstacles in the paths of those who are disadvantaged. They point to substantial differences in educational attainment across socioeconomic groups (a topic we take up later in this chapter) as evidence that socioeconomic class status is just as important as intellectual capability in influencing educational attainment within the institution of education (Bowles & Gintis, 1976).

Notably as well, although education may socialize students into society's norms and values, it also undermines societal authority by promoting a critical approach to dominant ideas. Education contributes substantially to the development of a capacity for "self-direction" (Miller, Kohn, & Schooler, 1986), and students often develop inquiring, critical spirits because they are exposed to views and ways of thinking that challenge their previously held ideas.

THE CONFLICT PERSPECTIVE

Conflict theorists agree that education trains people in the dominant norms and values of society and the work skills and habits demanded by the economic system. Nevertheless, they reject the functionalist notion that the system of education channels individuals into the positions for which they are best suited in terms of ambition, skills, and talents. Instead, they believe, it reproduces rather than reduces social stratification and, rather than ensuring that the best people train for and conscientiously perform the most socially important jobs (Davis & Moore, 1945), ensures that the discovery of talent will be limited (Tumin, 1953).

According to conflict theory, poor and working-class children have fewer opportunities to demonstrate their talents and abilities because they lack equal access to educational opportunities. Moreover, part of the "hidden curriculum" of the classroom is to socialize members of the working class to accept their class position (Bowles & Gintis, 1976). Children are taught at an early age to define their academic ambitions and abilities in keeping with the social class of their parents. Conflict theorists argue that lowered educational ambitions are reinforced through inferior educational opportunities, as well as labeling and discrimination in the classroom (Bowles & Gintis, 1976; Glazer, 1992; Kozol, 1991; Oakes, 1985; Willis, 1990). In the United States, this inequality has racial as well as economic dimensions.

Consider the experience of Malcolm X, a prominent champion of the rights of African Americans who was assassinated in 1965. In his autobiography, Malcolm X recounts how, despite being a top student, he was discouraged by his high school English teacher from becoming a lawyer:

> Mr. Ostrowski looked surprised, I remember. . . . He kind of half-smiled and said, "Malcolm, one of life's first needs is for us to be realistic. Don't misunderstand me, now. We all like you, you know that. . . . A lawyer—that's no realistic goal for a

> [Black man]. You need to think about something you can be. You're good with your hands—making things. . . . Why don't you plan on carpentry? People like you as a person—you'd get all kinds of work" (Haley & Malcolm X, 1964, p. 41).

More than a half century later, author Jonathan Kozol (2000) writes, poor and minority children continue to experience lower educational expectations and opportunities:

> Many people in Mott Haven [an impoverished neighborhood in the South Bronx] do a lot of work to make sure they are well-informed about the conditions in their children's public schools. Some also know a great deal more about the schools that serve the children of the privileged than many of the privileged themselves may recognize. They know that "business math" is not the same as calculus and that "job-readiness instruction" is not European history or English literature. They know that children of rich people do not often spend semesters of their teenage years in classes where they learn to type an application for an entry-level clerical position; they know that these wealthy children are too busy learning composition skills and polishing their French pronunciation and receiving preparation for the SATs. They come to understand the process by which a texture of enlightenment is stitched together for some children while it is denied to others. They also understand that, as the years go by, some of these children will appear to have deserved one kind of role in life, and some another. (pp. 100–101)

Today there continue to be disparities in education. Consider the issue of student access to Advanced Placement (AP) courses, which help prepare students for college-level work and, as well, offer a chance to earn college credit even before matriculation. Although thousands of students across the country enroll in AP courses every year, not all students have equal access to these accelerated and challenging classes: A Pro Publica study determined, for instance, that in New York, "many of the state's affluent school districts offer far more AP classes than do economically disadvantaged schools with high percentages of minority students" (Glorioso, 2011, para. 3). Researchers found that equity in AP offerings varied dramatically by state, with some states, such as Florida, providing broad access to AP courses, and others, including Kansas, Oklahoma, and Maryland, providing fewer opportunities in schools serving poorer families (Coutts & LaFleur, 2011). The Pro Publica study highlighted socioeconomic class as a determining variable in access, but racial and ethnic minorities are often enrolled in lower-income schools, suggesting that the effects of limited access to AP courses are experienced most acutely by Black and Hispanic students in the United States.

Among the most prominent conflict theorists in the sociology of education are Samuel Bowles and Herbert Gintis, whose 1976 book *Schooling in Capitalist America* posited three key arguments. First, the authors argued that schools not only impart cognitive skills but also "prepare people to function well and without complaint in the hierarchical structure of the modern corporation" (p. ix). Second, Bowles and Gintis used statistical data to support the argument that parental economic status is passed on to children, at least in part, through unequal educational opportunity, though the advantages conferred on children of higher-social-status families are not limited to their educational preparation. Finally, the authors suggested that the modern school system was not the product of the evolutionary perfection of democratic pedagogy, but rather primarily a reflection of the interests of raising profits for capitalist enterprises such as factories.

Frequently cited results of Bowles and Gintis's early work include a graph showing the powerful correlation between socioeconomic status (as measured by income) and educational attainment. The data, from a sample of men with similar childhood IQ scores, demonstrate an unmistakable relationship between the socioeconomic backgrounds of the subjects and the average number of years of education they completed (Figure 11.1). Although a precise update of Bowles and Gintis's data is not available, other data on the correlations among family income category, demonstrated academic potential, and educational attainment show that the same relationship identified by the theorists is relevant decades later. For example, Figure 11.2 shows bachelor's degree completion rates by both family income (socioeconomic status) and math achievement early in high school. Note that among the highest scoring students (fourth quartile), 74% of high-income students had graduated from college a decade later, whereas just 41% of low-income students had completed a degree. The graduation gap is consistent across score categories: In every category, students in the middle and top income categories were more likely to graduate than their lower-income counterparts.

Critics of conflict theories of education point out that education, even in highly stratified societies, offers

■ **FIGURE 11.1** Relationship Between U.S. Family Income and Years of Schooling for White Males Ages 35–44, 1962

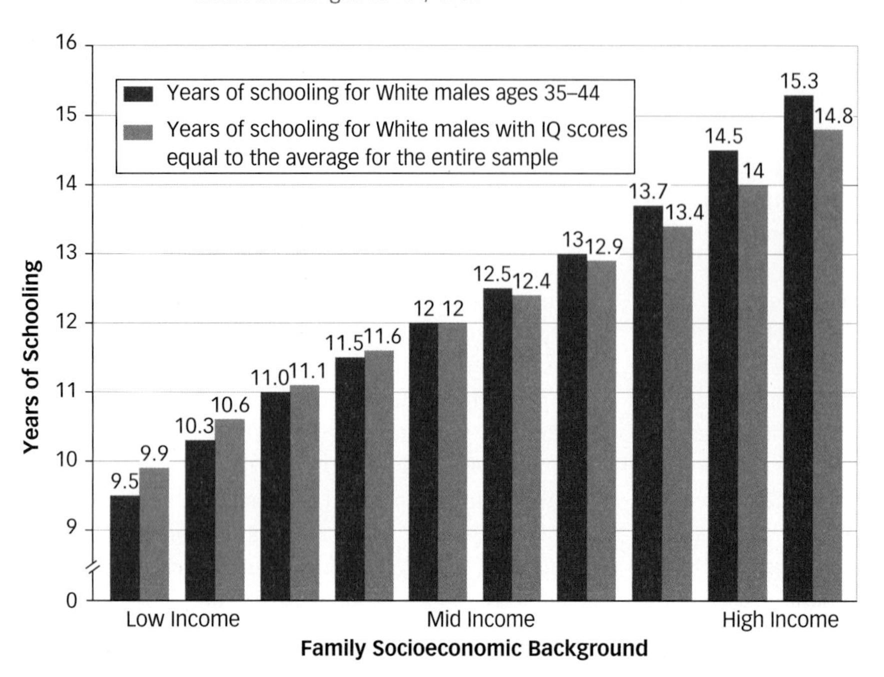

SOURCE: Bowles, Samuel, and Herbert Gintis. *Schooling in Capitalist America: Educational Reform and the Contradictions of Economic Life.* Copyright © 1976 Bowles, Samuel; Gintis, Herbert M. Reprinted by permission of Basic Books, a member of the Perseus Books Group.

an important way for poor and working-class people to improve their circumstances, and it remains the primary means of upward mobility. Education has been a crucial path by which generations of U.S. immigrants have escaped poverty. Thus, although it may contribute to the reproduction of an unequal socioeconomic structure, the educational system also provides meaningful opportunities for mobility and change.

THE SYMBOLIC INTERACTIONIST PERSPECTIVE

Symbolic interactionists study what occurs in the classroom, alerting us to subtle and not-so-subtle ways in which schools affect students' interactions and self-images. By looking at how students are labeled, for instance, symbolic interactionists shed light on the way schools help to reinforce and perpetuate differences among students.

In a classic study, Rosenthal and Jacobson (1968) conducted an intriguing experiment in which elementary school teachers were intentionally misinformed about the intelligence test scores of selected students. The teachers were told, in confidence, that certain students had scored unusually high on standardized tests the previous year. In fact, these students had been randomly selected and were no different in known intelligence from their peers. Rosenthal and Jacobson then observed the interactions between these students and their teachers and monitored the students' academic performance. The students labeled "exceptional" soon outperformed their peers, a difference that persisted for several years.

The teachers described the labeled students as "more curious" or "more interested" and communicated their heightened expectations of these learners through their voices, facial expressions, and use of praise. Enacting a *self-fulfilling prophecy,* the students came to see themselves through their teachers' eyes and began performing as if they were, in fact, more intelligent than their peers, earning still more positive attention from teachers. Younger students, whose self-images were more flexible, exhibited the greatest improvements in performance. Rosenthal and Jacobson concluded that the teachers behaved differently toward some students because the students had been labeled "exceptional."

The findings of other studies suggest similar conclusions. A study of student–teacher interaction in a largely African American kindergarten found that such labels as "fast" and "slow," which the teacher assigned by the eighth day of class, tended to stay with the labeled students throughout the year (Rist, 1970). More recent research has confirmed the harmful effects of teachers' stereotyped beliefs about minority students' competence on those students' performance (Garcia & Guerra, 2004). Another study found that female and Asian American students frequently received classroom grades higher than their actual test scores, while Latino, Black, and White males received lower grades (Farkas, Grobe, Sheehan, & Shuan, 1990; Farkas, Sheehan, & Grobe, 1990). The differences had to do with the teachers' perceptions of their students' "attitudes." Those who appeared to be attentive and cooperative were judged to be hard workers and good students, and were graded up; those who appeared to be indifferent or hostile were graded down (Rosenbloom & Way, 2004). A recent analysis of data from the Education Longitudinal

FIGURE 11.2 Percentage of Spring 2002 High School Sophomores Who Earned a Bachelor's Degree or Higher by 2012, by Socioeconomic Status and Mathematics Achievement Quartile in 2002

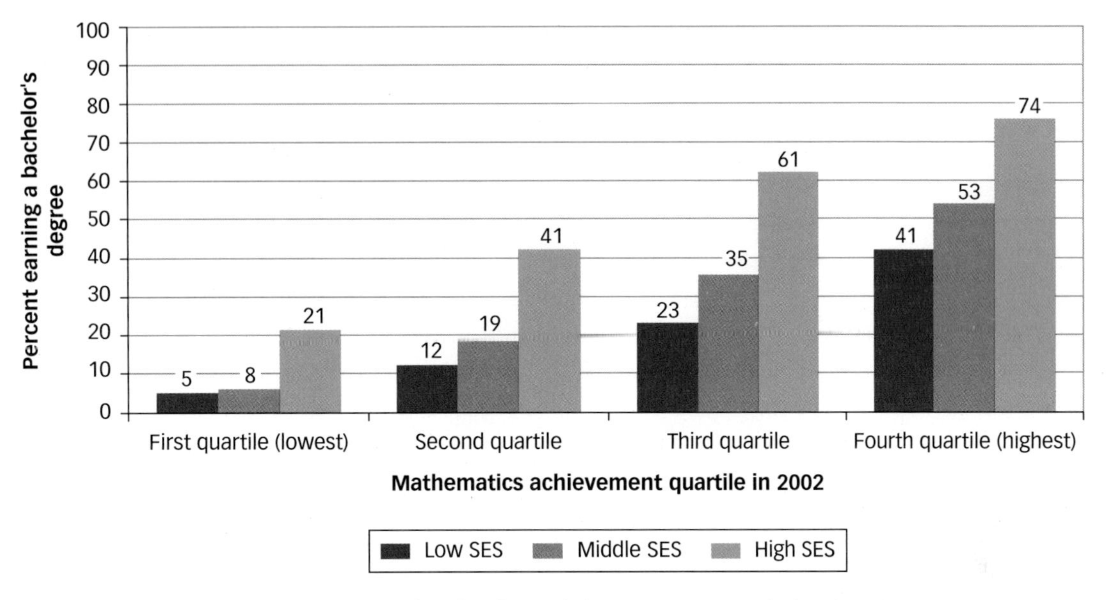

SOURCE: "The Condition of Education," National Center for Education Statistics, U.S. Department of Education, 2012.

Study, which followed 10th graders for a decade beginning in 2002 and ending in 2012, found that,

> even after accounting for other factors, teachers' expectations and students' college-going outcomes had a significant relationship, and teacher expectations were tremendously predictive of student college completion rates. In fact, after controlling for student demographics, teacher expectations were more predictive of college success than many major factors, including student motivation and student effort. These findings build on other research that suggests teacher expectations are powerful predictors of future success. (Boser, Wilhelm, & Hanna, 2014, "Teacher expectations are more predictive than other factors," para. 2)

Classroom labeling has been studied in other countries as well. In one influential study, Paul Willis (1990) found that British boys from working-class families were systematically labeled as low academic achievers and socialized to think of themselves as capable of doing only working-class jobs. The boys understood quite well that this labeling process worked against them, and they resisted it by the use of humor and other challenges to authority. These behaviors reinforced their teachers' perception that the boys would never make it and would eventually drop out of school and assume their "rightful position" in the working class. The boys thus accepted their teachers' labeling, creating a self-fulfilling prophecy in which they wound up in working-class jobs.

Symbolic interactionism is well suited to studying the ways in which teachers consciously or unintentionally affect their students, but a critic might note that because it focuses on social interaction, it cannot give us a picture of the role of the educational system in society as a whole or help us recognize and analyze structural problems such as unequal funding of schools across poor, middle-class, and wealthy areas.

EDUCATION, OPPORTUNITY, AND INEQUALITY

Functionalists argue that education is a vehicle for mobility and for filling the positions necessary for society to survive and thrive. Conflict theorists posit that the educational system reinforces existing inequalities by unequally according opportunities based on class, race, or gender. In fact, the U.S. educational system may operate to open avenues to mobility for all students—*and* to create obstacles to achievement among the less privileged. That is, it may both reduce and

INEQUALITY MATTERS

American Indian Schools

The 183 schools sited on American Indian reservations across 23 states are among the most decrepit and worst performing in the United States. Consider a description of one school offered in a journalistic investigation:

> Tucked into the desert hills on a Navajo reservation 150 miles east of the Grand Canyon, Crystal [Boarding School] has cracks running several feet down the walls, leaky pipes in the floors and asbestos in the basement. Students come from extremely troubled backgrounds, but there is no full-time counselor. Last year, a new reading coach took one look at the rundown cinder block housing and left the next day. Science and social studies have been cut to put more attention on the abysmal reading and math scores, but even so, in 2013 only 5 percent of students were considered to have grade-level math skills. (Severns, 2015, para. 4)

Few schools have after-school programs for children to support academic learning or to provide opportunities to do sports or art. In 2014, only 67% of American Indian students graduated from high school compared to the national average of 80%. Graduation rates among Native youth who attend schools run by the Bureau of Indian Education (BIE) are even worse: just 53% (Camera, 2015).

A 1928 report described the education provided to Native Americans, which had attempted to forcibly assimilate schoolchildren by, among others, changing their Native names and banning them from speaking their Native languages, as "grossly inadequate." Nearly a century later, forcible assimilation has ended, but the public education offered to American Indian children has scarcely improved. In 2015, President Barack Obama's Secretary of Education, Arne Duncan, described the American Indian school system as the poorest in the country: "It's just the epitome of broken. . . just utterly bankrupt" (Severns, 2015, para. 2). Many residents of American Indian reservations have been fighting to make their schools good places of learning, but bureaucratic and financial obstacles have made significant change difficult:

> While one office (which would later be called the Bureau of Indian Education) handled educational matters, other offices within the larger Bureau of Indian Affairs had say over school construction and maintenance, personnel and technology, all of which are major parts of school operations. The tribes also have some power and, particularly in the Southwest, so do school boards, which further diffuses the authority—and the accountability over the

Visions of America/Universal Images Group/Getty Images

schools' failures—across the country. (Severns, 2015, section 2, para 8)

Many of these schools exist in impoverished communities with almost no tax base to support even basic improvements (Mongeau, 2016).

In 2015, Duncan announced an award of more than $5.3 million in grants under the new Native Youth Community Projects program to help Native American youth become college- and career-ready (U.S. Department of Education, 2015). Since his first trip to Indian Country in 2009, Duncan has engaged with tribal officials on a range of educational issues. This initiative is an important step, but the condition of American Indian reservation schools is dire, and solving the dual problems of low opportunities and low achievement will require a significant investment of both money and attention:

"We have the worst of the worst statistics," said Aaron Payment, chairperson of the Sault Ste. Marie Tribe of Chippewa Indians in Michigan, speaking not only about graduation rates, but also rates of suicide, domestic violence and drug use. "The first Americans have become the last Americans," he said. (Camera, 2015)

THINK IT THROUGH

- The U.S. government created American Indian reservations and has overseen the schools on reservations for most or all of their existence. Does the federal government have a responsibility to ensure an adequate and equal education for American Indian children? Does it have a responsibility to ensure an adequate and equal education for all public school children?

reproduce inequality. In the following sections, we look at issues of education and inequality, focusing on questions about childhood and adult literacy, school segregation by race and income, and the college dropout phenomenon. We conclude the section with a look at the relationship between education and income in the United States.

WORD POVERTY AND ADULT ILLITERACY

Researcher Louisa Cook Moats uses the term *word poverty* to characterize the impoverished language environments in which some children grow up. Word poverty is a particular problem in economically disadvantaged homes: Research on a community in California found that by age 5, children in impoverished language environments had heard 32 million fewer words spoken to them than the average middle-class child. Perhaps not surprisingly, the fewer words that were spoken to children, the fewer they could actively use themselves: In a study of how many words children could produce at age 3, "children from impoverished environments used less than half the number of words already spoken by their more advantaged peers" (Wolf, 2008, pp. 102–103).

Word poverty is also linked to a deficit of books in the homes of many children. Research conducted in three Los Angeles communities found that in the most economically impoverished community in the study, it was common to find no children's books in the home. In low- to middle-income homes, an average of three books could be found. By contrast, in the most affluent families, there was an average of 200 books in each home (Wolf, 2008). According to a global study, the deficit or wealth of books in a home is of significance in children's later schooling: Being raised in a home without books is as likely to affect children's educational attainment as having parents with very low educational attainment. The researchers conclude that "growing up in a home with 500 books would propel a child 3.2 years further in education, on average" (Evans, Kelley, Sikora, & Treiman, 2010, p. 179). In the United States, the advantage to having an expansive library is an average of more than 2 years of education. Commenting on the study, an article on the website ScienceDaily noted, "The researchers were struck by the strong effect having books in the home had on children's educational attainment even above and beyond such factors as education level of the parents, the country's GDP [gross domestic product], the father's occupation or the political system of the country" (University of Nevada, Reno, 2010, para. 10).

Why is word poverty significant? The answer is that it is linked to low literacy. A fundamental necessity for any country in the modern world is a population that is functionally literate. No less important, literacy is necessary for individual success in education and the job market. The Program for the International Assessment of Adult Competencies (PIAAC) defines literacy as "understanding, evaluating, using and engaging with written text to participate in society, to achieve one's goals and to develop one's knowledge and potential" (Rampey et al., 2016, p. 2). PIAAC identifies six categories of literacy using a numerical scale (Figure 11.3). The PIAAC study, which was based on a sample of 8,670 people (even though the number in the cited figure is slightly smaller, as it excludes those over the age of 65) found that,

- About 17% of adults were at *level 1* (13%) or below *level 1* (4%) on the literacy test. At level 1, respondents performed simple tasks like locating information in a text. At this level, "Knowledge and skill in recognizing basic vocabulary, determining the meaning of sentences, and reading paragraphs of text is expected."
- Another 33% of respondents reached *level 2* on the test. "Tasks at this level require respondents to make matches between the text and information, and may require paraphrasing or low-level inferences."
- About 36% of respondents were at *level 3*. At this level, readers were expected to read "dense or lengthy" texts and to interpret, evaluate, and infer information. "Competing information is often present, but it is not more prominent than the correct information."
- Finally, about 13% of respondents were at *levels 4 and 5*. At these levels, readers were examining taking account of subtle rhetorical clues, evaluating evidence-based arguments, applying abstract ideas. (Rampey et al., 2016, p. B-3)

School segregation: The education of racial minorities in schools that are geographically, economically, and/or socially separated from those attended by Whites.

FIGURE 11.3 Literacy Level of U.S. Adults 16–65 (2012/2014)

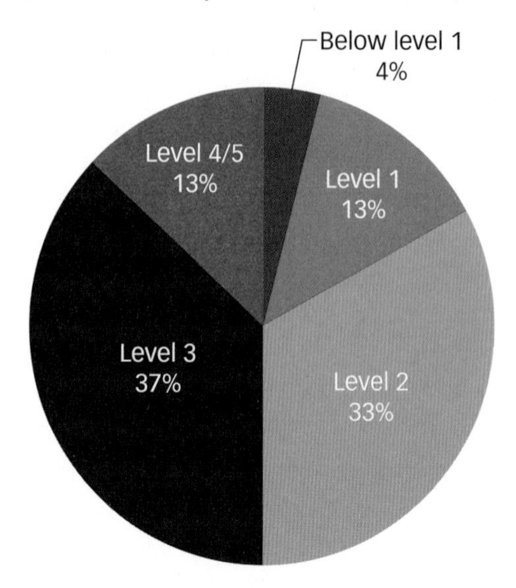

SOURCE: U.S. Department of Education, National Center for Education Statistics, Program for the International Assessment of Adult Competencies (PIAAC), U.S. PIAAC 2012/2014; Organization for Economic Cooperation and Development, PIAAC 2012.

Wolf (2008) suggests that a strong foundation in literacy is a key to later educational success. Students who enter high school with shaky foundations in literacy have a higher probability of school failure than do their peers who grew up in homes with books and parents who read to them at an early age. At the same time, failure to complete high school is likely to affect someone's ability to complete literacy activities successfully. If you were to research the correlation between literacy and high school completion, how would you proceed? What variables would you choose to study and why? What kind of relationship would you hypothesize?

SCHOOL SEGREGATION

School segregation, *the education of racial minorities in schools that are geographically, economically, and/or socially separated from those attended by the racial majority (Whites),* is a long-standing pattern that is worsening today, despite more than four decades of civil rights legislation intended to alleviate it and reduce its devastating effects. School segregation has long been linked to educational inequality in the United States.

Before slavery was abolished in the United States, it was a crime to teach slaves to read and write; formal education was reserved solely for Whites. Following the abolition of slavery and the end of the Civil War, Black students could be educated, but Jim Crow laws soon initiated a century of discrimination against Black Americans in the South. These laws determined, among other things, where Black Americans could live, where they could eat and shop, and where they would be educated. In the North, there were no laws segregating schools by race, but segregated schooling occurred nonetheless as a consequence of racial residential segregation.

Laws, customs, and discrimination created schools segregated by race in the United States until the 1950s (Jordan, 1992). Black activists challenged the constitutionality of segregation, but U.S. courts repeatedly found it did not violate the U.S. Constitution. For example, in its 1896 *Plessy v. Ferguson* decision, the U.S. Supreme Court upheld the states' rights to segregate public accommodations as long as they followed the principle of "separate but equal." In 1954, however, the Supreme Court reversed itself. Relying in part on social science research showing that segregated schools were not in fact equal, the Court ruled in *Brown v. Board of Education of Topeka* that laws segregating public schools were unconstitutional (Miller, 1995).

This decision met with considerable resistance, especially in the South, where schools were segregated by law. Governor George Wallace of Alabama personally blocked the entrance to the University of Alabama in an effort to stop Black students from enrolling, and a Black college student named James Meredith went to prison for trying to enroll and attend classes at the University of Mississippi. Black and White students who tried to integrate schools were beaten by police and fellow citizens (Branch, 1988; Chong, 1991; McCartney, 1992).

Court challenges, civil protests, and mass civil disobedience ultimately broke down barriers, and some racial integration of schools took place across the country. Although the Supreme Court decision in *Brown v. Board of Education* had prohibited purposeful discrimination on the basis of race, it did not provide for specific methods to achieve school integration. The fact that racial and ethnic groups were residentially segregated meant that, in fact, most Blacks would continue to attend schools that were predominantly Black, while Whites would continue to attend mostly White schools.

Subsequent court decisions provided one method of achieving integration: *school busing,* a court-ordered program of transporting public school students to schools outside their neighborhoods. Mandated busing proved highly controversial, provoking criticism among some academics and hostility among many parents and policy makers. Controversy erupted in 1974 when Black students were bused into poor Irish neighborhoods in South Boston, whose schools were among the worst in the state. Instead of providing equal educational opportunity, busing worsened racial conflict in some of Boston's most economically disadvantaged neighborhoods. Violence resulted, and over the next 10 years public school enrollment in the city plummeted (Frum, 2000).

Today, despite decades of civil rights activism and laws aimed at promoting integration, racial segregation persists in U.S. schools, and in some places it has even worsened. A recent article on Louisville, Kentucky, schools, which have gained attention for their desegregation efforts, points out that,

> nationwide, in 1954, zero percent of black students attended majority-white schools. By 1972, that number was 36.4 percent. . . . School integration reached its peak in 1988, when 43.5 percent of black students attended majority-white schools, but that number has declined since then, and in 2011, stood at just 23.2 percent. (Semuels, 2015, para. 64)

How is this possible? First, the movement over time of middle- and upper-class Whites into largely White school districts in suburban or outlying areas has left mostly poor minorities in U.S. inner-city schools, many of which are highly segregated (Coleman, Hoffer, & Kilgore, 1982; Kozol, 2005; Orfield & Eaton, 1996). Because they are often located in low-income neighborhoods, highly segregated schools also tend to be the most poorly funded (Figure 11.4). There are variations in state formulas for funding schools, but the source on which most U.S. school districts still depend most heavily is local property tax revenue. Although this system ensures that those who live in areas with high property values will generally accrue adequate—or even excellent—funds for the academic programs and physical maintenance of their schools, it also puts those who live in lower-income rural and urban areas at a distinct disadvantage, since even high property tax rates cannot bring in the level of resources that schools in middle- to upper-class areas enjoy (Ball, Bowe, & Gewirtz, 1995; Kozol, 2005).

Second, U.S. Supreme Court decisions such as *Board of Education of Oklahoma City v. Dowell, Freeman v. Pitts,* and *Missouri v. Jenkins* have limited the scope of previous laws aimed at promoting racial integration of schools. The Court has ruled that segregated schools resulting from "residential preferences" are a result of people making choices about where to reside and are therefore beyond the scope of the law. The Court declared in these cases that school districts that previously had made an effort to integrate schools could send students back to neighborhood schools even if those schools were segregated and inferior (Orfield & Eaton, 1996).

FIGURE 11.4 Racial Composition of U.S. Public Schools in Selected Cities, 2012

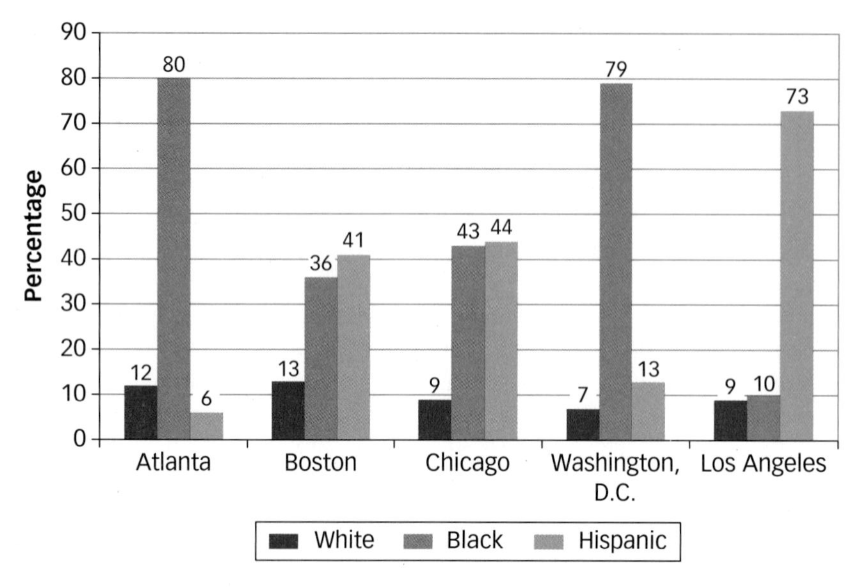

SOURCE: Data from Federal Education Budget Project, "Comparative Analysis of Funding, Student Demographics and Achievement Data," New America Foundation, 2012.

Latino and Black students are more likely to be in segregated schools today than in earlier decades (Figure 11.5). In Chicago in 2012, for instance, 44% of students enrolled in public school were Hispanic, 43% were Black, and just 9% were White. In Washington, D.C., public school enrollment is 79% African American and 13% Hispanic. In Los Angeles, fully three quarters of students are Hispanic and about 9% are White, while 10% are Black (New America Foundation, 2012). Many schools that operate under **de facto segregation** face daunting problems, including

> low levels of competition and expectation, less qualified teachers who leave as soon as they get seniority, more limited curricula, peer pressure against academic achievement and supportive of crime and substance abuse, high levels of teen pregnancy, few connections with colleges and employers who can assist students, less serious academic counseling and preparation for college, and powerless parents who themselves failed in school and do not know how to evaluate or change schools. (Orfield & Eaton, 1996, p. 54)

De facto segregation: School segregation based largely on residential patterns, which persists even though legal segregation is now outlawed in the United States.

By contrast, most Asian American students are integrated into schools with Whites. Asian American communities such as "Chinatowns" and "Little Saigons," which are populated with recent immigrants from China, Vietnam, Korea, and other Asian countries, are an exception, even though integration becomes more common in later generations (Chen, 1992; Loo, 1991; Zhou, 2009).

American Indians on reservations are the most segregated of all minorities (see the *Inequality Matters* box in this chapter). The various tribes are recognized by treaty as separate nations whose rights are governed by agreements between them and the U.S. government. Their schools are run by the Bureau of Indian Affairs, which employs teachers and sets the curriculum. Treaties between the U.S. government and Indian nations have sought to ensure education that recognizes the value of American Indian culture and tradition. Yet the teachers employed by the Bureau of Indian Affairs are ordinarily expected to cover the standard subjects of U.S. school curricula, and in English. Problems within the tribal communities have resulted, since Native Americans often see such instruction as failing to respect their linguistic and cultural differences.

DROPPING IN, DROPPING OUT: WHY ARE COLLEGE DROPOUT RATES SO HIGH?

Most high school graduates in the United States today go to college. According to data from the National Center for Education Statistics (2016a), in 2014, 68% of high school completers enrolled in college. This figure has grown over time: In 1960, it was just 45% and in 1990, 60%. Students of all racial and ethnic backgrounds are enrolling at high rates: Fully 85% of Asian American students, 68% of White students, 63% of Black students, and 62% of Hispanic students enrolled in college immediately after completing high school (National Center for Education Statistics, 2016a). Data suggest that education is more critical than ever for raising earning potential and strengthening competitiveness in the job market. In light of this, it is not surprising that most students are seeking to continue their education beyond high school.

FIGURE 11.5 Average Debt for College Graduates

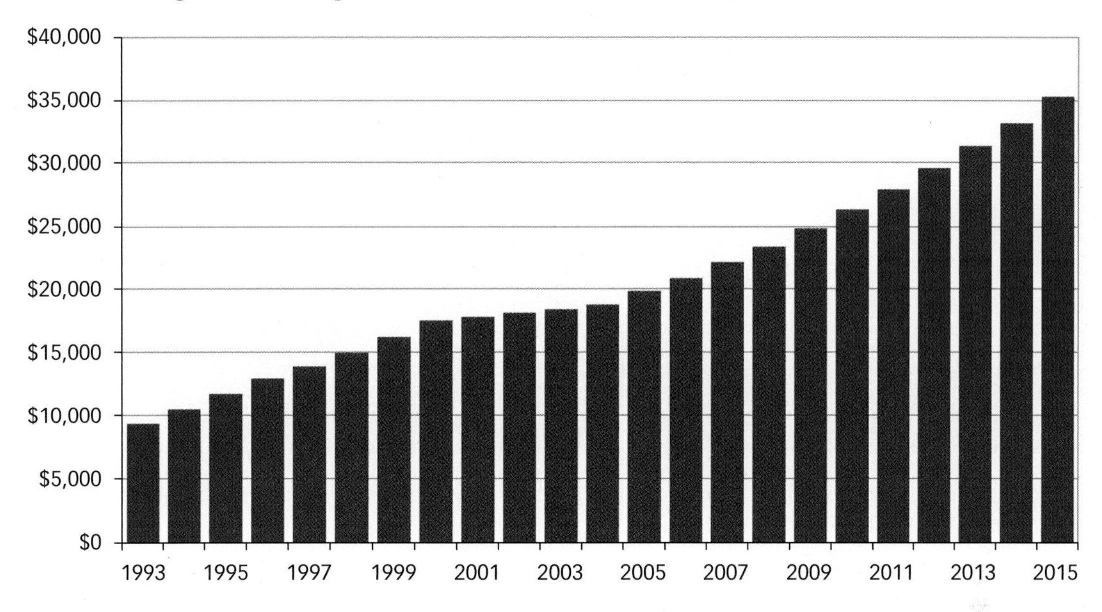

SOURCE: "Congratulations, Class of 2015. You're the Most Indebted Ever (For Now)," by Jeffrey Sparshot, *The Wall Street Journal,* May 8, 2015.

Some observers, however, point out that all is not well in U.S. higher education. In fact, they suggest, the high rate of enrollment obscures a troubling reality: Many students leave college with debt—and no degree. Journalist David Leonhardt (2009, para. 3) writes that "in terms of its core mission—turning teenagers into educated college graduates—much of the system is simply failing." Leonhardt argues that while the United States does an excellent job getting high school graduates to enroll in higher education, colleges have been far less successful in fostering timely graduation of students—or graduating them at all. Statistics suggest that many who enroll in college never finish with degrees, even though many end their college careers with substantial debt.

College attainment levels have remained flat for generations (Lewin, 2011a). About 59% of students enrolled in four-year institutions go on to graduate, but there are some significant differences in six-year completion rates by race and ethnicity. For example, for the class enrolled in a four-year college in the year 2006, there were notable differences in graduation rates four, five, and six years after enrollment (see Figure 11.6). There were also notable differences by institution: For example, although the six-year completion rate at the country's most selective schools (those that accept 25% or fewer applicants) is about 89%, this falls to about 62% for somewhat selective schools (those accepting 50% to 74% of applicants), and drops to 36% for open-admission schools (National Center for Education Statistics, 2016b). Dropouts are costly, both to the nation as a whole, which loses potentially educated and productive workers, and to individuals, whose earning potential is diminished by their failure to obtain degrees and whose financial security may be compromised when they leave college with debt but no degree.

Public domain- Library of Congress

Gender-segregated classrooms are uncommon in public schools today. Racially segregated classrooms, however, continue to be common.

Spencer Grant/Photo Researchers, Inc.

AP Photo/Paul Sancya

Across the country, unequal funding of public schools and the resulting inequalities in resources are problems that perpetuate disparities in education and upward mobility.

So what is behind the college dropout phenomenon? Several factors contribute. First, high college costs drive many students out of higher education. The cost of a four-year private college has outpaced inflation, as well as wage growth, and student borrowing has risen (Figure 11.6). Costs are a particularly acute issue for lower income students, who are more likely than their better-off peers to drop out before completing a degree. The financial burden of a college education falls more heavily on those with fewer resources, even when support, like federal Pell Grants, defray some tuition costs.

FIGURE 11.6 Six-Year College Completion by Race/Ethnicity for First-Time Students Starting in 2007 (four-year schools)

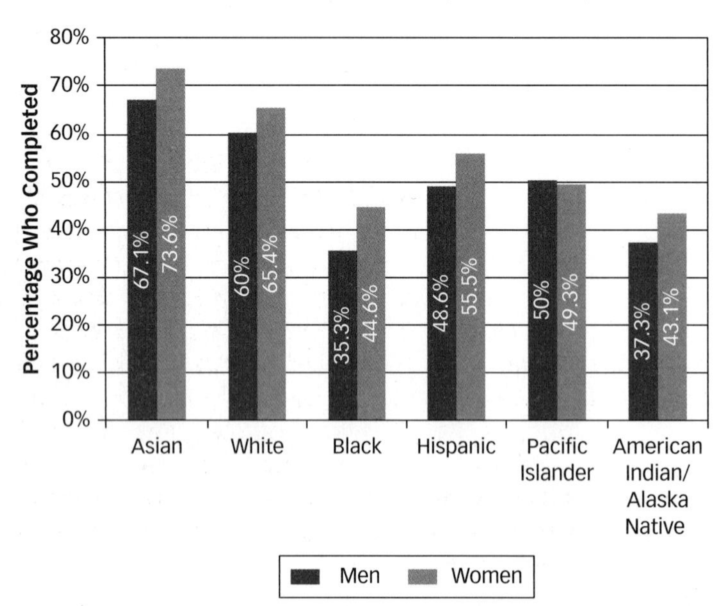

SOURCE: Digest of Education Statistics, National Center for Education Statistics, U.S. Department of Education.

Second, the rigors of college work lead some students to drop out. This factor is complex. With an increasing proportion of high school graduates enrolling in college, there may be more new students who are unready for the workload or the level of work. Half of students in associate degree programs and about a fifth of those in bachelor's programs are required by their institutions to enroll in remedial classes to address academic shortcomings. Some of these courses do not confer college credit, raising the cost of an education, lengthening the time needed to earn a degree, and increasing the likelihood that a student will leave without completing college. Advocates for students suggest that colleges can do more to help students stay and succeed with coaching, scheduling that meets the needs of working students, and accelerated programs that speed the time to degree with rigorous work offered in concentrated time periods (Lewin, 2011a). At the same time, budget cuts, particularly at state institutions, have reduced rather than expanded opportunities to provide targeted services to struggling students.

Third, part-time attendance raises the probability of noncompletion. Many students find

FIGURE 11.7 Earnings and Unemployment Rates by Educational Attainment in the United States, 2016

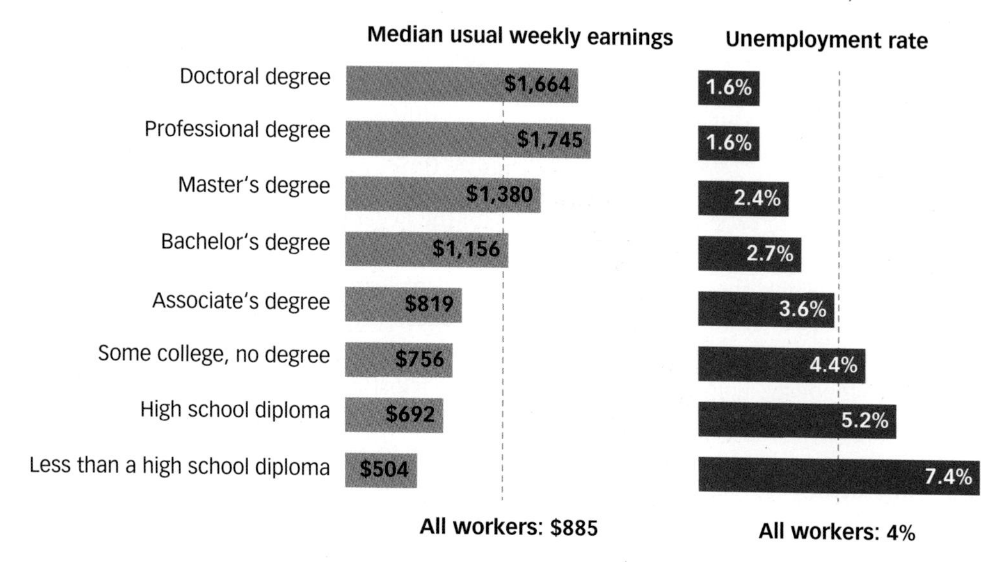

SOURCE: Bureau of Labor Statistics.

NOTE: Data are for persons age 25 and over. Earnings are for full-time wage and salary workers.

it challenging to balance the rigors of school and work. According to Complete College America (2011), the majority of community college students work more than 20 hours per week, and a substantial proportion also take care of families. The costs, as noted above, may also compel some students to choose part-time study. Alas, while attending college part-time seems like a viable solution, it substantially lowers the chance that a student will ever earn a degree: According to one study, just 13% of part-time students seeking a bachelor's degree had earned one in an 8-year time span. Only about a quarter of students today fit the stereotypical model of full-time, on-campus students, suggesting that the scope of the problem is bigger than it appears (Complete College America, 2011).

According to the Organisation for Economic Co-operation and Development (OECD, 2014), the United States ranks 19th in college degree attainment among 28 wealthy democratic countries. At one time, it was near the top of the list. Although everyone may not desire or even need a college degree, the competitive global economic environment has put a premium value on higher education, which offers greater security from unemployment and greater earning potential than a high school credential alone. Understanding why students drop out is the first step to addressing this problem effectively.

EDUCATION, EMPLOYMENT, AND EARNINGS

There is a strong relationship between educational attainment and the labor force participation rate, which shows the proportion of those of working age (usually 16–64) who are either employed or unemployed and actively seeking work. It does not include those who are institutionalized (in prison, for instance) or those who are serving in the armed forces; other groups who are not "participating" in the labor force include many full-time students and homemakers. In April 2017, labor force participation rates of adults varied significantly by education: The labor force participation rate for those with less than a high school education was 46%; for those with a high school education, it climbed to 58%; and for those with some college or an associate's degree, it was 66%. For adults with a bachelor's degree or higher degree, it rose to 74% (U.S. Bureau of Labor Statistics, 2017d).

In Figure 11.7, we also see a strong correlation between educational attainment and income, and between educational attainment and vulnerability to unemployment. We have seen in other chapters that educational attainment has grown in importance in the postindustrial era, as the living wage jobs of the industrial era in sectors such as automobile manufacturing, steel, and textiles have fallen victim to outsourcing and automation. What remains as the foundation of the U.S. economy are advanced professional occupations, which require higher education and often even graduate degrees, and service jobs, which are often part-time, low-pay, and low-benefit positions in sectors such as child and elder care, retail, and hospitality. Although some manufacturing has continued to be sited in the United States, new manufacturing jobs are far less likely to be unionized, more likely to involve short-term contracts, and characterized by a lower pay scale than similar jobs in the past. Several new manufacturing jobs demand proficiency with high-technology equipment, which may require either college education or other advanced training beyond high school.

In the wake of the Great Recession, which ended in 2009, many students still struggle to find postgraduation employment, but their prospects have improved with stronger job growth. Some experts caution, however, that the poorer employment prospects of graduates in the years 2009 to 2014 created a "backlog" of college completers seeking employment, which may raise competition for the entry-level jobs to which many new graduates aspire. The wages of young graduates (21–24) have recovered somewhat in the post-recession period, even though they continue to be volatile (Figure 11.8). Significantly, some entry-level jobs have evolved into unpaid internships, rendering the first step on the career ladder more tenuous for new graduates.

Although more recent graduates appear to be finding jobs in a stronger labor market (see Figure 11.9), many are also burdened by student loan debt. According to the Federal Reserve Bank of New York, between 2004 and 2014, there was a 92% increase in the number of student loan borrowers and a 74% rise in average loan balances (Davis, Kimball, & Gould, 2015). Notably, borrowing differs by race and ethnicity: An estimated 80% of Black students take on debt, compared to about 63% of White students. Among Hispanic students, the rate is similar to that of Whites attending public universities, even though they borrow more heavily when attending private schools (Huelsman, 2015). One key reason why this difference is significant is the fact that Black and Hispanic college graduates have higher rates of unemployment than their White peers: In the period between the spring of 2015 and the spring of 2016, the average rate of unemployment for young (21–24) Black college graduates was 9.4%; for Hispanic graduates it was 6.5%; and for White graduates it was 4.7% (Kroeger, Cooke, & Gould, 2016).

FIGURE 11.8 Real Average Hourly Wages of Young Workers, by Education, 1990–2017*

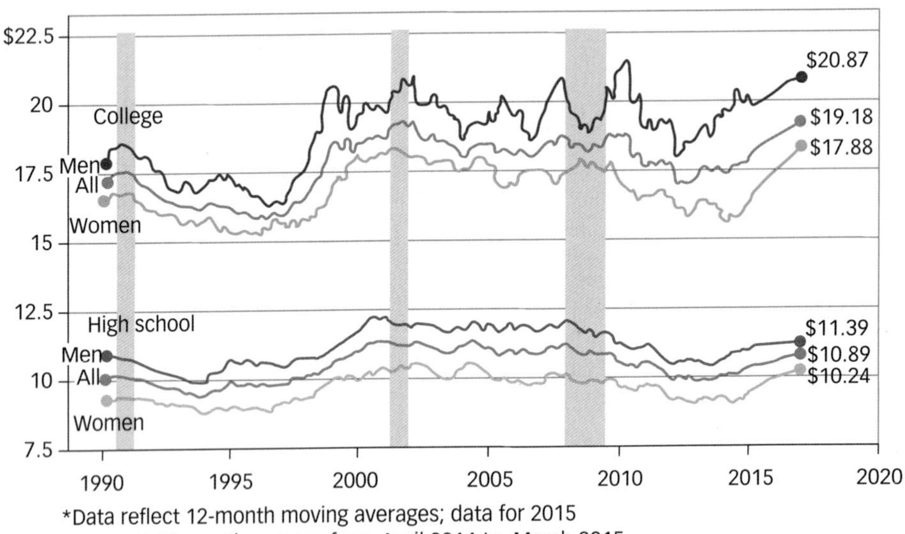

SOURCE: "The Class of 2017" by Teresa Kroeger, Elise Gould, May 4, 2017. Table 2. Washington, DC: Economic Policy Institute. Reprinted with permission.

NOTE: Data are for high school graduates age 17–20 and college graduates age 21–24 who are not enrolled in further schooling. Wages are in 2016 dollars.

FIGURE 11.9 Rates of Unemployment for Persons 16+, 2006–2016

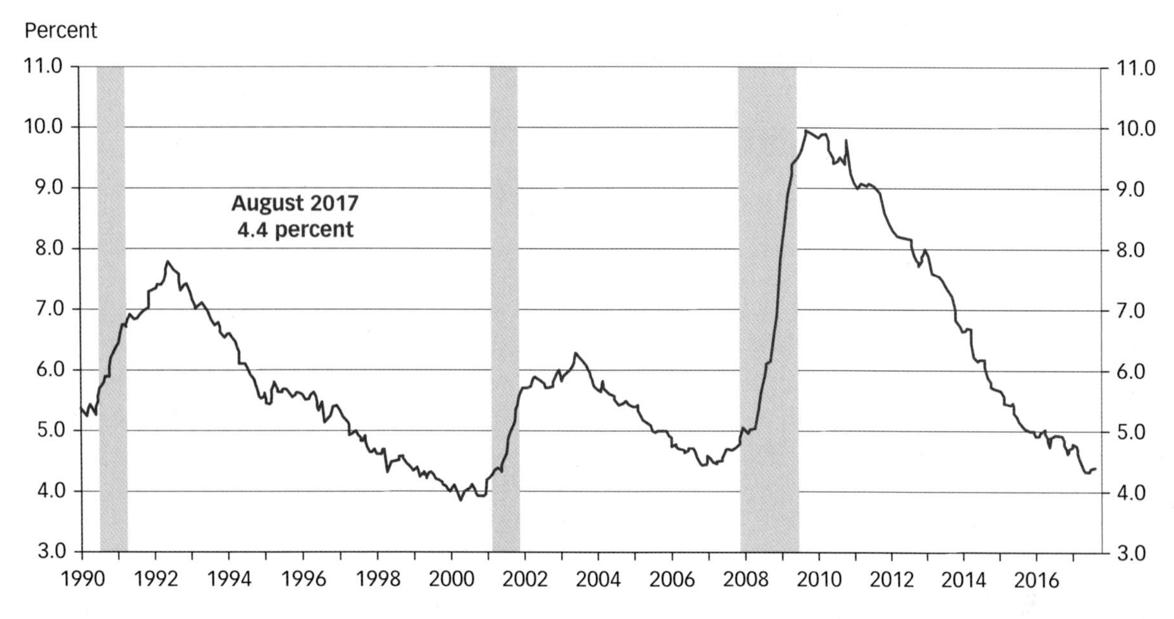

SOURCE: U.S. Bureau of Labor Statistics. (2016). LNS14000000, Retrieved from http://data.bls.gov/timeseries/LNS14000000.

At the same time, the assertion that higher education opens doors to employment and higher lifetime earnings remains essentially correct. According to the Center on Education and the Workforce at Georgetown University,

> By 2018, the economy will create 46.8 million openings—13.8 million brand-new jobs and 33 million "replacement jobs," positions vacated by workers who have retired or permanently left their occupations. Nearly two-thirds of these 46.8 million jobs—some 63 percent—will require workers with at least some college education. About 33 percent will require a Bachelor's degree or better, while 30 percent will require some college or a two-year Associate's degree. Only 36 percent will require workers with just a high school diploma or less. (Carnevale, Smith, & Strohl, 2010)

Although slow wage growth and the rise of student debt are critical concerns for students, their families, and the economy as a whole, educational attainment will continue to grow in importance as a pathway to professional careers and higher earning potential. Below we turn to a discussion of the economy, focusing in particular on historical and contemporary shifts in the economy and labor market, and asking what recent trends mean for workers in the years to come.

THE ECONOMY IN HISTORICAL PERSPECTIVE

The **economy** is *the social institution that organizes the ways in which a society produces, distributes, and consumes goods and services.* By **goods** we mean *objects that have an economic value to others,* whether they are the basic necessities for survival (a safe place to live, nutritious food to eat, weather-appropriate clothing) or things that people simply want (designer clothing, an Apple iPhone, popcorn at the movies). **Services** are *economically productive activities that do not result directly in physical products*; they can be relatively simple (shining shoes, working a cash register, waiting tables at a restaurant) or

Economy: The social institution that organizes the ways in which a society produces, distributes, and consumes goods and services.

Goods: Objects that have an economic value to others, whether they are the basic necessities for survival or things that people simply want.

Services: Economically productive activities that do not result directly in physical products; may be relatively simple or quite complex.

DISCOVER & DEBATE

Education and the Economy

Motion: Politicians and the public should support a $15 federal minimum wage.

Background

The minimum wage is the lowest wage that can legally be paid to workers, even though some exceptions exist, such as tipped workers and young or disabled workers. In the United States, the minimum wage was first set in 1938 by a federal law, the Fair Labor Standards Act. The first minimum wage was $0.25 cents per hour. It has been raised 22 times since 1938, most recently in 2009 when it was raised to $7.25. Some states have their own minimum wage laws: As of January 2017, 29 states and the District of Columbia had minimum wage floors higher than the federal minimum wage. There is a vigorous debate about the minimum wage and who may benefit or lose from a higher minimum wage.

Affirmative Arguments

- A higher minimum wage increases earnings, reducing workers' poverty and lowering their reliance on government benefits like food stamps.
- A higher minimum wage increases demand for goods, as poorer households spend a larger proportion of their income than do richer households. Greater demand can act as an economic stimulus, increasing hiring and profits.
- A higher minimum wage reduces employee turnover, which is costly to businesses.

Opposition Arguments

- A higher minimum wage increases prices, as employers pass on higher labor costs to consumers.
- A higher minimum wage reduces employment, as employers hire fewer workers or offer fewer hours to current workers.
- A higher minimum wage reduces business profits.

Questions for Consideration

- What are the characteristics of minimum wage workers in the United States today? What are the characteristics of industries paying the minimum wage in the United States today? How does this information help us to evaluate the necessity of a higher minimum wage?
- What do the experiences of states and cities with lower or higher minimum wages suggest about the strength of the affirmative and opposition arguments?
- Will increasing automation in industries like fast food and retail affect the minimum wage? Will the minimum wage affect the pace of automation in these industries?

Debate Tip

▶ Practice your arguments. Use clue cards for guidance if needed. This will also help with time management during the debate if your debate is timed.

quite complex (repairing an airplane engine or computer, conducting a medical procedure).

In human history, three technological revolutions have brought radically new forms of economic organization. The first led to the growth of agriculture several millennia ago, and the second to modern industry some 250 years ago. We have now reached the third revolution, which has carried us into a postindustrial age. Trends, however, suggest new changes are afoot as we shift into a digital or high technology economy characterized by the rising role of automation, robotics, and artificial intelligence.

Library of Congress

Karl Marx saw industrial workers as "instruments of labor" tethered to an exploitive system. One 19th-century British mother described her 7-year-old to a government commission: "He used to work 16 hours a day.... I have often knelt down to feed him, as he stood by the machine, for he could not leave it or stop" (quoted in Hochschild, 2003, p. 3).

THE AGRICULTURAL REVOLUTION AND AGRICULTURAL SOCIETY

The agricultural revolution vastly increased human productivity over that of earlier hunting, gathering, and pastoral societies. This achievement was spurred by the development of innovations such as irrigation and crop rotation methods, as well as by expanding knowledge about animal husbandry and the use of animals in agriculture. For example, the plow, which came into use about 5,000 years ago, had a transformational effect on agriculture when it was harnessed to a working animal. Greater productivity led to economic surplus. Although the majority of people in agricultural societies still engaged in subsistence farming, an increasing number could produce surplus crops, which they could then barter or sell.

Eventually, specialized economic roles evolved. Some people were farmers; others were landowners who profited from farmers' labor. Several families specialized in the making of handicrafts, working independently on items of their own design. This work gave rise to cottage industries—so called because the work was usually done at home.

The production of agricultural surpluses, as well as handicrafts, created an opportunity for yet another economic role to emerge—that of merchants, who specialized in trading surplus crops and crafted goods. Trading routes developed and permanent cities grew up along them, and the number and complexity of economic activities increased. By about the 15th century, early markets arose to serve as sites for the exchange of goods and services. Prices in markets were set (as they are in free markets today) at the point where *supply* (available goods and services) was balanced by *demand* (the degree to which those goods and services are wanted).

THE INDUSTRIAL REVOLUTION AND INDUSTRIAL SOCIETY

The Industrial Revolution, which began in England with the harnessing of water and steam power to run machines such as looms, increased productivity still further. Cottage industries were replaced by factories, the hallmark of industrial society, and urban areas became centers of economic activity, attracting rural laborers seeking work and creating growing momentum for urbanization. Industrialization spread through Europe and the United States, and then to the rest of the world. The change was massive. In 1810, about 84% of the U.S. workforce worked in agriculture and only 3% in manufacturing; by 1960, just 8% of all U.S. workers labored in agriculture, and fully a quarter of the total workforce was engaged in manufacturing (Blinder, 2006).

Industrial society is characterized by the increased use of machinery and mass production, the centrality of the modern industrial laborer, and the development of a class society rooted in the modern division of labor.

INCREASED USE OF MACHINERY AND MASS PRODUCTION Machines increase the productive capacity of individual laborers by enabling them to produce more goods efficiently at lower cost. New machines have historically required new sources of energy as well: Waterwheels gave way to steam engines, then the internal combustion engine, and eventually electricity and other modern forms of power.

In 1913, automobile mogul Henry Ford introduced a new system of manufacturing in his factories. **Mass production** is *the large-scale, highly standardized manufacturing of identical commodities on a mechanical assembly line.* Under Ford's new system, a continuous conveyor belt moved unfinished automobiles past individual workers, each of whom performed a specific operation on each automobile: One worker would attach the door, another the windshield, another the wheels. (The term *Fordism* is sometimes used to describe this system.) Mass production resulted in the development of large numbers of identical components and products that could be produced efficiently at lower cost. This linked system of production became a foundation for the evolution and expansion of productive industries that went far beyond auto manufacturing.

THE BIRTH OF THE INDUSTRIAL LABORER With the birth of industry came the rise of the industrial labor force, comprising mostly migrants from poorer rural areas or abroad seeking their fortunes in growing cities. Often the number of would-be workers competing for available jobs created a surplus of labor. Karl Marx described this as a **reserve army of labor,** *a pool of job seekers whose numbers outpace the available positions and thus contribute to keeping wages low and conditions of work tenuous* (those who do not like the conditions of work are easy to replace with those seeking work).

If it is possible to create an assembly line on which each worker performs a single, repetitive task, why not design those tasks to be as efficient as possible? This was the goal of **scientific management,** *a practice that sought to use principles of engineering to reduce the physical movements of workers.* Frederick Winslow Taylor's *Principles of Scientific Management,* published in 1911, gave factory managers the information they needed to greatly increase their control over the labor process by giving explicit instructions to workers regarding how they would perform their well-defined tasks. Although Taylor was focused on the goal of efficiency, "Taylorism" also had the consequence of further deskilling work. Deskilling rendered workers more vulnerable to layoffs, since they—like the components they were making—were standardized and therefore easily replaced (Braverman, 1974/1988).

CLASSES IN INDUSTRIAL CAPITALISM New economic classes developed along with the rise of industrial capitalist society. One important new class was composed of industrialists who owned what Marx called the *means of production*—for example, factories. Another was made up of wage laborers—workers who did not own land, property, or tools. They had only their labor power to sell at the factory gate. Work in early industrial capitalism was demanding, highly regimented, and even hazardous. Workers labored at tedious tasks for 14 to 16 hours a day, 6 or 7 days a week, and were at risk of losing their jobs if economic conditions turned unfavorable or if they raised too many objections (recall the concept of the reserve army of labor). The pool of exploitable labor was expanded by migrant workers from rural areas and abroad, and even children of poor families were sometimes forced to labor for wages.

Influenced by the poor conditions they saw in 19th-century English factories, Karl Marx and Friedrich Engels posited that these two classes, which they termed the *bourgeoisie,* or capitalists, and the *proletariat,* or working class, would come into conflict. They argued in the *Manifesto of the Communist Party* (1848/1998) that the bourgeoisie exploited the proletariat by appropriating the surplus value of their labor. That is, capitalists paid workers the minimum they could get away with and kept the remainder of the value generated by the finished products for themselves as profit, or as a means to gather more productive capital in their own hands. The exploitation of wage labor by capitalists would, they believed, end in revolution and the end of private ownership of the means of production.

Although some observers of early capitalism, including Marx and Engels, offered scathing critiques of the social and economic conditions of factory laborers, the early and middle decades of the 20th century (with the exception of the period of the Great Depression) witnessed improved conditions and opportunities for the blue-collar workforce in the United States. In the early 20th century, Henry Ford, the

Mass production: The large-scale, highly standardized manufacturing of identical commodities on a mechanical assembly line.

Reserve army of labor: A pool of job seekers whose numbers outpace the available positions and thus contribute to keeping wages low and conditions of work tenuous.

Scientific management: A practice that sought to use principles of engineering to reduce the physical movements of workers.

TABLE 11.1 Selected Characteristics of Industrial and Postindustrial Societies

Characteristic	Industrial Society	Postindustrial Society
Principal technology	Industrial machinery	Advanced technologies, including computers, automation of tasks
Key types of labor categories	Industrial workers and professionals	"Knowledge workers" and service workers
Type of production	Mass production	Flexible production
Labor control	"Scientific management"	Outsourcing, threatened and real; technological control of work
Selected social stratification characteristics	Development of a modern class society with a dominant economic class, an expanding middle class that may integrate workers, and an economic underclass	Segmentation of the middle class by educational attainment, concentration of wealth and income at the top, and an expanding stratum of working poor

patriarch of Fordist production, took the audacious step of paying workers on his Model T assembly line in Michigan fully $5 for an 8-hour day, nearly three times the wage of a factory employee in 1914. Ford reasoned that workers who earned a solid wage would become consumers of products such as his Model T. Indeed, his workers bought, his profits grew, and industrial laborers (and, eventually, the workers of the unionized U.S. car industry) set off on a slow but steady path to the middle class (Reich, 2010).

The class structure that emerged from advanced industrial capitalism in the United States, Europe, Japan, Canada, and other modern states boasted substantial middle classes composed of workers who ranged from well-educated teachers and managers to industrial workers and mechanics with a high school or technical education. The fortunes of blue-collar and semiprofessional workers were boosted by several factors. Among these were extended periods of low unemployment in which workers had greater leverage in negotiating job conditions (Uchitelle, 2007). Unions supported autoworkers, railroad workers, and workers in many other industries in the negotiation of contracts that ensured living wages, as well as job security and benefits. Unionization surged following the Great Depression and the 1935 passage of the Wagner Act, which "guaranteed the rights of workers to join unions and bargain collectively" (VanGiezen & Schwenk, 2001), growing to more than 27% of the labor force by 1940. At their peak in 1979, U.S. unions claimed 21 million members (Mayer, 2004).

Changes in the U.S. economy, including those we saw illustrated in this chapter's opening story, have shaken the relatively stable middle class that emerged around the middle of the 20th century. Since the 1970s, mass layoffs have grown across industries, even though manufacturing has been hit hardest (Uchitelle, 2007). As a result, today the industrial laborer is less likely to belong to a union, less likely to have appreciable job security, and more likely to have experienced a decline in wages and benefits. Income gains have slipped, and, for many, membership in the U.S. middle class has become tenuous (Table 11.1).

POSTINDUSTRIAL SOCIETY

During the past quarter century the "information revolution," which began with Intel's invention of the microchip in 1971, has altered economic life, accelerating changes in the organization of work that were already under way. Pressured by global competition that intensified by the end of the 1970s, U.S. firms began to move away from the inflexible Fordist system of mass production, seeking ways to accommodate rapid changes in products and production processes and to reduce high labor costs that were making U.S. products less competitive. Postindustrial economic organization is complex, so the sections below focus on just some of the key aspects, including the growth of automation and flexible production, reliance on "outsourcing" and "offshoring," and the growth of the service economy.

AUTOMATION AND FLEXIBLE PRODUCTION

Postindustrial production relies on ever-expanding **automation**, *the replacement of human labor by machines in the production process.* Today, robots can perform tedious and dangerous work that once required the labor of hundreds of workers. Although automation increases efficiency, it has also eliminated jobs.

Computer-driven assembly lines can be quickly reprogrammed, allowing manufacturers to shift to new products and designs rapidly and to shorten the time from factory

Automation: The replacement of human labor by machines in the production process.

to buyer. "Just-in-time" delivery systems also minimize the need for businesses to maintain warehouses full of parts and supplies; instead, parts suppliers ship components to factories on an as-needed basis so they move right to the production floor and into the products. Such reliance on more flexible, less standardized forms of production is sometimes termed *post-Fordism*.

Notably, while to this point automation has had its most visible impact on manufacturing jobs, it is becoming significant, as we saw in the opening story, in the large U.S. service industry as well. Consider, for instance, the mass expansion of self-checkout lines at supermarkets, drug stores, and home improvement stores, among many others. In many cities, one can easily go into a retail store, find the items one needs, and check out without ever speaking to another human being. Even though offering lower labor costs to employers and some convenience to consumers, self-ordering and self-checkout technologies are reducing the numbers of jobs available at dining and retail establishments. Further along in the chapter, we look at the potentially dramatic shifts in the future labor market as automation and artificial intelligence reach into other sectors of the labor market.

RELIANCE ON OUTSOURCING AND OFFSHORING Businesses can perform activities associated with producing and marketing a product "in house," or they can contract some of the work to outside firms, which in turn can do their own subcontracting to other firms. The term *outsourcing* often describes the use of low-cost foreign labor, but it can also mean contracting U.S. workers to do a job, typically for less pay than a company employee would earn.

According to a recent *Forbes* magazine article on the decline of union influence, between 20% and 40% of autoworkers at foreign-owned factories in the United States, most of which are in the South, are temporary hires (Muller, 2014). Striking today is the emergence of outsourcing across a wide spectrum of industries. For example, United Airlines used to rely on its own mechanics to service the company's planes. The mechanics were well paid and enjoyed benefits negotiated by their union. By the late 1990s, however, United increasingly turned to nonunionized mechanics operating from lower-cost, lower-wage hangars in the South. The terrorist attacks of September 11, 2001, which temporarily halted air travel, exacerbated the financial difficulties of airlines. In spite of billions in government aid and loans, airlines have continued to struggle. Major carriers have become even more reliant on outsourcing to cut costs (Uchitelle, 2007).

The phenomenon of contracted work—that is, temporary work that minimizes the commitment of employer and employee to a long-term economic relationship—is not limited to the blue-collar workforce. Computer giant Microsoft's use of "permatemps," initiated in the 1990s, is a striking example. During this time, 1,500 permatemps worked with the 17,000 regular domestic employees of the company. Although they performed comparable tasks, the permatemps, some of whom had been in their jobs for 5 years or more, not only were denied the same vacation, health, and retirement benefits as other workers but also were denied discounts at the Microsoft store, opportunities for further job training, and even use of the company basketball court. A class-action suit was filed against Microsoft, and the company agreed to an out-of-court settlement of $97 million (FACE Intel, 2000).

Offshoring refers more specifically to the practice among U.S. companies of contracting with businesses outside the country to perform services that would otherwise be done by U.S. workers. The movement of manufacturing jobs overseas to lower-wage countries, as noted earlier, has been taking place since the 1970s and 1980s. More recently, however, workers and policy makers have expressed concern about the offshoring of professional jobs, such as those in information technology. According to a recent Congressional Research Service paper on the topic, this trend has been fostered by the widespread adoption of technologies enabling rapid transmission of voice and data across the globe, economic crises in the United States that have created greater pressure to achieve economic "efficiencies" (such as lower labor costs), and the availability of a growing pool of well-educated and often English-speaking labor abroad (Levine, 2012).

TRANSFORMATION OF THE OCCUPATIONAL AND CLASS STRUCTURE Among the most highly compensated workers in the modern economy are those who invent or design new products, engineer new technologies, and solve problems. They are creative people who "make things happen," organizers who bring people together, administrators who make firms run efficiently, legal and financial experts who help firms to be profitable, and computer scientists who are driving digital networking innovations (Bell, 1973; Reich, 2010). Workers in this category are sometimes called "symbolic analysts" (Reich, 1991) or "knowledge workers." Most symbolic analysts are highly educated professionals who engage in mental labor and, in some way, the manipulation of symbols (numbers, computer codes, words). They include engineers, university professors, physicians, scientists, lawyers, and financiers and bankers, among others.

Although the ranks of symbolic analysts have grown overall in recent decades and the ranks of "routine production workers" in manufacturing have been falling, most job growth over this period has been concentrated in the service sector. Services constitute a diverse sector of the labor market. As of 2014, the service sector employed more than 120 million U.S. workers and accounted for almost 80% of the U.S. workforce (U.S. Bureau of Labor Statistics, 2015). Service occupations include some jobs that require higher education, including financial and private educational services, but also include retail sales, home health and nurses' aides, food service, and security services.

REUTERS/CHRIS KEANE

Some manufacturing jobs have returned to the United States after the dramatic decline of this job sector in the 1980s and 1990s. Today's industrial jobs, however, typically pay less and are more likely to be temporary contract positions rather than permanent jobs. ■

Many service positions do not require extensive education or training, and a growing fraction are part-time rather than full-time, are nonunionized, and have few or no benefits. Quite a few of these jobs require "people skills" stereotypically associated with females and are often viewed as "women's jobs" (but by no means invariably, since private security guards, a growing occupation, tend to be men). By contrast, many routine production jobs in the past were manufacturing jobs that commonly employed men. The decline in manufacturing employment opportunities, along with declines in educational attainment among men, has made unemployment and underemployment particularly acute for some demographic groups, including minority males (Autor, 2010).

Together, these diverse labor market trends point to significant shifts in the U.S. class structure. Economist David Autor (2010) argues that a polarization of job opportunities has taken place, particularly in the past two decades. Autor sees a modern economy characterized by "expanding opportunities in both high-skill, high-wage occupations and low-skill, low-wage occupations, coupled with contracting opportunities in middle-wage, middle-skill, white-collar and blue-collar jobs." He views this as the basis of a split in the middle class, with those whose membership in that group bolstered by, for instance, good manufacturing jobs now losing ground, and those who occupy the upper, professional rungs of the middle class maintaining their status amid growing opportunities.

Nevertheless, not all economists agree with this assessment. Economist Alan Blinder (2006) argues that "many people blithely assume that the critical labor-market distinction is, and will remain, between highly educated (or highly skilled) people and less-educated (or less-skilled) people—doctors versus call-center operators, for example. The supposed remedy for the rich countries, accordingly, is more education and a general 'upskilling' of the work force. But this view may be mistaken" (p. 118). Blinder suggests that the more critical social division in the future may not be between jobs that require high levels of education and those that do not, but rather between work that can be wirelessly outsourced and work that cannot. Consider the growth of online university education. Whereas a college professor may be able to accommodate 100 or even 500 students in a massive lecture hall, an online instructor can have thousands of students and teach them at a considerable cost savings to the institution—and, in some instances, to the students. Some universities, such as the Massachusetts Institute of Technology (MIT), are offering free college course lectures online (though these are not normally available for credit). Although this is not "outsourcing" as we typically define it, trends suggest that even many highly educated workers will be vulnerable to technological changes in the decades ahead, a topic we take up in more detail shortly.

THE SERVICE ECONOMY AND EMOTIONAL LABOR

As discussed above, recent decades have seen the expansion of the service sector of the U.S. economy. Many service jobs today require a substantial amount of "emotional labor."

BEHIND THE NUMBERS

Unemployment, Employment, and Underemployment in the United States

According to the U.S. Bureau of Labor Statistics (2017b), in August 2017 the U.S. labor force participation rate (that is, the labor force as a percentage of the civilian noninstitutional population) was almost 63%, and more than 159.8 million U.S. residents were *employed.* At the same time, about 4.4% of U.S. workers, or 7.1 million individuals, were counted by the BLS as *unemployed.* What do these numbers tell us? What do they illuminate, and what do they obscure?

Consider some of the most frequently cited BLS figures—unemployment in the United States. According to BLS, the **unemployed** are *people who are jobless, have actively looked for work in the prior 4 weeks, and are available for work.* The BLS figures are based on the monthly Current Population Survey, which uses a representative sample of 60,000 households and has been conducted every month since 1940. Although the BLS cannot count every U.S. household, the size of the sample and its configuration are believed to ensure a statistically accurate representation of the U.S. labor force.

Official unemployment figures, however, do not include those who, after a brief or extended period of joblessness, have given up looking for work, or whose job seeking is "passive"—for instance, limited to scanning newspaper or online classified ads. Those persons are categorized as **not in the labor force**, because they are *neither officially employed nor officially unemployed.* Persons who would like to work and have searched actively for a job in the past 12 months (but not in the prior 4 weeks) are categorized as **marginally attached to the labor force**: In August 2017, there were about 1.5 million such individuals. BLS also identifies a category they call *discouraged workers*, which includes those who would like to work but have given up searching, believing that no jobs are available for them: Recent data puts this figure at just over half a million U.S. residents. Widely cited official unemployment statistics omit these categories and may thus underestimate the numbers of those who need and want to work.

What about labor force participation rates? Who, according to BLS, is counted as *employed*? In BLS statistics, *employed persons are those who are 16 years of age or older in the civilian, noninstitutional population (that is, not in the military or in mental or penal institutions) who did any paid work—even as little as one hour—in the reference week or worked in their own businesses or farms*. This figure is a useful overview of economic activity and is valuable for examining labor market conditions over time, but it fails to capture the problem of underemployment.

Underemployment manifests in two key ways. First, the underemployed include workers forced to work part-time when they would like to work full-time. According to BLS, in August 2017, there were about 5.3 million involuntary part-time workers in the United States; these are workers who are in part-time positions because their hours have been reduced or they are unable to find a full-time job. Second, workers in jobs that are well below their skill level can also be considered underemployed. For example, some recent data looks at college graduates who are in jobs that do not require a university degree. How does one identify which jobs qualify for this designation? The Federal Reserve Bank of New York (Abel, Deitz, & Su, 2014) uses the following measure: "We consider a college education to be a requirement for a given occupation if at least 50 percent of the respondents working in that occupation indicated that a bachelor's degree is necessary to perform the job" (p. 3). A recent report by the New York City Comptroller's Office found that while "72% of New York City workers between the ages of 23 and 29 years old in 2014 had acquired at least some college education . . . 'the link between higher education and employment has weakened'" (Soergel, 2016, para. 4). The report noted that the percentage of low-wage workers with at least a bachelor's degree had risen to 33% by 2014, a 10-point rise since 2000 (Soergel, 2016).

Unemployment and employment figures are important measures that help to track trends over time and enable comparisons between demographic groups. At the same time, while they illuminate some aspects of the complex labor market, they obscure others.

THINK IT THROUGH

- As we saw, *underemployment* is an economic phenomenon that does not appear in unemployment numbers. Why is it economically significant? Why is it sociologically significant?

According to sociologist Arlie Hochschild (2003), **emotional labor** is the *commodification of emotions, including "the management of feeling to create a publicly observable facial and bodily display"* (p. 7). Like physical labor, the symbol of the industrial economy, emotional labor is also "sold for a wage and. . . has exchange value" (p. 7).

Hochschild (2003) uses the example of flight attendants, who do emotional labor in the management of airline passengers' comfort, good feelings, and sense of safety, but we could also use as examples customer service workers, retail sales associates, and restaurant servers. Although these workers may enjoy their jobs, they are also forced to feign positive feelings even when such feelings are absent and to labor to evoke positive feelings in their customers. The emotional laborer is, in a sense, compelled to "sell" his or her smile in exchange for a wage, just as the industrial laborer sells his or her physical labor. The emotional laborer's actions are programmed for profit and efficiency, as he or she is asked to perform emotions that maximize both. Consider, for instance, the common use of "scripts" for employees in sales jobs or restaurants that closely instruct workers on how to maintain a message and close a sale, even if it causes the employee (or the consumer) distress or discomfort. The strain between real and performed feelings, notes Hochschild, leads to an emotive dissonance—that is, a "disconnect"—between what the worker really feels and the emotions to be shown or suppressed. Hochschild posits that just as Marx's proletarian laboring in a mill was alienated from the work and from him- or herself, so too is the emotional laborer alienated from work and his or her emotional life.

In the next section of the chapter, we discuss some evolving aspects of the economy, returning to a theme introduced in our opening story: the current and potential future effects of automation and artificial intelligence on work and the workplace.

THE TECHNOLOGICAL REVOLUTION AND THE FUTURE OF WORK

In the previous section, we discussed some key characteristics of the economic eras that have taken us to the present. In this section, we consider possible paths of economic development in the years ahead, focusing in particular on ways in which expanded automation, robotics, and the rise of artificial intelligence may reshape the future labor market in the United States and the world.

Technological change has historically wrought both prosperity and pain in the economy and labor market. For example, while innovations like the mechanization of agriculture in the 19th century dramatically improved productivity and enabled some landowners and farmers to grow a surplus that could be sold at a profit, it also created significant disruptions for agricultural laborers. At the same time, new technological innovations in production created a mass

Emotional labor: The management of feelings or emotions to create a publicly observable facial and bodily display in return for a wage.

of new jobs in urban industry, spurring rural to urban migration and a new economic order heavily rooted in manufacturing. Put simply, in the past, technological innovations and accompanying economic shifts have put workers out of jobs, but in the words of economist Martin Ford (2015), "it never became systematic or permanent. New jobs were created and dispossessed workers found new opportunities" (p. x).

Today we are experiencing a new era of change and, potentially, disruption, as technology is changing how work and the workplace are structured. What are evolving trends in the economy and labor market? Below we discuss two key points.

BIG NAMES, FEW WORKERS: DIGITAL NETWORKING COMPANIES IN THE CONTEMPORARY ECONOMY

The most visible and well-known companies in the United States today do not employ large numbers of workers. Consider an observation made by computer scientist Jaron Lanier (2013):

> At the height of its power, the photography company Kodak employed more than 140,000 people and was worth $28 billion. They even invented the first digital camera. But today Kodak is bankrupt, and the new face of digital photography has become Instagram. When Instagram was sold to Facebook for a billion dollars in 2012, it employed only thirteen people. (p. 2)

Lanier's example points to a significant contemporary trend: We are seeing the dramatic rise of companies whose fortunes are tied to digital networking—Instagram, Facebook, WhatsApp, and Snapchat are just a few. Companies engaged in digital networking are among the most financially valued firms today. At the same time, the number of jobs they directly contribute to the labor market is relatively low. For example, in 2015, Snapchat had a valuation of $55 billion; at that time, it had 330 employees. When Facebook recently purchased WhatsApp at a cost of $22 billion, the company had a total of 55 employees. Figure 11.10 offers a visual representation of the "highest valuation per employee." That is, it helps us see that some companies have both high valuations and few employees: Snapchat's "valuation per employee" is $48 million. As one article noted, "Ultimately, software has proven to be one of the most headcount-efficient businesses in the world" (Chen, 2015, para. 6).

Although "headcount efficiency" is a boon for companies and shareholders, it may be less beneficial for jobseekers. In the heyday of U.S. manufacturing, prominent and technologically modern companies were providers of significant numbers of jobs: In 1955, for instance, General Motors had a workforce of over 576,000; U.S. Steel employed about 268,000 workers; and Chrysler had over 167,000 employees ("America's 5 Biggest Employers," 2010). The digitally networked economy is producing new, well-paying, and interesting jobs, but will there be enough of them to employ the workforce of the future?

RISE OF THE ROBOTS?

Economist Martin Ford (2015) writes that we are in a moment when the role of technology in the workplace is changing. Ford notes that

> [this] shift will ultimately challenge one of our basic assumptions about technology: that machines are tools that increase the productivity of workers. Instead machines themselves are turning into workers, and the line between the capability of labor and capital is blurring as never before. (p. xii)

Ford (2015) suggests that the change is underpinned by "the relentless acceleration of computer technology" (p. xii). When Ford writes that "machines themselves are turning into workers," he is recognizing the myriad ways in which technology has the potential to disrupt the contemporary labor market—and, by extension, society—in ways that are still difficult to fully grasp.

For example, consider the seemingly imminent introduction of self-driving cars on our roads. A recent article in the *Washington Post* looks at one company's efforts to bring this goal to fruition in the city of Pittsburgh:

> Uber is about to build a vast, high-tech playground in one of this city's poorest areas.
>
> The ride-hailing giant wants a protected place to test driverless Ubers, part of its effort to replace costly human drivers.
>
> So on the site of an abandoned steel mill south of the Hot Metal Bridge, the company will carve out a 20-plus-square block, Pac-Man-like maze lined with trapezoidal obstacles. It is the same place where thousands of workers once streamed in to take punishing jobs at the beehive-shaped ovens for baking coal and the furnaces that were fueled by it. (Laris, 2016, p. 1)

As self-driving cars become part of our world, "costly human drivers" may indeed be replaced. A key question, then, is what will those human drivers do? According to the U.S. Bureau of Labor Statistics (2017c), in 2014, the

FIGURE 11.10 Value of Tech Companies per Employee

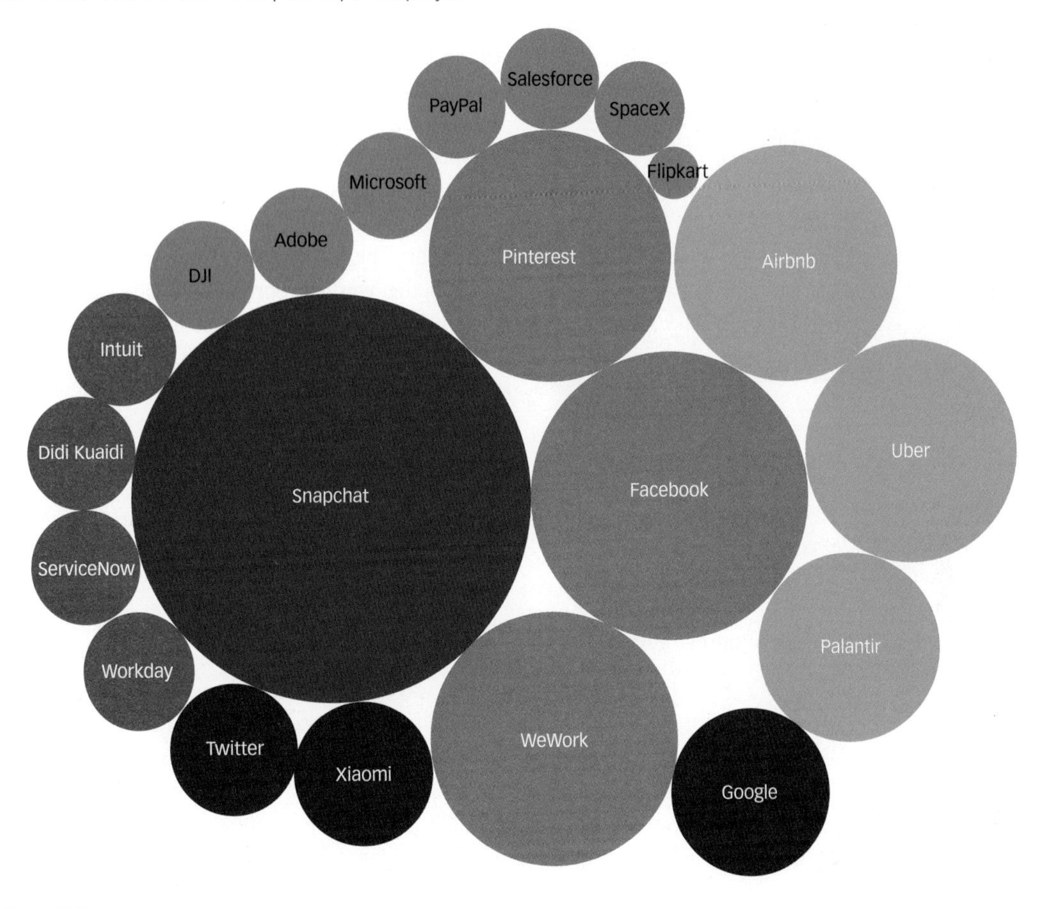

SOURCE: Chen, 2015.

country had about 1.4 million truck drivers and 800,000 delivery drivers. These are just two of the many occupations that are based on driving, including taxi and Uber drivers.

Significantly, the advent of artificial intelligence is also changing the labor market for those with advanced education. Consider the case of journalists. The effect of the Internet on journalism has been widely discussed. On the one hand, as more people get their news "for free" on the Internet, paid subscriptions to newspapers and magazines have fallen and the availability of jobs for reporters has contracted. On the other hand, the Internet has seen the birth of new online news sites that have opened opportunities for writers. The effects of artificial intelligence on journalism, however, are still nascent and may be even more disruptive. New technology is permitting media outlets to produce narrative without employing reporters. According to Ford (2015),

> Narrative Science's technology is used by top media outlets . . . to produce automated articles in a variety of areas, including sports, business, and politics. The company's software generates a news story every thirty seconds, and many of these are published on widely known websites that prefer not to acknowledge the use of their services. (pp. 84–85)

In 2015, the Associated Press, a major producer of news content, revealed that it has used a fully automated program for the production of some content since 2014: The "robot reporter" writes about 1,000 articles a month (Gleyo, 2015). When asked by a reporter to predict how many news articles would be written algorithmically within 15 years, the cofounder of Narrative Science estimated the proportion to be over 90% (Ford, 2015).

Significantly, some observers of artificial intelligence trends suggest that while human input is still needed in decision making, robots are *better* at many tasks than humans. A recent article on robot surgeons noted that "In experiments on pigs, surgical stitches made by autonomous robots were

ANGELO MERENDINO/AFP/Getty Images

The self-driving car, like this one being tested by Uber, is coming to a street near you. What will be the benefits of self-driving cars to individual drivers and society? What might be the costs? ■

as good or better than stitches made by skilled surgeons" (Seaman, 2016, p. E6). The author of the study is quoted as saying that "No matter how steady a surgeon's hands are, there is always some tremor." Hence, "Using autonomous robots in some of the 44.5 million soft tissue surgeries in the United States each year might reduce human errors and improve efficiency, surgical time and access to quality surgeons." Human physicians and surgeons will remain a central part of patient care and care decisions for the foreseeable future, but medicine is just one of many fields in which change is coming.

As artificial intelligence becomes capable of taking on both routine tasks (as it has been doing already) and more complex, analytical and technological tasks (as it is beginning to do), it is worth asking how decision makers and society will respond. Will advances in artificial intelligence create new jobs and new job sectors that enable society and the economy to flourish? Or will computer intelligence push "costly" human workers out of jobs permanently? What do you think?

WHY STUDY EDUCATION AND THE ECONOMY?

Education opens up the world to us. Through education, we gain new perspectives and build skills and knowledge to understand the world around us and to address key issues and problems. In an increasingly interdependent and interconnected world, education gives us advantages in navigating new challenges. Opportunities are not, however, equally distributed and factors including socioeconomic status and place of residence can profoundly affect access to a good education. That matters because undeveloped potential cannot improve the lives or prospects of individuals, communities, and the country.

The significance of education in determining one's prospects is growing as the economy and labor market are changing. Whether you were born in the 1960s, the 1970s, the 1980s, the 1990s, or earlier, the U.S. economy has experienced dramatic changes in your lifetime. In the 1960s, more than one third of the U.S. nonagricultural workforce was engaged in manufacturing. At the same time, more Americans were pursuing higher education and demand for skilled professionals was high. In the latter years of the 1970s, the United States experienced a steep rise in imports—U.S.-made goods and U.S. workers were forced to compete with lower-priced goods and lower-priced labor. From this period forward, the share of goods made in the United States and the number of workers making them fell (Uchitelle, 2007). Starting in the early 1980s, wages, which had increased for decades, stagnated. Manufacturing jobs continued to shrink, but the service sector expanded and demand for educated workers remained robust. By the 1990s, advances in computer technologies brought a new wave of outsourcing, not of manufacturing jobs, many of which had already moved offshore, but of information technology and, increasingly, customer service jobs (Erber & Sayed-Ahmed, 2005). Countries such as India, with large populations of educated and English-speaking workers, benefited from American firms' pursuit of lower cost labor not only in manufacturing but in service as well.

The shape of our economy and our economic fortunes has changed in myriad ways and continues to do so in the new millennium. Some of the early contours of a digitally networked economy are apparent in the United States: As noted early in the chapter, advanced technology is shifting its role from that of assisting workers to replacing them. This is already taking place in manufacturing, and it is seeping into the service sector. Even occupational sectors requiring advanced education are not immune to these dramatic changes. Will technology, particularly in the form of automation, robotics, and artificial intelligence, contribute to the creation of new jobs and opportunities? Will it diminish or destroy existing economic sectors? These questions remain to be answered.

Understanding the relationship between the skills and knowledge gained through education and the demands of the economy and labor market is critical to gaining a perspective on how we as individuals and as a country can both prepare for and shape our future.

GLOBAL ISSUES

The Digital Sweatshop

The exploitation of labor is a fundamental characteristic of industrial capitalism, according to Karl Marx. Although in Western countries today few industrial sites like those he and Upton Sinclair described exist, factories with strikingly poor conditions and large pools of low-wage labor flourish in other countries, including China and Thailand. Workers in developing countries bear many of the costs of the high technology we enjoy in the form of advanced computers, phones, and other necessities and amenities.

AFP/AFP/Getty Images

Apple and other global companies have been under scrutiny for the hazardous working conditions in some offshore factories. Some workers have responded with strikes. A small number have committed suicide on factory grounds. ■

In January 2012, the *New York Times* published an investigative article about Foxconn, one of Apple's key suppliers in China. The article points out that while "Apple and its high-technology peers—as well as dozens of other American industries—have achieved a pace of innovation nearly unmatched in modern history. . . the workers assembling iPhones, iPads and other devices often labor in harsh conditions, according to employees inside those plants, worker advocates and documents published by companies themselves" (Duhigg & Barboza, 2012, para. 6). Among documented issues noted by workers and their advocates are excessive employee overtime, difficult work conditions that include long hours standing, and work injuries resulting from poisonous chemicals used in the manufacture and cleaning of products such as iPads. The article adds that "under-age workers have helped build Apple's products, and the company's suppliers have improperly disposed of hazardous waste and falsified records."

Apple representatives argue that the company has conducted investigations into these conditions and has standards to which its manufacturers must conform (Duhigg & Greenhouse, 2012), but a recent British Broadcasting Corporation investigation at the Pegatron factory outside of Shanghai uncovered a variety of abuses, including forced overtime (Bilton, 2014). Like any modern capitalist enterprise, Apple exists in a deeply competitive economic environment, and holding costs down is a path to greater profit. Tightly controlled and rapid manufacturing is also key to maintaining the innovations that drive the technology marketplace.

The *New York Times* article points out that Apple is one of the most admired U.S. brands. A survey the newspaper conducted in 2011 found that fully 56% of respondents could not think of anything negative about the company. Negative opinions were far more likely to be linked to the cost of Apple products (14%) than to its overseas labor practices (2%). Without pressure for change from consumers or companies themselves, the voices of laborers are least likely to be heard and their interests least likely to be realized.

As an Apple executive interviewed for the story noted, "You can either manufacture in comfortable, worker-friendly factories, or you can reinvent the product every year, and make it better and faster and cheaper, which requires factories that seem harsh by American standards. . . . And right now, customers care more about a new iPhone than working conditions in China" (quoted in Duhigg & Barboza, 2012, "Hitting the Apple Lottery," para. 12–13).

THINK IT THROUGH

- Consider the interests that come into play in this environment: Apple and its manufacturers are interested in low labor costs, efficient and effective production, and high profits. Consumers are interested in new gadgets and technologies to increase their productivity and pleasure. Workers are interested in safe working conditions and good pay. Can all these interests be realized? What do you think?

WHAT CAN I DO WITH A SOCIOLOGY DEGREE?

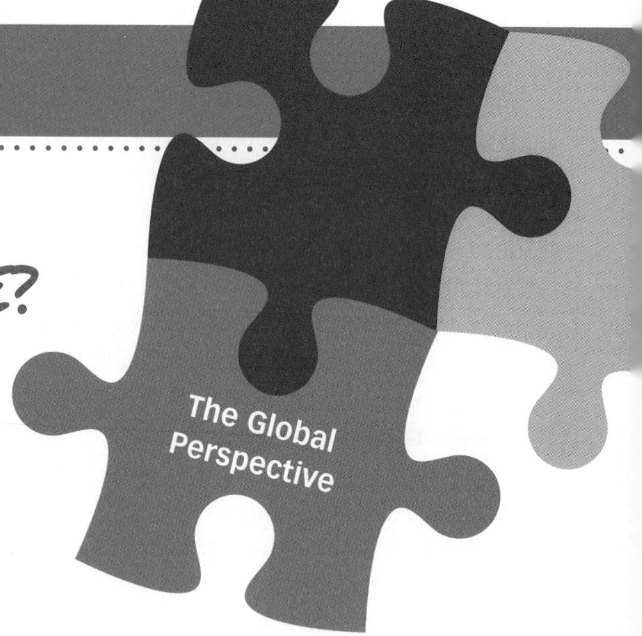

The Global Perspective

The study of sociology helps you develop a broad understanding of the social world, which includes relationships between cultures and countries over time and space and the ability to see the world from a variety of perspectives. A *global perspective* encompasses knowledge and skills. A global perspective evolves through study and experiences that lead to a strong understanding and appreciation of the significance of global cultural, economic, political, and social connections for individuals, communities, and countries. It also encompasses the development of skills for working effectively in intercultural environments.

Understanding different cultures, recognizing a diverse spectrum of legitimate political and economic interests, and having the ability to see issues from multiple perspectives are key elements in global efforts to deal cooperatively with environmental, health, and other threats to the planet. As a sociology student, you will have the opportunity to develop the kind of thoughtful global perspective that will enable to you make critical connections between decisions about, for instance, economic consumption or production, which are made at the individual or community or country level, and effects that are experienced globally.

Voltaire Xodus, Social Entrepreneur and Founder of Re-Up

DePaul University, BA in Sociology

When I graduated from DePaul University in 2007 with a background in sociology, I never thought about all the possibilities and ways I could apply my discipline to generate global solutions and personal opportunities. Currently, I'm a social entrepreneur who runs a tech startup (ReUp) in Amsterdam, Netherlands. Being 10 years removed from my graduation, I'm very pleased to have found the growing field of social enterprise. In short, social enterprises/social entrepreneurs are individuals who create businesses that have a core value base philosophy of "people first, financial profit second." This alternative value-based system empowers students majoring in the liberal arts (i.e., sociology, poly sci, anthropology, and philosophy) with a platform to innovate and create sustainable ideas that solve many of the economic, environmental, and global social justice issues of our time. If you're looking for examples of social enterprises, check out the work TOMS Shoes is doing for children around the world without shoes. Or the social and economic impact Radha Agrawal is having on women with her THINX underwear invention.

Social entrepreneurship allowed me to put my social justice values to work by combining sociology with entrepreneurship. Moreover, it helped me think and become global. Over the past 2 years, I've done behavioral research in 17 countries and 40 cities on people's passion, purpose, and goal achievement. My work led me to produce an app game called ReUp that measures people's willpower toward their goals in life. Because ReUp can measure individuals and groups, it can measure the productivity of cities and countries in real time. The big data generated from people playing the game helps users see how their small choices have value. For example, if 50,000 people in New Delhi don't smoke, we can see how that impacts the health care system in India. Or if 80,000 people in Los Angeles take their bike to work for 30 days, we'd be able to show how that impacts CO_2 admissions. Global issues such as these are problems that must be solved, and I'm a firm believer that social entrepreneurs will be the heroes of the 21st century that solve our big problems.

SUMMARY

- **Education** is the transmission of society's norms, values, and knowledge base by means of direct instruction.

- **Mass education** spread with industrialization and the need for widespread **literacy**. Today the need is not just for literacy but for specialized training as well. All industrial societies today, including the United States, have systems of **public education** that continue through the high school level, and frequently the university level as well. Such societies are sometimes termed **credential societies**, in that access to desirable jobs and social status depends on the possession of a certificate or diploma.

- Functionalist theories of education emphasize the role of the school in serving the needs of society by socializing students and filling positions in the social order, while conflict theories emphasize education's role in reproducing rather than reducing social inequality.
- Symbolic interactionist theory, by focusing on the classroom itself, reveals how teachers' perceptions of students—as well as students' self-perceptions—are important in shaping students' performance.
- Early literacy and later educational attainment are powerfully correlated. Access to books and early reading experiences are among the strongest predictors of basic literacy at an early age. Researchers measure multiple levels of literacy.
- U.S. public schools are highly segregated by race and ethnicity. Before the 1954 U.S. Supreme Court decision in *Brown v. Board of Education*, segregation was legal. Since that time, schools have continued to show **de facto segregation** because segregated residential patterns still exist, because many White parents decide to send their children to private schools, and because the courts have recently limited the scope of previous laws aimed at promoting full integration.
- Differences in school funding by race, ethnicity, and class reinforce existing patterns of social inequality. In general, the higher someone's social class, the more likely he or she is to complete high school and college. Low-income people, in contrast, are often trapped in a cycle of low educational attainment and poverty.
- There are strong demonstrable relationships between educational attainment and employment prospects and between educational attainment and income. There is also a correlation between the socioeconomic status of a family and the probability of its members' further educational attainment.
- The **economy**—the social institution that organizes the ways in which a society produces, distributes, and consumes **goods** and **services**—is one of the most important institutions in society.
- Three major technological revolutions in human history have brought radically new forms of economic organization. The first led to agriculture, the second to modern industry, and the third to the postindustrial society that characterizes the modern United States.
- Industrial society is characterized by **automation**, the modern factory, **mass production**, **scientific management**, and modern social classes. Postindustrial society is characterized by the use of computers, the increased importance of higher education for well-paying jobs, flexible forms of production, increased reliance on outsourcing, and the growth of the service economy.
- Although postindustrial society holds the promise of prosperity for people who work with ideas and information, automation and globalization have also allowed for new forms of exploitation of the global workforce and job loss and declining wages for some workers in manufacturing and other sectors.
- Artificial intelligence has the potential to transform the labor market, as machines shift from the role of being an instrument for human workers to being workers. This change may affect jobs for both less-educated and highly educated employees.

KEY TERMS

education, 345
formal education, 345
mass education, 345
literacy, 346
public education, 346
credential society, 347
school segregation, 354
de facto segregation, 356

economy, 361

goods, 361

services, 361

mass production, 364

reserve army of labor, 364

scientific management, 364

automation, 365

unemployed, 368

not in the labor force, 368

marginally attached to the labor force, 368

emotional labor, 369

DISCUSSION QUESTIONS

1. What are some of the key reasons students drop out of college? How can identifying the sociological roots of the problem help us to develop effective policies to address it?

2. What do contemporary data show us about the relationship between family income and academic achievement, as measured by variables like educational attainment or SAT scores? How do sociologists explain the relationship? What are strengths and weaknesses of their arguments?

3. What is the current state of racial segregation in U.S. public schools? How has it changed since the civil rights era of the 1960s? What sociological factors help explain high levels of racial segregation in schools? How can the United States address high levels of racial segregation in our schools?

4. How is unemployment in the United States measured? What aspects of this phenomenon does the unemployment rate measure and what aspects does it fail to capture?

5. What effects might the expansion of automation and artificial intelligence have on the U.S. and global workforce? What evidence of the effect is available today? What sectors of the labor market may be affected in the future?

SOCIAL MOVEMENTS AND SOCIAL CHANGE

12.1 Apply sociological perspectives to understand characteristics and paths of social change

12.2 Describe key sources of social change in society

12.3 Identify different types of social movements

AP Photo/Eric Gay

WHAT DO YOU THINK?

1. Are students on college campuses today socially or politically active? What are the issues driving campus activism today?
2. Do people behave differently in crowds than they do individually or in small groups? What sociological factors explain crowd behavior?
3. What are the functions of social media in movements for social change today?

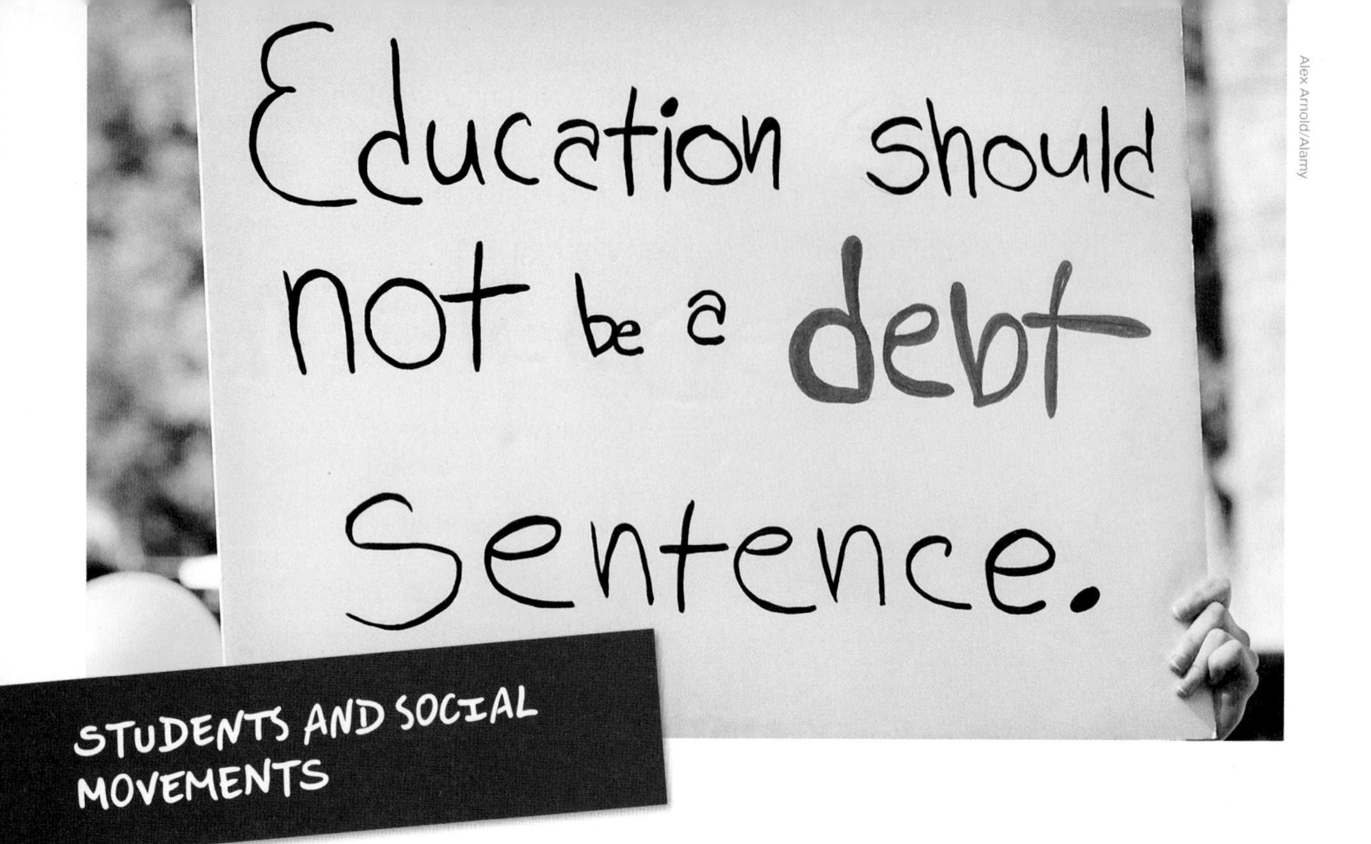

STUDENTS AND SOCIAL MOVEMENTS

In the 1960s, student protest movements experienced a heyday, encompassing a wide variety of issues and drawing in thousands of young activists. Many young people, as well as faculty, protested U.S. involvement in the Vietnam War (1964–1973). In 1965, for example, at the University of Michigan, antiwar activists held a "teach-in," heralded as a means for both making a political statement and educating people about war and the activists' objections to it. The teach-in was held at night, after classes, and thus did not disrupt the university's activities; it attracted administration and student support. Other protests, however, targeted university administrators and policies. In 1968, students staged a 3-day sit-in at the University of Georgia's administrative building, speaking out against the unequal treatment of male and female students at the school. Women students at the campus had a stricter dress code and curfew than their male peers; as well, they were not permitted to drink or to live off campus. Students challenged their universities on other fronts as well: The massive Berkeley free-speech movement of 1964 was born as a protest against a University of California rule that prohibited student groups operating on campus from engaging in any off-campus politics; even the distribution of leaflets was prohibited (Lang, 2016).

Today, student activism is returning to U.S. college campuses. Many issues are new, even though a concern for social justice continues to be central. One important issue driving campus activism has been the prevalence of sexual assault on campus and efforts to both prevent and punish sexual assault. Students have also spoken out widely against the presence of hostile racial climates on campuses: Among the most visible were the 2015 protests at the University of Missouri, which included hunger strikes, a boycott by the school's largely Black football team, and, ultimately, the resignation of the school president (Boghosian, 2015). Notably, activism in our era is also tied into social media, which is used to generate interest and organize activists. It may serve as a platform for protest, largely substituting online participation for physical presence. In a demonstration against the high levels of debt students incur in their studies, a group at New York University encouraged students to share their experiences using hashtags like #YouAreNotALoan (Engelberg, 2015).

Social movements have been a fundamental foundation of social change. The relative quiet on U.S. campuses in recent decades has been replaced by rising student engagement in campus activism. Can this engagement be sustained? Will it successfully translate into meaningful changes? What role will social media play in a new world of activism? These are just some of the questions sociologists will be seeking to answer in the years ahead. ■

We begin this chapter with an overview of sociological theorizing on social change. We continue with an examination of key sources of social change, focusing in particular on collective behavior and resources from which strikers such as those described above draw. Next we provide an overview of forms that social movements take, and we conclude with some reflections on the nature of social change going forward in a rapidly changing and globalized world.

SOCIOLOGICAL PERSPECTIVES ON SOCIAL CHANGE

The concept of social change is all-encompassing. It refers to small-group changes, such as a social club changing a long-standing policy against admitting women or minorities, and to global-level and national-level transformations, such as the outsourcing of jobs to low-wage countries and the rise of social movements that seek to address the threat of climate change.

When sociologists speak of social change, they are generally referring to changes that occur throughout the social structure of an entire society. *Societies* are understood sociologically as entities comprising those people who share a common culture and common institutions. *Social change* may refer to changes within small, relatively isolated communities such as those of the Amish or the small, culturally homogeneous tribes that dot the Amazon basin; changes across complex and modern societies such as the United States, Japan, or Germany; or changes common across similar societies, such as the economically advanced states of the West or the Arab countries of North Africa and the Middle East.

Three key types of social change theories in sociology are functionalist theories, conflict theories, and cyclical theories. Sociological perspectives on social change begin with particular assumptions about both the social world and basic processes of change. Below we briefly consider each theoretical perspective and discuss its utility for helping us understand the nature of social change in the world today.

THE FUNCTIONALIST PERSPECTIVE

Functionalist theories of social change assume that as societies develop, they become more complex and interdependent. Herbert Spencer (1892) argued that what distinguishes modern societies is **differentiation**—that is, *the development of increasing societal complexity through the creation of specialized social roles and institutions.* Spencer was referring to what Émile Durkheim conceptualized as the division of labor, which is characterized by the sorting of people into interdependent occupational and task categories (and, by extension, class categories). Think of medieval England, when craftsmen working at home made tools and shoes that they exchanged for food or clothing, using a broad range of skills to act relatively independently of one another. Compare this to modern society, where factory workers each produce parts of an automobile, managers sell completed cars to dealerships, and salespeople sell them to customers. Today people master a narrow range of tasks within a large number of highly specialized (differentiated) institutional roles and thus are highly interdependent. (Note the similarity here to Durkheim's notion

Differentiation: The development of increasing societal complexity through the creation of specialized social roles and institutions.

that societies evolve over time from *mechanical* to *organic solidarity*—the former being characteristic of traditional, homogeneous societies and the latter characteristic of diverse, modern societies.)

The earliest functionalist theories of social change were *evolutionary theories,* which assumed that all societies begin as "simple" or "primitive" and eventually develop into more "complicated" and "civilized" forms along a single, unidirectional evolutionary path (Morgan, 1877/1964). During the 20th century, however, this notion of unilinear development became increasingly shaky, as anthropologists came to believe that societies evolve in many different ways. More recent evolutionary theories (sometimes termed *multilinear*) argue that multiple paths to social change exist, depending on the particular circumstances of the society (Moore, 2004; Sahlins & Service, 1960). Technology, environment, population size, and social organization are among the factors that play roles in determining the path a society takes.

FPG/Archive Photos/Getty Images

Up to the early 20th century, it was commonly believed that women should not vote and should not be involved in politics. Women like Elizabeth Cady Stanton and Susan B. Anthony challenged both public beliefs and legal practices that prevented women from casting ballots. ■

Some evolutionary theorists viewed societies as eventually reaching an equilibrium state in which no further change would occur unless an external force set it in motion. For example, Durkheim believed that "primitive," or less developed, societies were largely unchanging unless population growth resulted in such a differentiation of social relationships that organic solidarity replaced mechanical solidarity. Talcott Parsons (1951) viewed societies as equilibrium systems that constantly seek to maintain balance, or the status quo, unless something external disrupts equilibrium, such as changes in technology or economic relationships with other societies. Parsons later came to argue, however, that societies do change by becoming more complicated systems that are better adapted to their external environments (Parsons & Shils, 2001).

Although no one can deny that modern societies contain many more specialized roles and institutions than earlier ones, evolutionary theories also assume that social changes are progressive and that "modern" (European) societies are more evolved than earlier "primitive" ones. Such beliefs appealed to countries whose soldiers, missionaries, and merchants were conquering or colonizing much of the rest of the world, since they helped justify those imperialist actions as part of the "civilizing" mission of a more advanced people. Anthropologists and sociologists eventually rejected these ideas (Nolan & Lenski, 2009).

On a more micro level, consider de-differentiation in the mainstream marital relationship. Traditionally, the man was the "head of the household" and often ruled his wife and children with an iron fist. Both the norm and the reality of marriage today are characterized by a de-differentiation of roles in which men take on domestic responsibilities and, increasingly, the wife is a major income producer for the family.

Since different parts of society undergo the processes of differentiation and de-differentiation to varying degrees and at different times, considerable conflict may arise between them (Alexander, 1998; Alexander & Colomy, 1990; Colomy, 1986, 1990). It is, however, the conflict perspective that assumes conflict as the foundation for social change. We look at that perspective below.

THE CONFLICT PERSPECTIVE

Conflict theories suggest that conflict is the product of divergent and perhaps irreconcilable social group interests and contradictory goals of social relationships. Even if a population or technology is in a state of stasis rather than change, conflict theorists see social change as inevitable, as people create ways of dealing with the conflicts and contradictions inherent in social life. Responding to the conflicts and contradictions can potentially bring a society to the brink of sharp and sometimes violent breaks with the past.

Unlike their functionalist peers in sociology, conflict theorists do not see social stability as the ultimate goal of social organization. They recognize conflict as a vital, transformative part of social life.

Karl Marx focused his research on the contradictions and conflicts built into capitalist societies, where the world is divided between owners of the means of production and workers, who own only their own labor power and must sell it under conditions not of their own making. In Marx's view, the revolutionary transformation of a society into a new type—from feudalism to capitalism, or from capitalism to socialism, for example—would occur when the consciousness of the people or the concentration of power in one social class was sufficient to create a social movement able to transform political and economic institutions into new sets of social relationships. As we have seen throughout this text, Marx's conflict theory adhered to its own evolutionary view of social change, in which all societies would advance to the same final destination: a classless, stateless society. We have earlier noted several weaknesses in this theory. Of particular importance is Marx's tendency to overemphasize economic conflict while underestimating cultural conflict and other noneconomic factors, such as gender, ethnicity, race, and nationalism, which have become increasingly important in the world today.

Later conflict theorists have addressed key questions about processes of social change, such as how groups come to want and pursue social change. Italian Marxist Antonio Gramsci (1971), for instance, highlighted the importance of ideas in maintaining order and oppression in society. He observed that the ruling class is often able to create *ideological hegemony,* a generally accepted view of what is of value and how people should relate to their economic and social status in society. Ideological hegemony may lead people to consent to their own domination by, for instance, socializing them to believe that the existing hierarchy of power is the best or only way to organize society. Consider, for example, that in the past women were socialized by schools, families, and religious institutions to believe they should not have jobs outside the home or vote. The idea that women should not hold positions outside the home could be considered a *hegemonic idea* of this period.

Gramsci also spoke of *organic intellectuals*—those who emerge from oppressed groups to create counter-hegemonies that challenge dominant (and dominating) ideas. In the mid-19th century, women's suffrage activists including Lucretia Mott, Susan B. Anthony, and Elizabeth Cady Stanton were organic intellectuals, challenging powerful beliefs that women should be excluded from politics. Over time and through the efforts of activists, the counter-hegemonic idea that women should have a voice in politics became, in fact, the hegemonic, or dominant, belief in Western society.

In the 1950s, in response to the dominant functionalist paradigm, sociologist Ralf Dahrendorf published an influential article titled "Out of Utopia" (1958). Dahrendorf argued that functionalist theory, with its emphasis on how social institutions exist to maintain the status quo, overlooks critically important characteristics of society that lead to social conflict, such as the role of power, social change, and the unequal distribution of resources. The distribution of authority in society, said Dahrendorf, is a

H.M. Herget/National Geographic Creative

Global military and political dominance, sophisticated technology, specialization and division of labor, political institutions, and the social class structure are all strikingly similar between the United States and the fallen Roman Empire. Is there a cautionary tale here about a possible future of the United States? ■

means of determining the probability of conflict. Where hierarchical structures such as states, private economic entities such as manufacturing firms, and even religious organizations are all dominated by the same elite, the potential for conflict is higher than in societies where authority is more dispersed. Put another way, if Group A dominates all or most key hierarchical authority structures and Group B is nearly always subordinate, conflict will be likely because Group B has little stake in the existing social order. Nevertheless, if Group B has authority in some hierarchical structures and Group A has authority in others, neither group has great incentive to challenge the status quo.

Marx emphasized control of the means of production as a source of power and conflict; Gramsci highlighted control of dominant ideas in society as an important source of power and change; and Dahrendorf put authority and its concentration or distribution at the center of his work. Conflict theorists differ in their beliefs about what sources are most likely to underlie social conflict and social change, but all agree that social conflict and social change are both inevitable and desirable components of society and progress.

RISE-AND-FALL THEORIES OF SOCIAL CHANGE

Rise-and-fall theories of social change deny that there is any particular forward direction to social change; rather, they *argue that change reflects a cycle of growth and decline.* Rise-and-fall or cyclical theories are common in the religious myths of many cultures, which view social life as a reflection of the life cycle of living creatures, or the seasons of the year, with the end representing some form of return to the beginning. Sociology, emerging in an era that equated scientific and technological advancement with progress, at first tended to reject such cyclical metaphors in favor of more evolutionary or revolutionary ones that emphasized the forward motion of progress.

There have been several significant exceptions, however, among historically oriented social theorists. Pitirim Sorokin (1957/1970, 1962), a historical sociologist of the mid-20th century, argued that societies alternate among three different kinds of mentalities: those that give primacy to the senses, those that emphasize religiosity, and those that celebrate logic and reason. Societies that value hedonism and the satisfaction of immediate pleasures more highly than the achievement of long-term goals give primacy to the senses; religiosity occurs in societies that value following the tenets of a religion over enjoying the senses or solving problems through logic and reason. We tend to think of modern societies as defined largely by the emphasis on logic and reason.

Societies everywhere have contained a mixture of religiosity, an emphasis on the senses, and the celebration of logic and reason. Sorokin's "ideal types" may nonetheless be useful for describing the *relative* emphasis of each of these modes of adaptation in different societies. For example, we might say that the modern Western world puts greater emphasis on logic and reason than on religion or giving primacy to the senses; it would be a mistake, however, to say that there is no emphasis on the senses or religion, because these traits too play important roles in shaping the modern Western world.

In *The Rise and Fall of the Great Powers* (1987), historian Paul Kennedy traces the conditions associated with national power and decline during the past five centuries. As nations grow in economic power, he argues, they often seek to become world military powers as well, a goal that in the long run proves to be their undoing. Wielding global military power eventually weakens a nation's domestic economy, undermining the prosperity that once fueled it. Kennedy forecasts that this might well be the fate of the United States. More recently, writer Cullen Murphy (2007) has pointed to parallels between the Roman Empire and the United States, noting that Rome too was characterized by an overburdened and costly military, a deep sense of exceptionalism, and a tendency to denigrate and misunderstand other cultures. He notes as well the Roman pattern of shifting the onus for providing services to citizens away from the public sector to the private sector, seeing this as a form of enrichment for the few but a disadvantage for the many. A key point in rise-and-fall narratives is that social change can be both progressive and regressive—power does not invariably beget more power; it may also beget decline.

The most renowned sociologist considered by some to be a cyclical theorist is Max Weber. Although he took an evolutionary view of society as increasingly moving toward a politically and economically legal-rational society governed by rules and regulations, Weber (1919/1946) also emphasized the role of irrational elements in shaping human behavior. For example, although he wrote about the growing formal rationality of the modern world, he also recognized

Rise-and-fall theories of social change: Theories that see social change as characterized by a cycle of growth and decline.

CNP/Hulton Archive/Getty Images

Dr. Martin Luther King Jr. had a transformational dream. His words and deeds inspired and continue to inspire social change. The actions of a single person can be truly significant.

the possibility that a society's path could be altered by the appearance of a charismatic figure whose singular personal authority transcended institutionalized authority structures. Leaders who drastically changed a nation's trajectory include Haile Selassie, who governed Ethiopia for half a century, Adolf Hitler in Germany, Mao Zedong in China, and Fidel Castro in Cuba. In the United States, Martin Luther King Jr. led the civil rights movement in the 1960s and fundamentally changed race relations.

Cyclical theories have not enjoyed great popularity among sociologists. Even Weber's theory is not truly cyclical; his idea of *charismatic authority* is a sort of wild card, providing an unpredictable twist in an otherwise predictable march of social change from one form of authority to another. The more far-reaching versions of cyclical theory, such as Sorokin's theory that society swings among three different worldviews, are framed in such broad terms that it is challenging to prove them right or wrong.

SOURCES OF SOCIAL CHANGE

Social change ultimately results from human action. Sociologists studying how change occurs often analyze the mass action of large numbers of people and the institutionalized behaviors of organizations. In this section we examine social change within the context of mass action by groups of people, focusing on theories of collective behavior and the role played by social movements.

COLLECTIVE BEHAVIOR

Collective behavior is *voluntary, goal-oriented action that occurs in relatively disorganized situations in which society's predominant social norms and values cease to govern individual behavior* (Oberschall, 1973; Turner & Killian, 1987). Although collective behavior is usually associated with disorganized aggregates of people, it may also occur in highly regimented social contexts when order and discipline break down.

Beginning with the writings of the 19th-century French sociologist Gustave Le Bon (1896/1960), the sociological study of collective behavior has been particularly concerned with the behavior of people in **crowds**—that is, *temporary gatherings of closely interacting people with a common focus.* People in crowds were traditionally seen as prone to being swept up in group emotions, losing their ability to make rational decisions as individuals. The "group mind" of the crowd has long been viewed as an irrational and dangerous aspect of modern societies, with crowds believed to consist of rootless, isolated individuals prone to herdlike behavior (Arendt, 1951; Fromm, 1941; Gaskell & Smith, 1981; Kornhauser, 1959).

More recently, however, it has become clear that there can be a fair degree of social organization in crowds. For example, the Occupy Wall Street movement of 2011–2012 and the Arab Spring revolutions, which began in late 2010, although representing spontaneous beginnings, quickly developed a degree of predictability and organization, and in turn became social movements. It is important to note that crowds alone do not constitute social movements, but they are a critical ingredient in most cases. In a social media age, however, sociologists may need to rethink the very notion of "spontaneity," as collective action today is often rooted in activist social media that contributes to informing and organizing collective behavior.

Collective behavior: Voluntary, goal-oriented action that occurs in relatively disorganized situations in which society's predominant social norms and values cease to govern individual behavior.

Crowds: Temporary gatherings of closely interacting people with a common focus.

Sports and Social Change

For many of us, sports play an important role in our lives: From watching the Olympics to rooting for our college teams to playing weekend games with friends, we take pleasure in the competition, the action, and the company. At some pivotal points in U.S. history, sports have also played an important role in driving social change. Consider the 1972 passage of Title IX, a federal law that prohibits discrimination on the basis of sex in any federally funded education program or activity. Title IX is credited with, among other things, opening up unprecedented opportunities for girls and young women to participate in organized sports, because it requires every school receiving federal funding to offer team sports to both male and female athletes and prohibits the denial of equal participation opportunities for women in organized sports. In the year prior to the implementation of Title IX, just a little more than 300,000 girls and women were playing high school and college sports across the United States. By 2012, the figure was well over 3 million ("Before and after Title IX," 2012).

Science Source

Baseball player Jackie Robinson was the first African American to play on a Major League Baseball team. He was recruited by the Brooklyn Dodgers and played for the team for the first time in 1947. In 1997, his uniform number, 42, was retired across major league baseball.

Before Title IX, however, a young athlete with big dreams was an important driver of social change in racial integration in the United States. Some sports sociologists suggest that Jackie Robinson, the first African American player to integrate Major League Baseball, drove the first significant change in Black and White relations in the 20th century. In the words of sociologist Richard Zamoff, "A year before President [Harry] Truman's executive order desegregating the military, seven years before *Brown v. Board of Education,* and more than ten years before most people in America had ever heard about Rosa Parks or Martin Luther King, Jr." (personal communication, 2014), Jackie Robinson and his Brooklyn Dodgers team initiated a sometimes fraught but entirely necessary dialogue in U.S. society about race relations and integration. In the words of Gerald Early (2011), we can divide Black–White relations in the 20th century into two periods: "before Robinson and after Robinson."

Before Robinson's integration of the minor leagues in 1946 and then the Major League in 1947, professional baseball had been segregated for more than half a century. Robinson's debut with the Dodgers was not welcomed in all quarters, and he suffered threats and abuse from fans, the press, and even other players. Notably, Robinson had agreed to the condition imposed by Dodgers general manager Branch Rickey that he not fight back in response to the racist taunts. By the end of the season, Robinson had not only endured the intense challenges of integrating the league but had also won the admiration of scores of fans with his grace under fire and his athletic achievements, which included helping to lead his team to the National League pennant and an appearance in the World Series in his first year with the Dodgers.

Jackie Robinson has been widely recognized for both his individual accomplishments and the contributions he made to the game of baseball and a society still struggling with racism in the middle of the 20th century. Interestingly, 25 years after his initial integration of baseball, he nearly refused to participate in a commemorative event because of his disappointment in the fact that Major League Baseball had yet to appoint a Black team manager. The first Black manager of a Major League Baseball team was hired by the Cleveland Indians in 1975, 3 years after Robinson's death.

Sports has been a driver of social change in the United States and across the globe. The progress it has wrought is, as Robinson saw, incomplete and imperfect but nonetheless of great significance.

THINK IT THROUGH

- What makes sports a potential vehicle for social change rather than "just a game"? Can you think of other instances in which sports or particular athletes have had a powerful social impact?

Sociologists seek to explain the conditions that may lead a group of people to engage in collective behavior, whether violent or peaceful. Below we examine three principal sociological approaches: contagion theories, which emphasize nonsocial factors such as instincts; emergent norm theories, which seek out some kind of underlying social organization that leads a group to generate norms governing collective action; and value-added theories, which combine elements of personal, organizational, and social conditions to explain collective behavior.

CONTAGION THEORIES Contagion theories assume that human beings can revert to herdlike behavior when they come together in large crowds. Herbert Blumer (1951), drawing on symbolic interactionism, emphasized the role of raw imitation, which leads people in crowds to "mill about" much like a group of animals, stimulating and goading one another into movement actions, whether peaceful or violent. Individual acts, therefore, become contagious; they are unconsciously copied until they eventually explode into collective action. A skilled leader can effectively manipulate such behavior, "working the crowd" until it reaches a fever pitch.

Sociologists have used the contagion theory perspective to study the panic flights of crowds, "epidemics" of bizarre collective behaviors such as uncontrollable dancing or fainting, and reports of satanic child abuse. In 1983, a local "panic" erupted in a small California city after a parent of a preschool child accused teachers at her child's school of raping and sodomizing dozens of students. The trial in the case stretched on for years, but no wrongdoing was ever proved and no defendant convicted. Accusations in the case, which drew on allegations from children and parents, included stories about teachers chopping up animals at the school, clubbing to death a horse, and sacrificing a baby. Public accounts of the trial unleashed a national panic about abuse and satanism in child-care facilities, even though there was no serious documentation of such activities (Haberman, 2014). Some sociologists believe that a few well-publicized cases of deviant behavior—including wild accusations like those described above—can trigger imitative behavior until a virtual "epidemic" emerges that then feeds on itself (Goode, 2009).

Baltimore resident Freddie Gray was arrested on April 12, 2015. While in police custody, he sustained serious neck and spine injuries and died a week later. Protests, most peaceful, but some violent, shook the city, as residents expressed their frustration with police actions. ■

How does the contagion actually spread? What are the mechanisms that affect whether people imitate one another's behavior in the interest of grabbing attention or promoting social change? In the case of the Occupy Wall Street movement, we might conclude that as increasing numbers of people realized there was an avenue they could use to protest the political and economic conditions in the United States, they began establishing Occupy camps all over the country. The decline of the movement over time was more gradual. What about student activist movements? Arguably, student protests on a few campuses and, in some instances, success in achieving goals, may encourage groups at other schools to become publicly active. Social media itself may drive a degree of contagion, as it is an ideal vehicle for the rapid dissemination of ideas and information.

Although copycat behavior may build momentum rapidly, an explanation limited to this factor is unlikely to account fully for collective behavior. Furthermore, such explanations are sometimes used to discredit particular instances of collective behavior as resulting from an irrational (and therefore dangerous) tendency of people to jump on the bandwagon. Critics of the Occupy movement often depicted participants as little more than copycats engaging in occupying city space, rather than as members of a movement with serious concerns about the state of contemporary society. In the 1960s, some people dismissed antiwar and civil rights protesters as misled "flower children" rather than recognizing them as people concerned about injustice and war. Sociologists, however, seek ways to determine *why* collective behavior occurs and to understand the rational and organizational basis for its emergence (Chafetz & Dworkin, 1983; Wright, 1993). We look next at what some other theories suggest.

EMERGENT NORM THEORIES Most sociologists prefer to look for norms and values that shape conscious human behavior rather than rely on the idea that instincts govern unconscious processes. Some have suggested that emergent norms offer an explanation for collective behavior. We can define **emergent norms** as *norms that are situationally created to support a collective action.* For example, Ralph H. Turner and Lewis M. Killian (1987) argue that even when crowd behavior appears chaotic and disorganized, norms emerge that explain the crowd's actions. Crowd members take stock of what is going on around them, are mindful of their personal motivations, and, in general, collectively define the situation in which they find themselves. In this respect, crowd behavior is not very different from ordinary behavior; there is no need to fall back on "instincts" or "contagion" to explain it.

The Tea Party political movement in the United States began as a collective protest against "big government." It soon developed a package of emergent norms that morphed into a political movement emphasizing the importance of getting like-minded politicians elected to office, as well as norms that emphasized the importance of adherence to the central ideas of the U.S. Constitution, lower taxes, more limited government, and reduced government spending.

The emergent norm approach offers only a partial explanation of collective behavior. First, all crowds do not develop norms that govern their actions; crowds often emerge out of shared sets of norms among the participants. Second, purely spontaneous emotional outbursts may also occur as people act on their immediate impulses. Furthermore, when norms governing crowd behavior do emerge, they are unlikely by themselves to account fully for collective behavior. When crowds gathered in Baltimore to protest after Freddie Gray, a Black man, died in police custody, they were responding to fear of and frustration with police violence against minorities, but their demonstrations were not just a result of emergent norms, even though some actions were spontaneous. The grievances being expressed were rooted in long-standing disaffection with the treatment of poor minority communities in the city.

VALUE-ADDED THEORY Both contagion and emergent norm theories focus primarily on the micro level of individual action and thought, largely ignoring macro-level factors—poverty, unemployment, governmental abuses of authority, and so on—that may explain the emergence of collective behavior. More than 50 years ago, Neil Smelser (1962) sought to develop what he termed a "value-added" approach to understanding collective behavior. He identified several both micro- and macro-level factors that each contribute something of value to the outcome and that form a foundation for collective behavior. Think about a revolution or social movement discussed in this chapter or that you have learned about elsewhere—can you identify the factors below in that context?

1. *Structural conduciveness* exists when the existing social structure favors the emergence of collective behavior.
2. *Structural strain* occurs when the social system breaks down.
3. *Generalized beliefs* are shared explanations of the conditions that are troubling people. People must define the problem, identify its causes, and—to use C. Wright Mills's phrase—come to see their personal troubles as public issues.
4. *Precipitating factors* are dramatic events that confirm the generalized beliefs of the group, thereby triggering action.
5. *Mobilization for action* occurs when leaders arise who encourage action.
6. *The failure of social control* leaves those charged with maintaining law and order unable to do so in the face of mounting pressures for collective action.

Smelser's approach has been used to analyze collective behavior in a variety of settings, including self-help groups (D. H. Smith & Pillemer, 1983), social welfare organizations (M. J. Smith & Moses, 1980), and nuclear-weapons-freeze activism (Tygart, 1987). The theory's strength is that it combines societal-, organizational-, and individual-level factors into one comprehensive theory. Yet it has also been criticized for emphasizing the part that people's *reactions* play in collective behavior more than the fact that people themselves are conscious agents creating the conditions that can bring about significant social change.

HOW DO CROWDS ACT?

We have all participated in some form of collective behavior in our social lives. Collective behavior comes in a spectrum of different forms, including riots, fads, fashions, panics, crazes, and rumors. We discuss each of these forms of collective behavior below.

RIOTS A **riot** is *an illegal, prolonged outbreak of violent behavior by a large group of people directed against individuals or property.* Riots represent a form of crowd behavior; often they are spontaneous, although sometimes they are

Emergent norms: Norms that are situationally created to support a collective action.

Riot: An illegal, prolonged outbreak of violent behavior by a sizable group of people directed against people or property.

motivated by a conscious set of concerns. Prison and urban riots are common examples. During a riot, conventional norms, including respect for the private property of others, are suspended and replaced with other norms developed within the group. For example, inmates may destroy property to force prison officials to adopt more humane practices, and the theft of property during an urban riot may reflect the participants' desire for a more equitable distribution of resources.

The very use of the term *riot* to characterize a particular action is often highly political. In 1773, a crowd of Bostonians protesting British taxation of the American colonies seized a shipment of tea from a British vessel and dumped it into Boston Harbor. Although the British Crown roundly condemned this action as the illegal act of a rioting mob, U.S. history books celebrate the "Boston Tea Party" as the noble act of inspired patriots and an opening salvo in the Revolutionary War.

FADS AND FASHIONS The desire to join others in being different (itself perhaps something of an irony) continually feeds the rise of new looks and sounds. **Fads**, or *temporary, highly imitated outbreaks of mildly unconventional behavior,* are particularly common responses to popular entertainment such as music, movies, and books and require social networks (electronic or otherwise) to spread (Iribarren & Moro, 2007). The fads of piercing body parts to wear ornaments and extensive body tattooing have captured several generations and seem to be continuing today. Other fads have included wearing blue jeans with holes in the knees, staging "panty raids" on sorority houses, and adopting the "hipster" style popularized by young people united by a common interest in alternative music and Pabst Blue Ribbon beer.

As fads become popular, they sometimes cease being fads and instead become **fashions**, that is, *somewhat long-lasting styles of imitative behavior or appearance.* Georg Simmel (1904/1971) first examined the sociological implications of fashions more than a century ago. He pointed out that fashions reflect a tension between people's desire to be different and their desire to conform. By adopting a fashion, a person initially appears to stand out from the group, yet the fashion itself reflects group norms. As the fashion catches on, more and more people adopt it, and it eventually ceases to express any degree of individuality. Its very success undermines its attractiveness, so the eventual fate of all fashions is to become unfashionable.

Simmel's observations offer another insight into fashions: Unlike fads, they often grow out of the continuous and well-organized efforts of those who work in design, manufacturing technology, marketing, and media to define what is in style. As "grunge" music became popular in the 1990s, it spawned a profitable clothing industry, and highly paid fashion designers created clothing that was grungy in everything but price. Today there are a variety of fashion trends that resonate with different audiences and subcultures. Whether it is the look of skinny or torn jeans, oversize sunglasses or owl-like reading spectacles, or brand-name yoga pants or basketball sneakers, manufacturers and marketers will spend millions of dollars attempting to convince youthful consumers that they must buy particular products to be fashionable and popular.

PANICS AND CRAZES A **panic** is *a massive flight from something feared.* The most celebrated example was created by an infamous radio broadcast on the night before Halloween in 1938: Orson Welles's Mercury Theatre rendition of H. G. Wells's science fiction novel *War of the Worlds.* The broadcast managed to convince thousands that Martians had landed in Grover's Mill, New Jersey, and were wreaking havoc with deadly laser beams. People panicked, flooded the telephone lines with calls, and fled to "safer" ground.

Panics are often ignited by the belief that something is awry in the corporate world or in consumer technology. As the year 2000 approached, panic over the Y2K problem, also known as the "millennium bug," gripped many people who believed reports that computer systems worldwide would crash when the year 2000 began (supposedly computers would be unable to distinguish the year 2000 from 1900, because they used only two digits to designate the year). A recent example of a panic involved the Mayan calendar, which was projected to "end" during our calendar equivalent of December 2012. The fact that the structure of the Mayan calendar and the Mayan system of counting and noting dates did not pass December 2012 led many to believe that the Mayans had predicted the end of the world.

Some panics, like that around Y2K, reflect the fear that, in modern industrial society, we are highly dependent on products and technological processes about which we have little knowledge and over which we have no control.

A **craze** is *an intense attraction to an object, a person, or an activity.* Crazes are like fads but more intense. Body

---

Fads: Temporary, highly imitated outbreaks of mildly unconventional behavior.

Fashions: Styles of imitative behavior or appearance that are of longer duration than fads.

Panic: A massive flight from something that is feared.

Craze: An intense attraction to an object, a person, or an activity.

disfigurement has been a periodic craze, ranging from nose piercing to putting rings through nipples, belly buttons, lips, and tongues. The fact that these practices instill horror in some people probably accounts in part for the attraction they hold for others. In many cultures, body disfigurement is considered a necessary condition of beauty or attractiveness. Although such practices would be regarded as crazes in the West, they are normal enhancements of beauty in other cultures (Brown, Edwards, & Moore, 1988).

RUMORS **Rumors** are *unverified forms of information that are transmitted informally, usually originating in unknown sources.* The classic study on rumors was conducted more than 65 years ago by Gordon W. Allport and Leo Postman (1947). In one version of this research, a White student was asked to study a photograph depicting an urban scene: two men on a subway car, one menacing the other. The student was then asked to describe the picture to a second White student, who in turn was asked to pass the information along to a third, and so on. Eventually, after numerous retellings, the information changed completely to reflect the students' previously held beliefs. For example, as the "rumor" in the study took shape, the person engaging in the menacing act was described as Black and the victim as White—even though in the actual photograph the reverse was true.

Allport and Postman's research revealed several features unique to rumors. The information they contain is continually reorganized according to the belief systems of those who are passing them along. Some information is forgotten, and some is altered to fit into more familiar frameworks, such as racist preconceptions in the example above. Furthermore, the degree of alteration varies according to the nature of the rumor; it is greatest for rumors that trigger strong emotions or that pass through large numbers of people.

For a rumor to have an effect, it must tap into collectively held beliefs, fears, or hopes. For some the rumor that the world will be ending imminently is a hopeful message; for others it is a source of great fear. Rumors often reinforce subcultural beliefs. The rumor that the Central Intelligence Agency and the National Security Agency are planting listening devices in everyone's homes feeds into the belief that the government is out to control us. Political campaigns are infamous for starting and perpetuating rumors: For example, the rumors that President Barack Obama is not a U.S. citizen, is a Muslim, and is trying to create European-style socialism in the United States have been around since he became a prominent political figure running for the presidency in 2008. Despite the fact that an abundance of evidence contradicts these rumors, some groups have embraced them.

Political activism swept the country in the 1960s and 1970s with widespread demonstrations focused on civil rights, women's rights, and the Vietnam War. The dramatic protests and social transformations of this period helped fuel the reformulation of theories on social change.

SOCIAL MOVEMENTS

Theories of collective behavior generally emphasize the passive, reactive side of human behavior. Social movement theory, in contrast, regards human beings as the active makers of their own history—agents who have visions and goals, analyze existing conditions, weigh alternative courses of action, and organize themselves as best they can to achieve success.

Rumors: Unverified forms of information that are transmitted informally, usually originating in unknown sources.

DISCOVER & DEBATE

Social Movements and Social Change

Motion: Online social activism is an effective way to foster social change.

Background

A common form of social activism today is what has been termed "hashtag activism" (Dewey, 2014). This kind of activism can be understood as a movement to spread awareness online about social issues. It is practiced by well-known public figures and organizations, as well as by ordinary individuals. Hashtag activism is prominent on Twitter, but similar online campaigns are spread on social media platforms like Facebook and Instagram.

Affirmative Arguments

- Social media is an effective way to spread information about important social issues, particularly among young people who are very connected to social media and less likely to read a newspaper or listen to television or radio news.
- Social media is a powerful platform for fostering change in countries with media censorship. For example, social media activism led to the #UmbrellaMovement in Hong Kong, a territory of China with a high level of censorship. Although mainstream media did not cover the protests, potential participants learned about protest activities through social media.
- Online activism is effective because it expands the number of people who can participate. For example, online activism is accessible to people with disabilities, as well as to others who cannot participate in in-person activism due to financial, health, or other constraints that limit mobility.

Opposition Arguments

- Online activism makes concerned citizens feel better, but there are more effective ways of fostering change like calling elected representatives, donating money to social causes, or participating in marches.
- Although it is easy to gather support for many issues on social media platforms, there is often a lack of organizational support to follow up on the demands made by online activists.
- Some research (Kristofferson, White, & Peloza, 2014a, 2014b) suggests that participation in symbolic public activism (like joining a Facebook group) may reduce the chance that an issue enthusiast takes further steps to foster social change: "once our need to act has been satisfied, we may not be motivated to do more" (Feldman, 2017: 40).

Questions for Consideration

- How do we measure the effectiveness of an online social issues campaign? How should we define success?
- What is the relationship between online issue activism and in-person activism, like participation in a march?
- Do motivations for online activism differ from those of in-person activism?

Debate Tip

▶ Be aware of your audience, and take care to articulate your argument in way that will be understood by your listeners. Avoid academic jargon and slang words. Use clear, straightforward language.

TABLE 12.1 Principal Types of Social Movements

Type	Principal Aims	Examples
Reformist	To bring about change within the existing economic and political system	• U.S. civil rights movement • Same-sex marriage rights movement • Climate change activism • Labor movements, including the low-wage worker movements • International human rights activism
Revolutionary	To fundamentally change the existing social, political, and/or economic system in light of a detailed alternative vision	• 1776 U.S. Revolutionary War • 1905 and 1917 Russian Revolutions • 1991 South African antiapartheid movement • 2010 Arab Spring
Rebellious	To fundamentally alter the existing political and/or economic system without a detailed alternative vision	• Nat Turner slave rebellion • Urban riots following the assassination of Martin Luther King Jr. • Rebellions against austerity measures in Greece, Spain, and Portugal
Reactionary	To restore an earlier social system—often based on a mythical past	• White supremacist organizations in the United States and Europe • German skinheads • Serbian nationalists
Utopian	To withdraw from society and create a utopian community	• Religious communities such as the Quakers, Mennonites, and Mormons • 1960s communes in the United States
New social movements	To make fundamental changes in values, culture, and private life	• Gay, lesbian, bisexual, and transgender rights movements • Environmental movements

A **social movement** is a large number of people who come together in a continuing and organized effort to bring about (or resist) social change, and who rely at least partially on noninstitutionalized forms of political action. Social movements thus have one foot outside the political establishment, and this is what distinguishes them from other efforts aimed at bringing about social change. Their political activities are not limited to such routine efforts as lobbying or campaigning; they include noninstitutionalized political actions such as boycotts, marches and other demonstrations, and civil disobedience.

Social movements often include some degree of formal organization oriented toward achieving longer-term goals, along with supporting sets of beliefs and opinions, but their strength often derives from their ability to disrupt the status quo by means of spontaneous, relatively unorganized political actions. As part of its support for the civil rights movement in the 1960s, the National Association for the Advancement of Colored People (NAACP) advocated the disruption of normal business activities, such as boycotting buses and restaurants, to force integration. The people who participate in social movements typically are outside the existing set of power relationships in society; such movements provide one of the few forms of political voice available to the relatively powerless (McAdam, McCarthy, & Zald, 1988; Tarrow, 1994). A recent example is the Dreamer movement, which has supported passage of the Dream Act. This immigration reform legislation allows undocumented young people who migrated to the United States with their families when they were children to have access to higher education and, over time, permanent residency or citizenship. An executive order signed by President Obama in 2012 allows the Dreamers to apply for deferred action permits and avoid deportation under certain conditions.

The body of research on social movements in the United States is partially the result of movements that began in the late 1950s and gained attention and support in the 1960s and early 1970s. Theories of collective behavior, with their emphasis on the seemingly irrational actions of

Social movement: A large number of people who come together in a continuing and organized effort to bring about (or resist) social change, and who rely at least partially on noninstitutionalized forms of political action.

AP Photo/Steven Senne

In 2017, large pro-immigrant demonstrations were held in many cities in the U.S. Protesters spoke against the deportation of undocumented migrants and the barring of refugees from some countries. This demonstration took place in Boston. ■

unorganized crowds, were ill equipped to explain the rise of well-organized efforts by hundreds of thousands of people to change government policies toward the Vietnam War and civil rights for African Americans. As these two social movements spawned others, including the second-wave feminist movement, which saw women demanding greater rights and opportunities in the workplace, sociologists had to rethink their basic assumptions and develop new theoretical perspectives. Below we examine different types of social movements, looking especially at sociological theories about why they arise.

TYPES OF SOCIAL MOVEMENTS

Social movements are typically classified according to the direction and degree of change they seek. For purposes of our discussion, we will distinguish five different kinds: reformist, revolutionary, rebellious, reactionary, and utopian (Table 12.1). In fact, these distinctions are not clear-cut, and the categories are not mutually exclusive. Rather, they represent ideal types. In the final section of the chapter, we will also consider some examples of a new sixth category: social movements that aim to change values and beliefs.

REFORMIST MOVEMENTS **Reformist social movements** seek to *bring about social change within the existing economic and political system* and usually address institutions such as the courts and lawmaking bodies and/or public officials. They are most often found in societies where democratic institutions make it possible to achieve social change within the established political processes. Yet even reformist social movements can include factions that advocate more sweeping, revolutionary social changes. Sometimes the government fails to respond, or it responds very slowly, raising frustrations. At other times, the government may actively repress a movement, arresting its leaders, breaking up its demonstrations, and even outlawing its activities.

The American Woman Suffrage Association, formed in 1869 by Susan B. Anthony and Elizabeth Cady Stanton, was a reformist organization that resulted in significant social changes. During the latter part of the 19th century, it became one of the most powerful political forces in the United States, seeking to liberate women from oppression and ensure them the right to vote (Vellacott, 1993), precipitating the first wave of the women's movement. In 1872, Victoria Woodhull helped to organize the Equal Rights Party, which nominated her for the U.S. presidency (even though, by law, no woman could vote for her); she campaigned on the issues of voting rights for women, the right of women to earn and control their own money, and free love (Underhill, 1995). After a half century of struggle by numerous social movement activists, women finally won the right to vote with the ratification of the Nineteenth Amendment to the U.S. Constitution in 1920.

The civil rights movement of the late 1950s and the 1960s called for social changes that would enforce the constitutionally mandated civil rights of African Americans; it often included nonviolent civil disobedience directed at breaking unjust laws. The ultimate aim of the civil rights movement was to change those laws, rather than to change society as a whole. Thus, for example, when Rosa Parks violated the laws of Montgomery, Alabama, by refusing to give up her seat on a city bus to a White person, she was challenging the city ordinance, but not the government itself.

Much early civil rights activism was oriented toward registering southern Blacks to vote, so that by exercising their legal franchise, they could achieve a measure of political power. Within the civil rights movement, however, there were activists who concluded that the rights of Black Americans would never be achieved through reformist activities alone. Like many social movements, the civil rights movement was marked by internal struggles and debates regarding the degree to which purely reformist activities were adequate to the movement's objectives (Branch, 1988). The Black Panther Party, for example, argued for far more radical changes in U.S. society, advocating "Black power" instead of merely fighting for an end to racial segregation. The Black Panthers

Reformist social movements: Movements seeking to bring about social change within the existing economic and political system.

BEHIND THE NUMBERS

There Were Millions . . . Or Not

How many demonstrators attended a protest action on a given day in a particular place? This can be a surprisingly contentious issue. For example, how many people attended the Million Man March, a massive 1995 grassroots gathering intended to highlight issues of concern to Black men and their families and communities? As Ira Flatow noted on the National Public Radio (2010) program *Science Friday*, "It depends on whom you ask. According to the U.S. Park Police, about 400,000. But the organizers of the march took issue with that number and asked for a recount. And using different images . . . a crowd counting expert at Boston University estimated the crowd to be closer to 800,000—almost twice the number that the Park Service had."

Once you become familiar with the importance of research methods, you find that the *method* of obtaining information can be at least as important as the information itself. When a statistic, fact, or figure is produced, it is always important to consider the process behind its production. We often hear media accounts that report numbers of demonstrators in given units of space or time (for instance, there were 200 protesters in front of the mayor's office in New York City, or 20,000 demonstrators on the streets of Baltimore). Where do these numbers come from? Who is keeping count?

In taking a critical look behind the numbers in the U.S. case, we find that the National Park Service does not conduct official head counts of the demonstrators in public spaces like the National Mall in Washington, DC, which has long been a popular venue for large gatherings. Journalists often rely on best-guess estimates for crowds. Satellite pictures have been common sources of information on crowds, even though each such photo captures just a few moments in time (National Public Radio, 2010).

Technology is bringing us closer to being able to get an accurate count of participants in a collective action. Whereas it may, until recently, have taken days to ascertain even a good estimate of a crowd, researchers at the University of Central Florida have introduced the world's first mass crowd-counting program. In September 2015, the software was used to count the number of demonstrators in Barcelona calling for the independence of the region of Catalonia. The computer program scanned 67 aerial images of the demonstrators, whose protest action stretched for 3.2 miles. The data, which was ready in just 30 minutes, led researchers to conclude that just over half a million people were in attendance, a figure significantly below that offered by the protest organizers (Science Daily, 2015).

Social media is also enabling new means of counting marchers through "crowdsourcing." The Women's March took place on January 21, 2017, in cities across the U.S. and the globe. How many people marched? The Washington, DC, march, together with marches in other U.S. cities, may have gathered from 3 to 4 million people, figures assembled in part through a Google spreadsheet tweeted by a political science professor. The public was invited to share information and sources to the spreadsheet: According to an account of the effort, "The spreadsheet currently has entries for nearly 550 cities and towns in the U.S., from the march in D.C. (470,000 to 680,000 participants) to a protest in Show Low, Arizona (one participant). The spreadsheet also tallies attendance at rallies in more than 100 cities around the world" (Waddell, 2017).

Clearly, counting participants is an important and improving process, but still an inexact science.

THINK IT THROUGH

- Why are counts of participants at public demonstrations and events potentially controversial and contested? What makes them significant?

often engaged in reformist activities, such as establishing community centers and calling for the establishment and support of more Black-owned businesses. At the same time, they also engaged in revolutionary activities, such as arming themselves against what they viewed to be a hostile police presence within Black neighborhoods.

The experience of U.S. labor unions, another example of a reformist social movement, shows the limits of the reformist approach to social change. Organized labor's principal demands have been for fewer hours, higher wages and benefits, job security, and safer working conditions. (In Europe, similar demands have been made, although workers there have sought political power as well.) Labor unions within the United States seldom appeal to a broad constituency beyond the workers themselves, and as a result, their success has depended largely on workers' economic power. U.S. workers have lost much of that power since the early 1970s, as economic globalization has meant the loss of many jobs to low-wage areas. Threats of strikes are no longer quite as menacing, as corporations can close factories down and reopen them elsewhere in the world.

Anadolu Agency/Contributor/Getty Images

On March 26, 2017, thousands of protesters in St. Petersburg, Russia, demonstrated against government corruption. Similar protests took place in about 100 cities. In Russia, activists risk detention and prosecution for challenging state power.

REVOLUTIONARY MOVEMENTS **Revolutionary social movements** seek to *fundamentally alter the existing social, political, and economic system in keeping with a vision of a new social order.* They frequently result from the belief that reformist approaches are unlikely to succeed because the political or economic system is too resistant. In fact, whether a social movement becomes predominantly reformist or revolutionary may well hinge on the degree to which its objectives can be achieved within the system.

Revolutionary movements call for basic changes in economics, politics, norms, and values, offering a blueprint for a new social order that can be achieved only through mass action, usually by fostering conflict between those who favor change and those who favor the status quo. They are directed at clearly identifiable targets, such as a system of government believed to be unjust or an economy believed to be based on exploitation. Yet even the most revolutionary of social movements is likely to have reformist elements, members or factions who believe some change is possible within the established institutions. In most social movements, members debate the relative importance of reformist and revolutionary activities. Although the rhetoric may favor revolution, most day-to-day activities are likely to support reform. Only when a social movement is suppressed and avenues to reform are closed off will its methods call for outright revolution.

Revolutionary social movements sometimes, although by no means always, include violence. In South Africa, for example, the movements that were most successful in bringing about an end to apartheid were largely nonviolent. Those that defeated socialism in the former Soviet Union and Eastern Europe did so with a minimal amount of bloodshed. Nevertheless, revolutionary movements associated with the Arab Spring, which began in 2010 in countries like Egypt, Tunisia, and Libya, resulted in considerable violence, most often perpetrated against the protesters by those already in power or their allies. It is unclear, however, whether the Arab Spring movements were truly revolutionary; most new governments are not radically more democratic than their predecessors. It takes time for political and economic conditions to change within any given country, however, and although some dictators have been removed from power, it remains to be seen whether these changes in political office will result in the changes desired by constituents.

REBELLIONS **Rebellions** seek to *overthrow the existing social, political, and economic systems but lack detailed plans for a new social order.* They are particularly common in societies where effective mobilization against existing structures is difficult or impossible because of the structures' repressive nature. The histories of European feudalism and U.S. slavery are punctuated by examples of rebellions.

Revolutionary social movements: Movements seeking to fundamentally alter the existing social, political, and economic system in keeping with a vision of a new social order.

Rebellions: Movements seeking to overthrow the existing social, political, and economic systems but lacking detailed plans for a new social order.

Nat Turner, a Black American slave, led other slaves in an 1831 uprising against their White owners in the state of Virginia. Before the uprising was suppressed, 55 Whites were killed, and subsequently Turner and 16 of his followers were hanged (Greenberg, 2003).

After the Civil War, the Ku Klux Klan instituted vigilante justice and lynched over 4,000 African Americans for alleged crimes, including looking "the wrong way" at a White woman. White supremacist groups exemplify a resistance or countermovement that rejects racial integration and expansion of civil rights.

REACTIONARY MOVEMENTS **Reactionary social movements** seek to restore an earlier social system—often based on a mythical past—along with the traditional norms and values that once presumably accompanied it. These movements are termed reactionary because they arise in reaction to recent social changes that threaten or have replaced the old order. They are also sometimes referred to as countermovements or resistance movements for the same reason.

For these groups, a mythical past is often the starting point for pursuing goals aimed at transforming the present. The Ku Klux Klan, the White Aryan Resistance, and other White supremacist organizations have long sought to return to a United States where Whites held exclusive political and economic power. Their methods have ranged from spreading discredited social and biological theories that expound the superiority of the "White race" to acts of violence against Black Americans, Asians, Latinos, Jews, gays and lesbians, and others deemed to be inferior or otherwise a threat to the "American way of life" (Gerhardt, 1989; Moore, 1991).

Whether a social movement is viewed as reactionary or revolutionary depends to some extent on the observer's perspective. In Iran, for example, a social movement led by the Ayatollah Khomeini overthrew the nation's pro-U.S. leader in 1979 and created an Islamic republic that quickly reestablished traditional Muslim laws. In the pronouncements of U.S. policy makers and the mass media, the new Iranian regime was reactionary: It required women to be veiled, turned its back on democratic institutions, and levied death sentences on those who violated key Islamic values or otherwise threatened the Islamic state. Yet from the point of view of the clerics who led the upheaval, the movement overthrew a corrupt and brutal dictator who had enriched his family at the expense of the Iranian people and had fostered an alien way of life offensive to traditional Iranian values. From this standpoint, the movement claimed to be revolutionary, promising to provide a better life for Iranians.

As globalization threatens traditional ways of life around the world, we might expect to see an increase in reactionary social movements. This is especially likely to be the case if threats to long-standing traditional values are accompanied by declines in standards of living. In Germany, for example, a decline in living standards for many working-class people has spawned a small but significant resurgence of Nazi ideology, and racial supremacist groups blame foreign immigrants for their economic woes. The result has been a vocal campaign by skinhead groups against immigrants, particularly in the states that made up the former East Germany, which have seen greater economic upheavals than other parts of the country.

UTOPIAN MOVEMENTS **Utopian social movements** seek to *withdraw from the dominant society by creating their own ideal communities.* The youth movements of the 1960s had a strong utopian impulse; many young (and a few older) people "dropped out" and formed their own communities, starting alternative newspapers, health clinics, and

Reactionary social movements: Movements seeking to restore an earlier social system—often based on a mythical past—along with the traditional norms and values that once presumably accompanied it.

Utopian social movements: Movements seeking to withdraw from the dominant society by creating their own ideal communities.

schools and in general seeking to live according to their own value systems outside the established social institutions. Some sought to live communally as well, pooling their resources and sharing tasks and responsibilities. They saw these efforts to create "intentional" communities, based on cooperation rather than competition, as the seeds of a revolutionary new society.

Although religious utopian movements have proved to be somewhat enduring, those based on social philosophy have not. Some "utopian socialist" communities were founded in the United States during the 19th century; some provided models for the socialist collectives of the 1960s. Few lasted for any length of time. The old ways of thinking and acting proved remarkably tenacious, and the presence of the larger society—which remained basically unchanged by the experimentation—was a constant temptation. "Alternative" institutions such as communally run newspapers and health clinics found they had to contend with well-funded mainstream competitors. Most folded or reverted to mainstream forms (Fairfield, 1972; Nordhoff, 1875/1975; Rothschild & Whitt, 1987).

WHY DO SOCIAL MOVEMENTS ARISE?

Although social movements have existed throughout history, modern society has created conditions in which they thrive and multiply. The rise of the modern democratic nation-state, along with the development of capitalism, has fueled their growth. Democratic forms of governance, which emphasize social equality and the right of political participation, legitimate the belief that people should organize themselves politically to achieve their goals. Democratic nation-states give rise to social movements—and often protect them as well. Capitalism, which raises universal economic expectations while producing some inequality, further spurs the formation of such movements.

Given these general historical circumstances, sociologists have advanced several theories to explain why people sometimes come together to create or resist social change. Some focus on the micro level, looking at the characteristics and motivations of the people who join social movements. Some focus on the organizational level, looking at the characteristics that result in successful social movement organizations. Some focus on the macro level, examining the societal conditions that give rise to social movements. More recently, theories have emphasized cultural dimensions of social movements, stressing the extent to which social movements reflect—as well as shape—larger cultural understandings. An ideal theory would bridge all these levels, and some efforts have been made to develop one.

MICRO-LEVEL APPROACHES Much research has focused on what motivates individuals to become active members of social movements. Psychological factors turn out to be poor predictors. Neither personality nor personal alienation adequately accounts for activist leanings. Rather, participation seems motivated more by psychological identification with others who are similarly afflicted (Marwell & Oliver, 1993; McAdam, 1982).

Sociology generally explains activism in such terms as having had prior contact with movement members, belonging to social networks that support movement activity, and having a history of activism (McAdam, 1986; Snow, Zurcher, & Ekland-Olson, 1980). Coming from a family background of social activism may also be important. One study, for example, found that many White male activists during the early 1960s social movements had parents who themselves had been activists 30 years earlier (Flacks, 1971). A lack of personal constraints may also be a partial explanation; it is obviously easier for individuals to engage in political activity if work or family circumstances afford them the necessary time and resources (McCarthy & Zald, 1973). Finally, a sense of moral rightness may provide a powerful motivation to become active, even when the work is difficult and the monetary rewards are small or nonexistent (Jenkins, 1983).

Social movements always suffer from the **free rider problem**, however—that is, *many people avoid the costs of social movement activism* (such as time, energy, and other personal resources) *and still benefit from its success* (Marwell & Oliver, 1993). Why not let others join the social movement and do the hard work, since if the movement succeeds everyone will benefit, regardless of degree of participation? Clearly it takes a great deal of motivation and commitment, as well as a conviction that their efforts may make a difference, for people to devote their time to mailing leaflets or organizing marches; building such motivation and commitment is a major challenge faced by all social movements.

ORGANIZATIONAL-LEVEL APPROACHES Some recent research has been devoted to understanding how social movements are consciously and deliberately organized to create

Free rider problem: The problem that many people avoid the costs of social movement activism (such as time, energy, and other personal resources) and still benefit from its success.

social change. This research focuses on **social movement organizations (SMOs)**, *formal organizations that seek to achieve social change through noninstitutionalized forms of political action.* The study of SMOs represents a major sociological step away from regarding social change as resulting from unorganized individuals and crowds. Instead, it places the study of social change within the framework of the sociology of organizations.

Because social movement organizations constitute a type of formal organization, sociologists use the same concepts and tools to study civil rights organizations and revolutionary groups as they do to study business firms and government bureaucracies. Researchers conceptualize SMOs' actions as rational, their goals as more or less clearly defined, and their organizational structures as bureaucratically oriented toward specific measurable goals (Jenkins, 1983; McCarthy & Zald, 1977).

Social movement organizations range from informal volunteer groups to professional organizations with full-time leadership and staff. A single social movement may sustain numerous such organizations: A partial list associated with the 1960s civil rights movement includes the NAACP, the Student Nonviolent Coordinating Committee (SNCC), the Congress of Racial Equality (CORE), the Southern Christian Leadership Conference (SCLC), Students for a Democratic Society (SDS), and the Black Panther Party. As social movements grow, so too do the number of SMOs associated with them, each vying for members, financial support, and media attention.

One influential approach to the study of social movement organizations is **resource mobilization theory**, a theory that focuses on the ability of social movement organizations to generate money, membership, and political support to achieve their objectives. This approach argues that since discontent and social strain are always present among some members of any society, these factors cannot explain the rise or the relative success of social movements. Rather, what matters are differences in the resources available to different groups and how effectively they use them. The task for sociologists, then, is to explain why some SMOs are better able to deploy scarce resources than others (Jenkins, 1983; McAdam, 1988). Among the most important resources are tangible assets such as money, facilities, and means of communication, as well as such intangibles such as a central core of dedicated, skilled, hardworking members (Jenkins, 1983).

Much like businesses, then, social movement organizations rise or fall on their ability to be competitive in a resource-scarce environment. Some scholars have even written of "social movement industries," with competing organizations engaging in "social marketing" to promote their particular "brands" of social change (Jenkins, 1983; Zald & McCarthy, 1980).

Governmental policies are important determinants of the success or failure of social movement organizations. The government may repress an organization, driving it underground so that it has difficulty in operating. Or the government may favor more moderate organizations (for example, Martin Luther King Jr.'s Southern Christian Leadership Conference) over other, more radical ones (such as the Black Panther Party). Other ways in which the government affects SMOs are through regulating them, providing favorable tax treatment for those that qualify, and refraining from excessive surveillance or harassment (McAdam et al., 1988).

The success or failure of social movement organizations also depends on their ability to influence the mass media. During the 1960s, the anti–Vietnam War organizations became very effective in commanding the television spotlight, although this effectiveness proved a mixed blessing: Media coverage frequently sensationalized demonstrations rather than presenting the underlying issues, thus contributing to rivalries and tensions within the antiwar movement (Gitlin, 1980). Today, arguably, social media exercise even greater influence on movement success.

Although some scholars have argued that larger, more bureaucratic social movement organizations are likely to be successful in the long run (Gamson, 1975), others have claimed that mass defiance, rather than formal organization, is the key to success (Piven & Cloward, 1977). Paradoxically, too much success may undermine social movements, since their strength derives partly from their being outside society's power structures as they make highly visible demands for social change. Once a group's demands are met, the participants are often drawn inside the very power structures they once sought to change. Movement leaders become bureaucrats, their fights are conducted by lawyers and government officials, and rank-and-file members disappear; the militant thrust of the organization is then blunted (Piven & Cloward, 1977).

Social movement organizations (SMOs): Formal organizations that seek to achieve social change through noninstitutionalized forms of political action.

Resource mobilization theory: A theory about social movement organizations that focuses on their ability to generate money, membership, and political support to achieve their objectives.

A related problem is goal displacement, which occurs when a social movement organization's original goals become redirected toward enhancing the organization and its leadership (McCarthy & Zald, 1973). The U.S. labor movement is an example: Once labor unions became successful, many of them became large and prosperous bureaucracies that were perceived as distanced from the needs of their rank-and-file members.

In the end, social movement organizations have to motivate people to support their causes, often with dollars as well as votes. Many groups engage in **grassroots organizing**, *attempts to mobilize support among the ordinary members of a community*. This organizing may range from door-to-door canvassing to leafleting to get people to attend massive demonstrations. Most social movements emerge from a group that has some grievance, and their active members consist largely of people who will directly benefit from any social change that occurs.

Some social movement organizations also depend on **conscience constituents**, people who provide resources for a social movement organization but who are not themselves members of the aggrieved group that the organization champions (McCarthy & Zald, 1973). Such supporters are motivated by strong ethical convictions rather than by direct self-interest in achieving the social movement's goals. The National Coalition for the Homeless, for example, consists primarily of public interest lawyers, shelter operators, and others who advocate on behalf of homeless people; only a relatively small number of homeless people are directly involved in the organization. Homeless advocacy groups raise money from numerous sources, including media celebrities and direct mailings to ordinary citizens (Blau, 1992).

MACRO-LEVEL APPROACHES Regardless of the efforts particular social movement organizations make, large-scale economic, political, and cultural conditions ultimately determine a movement's success or failure. For a social movement to arise and succeed, conditions must be such that people feel it is necessary and are willing to support it. Therefore, social movements emerge and flourish in times of other social change, particularly if people experience that change as disruptive of their daily lives (McAdam et al., 1988; Tilly, 1978). For example, the labor movement arose with the emergence of industrial capitalism, which brought harsh conditions to the lives of many people, and the women's movement reemerged in the 1960s, when expanded educational opportunities for women left many female college graduates feeling marginalized and alienated as full-time homemakers and workplace discrimination threw obstacles in the way of their workplace aspirations.

Some political systems encourage social movements, while others repress them (Gale, 1986). When a government is in crisis, it may respond by becoming more repressive, or it may create a space for social movements to flourish. The former action occurred in China in 1989, when thousands of students and workers, frustrated by deteriorating economic conditions and rigid government controls, took to the streets to demand greater economic and political freedom. The brutal crackdown at Beijing's Tiananmen Square, televised live to a global audience, ended the nascent social movement for democracy. Likewise, government crackdowns on demonstrators and social movement participants have been widespread throughout the Middle East and North Africa as the Arab Spring movements have progressed—Syria's protest movement has, as of this writing, deteriorated into a civil war between the authoritarian government and those who seek its replacement.

Just as economic and political collapse may facilitate the rise of social movements, so too may prosperity. Resources for social activism are more abundant, mass media and other means of communication are more likely to be readily available, and activists are more likely to have independent means of supporting themselves. Prosperous societies are also more likely to have large classes of well-educated people, a group that has historically provided the leadership in many social movements (McAdam et al., 1988; McCarthy & Zald, 1973; Zald & McCarthy, 1980).

Finally, even the spatial organization of society may have an impact on social movements. Dense, concentrated neighborhoods or workplaces facilitate social interaction and spur the growth of social movements. A century and a half ago, Karl Marx recognized that cities and factories were powerful breeding grounds for revolutionary insurgency against capitalism, since they brought previously isolated workers together in single locations. Subsequent

Grassroots organizing: Attempts to mobilize support among the ordinary members of a community.

Conscience constituents: People who provide resources for a social movement organization but who are not themselves members of the aggrieved group that the organization champions.

AP Photo/Jeff Widener

This iconic image shows one man standing in opposition to four tanks in Tiananmen Square, China, on June 5, 1989. Thousands of pro-democracy demonstrators sought political and economic changes in a weeks-long occupation of the square. Many were injured or killed in a government crackdown.

research has sustained his conclusion (Marx & Engels, 1848/1998; Tilly, 1975). The concentration of students on college campuses contributed to the rise of student activism in the 1960s (Lofland, 1985). As we saw in our opening story, it may be having a comparable effect on activism today.

CULTURAL-LEVEL STUDIES AND "FRAME ALIGNMENT" Much of the research we have discussed emphasizes the political, economic, and organizational conditions that either help or hinder the rise of social movements. Sociologists have often regarded social movements as by-products of favorable social circumstances rather than as the active accomplishments of their members. Today, however, instead of stressing how important it is for conditions to be ripe for social movements to thrive, many sociologists are thinking about how social movement organizations themselves are continually interpreting events so as to align themselves better with the cultural understanding of the wider society. The Tea Party movement is a good example. Although it has a long list of political goals it wants to achieve, it has succeeded in rallying people around the idea that "big government" and taxation are a threat to freedom and liberty. These are ideas that resonate with those who have some suspicion of intrusive government. The movement seeks to create a "good fit" between itself and the people who are its likely constituents.

Sociologists think of that fit in terms of **frame alignment**, the process by which the interests, understandings, and values of a social movement organization are shaped to match those in the wider society. If their members' understandings align with the understandings of others in a community or society, social movements are likely to be successful; otherwise they are likely to fail. Social movement organizations achieve frame alignment in a variety of ways, ranging from modifying the beliefs of members to attempting to change the beliefs of the entire society (Snow, Rochford, Worden, & Benford, 1986).

In one common situation, people already share the social movement's concerns and understandings but lack the means to bring about the desired changes. In this case, there is no need for the social movement organization to get people to change their thinking about the problem; rather, the task is to get people to support the movement's efforts to do something about it. The SMO must "get the word out," whether through informal networks, social media, or direct-mail campaigns.

Sometimes the social movement's concerns are only weakly shared by others. In this case, the challenge for the social movement organization is to get people engaged and concerned enough to take action, perhaps by amplifying their concern that something they strongly believe in requires political action. The environmental movement is a case in point. Many scientists and a large number of other people are convinced that the earth is warming at a rapid rate due to the emission of industrial gases into the atmosphere. The movement has grown rapidly, but it has also produced a large number of skeptics, including politicians, who deny that climate change is taking place. Groups such as the Sierra Club and Greenpeace and the owners of retail chains such as Patagonia and REI actively provide information on climate change to the public in the hope of spurring individuals to action.

Frame alignment: The process by which the interests, understandings, and values of a social movement organization are rendered congruent with those of the wider society.

Although environmental activism has a long history in the United States, in recent years it has been reignited and challenged in a debate over climate change. Scientists, academics, and activists are concerned by scientific evidence that global warming is being accelerated by human activity and presents a threat to ecosystems, countries, and communities. On Earth Day 2017, marchers in cities around the world sought to draw attention to the threat. ■

Finally, a social movement organization may seek to build support by attempting to change the way people think entirely. Revolutionary SMOs, for example, urge people to stop thinking of themselves as victims of bad luck, focusing attention instead on the faults of the political or economic system, which presumably requires a drastic overhaul.

To sum up, social movement organizations are competing for the hearts and minds of their constituents, with whom they must somehow bring their own beliefs and analyses into alignment if they are to succeed.

MICROMOBILIZATION CONTEXTS FOR BUILDING SOCIAL MOVEMENTS

Some conditions are ideal for social movement organizations to spring up. Sociologists call these *micromobilization contexts,* small-group settings in which people are able to generate a shared set of beliefs to explain some social problem, along with the necessary social organization to do something about it (McAdam et al., 1988). Both formal and informal social networks usually exist in these settings, making it easier for members to understand why a micro-level problem, such as a personal experience of racism, is in fact the result of macro-level social forces, such as institutional racism. The civil rights movement, for example, emerged at a time when the Black community was developing strong local organizations, including schools, churches, and political groups. These highly interconnected institutions provided fertile ground for the seeds of social activism (McAdam, 1982). Other examples are unions, student support groups, and even friendship networks, which are more elaborate in the age of Facebook, Twitter, and other social media (Bekkers, Edwards, & Moody, 2010).

Micromobilization contexts also create the basic organizational framework required to address a problem—including leadership, mass media, and other communications technologies—as well as specific roles for movement activists and motivation to get involved. These incentives range from the emotional rewards that come from belonging to a group dedicated to a common cause to paid salaries. Micromobilization contexts thus serve as the bridge that connects the personal concerns of individuals to collectives hoping to create large-scale social change (Abrahams, 1992; Scott, 1990).

Finally, micromobilization contexts provide the starting point for cycles of protest that begin in one place and then spread—to new locations as well as to new social movements (Tarrow, 1983). Members of social movement organizations learn from one another and copy one another's techniques, acquiring large repertoires of protest activities in the process (Bekkers et al., 2010; Tilly, 1978).

NEW SOCIAL MOVEMENTS

Social movements have often served as a means to an end: People come together to achieve specific objectives, such as improving the conditions of workers, gaining equality for the disadvantaged, or protesting a war. In the past, participation in such social movements was often separate from members' personal lives. Since the 1960s, however, many social movements have sought to break the boundary between politics and personal life. In addition to being a means for changing the world, the social movement organization has come to be seen as a vehicle for personal change and growth (Giugni & Passy, 1998).

In a sense, this progression reflects the *sociological imagination,* which calls for us to understand the relationship between our personal experiences and larger social forces. Social movements that have embraced this perspective have been labeled **new social movements**. Although they often address political and economic issues, they *are fundamentally concerned with the quality of private life, often advocating large-scale changes in the way people think and act.*

New social movements may be formally organized, with clearly defined roles (leadership, recruiting, and so on), or they may be informal and loosely organized, preferring spontaneous and confrontational methods to more bureaucratic approaches. Part of the purpose of new social movements in protesting, in fact, is not to force a distinction between "them" and "us" but to draw attention to the movement's own right to exist as equals with other groups in society (Gamson, 1991; Omvedt, 1992; Tucker, 1991).

The new social movements aim to improve life in a wide range of areas subject to governmental, business, or other large-scale institutional control, from the workplace to sexuality, health, education, and interpersonal relationships. Four characteristics set these movements apart from earlier ones (Melucci, 1989):

1. The new social movements focus not just on the distribution of material goods but also on the control of symbols and information—an appropriate goal for an "information society" in which the production and ownership of knowledge are increasingly valuable.
2. People join new social movement organizations not purely to achieve specific goals but also because they value participation for its own sake. For instance, LGBT (lesbian, gay, bisexual, and transgender) movements have provided safe havens for members in addition to pursuing social change.
3. Rather than large, bureaucratically run, top-down organizations, the new social movements are often networks of people engaged in routine daily activities. For example, a small online movement was begun by a woman who objected to an unannounced $5 charge on her credit card bill; her protest was joined by thousands of others, and the bank rescinded the charge. Groups trying to raise awareness of climate change and threats to the environment often are loosely organized and register their concerns online and through other media such as newspapers and television talk shows.
4. The new social movements strongly emphasize the interconnectedness of planetary life and may see their actions as tied to a vision of the planet as a whole, rather than centering on narrow self-interest. "Think globally, act locally" is the watchword and includes but is not limited to an awareness of environmental issues.

WHY STUDY SOCIAL CHANGE?

Human beings make their own history, but they do not make it out of thin air. Every generation inherits certain *constraints,* characteristics of the society that limit their vision and their choices, and *resources,* characteristics of the society that they can mobilize in new and creative ways. People are constrained by existing institutions and social relationships. Social structures provide the resources for human action, even as the actions themselves are oriented toward changing those structures (Giddens, 1985).

The sociologically significant processes of globalization and technological change provide both resources and constraints for people everywhere. Social movements themselves may become increasingly internationalized (Marx & McAdam, 1994). Economic globalization, like most social processes, has both positive and negative effects. On one hand, it opens up the possibility of a vast increase in global productive capacity, technological advances, global cooperation, and an increase in the standard of living for people around the world. On the other hand, globalization may also lead to lowered wages and to job losses in high-wage industrial countries, as well as to exploitative labor conditions in the low-wage countries of the world. Concerns about such problems have given rise to labor and environmental groups that operate across national borders (Barry & Sims, 1994).

We live at a moment in history that contains enormous possibilities as well as daunting problems. Without an understanding of these social forces, we will be unable to act intelligently to bring about the kind of world we most desire. Your understanding of the forces shaping social change today will enable you and tomorrow's citizens to act more effectively to shape your social world.

New social movements: Movements that have arisen since the 1960s and are fundamentally concerned with the quality of private life, often advocating large-scale cultural changes in how people think and act.

SOCIAL LIFE, SOCIAL MEDIA

Technology, Dystopia, and Social Change

As this and other chapters have shown, social activism has fostered social change across time and place. Fearless protest of injustice, fierce resistance to tyranny, and sustained challenges to oppression and inequality have often borne fruit. But what if technology—specifically, the enticing entertainment and interaction offered by technology like smartphones, computers, and virtual reality devices—is wearing down our will to engage with social and political issues and to pursue social change?

In George Orwell's classic dystopian novel, *1984*, published in 1949, the author describes a future in which people are controlled by an authoritarian state that Orwell calls "Big Brother." Big Brother uses propaganda to mislead and frighten, as well as devices like telescreens to distract citizens into submission. In a memorable line from *1984*, a character who works for the government dismisses the prospects for resistance to tyranny, stating that, "The people will not revolt. They will not look up from their screens long enough to notice what's happening" (Orwell, 1949/1961). Notably, scientific studies today point to a growing epidemic of technological dependency, even addiction. A *Newsweek* article on the issue notes, "In less than the span of a single childhood, Americans have merged with their machines, staring at a screen for at least eight hours a day, more time than we spend on any other activity including sleeping" (Dokoupil, 2012a, para. 9).

Significantly, people around the world appear to be spending increasing amounts of time pursuing entertainment. For instance, according to a 2015 Common Sense Media report, teens spend an average of 9 hours per day engaged in using media for enjoyment (Wallace, 2015). Author Jane McGonigal (2011) writes that worldwide at least half a billion people are playing computer games for at least an hour a day. Remarkably, she suggests that the average young person has spent as much as 10,000 hours of his or her life "gaming" by the age of 21. About 5 million players in the United States spend 40 hours per week or more engaged in games, a time commitment equivalent to a full-time job, even though McGonigal takes a largely positive rather than critical perspective on the global gaming rage.

Well before the advent of the Internet and the ever-growing spectrum of entertainment options it brings us, another author of dystopian fiction, Aldous Huxley, penned *Brave New World* (1932/2006), a novel that describes a future in which "soma," a fictitious drug of pleasure, pacifies the masses and hedonistic pleasures are a driving societal motivation. In his "negative utopia," political oppression and a stark social hierarchy are sustained by distraction and disinterest, as citizens trade freedom for amusement. As Huxley writes in Chapter 12, "most men and women will grow up to love their servitude and will never dream of revolution."

Modern technology is a paradox: It can inform and engage, and it can provide pleasures that pacify and distract. Did writers like Orwell and Huxley, writing in the middle of the 20th century, correctly foretell a dire future of domination through technology, or did they misunderstand the emancipatory potential of modern innovations? What do you think?

THINK IT THROUGH

- What might Orwell and Huxley say about today's technologies? How would you characterize their effects on social activism?

Follow us on Twitter to keep up with current sociological stories and research! We're at @Discoversoc1.

WHAT CAN I DO WITH A SOCIOLOGY DEGREE?

Understanding and Fostering Social Change

Social change comes about as a result of shifts in the social order of society. Although changes may be evolutionary or revolutionary in pace, change is inevitable. *Understanding social change* and the factors that underlie its dynamics is key to bringing about positive change, whether at the micro or the macro level. Sociologists study factors that bring about large-scale social change—for instance, shifts in population growth or health, technological innovations, economic and labor market changes, the mobilization of civil society, or the rise of a charismatic leader—and seek to understand barriers to normative or structural change. They are also interested in factors that affect change or resistance to change in smaller groups and communities. Skills in the areas of leadership, communications, strategic thinking, motivation and mobilization, and advocacy can evolve from knowledge gained in the study of social change. Students interested in social change may also take advantage of internships or practicums in community or political organizations involved in fostering positive change. Supervised practice and the opportunity for reflection on your work nurture skills in the area of social change.

Careers in social change may focus on specific areas, including the environment, labor, human rights, free speech, legal reform, social justice, conflict resolution, poverty, health care, gender equity, economic justice, and corporate ethics. They may be careers in public service (such as in federal, state, or local government) or in the private sector (with advocacy organizations or in research-focused organizations, for instance). An understanding of social change and the development of skills associated with fostering positive social change are important in a wide variety of occupational fields.

Holly Millet, Social Media Coordinator at Capstrat

James Madison University, BA in Sociology, minors in Women's and Gender Studies and Communication Studies

In my last year of college, I faced the classic question, "What do you hope to do with your life?" countless times. My response had always been, "I hope to change the world." While ambitious, this goal was very much true, and it was the defining factor of my career search. In college, learning about the social issues that we face in society was enlightening, frustrating, and most of all, motivating. As I considered career options, one thing was for certain: I knew that my choice must allow me to make a positive difference. In many of my courses, I studied the impact that the media has on our culture. From our norms to our gender roles to our beauty standards, the media greatly influences our daily life. A career in this field would allow me to become an agent of change.

This career is a nontraditional one, and it is empowering. I write social media posts and website content for clients big and small. I make sure that the content is inclusive and fair. For example, I recently worked with a group of coworkers to create an online survey for a client. The first question was "What is your gender?" The options were "Male" or "Female." After some explanation, I convinced the group that "Male" or "Female" are not the only answers that should be included. When we added an open space for users to write in their own answers, I knew that I made a meaningful impact. I am excited to continue to bring my sociological mind-set to the world of social media and looking forward to seeing what others who take this path can do, too!

Career Data: Public Relations Specialist

- 2016 Median Pay: $58,020 per year
- Typical Entry-Level Education: Bachelor's degree
- Projected Job Growth by 2024: 6% (As fast as average)

SOURCE: Bureau of Labor Statistics, Occupational Outlook Handbook, 2016.

SUMMARY

- Sociologists disagree about whether social change is gradual or abrupt, and about whether all societies are changing in roughly the same direction. The evolutionary, revolutionary, and **rise-and-fall theories of social change** are three approaches to these questions.
- Some early sociologists viewed **collective behavior** as a form of group contagion in which the veneer of civilization gave way to more instinctive, herdlike forms of behavior.
- A more sociological approach, **emergent norm** theory, examines the ways in which **crowds** and other forms of collective behavior develop their own rules and shared understandings.
- The most comprehensive theory of collective behavior, value-added theory, attempts to take into account the necessary conditions for collective behavior at the individual, organizational, and even societal levels.
- Social movements have been important historical vehicles for bringing about social change. They are usually achieved through **social movement organizations (SMOs)**, which we study using the tools and understandings of organizational sociology.
- We can classify social movements as **reformist**, **revolutionary**, **rebellious**, **reactionary**, **utopian**, or "**new**," depending on their vision of social change.
- **Resource mobilization theory** argues that we can explain the success or failure of SMOs not by the degree of social strain that may explain their origins but by their organizational ability to marshal the financial and personal resources they need.
- In recent years sociologists have sought to explain how **social movements** align their own beliefs and values with those of their potential constituents in the wider society. **Frame alignment** activities range from modifying the beliefs of the SMO to attempting to change the beliefs of the entire society.
- Many social movements depend heavily on **conscience constituents** for their support. Micromobilization contexts are also important incubators of social movements.
- Globalization has created an opportunity for the formation of global social movements, since many of the problems in the world today are global and require global solutions.
- **New social movements**, organized around issues of personal identity and values, differ from earlier social movements in that they focus on symbols and information as well as material issues, participation is frequently seen as an end in itself, the movements are organized as networks rather than bureaucratically, and they emphasize the interconnectedness of social groups and larger social entities.

KEY TERMS

differentiation, 381
rise-and-fall theories of social change, 384
collective behavior, 385
crowds, 385
emergent norms, 389
riot, 389
fads, 390
fashions, 390
panic, 390
craze, 390
rumors, 391
social movement, 393
reformist social movements, 394
revolutionary social movements, 396
rebellions, 396
reactionary social movements, 397
utopian social movements, 397
free rider problem, 398
social movement organizations (SMOs), 399
resource mobilization theory, 399
grassroots organizing, 400
conscience constituents, 400
frame alignment, 401
new social movements, 403

DISCUSSION QUESTIONS

1. Consider what you have learned about social movements and social change in this chapter. How is the global expansion of social media likely to change how people pursue social change? How has it done so already?
2. Under what kinds of societal conditions do movements for social change emerge? Describe a societal context that has brought about or could bring about the development of such a movement.
3. How do fads differ from fashions? Offer some examples of each, and consider whether and how setting phenomena in these different categories can shed light on their roots and functions.
4. What are the different types of social movements identified by sociologists? Does the growing influence of social media require the expansion of these categories?
5. Design a social movement. What problem or issue would you want to address? How would you disseminate information and engage other participants? How would you overcome the problems of social movements that were identified in this chapter?

edge.sagepub.com/eglitis

Want a better grade?

Get the tools you need to sharpen your study skills. Access practice quizzes, eFlashcards, video and multimedia at **https://edge.sagepub.com/eglitis**.

GLOSSARY

Achieved status: Social position linked to an individual's acquisition of socially valued credentials or skills.

Agency: The ability of individuals and groups to exercise free will and to make social changes on a small or large scale.

Alliance (or coalition): A subgroup that forms between group members, enabling them to dominate the group in their own interest.

Anomie: A social condition of normlessness; a state of normative uncertainty that occurs when people lose touch with the shared rules and values that give order and meaning to their lives.

Anticipatory socialization: Adoption of the behaviors or standards of a group one emulates or hopes to join.

Antimiscegenation laws: Laws prohibiting interracial sexual relations and marriage.

Ascribed status: Social position linked to characteristics that are socially significant but cannot generally be altered (such as race or gender).

Assimilation: The absorption of a minority group into the dominant culture.

Atavisms: Throwbacks to primitive early humans.

Automation: The replacement of human labor by machines in the production process.

Behaviorism: A psychological perspective that emphasizes the effect of rewards and punishments on human behavior.

Beliefs: Particular ideas that people accept as true.

Bias: A characteristic of results that systematically misrepresent the true nature of what is being studied.

Bourgeoisie: The capitalist (or property-owning) class.

Bureaucracies: Formal organizations characterized by written rules, hierarchical authority, and paid staff, intended to promote organizational efficiency.

Capital crime: Crimes, such as murder, which are severe enough to merit the death penalty.

Capital offenses: Crimes considered so heinous they are punishable by death.

Caste society: A system in which the social levels are closed, so that all individuals remain at the social level of their birth throughout life.

Causal relationship: A relationship between two variables in which one variable is the cause of the other.

Class: A person's economic position in society, usually associated with income, wealth, and occupation, and sometimes associated with political voice.

Class conflict: Competition between social classes over the distribution of wealth, power, and other valued resources in society.

Class-dominant theories: Theories that propose that what is labeled deviant or criminal—and therefore who gets punished—is determined by the interests of the dominant class in a particular culture or society.

Class society: A system in which social mobility allows an individual to change his or her socioeconomic position.

Coercive organizations: Organizations in which people are forced to give unquestioned obedience to authority.

Cognitive development: The theory, developed by Jean Piaget, that an individual's ability to make logical decisions increases as the person grows older.

Cohabitation: Living together as a couple without being legally married.

Collective behavior: Voluntary, goal-oriented action that occurs in relatively disorganized situations in which society's predominant social norms and values cease to govern individual behavior.

Collective conscience: The common beliefs and values that bind a society together.

Common-law marriage: A type of relationship in which partners live as if married but without marriage's formal legal framework.

Concepts: Ideas that describe several things that have something in common.

Conscience constituents: People who provide resources for a social movement organization but who are not themselves members of the aggrieved group that the organization champions.

Control theory: The theory that the cause of deviance lies in the arena of social control and, specifically, the life experiences and relationships that people form.

Conversation analysis: The study of how participants in social interaction recognize and produce coherent conversation.

Correlation: The degree to which two or more variables are associated with one another.

Craze: An intense attraction to an object, a person, or an activity.

Credential society: A society in which access to desirable work and social status depends on the possession of a certificate or diploma certifying the completion of formal education.

Crime: Any act defined in the law as punishable by fines, imprisonment, or both.

Critical thinking: The ability to evaluate claims about truth by using reason and evidence.

Crowds: Temporary gatherings of closely interacting people with a common focus.

Cultural capital: Wealth in the form of knowledge, ideas, verbal skills, and ways of thinking and acting.

Cultural inconsistency: A contradiction between the goals of ideal culture and the practices of real culture.

Cultural pluralism: The coexistence of different racial and ethnic groups, characterized by acceptance of one another's differences.

Cultural relativism: A worldview whereby the practices of a society are understood sociologically in terms of that society's norms and values, and not the norms and values of another society.

Culture: The beliefs, norms, behaviors, and products common to the members of a particular group.

De facto segregation: School segregation based largely on residential patterns or student choice, which persists even though legal segregation is now outlawed in the United States.

Deductive reasoning: The process of taking an existing theory and logically deducing that if the theory is accurate, we should discover other patterns of behavior consistent with it.

Dependency theory: The theory that the poverty of some countries is a consequence of their exploitation by wealthy states, which control the global capitalist system.

Dependent variables: Variables that change as a result of changes in other variables.

Deviance: Any attitude, behavior, or condition that violates cultural norms or societal laws and results in disapproval, hostility, or sanction if it becomes known.

Differential association theory: The theory that deviant and criminal behavior results from regular exposure to attitudes favorable to acting in ways that are deviant or criminal.

Differentiation: The development of increasing societal complexity through the creation of specialized social roles and institutions.

Discrimination: The unequal treatment of individuals on the basis of their membership in a group.

Document analysis: The examination of written materials or cultural products: previous studies, newspaper reports, court records, campaign posters, digital reports, films, pamphlets, and other forms of text or images produced by individuals, government agencies, or private organizations.

Domestic (or family) violence: Physical or sexual abuse committed by one family member against another.

Double consciousness: Among African Americans, an awareness of being both American and Black, never free of racial stigma.

Doxic: Taken for granted as "natural" or "normal" in society.

Dramaturgical approach: Developed by Erving Goffman, the study of social interaction as if it were governed by the norms of theatrical performance.

Dyad: A group consisting of two persons.

Economic capital: Money and material that can be used to access valued goods and services.

Economy: The social institution that organizes the ways in which a society produces, distributes, and consumes goods and services.

Education: The transmission of society's norms, values, and knowledge base by means of direct instruction.

Ego: According to Sigmund Freud, the part of the mind that is the "self," the core of what is regarded as a person's unique personality.

Egocentric: Experiencing the world as if it were centered entirely on oneself.

Emergent norms: Norms that are situationally created to support a collective action.

Emic perspective: The perspective of the insider, the one belonging to the cultural group in question.

Emotional labor: The management of feelings or emotions to create a publicly observable facial and bodily display in return for a wage.

Endogamous: A characteristic of marriages in which partners are limited to members of the same social group or caste.

Ethnicity: Characteristics of groups associated with national origins, languages, and cultural and religious practices.

Ethnocentrism: A worldview whereby one judges other cultures by the standards of one's own culture and regards one's own way of life as "normal" and better than others.

Ethnomethodology: A sociological method used to study the body of commonsense knowledge and procedures by which ordinary members of a society make sense of their social circumstances and interaction.

Etic perspective: The perspective of the outside observer.

Experiments: Research techniques for investigating cause and effect under controlled conditions.

Expulsion: The process of forcibly removing a population from a particular area.

Extended families: Social groups consisting of one or more parents, children, and other kin, often spanning several generations, living in the same household.

Fads: Temporary, highly imitated outbreaks of mildly unconventional behavior.

Falsifiability: The ability for a theory to be disproved; the logical possibility for a theory to be tested and proved false.

Family: Two or more individuals who identify themselves as being related to one another, usually by blood, marriage, or adoption, and who share intimate relationships and dependency.

Fashions: Styles of imitative behavior or appearance that are of longer duration than fads.

Feminism: The belief that social equality should exist between the sexes; also, the social movements aimed at achieving that goal.

Feminist perspective on deviance: A perspective that suggests that studies of deviance have been subject to gender bias and that both gender-specific cultural norms and the particular ways in which women are victimized by virtue of their gender help to account for deviance among women.

Fieldwork: A research method that relies on in-depth and often extended study of a group or community.

Folkways: Fairly weak norms that are passed down from the past, the violation of which is generally not considered serious within a particular culture.

Food deserts: Areas that lack sources of competitively priced healthy and fresh food.

Formal education: Education that occurs within academic institutions such as schools.

Formal organization: An organization that is rationally designed to achieve its objectives, often by means of explicit rules, regulations, and procedures.

Formal rationality: A context in which people's pursuit of goals is shaped by rules, regulations, and larger social structures.

Formal social control: Official attempts to discourage certain behaviors and visibly punish others; most often exercised by the state.

Frame alignment: The process by which the interests, understandings, and values of a social movement organization are rendered congruent with those of the wider society.

Free rider problem: The problem that many people avoid the costs of social movement activism (such as time, energy, and other personal resources) and still benefit from its success.

Gender: Behavioral characteristics that differ between males and females based on culturally enforced and socially learned norms and roles.

Gender roles: The attitudes and behaviors that are considered appropriately "masculine" or "feminine" in a particular culture.

Gender wage gap: The difference between the earnings of women who work full-time year-round as a group and those of men who work full-time year-round as a group.

Generalized other: The abstract sense of society's norms and values by which people evaluate themselves.

Genocide: The mass, systematic destruction of a people or a nation.

Glass ceiling: An artificial boundary that allows women to see the next occupational or salary level even as structural obstacles keep them from reaching it.

Glass escalator: The nearly invisible promotional boost that men gain in female-dominated occupations.

Global culture: A type of culture—some would say U.S. culture—that has spread across the world in the form of Hollywood films, fast-food restaurants, and popular music heard in virtually every country.

Global inequality: The systematic disparities in income, wealth, health, education, access to technology, opportunity, and power among countries, communities, and households around the world.

Globalization: The process by which people all over the planet become increasingly interconnected economically, politically, culturally, and environmentally.

Goods: Objects that have an economic value to others, whether they are the basic necessities for survival or things that people simply want.

Grassroots organizing: Attempts to mobilize support among the ordinary members of a community.

Gross national income–purchasing power parity per capita (GNI-PPP): A comparative economic measure that uses international dollars to indicate the amount of goods and services someone could buy in the United States with a given amount of money.

Groupthink: A process by which the members of a group ignore ways of thinking and plans of action that go against the group consensus.

Habitus: The internalization of objective probabilities and subsequent expression of those probabilities as choice.

Hidden curriculum: The unspoken classroom socialization into the norms, values, and roles of a society that schools provide along with the "official" curriculum.

High culture: The music, theater, literature, and other cultural products that are held in particularly high esteem in society.

Human capital: The skills and knowledge a person possesses that make him or her valuable in a particular workplace.

Hypotheses: Ideas about the world, derived from theories, which can be disproved when tested against observations.

I: According to George Herbert Mead, the part of the self that is the impulse to act; it is creative, innovative, unthinking, and largely unpredictable.

Id: According to Sigmund Freud, the part of the mind that is the repository of basic biological drives and needs.

Ideal culture: The values, norms, and behaviors that people in a given society profess to embrace.

Income: The amount of money a person or household earns in a given period of time.

Independent or experimental variables: Variables that cause changes in other variables.

Indirect labor costs: Costs in time, training, or money incurred when an employee takes time off to care for sick family members, opts for parental leave, arrives at work late, or leaves a position after receiving employer-provided training.

Individual discrimination: Overt and intentional unequal treatment, often based on prejudicial beliefs.

Inductive reasoning: The process of generalizing to an entire category of phenomena from a particular set of observations.

Inequality: Differences in wealth, power, and other valued resources.

Infant mortality rate: The number of deaths of infants younger than age 1 per 1,000 live births per year.

Informal social control: The unofficial mechanism through which deviance and deviant behaviors are discouraged in society; most often occurs among ordinary people during the course of their interactions.

Institutionalized discrimination: Unequal treatment that has become a part of the routine operation of such major social institutions as businesses, schools, hospitals, and the government.

International families: Families that result from globalization.

International governmental organization (IGO): An international organization established by treaties between governments for purposes of commerce, security, promotion of social welfare and human rights, or environmental protection.

International nongovernmental organization (INGO): An international organization established by agreements between the individuals or private organizations making up its membership and existing to fulfill an explicit mission.

Interview: A detailed conversation designed to obtain in-depth information about a person and his or her activities.

Iron law of oligarchy: Robert Michels's theory that there is an inevitable tendency for a large-scale bureaucratic organization to become ruled undemocratically by a handful of people.

Labeling theory: A symbolic interactionist approach holding that deviance is a product of the labels people attach to certain types of behavior.

Labor demand factors: Factors that highlight the needs and preferences of the employer.

Labor supply factors: Factors that highlight reasons that women or men may "prefer" particular occupations.

Language: A system of symbolic verbal, nonverbal, and written representations rooted within a particular culture.

Latent functions: Functions of an object, an institution, or a phenomenon that are not recognized or expected.

Laws: Codified norms or rules of behavior.

Leading questions: Questions that tend to elicit particular responses.

Legitimate authority: A type of power that is recognized as rightful by those over whom it is exercised.

Liberal feminism: The belief that women's inequality is primarily the result of imperfect institutions, which can be corrected by reforms that do not fundamentally alter society itself.

Life chances: The opportunities and obstacles a person encounters in education, social life, work, and other areas critical to social mobility.

Literacy: The ability to read and write at a basic level.

Looking-glass self: The concept developed by Charles Horton Cooley that our self-image results from how we interpret other people's views of us.

Macro-level paradigms: Theories of the social world that are concerned with large-scale patterns and institutions.

Mandatory minimum sentences: Legal requirements that persons found guilty of particular crimes must be sentenced to set minimum numbers of years in prison.

Manifest functions: Functions of an object, an institution, or a phenomenon that are obvious and intended.

Marginally attached to the labor force: Persons who would like to work and have searched actively for a job in the past 12 months.

Marriage: A culturally approved relationship, usually between two individuals, that provides a degree of economic cooperation, emotional intimacy, and sexual activity.

Mass education: The extension of formal schooling to wide segments of the population.

Mass media: Media of public communication intended to reach and influence a mass audience.

Mass production: The large-scale, highly standardized manufacturing of identical commodities on a mechanical assembly line.

Material culture: The physical objects that are created, embraced, or consumed by society that help shape people's lives.

Matrix of domination: A system of social positions in which any individual may concurrently occupy a status (for example, gender, race, class, or sexual orientation) as a member of a dominated group and a status as a member of a dominating group.

Me: According to George Herbert Mead, the part of the self through which we see ourselves as others see us.

Means of production: The sites and technology that produce the goods we need and use.

Meritocracy: A society in which personal success is based on talent and individual effort.

Micro-level paradigm: A theory of the social world that is concerned with small-group social relations and interactions.

Minorities: Less powerful groups who are dominated by a more powerful group and, often, discriminated against on the basis of characteristics deemed by the majority to be socially significant.

Mixed contacts: Interactions between those who are stigmatized and those who are "normal."

Modernization theory: A market-oriented development theory that envisions development as evolutionary and guided by "modern" institutions, practices, and cultures.

Monogamy: A form of marriage in which a person may have only one spouse at a time.

Mores: Strongly held norms, the violation of which seriously offends the standards of acceptable conduct of most people within a particular culture.

Multicultural feminism: The belief that inequality must be understood—and ended—for all women, regardless of race, class, nationality, age, sexual orientation, physical ability, or other characteristics.

Multiculturalism: A commitment to respecting cultural differences rather than trying to submerge them into a larger, dominant culture.

Negative correlation: A relation between two variables in which one increases as the other decreases.

Net financial assets: A measure of wealth that excludes illiquid personal assets such as home and car.

New social movements: Movements that have arisen since the 1960s and are fundamentally concerned with the quality of private life, often advocating large-scale cultural changes in how people think and act.

Nonmaterial culture: The abstract creations of human cultures, including language and social practices.

Normative organizations: Organizations that people join of their own will to pursue morally worthwhile goals without expectation of material reward; sometimes called *voluntary associations*.

Norms: Accepted social behaviors and beliefs.

Not in the labor force: Persons who are neither officially employed nor officially unemployed.

Nuclear families: Social groups consisting of one or two parents and their biological, dependent children, living in a household with no other kin.

Objectivity: The ability to represent the object of study accurately.

Occupation: A person's main vocation or paid employment.

Occupational segregation by gender: The concentration of men and women in different occupations.

Official poverty line: The dollar amount set by the government as the minimum necessary to meet the basic needs of a family.

Operational definition: A definition of a concept that allows the concept to be observed and measured.

Opportunity theory: The theory that people differ not only in their motivations to engage in deviant acts but also in their *opportunities* to do so.

Organization: A group with an identifiable membership that engages in concerted collective actions to achieve a common purpose.

Organized crime: Crime committed by criminal groups that provide illegal goods and services.

Panic: A massive flight from something that is feared.

Patriarchy: Any set of social relationships in which men dominate women.

Personal power: Power that derives from a leader's personality.

Phrenology: A theory that the skull shapes of deviant individuals differ from those of nondeviants.

Pluralistic societies: Societies made up of many diverse groups with different norms and values.

Political power: The ability to exercise influence on political institutions and/or actors to realize personal or group interests.

Polyandry: A form of marriage in which a woman may have multiple husbands.

Polygamy: A form of marriage in which a person may have more than one spouse at a time.

Polygyny: A form of marriage in which a man may have multiple wives.

Popular culture: The entertainment, culinary, and athletic tastes shared by the masses.

Population: The whole group of people studied in sociological research.

Positional power: Power that stems officially from the leadership position itself.

Positivist: Science that is based on facts alone.

Power: The ability to mobilize resources and achieve goals despite the resistance of others.

Prejudice: A belief about an individual or a group that is not subject to change on the basis of evidence.

Presentation of self: The creation of impressions in the minds of others to define and control social situations.

Primary deviance: A term developed by Edwin Lemert; the first step in the labeling of deviance, it occurs at the moment an activity is labeled deviant (see also *secondary deviance*).

Primary groups: Small groups characterized by intense emotional ties, face-to-face interaction, intimacy, and a strong, enduring sense of commitment.

Principle of falsification: The principle, advanced by philosopher Karl Popper, that a scientific theory must lead to testable hypotheses that can be disproved if they are wrong.

Proletariat: The working class; wage workers.

Property crimes: Crimes that involve the violation of individuals' ownership rights, including burglary, larceny/theft, arson, and motor vehicle theft.

Psychoanalysis: A psychological perspective that emphasizes the complex reasoning processes of the conscious and unconscious mind.

Public education: A universal education system provided by the government and funded by tax revenues rather than student fees.

Qualitative research: Research that is characterized by data that cannot be quantified (or converted into numbers), focusing instead on generating in-depth knowledge of social life, institutions, and processes.

Qualitative variables: Variables that express qualities and do not have numerical values.

Quantitative research: Research that gathers data that can be quantified and offers insight into broad patterns of social behavior and social attitudes.

Quantitative variables: Factors that can be counted.

Race: A group of people who share a set of characteristics (usually physical characteristics) deemed by society to be socially significant.

Racism: The idea that one racial group is inherently superior to another; often results in institutionalized relationships between dominant and minority groups that create a structure of economic, social, and political inequality based on socially constructed racial or ethnic categories.

Radical feminism: The belief that women's inequality underlies all other forms of inequality, including economic inequality.

Random sampling: Sampling in which everyone in the population of interest has an equal chance of being chosen for the study.

Rape culture: A social culture that provides an environment conducive to rape.

Reactionary social movements: Movements seeking to restore an earlier social system—often based on a mythical past—along with the traditional norms and values that once presumably accompanied it.

Real culture: The values, norms, and behaviors that people in a given society actually embrace and exhibit.

Rebellions: Movements seeking to overthrow the existing social, political, and economic systems but lacking detailed plans for a new social order.

Reference groups: Groups that provide standards for judging our attitudes or behaviors.

Reformist social movements: Movements seeking to bring about social change within the existing economic and political system.

Reliability: The extent to which researchers' findings are consistent with the findings of different studies of the same thing, or with the findings of the same study over time.

Replication: The repetition of a previous study using a different sample or population to verify or refute the original findings.

Research methods: Specific techniques for systematically gathering data.

Reserve army of labor: A pool of job seekers whose numbers outpace the available positions and thus contribute to keeping wages low and conditions of work tenuous.

Resocialization: The process of altering an individual's behavior through control of his or her environment, for example, within a total institution.

Resource mobilization theory: A theory about social movement organizations that focuses on their ability to generate money, membership, and political support in order to achieve their objectives.

Revolutionary social movements: Movements seeking to fundamentally alter the existing social, political, and economic system in keeping with a vision of a new social order.

Riot: An illegal, prolonged outbreak of violent behavior by a sizable group of people directed against people or property.

Rise-and-fall theories of social change: Theories that see social change as characterized by a cycle of growth and decline.

Role-taking: The ability to take the roles of others in interaction.

Rumors: Unverified forms of information that are transmitted informally, usually originating in unknown sources.

Sample: A portion of the larger population selected to represent the whole.

School segregation: The education of racial minorities in schools that are geographically, economically, and/or socially separated from those attended by Whites.

School to prison pipeline: The policies and practices that push students, particularly at-risk youth, out of schools and into the criminal justice system.

Scientific: A way of learning about the world that combines logically constructed theory and systematic observation.

Scientific management: A practice that sought to use principles of engineering to reduce the physical movements of workers.

Scientific method: A way of learning about the world that combines logically constructed theory and systematic observation to provide explanations of how things work.

Scientific theories: Explanations of how and why scientific observations are as they are.

Second shift: The unpaid housework that women typically do after they come home from their paid employment.

Secondary deviance: A term developed by Edwin Lemert; the second step in the labeling of deviance, it occurs when a person labeled deviant accepts the label as part of his or her identity and, as a result, begins to act in conformity with the label (see also *primary deviance*).

Secondary groups: Groups that are large and impersonal and characterized by fleeting relationships.

Segregation: The practice of separating people spatially or socially on the basis of race or ethnicity.

Serial monogamy: The practice of having more than one wife or husband, but only one at a time.

Services: Economically productive activities that do not result directly in physical products; may be relatively simple or quite complex.

Sex: The anatomical and other biological characteristics that differ between males and females and that originate in genetic differences.

Sex category: The socially required identification display that confirms someone's membership in a given category.

Sexism: The belief that one sex is innately superior to the other and is therefore justified in having a dominant social position.

Sexual division of labor in modern societies: The phenomenon of dividing production functions by gender and designating different spheres of activity, the "private" to women and the "public" to men.

Sexuality: The ways in which people construct their sexual identity, attraction, and relationships, including the norms governing sexual behavior.

Significant others: According to George Herbert Mead, the specific people who are important in children's lives and whose views have the greatest impact on the children's self-evaluations.

Social bonds: Individuals' connections to others (see also *control theory*).

Social capital: The social knowledge and connections that enable people to accomplish their goals and extend their influence.

Social categories: Categories of people sharing common characteristics without necessarily interacting or identifying with one another.

Social class reproduction: The way in which class status is reproduced from generation to generation, with parents "passing on" a class position to their offspring.

Social closure: The ability of a group to strategically and consciously exclude outsiders or those deemed "undesirable" from participating in the group or enjoying the group's resources.

Social conflict paradigm: A theory that seeks to explain social organization and change in terms of the conflict that is built into social relations; also known as *conflict theory*.

Social control: The attempts by certain people or groups in society to control the behaviors of other individuals and groups to increase the likelihood that they will conform to established norms or laws.

Social diversity: The social and cultural mixture of different groups in society and the societal recognition of difference as significant.

Social dynamics: The laws that govern social change.

Social embeddedness: The idea that economic, political, and other forms of human behavior are fundamentally shaped by social relations.

Social epidemiology: The study of communities and their social statuses, practices, and problems with the aim of understanding patterns of health and disease.

Social facts: Qualities of groups that are external to individual members yet constrain their thinking and behavior.

Social inequality: A high degree of disparity in income, wealth, power, prestige, and other resources.

Social learning: The way people adapt their behavior in response to social rewards and punishments.

Social mobility: The upward or downward status movement of individuals or groups over time.

Social movement: A large number of people who come together in a continuing and organized effort to bring about (or resist) social change, and who rely at least partially on noninstitutionalized forms of political action.

Social movement organizations (SMOs): Formal organizations that seek to achieve social change through noninstitutionalized forms of political action.

Social power: The ability to exercise social control.

Social solidarity: The bonds that unite the members of a social group.

Social statics: The way society is held together.

Social stratification: The systematic ranking of different groups of people in a hierarchy of inequality.

Socialist feminism: The belief that women's inequality results from the combination of capitalistic economic relations and male domination; argues that both must be transformed fundamentally before women can achieve equality.

Socialization: The process by which people learn the culture of their society.

Sociological imagination: The ability to grasp the relationship between individual lives and the larger social forces that help to shape them.

Sociological theories: Logical, rigorous frameworks for the interpretation of social life that make particular assumptions and ask particular questions about the social world.

Sociology: The scientific study of human social relations, groups, and societies.

Spurious relationship: A correlation between two or more variables that is the result of something else that is not being measured, rather than a causal link between the variables themselves.

Standpoint epistemology: A philosophical perspective that argues that what we can know is affected by the position we occupy in society.

Standpoint theory: A perspective that says the knowledge we create is conditioned by where we stand, or our subjective social position.

State crimes: Criminal or other harmful acts committed by state officials in the pursuit of their jobs as representatives of the government.

Statistical data: Quantitative information obtained from government agencies, businesses, research studies, and other entities that collect data for their own or others' use.

Status: The prestige associated with a social position.

Stereotype threat: A situation in which an individual is at risk of confirming a negative stereotype about his or her social group.

Stereotyping: The generalization of a set of characteristics to all members of a group.

Stigma: An attribute that is deeply discrediting to an individual or a group because it overshadows other attributes and merits the individual or group may possess.

Stigmatization: The branding of behavior as highly disgraceful (see also *labeling theory*).

Strain theory: The theory that when there is a discrepancy between the cultural goals for success and the means available to achieve those goals, rates of deviance will be high.

Stratified sampling: Dividing a population into a series of subgroups and taking random samples from within each group.

Structural contradiction theory: The theory that conflicts generated by fundamental contradictions in the structure of society produce laws defining certain acts as deviant or criminal.

Structural functionalism: A theory that seeks to explain social organization and change in terms of the roles performed by different social structures, phenomena, and institutions; also known as *functionalism*.

Structural strain: In Merton's reformulation of Durkheim's functionalist theory, a form of anomie that occurs when a gap exists between society's culturally defined goals and the means society makes available to achieve those goals.

Structuralism: The idea that an overarching structure exists within which culture and other aspects of society must be understood.

Structure: Patterned social arrangements that have effects on agency.

Subcultural theories: Theories that explain deviance in terms of the conflicting interests of more and less powerful segments of a population.

Subcultures: Cultures that exist together with a dominant culture but differ in some important respects from that dominant culture.

Superego: According to Sigmund Freud, the part of the mind that consists of the values and norms of society, insofar as they are internalized, or taken in, by the individual.

Survey: A research method that uses a questionnaire or interviews administered to a group of people in person or by telephone or e-mail to determine their characteristics, opinions, and behaviors.

Symbolic interactionism: A microsociological perspective that posits that both the individual self and society as a whole are the products of social interactions based on language and other symbols.

Symbols: Representations of things that are not immediately present to our senses.

Taboos: Powerful mores, the violation of which is considered serious and even unthinkable within a particular culture.

"Three Strikes" laws: State and federal laws that sentence an individual to life in prison who has been found guilty of committing three felonies, or serious crimes punishable by a minimum of a year in prison.

Total fertility rate (TFR): The average number of children a woman in a given country will have in her lifetime if age-specific fertility rates hold throughout her childbearing years.

Total institutions: Institutions that isolate individuals from the rest of society to achieve administrative control over most aspects of their lives.

Transactional leader: A leader who is primarily concerned with accomplishing the group's tasks, getting group members to do their jobs, and making certain that the group achieves its goals.

Transformational leader: A leader who is able to instill in the members of a group a sense of mission or higher purpose, thereby changing the nature of the group itself.

Transgender: An umbrella term used to describe those whose gender identity, expression, or behavior differs from their assigned sex or is outside the gender binary.

Transsexual: A term used to refer to people who use surgery and hormones to change their sex to match their preferred gender.

Triad: A group consisting of three persons.

Unemployed: Persons who are jobless, actively looked for work in the prior 4 weeks, and are available for work.

Utilitarian organizations: Organizations that people join primarily because of some material benefit they expect to receive in return for membership.

Utopian social movements: Movements seeking to withdraw from the dominant society by creating their own ideal communities.

Validity: The degree to which concepts and their measurements accurately represent what they claim to represent.

Value neutrality: The characteristic of being free of personal beliefs and opinions that would influence the course of research.

Values: The general standards in society that define ideal principles, like those governing notions of right and wrong.

Variable: A concept or its empirical measure that can take on multiple values.

Verstehen: The German word for interpretive understanding; Weber's proposed methodology for explaining social relationships by having the sociologist imagine how subjects might perceive a situation.

Violent crimes: Crimes that involve force or threat of force, including robbery, murder, assault, and rape.

"War on drugs": Actions taken by U.S. state and federal governments that are intended to curb the illegal drug trade and reduce drug use.

Wealth (or net worth): The value of everything a person owns minus the value of everything he or she owes.

White-collar crime: Crime committed by people of high social status in connection with their work.

World systems theory: The theory that the global capitalist economic system has long been shaped by a few powerful economic actors, who have ordered it in a way that favors their interests.

Zero tolerance policies: School or district policy that sets predetermined punishments for certain misbehaviors and punishes the same way no matter the severity or the context of the behavior.

REFERENCES

ABC News. (2015, April 24). The twelve biggest moments from Bruce Jenner: The interview. *ABC News* Retrieved from http://abcnews.go.com/Entertainment/12-biggest-moments-bruce-jenner-interview/story?id=30572364

Abdullah, H. (2016, April 5). HUD seeks to end housing discrimination against ex-offenders. *NBC News*. Retrieved from http://www.nbcnews.com/news/us-news/hud-seeks-end-housing-discrimination-against-ex-offenders-n550471

Abel, J. R., Deitz, R., & Su, Y. (2014). Are recent college graduates finding good jobs? *Current Issues in Economics and Finance, (20)*1, 1–8. Retrieved from https://www.newyorkfed.org/medialibrary/media/research/current_issues/ci20-1.pdf

Abrahams, N. (1992). Towards reconceptualizing political action. *Sociological Inquiry, 62,* 327–347.

Achen, A. C., & Stafford, F. P. (2005). *Data quality of housework hours in the Panel Study of Income Dynamics: Who really does the dishes?* (PSID Technical Series Paper 05-04). Ann Arbor: Institute for Social Research, University of Michigan. Retrieved from http://psidonline.isr.umich.edu/Publications/Papers/tsp/2005-04_Data_Qual_of_Household_Hours-_Dishes.pdf

Acierno, R., Hernandez-Tejada, M., Muzzy, W., & Steve, K. (2009). *Final report: The National Elder Mistreatment Study.* Report submitted to the U.S. Department of Justice, National Institute of Justice. Retrieved from https://www.ncjrs.gov/pdffiles1/nij/grants/226456.pdf

Ackbar, S. (2011). *Constructions and socialization of gender and sexuality in lesbian-/gay-headed families* (Doctoral dissertation, University of Windsor). Retrieved from ProQuest (NR77959).

Adachi, P. J. C., & Willoughby, T. (2011). The effect of video game competition and violence on aggressive behavior: Which characteristic has the greatest influence? *Psychology of Violence, 1*(4), 259–274.

Adams, J., Parkinson, L., Sanson-Fisher, R. W., & Walsh, R. A. (2008). Enhancing self-report of adolescent smoking: The effects of bogus pipeline and anonymity. *Addictive Behaviors, 33*(10), 1291–1296.

Addams, J. (1895). *Hull-House maps and papers*. Chicago: Hull-House Association.

Adler, F. (1975). *Sisters in crime: The rise of the new female criminal*. New York: McGraw-Hill.

Adorno, T. (1975). The culture industry reconsidered. *New German Critique, 6*(Fall), 12–19.

Advancement Project. (2010). *Test, punish, and push out: How "zero tolerance" and high-stakes testing funnel youth into the school-to-prison pipeline*. Retrieved from http://b.3cdn.net/advancement/d05cb2181a4545db07_r2im6caqe.pdf

Ahola, A. S., Christianson, S., & Hellstrom, A. (2009). Justice needs a blindfold: Effects of gender and attractiveness on prison sentences and attributions of personal characteristics in a judicial process. *Psychiatry, Psychology, and Law, 16*(S1), S90–S100.

Ahuja, M., Barnes, R., Chow, E., & Rivero, C. (2014, September 4). The changing landscape on same-sex marriage. *Washington Post*. Retrieved from http://www.washingtonpost.com/wp-srv/special/politics/same-sex-marriage/

Aina, O. E., & Cameron, P. A. (2011). Why does gender matter? Counteracting stereotypes with young children. *Dimensions of Early Childhood, 39*(1), 11–19.

Al Jazeera. (2016, May 27). UN: Plenty of civilians in danger of starvation. *Al Jazeera* Retrieved from http://www.aljazeera.com/news/2016/05/syria-160526162935029.html

Albanese, J. S. (1989). *Organized crime in America.* New York: Anderson.

Aldrich, H. E., & Marsden, P. V. (1988). Environments and organizations. In N. J. Smelser (Ed.), *Handbook of sociology* (pp. 361–392). Newbury Park, CA: Sage.

Alexander, J. C. (1998). *Neofunctionalism and after.* Malden, MA: Blackwell.

Alexander, J. C., & Colomy, P. (1990). *Differentiation theory and social change.* New York: Columbia University Press.

Alexander, M. (2010). *The new Jim Crow: Mass incarceration in the age of colorblindness*. New York: New Press.

Alfano, S. (2009, February 11). Poll: Women's movement worthwhile. *CBS News.* Retrieved from http://www.cbsnews.com/2100-500160_162-965224.html

Allen, V. L., & Levine, J. M. (1968). Social support, dissent and conformity. *Sociometry, 31,* 138–149.

Allport, G. W., & Postman, L. (1947). *The psychology of rumor.* New York: Holt.

American Academy of Child and Adolescent Psychiatry. (2011). Children and watching TV. *Facts for Families, 54*(4). Retrieved from https://www.aacap.org/App_Themes/AACAP/docs/facts_for_families/54_children_and_watching_tv.pdf

American Association of University Women (AAUW). (2016, Spring). *The simple truth about the gender pay gap.* Washington, DC: Author. Retrieved from http://www.aauw.org/research/the-simple-truth-about-the-gender-pay-gap/

American Bar Association. (2014, July). *A current glance at women in the law*. Chicago: American Bar Association, Commission on Women in the Profession. Retrieved from https://www.americanbar.org/content/dam/aba/marketing/women/current_glance_statistics_july2014.authcheckdam.pdf

American Civil Liberties Union. (n.d.). *School-to-prison pipeline*. Retrieved from https://www.aclu.org/issues/juvenile-justice/school-prison-pipeline

America's 5 biggest employers—then and now. (2010, September 23). *Huffington Post*. Retrieved from http://www.huffingtonpost.com/2010/09/23/americas-5-biggest-employ_n_736215.html

Amnesty International. (2004, October 26). *Democratic Republic of Congo: Mass rape—Time for remedies*. Retrieved from http://www.amnesty.eu/en/news/statements-reports/eu/poverty-and-human-rights/democratic-republic-of-congo-mass-rape-time-for-remedies-0093/#.WbaF0BlhmUl

Amnesty International. (2012). *Death penalty facts*. Retrieved from http://www.amnestyusa.org/pdfs/DeathPenaltyFactsMay2012.pdf

Amnesty International. (2014). *Struggle for maternal health: Barriers to antenatal care in South Africa*. Retrieved from http://www.amnesty.ca/sites/amnesty/files/south_africa_maternal_health_report_pdf.pdf

Amnesty International. (2015, March 19). *Nigeria: Hundreds of oil spills continue to blight Niger delta*. Retrieved from https://www.amnesty.org/en/latest/news/2015/03/hundreds-of-oil-spills-continue-to-blight-niger-delta/

Andersen, M. L., & Collins, P. H. (Eds.). (1992). *Race, class, and gender: An anthology*. Stamford, CT: Wadsworth.

Anderson, C., Berkowitz, L., Donnerstein, E., Huesmann, L. R., Johnson, J., Linz, D., . . . Wartella, E. (2003). The influence of media violence on youth. *Psychological Science in the Public Interest, 4*(3), 81–110.

Anderson, E. (1999). *Code of the street: Decency, violence and the moral life of the inner city*. New York: Norton.

Anderson, N. (1940). *Men on the move*. Chicago: University of Chicago Press.

Anderson, T. D. (2000). Sex-role orientation and care-oriented moral reasoning: An online test of Carol Gilligan's theory. *Dissertation Abstracts International, 61*(4), 1618-A. Retrieved from http://search.proquest.com.proxygw.wrlc.org/socabs/docview/60390650/13C8E238511536831E/1?accountid=11243

Angier, N. (2000, August 22). Do races differ? Not really, genes show. *New York Times*. Retrieved from http://www.nytimes.com/2000/08/22/science/do-races-differ-not-really-genes-show.html?pagewanted= all&src=pm

Anupam, B., Olenski, A. R., & Blumenthal, D. M. (2016, July 11). Sex differences in physician salary in U.S. public medical schools. *The JAMA Network*. Retrieved from http://archinte.jamanetwork.com/article.aspx?articleid=2532788#Results

Anzaldúa, G. (Ed.). (1990). *Making face, making soul: Haciendo caras*. San Francisco: Aunt Lute Foundation.

Appelbaum, B. (2015). Out of trouble, but criminal records keep men out of work. *New York Times*. Retrieved from http://www.nytimes.com/2015/03/01/business/out-of-trouble-but-criminal-records-keep-men-out-of-work.html?_r=0

Appelo, T. (2012). THR poll: "Glee" and "Modern Family" drive voters to favor gay marriage—even many Romney voters. *The Hollywood Reporter*. Retrieved from http://www.hollywoodreporter.com/news/thr-poll-glee-modern-family-386225

Arab American Institute. (2012). *Arab Americans*. Retrieved from http://www.aaiusa.org/arab-americans

Arab American Institute Foundation. (2011). *Quick facts about Arab Americans*. Retrieved from https://b.3cdn.net/aai/fcc68db3efdd45f613_vim6ii3a7.pdf

Archer, D., & Gartner, R. (1984). *Violence and crime in cross-national perspective*. New Haven, CT: Yale University Press.

Arendt, H. (1951). *The origins of totalitarianism*. New York: Harcourt, Brace.

Armstrong, L., Phillips, J. G., & Saling, L. L. (2000). Potential determinants of heavier Internet use. *International Journal of Human-Computer Studies, 53*(4), 537–550.

Asch, S. (1952). *Social psychology*. Englewood Cliffs, NJ: Prentice-Hall.

Asencio, E. K., & Burke, P. J. (2011). Does incarceration change the criminal identity? A synthesis of labeling and identity theory perspectives on identity change. *Sociological Perspectives, 54*(20), 163–182.

Associated Press. (2015, December 16). 2014 World Cup final attracted 1.01 billion viewers, FIFA says. *Associated Press* Retrieved from http://www.espnfc.us/fifa-world-cup/story/2759180/fifa-reports-101-billion-viewers-for-2014-world-cup-final

Aubrey, J. S., & Frisby, C. M. (2011). Sexual objectification in music videos: A content analysis comparing gender and genre. *Mass Communication and Society, 14*(4), 475–501.

Aubrey, J. S., & Harrison, K. (2004). The gender-role content of children's favorite television programs and its links to their gender-related perceptions. *Media Psychology, 6*, 111–146.

Austin, J., Dimas, J., & Steinhart, D. (1992). *Over-representation of minority youth in the California juvenile justice system* (Report prepared for the California State Advisory Group on Juvenile Justice and the California Office of Criminal Justice Planning). Washington, DC: National Council on Crime and Delinquency.

Autor, D. (2010, April). *The polarization of job opportunities in the U.S. labor market: Implications for employment and earnings*. Washington, DC: Center for American Progress and the Hamilton Project. Retrieved from http://www.scribd.com/doc/52779456/The-Polarization-of-Job-Opportunities-in-the-U-S-Labor-Market

Aviel, D. (1997). Issues in education: A closer examination of American education. *Childhood Education, 73*(3), 130–132.

Babbie, E. R. (1998). *The practice of social research*. Belmont, CA: Wadsworth.

Babcock, P., & Marks, M. (2010, August 5). *Leisure college, USA: The decline in student study time* (Research Education Outlook No. 7). Washington, DC: American Enterprise Institute for Public Policy. Retrieved from http://www.aei.org/publication/leisure-college-usa/

Badger, E. (2014, April 15). Pollution is segregated too. *Washington Post*. Retrieved from https://www.washingtonpost.com/news/wonk/wp/2014/04/15/pollution-is-substantially-worse-in-minority-neighborhoods-across-the-u-s/

Badger, E. (2016, May 2). 'This can't happen by accident.' *Washington Post*. Retrieved from https://www.washingtonpost.com/graphics/business/wonk/housing/atlanta/

Badger, E., & Eilperin J. (2016, March 14). The cruelest thing about buying diapers. *Washington Post*. Retrieved from https://www.washingtonpost.com/news/wonk/wp/2016/03/14/the-cruelest-thing-about-buying-diapers/

Bailey, K., West, R., & Anderson, C. A. (2011). The influence of video games on social, cognitive, and affective information processing. In J. Decety & J. Cacioppo (Eds.), *Handbook of social neuroscience* (pp. 1001–1011). New York: Oxford University Press.

Baldwin, J. D., & Baldwin, J. I. (1986). *Behavior principles in everyday life*. Englewood Cliffs, NJ: Prentice Hall.

Baldwin, J. D., & Baldwin, J. I. (1988). Factors affecting AIDS-related sexual risk-taking behavior among college students. *Journal of Sex Research, 25*(2), 181–196.

Ball, S. J., Bowe, R., & Gewirtz, S. (1995). Circuits of schooling: A sociological exploration of parental choice of school in social class contexts. *Sociological Review, 43*(1), 52–77.

Balzac, H. de. (1985). *Les employés*. Paris: French & European Publications. (Original work published 1841)

Bandura, A. (1977). *Social learning theory*. Englewood Cliffs, NJ: Prentice Hall.

Bandura, A., & Walters, R. H. (1963). *Social learning and personality development*. New York: Holt, Rinehart & Winston.

Barber, B. K. (1992). Family, personality, and adolescent problem behaviors. *Journal of Marriage and the Family, 54*(2), 69–79.

Bare branches, redundant males. (2015, April 18). *The Economist*. Retrieved from http://www.economist.com/news/asia/21648715-distorted-sex-ratios-birth-generation-ago-are-changing-marriage-and-damaging-societies-asias

Barner, M. (1999). Sex-role stereotyping in FCC-mandated children's educational television. *Journal of Broadcasting & Electronic Media, 43*(4), 551–564.

Barnes, R. (2012, November 26). Justices decline to consider whether Constitution requires insanity defense. *Washington Post*. Retrieved from https://www.washingtonpost.com/politics/justices-decline-to-consider-whether-constitution-requires-insanity-defense/2012/11/26/d7a3cc62-3816-11e2-8a97-363b0f9a0ab3_story.html?utm_term=.4c83389ec92e

Barr, J. (2017, September 23). Trump Says N.F.L. players who take a knee during national anthem should be fired. *New York Times*. Retrieved from https://www.nytimes.com/2017/09/23/sports/football/trump-nfl-kaepernick.html

Barrera, M. (1979). *Race and class in the Southwest*. Notre Dame, IN: University of Notre Dame Press.

Barry, K. (1979). *Female sexual slavery*. Englewood Cliffs, NJ: Prentice Hall.

Barry, T., & Sims, B. (1994). *The challenge of cross-border environmentalism: The U.S.–Mexico case*. Albuquerque, NM: Resource Center Press.

Basow, S. (2004). The hidden curriculum: Gender in the classroom. In M. Paludi (Ed.), *Praeger guide to the psychology of gender* (pp. 117–132). Westport, CT: Praeger.

Bauman, K., & Ryan, C. (2015, October 7). Women now at the head of the class, lead men in college attainment [Web log post]. *U.S. Census Bureau*. Retrieved from https://www.census.gov/newsroom/blogs/random-samplings/2015/10/women-now-at-the-head-of-the-class-lead-men-in-college-attainment.html

Bauman, Z. (2001). *Modernity and the Holocaust*. Ithaca, NY: Cornell University Press.

BBC. (2005, October 17). 1968: Black athletes make silent protest. *BBC News* Retrieved from http://news.bbc.co.uk/onthisday/hi/dates/stories/october/17/newsid_3535000/3535348.stm

BBC. (2008, December 18). Rwanda: How the genocide happened. *BBC News* Retrieved from http://news.bbc.co.uk/2/hi/1288230.stm

BBC. (2014a, February 17). Former Barclays employees named in Libor criminal case. *BBC News* Retrieved from http://www.bbc.co.uk/news/business-26228635

BBC. (2014b). History: The troubles, 1968–1998. *BBC News* Retrieved from http://www.bbc.co.uk/history/troubles

BBC. (2014c, June 5). Softbank unveils "human-like" robot Pepper. *BBC News* Retrieved from http://www.bbc.com/news/technology-27709828

Beaver, K. M., Wright, J. P., DeLisi, M., & Vaughn, M. G. (2008). Genetic influences on the stability of low self-control: Results from a longitudinal sample of twins. *Journal of Criminal Justice, 36*, 478–485.

Beck, J. (2016, March 1). The Instagrams of food deserts. *The Atlantic*. Retrieved from http://www.theatlantic.com/health/archive/2016/03/the-instagrams-of-food-deserts/471540/

Before and after Title IX: Women in sports. (2012, June 16). *New York Times*. Retrieved from http://www.nytimes.com/interactive/2012/06/17/opinion/sunday/sundayreview-titleix-timeline.html?_r=0#/#time12_264

Beiner, T. M. (2007). Sexy dressing revisited: Does target dress play a part in sexual harassment cases? *Duke Journal of Gender Law & Policy, 14*, 125–152.

Bekkers, V., Edwards, A., & Moody, R. (2010, September 16–17). *Micro-mobilization, social media and coping strategies: Some Dutch experiences*. Paper presented at the Internet and Public Policy Conference, St. Anne's College, Oxford University, Oxford, England.

Bell, D. (1973). *The coming of post-industrial society: A venture in social forecasting*. New York: Basic Books.

Bellstrom, K. (2015, June 29). GM's Mary Barra sets a Fortune 500 record for female CEOs. *Fortune*. Retrieved from http://fortune.com/2015/06/29/female-ceos-fortune-500-barra/

Bennett, J. (2015, August 8). A master's degree in. . . masculinity? *New York Times*. Retrieved from http://www.nytimes.com/2015/08/09/fashion/masculinities-studies-stonybrook-michael-kimmel.html

Bergen, T. J., Jr. (1996). The social philosophy of public education. *School Business Affairs, 62*(6), 22–27.

Berkowitz, B., Gamio, L., Lu, D., Uhrmacher, K., & Lindeman, T. (2016, July 27). The math of mass shootings. *Washington Post*. Retrieved from https://www.washingtonpost.com/graphics/national/mass-shootings-in-america/

Berman, M. (2014, December 31). The most recent state to abolish the death penalty is about to empty its death row. *Washington Post*. Retrieved from https://www.washingtonpost.com/news/post-nation/wp/2014/12/31/the-most-recent-state-to-abolish-the-death-penalty-is-about-to-empty-its-death-row/?utm_term=.afcca9cc6fa1

Bernard, J. (1981). *The female world*. New York: Free Press.

Bernard, J. (1982). *The future of marriage*. New Haven, CT: Yale University Press.

Berns, R. (1989). *Child, family, community: Socialization and support*. New York: Holt, Rinehart & Winston.

Bettelheim, B. (1979). *Surviving, and other essays*. New York: Knopf.

Bettelheim, B. (1982). Difficulties between parents and children: Their causes and how to prevent them. In N. Stinnett et al. (Eds.), *Family strengths 4: Positive support systems* (pp. 5–14). Lincoln: University of Nebraska Press.

Bhanot, R. T., & Jovanovic, J. (2005). Do parents' academic gender stereotypes influence whether they intrude on their children's homework? *Sex Roles, 52*(9–10), 597–607.

Bigio, J. (2016, December 9). Fighting corruption by combatting sexual extortion (blog). *Council on Foreign Relations*. Retrieved from https://www.cfr.org/blog/fighting-corruption-combating-sexual-extortion

Bilal, M., Zia-ur-Rehman, M., & Raza, I. (2010). Impact of family friendly policies on employees' job satisfaction and turnover intention (A study on work–life balance at workplace). *Interdisciplinary Journal of Contemporary Research in Business, 2*(7), 378–395.

Bilton, R. (2014, December 18). Apple 'failing to protect Chinese factory workers.' *BBC News*. Retrieved from http://www.bbc.com/news/business-30532463

Bishaw, A. (2014, June). *Changes in areas with concentrated poverty: 2000 to 2010* (American Community Survey Report 27). Washington, DC: U.S. Census Bureau. Retrieved from http://www.census.gov/content/dam/Census/library/publications/2014/acs/acs-27.pdf

Bishop, C. J., Kiss, M., Morrison, T. G., Rushe, D. M., & Specht, J. (2014). The association between gay men's stereotypic beliefs about drag queens and their endorsement of hypermasculinity. *Journal of Homosexuality, 62*(4), 554–567.

Bishop, K. (2009). Dead man still walking: Explaining the zombie renaissance. *Journal of Popular Film and Television, 37*(1), 16–25.

Bishop, K. (2010). *American zombie gothic: The rise and fall (and rise) of the walking dead in popular culture*. Jefferson, NC: McFarland.

Bishop, M., & Hicks, S. L. (Eds.). (2009). *Hearing, mother father deaf*. Washington, DC: Gallaudet University Press.

Bissinger, B. (2015, July). Caitlyn Jenner: The full story. *Vanity Fair*. Retrieved from http://www.vanityfair.com/hollywood/2015/06/caitlyn-jenner-bruce-cover-annie-leibovitz

Blalock, H. (1967). *Toward a theory of minority group relations*. New York: Wiley.

Blau, J. (1992). *The visible poor: Homelessness in the United States*. New York: Oxford University Press.

Blau, P. M. (1964). *Exchange and power in social life*. New York: Wiley.

Blau, P. M. (1977). *Inequality and heterogeneity: A primitive theory of social structure*. New York: Free Press.

Blau, P. M., & Meyer, M. (1987). *Bureaucracy in modern society* (3rd ed.). New York: Random House.

Blinder, A. S. (2006). Offshoring: The next industrial revolution? *Foreign Affairs, 85*(2), 113–128.

Block, A., & Chambliss, W. J. (1981). *Organizing crime*. New York: Elsevier.

Block, A., & Weaver, A. (2004). *All is clouded by desire: Global banking, money laundering, and international organized crime*. Westport, CT: Praeger.

Block, J. J. (2008). Issues for *DSM-V*: Internet addiction. *American Journal of Psychiatry, 165*(3), 306–307.

Block, M., Cox, A., & Giratiknon, T. (2015, July 8). Mapping segregation. *New York Times*. Retrieved from http://www.nytimes.com/interactive/2015/07/08/us/census-race-map.html

Blow, C. M. (2015, July 30). The shooting of Samuel Du Bose. *New York Times*. Retrieved from http://www.nytimes.com/2015/07/30/opinion/charles-blow-the-shooting-of-samuel-dubose.html

Blumberg, J. (2007, October 23). A brief history of the Salem witch trials. *Smithsonian*. Retrieved from http://www.smithsonianmag.com/history-archaeology/brief-salem.html

Blumer, H. (1951). Collective behavior. In A. M. Lee (Ed.), *Principles of sociology* (pp. 166–222). New York: Barnes & Noble.

Blumer, H. (1969). *Symbolic interactionism: Perspective and method*. Englewood Cliffs, NJ: Prentice Hall.

Blumer, H. (1970). *Movies and conduct*. New York: Arno Press.

Boghosian, A. (2015, November 29). 8 important social movements on college campuses today. *Fresh U*. Retrieved from https://www.freshu.io/alison-boghosian/social-movements-on-college-campuses

Bohnert, D., & Ross, W. H. (2010). The influence of social networking Web sites on the evaluation of job candidates. *Cyberpsychology, Behavior, and Social Networking, 13*, 341–347.

Booker, M. K. (2001). *Monsters, mushroom clouds, and the Cold War: American science fiction and the roots of postmodernism, 1946–1964*. Westport, CT: Greenwood.

Bos, H., & Sandfort, T. G. M. (2010). Children's gender identity in lesbian and heterosexual two-parent families. *Sex Roles, 62*(1–2), 114–126.

Boser, U., Wilhelm, M., & Hanna, R. (2014, October 6). The power of the Pygmalion effect: Teacher expectations strongly predict college outcomes. *Center for American Progress*. Retrieved from https://www.americanprogress.org/issues/education/report/2014/10/06/96806/the-power-of-the-pygmalion-effect/

Boswell, A. A., & Spade, J. Z. (1996). Fraternities and collegiate rape culture: Why are some fraternities more dangerous places for women? *Gender & Society, 10*, 133–147.

Bottomore, T. (2002). *The Frankfurt School and its critics*. New York: Routledge.

Bourdieu, P. (1977). *Outline of a theory of practice*. New York: Cambridge University Press.

Bourdieu, P. (1984). *Distinction: A social critique of the judgment of taste*. Cambridge, MA: Harvard University Press.

Bourdieu, P. (1991). *Language and symbolic power*. New York: Cambridge University Press.

Bourdieu, P., & Coleman, J. S. (1991). *Social theory for a changing society*. Boulder, CO: Westview Press.

Bowles, H. R. (2014, June 19). Why women don't negotiate their job offers. *Harvard Business Review*. Retrieved from https://hbr.org/2014/06/why-women-dont-negotiate-their-job-offers/

Bowles, S., & Gintis, H. (1976). *Schooling in capitalist America: Educational reform and the contradictions of economic life*. New York: Basic Books.

Bowling Green State University. (2012, February 11). Finding love has no expiration date: People over 60 are fastest growing demographic in online dating. *Science Daily*. Retrieved from www.sciencedaily.com/releases/2012/02/120211095051.htm

Branch, T. (1988). *Parting the waters: America in the King years, 1954–1963*. New York: Simon & Schuster.

Branson, C., & Cornell, D. (2009). A comparison of self and peer reports in the assessment of middle school bullying. *Journal of Applied School Psychology, 25*, 5–27.

Braverman, H. (1988). *Labor and monopoly capital: The degradation of work in the 20th century*. New York: Monthly Review Press. (Original work published 1974)

Bremer, C. (2012, March). *Economic commentary* (T. Vaughn, managing director). Retrieved from http://www.tom-vaughn.com/Economic-Commentary-March-2012.c3472.htm

Bremer, J., & Rauch, P. K. (1998). Children and computers: Risks and benefits. *Journal of the American Academy of Child and Adolescent Psychiatry, 37*, 559–560.

Brennan, W. (2015, November). How to make money in music. *The Atlantic*. Retrieved from http://www.theatlantic.com/magazine/archive/2015/11/how-to-make-money-in-music/407875/

Brock, J., & Cocks, T. (2012, March 8). Insight: Nigeria oil corruption highlighted by audits. *Reuters*. Retrieved from http://www.reuters.com/article/2012/03/08/us-nigeria-corruption-oil-idUSBRE8270GF20120308

Brook, T. (2014, October 21). How the global box office is changing Hollywood. *BBC*. Retrieved from http://www.bbc.com/culture/story/20130620-is-china-hollywoods-future

Brown, D. (2010, September 16). A mother's education has a huge effect on a child's health. *Washington Post*. Retrieved from http://www.washingtonpost.com/wp-dyn/content/article/2010/09/16/AR2010091606384.html

Brown, D. E., Edwards, J. W., & Moore, R. B. (1988). *The penis inserts of Southeast Asia*. Berkeley, CA: Center for South and Southeast Asian Studies.

Brumberg, J. J. (1997). *The body project: An intimate history of American girls*. New York: Vintage Books.

Buchwald, E., Fletcher, P. R., & Roth, M. (2005). *Transforming a rape culture* (Rev. ed.). Minneapolis: Milkweed Editions.

Buechler, S. M. (1990). *Women's movements in the United States: Women's suffrage, equal rights, and beyond*. New Brunswick, NJ: Rutgers University Press.

Bureau of Labor Statistics, U.S. Department of Labor. (2016). *Earnings and unemployment rates by educational attainment in the United States*. Retrieved from https://www.bls.gov/emp/ep_chart_001.htm

Bureau of Labor Statistics, U.S. Department of Labor. (2017, February 7). *The economics daily, unemployment rate 2.5 percent for college grads, 7.7 percent for high school dropouts, January 2017*. Retrieved from https://www.bls.gov/opub/ted/2017/unemployment-rate-2-point-5-percent-for-college-grads-7-point-7-percent-for-high-school-dropouts-january-2017.htm

Burgess, R. L., & Akers, R. L. (1966). A differential association-reinforcement theory of criminal behavior. *Social Problems, 14*(2), 128–147.

Burns, J. M. (1978). *Leadership*. New York: Harper & Row.

Business Wire. (2016, March 10). Calvin Klein announced as exclusive apparel partner of Justin Bieber's Purpose world tour. *Business Wire*. Retrieved from http://www.businesswire.com/news/home/20160310005916/en/Calvin-Klein-Announced-Exclusive-Apparel-Partner-Justin\

Cabeza, M. F., Johnson, J. B., & Tyner, L. J. (2011). Glass ceiling and maternity leave as important contributors to the gender wage gap. *Southern Journal of Business and Ethics, 3*, 73–85.

Camarota, S. (2005). *Birth rates among immigrants in America: Comparing fertility in the U.S. and home countries*. Washington, DC: Center for Immigration Studies. Retrieved from https://cis.org/Birth-Rates-Among-Immigrants-America

Camera, L. (2015, November 6). Native American students left behind. *U.S. News & World Report*. Retrieved from http://www.usnews.com/news/articles/2015/11/06/native-american-students-left-behind

Campbell, A. (1984). *The girls in the gang*. New Brunswick, NJ: Rutgers University Press.

Campbell, A., & Muncer, S. (Eds.). (1998). *The social child.* East Sussex, England: Psychology Press.

Campbell, K., Klein, D. M., & Olson, K. (1992). Conversation activity and interruptions among men and women. *Journal of Social Psychology, 132,* 419–421.

Caputi, J. (2014). The real "hot mess": The sexist branding of female pop stars [Review of the book *Gender, branding, and the modern music industry: The social construction of female popular music stars,* by K. J. Lieb]. *Sex Roles, 70*(9–10), 439–441.

CareerBuilder. (2015). *Employers reveal biggest resume blunders in annual CareerBuilder survey.* Retrieved from http://www.careerbuilder.com/share/aboutus/pressreleasesdetail.aspx?sd=8/13/2015&id=pr909&ed=12/31/2015

Carnevale, A. P., Smith, N., & Strohl, J. (2010, June). *Help wanted: Projections of jobs and education requirements through 2018.* Washington, DC: Georgetown University, Center on Education and the Workforce. Retrieved from https://cew.georgetown.edu/wp-content/uploads/2014/12/HelpWanted.ExecutiveSummary.pdf

Carpenter, Z. (2015, November 4). Think it's hard finding a place to live? Try doing so with a criminal record. *The Nation.* Retrieved from https://www.thenation.com/article/public-housing-criminal-record/

Carrell, S. E., Sacerdote, B. I., & West, J. E. (2011). *From natural variation to optimal policy? The Lucas critique meets peer effects* (Working Paper 16865). Cambridge, MA: National Bureau of Economic Research.

Carson, E. A. (2015). *Prisoners in 2014.* Washington, DC: U.S. Department of Justice, Bureau of Justice Statistics. Retrieved from http://www.bjs.gov/content/pub/pdf/p14.pdf

Carson, E. A., & Anderson E. (2016). *Prisoners in 2015* (BJS Bulletin NCJ 250229). Washington, DC: US Department of Justice, Bureau of Justice Statistics. Retrieved from https://www.bjs.gov/content/pub/pdf/p15.pdf

Carson, E. A., & Golinelli, D. (2013). *Prisoners in 2012: Trends in admissions and releases, 1991–2012* (BJS Bulletin NCJ 243920). Washington, DC: U.S. Department of Justice, Bureau of Justice Statistics. Retrieved from http://www.bjs.gov/content/pub/pdf/p12tar9112.pdf

Cassidy, C. (2016, June 5). Patchy reporting undercuts national hate crimes count. *Associated Press.* Retrieved from http://bigstory.ap.org/article/8247a1d2f76b4baea2a121186dedf768/ap-patchy-reporting-undercuts-national-hate-crimes-count

Catalano, S. (2012). *Intimate partner violence, 1993–2010* (NCJ 239203). Washington, DC: U.S. Department of Justice, Bureau of Justice Statistics. Retrieved from http://bjs.ojp.usdoj.gov/content/pub/pdf/ipv9310.pdf

Caumont, A. (2013, August 16). *Most of today's single mothers have never been married.* Washington, DC: Pew Research Center. Retrieved from http://www.pewresearch.org/fact-tank/2013/08/16/more-of-todays-single-mothers-have-never-been-married/

Cavalli-Sforza, L. L., Menozzi, P., & Piazza, A. (1994). *The history and geography of human genes.* Princeton, NJ: Princeton University Press.

Cawley, J. (2001). The impact of obesity on wages. *Journal of Human Resources, 39,* 451–474.

Centers for Disease Control and Prevention. (2010). *National intimate partner and sexual violence survey.* Atlanta, GA: Author. Retrieved from http://www.cdc.gov/ViolencePrevention/pdf/NISVS_FactSheet-a.pdf

Centers for Disease Control and Prevention. (2012). *Overweight and obesity: Adult obesity facts.* Retrieved from https://www.cdc.gov/obesity/data/adult.html

Centers for Disease Control and Prevention. (2017). *Marriages and divorces.* Atlanta, GA: CDC, National Center for Health Statistics, National Vital Statistics System. Retrieved from https://www.cdc.gov/nchs/nvss/marriage-divorce.htm

Chafetz, J. S. (1984). *Sex and advantage: A comparative, macro-structural theory of sex stratification.* Totowa, NJ: Rowman & Allanheld.

Chafetz, J. S. (1997). Feminist theory and sociology: Underutilized contributions for mainstream theory. *Annual Review of Sociology, 23,* 97–120.

Chafetz, J. S., & Dworkin, A. G. (1983). Macro and micro process in the emergence of feminist movements: Toward a unified theory. *Western Sociological Review, 14*(1), 27–45.

Chaffey, D. (2015, April 27). Social network popularity by country. *Smart Insights.* Retrieved from http://www.smartinsights.com/social-media-marketing/social-media-strategy/new-global-social-media-research/attachment/2015-social-network-popularity-by-country/

Chaffey, D. (2016). Global social media research summary 2016. *Smart Insights.* Retrieved from http://www.smartinsights.com/social-media-marketing/social-media-strategy/new-global-social-media-research/

Chalk, F., & Jonassohn, K. (1990). *The history and sociology of genocide: Analyses and case studies.* New Haven, CT: Yale University Press.

Chambliss, W. J. (1973). The Saints and the Roughnecks. *Society 11*(1), 24–31.

Chambliss, W. J. (1988a). *Exploring criminology.* New York: Macmillan.

Chambliss, W. J. (1988b). *On the take: From petty crooks to presidents.* Bloomington: Indiana University Press.

Chambliss, W. J. (2001). *Power, politics, and crime.* Boulder, CO: Westview Press.

Chambliss, W. J., & Hass, A. (2011). *Criminology: Connecting theory, research, and practice.* New York: McGraw-Hill.

Chambliss, W. J., & King, H. (1984). *Boxman: A professional thief's journey.* New York: Macmillan.

Chambliss, W. J., Michalowski, R., & Kramer, R. C. (Eds.). (2010). *State crime in the global age.* London: Willan.

Chambliss, W. J., & Zatz, M. S. (1994). *Making law: The state, the law, and structural contradictions.* Bloomington: Indiana University Press.

Charity Navigator. (2016). *Islamic relief USA.* Retrieved from http://www.charitynavigator.org/index.cfm?bay=search.summary&orgid=3908#.Vryv7jbYXEw

Chen, H. S. (1992). *Chinatown no more: Taiwan immigrants in contemporary New York.* Ithaca, NY: Cornell University Press.

Chen, L. (2015, August 11). The most valuable employees: Snapchat doubles Facebook. *Forbes.* Retrieved from http://www.forbes.com/sites/liyanchen/2015/08/11/the-most-valuable-employees-snapchat-doubles-facebook/#1ba06be3f754

Chesney-Lind, M. (1989). Girls' crime and woman's place: Toward a feminist model of female delinquency. *Crime & Delinquency, 33*(1), 5–29.

Chesney-Lind, M. (2004). Beyond bad girls: Feminist perspectives on female offending. In C. Sumner (Ed.), *The Blackwell companion in criminology.* Oxford: Blackwell.

Chia, R. C., Allred, L. J., Grossnickle, W. F., & Lee, G. W. (1998). Effects of attractiveness and gender on the perception of achievement-related variables. *Journal of Social Psychology, 138*(4), 471–477.

Chiang, S. (2009). Personal power and positional power in a power-full "I": A discourse analysis of doctoral dissertation supervision. *Discourse and Communication, 3*(3), 255–271.

Child Trends. (2014, November). *Attitudes toward spanking.* Retrieved from http://www.childtrends.org/wp-content/uploads/2012/10/51_Attitudes_Toward_Spanking.pdf

Child Trends. (2015). *Databank: Late or no prenatal care.* Retrieved from http://www.childtrends.org/?indicators=late-or-no-prenatal-care

Childhelp. (2010). *National child abuse statistics: Child abuse in America.* Retrieved from http://www.childhelp.org/pages/statistics#gen-stats

ChildStats. (2013). *America's children: Key national indicators of well-being, 2013*. Retrieved from https://www.childstats.gov/pdf/ac2013/ac_13.pdf

Chodorow, N. (1999). *The reproduction of mothering: Psychoanalysis and the sociology of gender*. Berkeley: University of California Press.

Chong, D. (1991). *Collective action and the civil rights movement*. Chicago: University of Chicago Press.

Christiansen, K. O. (1977). Preliminary study of criminality among twins. In S. A. Mednick & K. O. Christiansen (Eds.), *Biosocial bases of criminal behavior*. New York: Gardner Press.

Church, W. T. II, Jaggers, J. W., & Taylor, J. K. (2012). Neighborhood, poverty, and negative behavior: An examination of differential association and social control theory. *Children and Youth Services Review, 34*(5), 1035–1041.

Cichowski, L., & Nance, W. E. (2004, April 27). More marriages among the deaf may have led to doubling of common form of genetic deafness in the U.S. *Virginia Commonwealth University News Center*. Retrieved from http://www.news.vcu.edu/article/More_marriages_among_the_deaf_may_have_led_to_doubling_of_common

Clark, H. (2006, March 8). Are women happy under the glass ceiling? *Forbes*. Retrieved from https://www.forbes.com/2006/03/07/glass-ceiling-opportunities--cx_hc_0308glass.html

Cline, E. L. (2013). *Overdressed: The shockingly high cost of cheap fashion*. New York: Portfolio.

Cloward, R. A., & Ohlin, L. E. (1960). *Delinquency and opportunity: A theory of delinquent gangs*. Glencoe, IL: Free Press.

Coates, T. (2015, April). The Black family in the age of mass incarceration. *The Atlantic*. Retrieved from https://www.theatlantic.com/magazine/archive/2015/10/the-black-family-in-the-age-of-mass-incarceration/403246/

Cohen, A. K. (1955). *Delinquent boys: The culture of the gang*. Glencoe, IL: Free Press.

Cohn, D., Livingston, G., & Wang, W. (2014, April 8). *After decades of decline, a rise in stay-at-home mothers*. Washington, DC: Pew Research Center. Retrieved from http://www.pewsocialtrends.org/2014/04/08/after-decades-of-decline-a-rise-in-stay-at-home-mothers

Coleman, J. M., & Hong, Y.-Y. (2008). Beyond nature and nurture: The influence of lay gender theories on self-stereotyping. *Self and Identity, 7*(1), 34–53.

Coleman, J. S. (1990). *The foundations of social theory*. Cambridge, MA: Harvard University Press.

Coleman, J. S., Hoffer, T., & Kilgore, S. (1982). *High school achievement: Public, Catholic, and private schools compared*. New York: Basic Books.

Colen, C. G., Geronimus, A. T., Bound, J., & James, S. A. (2006). Maternal upward socioeconomic mobility and Black–White disparities in infant birthweight. *American Journal of Public Health, 96*(11), 2032–2039.

Collins, P. H. (1990). *Black feminist thought: Knowledge, consciousness and the politics of empowerment*. New York: Routledge.

Collins, R. (1979). *The credential society: An historical sociology of education and stratification*. New York: Academic Press.

Colomy, P. (1986). Recent developments in the functionalist approach to change. *Sociological Focus, 19,* 139–158.

Colomy, P. (Ed.). (1990). *Functionalist sociology*. Brookfield, VT: Elgar.

Coltrane, S., & Ishii-Kuntz, M. (1992). Remarriage, stepparenting, and household labor. *Journal of Family Issues, 13*(2), 215–233.

Complete College America. (2011, September). *Time is the enemy*. Washington, DC: Author. Retrieved from http://completecollege.org/docs/Time_Is_the_Enemy.pdf

Comte, A. (1975). *Auguste Comte and positivism: The essential writings* (G. Lenzer, Ed.). New York: Harper Torchbooks.

Condron, D. J. (2009). Social class, school and non-school environments, and Black/White inequalities in children's learning. *American Sociological Review, 74,* 685–708.

Condry, J. C. (1989). *The psychology of television*. Hillsdale, NJ: Erlbaum.

Conley, D. (1999). *Being Black, living in the red: Race, wealth, and social policy in America*. Berkeley: University of California Press.

Connell, R. W. (2005). Change among the gatekeepers: Men, masculinities, and gender equality in the global arena. *Signs, 30*(3), 1801–1826.

Connell, R. W. (2010). *Masculinities*. Retrieved from http://www.raewynconnell.net/p/masculinities_20.html

Connell, R. W., & Messerschmidt, J. W. (2005). Hegemonic masculinity: Rethinking the concept. *Gender & Society, 19*(6), 829–859.

Consumer Financial Protection Bureau. (2015, July 21). *CFPB orders Citibank to pay $700 million in consumer relief for illegal credit card practices*. Retrieved from http://www.consumerfinance.gov/about-us/newsroom/cfpb-orders-citibank-to-pay-700-million-in-consumer-relief-for-illegal-credit-card-practices/

Cooley, C. H. (1909). *Social organization: A study of the larger mind*. New York: Charles Scribner's Sons.

Cooley, C. H. (1964). *Human nature and the social order*. New York: Schocken Books. (Original work published 1902)

Coontz, S. (2000). Historical perspectives on family studies. *Journal of Marriage and the Family, 62*(2), 283–297.

Coontz, S. (2005). *Marriage, a history: From obedience to intimacy, or how love conquered marriage*. New York: Penguin Books.

Cosgrove, B. (2014, September 27). The Black power salute that rocked the 1968 Olympics. *Time*. Retrieved from http://time.com/3880999/black-power-salute-tommie-smith-and-john-carlos-at-the-1968-olympics/

Coutts, S., & LaFleur, J. (2011). Some states still leave low-income students behind; others make surprising gains. *ProPublica*. Retrieved from https://www.propublica.org/article/opportunity-gap-schools-data

Criminalizing children at school. (2013, April 18). *New York Times*. Retrieved from http://www.nytimes.com/2013/04/19/opinion/criminalizing-children-at-school.html

Crocker, W. H. (1986). Canela body painting. *Review: Latin American Literature and Arts, 36,* 24–26.

Crocker, W. H. (1990). The Canela (Eastern Timbira), I: An ethnographic introduction. *Smithsonian Contributions to Anthropology, 33.* Washington, DC: Smithsonian Institution Press.

Crocker, W. H. (1994). *The Canela: Bonding through kinship, ritual, and sex* (Case studies in cultural anthropology). Fort Worth, TX: Harcourt Brace College.

Culhane, D. (2010, July 11). Five myths about America's homeless. *Washington Post*. Retrieved from http://www.washingtonpost.com/wp-dyn/content/article/2010/07/09/AR2010070902357.html

Curtiss, S. (1977). *Genie: A psycholinguistic study of a modern-day "wild child."* Boston: Academic Press.

Cutright, P., & Fernquist, R. M. (2000). Effects of societal integration, period, region, and culture of suicide on male age-specific suicide rates: 20 developed countries, 1955–1989. *Social Science Research, 29,* 148–172.

Dahrendorf, R. (1958). *Out of utopia*. New York: Ardent Media.

Daniels, R. (2002). Incarceration of the Japanese Americans: A sixty-year perspective. *History Teacher, 35*(3), 297–310.

Davey, M., & Smith, M. (2016, April 8). Hastert molested at least four boys, prosecutors say. *New York Times*. Retrieved from http://www.nytimes.com/2016/04/09/us/dennis-hastert-molested-at-least-four-boys-prosecutors-say.html

David, D. S., & Brannon, R. (1976). *The forty-nine percent majority: The male sex role*. New York: Random House.

Davis, A., Kimball, W., & Gould, E. (2015, May 27). *The class of 2015* (Briefing Paper #401).

Washington, DC: Economic Policy Institute. Retrieved from http://www.epi.org/publication/the-class-of-2015/

Davis, K., & Moore, W. (1945). Some principles of stratification. *American Sociological Review, 10,* 242–249.

Davis, S. N., Greenstein, T. N., & Marks, J. P. (2007). Effects of union type on division of household labor: Do cohabitating men really perform more housework? *Journal of Family Issues, 28*(9), 1246–1272.

de Vise, D. (2012, May 21). Is college too easy? As study time falls, debate rises. *Washington Post.* Retrieved from http://www.washingtonpost.com/local/education/is-college-too-easy-as-study-time-falls-debate-rises/2012/05/21/gIQAp7uUgU_story.html

Death Penalty Information Center. (2016a). *States with and without the death penalty.* Retrieved from http://www.deathpenaltyinfo.org/states-and-without-death-penalty

Death Penalty Information Center. (2016b). *The Death Penalty in 2016: Year End Report.* Washington, DC: Author. Retrieved from https://deathpenaltyinfo.org/documents/2016YrEnd.pdf

Death Penalty Information Center. (n.d.). *Executions in the United States.* Retrieved from http://www.death penaltyinfo.org/executions-united-states

DeBeaumont, R. (2009). Occupational differences in the wage penalty for obese women. *Journal of Socio-Economics, 38,* 344–349.

DeChoudhury, M., Sharma, S., & Kiciman, E. (2016, February). *Characterizing dietary choices, nutrition, and language in food deserts via social media.* Paper presented at Computer-Supported Cooperative Work and Social Computing 2016, San Francisco, California. Retrieved from http://dx.doi.org/10.1145/2818048.2819956

DeFrancisco, V. L. (1991). The sounds of silence: How men silence women in marital relations. *Discourse & Society, 2*(4), 412–423.

DeNavas-Walt, C., & Proctor, B. D. (2014). *Income and poverty in the United States: 2013* (Current Population Reports P60-249). Washington, DC: U.S. Census Bureau. Retrieved from https://www.census.gov/content/dam/Census/library/publications/2014/demo/p60-249.pdf

DeNavas-Walt, C., & Proctor, B. D. (2015). *Income and poverty in the United States: 2014* (Current Population Reports P60-252). Washington, DC: U.S. Census Bureau. Retrieved from https://www.census.gov/content/dam/Census/library/publications/2015/demo/p60-252.pdf

Denno, B. W. (1990). *Biology and violence from birth to adulthood.* Cambridge, England: Cambridge University Press.

DePillis, L. (2015, August 16). Minimum-wage offensive could speed arrival of robot-powered restaurants. *Washington Post.* Retrieved from https://www.washingtonpost.com/business/capitalbusiness/minimum-wage-offensive-could-speed-arrival-of-robot-powered-restaurants/2015/08/16/35f284ea-3f6f-11e5-8d45-d815146f81fa_story.html?utm_term=.8d8d18ce976f

DeSantis, A., & Kayson, W. A. (1997). Defendants' characteristics of attractiveness, race, sex and sentencing decisions. *Psychological Reports, 81,* 679–683.

Desmond, M. (2015, March). *Unaffordable America: Poverty, housing, and eviction* (Fast Forward, No. 22). Madison: University of Wisconsin, Institute for Research on Poverty. Retrieved from http://www.irp.wisc.edu/publications/fastfocus/pdfs/FF22-2015.pdf

Desmond, M. (2016a). *Evicted: Poverty and profit in the American city.* New York: Crown.

Desmond, M. (2016b, June 9). *Evicted: Housing, poverty, and policy.* Presentation at Georgetown Law School, Washington, DC.

Dewey, C. (2014, May 9). Is tweeting a hashtag better than doing nothing? Or about the same? *Washington Post,* pp. C1, C4.

DeWitt, A. L., Cready, C. M., & Seward, R. R. (2013). Parental role portrayal in twentieth century children's picture books: More egalitarian or ongoing stereotyping? *Sex Roles, 69*(1–2), 89–106.

Diaz, J. D. (1999). *Suicide in the Las Vegas homeless population: Applying Durkheim's theory of suicide* (Doctoral dissertation, University of Nevada, Las Vegas).

Dilmac, B. (2009). Psychological needs as a predictor of cyberbullying: A preliminary report on college students. *Educational Sciences: Theory and Practice, 9*(3), 1308–1325.

DiMaggio, P. J., & Powell, W. (1983). The iron cage revisited: Institutional isomorphism and collective rationality in organizational fields. *American Sociological Review, 48,* 147–160.

Dion, K., Berscheid, E., & Walster, E. (1972). What is beautiful is good. *Journal of Personality and Social Psychology, 24*(3), 285–290.

Dishion, T. J., McCord, J., & Poulin, F. (1999). When interventions harm: Peer groups and problem behavior. *American Psychologist, 54,* 755–764.

Doey, L., Coplan, R. J., & Kingsbury, M. (2013). Bashful boys and coy girls: A review of gender differences in childhood shyness. *Sex Roles,* 70(7–8), 255–266.

Dokoupil, T. (2012a, July 9). Is the Internet making us crazy? What the new research says. *Newsweek.* Retrieved from http://www.newsweek.com/internet-making-us-crazy-what-new-research-says-65593

Dokoupil, T. (2012b, July 16). Tweets, texts, email, posts: Is the onslaught making us crazy? *Newsweek,* pp. 24–30.

Dollard, J. (1957). *Caste and class in a Southern town* (3rd ed.). New York: Anchor Books.

Dolnick, E. (1993, September). Deafness as culture. *Atlantic Monthly,* pp. 37–53.

Domhoff, G. W. (2009). *Who rules America? Challenges to corporate and class dominance* (6th ed.). New York: McGraw-Hill.

Dominus, S. (2017, May 11). "Is an open marriage a happier marriage?" *The New York Times Magazine.* Retrieved from https://www.nytimes.com/2017/05/11/magazine/is-an-open-marriage-a-happier-marriage.html

Douglas, D. (2013, March 6). Attorney general says big banks' size may inhibit prosecution. *Washington Post,* p. A12.

Downs, E., & Smith, S. (2010). Keeping abreast of hypersexuality: A video game character content analysis. *Sex Roles, 62*(11), 721–733.

Drake, B. (2014, January 7). *Number of older Americans in the workforce is on the rise.* Washington, DC: Pew Research Center. Retrieved from http://www.pewresearch.org/fact-tank/2014/01/07/number-of-older-americans-in-the-workforce-is-on-the-rise/

Drew, J. (2015, April 6). A list of tribal laws prohibiting gay marriage. *Yahoo!* Retrieved from https://www.yahoo.com/news/list-tribal-laws-prohibiting-gay-marriage-162248831.html?ref=gs

Drug Policy Alliance. (n.d.). *Marijuana legalization and regulation.* Retrieved from http://www.drugpolicy.org/marijuana-legalization-and-regulation

Du Bois, W. E. B. (2008). *The souls of Black folk.* Rockville, MD: Arc Manor. (Original work published 1903)

Duggan, M. (2015, December 5). Who plays video games and identifies as a "gamer." *Pew Research Center Internet & Technology.* Retrieved from http://www.pewinternet.org/2015/12/15/who-plays-video-games-and-identifies-as-a-gamer/

Duggan, M., Ellison, N. B., Lampe, C., Lenhart, A., & Madden, M. (2015, January 9). *Social media update 2014.* Washington, DC: Pew Research Center. Retrieved from http://www.pewinternet.org/2015/01/09/social-media-update-2014/

Duhigg, C., & Barboza, D. (2012, January 25). In China, human costs are built into an iPad. *New York Times.* Retrieved from http://www.nytimes.com/2012/01/26/business/ieconomy-apples-ipad-and-the-human-costs-for-workers-in-china.html?_r=2& pagewanted=print

Duhigg, C., & Greenhouse, S. (2012, March 29). Electronic giant vowing reforms in China plants. *New York Times.* Retrieved from https://mobile.nytimes.com/comments/2012/03/30/business/apple-supplier-in-china-pledges-changes-in-working-conditions.html?mcubz=1

Dunner, D. L., Gershon, E. S., & Barrett, J. S. (1988). *Relatives at risk for mental disorder.* New York: Ravens Press.

Durkheim, É. (1951). *Suicide.* New York: Free Press. (Original work published 1897)

Durkheim, É. (1956). *Education and sociology* (S. L. Fox, Trans.). New York: Free Press. (Original work published 1922)

Durkheim, É. (1964). *The rules of sociological method.* New York: Free Press. (Original work published 1895)

Durkheim, É. (1973a). *Émile Durkheim on morality and society.* Chicago: University of Chicago Press. (Original work published 1922)

Durkheim, É. (1973b). *Moral education: A study in the theory and application of the sociology of education.* New York: Free Press. (Original work published 1922)

Durkheim, É. (1997). *The division of labor in society.* New York: Free Press. (Original work published 1893)

Dworkin, A. (1981). *Pornography: Men possessing women.* New York: Pedigree.

Dworkin, A. (1987). *Intercourse.* New York: Free Press.

Dworkin, A. (1989). *Letters from the war zone: Writings, 1976–1987.* New York: Dutton.

Dwoskin, E. (2012, March 28). Will you marry me (after I pay off my student loans)? *Bloomberg Businessweek.* Retrieved from http://www.businessweek.com/articles/2012-03-28/will-you-marry-me-after-i-pay-off-my-student-loans

Dwyer, C. (1976). *Research report.* Princeton, NJ: Educational Testing Service.

Dwyer, R. E., Hodson, R., & McCloud, L. (2013). Gender, debt, and dropping out of college. *Gender & Society, 27*(1), 30–55.

Early, G. (2011). *A level playing field: African American athletes and the republic of sports.* Cambridge, MA: Harvard University Press.

Eccles, J. S., & Barber, B. L. (1999). Student council, volunteering, basketball, or marching band: What kind of extracurricular involvement matters? *Journal of Adolescent Research, 14*(1), 10–43.

Eckholm, E. (2010, February 19). A sight all too familiar in poor neighborhoods. *The New York Times.* Retrieved from http://www.nytimes.com/2010/02/19/us/19evict.html

Edin, K., & Kefalas, M. (2005). *Promises I can keep: Why poor women put motherhood before marriage.* Berkeley: University of California Press.

Edwards, A. N. (2014). *Dynamics of economic well-being: Poverty, 2009–2011* (Household Economic Studies P70-137). Washington, DC: U.S. Census Bureau.

Edwards, K. E. (2007). *"Putting my man face on": A grounded theory of college men's gender identity development* (Doctoral dissertation, University of Maryland—College Park). Retrieved from ProQuest (3260431).

Effinger, A., & Burton, K. (2014, May 10). The next mobile frontier: Trailer parks lure white-collar types seeking double-wide profits. *Washington Post.* Retrieved from https://www.washingtonpost.com/business/the-next-mobile-frontier-trailer-parks-lure-white-collar-types-seeking-double-wide-profits/2014/05/08/b58f2df2-cee1-11e3-937f-d3026234b51c_story.html?utm_term=.c370e13fa67e

Ehrenreich, B. (2001). *Nickel and dimed: On (not) getting by in America.* New York: Metropolitan Books.

Ehrenreich, B. (2016, February 26). Matthew Desmond's "Evicted: Poverty and Profit in the American City." *New York Times.* Retrieved from https://www.nytimes.com/2016/02/28/books/review/matthew-desmonds-evicted-poverty-and-profit-in-the-american-city.html?mcubz=1

Ehrenreich, B., & Hochschild, A. R. (2002). Introduction. In B. Ehrenreich & A. R. Hochschild (Eds.), *Global woman: Nannies, maids, and sex workers in the new economy* (pp. 1–14). New York: Metropolitan Books.

Eichler, A. (2012, May 30). Unpaid overtime: Wage and hour lawsuits have skyrocketed in the last decade. *Huffington Post.* Retrieved from http://www.huffingtonpost.com/2012/05/30/wage-hour-lawsuits_n_1556484.html

Eliot, L. (2009). *Pink brain, blue brain: How small differences grow into troublesome gaps—and what we can do about it.* New York: Houghton Mifflin Harcourt.

Elliott, J., & Sullivan, L. (2015, June 3). How the Red Cross raised half a billion dollars for Haiti and built six homes. *ProPublica.* Retrieved from https://www.propublica.org/article/how-the-red-cross-raised-half-a-billion-dollars-for-haiti-and-built-6-homes

Ellison, M. (2015, May 29). The girls of the Lord's Resistance Army. *Al Jazeera.* Retrieved from http://www.aljazeera.com/indepth/features/2015/05/magazine-girls-lord-resistance-army-150527110756222.html

Emerson, R. M. (1962). Power-dependence relations. *American Sociological Review, 27,* 31–41.

Emmanuel, A. (1972). *Unequal exchange: A study of the imperialism of trade.* New York: Monthly Review Press.

Engelberg, I. (2015, May 12). NYU SLAM protests the student debt crisis. *NYU Local.* Retrieved from http://nyulocal.com/on-campus/2015/05/12/nyu-slam-protests-the-student-debt-crisis/

Engels, F. (1942). *The origins of family, private property, and the state.* New York: International. (Original work published 1884)

Erber, G., & Sayed-Ahmed, A. (2005). Offshore outsourcing: A global shift in the present IT industry. *Intereconomics, 40*(2), 100–112.

Erikson, E. H. (1950). *Childhood and society.* New York: Norton.

Etter, G. (1998). Common characteristics of gangs: Examining the cultures of the new urban tribes. *Journal of Gang Research, 5*(2), 19–33.

Etzioni, A. (1975). *A comparative analysis of complex organizations: On power, involvement, and their correlates.* New York: Free Press.

Evans, M. D. R., Kelley, J., Sikora, J., & Treiman, D. J. (2010). Family scholarly culture and educational success: Books and schooling in 27 nations. *Research in Social Stratification and Mobility, 28*(2), 171–197.

FACE Intel (Former and Current Employees of Intel). (2000). *Related class action lawsuits: A huge victory for the worker.* Retrieved May 5, 2015, from http://www.faceintel.com/relatedclass actions.htm

Fainaru-Wada, M., & Fainaru, S. (2014). *League of denial: The NFL, concussions, and the battle for truth.* New York: Three Rivers Press.

Fairfield, R. (1972). *Communes USA.* Baltimore: Penguin Books.

Faiths unite for day of dignity to help homeless. (2015, October 18). *Channel 3 News Las Vegas.* Retrieved from http://news3lv.com/archive/faiths-unite-for-day-of-dignity-to-help-homeless

Faludi, S. (1991). *Backlash: The undeclared war against American women.* New York: Crown.

Farkas, G., Grobe, R. P., Sheehan, D., & Shuan, Y. (1990). Cultural resources and school success: Gender, ethnicity, and poverty groups within an urban school district. *American Sociological Review, 55,* 127–142.

Farkas, G., Sheehan, D., & Grobe, R. P. (1990). Coursework mastery and school success: Gender, ethnicity, and poverty groups within an urban school district. *American Educational Research Journal, 27*(4), 807–827.

Federal Bureau of Investigation. (2015a, November 16). *Latest hate crime statistics available*. Retrieved from https://www.fbi.gov/news/stories/2015/november/latest-hate-crime-statistics-available

Federal Bureau of Investigation. (2015b). Persons arrested. In *Crime in the United States 2015* (Uniform Crime Reports). Washington, DC: Author. Retrieved from https://ucr.fbi.gov/crime-in-the-u.s/2015/crime-in-the-u.s.-2015/persons-arrested/arrestmain_final.pdf

Federal Bureau of Investigation. (2015c). Property crime. In *Crime in the United States 2014* (Uniform Crime Reports). Washington, DC: Author. Retrieved from https://www.fbi.gov/about-us/cjis/ucr/crime-in-the-u.s/2014/crime-in-the-u.s.-2014/offenses-known-to-law-enforcement/property-crime/property-crime

Federal Bureau of Investigation. (2015d). Violent crime. In *Crime in the United States 2014* (Uniform Crime Reports). Washington, DC: Author. Retrieved from https://www.fbi.gov/about-us/cjis/ucr/crime-in-the-u.s/2014/crime-in-the-u.s.-2014/offenses-known-to-law-enforcement/violent-crime/violent-crime

Federal Bureau of Investigation. (n.d.). *UCR frequently asked questions*. Washington, DC: Author. Retrieved from https://www2.fbi.gov/ucr/ucr_general.html

Federal Reserve System & Brookings Institution. (2008). *The enduring challenge of concentrated poverty in America: Case studies from communities across the U.S.* Washington, DC: Authors. Retrieved from http://www.frbsf.org/community-development/files/cp_fullreport.pdf

Feldman, A. (1991). *Formations of violence: The narrative of the body and political terror in Northern Ireland*. Chicago: University of Chicago Press.

Feldman, D. (2017). "Safety Pins for Slackers." *Psychology Today, 50*(4): 40–41.

Fenstermaker Berk, S. (1985). *The gender factory: The apportionment of work in American households*. New York: Plenum Press.

Fenstermaker, S., & West, C. (2002). *Doing gender, doing difference: Inequality, power, and institutional change*. New York: Routledge.

Ferment, C. A. (1989). Political practice and the rise of an ethnic enclave: The Cuban American case. *Theory and Society, 18*(January), 47–48.

Figlio, D. N. (2005). *Testing, crime and punishment* (NBER Working Paper 11194). Cambridge, MA: National Bureau of Economic Research.

Financial Crimes Enforcement Network. (2014, January 7). *JPMorgan admits violation of the Bank Secrecy Act* (Press release). Retrieved from http://www.fincen.gov/news_room/nr/pdf/20140107.pdf

Finckenauer, J. O., & Waring, E. (1996). Russian emigre crime in the U.S.: Organized crime or crime that is organized? *Transnational Organized Crime, 2*(2–3), 139–155.

Fine, L. (2012). *Sexual identity and postsecondary education: Outcomes, institutional factors, and narratives* (Electronic thesis or dissertation, Ohio State University, Ohio).

Firestone, S. (1971). *The dialectic of sex*. London: Paladin.

Fischer, W., & Sard, B. (2016, June 8). *Chart book: Federal housing spending is poorly matched to need*. Washington, DC: Center on Budget and Policy Priorities. Retrieved from http://www.cbpp.org/research/housing/chart-book-federal-housing-spending-is-poorly-matched-to-need

Fishman, P. (1978). Women's work in interaction. *Social Problems, 25*(4), 397–406.

Flacks, R. (1971). *Youth and social change*. Chicago: Markham.

Ford, D. (2015, July 24). Who commits mass shootings? *CNN*. Retrieved from http://www.cnn.com/2015/06/27/us/mass-shootings/

Ford, M. (2015). *Rise of the robots: Technology and the threat of a jobless future*. New York: Basic Books.

Forsythe-Brown, I. (2007). *An exploratory analysis of gender, kinscripts and the work of transnational kinship among Afro-Caribbean immigrant families* (Doctoral dissertation, University of Maryland—College Park). Retrieved from ProQuest (3307758).

Frank, A. G. (1966). The development of underdevelopment. *Monthly Review, 18*(4), 17–31.

Frank, A. G. (1979). *Dependent accumulation and underdevelopment*. London: Macmillan.

Frederick, S., & AWARE (Association of Women for Action and Research) Committee on Rape. (2001). *Rape: Weapon of terror.* River Edge, NJ: Global.

Freire, P. (1972). *Pedagogy of the oppressed*. New York: Herder & Herder.

Freud, S. (1905). Three essays on sexuality. In *Standard Edition* (Vol. 7). London: Hogarth.

Freud, S. (1929). Civilization and its discontents. In *Standard Edition* (Vol. 21). London: Hogarth.

Freud, S. (1933). *New introductory lectures on psychoanalysis*. New York: Norton.

Freund, C. P. (2002). In praise of vulgarity. *Reason, 33*(10), 24–35.

Friedan, B. (1963). *The feminine mystique*. New York: Norton.

Friedan, B. (1981). *The second stage*. New York: Summit.

Friedl, E. (1975). *Women and men: An anthropologist's view*. New York: Holt, Rinehart & Winston.

Friedman, H. L. (2013). Tiger girls on the soccer field. *Contexts, 12*(4), 30–35.

Friedman, S., Squires, G. D., & Galvan, C. (2010). *Cybersegregation in Dallas and Boston: Is Neil a more desirable tenant than Tyrone or Jorge?* Paper presented at the annual meeting of the Population Association of America, Dallas, TX.

Friedman, T. L. (2000). *The Lexus and the olive tree: Understanding globalization*. New York: Anchor Books.

Fromm, E. (1941). *Escape from freedom*. New York: Farrar & Rinehart.

Frum, D. (2000). *How we got here: The '70s*. New York: Basic Books.

Frye, N. K., & Breaugh, J. A. (2004). Family-friendly policies, supervisor support, work–family conflict, family–work conflict, and satisfaction: A test of a conceptual model. *Journal of Business and Psychology, 19*(2), 197–220.

Gale, R. P. (1986). Social movements and the state: The environmental movement, counter movement, and governmental agencies. *Sociological Perspectives, 29,* 202–240.

Gallaudet Research Institute. (2005). *A brief summary of estimates for the size of the deaf population in the USA based on available federal data and published research*. Retrieved from http://research.gallaudet.edu/Demographics/deaf-US.php

Gallaudet University. (2012). *Local and regional deaf populations*. Retrieved from http://libguides.gallaudet.edu/content.php?pid=119476&sid=1029190

Gamble, J. L., & Hess, J. J. (2012). Temperature and violent crime in Dallas, Texas: Relationships and implications of climate change. *Western Journal of Emergency Medicine, 13*(3), 239–246.

Gamson, J. (1991). Silence, death, and the invisible enemy: AIDS activism and social movement "newness." *Social Problems, 36*(4), 351–367.

Gamson, W. (1975). *The strategy of social protest*. Homewood, IL: Dorsey Press.

Gans, H. J. (1972). The positive functions of poverty. *American Journal of Sociology, 78*(2), 275–289.

Garcia, S. B., & Guerra, P. L. (2004). Deconstructing deficit thinking: Working with educators to create more equitable learning environments. *Education and Urban Society, 36*(2), 150–168.

Gardiner, B., Mansfield, M., Anderson, I., Holder, J., Louter, D., & Ulmanu, M. (2016, April 12). The dark side of Guardian comments. *The Guardian*. Retrieved from https://www.theguardian.com/technology/2016/apr/12/the-dark-side-of-guardian-comments

Garfinkel, H. (1963). A conception of, and experiments with, "trust" as a condition of stable concerted actions. In O. J. Harvey (Ed.), *Motivation and social interaction* (pp. 187–238). New York: Ronald Press.

Garfinkel, H. (1985). *Studies in ethnomethodology*. New York: Blackwell.

Gaskell, G., & Smith, P. (1981, August 20). The crowd in history. *New Society*, pp. 303–304.

Gates, G. J. (2011). *How many people are lesbian, gay, bisexual, and transgender?* Los Angeles, CA: The Williams Institute, University of California—Los Angeles. Retrieved from http://williamsinstitute.law.ucla.edu/wp-content/uploads/Gates-How-Many-People-LGBT-Apr-2011.pdf

Gauntlett, D. (2008). *Media, gender, and identity: An introduction* (2nd ed.). New York: Taylor & Francis.

Gaynor, T. (2015, December 18). 2015 likely to break records for forced displacement—study. *United Nations High Commissioner for Refugees*. Retrieved from http://www.unhcr.org/en-us/news/latest/2015/12/5672c2576/2015-likely-break-records-forced-displacement-study.html

Gerding, A., & Signorielli, N. (2014). Gender roles in tween television programming: A content analysis of two genres. *Sex Roles, 70*(1–2), 43–56.

Gerhardt, K. F. G. (1989). *The silent brotherhood: Inside America's racist underground*. New York: Free Press.

Geronimus, A. (1992). The weathering hypothesis and the health of African-American women and infants: Evidence and speculations. *Ethnicity and Disease, 2*(3), 207–221.

Gershoff, E. T., & Grogan-Kaylor, A. (2016, June). Spanking and child outcomes: Old controversies and new meta-analyses. *Journal of Family Psychology, 30*(4), 453–469. Retrieved from http://dx.doi.org/10.1037/fam0000191

Gerstel, N., & Gallagher, S. (1994). Caring for kith and kin: Gender, employment, and the privatization of care. *Social Problems, 41*(4), 519–539.

Gharib, M. (2015, November 30). Love it or hate it, #Givingtuesday has become "a thing." *NPR*. Retrieved from http://www.npr.org/sections/goatsandsoda/2015/11/30/457881058/love-it-or-hate-it-givingtuesday-has-become-a-thing

Ghosh, B. N. (2001). *Dependency theory revisited*. London: Ashgate.

Gibbs, N. (2009, October 14). The state of the American woman: What women want now. *Time*. Retrieved from http://content.time.com/time/specials/packages/article/0,28804,1930277_1930145,00.html

Giddens, A. (1985). *The constitution of society*. Berkeley: University of California Press.

Giedd, J. N. (2004). Structural magnetic resonance imaging of the adolescent brain. *Annals of the New York Academy of Sciences, 1021*, 77–85.

Gilbert, D. L. (2011). *The American class structure in an age of growing inequality* (8th ed.). Thousand Oaks, CA: Pine Forge.

Gilbertson, G. A., & Gurak, D. T. (1993). Broadening the enclave debate: The labor market experiences of Dominican and Colombian men in New York City. *Sociological Forum, 8*(June), 205–220.

Gilligan, C. (1982). *In a different voice: Psychological theory and women's development*. Cambridge, MA: Harvard University Press.

Gilligan, C., Ward, J. V., & Taylor, J. M. (Eds.). (1989). *Mapping the moral domain: A contribution of women's thinking to psychological theory and education*. Cambridge, MA: Harvard University Press.

Gilman, C. P. (1892). The yellow wallpaper (Short story). *The New England Magazine*.

Gilman, C. P. (2006). *Women and economics: A study of the economic relation between men and women as a factor in social evolution*. New York: Cosimo. (Original work published 1898)

Gitlin, T. (1980). *The whole world is watching: Mass media in the making and unmaking of the new left*. Berkeley: University of California Press.

Giugni, M., & Passy, F. (1998). *Social movements and policy change: Direct, mediated, or joint effect?* American Sociological Association Section on Collective Behavior and Social Movements Working Paper Series, 9(4).

Glassdoor. (2015, August 25). *Here's how much more CEOs earn than their employees*. Retrieved from https://www.glassdoor.com/blog/heres-ceos-earn-employee/

Glaze, L. E., & Herberman, E. J. (2013, December). *Correctional populations in the United States, 2012* (BJS Bulletin NCJ 243936). Washington, DC: U.S. Department of Justice, Bureau of Justice Statistics. Retrieved from http://www.bjs.gov/content/pub/pdf/cpus12.pdf

Glazer, N. (1992). The real world of education. *The Public Interest* (Winter), 57–75.

Glazer, N. (1997). *We are all multiculturalists now*. Cambridge, MA: Harvard University Press.

Glenny, M. (2009). *McMafia: A journey through the global criminal underworld*. New York: Knopf.

Glewwe, P. (1999). Why does mother's schooling raise child health in developing countries? Evidence from Morocco. *Journal of Human Resources, 34*, 124–159.

Gleyo, F. (2015, October 10). AP has a robot journalist that writes a thousand articles per month. *Tech Times*. Retrieved from http://www.techtimes.com/articles/93473/20151010/ap-has-a-robot-journalist-that-writes-a-thousand-articles-per-month.htm

Glorioso, C. (2011, September 27). AP opportunity gap: NY's poor students enroll in fewer college-prep courses. *NBC New York*. Retrieved from http://www.nbcnewyork.com/news/local/Advanced-Placement-AP-Classes-College-Prep-New-York-State-130672323.html

Goffman, E. (1959). *The presentation of self in everyday life*. New York: Doubleday.

Goffman, E. (1961). *Asylums: Essays on the social situation of mental patients and other inmates*. Garden City, NY: Anchor Books.

Goffman, E. (1963a). *Behavior in public place*. New York: Free Press.

Goffman, E. (1963b). *Stigma: Notes on the management of spoiled identity*. Englewood Cliffs, NJ: Prentice Hall.

Goffman, E. (1967). *Interaction ritual: Essays on face to face behavior*. Garden City, NY: Anchor.

Goffman, E. (1972). *Relations in public: Microstudies of the public order*. New York: Harper & Row.

Gokcearslan, A. (2010). The effect of cartoon movies on children's gender development. *Procedia: Social and Behavior Sciences, 2*(2), 5202–5207.

Goldhagen, D. J. (1997). *Hitler's willing executioners*. New York: Vintage Books.

Goldin, C. (2014). A grand gender convergence: Its last chapter. *American Economic Review, 104*(4), 1091–1119.

Goldin, C., Katz, M. F., & Kuziemko, I. (2006). *The homecoming of American college women: The reversal of the college gender gap* (Working Paper 12130). Cambridge, MA: National Bureau of Economic Research. Retrieved from http://faculty.smu.edu/millimet/classes/eco7321/papers/goldin%20et%20al.pdf

Golding, W. (1954). *Lord of the flies*. London: Faber and Faber.

Goldscheider, F. K., & Waite, L. J. (1991). *New families, no families? The transformation of the American home*. Berkeley: University of California Press.

Goldstone, J. A. (2001). Towards a fourth generation of revolutionary theory. *Annual Review of Political Science, 4*, 139–187.

Goode, E. (2009). *Moral panics: The social construction of deviance*. Chichester, England: Wiley-Blackwell.

Goodier, R. (2013, September 17). TV may reinforce stereotypes about men in nursing. *Reuters*. Retrieved from http://www.reuters.com/article/us-tv-nurses-idUSBRE98G18G20130917

Goody, J. (1983). *The development of the family and marriage in Europe*. Cambridge: Cambridge University Press.

Gottfredson, M. R., & Hirschi, T. (2004). *A general theory of crime.* Stanford, CA: Stanford University Press. (Original work published 1990)

Gottlieb, L. (2011, July/August). How to land your kid in therapy. *Atlantic Monthly*. Retrieved from https://www.theatlantic.com/magazine/archive/2011/07/how-to-land-your-kid-in-therapy/308555/

Gourevitch, P. (1999). *We wish to inform you that tomorrow we will be killed with our families: Stories from Rwanda*. New York: Farrar, Straus and Giroux.

Gracey, H. L. (1991). Learning the student role: Kindergarten as academic boot camp. In J. M. Henslin (Ed.), *Down to earth sociology: Introductory readings* (6th ed.). New York: Free Press.

Gramsci, A. (1971). *Selections from the prison notebooks* (Q. Hoare & G. N. Smith, Eds. and Trans.). London: Lawrence & Wishart.

Grant, R. (1991). The sources of gender bias in international relations theory. In R. Grant & K. Newland (Eds.), *Gender and international relations* (pp. 8–26). Bloomington: Indiana University Press.

Great Nonprofits. (2016). *Islamic relief USA*. Retrieved from http://greatnonprofits.org/org/islamic-relief-usa

Green, P., & Ward, T. (2004). *State crime: Governments, violence and corruption.* London: Pluto Press.

Greenberg, A. (2015, June 2). The dark web drug lords who got away. *Wired*. Retrieved from https://www.wired.com/2015/06/dark-web-drug-lords-got-away/

Greenberg, K. S. (1996). *The confessions of Nat Turner and related documents*. Boston: Bedford Books.

Greenberg, K. S. (2003). *Nat Turner: A slave rebellion in history and memory.* New York: Oxford University Press.

Greene, K., & Krcmar, M. (2005). Predicting exposure to and liking of media violence: A uses and gratification approach. *Communication Studies, 56*(1), 71–93.

Grey, S. (2006). *Ghost plane: The true story of the CIA torture program*. New York: Macmillan.

Griffin, S. (1978). *Woman and nature: The roaring inside her.* New York: Harper & Row.

Griffin, S. (1979). *Rape, the power of consciousness.* New York: Harper & Row.

Griffin, S. (1981). *Pornography as silence: Culture's revenge against nature*. New York: Harper & Row.

Grimes, S. (2014, November 20). The selfie exchange. *Contexts*. Retrieved from https://contexts.org/articles/the-selfie-exchange/

Grogan, S. (2008). *Body image: Understanding body dissatisfaction in men, women, and children*. New York: Routledge.

Grusky, O., Bonacich, P., & Webster, C. (1995). The coalition structure of the four person family. *Current Research in Social Psychology, 2,* 16–28.

Guerino, P., & Beck, A. J. (2011). *Sexual victimization reported by adult correctional authorities, 2007–2008* (BJS Special Report NCJ 231172). Washington, DC: U.S. Department of Justice, Bureau of Justice Statistics. Retrieved from http://bjs.ojp.usdoj.gov/content/pub/pdf/svraca0708.pdf

Guilmoto, C. Z. (2012). *Sex imbalances at birth*. New York: United Nations Population Fund Asia and Pacific Regional Office. Retrieved from http://www.unfpa.org/publications/sex-imbalances-birth

Gump, L. S., Baker, R. C., & Roll, S. (2000). Cultural and gender differences in moral judgment: A study of Mexican Americans and Anglo-Americans. *Hispanic Journal of Behavioral Sciences, 22*(1), 78–93.

Gunnell, J. J., & Ceci, S. J. (2010). When emotionality trumps reason: A study of individual processing style and juror bias. *Behavioral Sciences & the Law, 28*(6), 850–877.

Gunnoe, M. L. (1997). Toward a developmental contextual model of the effects of parental spanking on children's aggression. *Archives of Pediatrics and Adolescence, 151*(8), 768–775.

Guo, J. (2016, January 25). Researchers have found a major problem with 'The Little Mermaid' and other Disney movies. *Washington Post*. Retrieved from https://www.washingtonpost.com/news/wonk/wp/2016/01/25/researchers-have-discovered-a-major-problem-with-the-little-mermaid-and-other-disney-movies/

Haberman, C. (2014, March 9). The trial that unleashed hysteria over child abuse. *New York Times.* Retrieved from http://www.nytimes.com/2014/03/10/us/the-trial-that-unleashed-hysteria-over-child-abuse.html?_r=0

Habermas, J. (1989). The structural transformation of the public sphere: An inquiry into a category of bourgeois society. Cambridge: MIT Press. (Original work published 1962)

Haggerty, R. A. (Ed.). (1991). *Dominican Republic and Haiti: Country studies* (2nd ed.). Washington, DC: Federal Research Division, Library of Congress.

Haj-yahia, M. M., & Cohen, H. C. (2009). On the lived experience of battered women residing in shelters. *Journal of Family Violence, 24*(2), 95–109.

Haley, A., & Malcolm X. (1964). *The autobiography of Malcolm X.* New York: Ballantine Books.

Hall, E. (1973). *The silent language.* New York: Doubleday.

Hall, P. M. (2003). Interactionism, social organization, and social processes: Looking back there, reflecting now here, and moving ahead then. *Symbolic Interaction, 26,* 33–55.

Hamblin, J. (2016, June 16). Toxic masculinity and murder. *The Atlantic*. Retrieved from http://www.theatlantic.com/health/archive/2016/06/toxic-masculinity-and-mass-murder/486983/

Hamel, L., Rao, M., Levitt, L., Claxton, G., Cox, C., Pollitz, K., & Brodie, M. (2014). *Survey of non-group health insurance enrollees: A first look at people buying their own health insurance following implementation of the Affordable Care Act*. Menlo Park, CA: Kaiser Family Foundation. Retrieved from http://kaiserfamilyfoundation.files.wordpress.com/2014/06/survey-of-non-group-health-insurance-enrollees-findings-final1.pdf

Hamermesh, D. S. (2011). *Beauty pays: Why attractive people are more successful.* Princeton, NJ: Princeton University Press.

Hamermesh, D. S., & Parker, A. (2005). Beauty in the classroom: Professorial pulchritude and putative pedagogical productivity. *Economics of Education Review, 24,* 369–376.

Hamm, M. S. (2002). Apocalyptic violence: The seduction of terrorist subcultures. *Theoretical Criminology, 8*(3), 323–339.

Hammond, E. M., Berry, M. A., & Rodriguez, D. N. (2011). The influence of rape myth acceptance, sexual attitudes, and belief in a just world on attributions of responsibility in a date rape scenario. *Legal and Criminological Psychology, 16*(2), 242–252.

Handlin, O. (1991). *Boston's immigrants, 1790–1880: A study in acculturation*. Cambridge, MA: Belknap Press.

Haney, C., Banks, W. C., & Zimbardo, P. G. (1973). Interpersonal dynamics in a simulated prison. *International Journal of Criminology and Penology, 1,* 69–97.

Haninger, K., & Thompson, K. M. (2004). Content and ratings of teen-rated video games. *Journal of the American Medical Association, 291*(7), 856–865.

Hardoon, D., Fuentes-Nieva, R., & Ayele, S. (2016, January 18). An economy for the 1%: How privilege and power in the economy drive extreme inequality and how this can be stopped. *Oxfam International*. Retrieved from http://policy-practice.oxfam.org.uk/publications/an-economy-for-the-1-how-privilege-and-power-in-the-economy-drive-extreme-inequ-592643

Harkinson, J. (2014, August 13). 4 unarmed black men have been killed by police in the last month. *Mother Jones*. Retrieved from http://www.motherjones.com/politics/2014/08/3-unarmed-black-african-american-men-killed-police

Harper, B. (2000). Beauty, stature and the labour market: A British cohort study. *Oxford*

Bulletin of Economics and Statistics, 62, 771–800.

Harring, H. A., Montgomery, K., & Hardin, J. (2011). Perceptions of body weight, weight, weight management strategies, and depressive symptoms among US college students. *Journal of American College Health, 59*(1), 43–50.

Harrington, M. (1963). *The other America: Poverty in the United States.* New York: Simon & Schuster.

Harris Poll. (2014). Doctors, military officers, firefighters, and scientists seen as among America's most prestigious occupations. Retrieved from http://www.theharrispoll.com/politics/Doctors__Military_Officers__Firefighters__and_Scientists_Seen_as_Among_America_s_Most_Prestigious_Occupations.html

Harris, J. R. (2009). *The nurture assumption: Why children turn out the way they do* (2nd ed.). New York: Free Press.

Harris, K. (2016, April 5). Over sixty percent of millennial women don't know how to ask for more. *Levo.* Retrieved from http://www.levo.com/articles/news/millennial-women-arent-negotiating

Harth, E. (2001). *Last witnesses: Reflections on the wartime internment of Japanese Americans.* London: Palgrave Macmillan.

Hartmann, H. (1984). The unhappy union of Marxism and feminism: Toward a more progressive union. In A. M. Jaggar & P. S. Rothenberg (Eds.), *Feminist frameworks: Alternative theoretical accounts of the relations between women and men* (2nd ed., pp. 172–188). New York: McGraw- Hill.

Harvard Medical School. (2010, July). Marriage and men's health. *Harvard Men's Health Watch Newsletter.* Retrieved from http://www.health.harvard.edu/newsletters/Harvard_Mens_Health_Watch/2010/July/marriage-and-mens-health

Hattery, A. J. (2001). *Families in crisis: Men and women's perceptions of violence in partner relationships.* Blacksburg, VA: Southern Sociological Society.

Hatzenbuehler, P. L., Gillespie, J. M., & O'Neil, C. E. (2012, April). Does healthy food cost more in poor neighborhoods? An analysis of retail food cost and spatial competition. *Agricultural and Resource Economics Review, 41*(1), 43–56.

Hausmann, R., Tyson, L. D., & Zahidi, S. (2011). *The global gender gap report 2011.* Geneva, Switzerland: The World Economic Forum.

Hedwig, L. (2011). Inequality as an explanation for obesity in the United States. *Sociology Compass, 5*(3), 215–232.

Hegewisch, A., & Liepmann, H. (2012). *Fact sheet: The gender wage gap by occupation.* Washington, DC: Institute for Women's Policy Research. Retrieved from http://www.iwpr.org/publications/pubs/the-gender-wage-gap-by-occupation

Hegewisch, A., & Matite, M. (2013). *Fact sheet: The gender wage gap by occupation.* Washington, DC: Institute for Women's Policy Research. Retrieved from http://www.iwpr.org/publications/pubs/the-gender-wage-gap-by-occupation-2

Helin, K. (2016, July 21). NBA makes it official: 2017 All-Star Game pulled from Charlotte due to "Bathroom Law." *NBC Sports.* Retrieved from http://nba.nbcsports.com/2016/07/21/nba-makes-it-official-2017-all-star-game-pulled-from-charlotte-due-to-bathroom-law/

Heppner, C. M. (1992). *Seeds of disquiet: One deaf woman's experience.* Washington, DC: Gallaudet University Press.

Herbert, B. (2010, March 5). Cops vs. kids. *New York Times.* Retrieved from http://www.nytimes.com/2010/03/06/opinion/06herbert.html?_r=0

Heritage, J., & Greatbatch, D. (1991). On the institutional character of institutional talk: The case of news interviews. In D. H. Zimmerman & D. Boden (Eds.), *Talk and social structure* (pp. 93–137). Cambridge: Polity Press.

Hersey, P., Blanchard, K., & Natemeyer, W. (1987). *Situational leadership, perception, and the use of power.* Escondido, CA: Leadership Studies.

Hess, H. (1973). *Mafia and mafiosi: The structure of power.* Farnborough, England: Saxon House.

Hesse-Biber, S. (1997). *Am I thin enough yet? The cult of thinness and the commercialization of identity.* New York: Oxford University Press.

Hill, L. E., & Johnson, H. P. (2002). *How fertility changes across immigrant generations.* San Francisco: Public Policy Institute of California. Retrieved from http://www.ppic.org/content/pubs/rb/RB_402LHRB.pdf

Hillin, T. (2016, May 24). Facebook apologized after fat-shaming a model—but the damage was already done. *Fusion.* Retrieved from http://fusion.net/story/306275/facebook-apologized-after-fat-shaming-model-tess-holliday/

Hine, T. (2000). *The rise and fall of the American teenager.* New York: Bard/Avon.

Hirschi, T. (1969). *Causes of delinquency.* Berkeley: University of California Press.

Hirschi, T. (2004). Self-control and crime. In R. F. Baumeister & K. D. Vohs (Eds.), *Handbook of self-regulation: Research, theory, and applications* (pp. 537–552). New York: Guilford.

Ho, C. (1993). The internationalization of kinship and the feminization of Caribbean migration: The case of Afro-Trinidadian immigrants in Los Angeles. *Human Organization, 52*(1), 32–40.

Hochschild, A. (2001a, December 19). The nanny chain. *The American Prospect.* Retrieved from http://prospect.org/article/nanny-chain

Hochschild, A. R. (2001b). *The time bind: When work becomes home and home becomes work.* New York: Holt.

Hochschild, A. R. (2003). *The managed heart: Commercialization of human feeling.* Berkeley: University of California Press.

Hochschild, A. R. (with Machung, A.). (2012). *The second shift: Working families and the revolution at home* (rev. ed.). New York: Penguin Books.

Holt, T. (1977). *Black over White: Negro political leadership in South Carolina during Reconstruction.* Urbana: University of Illinois Press.

Hooton, E. A. (1939). *The American criminal: An anthropological study.* Cambridge, MA: Harvard University Press.

Hopkins, D. J. (2009). No more Wilder effect, never a Whitman effect: When and why polls mislead about black and female candidates. *Journal of Politics, 71,* 769–781.

Hopper, R. (1991). Hold the phone. In D. H. Zimmerman & D. Boden (Eds.), *Talk and social structure* (pp. 217–231). Cambridge: Polity Press.

Horan, P. M., & Hargis, P. G. (1991). Children's work and schooling in the late nineteenth century family economy. *American Sociological Review, 56,* 583–596.

Horkheimer, M. (1947). *The eclipse of reason.* Oxford: Oxford University Press.

Horkheimer, M., & Adorno, T. (2007). *The dialectic of enlightenment.* Stanford, CA: Stanford University Press. (Original work published 1944)

Houghton, S., Hunter, S. C., Rosenberg, M., Wood, L., Zadow, C., Martin, K., & Shilton, T. (2015). *Virtually impossible: Limiting Australian children and adolescents daily screen based media use.* BMC Public Health. doi:10.1186/1471-2458-15-5

Huber, J. (1990). Macro-micro links in gender stratification: 1989 presidential address. *American Sociological Review, 55,* 1–10.

Huber, J. (1993). Gender role change in families: A macrosociological view. In T. Brubaker (Ed.), *Family relations: Challenges for the future.* Newbury Park, CA: Sage.

Huber, J. (2006). Comparative gender stratification. In J. S. Chafetz (Ed.), *Handbook of the sociology of gender* (pp. 65–80). New York: Springer.

Hudson, J. I., Hiripi, E., Pope, H. G., & Kessler, R. C. (2007). The prevalence and correlates of eating disorders in the National Comorbidity Survey Replication. *Biological Psychiatry, 61,* 248–258.

Huelsman, M. (2015, May 19). The debt divide: The racial and class bias behind the "new normal" of student borrowing. *Demos*. Retrieved from http://www.demos.org/publication/debt-divide-racial-and-class-bias-behind-new-normal-student-borrowing

Huffman, M. L., & Torres, L. (2002). It's not only "who you know" that matters: Gender, personal contacts, and job lead quality. *Gender & Society, 16,* 793–813.

Hunter, L. (2016, June 28). The gender pay gap is even worse at the top. *Fast Company*. Retrieved from http://www.fastcompany.com/3061213/the-gender-pay-gap-is-even-worse-at-the-top

Hutcheon, D. (1999). *Building character and structure*. Westport, CT: Praeger.

Hutchinson, A. (2016, March 18). Here's why Twitter is so important, to everyone. *Social Media Today*. Retrieved from http://www.socialmediatoday.com/social-networks/heres-why-twitter-so-important-everyone

Huxley, A. (2006). *Brave new world*. New York: Harper Perennial. (Original work published 1932).

Hvistendahl, M. (2011). *Unnatural selection: Choosing boys over girls, and the consequences of a world full of men*. New York: Public Affairs.

Hyman, H. H. (1942). The psychology of status. *Archives of Psychology, 38*(15), 147–165.

IBISWorld. (2017, August). *Wedding Services in the U.S.: Market Research Report*. Retrieved from https://www.ibisworld.com/industry/default.aspx?indid=2008

Immerwahr, D. (2007). Caste or colony? Indianizing race in the United States. *Modern Intellectual History, 4*(2), 275–301.

In the trenches of a language war. (2013, December 21). *The Economist,* pp. 86–87.

Ingraham, C. (1999). *White weddings: Romancing heterosexuality in popular culture*. New York: Routledge.

Institute for Women's Policy Research. (2015). *The gender wage gap by occupation 2015 and by race and ethnicity* (IWPR #C431 Tables 1 and 2). Washington, DC: Author.

International Association of Women Judges (IAWJ). (n.d.). *Sextortion*. Retrieved from http://www.iawj.org/Sextortion.html

International Development Research Centre. (n.d.). *The daughter deficit: Exploring declining sex ratios in India.* Ottawa, ON, Canada: Women's Rights and Citizenship. Retrieved from https://www.idrc.ca/en/article/daughter-deficit-exploring-declining-sex-ratios-india

International Labour Organization. (n.d.). Forced labour, modern slavery, and human trafficking. Retrieved from http://www.ilo.org/global/topics/forced-labour/lang—en/index.htm

Iribarren, J. L., & Moro, E. (2007). Information diffusion epidemics in social networks. *Physical Review Letters, 103.*

Isidore, C. (2012, September 6). 3 answers to the auto bailout debate. *CNNMoney*. Retrieved from http://money.cnn.com/2012/09/06/autos/auto-bailout

Jacob, B. A. (2002). *Where the boys aren't: Non-cognitive skills, returns to school, and the gender gap in higher education* (Working Paper 8964). Cambridge, MA: National Bureau of Economic Research. Retrieved from http://www.nber.org/papers/w8964.pdf

Jaffee, S., & Hyde, J. (2000). Gender differences in moral orientation: A meta analysis. *Psychological Bulletin, 126*(5), 703–726.

Jaggar, A. M. (1983). *Feminist politics and human nature.* Totowa, NJ: Rowman & Allanheld.

Janis, I. L. (1972). *Victims of groupthink.* Boston: Houghton Mifflin.

Janis, I. L. (1989). *Crucial decisions: Leadership in policy making and crisis management*. New York: Free Press.

Janis, I. L., & Mann, L. (1977). *Decision making: A psychological analysis of conflict, choice, and commitment*. New York: Free Press.

Jargowsky, P. (2015, August 7). Architecture of segregation: Civil unrest, the concentration of poverty, and public policy. *The Century Foundation*. Retrieved from https://tcf.org/content/report/architecture- of-segregation/

Jenkins, C. D. (1983). Social environment and cancer mortality in men. *New England Journal of Medicine, 308,* 395–408.

Johns, M., Schmader, T., & Martens, A. (2005). Knowing is half the battle: Teaching stereotype threat as a means of improving women's math performance. *Psychological Science, 16*(3), 175–179.

Johnson, J. M., & Ferraro, K. J. (1984). The victimized self: The case of battered women. In J. A. Kotarba & A. Fontana (Eds.), *The existential self in society* (pp. 119–130). Chicago: University of Chicago Press.

Johnson, M. (2013, January 23). The history of Twitter. *Socialnomics*. Retrieved from http://socialnomics.net/2013/01/23/the-history-of-twitter/

Johnston, J. (2014, January 16). Outsourcing Haiti. *Boston Review*. Retrieved from https://bostonreview.net/world/jake-johnston-haiti-earthquake-aid-caracol

Johnston, L. D., O'Malley, P. M., Bachman, J. G., Schulenberg, J. E., & Miech, R.A. (2014). Demographic subgroup trends among adolescents in the use of various licit and illicit drugs, 1975–2014. *Monitoring the Future Occasional Paper No. 83*. Ann Arbor, MI: Institute for Social Research.

Jones, C. (2016, November 20). Giving Tuesday charitable tally rises 44% to smash record. *USA Today*. Retrieved from https://www.usatoday.com/story/money/2016/11/29/giving-tuesday-twitter-donations/94616650/

Jones, J. (2013, August 9). Most in U.S. say it's essential that immigrants learn English. *Gallup*. Retrieved from http://www.gallup.com/poll/163895/say-essential-immigrants-learn-english.aspx

Jones, N. A., & Bullock, J. (2012). *The two or more races population: 2010* (Census Brief C2010BR-13). Washington, DC: U.S. Census Bureau. Retrieved from http://www.census.gov/prod/cen2010/briefs/c2010br-13.pdf

Jones, R. P., & Cox D. (2015). *How race and religion shape millennial attitudes on sexuality and reproductive health*. Washington, DC: Public Religion Research Institute. Retrieved from http://www.prri.org/wp-content/uploads/2015/03/PRRI-Millennials-Web-FINAL.pdf

Jordan, M. (1992, January 9). Big city schools become more segregated in the 1980s, a study says. *Washington Post,* p. A3.

Josephson Institute Center for Youth Ethics. (2012). *2012 Report card on the ethics of American youth*. Los Angeles: Author. Retrieved from http://charactercounts.org/programs/reportcard/2012/index.html

Josephson Institute of Ethics. (2009). *A study of values and behavior concerning integrity: The impact of age, cynicism and high school character*. Los Angeles: Author.

Junco, R. (2012). Too much face and not enough books: The relationship between multiple indices of Facebook use and academic performance. *Computers in Human Behavior, 28*(1), 187–198.

Kaeble, D., & Glaze L. (2016, December). *Correctional populations in the United States, 2015.* Washington, DC: U.S. Department of Justice, Bureau of Justice Statistics. Retrieved from https://www.bjs.gov/content/pub/pdf/cpus15.pdf

Kagay, M. R. (1994, July 8). Poll on doubt of Holocaust is corrected: Roper says 91% are sure it occurred. *New York Times.*

Kahlenberg, S. G., & Hein, M. M. (2010). Progression on Nickelodeon? Gender-role stereotypes in toy commercials. *Sex Roles, 62*(11–12), 830–847.

Kahlor, L. A., & Morrison, D. (2007). Television viewing and rape myth acceptance among college women. *Sex Roles, 56*(11–12), 729–739.

Kaiser Family Foundation. (1998). *American values: 1998 national survey of Americans on values*. Retrieved from http://www.kff.org/kaiserpolls/1441-index.cfm

Kaiser Family Foundation. (2008, October). *Eliminating racial/ethnic disparities in health care: What are the options?* (Health Care and the 2008 Elections). Menlo Park, CA: Author. Retrieved from https://kaiserfamilyfoundation.files.wordpress.com/2013/01/7830.pdf

Kaiser Family Foundation. (2015). *Distribution of medical school graduates by gender*. Retrieved from http://kff.org/other/state-indicator/medical-school-graduates-by-gender/

Kaiser Family Foundation. (2017). *Population distribution by race/ethnicity*. Retrieved from http://www.kff.org/other/state-indicator/distribution-by-raceethnicity/?currentTimeframe=0&sortModel=%7B%22colId%22:%22Location%22,%22sort%22:%22asc%22%7D

Kalmijn, M., 2017. The ambiguous link between marriage and health: A dynamic reanalysis of loss and gain effects. *Social Forces, 95*(4), 1607–1636.

Kalogeropoulos, D. (2015, March 15). The average American watches this much TV every day: How do you compare? [Blog post]. *The Motley Fool*. Retrieved from http://www.fool.com/investing/general/2015/03/15/the-average-american-watches-this-much-tv-every-da.aspx

Kanazawa, S., & Still, M. C. (2000). Parental investment as a game of chicken. *Politics and the Life Sciences, 19,* 17–26.

Kandal, T. R. (1988). *The woman question in classical sociological theory*. Gainesville: University of Florida Press.

Kanter, R. M. (1983). *The change masters: Innovation for productivity in the American corporation*. New York: Simon & Schuster.

Kaplan, S. (2016, February 8). FBI arrests nearly all of the top officials of Crystal City, Texas. *Washington Post*. Retrieved from https://www.washingtonpost.com/news/morning-mix/wp/2016/02/08/theres-only-one-person-left-on-this-texas-city-council-after-fbi-arrests-top-officials-on-corruption-charges/

Kappeler, V. E., Sluder, R. D., & Alpert, G. P. (1998). *Forces of deviance: Understanding the dark side of policing*. Prospect Heights, IL: Waveland Press.

Kapuscinski, R. (2001). *The shadow of the sun*. New York: Vintage Books.

Kara, S. (2009). *Sex trafficking: Inside the business of modern slavery*. New York: Columbia University Press.

Karpinski, A. C., & Duberstein, A. (2009). *A description of Facebook use and academic performance among undergraduate and graduate students*. Columbus: Ohio State University, College of Education and Human Ecology. Retrieved from http://researchnews.osu.edu/archive/facebook2009.jpg

Kasarda, J. (1993). Urban industrial transition and the underclass. In W. J. Wilson (Ed.), *The ghetto underclass* (pp. 43–64). Newbury Park, CA: Sage.

Katz, J. (2006). *The macho paradox*. Naperville, IL: Sourcebooks.

Katz, J., & Chambliss, W. J. (1995). Biology and crime. In J. F. Sheley (Ed.), *Criminology: A contemporary handbook* (2nd ed.). Belmont, CA: Wadsworth.

Katz, J., & Jhally, S. (2000a, February 13). Manhood on the mat: The problem is not that pro wrestling makes boys violent: The real lesson of the wildly popular pseudo-sport is more insidious. *Boston Globe*. Retrieved from http://www.jacksonkatz.com/publication/pub_manhood/

Katz, J., & Jhally, S. (2000b, June 25). Put the blame where it belongs: On men. *Los Angeles Times*. Retrieved from http://articles.latimes.com/2000/jun/25/opinion/op-44616

Kaufman, J. M. (2009). Gendered responses to serious strain: The argument for a general strain of deviance. *Justice Quarterly, 26*(3), 410–444.

Kavner, L. (2012, August 15). Compliance, a low budget Indie, might be the most disturbing movie ever made. *Huffington Post*. Retrieved from http://www.huffingtonpost.com/2012/08/15/compliance-movie-film_n_1779123.html

Kell, J. (2015, May 22). Lean times for the diet industry. *Fortune*. Retrieved from http://fortune.com/2015/05/22/lean-times-for-the-diet-industry/

Kelley, B., & Carchia, C. (2013, July 11). "Hey, data data—swing!": The hidden demographics of youth sports. *ESPN The Magazine*. Retrieved from http://espn.go.com/espn/story/_/id/9469252/hidden-demographics-youth-sports-espn-magazine

Kellner, D. (1990). *Television and the crisis of democracy*. Boulder, CO: Westview Press.

Kelly, M. (2012, June 13). Hollywood's problem with senior citizen sex. *The Atlantic*. Retrieved from http://www.theatlantic.com/entertainment/archive/2012/06/hollywoods-problem-with-senior-citizen-sex/258444/

Kennedy, P. (1987). *The rise and fall of the great powers: Economic change and military conflict from 1500 to 2000*. New York: Random House.

Kennedy-Pipe, C. (1997). *The origins of the present troubles in Northern Ireland*. New York: Longman.

Kenning, C., & Halladay, J. (2008, January 25). Cities study dearth of healthy food. *USA Today*. Retrieved from http://usatoday30.usatoday.com/news/health/2008-01-24-fooddesert_N.htm

Kessler, E.-M., Racoczy, K., & Staudinger, U. (2004). The portrayal of older people in prime time television series: The match with gerontological evidence. *Ageing and Society, 24*(4), 531–552.

Khanna, N. (2011). *Biracial in America: Forming and performing racial identity*. Lanham, MD: Lexington Books.

Kimmel, M. S. (1986). Toward men's studies. *American Behavioral Scientist, 29*(5), 517–529.

Kimmel, M. S. (1996). *Manhood in America: A cultural history*. New York: Free Press.

Kimmel, M. S. (2000). *The gendered society*. New York: Oxford University Press.

Kimmel, M. S. (2013). *Angry white men: Masculinity in America at the end of an era*. New York: Nation Books.

King, H., & Chambliss, W. J. (1984). *Harry King: A professional thief's journey*. New York: Macmillan.

Kluckhohn, F. R., & Strodtbeck, F. L. (1961). *Variations in value orientations*. Evanston, IL: Row, Peterson.

Knight, G. P., Berkel, C., Umaña-Taylor, A. J., Gonzales, N. A., Ettekal, I., Jaconis, M., & Boyd, B. M. (2011). The familial socialization of culturally related values in Mexican American families. *Journal of Marriage and Family, 73*, 913–925. doi:10.1111/j.1741-3737.2011.00856.x

Knox, R. (2015, January 12). 5 years after Haiti's earthquake, where did the $13.5 billion go? *NPR*. Retrieved from http://www.npr.org/sections/goatsandsoda/2015/01/12/376138864/5-years-after-haiti-s-earthquake-why-aren-t-things-better

Kochhar, R. (2015, July 8). *A global middle class is more promise than reality*. Washington, DC: Pew Research Center. Retrieved from http://www.pewglobal.org/2015/07/08/a-global-middle-class-is-more-promise-than-reality/

Kochhar, R., & Fry, R. (2014, December 12). *Wealth inequality has widened along racial, ethnic lines since end of Great Recession*. Washington, DC: Pew Research Center. Retrieved from http://www.pewresearch.org/fact-tank/2014/12/12/racial-wealth-gaps-great-recession/

Kochhar, R., Fry, R., & Taylor, P. (2011). *Wealth gaps rise to record highs between Whites, Blacks, Hispanics*. Washington, DC: Pew Research Center. Retrieved from http://www.pewsocialtrends.org/files/2011/07/SDT-Wealth-Report_7-26-11_FINAL.pdf

Kohlberg, L. (1969). Stage and sequence: The cognitive-developmental approach to socialization. In A. Goslin (Ed.), *Handbook of socialization theory and research* (pp. 347–480). Chicago: Rand McNally.

Kohlberg, L. (1983). *The philosophy of moral development*. New York: Harper & Row.

Kohlberg, L. (1984). *The psychology of moral development*. New York: Harper & Row.

Kohn, M. L. (1989). *Class and conformity: A study in values* (2nd ed.). Chicago: University of Chicago Press.

Kolowich, S. (2011, August 22). What students don't know. *Inside Higher Ed*. Retrieved from http://www.insidehighered.com/news/2011/08/22/erial_study_of_

student_research_habits_at_illinois_university_libraries_reveals_alarmingly_poor_information_literacy_and_skills

Kornhauser, W. (1959). *The politics of mass society*. Glencoe, IL: Free Press.

Kornrich, S., & Furstenberg, F. (2013). Investing in children: Changes in parental spending on children, 1972–2007. *Demography, 50*(1), 1–23.

Kozol, J. (1991). *Savage inequalities: Children in American schools*. New York: HarperCollins.

Kozol, J. (1995). *Amazing grace: Lives of our children and the conscience of a nation*. New York: Crown.

Kozol, J. (2000). *Ordinary resurrections: Children in the years of hope*. New York: Crown.

Kozol, J. (2005). *The shame of the nation: The restoration of apartheid schooling in America*. New York: Three Rivers Press.

Kozol, J. (2013). *Fire in the ashes: Twenty-five years among the poorest children in America*. New York: Broadway Books.

Kraft, A. (2016, April 18). Chinese restaurant fires subpar robot waiters. *CBS News*. Retrieved from http://www.cbsnews.com/news/chinese-restaurant-fires-subpar-robot-waiters/

Kramer, A. (2013, May 13). How are savings groups changing lives? *Oxfam America*. Retrieved from http://firstperson.oxfamamerica.org/2013/05/how-are-savings-groups-changing-lives/

Kramer, R. C., & Michalowski, R. J. (2005). War, aggression and state crime: A criminological analysis of the invasion and occupation of Iraq. *British Journal of Criminology, 45,* 446–469.

Kraut, R., Patterson, M., Lundmark, V., Kiesler, S., Mukopadhayay, T., & Scherlis, W. (1998). Internet paradox: A social technology that reduces social involvement and psychological well-being? *American Psychologist, 53,* 1017–1032.

Kristof, N., & WuDunn, S. (2009). *Half the sky: Turning oppression into opportunity for women worldwide*. New York: Knopf.

Kristofferson, K., White, K., and Peloza, J. (2014a). Observability of an initial act of token support affects subsequent prosocial action. *Journal of Consumer Research 40*(6): 1149–1166.

Kristofferson, K., White, K., & Peloza, J. (2014b). The nature of slacktivism: How the social observability of an initial act of token support affects subsequent prosocial action. *Journal of Consumer Research, 40*(6), 1149–1166.

Kroeger, T., Cooke, T., & Gould, E. (2016). *The class of 2016: The labor market is still far from ideal for young graduates*. Washington, DC: Economic Policy Institute. Retrieved from http://www.epi.org/publication/class-of-2016/#epi-toc-6

Kroeger, T., & Gould, E. (2017, May 4). The class of 2017. *Economic Policy Institute*. Retrieved from http://www.epi.org/publication/the-class-of-2017/

Krogstad, J. M., & Lopez, M. H. (2014, April 29). *Hispanic nativity shift*. Washington, DC: Pew Research Center. Retrieved from http://www.pewhispanic.org/2014/04/29/hispanic-nativity-shift/

Kronk, E. A. (2013, April 16). One statute for two spirits: Same-sex marriage in Indian country. *Jurist Forum*. Retrieved from https://papers.ssrn.com/sol3/papers.cfm?abstract_id=2263441

Kubota, Y. (2009, June 8). Tokyo firm rents fake family, friends for weddings. *Reuters*. Retrieved from http://www.reuters.com/article/2009/06/08/us-japan-weddings-idUSTRE5571IY20090608

Kubrin, C. E. (2005). Gangstas, thugs, and hustlas: Identity and the code of the street in rap music. *Social Problems, 52*(3), 360–378.

Kurdek, L. A. (2007). The allocation of household labor by partners in gay and lesbian couples. *Journal of Family Issues, 28,* 132–148.

Lane, H. (1992). *The mask of benevolence: Disabling the deaf*. New York: Random House.

Lane, H. (2005). Ethnicity, ethics, and the deaf world. *Journal of Deaf Studies and Deaf Education, 10*(3), 291–310.

Lang, T. (2016, January 6). 11 past and present social movements led by college students. *Fresh U*. Retrieved from https://www.freshu.io/taylor-lang/the-biggest-social-movements-led-by-college-students-in-history

Langton, L., Planty, M., & Sandholtz, N. (2013). *Hate crime victimization, 2003–2011* (NCJ 241291). Washington, DC: U.S. Department of Justice, Bureau of Justice Statistics. Retrieved from http://www.bjs.gov/index.cfm?ty=pbdetail&iid=4614

Lanier, J. (2013). *Who owns the future?* New York: Simon & Schuster.

Lareau, A. (2002). Invisible inequality: Social class and childrearing in Black families and White families. *American Sociological Review, 67,* 747–776.

Laris, M. (2016, June 9). This government competition could completely change the American city. *Washington Post*. Retrieved from https://www.washingtonpost.com/local/trafficandcommuting/can-a-wonked-out-reality-competition-help-save-the-american-city/2016/06/08/f5f0b3d8-112f-11e6-8967-7ac733c56f12_story.html

Latimer, L. A., C. E. Velazquez, & Pasch, K. E. (2013). Characteristics and behaviors of non-overweight college students who are trying to lose weight. *Journal of Primary Prevention, 34*(4), 251–260. Retrieved from http://dx.doi.org.proxygw.wrlc.org/10.1007/s10935-013-0309-0

Laub, J., & Sampson, R. J. (2003). *Shared beginnings, divergent lives*. Cambridge, MA: Harvard University Press.

Lauzen, M., Dozier, D., & Horan, N. (2008). Constructing gender stereotypes through social roles in primetime television. *Journal of Broadcasting & Electronic Media, 52*(2), 200–214.

Lawson, K. M., Crouter A. C., & McHale, S. M. (2015, October). Links between family gender socialization experiences in childhood and gendered occupational attainment in young adulthood. *Journal of Vocational Behavior, 90*, 26–35.

Le Bon, G. (1960). *The crowd: A study of the popular mind*. New York: Viking Press. (Original work published 1896)

Leaper, C., Breed, L., Hoffman, L., & Perlman, C. A. (2002). Variations in the gender-stereotyped content of children's television cartoons across genres. *Journal of Applied Social Psychology, 32*(8), 1653–1662.

Leaper, C., & Robnett, R. D. (2011). Women are more likely than men to use tentative language, aren't they? A meta-analysis testing for gender differences and moderators. *Psychology of Women Quarterly, 35*(1), 129–142.

Lee, M. M., Carpenter, B., & Meyers, L. S. (2007). Representations of older adults in television advertisements. *Journal of Aging Studies, 21*(1), 23–30.

Leibbrandt, A., & List, J. A. (2012, November). *Do women avoid salary negotiations? Evidence from a large scale natural field experiment* (NBER Working Paper No. 18511). Cambridge, MA: National Bureau of Economic Research. Retrieved from http://www.nber.org/papers/w18511

Lemann, N. (1991). *The promised land: The great Black migration and how it changed America*. New York: Vintage Books.

Lemert, E. (1951). *Social pathology*. New York: McGraw-Hill.

Lempert, D. (2007). *Women's increasing wage penalties from being overweight and obese*. Washington, DC: U.S. Bureau of Labor Statistics. Retrieved from http://www.bls.gov/osmr/abstract/ec/ec070130.htm

Lenning, E. (2007). Execution for body parts: A case of state crime. *Contemporary Justice Review, 10*(2), 173–191.

Leonhardt, D. (2009, September 8). Colleges are failing in graduation rates. *New York Times*. Retrieved from http://www.nytimes.com/2009/09/09/business/economy/09leonhardt.html

Lester, D. (Ed.). (2000). *Suicide prevention: Resources for the millennium*. Philadelphia: Brunner-Routledge.

Levine, L. (2012, December 17). *Offshoring (or offshore outsourcing) and job loss among U.S. workers* (CRS 7-5700; RL32292). Washington, DC: Congressional Research Service. Retrieved from http://fas.org/sgp/crs/misc/RL32292.pdf

Levine, M., & Crowther, S. (2008). The responsive bystander: How social group membership and group size can encourage as well as inhibit bystander intervention. *Journal of Interpersonal Psychology, 95*(6), 1429–1439.

LeVine, R. A., LeVine, S., Schnell-Anzola, B., Rowe, M. L., & Dexter, E. 2012. *Literacy and mothering: How women's schooling changes the lives of the world's children.* New York: Oxford University Press.

Levine, S., & Laurie, N. O. (Eds.). (1974). *The American Indian today.* Baltimore: Penguin Books.

Levintova, H. (2015, October 1). Girls are the fastest-growing group in the juvenile justice system. *Mother Jones*. Retrieved from http://www.motherjones.com/politics/2015/09/girls-make-ever-growing-proportion-kids-juvenile-justice-system

Levitt, P. (2004, October 1). Transnational migrants: When "home" means more than one country. *Migration Policy Institute.* Retrieved from http://www.migrationpolicy.org/article/transnational-migrants-when-home-means-more-one-country

Lewin, T. (2011a, September 27). College graduation rates are stagnant even as enrollment rises, a study finds. *New York Times.* Retrieved from http://www.nytimes.com/2011/09/27/education/27remediation.html

Lewin, T. (2011b, October 25). Screen time higher than ever for children. *New York Times.* Retrieved from http://www.nytimes.com/2011/10/25/us/screen-time-higher-than-ever-for-children-study-finds.html

Lienert, P., & Thompson, M. (2014, April 2). GM avoided defective switch redesign in 2005 to save a dollar each. *Reuters.* Retrieved from http://www.reuters.com/article/2014/04/02/us-gm-recall-delphi-idUSBREA3105R20140402

Light, H. K., & Martin, R. E. (1986). American Indian families. *Journal of American Indian Education, 26*(1), 1–5.

Lindsey, E. W., & Mize, J. (2001). Contextual differences in parent–child play: Implications for children's gender role development. *Sex Roles, 44,* 155–176.

Lips, H. (2008). *Sex and gender: An introduction* (6th ed.). Boston: McGraw-Hill.

Living Tongues Institute for Endangered Languages. (n.d.). *Who we are*. Retrieved from http://www.livingtongues.org/aboutus.html

Livingston, G. (2014). *Growing number of dads home with the kids.* Washington, DC: Pew Research Center. Retrieved from http://www.pewsocialtrends.org/2014/06/05/growing-number-of-dads-home-with-the-kids

Livingstone, S., & Brake, D. R. (2010). On the rapid rise of social networking sites: New findings and policy implications. *Children and Society, 24,* 75–83.

Lofland, J. (1985). *Protest: Studies of collective behavior and social movements.* New Brunswick, NJ: Transaction.

Lofquist, D., Lugaila, T., O'Connell, M., & Feliz, S. (2012). *Households and families: 2010* (Census Brief C2010BR-14). Washington, DC: U.S. Census Bureau. Retrieved from http://www.census.gov/prod/cen2010/briefs/c2010br-14.pdf

Logan, J. R., Minca, E., & Adar, S. (2012). The geography of inequality: Why separate means unequal in American public schools. *Sociology of Education, 85*(3), 287–301.

Lombroso, C. (1896). *L'homme criminel.* Paris: F. Alcan.

Lonsway, K. A., Banyard, V. L., Berkowitz, A. D., Gidycz, C. A., Katz, J. T., Koss, M. P., Schewe, P. A., & Ullman, S. E. (2009). *Rape prevention and risk reduction: Review of the literature for practitioners.* Harrisburg, PA: VAWnet. Retrieved from http://oregonsatf.org/wp-content/uploads/2012/05/AR_RapePrevention.pdf

Loo, C. M. (1991). *Chinatown: Most time, hard time.* New York: Praeger.

Lough, R., & Denholm, E. (2005, July 17). *Violence against women in Northern Uganda.* London: Amnesty International. Retrieved from https://www.amnestyusa.org/reports/uganda-violence-against-women-in-northern-uganda/

Lubeck, S. (1985). *Sandbox society: Early education in Black and White America.* London: Falmer.

Lucas, J. W., & Lovaglia, M. J. (1998). Leadership status, group size, and emotion in face-to-face groups. *Sociological Perspectives, 41*(3), 617–637.

Maas, P. (1997). *Serpico.* New York: HarperTorch.

Mac Ionnrachtaigh, F. (2013). *Language, resistance and revival: Republican prisoners and the Irish language in the North of Ireland.* London: Pluto Press.

MacKinnon, C. A. (1982). Feminism, Marxism, method and the state: An agenda for theory. *Signs, 7*(3), 515–544.

MacKinnon, C. A. (1989). *Toward a feminist theory of the state.* Cambridge, MA: Harvard University Press.

Madlock, P. E., & Westerman, D. (2011). Hurtful cyber-teasing and violence: Who's laughing out loud? *Journal of Interpersonal Violence, 26*(17), 3542–3560.

Maher, J. K., Herbst, K. C., Childs, N. M., & Finn, S. (2008). Racial stereotypes in children's television commercials. *Journal of Advertising Research, 48*(3), 80–93.

Maher, L. (1997). *Sexed work: Gender, race, and resistance in a Brooklyn drug market.* New York: Oxford University Press.

Makoye, K. (2015, April 24). Tanzania cracks down on sextortion by public officials. *Reuters.* Retrieved from http://uk.reuters.com/article/uk-tanzania-sextortion/tanzania-cracks-down-on-sextortion-by-public-officials-idUKKBN0NF1LG20150424

Malacrida, C. (2005). Discipline and dehumanization in a total institution: Institutional survivors' descriptions of time-out rooms. *Disability & Society, 20*(5), 523–537.

Malinauskas, B. M., Raedeke, T. D., Aeby, V. G., Smith, J. L., & Dallas, M. B. (2006). Dieting practices, weight perceptions, and body composition: A comparison of normal weight, overweight, and obese college females. *Nutrition Journal, 5*(11).

Mann, C. R., & Zatz, M. S. (Eds.). (1998). *Images of color, images of crime.* Los Angeles: Roxbury.

Marcuse, H. (1964). *One-dimensional man.* Boston: Beacon Press.

Margolis, E. (2001). *The hidden curriculum in higher education.* New York: Routledge.

Marini, M. M. (1990). Sex and gender: What do we know? *Sociological Forum, 5*(1), 95–120.

Markert, J. (2010). The changing face of racial discrimination: Hispanics as the dominant minority in the United States—A new application of power-threat theory. *Critical Sociology, 36*(2), 307–327.

Marks, P. (2016, June 12). 'Hamilton' doesn't hit a record at the Tonys, but dominates the night. *Washington Post.* Retrieved from https://www.washingtonpost.com/entertainment/theater_dance/hamilton-doesnt-hit-a-record-at-the-tonys-but-dominates-the-night/2016/06/12/5f639dd2-30b9-11e6-8758-d58e76e11b12_story.html

Markusen, E. (2002). Mechanisms of genocide. In C. Rittner, J. K. Roth, & J. M. Smith (Eds.), *Will genocide ever end?* (pp. 83–90). St. Paul, MN: Paragon House.

Marlowe, C. M., Schneider, S. L., & Nelson, C. E. (1996). Gender and attractiveness biases in hiring decisions: Are more experienced managers less biased? *Journal of Applied Psychology, 81,* 11–21.

Martin, C. L., & Fabes, R. A. (2001). The stability and consequences of young children's same-sex peer interactions. *Developmental Psychology, 37,* 431–446.

Martin, D. S. (2012, March 1). Vets feel abandoned after secret drug experiments. *CNN.* Retrieved from http://edition.cnn.com/2012/03/01/health/human-test-subjects

Martin, K. A., & Kazyak, E. (2009). Hetero-romantic love and heterosexiness in children's G-rated films. *Gender & Society, 23*(3), 315–336.

Martineau, H. (1837). *Society in America.* New York: Saunders & Otley.

Marwell, G., & Oliver, P. (1993). *The critical mass in collective action: A micro-social theory.* New York: Cambridge University Press.

Marx, G. T., & McAdam, D. (1994). *Collective behavior and social movements: Process and structure.* Englewood Cliffs, NJ: Prentice Hall.

Marx, K. (1992a). *Capital: A critique of political economy* (Vol. 1). New York: Penguin Classics. (Original work published 1867)

Marx, K. (1992b). *Capital: A critique of political economy* (Vol. 2). New York: Penguin Classics. (Original work published 1885)

Marx, K. (1992c). *Capital: A critique of political economy* (Vol. 3). New York: Penguin Classics. (Original work published 1894)

Marx, K., & Engels, F. (1998). *The communist manifesto.* New York: Verso. (Original work published 1848)

Massey, D. S. (2011). Epilogue: The past and future of Mexico–U.S. migration. In O.-V. Mark (Ed.), *Beyond la frontera: The history of Mexico–U.S. migration* (pp. 241–265). New York: Oxford University Press.

Massey, D. S., & Denton, N. A. (1993). *American apartheid: Segregation and the making of the underclass.* Boston: Harvard University Press.

Masucci, M., & Langton, L. (2017). *Hate Crime Victimization, 20014-2015.* Washington, DC: Bureau of Justice Statistics. Retrieved from https://www.bjs.gov/content/pub/pdf/hcv0415.pdf.

Mayer, G. (2004, August 31). *Union membership trends in the United States.* Washington, DC: Congressional Research Service. Retrieved from http://digitalcommons.ilr.cornell.edu/cgi/viewcontent.cgi?article=1176&context=key_workplace

Mazur, E., & Richards, L. (2011). Adolescents' and emerging adults' social networking online: Homophily or diversity? *Journal of Applied Developmental Psychology, 32*(4), 180–188.

Mazzella, R., & Feingold, A. (1994). The effects of physical attractiveness, race, socioeconomic status, and gender of defendant and victims on judgments of mock jurors: A meta-analysis. *Journal of Applied Social Psychology, 24,* 1315–1344.

McAdam, D. (1982). *Political process and the development of Black insurgency, 1930–1970.* Chicago: University of Chicago Press.

McAdam, D. (1986). Recruitment to high-risk activism: The case of freedom summer. *American Journal of Sociology, 92,* 64–90.

McAdam, D. (1988). *Freedom summer: The idealists revisited.* New York: Oxford University Press.

McAdam, D., McCarthy, J. D., & Zald, M. N. (1988). Social movements. In N. J. Smelser (Ed.), *Handbook of sociology* (pp. 695–737). Newbury, Park, CA: Sage.

McCarthy, J. D., & Zald, M. N. (1973). *The trend of social movements in America: Professionalization and resource mobilization.* Morristown, NJ: General Learning.

McCarthy, J. D., & Zald, M. N. (1977). Resource mobilization and social movements: A partial theory. *American Journal of Sociology, 82,* 1212–1241.

McCartney, J. T. (1992). *Black power ideologies: An essay in African American political thought.* Philadelphia: Temple University Press.

McCoy, A. W. (1991). *The politics of heroin: CIA complicity in the global drug trade.* New York: Lawrence Hill.

McDonald, S., & Day, J. C. (2010). Race, gender, and the invisible hand of social capital. *Sociology Compass, 4*(7), 532–543.

McDonald, S., Lin, N., & Ao, D. (2009). Networks of opportunity: Gender, race, and job leads. *Social Problems, 56*(3), 385–402.

McDonald, S., & Mair, C. A. (2010). Social capital across the life course: Age and gendered patterns of network resources. *Sociological Forum, 25,* 335–359.

McGonigal, J. (2011). *Reality is broken: Why games make us better and how they can change the world.* New York: Penguin.

McGregor, J. (2014, January 3). Zappos says goodbye to bosses. *Washington Post.* Retrieved from http://www.washingtonpost.com/blogs/on-leadership/wp/2014/01/03/zappos-gets-rid-of-all-managers

McGuire, L. C., Okoro, C. A., Goins, R. T., & Anderson, L. A. (2008). Characteristics of American Indian and Alaska native adult caregivers: Behavioral Risk Factor Surveillance System, 2000. *Ethnicity & Disease, 18*(4), 520.

McIntosh, P. (1990). White privilege: Unpacking the invisible knapsack. *Independent School, 49*(2), 31–36.

McKenna, K. Y. A., & Bargh, J. A. (1998). Coming out in the age of the Internet: Identity "demarginalization" through virtual group participation. *Journal of Personality and Social Psychology, 75*(3), 681–694.

McLean, B., & Elkind, P. (2003). *The smartest guys in the room: The amazing rise and scandalous fall of Enron.* New York: Penguin/Portfolio.

McLean, B., & Nocera, J. (2010). *All the devils are here: The hidden history of the financial crisis.* New York: Penguin/Portfolio.

McLoyd, V. C., & Smith, J. (2002). Physical discipline and behavior problems in African American, European American, and Hispanic children: Emotional support as a moderator. *Journal of Marriage and Family, 64*(1), 40–53.

McLuhan, M. (1964). *Understanding media: The extensions of man.* New York: McGraw-Hill.

McMillan, S. (2001, October/November). What time is dinner? *History Magazine.* Retrieved from http://www.history-magazine.com/dinner2.html

McNeely, C. L. (1995). *Constructing the nation-state: International organization and prescriptive action.* Westport, CT: Greenwood.

Mead, G. H. (1934). *Mind, self, and society.* Chicago: University of Chicago Press.

Mead, G. H. (1938). *The philosophy of the act.* Chicago: University of Chicago Press.

Mednick, S. A., Gabrielli, W. F., Jr., & Hutchings, B. (1987). Genetic factors in the etiology of criminal behavior. In S. A. Mednick, T. E. Moffitt, & S. A. Stack (Eds.), *The causes of crime: New biological approaches.* Cambridge, England: Cambridge University Press.

Mednick, S. A., Moffitt, T. E., & Stack, S. A. (1987). *The causes of crime: New biological approaches.* Cambridge, England: Cambridge University Press.

Mehra, A., Dixon, A. L., Brass, D. J., & Robertson, B. (2006). The social network ties of group leaders: Implications for group performance and leader reputation. *Organization Science, 17*(1), 64–79.

Melucci, A. (1989). *Nomads of the present: Social movements and individual needs in contemporary society.* Philadelphia: Temple University Press.

Melvin, D., Walsh, N. P., & Hume, T. (2016, January 15). Starvation in Syria a "war crime," U.N. chief says. *CNN.* Retrieved from http://www.cnn.com/2016/01/15/middleeast/syria-madaya-starvation/

Merry, S. (2016, March 4). People hate the Ghostbusters trailer and yes, it's because it stars women. *Washington Post.* Retrieved from https://www.washingtonpost.com/news/arts-and-entertainment/wp/2016/03/04/people-are-hating-the-ghostbusters-trailer-guess-why/?utm_term=.b9fbe3b9c752 /

Merton, R. K. (1938). Social structure and anomie. *American sociological review, 3*(5), 672–682.

Merton, R. K. (1968). *Social theory and social structure.* New York: Free Press.

Merton, R. K. (1996). *On social structure and science.* Chicago: University of Chicago Press.

Messerschmidt, J. W. (1986). *Capitalism, patriarchy and crime: Towards a socialist feminist criminology.* Totowa, NJ: Rowman & Littlefield.

Messerschmidt, J. W. (1993). *Masculinities and crime: Critique and reconceptualization of theory.* Lanham, MD: Rowman & Littlefield.

Meyrowitz, J. (1985). *No sense of place: The impact of electronic media on social behavior.* Oxford: Oxford University Press.

Michalowski, R., & Dubisch, J. (2001). *Run for the wall: Remembering Vietnam on a motorcycle pilgrimage*. New Brunswick, NJ: Rutgers University Press.

Migration Policy Institute. (2015). *Largest U.S. immigrant groups over time, 1960-present*. Retrieved from http://www.migrationpolicy.org/programs/data-hub/charts/largest-immigrant-groups-over-time

Milgram, S. (1963). Behavioral studies in obedience. *Journal of Abnormal Psychology, 67,* 371–378.

Miller, K. A., Kohn, M. A., & Schooler, C. (1986). Educational self-direction and personality. *American Sociological Review, 5,* 372–390.

Miller, K. E., Melnick, M. J., Barnes, G. M., Farrell, M. P., & Sabo, D. F. (2005). Untangling the links among athletic involvement, gender, race, and adolescent academic outcomes. *Sociology of Sport Journal, 22*(2), 178–193.

Miller, L. P. (1995). Tracking the progress of *Brown*. *Teachers College Record, 96*(4), 609–613.

Miller, T., Govil, N., McMurria, J., & Maxwell, R. (2002). *Global Hollywood*. London: British Film Institute.

Millett, K. (1970). *Sexual politics*. Garden City, NY: Doubleday.

Mills, C. W. (2000a). *The power elite*. New York: Oxford University Press. (Original work published 1956)

Mills, C. W. (2000b). *The sociological imagination* (40th anniversary ed.). New York: Oxford University Press. (Original work published 1959)

Miner, H. (1956). Body ritual among the Nacirema. *American Anthropologist, 58*(3), 503–507.

Mitchiner, J., & Sass-Lehrer, M. (2011). My child can have more choices: Reflections of deaf mothers on cochlear implants for their children. In R. Paludneviciene & I. W. Leigh (Eds.), *Cochlear implants: Evolving perspectives*. Washington, DC: Gallaudet University Press.

Mizruchi, M. S., & Potts, B. B. (1998). Centrality and power revisited: Actor success in group decision making. *Social Networks, 20*(4), 353–387.

Moloney, C. J. (2012). *The buffalo slaughter and the conquest of the West* (Master's thesis, George Washington University).

Moloney, C. J., & Chambliss, W. J. (2014). Slaughtering the bison, controlling Native Americans: A state crime and green criminology synthesis. *Critical Criminology, 22,* 319–338.

Molotch, H. L. (1972). *Managed integration: Dilemmas of doing good in the city*. Berkeley: University of California Press.

Molotch, H. L., & Boden, D. (1985). Talking social structure: Discourse, dominance, and the Watergate hearings. *American Sociological Review, 50,* 273–288.

Monaghan, A. (2014, November 13). US wealth inequality—top 0.1% worth as much as the bottom 90%. *The Guardian*. Retrieved from https://www.theguardian.com/business/2014/nov/13/us-wealth-inequality-top-01-worth-as-much-as-the-bottom-90

Mongeau, L. (2016). Pulling reservation schools back from the brink. *The Hechinger Report*. Retrieved from http://hechingerreport.org/pulling-reservation- schools-back-brink/

Monroe, P. (1940). *Founding of the American public school system*. New York: Macmillan.

Moore, J. (2010, June 30). Congo war leaves legacy of sexual violence against women. *Christian Science Monitor.* Retrieved from http://www.csmonitor.com/World/Africa/2010/0630/Congo-war-leaves-legacy-of-sexual-violence-against-women

Moore, J. D. (2004). *Visions of culture: An introduction to anthropological theories and theorists* (2nd ed.). Walnut Creek, CA: AltaMira Press.

Moore, J. W. (1991). *Going down to the barrio: Homeboys and homegirls in change*. Philadelphia: Temple University Press.

Moore, J., & Pinderhughes, R. (2001). The Latino population: The importance of economic restructuring. In M. L. Andersen & P. H. Collins (Eds.), *Race, class, and gender: An anthology* (4th ed., pp. 251–258). Belmont, CA: Wadsworth.

Moore, P. (2016, April 26). Most Americans think released felons should have the vote. *YouGov*. Retrieved from https://today.yougov.com/news/2016/04/26/most-americans-think-released-felons-should-have-v/

Morath, E. (2016, July 19). Narrow the pay gap? There are apps for that. *Wall Street Journal*. Retrieved from http://blogs.wsj.com/economics/2016/07/19/narrow-the-gender-pay-gap-there-are-apps-for-that/

Morgan, J. (1999). *When chickenheads come home to roost: A hip hop feminist breaks it down*. New York: Touchstone.

Morgan, L. H. (1964). *Ancient society, or researches in the lines of human progress, from savagery through barbarism to civilization*. Cambridge, MA: Harvard University Press. (Original work published 1877)

Morgenstern, J. (2008, November 14). "Slumdog" finds rare riches in poor boy's tale. *Wall Street Journal.* Retrieved from http://online.wsj.com/article/SB122661670370126131.html

Morrison, M. K. C. (1987). *Black political mobilization: Leadership, power, and mass behavior*. Albany: State University of New York Press.

Moynihan, D. P. (1965). *The Negro family: The case for national action.* Washington, DC: U.S. Government Printing Office.

Mudde, C. (2011). *The relationship between immigration and nativism in Europe and North America.* Washington, DC: Migration Policy Institute. Retrieved from http://www.migrationpolicy.org/pubs/Immigration-Nativism.pdf

Mukhopadhyay, C. C., & Higgins, P. (1988). Anthropological studies of women's status revisited: 1977–87. *Annual Review of Anthropology, 17,* 461–495.

Muller, J. (2014, February 15). UAW's loss and what it means for your paycheck. *Forbes*. Retrieved from http://www.forbes.com/sites/joannmuller/2014/02/15/uaws-loss-and-what-it-means-for-your-paycheck

Muller, T., & Espenshade, T. J. (1985). *The fourth wave: California's newest immigrants.* Washington, DC: Urban Institute Press.

Muncer, S. J., & Campbell, A. (2000). Comments on "Sex differences in beliefs about aggression: Opponent's sex and the form of aggression" by J. Archer and A. Haigh. *British Journal of Social Psychology, 39*(2), 309–311.

Murdock, G. P. (1949). *Social structure.* New York: Macmillan.

Murphy, C. (2007). *Are we Rome? The fall of an empire and the fate of America*. New York: Houghton Mifflin Harcourt.

Murphy, M. (2012, December 18). But what about the men? Masculinity and mass shootings. *Feminist Current*. Retrieved from http://www.feministcurrent.com/2012/12/18/but-what-about-the-men-on-masculinity-and-mass-shootings/

Murphy, R. (1988). *Social closure: The theory of monopolization and exclusion*. Oxford: Clarendon.

Musick, K., & Meier, A. (2012). Assessing causality and persistence in associations between family dinners and adolescent well-being. *Journal of Marriage and Family 74*(3), 476–493.

Mutchler, J. E., Baker, L. E., & Lee, S. (2007). Grandparents responsible for grandchildren in Native-American families. *Social Science Quarterly, 88*(4), 990–1009.

Mutharayappa, R., Choe, M. K., Arnold, F., & Roy, T. K. (1997, March). *Son preference and its effect on fertility in India* (National Family Survey Subject Reports No. 3). Honolulu: East-West Center Program on Population. Retrieved from http://scholarspace.manoa.hawaii.edu/bitstream/handle/10125/3475/NFHSsubjrpt003.pdf? sequence=1

Myrdal, G. (1963). *Challenge to affluence.* New York: Random House.

Narayan, U., & Harding, S. (2000). *Decentering the center: Philosophy for a multicultural, postcolonial, and feminist world.* Bloomington: Indiana University Press.

National Association of Realtors. (2012). *The digital house hunt: Consumer and market trends in real estate*. Retrieved from http://www.realtor.org/sites/default/files/Study-Digital-House-Hunt-2013-01_1.pdf

National Association of the Deaf. (2000). *NAD position statement on cochlear implants*. Retrieved from http://www.nad.org/issues/technology/assistive-listening/cochlear-implants

National Center for Charitable Statistics. (2013). *Quick facts about nonprofits*. Retrieved from http://nccs.urban.org/statistics/quickfacts.cfm

National Center for Education Statistics. (2009). Gender: Grade point average. *Nation's Report Card, National Assessment of Educational Progress*. Retrieved from http://www.nationsreportcard.gov/hsts_2009/gender_gpa.asp

National Center for Education Statistics. (2016a, May). *Immediate college enrollment rate*. Retrieved from http://nces.ed.gov/programs/coe/indicator_cpa.asp

National Center for Education Statistics. (2016b). *Undergraduate retention and graduation rates*. Retrieved from https://nces.ed.gov/programs/coe/indicator_ctr.asp

National Center for Health Statistics. (2015). *Aggregate data 1950–2014*. Atlanta, GA: Centers for Disease Control and Prevention.

National Commission on Excellence in Education. (1983). *A nation at risk: The imperative for educational reform*. Washington, DC: Author.

National Conference of State Legislatures. (2016, September 29). *Felon voting rights*. Retrieved from http://www.ncsl.org/research/elections-and-campaigns/felon-voting-rights.aspx

National Employment Law Project. (2014, April). *The low-wage recovery: Industry employment and wages four years into the recovery* (Data Brief). New York: Author. Retrieved from http://www.nelp.org/page/-/reports/low-wage-recovery-industry-employment-wages-2014-report.pdf?nocdn=1

National Institute of Mental Health. (2010). *The numbers count: Mental disorders in America*. Retrieved from http://www.nimh.nih.gov/health/publications/the-numbers-count-mental-disorders-in-america/index.shtml#Hudson

National Organization for Women. (n.d.). *Education and Title IX*. Retrieved May 15, 2015, from http://www.now.org/issues/title_ix/index.html

National Public Radio. (2010, November 5). Counting crowds: Results may vary. *Science Friday*. Retrieved from http://www.npr.org/templates/story/story.php?storyId=131099075

National Public Radio. (2011, June 20). *How an athlete's death led to shoddy drug laws*. Retrieved from http://www.npr.org/2011/06/20/137302172/op-ed-bias-death-prompted-shoddy-legislation

National Public Radio. (2016, April 18). *Why America's schools have a money problem*. Retrieved from http://www.npr.org/2016/04/18/474256366/why-americas-schools-have-a-money-problem

National Survey of Student Engagement (NSSE). (2012). *Fostering student engagement campuswide: Annual results 2012*. Bloomington: Indiana University Center for Postsecondary Research. Retrieved May 15, 2015, from http://nsse.iub.edu/html/annual_results.cfm

Naylor, N. T. (2002). *Wages of crime: Black markets, illegal finance, and the underworld economy*. Ithaca, NY: Cornell University Press.

Neate, R. (2015, May 3). America's trailer parks: The residents may be poor but the owners are getting rich. *The Guardian*. Retrieved from http://www.theguardian.com/lifeandstyle/2015/may/03/owning-trailer-parks-mobile-home-university-investment

Neuman, W. L. (2000). *Social research methods: Qualitative and quantitative approaches*. Toronto: Allyn & Bacon.

New America Foundation. (2012). *Federal education budget project*. Retrieved from http://febp.newamerica.net/k12

Newcomb, T. C. (2008). *Parameters of parenting in Native American families* (Doctoral dissertation, Oklahoma State University). Retrieved from ProQuest (3320882).

Neyazi, T. A. (2010). Cultural imperialism or vernacular modernity? Hindi newspapers in a globalizing India. *Media, Culture & Society, 32*(6), 907–924.

Niarchos, C. N. (1995). Women, war, and rape: Challenges facing the International Tribunal for the Former Yugoslavia. *Human Rights Quarterly, 17*(4), 649–690.

Nicholas, S. E. (2009). "I live Hopi, I just don't speak it": The critical intersection of language, culture and identity in the lives of contemporary Hopi youth. *Journal of Language, Identity & Education, 8*(5), 321–334.

Nielsen. (2014, February 10). *What's empowering the new digital consumer?* Retrieved from http://www.nielsen.com/us/en/insights/news/2014/whats-empowering-the-new-digital-consumer.html

Nisbet, R. (1970). *The social bond: An introduction to the study of society*. New York: Knopf.

Nolan, P., & Lenski, G. (2009). *Human societies: An introduction to macrosociology*. Boulder, CO: Paradigm.

Nordhoff, C. (1975). *The communistic societies of the United States*. New York: Harper & Row. (Original work published 1875)

Norris, M. (2011, July 8). Why Black women, infants lag in birth outcomes. *NPR*. Retrieved from http://www.npr.org/2011/07/08/137652226/-the-race-gap

NPD Group. (2011). *Kids and gaming 2011*. Retrieved September 2015, from https://www.npd.com/latest-reports/video-games-kids-gaming/

O'Leary, A. (2012, August 2). In virtual play, sex harassment is all too real. *New York Times*. Retrieved from http://www.nytimes.com/2012/08/02/us/sexual-harassment-in-online-gaming-stirs-anger.html

O'Neill, T. (2007, February). Curse of the black gold: Hope and betrayal on the Niger Delta. *National Geographic*. Retrieved from http://ngm.nationalgeographic.com/2007/02/nigerian-oil/oneill-text

Oakes, J. (1985). *Keeping track: How schools structure inequality*. New Haven, CT: Yale University Press.

ObamaCare Facts. (2016). *ObamaCare Medicaid expansion*. Retrieved from http://obamacarefacts.com/obamacares-medicaid-expansion/

Oberschall, A. (1973). *Social conflict and social movements*. Englewood Cliffs, NJ: Prentice Hall.

Ogunwole, S. U., Drewery, M. P., Jr., & Rios-Vargas, M. (2012). *The population with a bachelor's degree or higher by race and Hispanic origin: 2006–2010* (American Community Survey Brief 10-19). Washington, DC: U.S. Census Bureau. Retrieved from http://www.census.gov/prod/2012pubs/acsbr10-19.pdf

Okun, A. (2013, October 9). Some terrible people on Twitter have decided that it's "Fat Shaming Week." *BuzzFeed*. Retrieved from https://www.buzzfeed.com/alannaokun/some-terrible-people-on-twitter-have-decided-that-its-fat-sh?utm_term=.cxw62AABWz#.ogZvdDDLjw

Olivieri, E. (2014). *Occupational choice and the college gender gap* (Working Paper). Retrieved from https://docs.google.com/viewer?a=v&pid=sites&srcid=ZGVmYXVsdGRvbWFpbnxlbGlzYW9saXZpZXJpfGd4OjhkNmI5NTg2NTgyOTYx

Omvedt, G. (1992). "Green earth, women's power, human liberation": Woman in peasant movements in India. *Development Dialogue, 1*(2), 116–130.

Orfield, G., & Eaton, S. E. (1996). *Dismantling desegregation: The quiet reversal of* Brown v. Board of Education. New York: Norton.

Organisation for Economic Co-operation and Development (OECD). (2014). *Education at a glance 2014*. Washington, DC: OECD. Retrieved from https://www.oecd.org/edu/Education-at-a-Glance-2014.pdf

Orwell, G. (1961). *1984*. New York: Signet Classic. (Original work published 1949).

Osborne, D., & Wagner, W. E. (2007). Exploring the relationship between homophobia and participation in core sports among high school students. *Sociological Perspectives, 50*(4), 597–613.

Oxfam. (2015). *A decade of saving for change* (Brochure). Retrieved from https://www.oxfamamerica.org/static/media/files/SFC timeline-final-AA.pdf

Oxford English Dictionary, O. E. (2010). OED (Online edition). Retrieved from http://dictionary.oed.com.gate.lib.buffalo.edu/entrance.dtl

Paglen, T., & Thompson, A. C. (2006). *Torture taxi: On the trail of the CIA's rendition flights.* Hoboken, NJ: Melville House.

Paoli, L. (2003). *Mafia brotherhoods: Organized crime Italian style*. Oxford: Oxford University Press.

Paquette, D. (2016, March 10). Pay doesn't look the same for men and women at top newspapers. *Washington Post*. Retrieved from https://www.washingtonpost.com/news/wonk/wp/2016/03/10/pay-doesnt-look-the-same-for-men-and-women-at-top-newspapers/

Park, P. (1993). *Voices of change: Participatory research in the United States and Canada*. Westport, CT: Bergin & Garvey.

Park, R. E., & Burgess, E. W. (1921). *Introduction to the science of sociology*. Chicago: University of Chicago Press.

Parker-Pope, T. (2010, April 14). Is marriage good for your health? *New York Times Magazine.* Retrieved from http://www.nytimes.com/2010/04/18/magazine/18marriage-t.html?pagewanted=all

Parkin, F. (1979). Social closure and class formation. In A. Giddens & D. Held (Eds.), *Classes, power, and conflict* (pp. 175–184). Los Angeles: University of California Press.

Parrado, E. A., & Morgan, S. P. (2008). Intergeneration fertility among Hispanic women: New evidence of immigrant assimilation. *Demography, 45*(3), 651–671.

Parsons, T. (1951). *The social system.* New York: Free Press.

Parsons, T. (1954). The kinship system of the contemporary United States. In *Essays in sociological theory* (pp. 189–194). New York: Free Press.

Parsons, T. (1967). *The structure of social action.* New York: Free Press.

Parsons, T. (1970). On building social system theory: A personal history. *Daedalus, 99*(4), 826–881.

Parsons, T. (2007). *Social structure and personality.* New York: Free Press. (Original work published 1964)

Parsons, T., & Bales, R. F. (1955). *Family, socialization and interaction process.* Glencoe, IL: Free Press.

Parsons, T., & Mayhew, H. D. (1982). *On institutions and social evolution: Selected writings.* Chicago: University of Chicago Press.

Parsons, T., & Shils, E. (2001). *Toward a general theory of action: Theoretical foundations for the social sciences*. New Brunswick, NJ: Transaction.

Parsons, T., & Smelser, N. J. (1956). *Economy and society.* New York: Free Press.

Pascoe, C. J. (2007). *Dude, you're a fag: Masculinity and sexuality in high school.* Berkeley: University of California Press.

Patel, A. (2013, November 23). Horrors of India's brothels documented. *BBC.* Retrieved from http://www.bbc.com/news/world-asia-india-24530198

Patterson, D. (1989). *Power in law enforcement: Subordinate preference and actual use of power base in special weapons teams (SWAT)* (Doctoral dissertation, Fielding Institute, Santa Barbara, CA).

PBS. (2011). Caught in the crossfire: Arab Americans. *9/11 stories.* Retrieved from http://www.pbs.org/itvs/caughtinthecrossfire/arab_americans.html

Pearlstein, S. (2010, October 6). The costs of rising economic inequality. *Washington Post.* Retrieved from http://www.washingtonpost.com/wp-dyn/content/article/2010/10/05/AR2010100505535.html

Peek, K. L. (1999). *The good, the bad, and the "misunderstood": A study of the cognitive moral development theory and ethics in the public sector*. Fort Lauderdale, FL: Nova Southeastern University.

Perrin, A. (2015, October 8). *Social media usage: 2005 to 2015.* Washington, DC: Pew Research Center. Retrieved from http://www.pewinternet.org/2015/10/08/social-networking-usage-2005-2015/

Peters, M. (2017, April 16). *The Fate of the Furious* had the biggest global opening weekend ever. *Comicbook.com*. Retrieved from http://comicbook.com/2017/04/16/fate-of-the-furious-global-box-office-record-star-wars/

Peterson, H. (2016, February 23). This is the first fast-food chain in America that requires zero human interaction. *Business Insider*. Retrieved from http://www.businessinsider.com/eatsa-fully-automated-restaurant-chain-2016-2

Pettit, K. L. S., & Reuben, K. (2010). *Investor-owners in the boom and bust.* Washington, DC: Urban Institute.

Pew Charitable Trusts. (2016, December 29). *National imprisonment and crime rates continue to fall* (Fact Sheet). Retrieved from http://www.pewtrusts.org/en/research-and-analysis/fact-sheets/2016/12/national-imprisonment-and-crime-rates-continue-to-fall

Pew Forum on Religion and Public Life. (2015, May 12). *America's changing religious landscape*. Washington, DC: Pew Research Center. Retrieved from http://www.pewforum.org/2015/05/12/americas-changing-religious-landscape/

Pew Research Center. (2008, July 13). *Hispanic Trends Project: 2008 national survey of Latinos*. Retrieved from http://www.pewhispanic.org/2008/07/13/2008-national-survey-of-latinos

Pew Research Center. (2011, June 2). *Republican candidates stir little enthusiasm.* Washington, DC: Author. Retrieved from http://www.people-press.org/files/legacy-pdf/06-02-11%202012%20Campaign%20Release.pdf

Pew Research Center. (2012, June 4). *Partisan polarization surges in Bush, Obama years.* Washington, DC: Author. Retrieved from http://www.people-press.org/2012/06/04/partisan-polarization-surges-in-bush-obama-years/

Pew Research Center. (2014a). *Finances are keeping many young adults from marrying.* Washington, DC: Author. Retrieved from http://www.pewsocialtrends.org/2014/09/24/record-share-of-americans-have-never-married/st-2014-09-24-never-married-23/

Pew Research Center. (2014b). *For young, never-married women, the pool of employed young men has shrunk*. Washington, DC: Author. Retrieved from http://www.pewsocialtrends.org/2014/09/24/record-share-of-americans-have-never-married/st-2014-09-24-never-married-04/

Pew Research Center. (2014c, March 7). *Millennials in adulthood.* Washington, DC: Author. Retrieved from http://www.pewsocialtrends.org/2014/03/07/millennials-in-adulthood/

Pew Research Center. (2014d, April 3). *Older adults and technology use.* Washington, DC: Author. Retrieved from http://www.pewinternet.org/files/2014/04/PIP_Seniors-and-Tech-Use_040314.pdf

Pew Research Center. (2015a, December 17). *Parenting in America: Outlook, worries, aspirations are strongly linked to financial situation.* Washington, DC: Author. Retrieved from http://www.pewsocialtrends.org/2015/12/17/parenting-in-america/

Pew Research Center. (2015b, December 14). *Use of spanking differs across racial and education groups.* Washington, DC: Author. Retrieved from http://www.pewsocialtrends.org/2015/12/17/parenting-in-america/st_2015-12-17_parenting-09/

Pew Research Center. (2017a, June 26). *Changing attitudes on gay marriage*. Washington, DC: Author. Retrieved from http://www.pewforum.org/fact-sheet/changing-attitudes-on-gay-marriage/

Pew Research Center. (2017b, January 12). Social media fact sheet. Retrieved from http://www.pewinternet.org/fact-sheet/social-media/

Phelan, A. M., & McLaughlin, H. J. (1995). Educational discoveries: The nature of the child and practices of new teachers. *Journal of Teacher Education, 46*(3), 165–174.

Piaget, J. (1926). *The language and thought of the child.* New York: Harcourt, Brace.

Piaget, J. (1928). *Judgment and reasoning in the child.* New York: Harcourt, Brace.

Piaget, J. (1930). *The child's conception of physical causality.* New York: Harcourt, Brace.

Piaget, J. (1932). *The moral judgment of the child.* New York: Harcourt, Brace.

PiperJaffray. (2016, Spring). *Talking stock with teens.* Retrieved from http://www.piperjaffray.com/3col.aspx?id=4035

Pipes, D., & Durán, K. (2002, August). *Muslim immigrants in the United States.* Washington, DC: Center for Immigration Studies. Retrieved from http://www.cis.org/sites/cis.org/files/articles/2002/back802.pdf

Piven, F. F., & Cloward, R. A. (1977). *Poor people's movements: Why they succeed, how they fail.* New York: Random House.

Podsakoff, P., & Schriesheim, C. (1985). Field studies of French and Raven's bases of power: Critique, reanalysis, and suggestions for future research. *Psychological Bulletin, 97*(3), 387–411.

Polaris Project. (n.d.). *Human trafficking statistics.* Retrieved from http://www.polarisproject.org

Polivy, J., & Herman, P. (2007). Is the body the self? Women and body image. *Collegium Anthropologicum, 31,* 63–67.

Ponton, L. (2000). *The sex lives of teenagers.* New York: Dutton.

Popper, K. (1959). *The logic of scientific discovery.* New York: Basic Books.

Population Reference Bureau. (2013). *2013 world population data sheet.* Washington, DC: Author. Retrieved from http://www.prb.org/pdf13/2013-population-data-sheet_eng.pdf

Population Reference Bureau. (2015). *2015 world population data sheet.* Washington, DC: Author. Retrieved from http://www.prb.org/pdf15/2015-world-population-data-sheet_eng.pdf

Population Reference Bureau. (2016). *World Population Data Sheet 2016.* Washington, DC, Author. Retrieved from http://www.prb.org/Publications/Datasheets/2016/2016-world-population-data-sheet.aspx.

Population Reference Bureau. (2017). *2017 world population data sheet.* Washington, DC: Author. Retrieved from http://www.prb.org/Publications/Datasheets/2017/2017-world-population-data-sheet.aspx

Poteet, G. A. (2007). *Perceptions of pretty people: An experimental study of interpersonal attractiveness* (Master's thesis, Washington State University). Retrieved from http://www.dissertations.wsu.edu/Thesis/Spring2007/a_poteet_050307.pdf

Potok, M. (2015, November 16). FBI: Reported hate crimes down nationally except against Muslims. *SPLC.* Retrieved from https://www.splcenter.org/hatewatch/2015/11/16/fbi-reported-hate-crimes-down-nationally-except-against-muslims

Pough, G. D. (2004). *Check it while I wreck it: Black womanhood, hip hop culture, and the public sphere.* Boston: Northeastern University Press.

Powell, R. (2013). Social desirability bias in polling on same-sex marriage ballot initiatives. *American Politics Research, 41*(6), 1052–1070.

Power, S. (2002). *"A problem from hell": America and the age of genocide.* New York: Basic Books.

Prell, R. (1999). *Fighting to become Americans: Jews, gender, and the anxiety of assimilation.* Boston: Beacon Press.

Presser, S. (1990). Can changes in context reduce vote overreporting in surveys? *Public Opinion Quarterly, 54,* 586–593.

Preston, P. (1994). *Mother father deaf: Living between sound and silence.* Cambridge, MA: Harvard University Press.

Preves, S. E. (2003). *Intersex and identity: The contested self.* New Brunswick, NJ: Rutgers University Press.

ProCon. (2017). *State felon voting laws.* Retrieved from http://felonvoting.procon.org/view.resource.php?resourceID=000286

Proulx C. M., & Snyder-Rivas, L. A. (2013). The longitudinal associations between marital happiness, problems, and self-rated health. *Journal of Family Psychology, 27*(2), 194–202. http://dx.doi.org/10.1037/a0031877

Putnam, R. (2000). *Bowling alone: The collapse and revival of American community.* New York: Simon & Schuster.

Queen, S. A., Habenstein, R. W., & Adams, J. B. (1961). *The family in various cultures* (2nd ed.). Philadelphia: J. B. Lippincott.

Questioningly winner: Twitter in a tweet. (2012, October 15). *The New Yorker.* Retrieved from http://www.newyorker.com/culture/culture-desk/questioningly-winner-defining-twitter-in-a-tweet

Quinney, R. (1970). *Crime and justice in America.* New York: Little, Brown.

Rampey, B. D., Finnegan, R., Goodman, M., Mohadjer, L., Krenzke, T., Hogan, J., . . . Xie, H. (2016, March). *Skills of U.S. unemployed, young, and older adults in sharper focus: Results from the Program for the International Assessment of Adult Competencies (PIAAC) 2012/2014: First Look.* Washington, DC: National Center for Education Statistics. Retrieved from https://nces.ed.gov/pubs2016/2016039.pdf

Rana Plaza collapse: 38 charged with murder over garment factory disaster. (2016, July 18). *The Guardian.* Retrieved from https://www.theguardian.com/world/2016/jul/18/rana-plaza-collapse-murder-charges-garment-factory

Rashbaum, W. K., & Goldstein, J. (2016, June 20). Three N.Y.P.D. commanders are arrested in vast corruption case. *New York Times.* Retrieved from https://www.nytimes.com/2016/06/21/nyregion/nypd-arrests.html?mcubz=1

Ratner, M., & Ray, E. (2004). *Guantánamo: What the world should know.* New York: Chelsea Green.

Raven, B., & Kruglianski, W. (1975). Conflict and power. In P. Swingle (Ed.), *Structure of conflict* (pp. 177–219). New York: Academic Press.

Reaney, P., & Goldsmith, B. (2008, April 4). Husbands create 7 hours of extra housework a week: Study. *Reuters.* Retrieved from http://www.reuters.com/article/2008/04/04/us-housework-husbands-idUSN0441782220080404

Reich, R. (1991). *The work of nations: Preparing ourselves for 21st century capitalism.* New York: First Vintage Books.

Reich, R. (2001, April 9). The case (once again) for universal health insurance. *American Prospect.* Retrieved from http://prospect.org/article/case-once-again-universal-health-insurance

Reich, R. (2010). *Aftershock: The next economy and America's future.* New York: Knopf.

Reiman, J., & Leighton, P. (2012). *The rich get richer and the poor get prison.* New York: Prentice Hall.

Reinders, G. (2006). *Women's reactions to a realistic rape portrayal and the influence of feminist identity and rape myth acceptance* (Doctoral dissertation, University of Missouri). Retrieved from https://mospace.umsystem.edu/xmlui/bitstream/handle/10355/4482/research.pdf?sequence=3

Reingold, J. (2016, March 4). How a radical shift to "self-management" left Zappos reeling. *Fortune.* Retrieved from http://fortune.com/zappos-tony-hsieh-holacracy/

Renjini, D. (2000). *Nayar women today: Disintegration of matrilineal system and the status of Nayar women in Kerala.* India: India Classical.

Renzetti, C. M., & Curran, D. J. (1992). *Women, men, and society* (2nd ed.). Boston: Allyn & Bacon.

Reskin, B., & Padavic, I. (2002). *Women and men at work* (2nd ed.). Thousand Oaks, CA: Sage.

Reuters. (2015, December 2). Giving Tuesday raised $118 million for charities, early figures show. *NBC News*. Retrieved from http://www.nbcnews.com/feature/season-of-kindness/giving-tuesday-raised-118-million-charities-early-figures-show-n473131

Richards, C. (2012). Playing under surveillance: Gender performance and the conduct of the self in a primary school playground. *British Journal of Sociology of Education, 33,* 373–390.

Rideout, V. J., Foehr, U. G., & Roberts, D. F. (2010). *Generation M2: Media in the lives of 8–18 year olds*. Menlo Park, CA: Henry J. Kaiser Foundation.

Ridgeway, C. L., & Correll, S. J. (2004). Unpacking the gender system: A theoretical perspective on gender beliefs and social relations. *Gender & Society, 18*(4), 510–531.

Ridgeway, C. L., & Smith-Lovin, L. (1999). The gender system and interaction. *Annual Review of Sociology, 25,* 191–217.

Ridley, M. (1998). *The origins of virtue: Human instincts and the evolution of cooperation*. New York: Viking Press.

Riordan, C. (1990). *Girls and boys in school: Together or separate?* New York: Teachers College Press.

Rist, R. S. (1970). Student, social class, and teacher expectations: The self-fulfilling prophecy in ghetto education. *Harvard Educational Review, 40,* 411–451.

Ritzer, G. (2007). *The globalization of nothing*. Thousand Oaks, CA: Pine Forge.

Riverson, J., Kunieda, M., Roberts, P., Lewi, N., & Walker, W. M. (2006). *The challenges in addressing gender dimensions of transport in developing countries: Lessons from the World Bank's projects.* Paper presented at the annual meeting of the Transportation Research Board. Retrieved from http://siteresources.worldbank.org/INTTSR/Resources/462613-1152683444211/06-0592.pdf

Roquemore, K., & Brunsma, D. L. (2008). *Beyond Black: Biracial identity in America*. Lanham, MD: Rowman & Littlefield.

Roschelle, A. R., & Kaufman, P. (2004). Fitting in and fighting back: Stigma management strategies among homeless kids. *Symbolic Interaction, 27*(1), 23–46. Retrieved from http://onlinelibrary.wiley.com/doi/10.1525/si.2004.27.1.23/abstract

Rosen, J. (2014, September 5). Animal traffic. *The New York Times Magazine*. Retrieved from https://www.nytimes.com/2014/09/05/t-magazine/animal-trafficking-black-market.html?mcubz=1

Rosenbloom, S. R., & Way, N. (2004). Experiences of discrimination among African American, Asian American, and Latino adolescents in an urban high school. *Youth & Society, 35*(4), 420–451.

Rosenfeld, M. J., Thomas, R. J., & Falcon, M. (2015). *How couples meet and stay together, waves 1, 2, and 3* (Public version 3.04, plus wave 4 supplement version 1.02 and wave 5 supplement version 1.0 [Computer files]). Stanford, CA: Stanford University Libraries.

Rosenthal, R., & Jacobson, L. (1968). *Pygmalion in the classroom.* New York: Holt, Rinehart & Winston.

Rosenwald, M. S. (2016, May 17). Youth sports participation is up slightly, but many kids are still left behind. *Washington Post*. Retrieved from https://www.washingtonpost.com/news/local/wp/2016/05/17/youth-sports-participation-is-up-slightly-but-many-kids-are-still-left-behind/?utm_term=.3639b32030cd

Rosoff, S., Pontell, H., & Tillman, R. (2010). *Profit without honor: White-collar crime and the looting of America.* Upper Saddle River, NJ: Prentice Hall.

Rostow, W. W. (1961). *The stages of economic growth.* Cambridge, England: Cambridge University Press.

Rothe, D. L. (2009). *State criminality: The crime of all crimes.* Lanham, MD: Lexington Books.

Rothschild, J., & Whitt, A. (1987). *The cooperative workplace: Potentials and dilemmas of organizational democracy and participation.* New York: Cambridge University Press.

Rothschild-Whitt, J. (1979). The collectivist organization: An alternative to rational-bureaucratic models. *American Sociological Review, 44,* 509–527.

Rowbotham, S. (1973). *Woman's consciousness, man's world.* Middlesex, England: Pelican.

Rubin, B. (1996). *Shifts in the social contract: Understanding change in American society*. Thousand Oaks, CA: Pine Forge.

Rubin, L. B. (2006). What am I going to do with the rest of my life? *Dissent, 53*(4), 88–94.

Rugh, J. S., & Massey, D. S. (2014). Segregation in post-civil rights America: Stalled integration or the end of the segregated century? *Du Bois Review: Social Science Research on Race, 11*(2), pp. 205–232.

Ruppanner, L., & Maume, D. J. (2016). The state of domestic affairs: Housework, gender, and state-level institutional logics. *Social Science Research, 60,* 15–28.

Ryan, R. A. (1981). Strengths of the American Indian family: State of the art. In F. Hoffman (Ed.), *The American Indian family: Strengths and stresses.* Isleta, NM: American Indian Social Research and Development Associates.

Rymer, R. (1993). *Genie: A scientific tragedy.* New York: HarperCollins.

Rymer, R. (2012, July). Vanishing voices. *National Geographic,* pp. 60–93.

Sabo, D. F., Miller, K. E., Farrell, M. P., Melnick, M. J., & Barnes, G. M. (1999). High school athletic participation, sexual behavior, and adolescent pregnancy: A regional study. *Journal of Adolescent Health, 25*(2), 597–613.

Sadker, D. M., & Sadker, M. P. (1997). *Failing at fairness: How our schools cheat girls.* New York: Scribner.

Sadker, D. M., & Zittleman, K. (2009). *Still failing at fairness: How gender bias cheats girls and boys in school and what we can do about it.* New York: Scribner.

Sadker, D. M., Zittleman, K., & Sadker, M. P. (2003). *Teachers, schools, and society.* New York: McGraw-Hill.

Saez, E. (2010, July 17). *Striking it richer: The evolution of top incomes in the United States (updated with 2008 estimates).* Berkeley: Econometrics Laboratory, University of California—Berkeley. Retrieved from http://elsa.berkeley.edu/~saez/saez-UStopincomes-2008.pdf

Saez, E., & Zucman, G. (2014). *Wealth inequality in the United States since 1913: Evidence from capitalized income tax data* (NBER Working Paper 201625). Cambridge, MA: National Bureau of Economic Research. Retrieved from http://gabriel-zucman.eu/files/SaezZucman2014.pdf

Sahlins, M. D., & Service, E. R. (1960). *Evolution and culture*. Ann Arbor, MI: Ann Arbor Paperbacks.

Salaita, S. (2005). Ethnic identity and imperative patriotism: Arab Americans before and after 9/11. *College Literature, 32*(2), 146–168.

Sampson, R. J., & Laub, J. H. (1990). Crime and deviance over the life course: The salience of adult social bonds. *American Sociological Review, 55,* 609–627.

Sanday, P. R. (1990). *Fraternity gang rape: Sex, brotherhood, and privilege on campus*. New York: New York University Press.

Sandoz, M. (1961). *These were the Sioux.* New York: Dell.

Sangweni, Y. (2017, February 26). The way too short list of Black Oscar winners. *Essence*. Retrieved from http://www.essence.com/galleries/way-too-short-list-black-oscar-winners#1106521

Schaefer, D. R. (2011). Resource characteristics in social exchange networks: Implications for positional advantage. *Social Networks, 33*(2), 143–151.

Schaefer, R. T. (2009). *Race and ethnicity in the United States* (5th ed.). Upper Saddle River, NJ: Pearson Prentice Hall.

Schafft, K. A., Jensen, E. B., & Hinrichs, C. C. (2009). Food deserts and overweight schoolchildren: Evidence from Pennsylvania. *Rural Sociology, 74*(2), 153–177.

Scheff, T. J. (1966). *Being mentally ill: A sociological theory*. Chicago: Aldine.

Scheff, T. J. (1988). Shame and conformity: The deference/emotion system. *American Sociological Review, 53,* 395–406.

Schegloff, E. (1990). On the organization of sequences as a source of "coherence" in talk-in-interaction. In B. Dorval (Ed.), *Conversational organization and its development* (pp. 55–77). Norwood, NJ: Ablex.

Schegloff, E. (1991). Reflections on talk and social structure. In D. H. Zimmerman & D. Boden (Eds.), *Talk and social structure* (pp. 44–70). Cambridge, England: Polity Press.

Schneider, D. M., & Gough, K. (1974). *Matrilineal kinship*. Berkeley: University of California Press.

Schofield, J. W. (2010). International evidence on ability grouping with curriculum differentiation and the achievement gap in secondary schools. *Teachers College Record, 112*(5), 1492–1528.

Schuessler, J. (2016, February 20). A Harvard sociologist on watching families lose their homes. *New York Times*. Retrieved from https://www.nytimes.com/2016/02/20/books/a-harvard-sociologist-on-watching-families-lose-their-homes.html?mcubz=3

Schulhofer, S. J. (2000). *Unwanted sex: The culture of intimidation and the failure of law*. Cambridge, MA: Harvard University Press.

Schulte, B. (2015, May 17). Why parents should stop hoping their kids will get married. *Washington Post*. Retrieved from https://www.washingtonpost.com/news/wonk/wp/2015/05/17/why-parents-should-stop-expecting-their-kids-to-get-married/

Schuman, H., & Presser, S. (1981). *Questions and answers in attitude surveys: Experiments on question form, wording, and context*. New York: Academic Press.

Schuppe, J. (2016, June 19). 30 years after basketball star Len Bias' death, its drug war impact endures. *NBC News*. Retrieved from http://www.nbcnews.com/news/us-news/30-years-after-basketball-star-len-bias-death-its-drug-n593731

Schwarz, H. (2015, April 28). There are 390,000 gay marriages in the U.S. The Supreme Court could quickly make it half a million. *Washington Post*. Retrieved from https://www.washingtonpost.com/news/the-fix/wp/2015/04/28/heres-how-many-gay-marriages-the-supreme-court-could-make-way-for/

Schwarz, O. (2010). On friendship, boobs and the logic of the catalogue. Online self-portraits as a means for the exchange of capital. *Convergence: The International Journal of Research on New Media Technologies, 16*(2), 163–183.

Science Daily. (2015, October 15). *World's first automated mass-crowd count*. Retrieved from https://www.sciencedaily.com/releases/2015/10/151015120025.htm

Scott, A. (1990). *Ideology and the new social movements.* London: Unwin Hyman.

Scott, J. (2005, May 16). Life at the top in America isn't just better, it's longer. *New York Times.* Retrieved from http://www.nytimes.com/2005/05/16/national/class/HEALTH-FINAL.html?pagewanted=all

Scott, J. C., Tehranian, J., & Mathias J. (2002). The production of legal identities proper to states: The case of the permanent family surname. *Comparative Studies in Society and History, 44*(1), 4–44.

Scott, W. R., & Meyer, J. W. (1994). *Institutional environments and organizations: Structural complexity and individualism*. Thousand Oaks, CA: Sage.

Seager, J. (2003). *The Penguin atlas of women in the world.* New York: Penguin Books.

Seaman, A. M. (2016, June 14). Robots may push surgeons to the sidelines – but not soon. *Washington Post*, p. E6.

Sebald, H. (2000). *Adolescence: A social psychological approach* (4th ed.). Englewood Cliffs, NJ: Prentice Hall.

Seemayer, Z., & Chestang, R. (2015, December 31). The 12 biggest celebrity arrests of 2015. *ET Online*. Retrieved from http://www.etonline.com/news/179007_the_12_biggest_celebrity_arrests_of_2015/

Sellin, T. (1938). *Culture, conflict and crime.* New York: Social Science Research Council.

Semenga, J. L., Fontent, K. R., & Kollar, M. A., 2017. *Income and poverty in the United States* (Report P60-259). Washington, DC: U.S. Census Bureau. Retrieved from https://www.census.gov/content/dam/Census/library/publications/2017/demo/P60-259.pdf

Semuels, A. (2015, March 27). The city that believed in desegregation. *The Atlantic*. Retrieved from http://www.theatlantic.com/business/archive/2015/03/the-city-that-believed-in-desegregation/388532/

Sender, H. (2015). Oscars 2015 infographic: How white are the 87th Academy Awards? *International Business Times*. Retrieved from http://www.ibtimes.com/oscars-2015-infographic-how-white-are-87th-academy-awards-1824028

Senior, J. (2016, February 21). Review: In "Evicted," home is an elusive goal for America's poor. *New York Times*. Retrieved from http://www.nytimes.com/2016/02/22/books/evicted-book-review-matthew-desmond.html

Sennett, R. (1998). *The corrosion of character: The personal consequences of work in the new capitalism*. New York: Norton.

Sentencing Project. (2011). *Felony disenfranchise ment*. Retrieved from http://www.sentencingproject.org/template/page.cfm?id=133

Sentencing Project. (2017, August). *Facts about prisons and people in prison*. Washington, DC: Author. Retrieved from http://www.sentencingproject.org/wp-content/uploads/2016/02/Facts-About-Prisons.pdf

Setoodeh, R. (2016, January 19). George Clooney on white Oscars: "We're moving in the wrong direction." *Variety*. Retrieved from http://variety.com/2016/film/news/george-clooney-white-oscars-1201682504/

Severns, M. (2015, November 25). How Washington created some of the worst schools in America. *Politico*. Retrieved from http://www.politico.com/story/2015/11/how-washington-created-the-worst-schools-in-america-215774

Shahani-Denning, C. (2003). *Physical attractiveness bias in hiring: What is beautiful is good.* Hempstead, NY: Hofstra University Office for Research and Sponsored Programs. Retrieved from http://www.hofstra.edu/pdf/orsp_shahani-denning_spring03.pdf

Shamir, R. (2011). Mind the gap: The commodification of corporate social responsibility. *Symbolic Interaction, 28*(2), 229–253. Retrieved from http://onlinelibrary.wiley.com/doi/10.1525/si.2005.28.2.229/abstract

Sharkey, J. (2014, May 7). Forget 1960, the golden age is now. *New York Times.* Retrieved from http://www.nytimes.com/2014/05/08/business/forget-1960-the-golden-age-is-now.html?_r=0

Shattuck, R. (1980). *The forbidden experiment.* New York: Farrar, Straus and Giroux.

Shaw, M. (2010). Sociology and genocide. In D. Bloxham & A. D. Moses (Eds.), *The Oxford handbook of genocide studies* (pp. 142–161). New York: Oxford University Press.

Sheinin, D., Thompson, K., McDonald, S. N., & Clement, S. (2016, January 31). New wave feminism. *Washington Post,* pp. A1, A17.

Sheldon, W. H. (1949). *Varieties of delinquent youth: An introduction to constitutional psychiatry*. New York: Harper.

Shipler, D. K. (2005). *The working poor: Invisible in America*. New York: Vintage Books.

Silva, E. B. (2001). *White supremacy and racism in the post–civil rights era*. Boulder, CO: Lynne Rienner.

Silver, N. (2015, May 1). The most diverse cities are often the most segregated. *FiveThirtyEight*.

Retrieved from http://fivethirtyeight.com/features/the-most-diverse-cities-are-often-the-most-segregated/

Silverman, R. M. (2005). Community socioeconomic status and disparities in mortgage lending: An analysis of metropolitical Detroit. *Social Science Journal, 42,* 479–486.

Simmel, G. (1955). *Conflict and the web of group affiliations* (K. Wolf, Trans.). Glencoe, IL: Free Press.

Simmel, G. (1971). Fashion. In D. Levine (Ed.), *Georg Simmel* (pp. 324–339). Chicago: University of Chicago Press. (Original work published 1904)

Simpson, M. E., & Conklin, G. H. (1989). Socioeconomic development, suicide, and religion: A test of Durkheim's theory of religion and suicide. *Social Forces, 67,* 945–964.

Sipes, L. A., Jr. (2012, February 6). Statistics on women offenders. *Corrections.com.* Retrieved from http://www.corrections.com/news/article/30166-statistics-on-women-offenders

Skinner, B. F. (1938). *The behavior of organisms.* Cambridge, MA: B. F. Skinner Foundation.

Skinner, B. F. (1953). *Science and human behavior.* Cambridge, MA: B. F. Skinner Foundation.

Slaughter, A. M. (2015). *Unfinished business: Women men work family.* New York: Random House.

Slovak, K., & Singer, J. B. (2011). School social workers' perceptions of cyberbullying. *Children & Schools, 33*(1), 1–16.

Smelser, N. J. (1962). *The theory of collective behavior.* New York: Free Press.

Smith, B. (1990). Racism and women's studies. In G. Anzaldúa (Ed.), *Making face, making soul: Haciendo caras.* San Francisco: Aunt Lute Foundation.

Smith, D. (1987). *The everyday world as problematic: A feminist sociology.* Boston: Northeastern University Press.

Smith, D. (1990). *The conceptual practices of power: A feminist sociology of knowledge.* Boston: Northeastern University Press.

Smith, D. (2005). *Institutional ethnography: A sociology for people.* Walnut Creek, CA: AltaMira Press.

Smith, D. H., & Pillemer, K. (1983). Self-help groups as social movement organizations: Social structure and social change. In L. Kriesberg (Ed.), *Research in social movements, conflicts and change* (Vol. 5, pp. 203–233). Greenwich, CT: JAI Press.

Smith-Greenaway, E. (2013). Maternal reading skills and child mortality in Nigeria: a reassessment of why education matters. *Demography, 50*(5), 1551–1561.

Smith, K. (2005). Prebirth gender talk: A case study in prenatal socialization. *Women & Language, 28*(1), 49–53.

Smith, M. J., & Moses, B. (1980). Social welfare agencies and social reform movements: The case of the single-parent family. *Journal of Sociology and Social Welfare, 7,* 125–136.

Smith, P. K. (2009). *Obesity among poor Americans: Is public assistance the problem?* Nashville, TN: Vanderbilt University Press.

Smith, P. K., Mahdavi, J., Carvalho, M., Fisher, S., Russell, S., & Tippett, N. (2008). Cyberbullying: Its nature and its impact in secondary school pupils. *Journal of Child Psychology and Psychiatry, 49*(4), 376–385.

Smith, R. W. (2002). As old as history. In C. Rittner, J. K. Roth, & J. M. Smith (Eds.), *Will genocide ever end?* (pp. 31–34). St. Paul, MN: Paragon House.

Smith, S. (2001). *Allah's mountains: The battle for Chechnya.* London: I. B. Tauris.

Smith, S. (2017). *Why people are rich and poor: Republicans and Democrats have very different views.* Washington, DC: Pew Research Center. Retrieved from http://www.pewresearch.org/fact-tank/2017/05/02/why-people-are-rich-and-poor-republicans-and-democrats-have-very-different-views/

Smith, S. C., Choueiti, M., & Pieper, K. (2014). *Race/Ethnicity in 600 popular films: Examination of on screen portrayals and behind the camera diversity.* Los Angeles: Annenberg School for Communication and Journalism, University of Southern California. Retrieved from http://annenberg.usc.edu/pages/~/media/MDSCI/Racial%20Inequality%20in%20Film%202007-2013%20Final.ashx

Smits, D. (1994). The frontier army and the destruction of the buffalo: 1865–1883. *Western Historical Quarterly, 25*(3), 312–338.

Smock, P. J., Manning, W. D., & Porter, M. (2005). "Everything's there except money": How money shapes decisions to marry among cohabitating adults. *Journal of Marriage and Family, 67*(3), 680–696.

Snow, D. A., Rochford, E. B. Jr., Worden, S. K., & Benford, R. D. (1986). Frame alignment processes, micromobilization, and movement participation. *American Sociological Review, 51,* 464–481.

Snow, D. A., Zurcher, L. A. Jr., & Ekland-Olson, S. (1980). Social networks and social movements: A microstructural approach to differential recruitment. *American Sociological Review, 45,* 787–801.

Soergel, A. (2016, April 26). Study: Overqualified millennials languish in low-wage jobs. *U.S. News.* Retrieved from http://www.usnews.com/news/articles/2016-04-26/overqualified-new-york-millennials-languish-in-low-wage-jobs

Sokoloff, N. J., & Raffel, B. (1995). *The criminal justice system and women: Offenders, victims, workers* (2nd ed.). New York: McGraw-Hill.

Somashekhar, S., Lowery, W., Alexander, K. L., Kindy, K., & Tate, J. (2015, August 8). Black and unarmed. *Washington Post.* Retrieved from http://www.washingtonpost.com/sf/national/2015/08/08/black-and-unarmed/

Sommers, C. H. (2000, May). The war against boys. *Atlantic Monthly.* Retrieved from http://www.theatlantic.com/magazine/archive/2000/05/the-war-against-boys/304659

Sorokin, P. (1962). *Society, culture, and personality: Their structure and dynamics.* New York: Cooper Square.

Sorokin, P. (1970). *Social and cultural dynamics: A study of change in major systems of art, truth, ethics, law and social relationships.* Boston: Extending Horizons Books, Porter Sargent Publishers. (Original work published 1957)

Sparrow, R. (2005). Defending deaf culture: The case of cochlear implants. *Journal of Political Philosophy, 13*(2), 135–152.

Spencer, H. (1892). *Essays, scientific, political and speculative* (2 vols.). New York: Appleton.

Spicher, C. H., & Hudak, M. A. (1997, August). *Gender role portrayal on Saturday morning cartoons: An update.* Paper presented at the annual meeting of the American Psychological Association, Chicago.

Spitzer, S. (1975). Toward a Marxian theory of deviance. *Social Problems, 22*(5), 641–651.

Sports Illustrated. (2014, September 11). *15 NFL players arrested for violence against women in last two years.* Retrieved from http://www.si.com/nfl/2014/09/11/nfl-players-arrested-domestic-violence-assault

Squires, G. D. (2003). Racial profiling, insurance style: Insurance redlining and the uneven development of metropolitan America. *Journal of Urban Affairs, 24*(4), 391–410.

Squires, G. D., Friedman, S., & Saidat, C. E. (2002). Experiencing residential segregation: A contemporary study of Washington, DC. *Urban Affairs Review, 38*(2), 155–183.

Stearns, E., & Glennie, E. J. (2006). When and why dropouts leave high school. *Youth and Society, 38*(1), 29–57.

Stedman, A. (2015, October 25). Kristin Wiig on Ghostbusters backlash: "It just bummed me out." *Variety.* Retrieved from http://variety.com/2015/film/news/kristen-wiig-ghostbusters-backlash-women-1201626285/

Steele, C. M., & Aronson, J. (1995). Stereotype threat and the intellectual test performance of African Americans. *Journal of Personality and Social Psychology, 69*(5), 797–811.

Steffensmeier, D., & Allen, E. (1998). The nature of female offending: Patterns and explanations. In R. T. Zaplin (Ed.), *Female offenders: Critical perspectives and effective intervention.* Gaithersburg, MD: Aspen.

Steinmetz, K. (2014). Clickbait, normcore, mansplain: Runners-up for Oxford's word of the year. *Time*. Retrieved from http://time.com/3590980/clickbait-normcore-mansplain-oxford-word-runners-up/

Stephens, T., Kamimura, A., Yamawaki, N., Bhattacharya, H., Mo, W., Birkholz, R., Makomenaw, A., & Olson, L. M. (2016). Rape myth acceptance among college students in the United States, Japan, and India. *SAGE Open*. Retrieved from http://journals.sagepub.com/doi/pdf/10.1177/2158244016675015

Stephenson, W. (2014, June 3). Welcome to West Port Arthur, Texas, ground zero in the fight for climate justice. *The Nation*. Retrieved from https://www.thenation.com/article/welcome-west-port-arthur-texas-ground-zero-fight-climate-justice/

Stepick, A. III, & Grenier, G. (1993). Cubans in Miami. In J. Moore & R. Pinderhughes (Eds.), *In the barrios: Latinos and the underclass debate* (pp. 79–100). New York: Russell Sage Foundation.

Stevenson, B. (2010). Beyond the classroom: Using Title IX to measure the return to high school sports. *Review of Economics & Statistics, 92*(2), 284–301.

Stiglitz, J. E. (2012). *The price of inequality: How today's divided society endangers our future*. New York: Norton.

Stokes, R., & Chevan, A. (1996). Female-headed families: Social and economic context of racial differences. *Journal of Urban Affairs, 8*(3), 245–268.

Stolle, D. (1998). Why do bowling and singing matter? Group characteristics, membership, and generalized trust. *Political Psychology, 19*(3), 497–525.

Stowe, H. B. (1852). *Uncle Tom's cabin*. Boston: John P. Jewett.

Strauss, C., & Scott, N. (2014, December 8). LeBron James, Kyrie Irving and Nets players wear "I can't breathe" shirts before Cavs game. *USA Today*. Retrieved from http://ftw.usatoday.com/2014/12/kyrie-irving-i-cant-breathe-t-shirt-before-cavaliers-eric-garner-lebron-james

Straus, M. A., & Gelles, R. J. (Eds.). (1990). *Physical violence in American families: Risk factors and adaptations to violence in 8,145 families*. New Brunswick, NJ: Transaction.

Straus, M. A., Gelles, R. J., & Steinmetz, S. K. (1988). *Behind closed doors: Violence in the American family.* Newbury Park, CA: Sage.

Straus, M. A., Sugarman, D. B., & Giles-Sims, J. (1997). Spanking by parents and subsequent antisocial behavior of children. *Archives of Pediatrics and Adolescence, 151,* 761–767.

Subrahmanyam, K., & Lin, G. (2007). Adolescents on the net: Internet use and well-being. *Adolescence, 42*(168), 659–677.

Supple, A. J., Ghazarian, S. R., Frabutt, J. M., Plunkett, S. W., & Sands, T. (2006). Contextual influences on Latino adolescent ethnic identity and academic outcomes. *Child Development, 77,* 1427–1433. doi:10.1111/j.1467-8624.2006.00945.x

Sutherland, E. H. (1929). The person v. the act in criminology. *Cornell Law Quarterly, 14,* 159–167.

Sutherland, E. H. (1983). *White collar crime: The uncut version.* New Haven, CT: Yale University Press. (Original work published 1949)

Sutter, J. (2016). We need a restroom revolution. *CNN*. Retrieved from http://www.cnn.com/2016/05/09/opinions/sutter-gender-neutral-restrooms/

Swanson, E. (2014, February 8). Most Americans OK with Coke's Super Bowl ad, but still think we should all speak English. *Huffington Post*. Retrieved from http://www.huffingtonpost.com/2014/02/08/english-official-language-poll_n_4748094.html

Tankersley, J. (2016, January 6). What top researchers discovered when they re-ran the numbers of income inequality. *Washington Post*. Retrieved from https://www.washingtonpost.com/news/wonk/wp/2016/01/06/what-top-researchers-discovered-when-they-re-ran-the-numbers-of-income-inequality/

Tannen, D. (2001). *You just don't understand: Women and men in conversation*. New York: HarperCollins.

Tannenbaum, F. (1938). *Crime and the community.* New York: Columbia University Press.

Tarrow, S. G. (1983). *Struggling to reform: Social movements and policy changes during cycles of protest*. Ithaca, NY: Cornell University Press.

Tarrow, S. G. (1994). *Power in movement: Social movements, collective action, and politics*. New York: Cambridge University Press.

Taslitz, A. E. (1999). *Rape and the culture of the courtroom.* New York: New York University Press.

Taylor, C. E., Newman, J. S., & Kelly, N. U. (1976). The child survival hypothesis. *Population Studies, 30*(2), 263–278.

Taylor, F. W. (1911). *Principles of scientific management*. New York: Harper & Brothers.

Taylor, K. (2016, March 16). Fast-food CEO says he's investing in machines because the government is making it difficult to afford employees. *Business Insider*. Retrieved from http://www.businessinsider.com/carls-jr-wants-open-automated-location-2016-3

Taylor, P., & Lopez, M. H. (2013, May 8). *Six take-aways from the Census Bureau's voting report*. Washington, DC: Pew Research Center. Retrieved from http://www.pewresearch.org/fact-tank/2013/05/08/six-take-aways-from-the-census-bureaus-voting-report/

Taylor, S., & Butcher, M. (2007). *Extra-legal defendant characteristics and mock juror ethnicity re-examined.* Paper presented at the annual conference of the British Psychological Society, York Conference Park, York, England.

Tenenbaum, H., & Leaper, C. (2003). Parent–child conversations about science: The socialization of gender inequities? *Developmental Psychology, 39*(1), 34–47.

Tews, M. J., Stafford, K., & Zhu, J. (2009). Beauty revisited: The impact of attractiveness, ability, and personality in the assessment of employment suitability. *International Journal of Selection and Assessment, 17*(1), 92–100.

The New York Times (2013, August 10). *California's Continuing Prison Crisis*. Retrieved from http://www.nytimes.com/2013/08/11/opinion/sunday/californias-continuing-prison-crisis.html?mcubz=1

Thomas, D. Q., & Ralph, R. E. (1999). Rape in war: The case of Bosnia. In S. P. Ramet (Ed.), *Gender politics in the Western Balkans: Women and society in Yugoslavia and the Yugoslav successor states* (pp. 203–218). University Park: Pennsylvania State University Press.

Thomas, G. M., Meyer, J. W., Ramirez, F. O., & Boli, J. (1987). *Institutional structure: Constituting state, society, and the individual.* Newbury Park, CA: Sage.

Thomas, W. I., & Thomas, D. S. (1928). *The child in America: Behavior problems and programs.* New York: Knopf.

Thompson, T. L., & Scantlin, R. M. (2007). Gender representation in cartoons. In J. J. Arnett (Ed.), *Encyclopedia of children, adolescents, and the media* (pp. 141–144). Thousand Oaks, CA: Sage.

Thorne, B. (1993). *Gender play: Girls and boys in school.* New Brunswick, NJ: Rutgers University Press.

Tilly, C. (1975). *The formation of national states in Europe.* Princeton, NJ: Princeton University Press.

Tilly, C. (1978). *From mobilization to revelation*. Reading, MA: Addison-Wesley.

Tolan, P., Gorman-Smith, D., & Henry, D. (2005). Family violence. *Annual Review of Psychology 57,* 557–583.

Transparency International. (2011). *Corruption perceptions index 2011.* Retrieved from http://cpi.transparency.org/cpi2011/results

Trimble, L. B., & Kmec, J. A. (2011). The role of social networks in the job attainment process. *Sociology Compass, 5,* 165–178.

Trivedy, S. (2015, May 30). India's missing girls: A tale of healthcare neglect faced by girls. *Oxfam India*. Retrieved from https://www.oxfamindia.org/blog/979/india%E2%80%99s-missing-girls%3A-tale-healthcare-neglect-faced-girls

Truman, J. L., & Morgan, R. E. (2014, April). *Nonfatal domestic violence, 2003–2012*. U.S. Department of Justice, Office of Justice Programs, Bureau of Justice Statistics. Retrieved from http://www.bjs.gov/content/pub/pdf/ndv0312.pdf

Truman, J. L., & Morgan R. E. (2016, October). *Criminal victimization, 2015.* Washington, DC: U.S. Department of Justice, Bureau of Justice Statistics. Retrieved from https://www.bjs.gov/content/pub/pdf/cv15.pdf

Tucker, K. H. (1991). How new are the new social movements? *Theory, Culture and Society, 8*(2), 75–98.

Tumin, M. M. (1953). Some principles of stratification: A critical analysis. *American Sociological Review, 18,* 387–393.

Tumin, M. M. (1963). On inequality. *American Sociological Review, 28,* 19–26.

Tumin, M. M. (1985). *Social stratification: The forms and functions of inequality* (2nd ed.). Englewood Cliffs, NJ: Prentice Hall.

Turner, J. S. (2011). Sex and the spectacle of music videos: An examination of the portrayal of race and sexuality in music videos. *Sex Roles, 64*(3–4), 173–191.

Turner, M. A., Popkin, S. J., & Rawlings, L. (2009). *Public housing and the legacy of segregation.* Washington, DC: Urban Institute Press.

Turner, R. H., & Killian, L. M. (1987). *Collective behavior* (3rd ed.). Englewood Cliffs, NJ: Prentice Hall.

Tyack, D., & Hansot, E. (1982). *Managers of virtue: Public school leadership in America, 1820–1980*. New York: Basic Books.

Tygart, C. E. (1987). Social structure linkages among social movement participants: Toward a synthesis of micro and macro paradigms. *Sociological Viewpoints, 3*(1), 71–84.

Tyman, K., Saylor, C., Taylor, L. A., & Comeaux, C. (2010). Comparing children and adolescents engaged in cyberbullying with matched peers. *Cyberpsychology, Behavior, and Social Networking, 13*(2), 195–199.

U.S. Bureau of Justice Statistics, Office of Justice Programs. (n.d.). *Data collection: National Crime Victimization Survey*. Retrieved from http://www.bjs.gov/index.cfm?ty=dcdetail&iid=245

U.S. Bureau of Labor Statistics. (2015, December 15). *Employment by major industry sector*. Retrieved from http://www.bls.gov/emp/ep_table_201.htm

U.S. Bureau of Labor Statistics. (2016a, January 15). *Women's earnings 83 percent of men's, but vary by occupation*. Retrieved from http://www.bls.gov/opub/ted/2016/womens-earnings-83-percent-of-mens-but-vary-by-occupation.htm

U.S. Bureau of Labor Statistics. (2017a, April 20). *Employment projections*. Retrieved from http://www.bls.gov/emp/ep_chart_001.htm

U.S. Bureau of Labor Statistics. (2017b, September 1). *Employment situation summary*. Retrieved from https://www.bls.gov/news.release/pdf/empsit.pdf

U.S. Bureau of Labor Statistics. (2017c, March 31). *May 2016 national occupational employment and wage estimates*. Retrieved from http://www.bls.gov/oes/current/oes_nat.htm

U.S. Bureau of Labor Statistics. (2017d, September 1). Table A-4. Employment status of the civilian population 25 years and over by educational attainment. Retrieved from http://www.bls.gov/news.release/empsit.t04.htm

U.S. Bureau of Labor Statistics. (2017e, March 8). Women's median earnings 82 percent of men's in 2016. *TED: The Economics Daily*. Retrieved from https://www.bls.gov/opub/ted/2017/womens-median-earnings-82-percent-of-mens-in-2016.htm

U.S. Census Bureau. (2011). *Profile America facts for features: American Indian and Alaska Native Heritage Month: November 2011*. Retrieved from http://www.census.gov/newsroom/releases/archives/facts_for_features_special_editions/cb11-ff22.html

U.S. Census Bureau. (2012a). *Income, poverty, and health insurance coverage: 2012* (Current population reports). Washington, DC: Author. Retrieved from https://www.census.gov/prod/2013pubs/p60-245.pdf

U.S. Census Bureau. (2013). *America's families and living arrangements: 2013: Children* (C table series). Retrieved from https://www.census.gov/data/tables/2013/demo/families/cps-2013.html

U.S. Census Bureau. (2015a). *America's families and living arrangements: 2015: Adults* (A table series): Table A1. Retrieved from https://www.census.gov/data/tables/2015/demo/families/cps-2015.html.

U.S. Census Bureau. (2017, April 4). Table MS-2: Estimated median age at first marriage, by sex: 1890 to the present. Retrieved from https://www.census.gov/data/tables/time-series/demo/families/marital.html

U.S. Department of Commerce, Economics and Statistics Administration. (2010, January). *Middle class in America* (Prepared for the Office of the Vice President of the United States Middle Class Task Force). Washington, DC: Author. Retrieved from http://www.esa.doc.gov/sites/default/files/middleclassreport.pdf

U.S. Department of Education. (2015). *U.S. Department of Education releases report on first-ever school environment listening tour for Native American students*. Washington, DC: Author. Retrieved from http://www.ed.gov/news/press-releases/us-department-education-releases-report-first-ever-school-environment-listening-tour-native-american-students

U.S. Department of Education Office for Civil Rights. (2014, March). *Data snapshot: School discipline* (Issue brief No. 1). Washington, DC: Author. Retrieved from http://ocrdata.ed.gov/Downloads/CRDC-School-Discipline-Snapshot.pdf

U.S. Department of Health and Human Services. (2010). *Statistics and research: Child maltreatment 2010*. Washington, DC: Author. Retrieved from https://www.acf.hhs.gov/cb/resource/child-maltreatment-2010

U.S. Department of Justice. (n.d.). *Prisoners and prisoner re-entry*. Retrieved from https://www.justice.gov/archive/fbci/progmenu_reentry.html

U.S. Department of Justice Office of Public Affairs. (2017, January 11). *New release: Volkswagen AG agrees to plead guilty and pay $4.3 billion in criminal and civil penalties; Six Volkswagen executives and employees are indicted in connection with conspiracy to cheat U.S. emissions tests*. Retrieved from https://www.justice.gov/opa/pr/volkswagen-ag-agrees-plead-guilty-and-pay-43-billion-criminal-and-civil-penalties-six

U.S. Department of State. (2012). *2012 trafficking in persons report*. Washington, DC: U.S. Government Printing Office. Retrieved from http://www.state.gov/j/tip/rls/tiprpt/2012

U.S. Government Accountability Office. (2011). *Child maltreatment: Strengthening national data on child fatalities could aid in prevention* (GAO-11-599). Washington, DC: U.S. Government Printing Office. Retrieved from http://www.gao.gov/new.items/d11599.pdf

U.S. Government Accountability Office. (2016). *K–12 Education: Better use of information could help agencies identify disparities and address racial discrimination* (GAO-16-345). Washington, DC: U.S. Government Printing Office. Retrieved from http://www.gao.gov/products/GAO-16-345

U.S. Securities and Exchange Commission. (2015). *SEC adopts rule for pay ratio disclosure*. Washington, DC: Author. Retrieved from http://www.sec.gov/news/pressrelease/2015-160.html

Uchitelle, L. (2007). *The disposable American: Layoffs and their consequences*. New York: Vintage Books.

Underhill, B. (1995). *The woman who ran for president: The many lives of Victoria Woodhull*. New York: Bridge Works.

Union of International Associations. (2011). Historical overview of number of international organizations by type, 1909–2011. In *Yearbook of international organizations, 2011/2012 edition*. Herndon, VA: Brill.

United Nations. (2015). *The Millennium Development Goals report 2015*. New York: Author. Retrieved from http://www.un.org/millenniumgoals/2015_MDG_Report/pdf/MDG%202015%20rev%20(July%201).pdf

United Nations Educational, Scientific and Cultural Organization (UNESCO). (2014b). *Teaching and learning: Achieving quality for all* (Education for All Global Monitoring Report). Paris: Author. Retrieved from http://unesdoc.unesco.org/images/0022/002256/225654e.pdf

United Nations Educational, Scientific and Cultural Organization (UNESCO). (2015a, July). *A growing number of children and adolescents are out of school as aid fails to meet the mark* (Policy Paper 22/Fact Sheet 31). Retrieved from http://www.uis.unesco.org/Education/Documents/fs-31-out-of-school-children-en.pdf

United Nations Educational, Scientific and Cultural Organization (UNESCO). (2015b, September). *Adult and youth illiteracy* (UIS Fact Sheet). Retrieved from http://www.uis.unesco.org/literacy/Documents/fs32-2015-literacy.pdf

United Nations International Children's Emergency Fund. (2013). *Improving Child Nutrition: The Achievable Imperative for Global Progress*. New York: UNICEF. Retrieved from https://www.unicef.org/gambia/Improving_Child_Nutrition_-_the_achievable_imperative_for_global_progress.pdf.

United Nations Population Fund. (2014). *The state of the world's midwifery 2014*. New York: Author. Retrieved from http://www.unfpa.org/sowmy

University of Nevada, Reno. (2010, May 21). Books in home as important as parents' education in determining children's education level. *Science Daily*. Retrieved from http://www.sciencedaily.com/releases/2010/05/100520213116.htm

Valentine, G. (2006). Globalizing intimacy: The role of information and communication technologies in maintaining and creating relationships. *Women's Studies Quarterly, 34*(1), 365–393.

Valenzuela, J. M. (1992). Permanencia y cambio en las identidades étnicas: La población de origen mexicano en Estados Unidos. *Estudios Sociológicos, 10*(28), 103–125.

Valette, A. (1893). *Socialism and sexualism*. Paris: Verneuil.

Van DeBosch, H., & Van Cleemput, K. (2008). Defining cyberbullying: A qualitative research into the perceptions of youngsters. *CyberPsychology & Behavior, 11*(4), 499–503.

van Dijke, M., & Poppe, M. (2006). Striving for personal power as a basis for social power dynamics. *European Journal of Social Psychology, 36*(4), 537–566.

Van Wees, H. (2010). Genocide in the ancient world. In D. Bloxham & A. D. Moses (Eds.), *The Oxford handbook of genocide studies* (pp. 239–258). New York: Oxford University Press.

VanGiezen, R., & Schwenk, A. E. (2001, Fall). Compensation before World War I through the Great Depression. *Compensation and Working Conditions* (U.S. Department of Labor, Bureau of Labor Statistics). Retrieved from http://www.bls.gov/opub/mlr/cwc/compensation-from-before-world-war-i-through-the-great-depression.pdf

Vasel, Kathryn. (2017, February 2). Couples are spending a record amount to get married. *CNN Money*. Retrieved from http://money.cnn.com/2017/02/02/pf/cost-of-wedding-budget-2016-the-knot/

Vatz, S. (2013, May 24). Why America stopped making its own clothes. *KQED News*. Retrieved from http://ww2.kqed.org/lowdown/2013/05/24/madeinamerica/

Veblen, T. (1899). *The theory of the leisure class*. New York: Macmillan.

Vega, T. (2015, October 30). Out of prison and out of work: Jobs out of reach for former inmates. *CNN Money*. Retrieved from http://money.cnn.com/2015/10/30/news/economy/former-inmates-unemployed/

Vellacott, J. (1993). *From Liberal to Labour with women's suffrage: The story of Catherine Marshall*. Montreal, QB, Canada: McGill-Queen's University Press.

Ventura, S. J., Curtin, S. C., Abma, J. C., & Henshaw S. K. (2012, June 20). Estimated pregnancy rates and rates of pregnancy outcomes for the United States, 1990–2008. *National Vital Statistics Reports, 60*(7). Retrieved from http://www.cdc.gov/nchs/data/nvsr/nvsr60/nvsr60_07.pdf

Vinovskis, M. A. (1992). Schooling and poor children in 19th-century America. *American Behavioral Scientist, 35*(3), 313–331.

Vinovskis, M. A. (1995). *Education, society, and economic opportunity: A historical perspective on persistent problems*. New Haven, CT: Yale University Press.

Voice of America News. (2015, January 12). *Haiti still struggling 5 years after earthquake*. Retrieved from http://m.voanews.com/a/2594607.html

Wacquant, L. (2002). From slavery to mass incarceration. *New Left Review, 13*(2), 40–61.

Waddell, K. (2017, January 23). The exhausting work of tallying America's largest protest. *The Atlantic Monthly*. Retrieved from https://www.theatlantic.com/technology/archive/2017/01/womens-march-protest-count/514166/

Wade, C., & Tavris, C. (1997). *Psychology*. New York: Longman.

Wagner, L. (2016, January 22). Film academy votes to increase diversity. *NPR*. Retrieved from http://www.npr.org/sections/thetwo-way/2016/01/22/464016379/film-academy-votes-to-increase-diversity

Wald, M. L. (2014, March 30). U.S. agency knew about G.M. flaw but did not act. *New York Times*. Retrieved from http://www.nytimes.com/2014/03/31/business/us-regulators-declined-full-inquiry-into-gm-ignition-flaws-memo-shows.html?_r=0

Wallace, K. (2015, November 3). Teens spend a "mind-boggling" 9 hours a day using media, report says. *CNN*. Retrieved from http://www.cnn.com/2015/11/03/health/teens-tweens-media-screen-use-report/

Wallenstein, A. (2014, February 10). How *The Walking Dead* breaks every rule we know about TV hits. *Variety*. Retrieved from http://variety.com/2014/tv/news/how-the-walking-dead-breaks-every-rule-we-know-about-tv-hits-1201089433

Wallerstein, I. (1974). *The modern world-system*. New York: Academic Press.

Wallerstein, I. (2011a). *The modern world-system I: Capitalist agriculture and the origins of the European world-economy in the sixteenth century*. Berkeley: University of California Press. (Original work published 1974)

Wallerstein, I. (2011b). *The modern world-system II: Mercantilism and the consolidation of the European world-economy, 1600–1750*. Berkeley: University of California Press. (Original work published 1980)

Wallerstein, I. (2011c). *The modern world-system III: The second era of great expansion of the capitalist world-economy, 1730–1840s*. Berkeley: University of California Press. (Original work published 1989)

Wallerstein, I. (2011d). *The modern world system IV: Centrist liberalism triumphant, 1789–1914*. Berkeley: University of California Press.

Wallis, C. (2011). Performing gender: A content analysis of gender display in music videos. *Sex Roles, 64*(3–4), 160–172.

Walters, P. B., & James, R. J. (1992). Schooling for some: Child labor and school enrollment of Black and White children in the early 20th century South. *American Sociological Review, 57,* 635–650.

Wang, W. (2012, February 16). *The rise of intermarriage: Rates, characteristics vary by race, gender*. Washington, DC: Pew Research Center. Retrieved from http://www.pewsocialtrends.org/2012/02/16/the-rise-of-intermarriage/

Wang, W., & Parker, K. (2011). *Women see value and benefits of college: Men lag on both fronts, survey finds.* Washington, DC: Pew Research Center. Retrieved from http://www.pewsocialtrends.org/files/2011/08/Gender-and-higher-ed-FNL-RPT.pdf

Wang, W., & Parker, K. (2014, September 24). *Record number of Americans have never married.* Washington, DC: Pew Research Center. Retrieved from http://www.pewsocialtrends.org/2014/09/24/record-share-of-americans-have-never-married/

Wasserman, I. M. (1999). *African Americans and the criminal justice system: An explanation for changing patterns of Black male suicide.* Paper presented at the annual conference of the Midwest Sociological Society, Minneapolis.

Watanabe, T. (1992, May 13). Rent-a-family fills emotional need in busy Japan. *Los Angeles Times.* Retrieved from http://community.seattletimes.nwsource.com/archive/?date=19920513&slug=1491524

Watson, J. B. (1924). *Behaviorism.* New York: People's Institute.

Weber, M. (1946). *From Max Weber: Essays in sociology* (H. Gerth & C. W. Mills, Eds. & Trans.). New York: Oxford University Press. (Original work published 1919)

Weber, M. (1979). *Economy and society: An outline of interpretive sociology* (2 vols.). Berkeley: University of California Press. (Original work published 1921)

Weber, M. (2002). *The Protestant ethic and the spirit of capitalism, and other writings.* New York: Penguin Books. (Original work published 1904–1905)

Weber, M. (2012). *The theory of social and economic organization.* Eastford, CT: Martino Fine Books. (Original work published 1921)

Webster, H. (2014, July 14). What parents and kids should know about selfies. *U.S. News & World Report*. Retrieved from http://health.usnews.com/health-news/health-wellness/articles/2014/07/14/what-parents-and-kids-should-know-about-selfies

Weinberg, R. (2004, August 5). 34: Len Bias dies of cocaine overdose. *ESPN*. Retrieved from http://espn.go.com/espn/espn25/story?page=moments/34

Weiss-Wendt, A. (2010). The state and genocide. In D. Bloxham & A. D. Moses (Eds.), *The Oxford handbook of genocide studies* (pp. 81–101). New York: Oxford University Press.

Weitzer, R., & Kubrin, C. E. (2009). Misogyny in rap music: A content analysis of prevalence and meanings. *Men and Masculinities, 12*(1), 3–29.

Wellman, B., & Hampton, K. (1999). Living networked on and offline. *Contemporary Sociology, 28*(6), 648–654.

Welsh, R. (1998). Severe parental punishment and aggression: The link between corporal punishment and delinquency. In I. A. Hyman & J. H. Wise (Eds.), *Corporal punishment in American education: Readings in history, practice and alternatives* (pp. 126–142). Philadelphia: Temple University Press.

Werdigier, J. (2010, June 4). J. P. Morgan penalized by regulator in Britain. *New York Times,* p. B3.

Wertheimer, B. (1977). *We were there: The story of working women in America*. New York: Pantheon.

West, C. (1979). Against our will: Male interruptions of females in cross-sex conversations. *Annals of the New York Academy of Sciences, 327,* 81–97.

West, C., & Zimmerman, D. H. (1977). Woman's place in everyday talk: Reflections on parent–child interactions. *Social Problems, 24,* 521–529.

West, C., & Zimmerman, D. H. (1983). Small insults: A study of interruptions in conversations between unacquainted persons. In B. Thorne, C. Kramarae, & N. Henley (Eds.), *Language, gender, and society* (pp. 102–117). Rowley, MA: Newbury House.

West, C., & Zimmerman, D. H. (1987). Doing gender. *Gender & Society, 1*(2), 125–151.

Western, B., & Pettit, B. (2010). Incarceration and social inequality. *Daedalus, 139*(3), 8–19.

Whalen, J., & Zimmerman, D. H. (1987). Sequential and institutional contexts in calls for help. *Social Psychology Quarterly, 50,* 172–185.

Whalen, J., & Zimmerman, D. H. (1990). Describing trouble: Epistemology in citizen calls to the police. *Language in Society, 19,* 465–492.

Whalen, J., Zimmerman, D. H., & Whalen, M. R. (1990). When words fail: A single case analysis. *Social Problems, 35,* 335–362.

Whelan, A., Wrigley, N., Warm, D., & Cannings, E. (2002). Life in a "food desert." *Urban Studies, 39*(11), 2083–2100.

Whyte, W. F. (1943). *Street corner society: The social structure of an Italian slum*. Chicago: University of Chicago Press.

Whyte, W. F. (1991). *Participatory action research.* Newbury Park, CA: Sage.

Williams, A. (2010, February 7). The new math on campus. *New York Times.* Retrieved from http://www.nytimes.com/2010/02/07/fashion/07campus.html?pagewanted=all

Williams, C. (1995). *Still a man's world: Men who do women's work.* Berkeley: University of California Press.

Williams, J. P., & Kirschner, D. (2012). Coordinated action in the massively multiplayer online game *World of Warcraft. Symbolic Interaction, 35,* 340–367.

Williams, R. M., Jr. (1970). *American society: A sociological interpretation* (3rd ed.). New York: Knopf.

Williams-Meyers, A. J. (1996). Slavery, rebellion, and revolution in the Americas: A historiographical scenario on the theses of Genovese and others. *Journal of Black Studies, 26*(4), 381–400.

Willis, P. (1990). *Common culture: Symbolic work at play in the everyday cultures of the young.* Boulder, CO: Westview Press.

Willoughby, T., Adachi, P. J. C., & Good, M. (2012). A longitudinal study of the association between violent video game play and aggression among adolescents. *Developmental Psychology, 48*(4), 1044–1057.

Wilson, B. J. (2008). Media violence and aggression in youth. In S. Calvert & B. Wilson (Eds.), *The handbook of children, media, and development*. West Sussex, England: Blackwell.

Wilson, D. C., Moore, D. W., McKay, P. F., & Avery, D. R. (2008). Affirmative action programs for women and minorities: Expressed support affected by question order. *Public Opinion Quarterly, 72*(3), 514–522.

Wilson, T. P. (1991). Social structure and the sequential organization of interaction. In D. H. Zimmerman & D. Boden (Eds.), *Talk and social structure* (pp. 22–43). Cambridge: Polity Press.

Wilson, W. J. (1978). *The declining significance of race: Blacks and changing American institutions*. Chicago: University of Chicago Press.

Wilson, W. J. (1987). *The truly disadvantaged: The inner city, the underclass, and public policy*. Chicago: University of Chicago Press.

Wilson, W. J. (1996). *When work disappears: The world of the new urban poor*. New York: Vintage Books.

Wilson, W. J. (2010). *More than just race: Being Black and poor in the inner city*. New York: Norton.

Wingfield, A. H. (2008). Racializing the glass escalator: Reconsidering men's experiences with women's work. *Gender & Society, 23*(1), 5–26.

Winterman, D. (2012, November 15). Breakfast, lunch, and dinner: Have we always eaten them? *BBC*. Retrieved from http://www.bbc.com/news/magazine-20243692

Wirth, L. (1945). The problem of minority groups. In R. Linton (Ed.), *The science of man in the world crisis* (pp. 347–372). New York: Columbia University Press.

Wittstock, L. W., & Salinas, E. J. (1998). A brief history of the American Indian Movement. *American Indian Movement Grand Governing Council*. Retrieved from http://www.aimovement.org/ggc/history.html

Woldoff, R. A. (2011). *White flight/Black flight: The dynamics of racial change in an American neighborhood.* Ithaca, NY: Cornell University Press.

Wolf, M. (2008). *Proust and the squid: The story and science of the reading brain*. New York: Harper Perennial.

Wolfson, A. (2005, October 9). A hoax most cruel: Caller coaxed McDonald's managers into strip-searching a worker. *Courier Journal.* Retrieved from http://www.courier-journal.com/apps/pbcs.dll/article?AID=/20051009/NEWS01/510090392&loc=interstitialskip&nclick_check=1

Wollstonecraft, M. (1792). *A vindication of the rights of women: With strictures on political and moral subjects*. Boston: Peter Edes.

Wonacott, M. E. (2002). *Gold-collar workers* (Eric Digest EDO-CE-02-234). Retrieved from http://www.calpro-online.org/ERIC/docs/dig234.pdf

Wood, G. S. (1993). *The radicalism of the American Revolution.* New York: Vintage Books.

Wood, R. G., Goesling, B., & Avellar, S. (2007). *The effects of marriage on health: A synthesis of recent research evidence.* Princeton, NJ: Mathematica Policy Research. Retrieved from https://www.mathematica-mpr.com/our-publications-and-findings/publications/the-effects-of-marriage-on-health-a-synthesis-of-recent-research-evidence

Woodiwiss, M. (2000). Organized crime: The dumbing of discourse. In G. Mair & R. Tarling (Eds.), *British Criminology Conference: Selected proceedings* (Vol. 3). London: British Society of Criminology. Retrieved from http://www.britsoccrim.org/volume1/017.pdf

Workman, J. E., & Freeburg, E. W. (1999). An examination of date rape, victim dress and perceiver variables within the context of attribution theory. *Sex Roles, 41*, 261–277.

World Bank. (2017). WDI 2017 maps: The world by income, 2017. Retrieved from http://data.worldbank.org/products/wdi-maps

World Health Organization. (2011). Health workforce—Aggregated data, density per 1,000. *Data Repository: World Health Statistics.*

World Health Organization. (2015). *Global Health Observatory data: Maternal mortality country profiles*. Retrieved from http://www.who.int/gho/maternal_health/countries/en/

Wright, E. O. (1994). *Interrogating inequality: Essays on class analysis, socialism and Marxism*. New York: Verso.

Wright, E. O. (1998). *Classes* (2nd ed.). New York: Verso.

Wright, J. P., Tibbetts, S. G., & Daigle, L. E. (2008). *Criminals in the making: Criminality across the life course.* Thousand Oaks, CA: Sage.

Wright, L. (1993, May 24). Remember Satan: Part II. *New Yorker,* pp. 54–76.

Wrong, D. H. (1959). The functional theory of stratification: Some neglected considerations. *American Sociological Review, 24,* 772–782.

Wuthnow, R. (1989). *Communities of discourse: Ideology and social structure in the Reformation, the Enlightenment, and European socialism*. Cambridge, MA: Harvard University Press.

Wyman, A. (1997). *Rural women teachers in the United States: A sourcebook*. Lanham, MD: Scarecrow Press.

Wyss, S. (2007). "This was my hell": The violence experienced by gender non-conforming youth in US high schools. *International Journal of Qualitative Studies in Education, 17*(5), 709–730.

Yen, C.-F., Yen, J.-Y., & Ko, C.-H. (2010). Internet addiction: Ongoing research in Asia. *World Psychiatry, 9*(2), 97. Retrieved from http://www.ncbi.nlm.nih.gov/pmc/articles/PMC2911088

Young, S., & Martin, D. S. (2012, March 9). CNN readers share stories about secret army drug testing program. *CNN*. Retrieved from http://edition.cnn.com/2012/03/09/health/soldier-guinea-pigs/index.html

Zald, M., & McCarthy, J. D. (1980). Social movement industries: Competition and cooperation among movement organizations. In L. Kriesberg (Ed.), *Research in social movements, conflicts and change* (Vol. 3). Greenwich, CT: JAI Press.

Zeitchik, S. (2016, July 4). Jesse Williams and the academy just changed Hollywood's race conversation. What's next? *Los Angeles Times*. Retrieved from http://www.latimes.com/entertainment/movies/la-et-mn-oscars-so-white-academy-jesse-williams-birth-loving-20160701-snap-story.html

Zenker, O. (2010). Language matters: Reflexive notes on representation of the Irish language revival in Catholic West Belfast. In O. Zenker & K. Kumoll (Eds.), *Beyond writing culture: Current intersections of epistemologies and representational practices* (pp. 121–138). New York: Berghahn Books.

Zhou, M. (2009). *Contemporary Chinese America: Immigration, ethnicity, and community transformation*. Philadelphia: Temple University Press.

Zimbardo, P. G. (1974). On "obedience to authority." *American Psychologist, 29*(7), 566–567.

Zimmerman, D. H. (1984). Talk and its occasion: The case of calling the police. In D. Schiffrin (Ed.), *Meaning, form, and use in context: Linguistic applications* (pp. 210–228). Washington, DC: Georgetown University Press.

Zimmerman, D. H. (1992). The interactional organization of calls for emergency assistance. In P. Drew & J. Heritage (Eds.), *Talk at work: Interaction in institutional settings* (pp. 418–469). New York: Cambridge University Press.

Zimmerman, D. H., & West, C. (1975). Sex roles, interruptions, and silences in conversations. In B. Thorne & N. Henley (Eds.), *Language and sex: Difference and dominance* (pp. 105–129). Rowley, MA: Newbury House.

Zimmerman, D. H., & West, C. (1980). Language and social interaction. *Sociological Inquiry, 50,* 3–4.

Zinn, M. B., Weber, L., Higginbotham, E., & Dill, B. T. (1986). The costs of exclusionary practices in women's studies. *Signs, 11*(2), 290–303.

Zinsser, J. (1993). *History and feminism: A glass half full (The feminist impact on the arts and sciences)*. Woodbridge: CT: Twayne.

INDEX

Abzug, Bella, 293
Academic ability grouping, 132–133
Accomplishment of natural growth, 328
Achayo, Rose, 299
Achieved status, 195
Addams, Jane, 21–22
Administrative staff, bureaucracies and, 143
Adorno, Theodor, 82–83
Adult illiteracy, word poverty and, 353–354
Adult stage, of socialization, 101–102, 104
Advanced Placement (AP) courses, access to, 349
Advertising, melding with culture, 82–83
Affordable Care Act (ACA), 203
African American men, disenfranchisement of, 244
African Americans. *See also* Race
  athletes and racial equality, 230–231, 386–387
  civil rights movement, 235–236, 249, 251, 393, 394, 396, 399
  crack cocaine epidemic and, 158–159, 181
  decline in marriage and increase in nonmarital births among, 329–330
  discrimination against, 241–244
  fragmentation of family among, 329–330
  historical overview, 249–251
  incarceration rates of, 181, 183
  neighborhood poverty and, 210
  school segregation and, 356
  slavery, 193–194, 238–239, 249
  spanking and, 105, 106–107
African American women
  birth outcomes of, 245–246
  eviction of, 195, 242–243
  standpoint epistemology and, 293
Age
  at first marriage in United States, 318
  social media use and, 96–97
Agency, 5–6
  defined, 5
  social reproduction and, 85–86
Agents of gender socialization, 270
Aggregate income, 199–200
Aging, socialization and, 114–115
Agrawal, Radha, 375
Agricultural revolution and agricultural society, 363
Ahola, A. S., 71
Aina, O. E., 271
Aka language, 76
Albright, Madeleine, 297
Alcatraz, occupation of, 248–249
Alexander, Michelle, 244–245
Alliance, 131, 133
Allport, Gordon W., 391
American Community Survey, 284
American Council on Education, 266
American Indian Movement (AIM), 250
American Indians, 248–249
  expulsion and, 233
  families, 322–324
  reservations, 233
  reservation schools, 352–353, 356
  team mascots/names and, 240, 250
  tribal names, 250
American Jewish Committee/ Roper poll, on beliefs about the Holocaust, 46–47
American Sociological Association Code of Ethics, 56
American Sociological Review, 44
American Women Suffrage Association, 394
Amish, 76, 109
Amnesty International, 299
Anecdotal evidence, critical thinking and, 7
Anomie, 10–11, 13, 162
"An Open Marriage A Happier Marriage" (Dominus), 171
Anthony, Susan B., 382, 383, 394
Anticipatory socialization, 108, 114
Anti-miscegenation laws, 311
Anwar, Aniqa, 91
Apartheid, 235, 236, 396
Apple, Inc., labor conditions in Chinese factories and, 373–374
Arab Americans, 253
Arab Spring, 385, 396, 400
Argot, 108
Argument, debate *vs.,* 8
Aristotle, 9
Artificial intelligence, 371–372
Asch, Solomon, 135–136
Ascribed status, 195
Asian Americans
  historical overview, 252–253
  school integration and, 356
Assimilation, 237
Atavisms, 161
Athletes, racial equality and, 230–321, 386–387
Atlanta University, 19
Attractiveness, benefits of, 70–71
Aubrey, J. S., 272–273
Authority
  legitimate, 135
  obedience to, 136–137
  positional, 135
Automation, 365–366
Autor, David, 367

Back stage, 120
Baganda tribe, 311
Balzac, Honoré de, 146
Ban Ki-moon, 216
Bank of America, 212
Bank Secrecy Act, 176
"Ban the box" movement, 183
Barra, Mary, 285
Barron's, 285
Bathrooms, transgender people and, 269
Bauman, Zygmunt, 240
Bay of Pigs invasion, groupthink and, 137–138
Beaufoy, Simon, 87
Beautiful is good hypothesis, 71
Beaver, Kevin, 162

Behaviorism, 99–100
Beliefs
characteristics of, 66
defined, 66
Bernard, Jessie, 313–314
Berry, Halle, 246
Bias, 43–44
critical thinking and, 7
social desirability, 48–49
surveys and, 52
Bias, Len, 158–159, 181
Biden, Joe, 196
Bieber, Justin, 82
Bigio, Jamille, 296
Biological constraints, in development, 103–104
Biological perspective on deviance, 161–162
Birth outcomes, racial disparities in, 245
Birthrates, immigrant, 321
Bishop, Kyle W., 65
Black Panther Party, 394, 396, 399
Blacks. *See* African Americans
Black underclass, 196
Blake, William, 10
Blau, Peter, 146
Blended families, 105
Blinder, Alan, 367
Blue-collar occupations, 198
Blumer, Herbert, 29, 387
Board of Education of Oklahoma City v. Dowell, 355
Bogumil, Elizabeth, 123–124
Bono, 82
Bosnia-Herzegovina, 259
Boston Tea Party, 390
Bourdieu, Pierre
doxic and, 74
on language, 250, 257
on social class reproduction, 85–86
structuralism and, 138
Bourgeoisie, 15, 212, 364
Bowles, Samuel, 349
Boycotts, over North Carolina bathroom bill, 269
Boyle, Danny, 87
Bracero program, 252
Brain-womb conflict, 278, 292
Brannon, R., 293
Brave New World (Huxley), 404
Brennan, William, 82
British East India Company, 147
Brown v. Board of Education of Topeka, 355, 386
Brunch, 113
Buffet, Warren, 192
Bullying, 40
cyberbullying, 111, 144–145
Bureaucracies, 16–17, 129, 141–147. *See also* Organizations
critical evaluation of, 143–146
defined, 141
democracy and, 146–147
groups, organizations, and, 144–145
ideal type, 142, 143
written rules and regulations and, 142–143
Bureau of Labor Statistics, 31
Burgess, Ernest, 20
Burial practices, 74, 75
Bush, George W., 300

Caldwell, Jessie, 205
Calhoun, John, 239
Cameron, P. A., 271
Cameroon, maternal mortality in, 295–297
Canela people, 270
Capital crime, 183–184
Capitalism
Marx's view of, 15–16
Protestantism and, 16
Capitalist class, 196
Capital offenses, 160–161
Caputi, J., 273
Careers using sociology degrees, 31
community resources and service skills and, 224–225
critical thinking and, 90–91
ethical decision making and, 302–303
evidence-based argument and, 261–262
global perspective and, 374–375
leadership skills and teamwork and, 151–152
problem solving and, 338–339
qualitative research skills and, 123–124
quantitative research skills and, 59
social change and, 405–406
written communication skills and, 186–187
Carlos, John, 230–231
Cartoons, gendered images in, 272
Cassidy, C., 84
Caste societies, 193–194
Castro, Fidel, 138, 252, 385
Causal relationship, 41
Causation, correlation and, 41
Centers for Disease Control and Prevention, 64
CEO pay, 197
Chalk, F., 260
Chambliss, William J., 49, 166–167, 169, 185
Chapman, Piper, 180
Charismatic authority, 385
Charity organizations, 141
social media and, 140
Cheating among high school students, 73
Chernow, John, 247
Chicago
racial segregation in, 236, 237
school segregation in, 356
Chicago School, 19–20
Child abuse, 326
Child care in United States, 319–321
Childhelp, 326
Child labor, 373
Child mortality, 216, 302
Child-rearing practices
ethnicity, race, and social class and, 105, 106–107
gender socialization and, 270–271
social class and, 311, 326–329, 331
Child survival hypothesis, 295
China
Apple's production in, 373–374
son preference and problem of marriage in, 336–337
Tiananmen Square protests, 400, 401
Chinese Americans, 253
Chodorow, Nancy, 314, 315
Christiansen, Karl, 161
Christianson, S., 71
Chrysler, 370
Churchill, Winston, 257
Citibank, 176
Civil rights movement, 235–236, 249, 251, 393, 394, 396, 399
Clarke, Edward, 278, 292
Class, defined, 195. *See also* Social class
Class conflict, 13
Class-dominant theory, 166–167
Classical sociological approaches to gender, 286–290
Class societies, 194
stratification and poverty persistence in, 211–213
Class status
in class societies, 194
reproduction of, 329

Class structure in postindustrial society, 366–367
Clinton, Bill, 318
Clinton, Hillary, 52
Clique, 134
Clooney, George, 247
Cloward, Richard, 162, 163, 166
Coalition, 131, 133
Coca-Cola, 86
Cochlear implants, 324
Coercive organizations, 141
Cognitive development, 102
Cognitive dissonance, 239
Cohabitation, 310, 316–317, 334
Collective behavior, 385–389
  defined, 385
Collective conscience, 13
Collectives, 146–147
Colleges and universities. *See* Higher education
Collins, Barbara Hicks, 235
Collins, Patricia Hill, 292–293
Commission, 175
Common-law marriage, 316–317
Common wisdom, sociological research and, 38–39
Communication
  gender and, 121, 122
  social interaction and, 120–122
  Twitter, 18–19
Communication skills, careers and written, 186–187
Community organizers, 338–339
Community resources and service skills, careers using, 224–225
Competitive kid capital, 331
Compliance (film), 137
Comte, Auguste, 10, 11–12, 238, 287
Concepts, 40
Concerted cultivation, 328–329
Conflict perspectives
  on education, 348–350
  on ethnicity, racism, and minority status, 238–239
  on the family, 312–315, 335
  on globalization, 89
  on pornography, 171
  on social change, 382–384
Conflict perspectives on deviance, 29, 165–168
  class-dominant theory, 166–167
  feminist theory, 167–168
  structural contradiction theory, 167
  subcultures and deviance, 166
Conformity
  to groups, 135–138
  success and, 163
Connell, Raewyn, 293
Connor, Bull, 176
Conscience constituents, 400
Consumer Financial Protection Bureau, 176
Consumer goods, inequalities in access to, 204–205
Consumption, global production and local, 26–27
Contagion theories, 387–388
Content analysis, 51
Contract labor market, 285, 366
Control group, 50
Control theory, 163–165
Convenience sample, 46
Conventional stage of moral development, 102
Convention on the Prevention and Punishment of the Crime of Genocide, 256–257
Conversation, between men and women, 121
Conversation analysis, 122
Cooley, Charles Horton, 100, 130
Coontz, Stephanie, 315, 316, 319
Coquille tribe, 322
Core countries, 221
Correlation, 41, 42
  negative, 43
  positive, 42–43
Cosby, Bill, 172
Cotton, Jarvious, 244
Counterculture, 76
Crack cocaine epidemic, 158–159, 181
Craigslist, 246
Crazes, 390–391
Credential society, 347
Crime, 160, 172–178. *See also* Deviance
  analysis of, 28–29
  capital, 183–184
  conflict theory interpretation of, 29
  Durkheim on, 28–29
  functionalist interpretation of, 28–29
  globalization and, 164–165
  organized, 173
  police corruption and policy brutality, 176–177
  state, 178
  statistics on, in United States, 174–175
  symbolic interactionist interpretation of, 29
  violent and property, 172–173
  white-collar, 29, 173, 175–176
Crime rate, validity of, 43, 174–175
Critical consumers of information, 9, 58
Critical thinking, 3, 6–9
  careers using, 90–91
  defined, 6
  rules for, 6–7
Crowd counting, 395
Crowds, 386–387
  behavior of, 389–391
  contagion theory on, 387–388
  defined, 385
  emergent norm theories on, 388–389
  value-added theory on, 389
Crowdsourcing, 395
Crowley, Candy, 71
Cuban Americans, 252
Cultural capital, 85
  groups and, 138–139
Cultural inconsistency, 70–74
Cultural labor, international division of, 87
Cultural-level studies, frame alignment and, 401–402
Cultural pluralism, 237
Cultural relativism, 74–75
Culture
  beliefs and, 66
  class, inequality, and, 85–86
  concepts and applications, 65–76
  defined, 65
  economy, family formation, and, 329–331
  global, 87
  globalization and, 86–90
  high, 79
  ideal and real, in U.S. society, 70–74
  language and, 76–78
  mass media and, 79–84, 88–89
  material, 66
  melding with advertising, 82–83
  nonmaterial, 66
  norms and, 66–69
  popular, 79
  rape, 83
  studying media and, through sociological lens, 90
  subcultures, 75–76
  values and, 66, 69–70
Culture industry, 82–83

Culture of thinness, in United States, 72–73
Cyberbullying, 111, 144–145
Cyclical theorists, 384–385

Dahrendorf, Ralf, on social change, 383–384
Dark web, 164
Data, evaluation of, 58
Data analysis, 56
Data analyst, 262
Data collection, 56
Daubié, Julie, 21
David, D. S., 293
Davis, K., 224
Davis, Kingsley, 211–212
Davis, Viola, 246
Deaf culture, family life and, 324–325
Death penalty, 160–161, 183–185
Debate
  argument *vs.*, 8
  defined, 8
  sociological, 9
de Beauvoir, Simone, 199
Deductive reasoning, 37
De facto segregation, 356
Delinquency, 165, 168
Democracy, bureaucracies and, 146–147
Democratic Republic of Congo, rape in war in, 299
Dependency relationship, 220
Dependency theory, 220
Dependent variables, 50, 57
Desmond, Matthew, 36–37, 38, 47, 242–243
Detached observation, 46, 47, 48
Devaluation of the feminine, 315
Development, stages of, 102–103
Deviance, 160–161. *See also* Crime
  analysis of, 28–29
  biological perspectives on, 161–162
  class-dominant theory and, 166–167
  conflict perspectives on, 29, 165–167
  defined, 160
  differential association theory and, 169
  everyday, 171
  feminist theory and, 167–168
  functionalist perspectives on, 29, 162–165
  interactionist perspectives on, 168–169
  Merton's theory of, 20
  of the powerful, 171–172
  primary, 168
  reasons to study, 185
  secondary, 168
  sexual, 171
  social control of, 170, 178–185
  sociological explanations for, 161–171
  structural contradiction theory and, 167
  subcultures and, 166
  symbolic interactionist interpretation of, 29
  types of, 171–178
Dewey, Thomas, 52, 53
DiCaprio, Leonardo, 86
Dickens, Charles, 10
Diderot, 10
Differential association theory, 169, 177
Differentiation, 381
Digital networking companies, 370
Dineh/Navajo, 250, 322, 324
Dinner, family, 114
Disaster preparedness campaign, zombies and, 64
Discipline
  in schools, 179–180
  spanking, 105, 106–107
Discouraged workers, 368
Discrimination
  in the classroom, 348–349
  consequences for health, 245–246
  defined, 241
  individual, 241
  institutionalized, 241–244
  technologies of, 246
Disney films, gendered images in, 272–273
Diversity, globalization and, 30
Division of labor
  household, 276
  sexual, 312
Divorce
  in modern United States, 316–319
  rates of, 105
  reasons for, 14–15
Diwali, 97
Doctors Without Borders (Médecins sans Frontières), 150
Document analysis, 51
"Doing Gender" (West & Zimmerman), 274
Domestic violence, 325–326
Domestic violence research, 118
Dorsey, Jack, 18
Double consciousness, 20
Downs, E., 273
Doxic, 74
Dramatic realization, 119
Dramaturgical approach, 119–120
Dreamer movement, 393
Drug use
  annual prevalence rate among 12th-graders, 38
  mandatory minimum sentences and, 170
Du Bois, W. E. B., 17, 20, 249
Du Bose, Samuel, 177
Duncan, Arne, 352–353
Durkheim, Émile
  analysis of crime and deviance, 28–29, 162
  on division of labor and evolution of society, 381–382
  on education, 347
  on function of social classes, 211
  on gender roles, 287
  mechanical and organic solidarity and, 238
  norms and anomie, 10–11
  photo of, 12
  religion and, 109
  social facts, social solidarity, and, 12–13, 335
  structural functionalism and, 23
Dwyer, Carol, 277
Dyad, 131
Dystopia, 404

Early, Gerald, 386
Earnings. *See also* Wages
  educational attainment and, 41, 359–361
  federal minimum wage, 362
Eating disorders, culture of thinness and, 72–73
Eatsa restaurant, 344–345
Economic capital, groups and, 138–139
Economic inequality, political party affiliation and, 69. *See also* Inequality
Economy
  culture, family formation, and, 329–331
  defined, 361
  in historical perspective, 361–369
  reasons to study, 372
  technological revolution and future of work, 369–372

Edgewood Arsenal, obedience to authority at, 137
Edin, Kathryn, 330, 331
Education. *See also* Higher education; Schools
defined, 345
formal, 345
global inequality and, 217–219
hourly wages of U.S. college and high school graduates, 201
industrialization, credential society, and, 345–347
labor force participation rates and, 359–361
mass, 345
median earnings and, 41
moral, 347
opportunity, inequality, and, 351–361
public, 346–347
reasons to study, 372
social mobility and, 39
theoretical perspectives on, 347–351
women and, 295
Educational attainment
earnings and, 41, 359–361
employment and, 359–361
individuals, groups, and, 132–133
socioeconomic status and, 349, 350, 351
women and divorce and, 14–15
Educational Longitudinal Study, 350–351
Ego, 103–104
Egocentric, 102
Ehrenreich, Barbara, 205, 334–335
Elder abuse, 326
Ellison, Marc, 299
Emergent norms, defined, 389
Emergent norm theories, 388–389
Emic perspective, 74
Emotional labor, 367, 369
Empirical data, 22
Employees, robot, 344–345
Les Employés (Balzac), 146
Employment
educational attainment and, 359–361
ex-offenders and, 182–183
rates of marriage and, 330, 334
Endogamous, 311
Engels, Friedrich, 287, 291, 364
English-only movement, 77–78
Enlightenment, 10
Entertainment, time spent pursuing, 404
Entertainment industry, race and ethnicity and, 246–247
Environmental activism, 401
Equal Pay Act (1963), 281, 285
Erikson, Erik, 109
Ethical decision making, careers using, 302–303
Ethical implications of research, weighing, 56
Ethnicity. *See also* Latinas/Latinos; Race and ethnicity
college gap and, 267
defined, 232
entertainment industry and, 246–247
median annual earnings by, 280
median household income by, 197
neighborhood poverty and, 210
nonmarital births and, 330
poverty in United States and, 207
wealth gap by, 202
Ethnic subcultures, 76
Ethnocentrism, 30, 74–75
Ethnography, 47
Ethnomethodology, 120–122
Etic perspective, 74
Etzioni, Amitai, 139–140
Europe, migration to, 256
European Union, 149
Everyday deviance, 171
Evicted: Poverty and Profit in the American City (Desmond), 36–37, 243
Eviction, poverty, race, and, 36–37, 195, 242–243
Evidence, critical thinking and, 7
Evidence-based argument, 261–262
Evolutionary theories, 382
Experimental group, 50
Experimental variables, 50
Experimentation, 46, 50
Experiments, defined, 50
Expulsion
of American Indians, 233
school, 179–180
Extended families, 311
Eye contact, 118

Fabes, R. A., 271
Facebook, 54, 96, 115, 151, 370, 402
Fact checkers, 73
Fads, 390
Failing at Fairness (Sadker & Sadker), 274
Fair Housing Act, 246
Falsifiability, 43
Family, 129. *See also* Divorce; Marriage
as agent of socialization, 104–105
American Indian, 322–324
changes in U.S., 315–326
child care and, 319–321
child rearing and, 311
deaf culture and, 324–325
defined, 309
economy, culture, and family formation, 329–331
extended, 311
fragmentation of black, 329–330
functional alternatives to, in modern Japan, 323
gender socialization and, 270–271
globalization and, 333–335
immigration and family patterns, 321–322
international, 334
middle-class family life, 331–333
nuclear, 311, 315
as reference group, 130
socioeconomic class and, 326–333
study of, 309–311
theoretical perspectives on, 311–315
trends in family living arrangements, 310
violence and, 325–326
Family dinner, 114
Family life, gender and, 275–276
Fashions, 390
Fast and Furious film series, 86
Fast food, globalization of, 89
Fear, zombies and contemporary, 65
Federal minimum wage, 362
Feig, Paul, 288, 289
Female assigned at birth (FAAB), 268
Female to man (FTM), 268
Feminine, 270
The Feminine Mystique (Friedan), 290, 316
Femininity, 315
Feminism
defined, 290
liberal, 290–291
multicultural, 291
radical, 291
second-wave, 290
socialist, 291
third-wave, 291–292
Feminist perspectives
on deviance, 167–168
on doing sociology, 292–293

on family, 312–315
on gender in contemporary United States, 290–292
Fertility
marriage squeeze and, 337
in poor countries, 215–217
Fieldwork, 46, 47–49
defined, 47
Fifty Shades of Grey (James), 171
Films, violence in, 84
Financial Crimes Enforcement Network, 176
Flag burning, 67
Flatow, Ira, 395
Flexible production, 365–366
Folkways, 67–68
characteristics of, 66
Food deserts, 203, 204–205
Football players, deviance and, 172, 230, 231
Ford, Henry, 364–365
Ford, Martin, 370, 371
Fordism, 364
Formal education, 345
Formal organizations
defined, 139
types of, 139–141
Formal rationality, 16
Formal social control, 178
imprisonment in United States and, 180–183
Foxconn, 373
Frame alignment, 401–402
France, Muslims in, 256
Freeburg, E. W., 84
Freeman v. Pitts, 355
Free rider problem, 398
Freud, Sigmund, 103–104, 268, 314–315
Friedan, Betty, 290, 316
Friedman, Hilary Levey, 331
Friedman, Thomas, 89
Frisby, C. M., 272–273
Front stage, 119–120
Functionalist perspectives. *See also* Structural functionalism
on deviance, 29, 162–165
on education, 347–348
on English-only movement, 77–78
on ethnicity, racism, and minority status, 238
on the family, 312, 335
on globalization, 87
on persistence of stratification and poverty, 211–212
on social change, 381–382
Functionalist perspectives on deviance, 162–165
control theory, 163–165
deviance and social solidarity, 162
opportunity theory, 163
structural strain theory, 163
The Future of Marriage (Bernard), 313

Gallaudet University, 324, 325
Game stage, in socialization, 101, 102, 104
Gang members, observation of, 49
Gangsta rap, content analysis of, 51
Gans, Herbert, 212, 213
Garfinkel, Harold, 120, 122
Garner, Eric, 231
Gender
classical sociological approaches to, 286–290
communication and, 121, 122
concepts of sex, gender, and sexuality, 267–270
constructing gendered selves, 269–275
contemporary U.S. feminist thinking on, 290–292
defined, 268
doing gender, 274–275
as dynamic concept, 268
incarceration rates and, 181
median earnings by, 280, 282
reasons to study from sociological perspective, 302
unemployment rates of college graduates by, 4–5
women's lives in global perspective, 295–302
Gender and economics, 281–286
gender occupational segregation, 282–286
gender wage gap, 281–282, 284–285
most common occupations for men/women in United States, 287
Gender and society, 275–281
college gap, 266–267
gender and family life, 275–276
gender and higher education, 277–281
gender in high school, 276–277
Gender displays, 270
Gendered institution, marriage as, 314
Gender roles
defined, 267
Parsons on, 25, 27, 287, 291, 312
social interaction and, 270
Gender socialization, 269–275
Gender stratification, 275
Gender wage gap, 38, 281–282, 284–285
defined, 281
Generalized other, 101–102
General Motors Corporation, 175–176, 370
"Genie," 98–99
Genocide, 256–259
defined, 256
explanations for, 259–260
Genocide Watch, 259
Gentrification, 223
Gen Xers, marriage and parenthood and, 316–317
Geronimus, Arline, 245–246
Ghostbusters: Answer the Call (film), 288–289
Ghostbusters (film), 288–289
Gig labor market, 285
Gig work, 366
Gilbert, D. L., 195, 196
Gilligan, Carol, 103
Gilman, Charlotte Perkins, 20, 287
Gintis, Herbert, 349
Girls
delinquency and, 168
organized sports and, 109
#Giving Tuesday, 140
Glass ceiling, 286
Glass escalator, 286
Global business organizations (GBOs), 150
Global culture, 87
Global Hollywood (Miller et al.), 87
Global inequality, 213–219. *See also* Inequality
defined, 213
indicators of, 216
Nigerian oil wealth, 221–224
theoretical perspectives on, 219–224
Globalization
criminal opportunities and, 164–165
culture and, 86–90
defined, 30
diversity and, 30
families and, 333–335
reactionary movements and, 397
social change and, 403
structural contradictions and, 167
The Globalization of Nothing (Ritzer), 89
Global organizations, 147
international governmental organizations, 147–150

international nongovernmental organizations, 150–151
Global perspective
career prospects and, 374–375
on race and ethnicity, 256–260
women's lives in, 295–302
Global production, local consumption and, 26–27
Global village, 79
Global woman, 334–335
Glocalization, 89
Goal displacement, bureaucracies and, 145–146
Goffman, Erving
doing gender and, 274–275
dramaturgical approach and, 118, 119–120
on misrepresentation, 73
on resocialization, 116
on stigma and mixed contacts, 240
Gold collar occupations, 198
Goldin, Claudia, 286
Golding, William, 128–129
Goldscheider, F. K., 276
Goods, 361
Gottfredson, M. R., 162, 163, 165
Government
policies supporting marriage, 327
social movement organizations and, 399
Government data, 51
Gracey, Harry, 347
Grades, sleep and, 41–42, 43
Graduation gap, class and, 349, 350
Gramsci, Antonio, 383, 384
Grassroots organizing, 400
Gray, Freddie, 388, 389
Great Recession, 202, 206, 251, 360
Grimes, S., 96
Grobalization, 89
Grogan, Sarah, 73
Gross national income-purchasing power parity per capita (GNI-PPP), 215
Group cooperation, 129
Group dynamics, 128–129
Groups. *See also* Bureaucracies; Organizations
academic achievement and, 132–133
conformity to, 135–138
economic, cultural, and social capital, and, 138–139
effect of size, 130–134
nature of, 129–130
organizations, bureaucracies, and, 144–145
power of, 130–138
primary, 100, 129, 130
reasons to study, 151
reference, 100–101, 130
relations between minority and dominant, 232–237
secondary, 100, 129, 130
types of group leadership, 134–135
Groupthink, 137–138
Guantanamo Bay prison, 178
Guilmoto, C. Z., 336–337
Gunnoe, Marjorie Lindner, 107

Habermas, Jürgen, 79, 81
Habitus, 86
Habyarimana, Juvénal, 259
Haiti, international response to disaster in, 148–149
Hamblin, James, 294
Hamilton (musical), 246, 247
Haninger, K., 273
Hanseatic League, 147
Harrington, Michael, 207
Harris, Judith Rich, 108
Hastert, Dennis, 172
Hate crimes, in United States, 234–235
Headcount efficiency, 370
Health
consequences of prejudice and discrimination for, 245–246
inequalities in, 203–204
marital status and, 313–314
Health care, inequalities in, 202–203
Health educator/community health worker, 225
Hegemonic masculinity, 293–294
Hellstrom, A., 71
Henderson, Amber, 59
Hendrix, Jimi, 82
Hesse-Biber, Sharlene, 73
Heteronormative, 268
Heterosexuality in media, 272
Hidden curriculum, 107, 273, 348
Hierarchy, bureaucracies and, 142–143
High culture, 79
Higher education
agency *vs.* structure and college attendance, 6
college debt, 279, 281
college dropout rates, 356–359
college enrollment gap, 278–279
college gap, 266–267
gender and, 277–281
student debt and, 317, 357, 360
unemployment rates among college graduates, 4–5
High-income countries, 213, 215
High mass consumption and high living standards stage, 220
High school
cheating in, 73
drug use in, 38
gender in, 276–277
Hip-hop, misogynistic lyrics of, 84
Hirschi, T., 162, 163, 165
His and her marriage, 313–314
Historical research, 51
Hitler, Adolf, 385
Ho, Christine, 334
Hochschild, Arlie Russell
on emotional labor, 369
on global woman, 334–335
on second shift, 276
on work-life balance, 331, 333
Holacracy, 147
Holliday, Tess, 71
Holocaust
denial of, 240
poll on beliefs about, 46–47
Homelessness, 38–39, 43–44
Homework, appropriateness of amounts of, 117–118
Homophobia, organized sports and, 109
Honesty, cultural inconsistency about, 71, 73
Horkheimer, Max, 82–83
Horn, Mike, 176
Household division of labor, 276
Household income, 197
Household poverty, 208
Housing
discrimination in, 246
ex-offenders and, 182
Hubbard, Jillian, 152
Hubbard, Leah, 303
Huffman, Matt, 139
Hull House, 21–22
Hull-House Maps and Papers (Addams), 22
Human capital, 283
Human experimentation directives, 56
Human Genome Project, race and, 231
Hunger, in poor countries, 215–217
Hurrell, 84
Hussein, Saddam, 259
Huxley, Aldous, 404

Hyman, Herbert, 130
Hypotheses
  defined, 37
  testing, 42–43

I, 101
Ibn Khaldun, 9
Id, 103–104
Ideal culture, 70–74
  defined, 70
Idealization, 119, 274
Ideal type of bureaucracy, 142, 143
Ideological hegemony, 383
Immigrants. *See also* Migration/ migrants
  deviance and, 166
  global woman, 334–335
  top feeder countries for migration to United States, 322
  top 10 largest U.S. immigrant groups, 322
Impersonality in record keeping, bureaucracies and, 143
Impression management, 119–120, 274
Imprisonment. *See also* Prisons
  stigma of, 182–183
  in United States, 180–183
Incest taboo, 68
Income, 197
  aggregate, 199–200
  wealth *vs.*, 197
  world by, 214
Income inequality, 199–201
Incompetence, bureaucracies and, 145
Independent variables, 50, 57
India
  caste system in, 194
  sex trafficking in, 297–298
  son preference and problem of marriage in, 336–337
Indians of All Tribes (IAT), 248–249
Indirect labor costs, 283
Individual discrimination, 241
Inductive reasoning, 37
Industrialization, 220, 345
Industrial laborer, 363, 364
Industrial Revolution, 10, 363
Industrial society, 363–365
  characteristics of, 365
Inequality. *See also* Global inequality; Social class and inequality
  class, culture, and, 85–86
  defined, 30
  education and, 351–361
  income, 199–201
  wealth, 24–25, 201–202
Infant mortality rate, 216
In flight stage with technological progress and cultural modernity, 220
Informal social control, 178
Information, critical consumer of, 9, 58
Instagram, 96, 370
Institute for Women's Policy Research (IWPR), 262
Institutionalized discrimination, 241–244
Institutions
  genocidal, 260
  total, 115–116
Intelligence, attractiveness and, 71
Interactionist perspectives on deviance, 168–169
  differential association theory, 169
  labeling theory, 168–169
Intermarriage, 311
Internally displaced persons, 233
International Crisis Group, 222
International families, 334
International governmental organizations (IGOs), 147–150
International Labour Organization, 297
International nongovernmental organizations (INGOs), 150–151
Internet
  addiction to, 110
  as agent of socialization, 110–111
  primary and secondary groups and, 130
Interracial marriages, 319
Intersectionality, 292
Interviews, 45
  defined, 47
Intimate partner violence (IPV), 325
An Introduction to the Science of Sociology (Park & Burgess), 19–20
Iran, reactionary movement in, 397
Irish Catholics, discrimination against, 254
Irish language, 80–81
Iron cage, bureaucracies and, 145
Iron law of oligarchy, 146
Irrationalities of rationality, 145
Irving, Kyrie, 231
Islamic Relief USA (IRUSA), 150–151
Islamic Relief Worldwide (IRW), 150
Itard, Jean-Marc-Gaspard, 98
Jacobson, L., 350
James, LeBron, 231
Janis, Irving L., 137–138
Japan, functional alternatives to family in, 323
Japanese Americans, 252, 253
Jefferson, Thomas, 6, 7
Jenner, Bruce/Caitlyn, 269
Jim Crow laws, 239, 245, 249, 354–355
Johnson, Lyndon B., 207
Jonassohn, K., 260
Jones, Leslie, 288
Journal of Health and Social Behavior, 44
JPMorgan Chase, 175, 176

Kaepernick, Colin, 230, 231
Katz, Jackson, 294
Kaufman, J. M., 163
Kefalas, Maria, 330, 331
Kellner, Douglas, 81
Kennedy, John F., 138, 207, 220
Kennedy, Paul, 384
Khan, Ali, 64
Khmer Rouge genocide, 259
Khomeini, Ayatollah, 397
Kiehl, Laura, 186–187
Killian, Lewis M., 389
Kimmel, Michael, 293, 294
King, Harry, 112
King, Martin Luther, Jr., 385, 386, 399
King, Rodney, 176
Kluger, Adam, 82
Kmec, J. A., 139
Knowledge workers, 366–367
Kohlberg, Lawrence, 102–103
Kohn, Melvin, 328
Kosovo, 259
Kozol, Jonathan, 349
Kristof, N., 295–296, 298
Ku Klux Klan, 397
Kurds, genocide against, 259

Labeling in the classroom, 348, 350–351
Labeling theory, 168–169, 171
Labor demand factors, 282, 283
Labor force participation rates, 368
Labor supply factors, 282–283
Lagarde, Christine, 297
Language(s)
  culture and, 76–78
  defined, 76
  endangered, 76–77

resistance, power, and, in Northern Ireland, 80–81
social integration and, 77–78
socialization and, 98
Lanier, Jaron, 370
Lareau, Annette, 328–329
Larrimore, Skyler, 338–339
Latent functions, 20, 27
of education, 347
Latinas/Latinos. *See also* Ethnicity; Race and ethnicity
child-rearing practices among, 104
incarceration rates among, 181, 183
marriage and nonmarital births among, 330
neighborhood poverty and, 210
overview, 251
school segregation and, 356
Laws, 68–69
characteristics of, 66
defined, 68
Leadership, types of group, 134–135
Leadership skills and teamwork, careers using, 151–152
Leading questions, 47
League of Nations, 147, 149
Le Bon, Gustave, 385
Legitimate authority, 135
Lemert, Edwin, 168
Lemkin, Raphael, 257
Leonhardt, David, 357
Levo.com, 284
The Lexus and the Olive Tree (Friedman), 89
Liberal feminism, 290–291
Life changes, 195
Light, Harriett, 322
LinkedIn, 139
Lips, Hilary, 270
Literacy
defined, 346, 354
word poverty and adult illiteracy, 353–354
Literature review, 55
Livingston, G., 319–320
Lombroso, Cesare, 162
Looking-glass self, 100, 130
Lord of the Flies (Golding), 128–129, 133
Lord's Resistance Army (LRA), 299
Los Angeles, school segregation in, 356
Lost (television program), 128, 129, 133
Lower middle-income countries, 213, 215
Low-income communities, nonmarital births in, 330
Low-income countries, 213, 215
hunger, mortality, and fertility in, 215–217

Mac Ionnrachtaigh, Feargal, 81
MacKinnon, Catharine, 83
Macro-level approaches, to social movements, 400–401
Macro-level paradigms, 23
Madoff, Bernie, 165, 175–176
Mair, C. A., 139
Malcolm X, 348–349
Male assigned at birth (MAAB), 268
Male to female (MTF), 268
Mali, microfinance program for women in, 301
Mandatory minimum sentences, 159, 170, 181
Mandela, Nelson, 134, 135, 233, 235
Manhood, rules of, 293
Manifest functions, 20, 27, 347
Manifesto of the Communist Party (Marx & Engels), 364
Mansplaining, 121
Manufacturing, 363, 364, 366–367
Mao Zedong, 385
Marginally attached to the labor force, 368
Marijuana, shifting legal status of, 161
Market research analysts, 91
Marriage
common-law, 316–317
decline of among working class, 30–31
defined, 309–310
employment and, 330, 334
Gilman on, 287
his and her, 313–314
intermarriage, 311
millennials and, 308–309
in modern United States, 316–319
parenthood and, 309
race and decline in, 329–330
same-sex, 48–49, 68, 271, 318
son preference in China and India and problem of, 336–337
state policies supporting, 327
Martin, C. L., 271
Martin, Ruth, 322
Martineau, Harriet, 11, 12
Marx, Karl, 10, 13–16
on economic capital, 85
on exploitation of labor, 373
grobalization and, 89
on industrial workers, 363, 364
on inequality and women, 291
on means of production, 364
Mills and, 21
on ruling ideas of society, 81
on social change, 383, 384
social conflict theory and, 23, 28, 212
on social movements, 400
Masculine, 269–270
Masculinities, sociology of, 293–295
Masculinity
Chodorow on development of, 315
hegemonic, 293–294
violent, 84
Mass education, 345
Mass media. *See also* Media
as agent of socialization, 110–111
culture and, 79–84, 88–89
defined, 79
Mass production, 364
Mass shootings, 294
Material culture, 66
Maternal mortality, 295–297, 298, 302
Matrix of domination, 293
Maume, D. J., 276
Mayer, Marissa, 285
McCarthy, Melissa, 288
McDonald, S., 139
McDonald's, 86, 87
McGonigal, Jane, 404
McIntosh, Peggy, 254–255
McKinnon, Kate, 288
McLaughlin, H. J., 348
McLuhan, Marshall, 79
McMillan, Sharrie, 113
Me, 101
Mea, Bill, 269
Mead, George Herbert, 23, 29, 101–102, 104
Mealtimes, 113–114
Means of production, 16, 212, 364
Mechanical solidarity, 13, 238, 382
Media. *See also* Mass media; Social media
culture, violence, and, 83–84
culture of thinness and, 72–73
reflecting and reinforcing gender, 272–273
as socialization agent, 88
Media violence, impact on children, 110
Men. *See also* Gender
conversation with women, 121
displays of intimacy between, 118
incarceration rates for, 181, 183

Meredith, James, 355
Meritocracy, 211
Merkel, Angela, 297
Merton, Robert K., 20, 27, 130, 162, 163, 323
Mexican Americans, 252
Meyrowitz, J., 112
Michels, Robert, 146
Microfinance programs, 301
Micro-level approaches, to social movements, 398
Micro-level paradigms, 23
Micromobilization contexts, 402
Microsoft, 366
Middle class, 196
  decline of, 193
  family life in, 331–333
  industrial capitalism and, 365
Middle-class parents, child rearing and, 326–329
Middle-income countries, 213, 215
Midwifery, 295
Migration/migrants. *See also* Immigrants
  deviance and, 166
  population growth in United States and, 248
  push and pull factors for, 256
  to United States by region of origin, 254
Milgram, Stanley, 136–137
Military
  as coercive organization, 141
  gender and service in, 269
Military international governmental organizations, 149–150
Millennials
  attitudes toward same-sex marriage and, 271
  marriage and parenthood and, 308–309, 316–317
Millet, Holly, 405–406
Million Man March, 395
Mills, C. Wright, 83
  overview, 21
  on power elite, 199
  sociological imagination and, 3–4, 5
Miner, Herbert, 74–75
Minimum wage, federal, 362
Minorities
  defined, 232
  model, 253
  symbolic interactionist perspective on, 239–240
Minority and dominant group relations, 232–237
Miranda, Lin-Manuel, 247
Misogyny, *Ghostbusters* remake and, 288–289
Misrepresentation, 73, 119
Missouri v. Jenkins, 355
Mixed contacts, 240
Moana (film), 273
Moats, Louisa Cook, 353
Model minority, 253
Modernization theory, 219–220
Monogamy, 310
  serial, 310
Montesquieu, 10
Moore, W., 224
Moore, Wilbert, 211–212
Moral development, 102–103
Moral education, 347
Mores, 68
  characteristics of, 66
More Than Just Race (Wilson), 331
Mormon Church, 310
Mortality, in poor countries, 215–217
Mortgage lending, discrimination in, 244
Mott, Lucretia, 290, 383
Moynihan, Daniel Patrick, 329, 330
Multicultural feminism, 291
Multiculturalism, 78
Multilinear theories, 382
Multiracial Americans, 255–256
Murdock, George Peter, 310
Murphy, Cullen, 384
Myrdal, Gunnar, 195–196
Mystification, 119–120

NAACP (National Association for the Advancement of Colored People), 393
Nacirema people, 74–75
Naming, power to, 250
Nanny chain, 334–335
National Basketball Association (NBA), North Carolina boycott over bathroom bill, 269
National Bureau of Economic Research, 180
National Coalition for the Homeless, 400
National Congress of American Indians, 250
National Crime Victimization Survey (NCVS), 43, 83, 172, 174–175
National Football League (NFL), 231, 294
National Intimate Partner and Sexual Violence Survey, 325
National Longitudinal Study of Adolescent Health, 162
National Opinion Research Center, 45
National Park Service, 395
National Survey of Student Engagement (NSSE), 54
A Nation at Risk (report), 117
Navajo/Dineh, 250
Navajo Nation, 322, 324
Nayar people, 311
Negative correlation, 43
Negotiation skills, gender wage gap and, 284
The Negro Family (Moynihan), 329
Neighborhood poverty, 208–211
Net financial assets, 197
Netizens, 151
Net worth, 197–198
The New Jim Crow (Alexander), 244
New social movements, 393, 402–403
Nigerian oil wealth, 221–224
1984 (Orwell), 404
Nisbet, Robert, 67
Nonmarital births, 329–331
Nonmaterial culture, 66
  beliefs, 66
  norms, 66–69
  values, 66, 69–70
Normalizing violence, 84
Normative organizations, 141
Norms, 10, 66–69
  characteristics of, 66
  defined, 66
  social interaction and, 118
North Atlantic Treaty Organization (NATO), 149
North Carolina bathroom bill, 269
Northern Ireland, language, resistance, and power in, 80–81
Not in the labor force, 368
Nuclear family, 311, 315
Nuremberg Code, 56, 58

Obama, Barack, 203, 251, 300, 352, 391, 393
Obedience to authority, 136–137
Obergefell v. Hodges, 318
Obesity
  correlation between poverty and, 42–43
  pay penalty and, 70–71
Objectivity in scientific research, 44

Observation
detached, 46, 47, 48
participant, 46, 47, 48
Occupational segregation by gender, 282–286
Occupational structure, in postindustrial society, 366–367
Occupations
defined, 198
prestige ranking of, 198
Occupy Wall Street movement, 385, 388
Official poverty, 208
Official poverty line, 208
Offshoring, 366
Ohlin, Lloyd, 162, 163, 166
Oligarchy, iron law of, 146
Olivieri, E., 279
O'Malley, Martin, 185
Omission, 175
O'Neill, Thomas, 158
Operational definition, 40
Operations research analyst, 123–124
Opportunity theory, 163
Orange Is the New Black (television program), 180
Organic intellectuals, 383
Organic solidarity, 13, 238, 382
Organizational-level approaches, to social movements, 398–400
Organizations, 139–141. *See also* Bureaucracies
coercive, 141
defined, 139
formal, 139–141
groups, bureaucracies, and, 144–145
normative, 141
reasons to study, 151
utilitarian, 140–141
Organized crime, 49, 173
Organized sports, as agent of socialization, 109
Orshansky, Mollie, 209
Orwell, George, 404
Osborne, D., 109
Oscars, race and, 246–247
Other
generalized, 101–102
significant, 101
The Other America (Harrington), 207
"Out of Utopia" (Dahrendorf), 383–384
Outreach specialists, 225
Outsourcing, 366
Ovarian determinism, 278
Overparenting, 328
Oxfam America, 299, 301
Oxford English Dictionary, 8, 121

Panics, 390
Parenthood, marriage and, 309
Parenting, in poverty, 332–333
Park, Robert Ezra, 19–20
Parks, Rosa, 386, 394
Parsons, Talcott
on the family, 312
on religion, 109
on sex-role differences, 25, 27, 288, 291, 312
on societies and status quo, 382
structural functionalism and, 23, 25, 27
on values, 70
Participant observation, 46, 47, 48
Participatory research, 46, 51
Pascoe, C. J., 271
Patriarchy, 291
Pavlov, Ivan, 99
Payment, Aaron, 353
Pay penalty, obesity and, 70–71
Peace Corps, 220
Peer review, 44
Peer socialization, 107–108
gender socialization and, 271–272
Pepper (robot), 323
Peripheral countries, 221
Permatemps, 366
Personality stabilization, 312
Personal power, 135
Personal troubles, sociological imagination and, 3
Phelan, A. M., 348
Phrenology, 161
Piaget, Jean, 102
Piketty, Thomas, 200
Pink collar occupations, 198
Plagiarism among high school students, 73
Plato, 9
Play stage, in socialization, 101, 104
Plessy v. Ferguson, 243, 355
Plummer, Gary, 294
Pluralistic societies, 160
Pluralist perspective on U.S. democracy, 199
Police
police corruption and police brutality, 176–177
presence in schools, 180
Political party affiliation
beliefs about economic inequality and, 69
support for social welfare and, 68
Political power, 199
African Americans and, 251
Political voice, 199
Politics
equal gender representation in, 300–301
prison, power, and, 244–245
Polling, 46–47, 52–53
Pollutants, segregation and, 236, 238
Polyandry, 310
Polygamy, 310
Polygyny, 310
"Poor Women in the Nineteenth Century" (Daubié), 21
Popper, Karl, 43, 44, 99
Popular culture, 79
Popular music industry, gender stereotypes and, 272–273
Population, defined, 45
Pornography, 84, 171
Port Harcourt (Nigeria), 222
Positional power, 135
Positive correlation, 42–43
Positivist, 11
Postconventional stage of moral development, 103
Post-Fordism, 366
Postindustrial society, 365–369
characteristics of, 365
Postman, Leo, 391
Poverty
correlation between obesity and, 42–43
eviction and, 36–37, 243
global, 213–219
neighborhood, 208–211
official, 208
parenting in, 332–333
persistence of, 211–213
single-parent families and, 330–331
transportation and, 218–219
in the United States, 24, 207–208, 209
Poverty areas, defined, 210
Powell, R., 49
Power
bureaucracies and concentration of, 146
defined, 29–30
deviance of the powerful, 171–172
of groups, 130–138
language, resistance, and, in Northern Ireland, 80–81

leaders and, 135
to name, 250
personal, 135
political, 199, 251
prison, politics, and, 244–245
social, 178
Power, Samantha, 260
Power elite, 199
Preconventional stage of moral development, 102
Prejudice
consequences for health, 245–246
defined, 240
Preparatory stage, in socialization, 101, 104
Presentation of self, 119
Presentence investigator, 186–187
Primary deviance, 168
Primary groups, 100, 129
characteristics of, 130
Principle of falsification, 43, 44, 99
Principles of Scientific Management (Taylor), 364
Prisons. *See also* Imprisonment
race and, 244–245
resocialization and, 116
riots in, 390
school to prison pipeline, 179–180
sexual victimization in, 168
stigma of, 182–183
U.S., 180–183
U.S. state and federal prison population, 1925-2015, 159
Private detectives and investigators, 187
Private troubles, 15
Problem solving, careers using, 338–339
Production
flexible, 365–366
mass, 364
means of, 16, 212, 364
Product placements, lyrical, 82
Program for the International Assessment of Adult Competencies (PIAAC), 354
Proletariats, 13–14, 212, 364
Property crime, 172–173
Protestantism, capitalism and, 16
Psychoanalysis, 103
Psychodynamic feminist perspective on the family, 314–315, 335
Public education, 346–347
Public issues, 3, 15
Public relations specialist, 406
Public sphere, 79, 81
Pull factors, 256, 335
Punishment, spanking and, 105, 106–107
Push factors, 256, 335

Qualitative research, 37
defined, 38
Qualitative research skills, careers using, 123–124
Qualitative variables, 41
Quantitative research, defined, 37–38
Quantitative research skills, careers using, 59
Quantitative variables, 40–41
Questionnaires, 45
Question order effects, 48
Questions
framing research, 53
leading, 47
Quintiles, 199–200

Race. *See also* African Americans
academic performance and, 39
anti-miscegenation laws, 311
child-rearing practices and, 105, 106–107
college gap and, 267
death penalty and, 185
defined, 232
discrimination in the classroom and, 348–349
entertainment industry and, 246–247
health and, 245–246
health inequality and, 203–204
incarceration rates and, 181, 183
median annual earnings by, 280
median household income by, 197
neighborhood poverty and, 210
nonmarital births and, 329–330
policy brutality and, 176–177
poverty in United States and, 207
suspension and expulsion from schools and, 180
wealth inequality and, 201–202
Race and ethnicity
global perspective on, 256–260
minority and dominant group relations, 232–237
prejudice, stereotyping, and discrimination, 240–247
racial and ethnic groups in the United States, 247–256
reasons to study, 260–261
social construction of, 231–232
theoretical approaches to, 238–240
Racial equality, athletes standing/kneeling for, 230–231
Racism
conflict perspective on, 238–239
defined, 238
Du Bois on, 20
functional perspective on, 238
Radical feminism, 291
Random sampling, 46
Rape, 295
in war, 298–299
Rape culture, 83
Rational bureaucracy, 142
Rationality, formal, 16
Reactionary movements, 393, 397
Real culture, 70–74
defined, 70
Reasoning
deductive, 37
inductive, 37
Rebellious movements, 393, 396–397
Red Cross, 149
Reference groups, 100–101, 130
Reformist movements, 393, 394, 396
Refugee Convention, 258
Refugees, 233, 258–259
Regulations, bureaucracies and, 142–143
Reich, Robert, 206
Reliability, 43–44
Religion, as agent of socialization, 109–110
Religious utopian movements, 398
Rental families, 323
Replication, 44
Research approval, 56
Research methods, 3, 45–54
experimentation, 46, 50
fieldwork, 46, 47–49
participatory research, 46, 51
polling, 46–47, 52–53
selecting, 55
survey research, 45–47
working with existing information, 46, 50–51
Research questions, framing, 53
Reservations, American Indian, 248, 249
Reserve army of labor, 364
Resistance, in Northern Ireland, 80–81
Resocialization, total institutions and, 115–116
Resource mobilization theory, 399
Restaurant industry, robots and, 344–345
Results, sharing, 56, 58
Retail industry, local and corporate, 16

Retreatist lifestyle, 76
ReUp, 375
Revolutionary movements, 393, 396
Rice, Condoleezza, 297
Rickey, Branch, 387
Riots, 389–390
The Rise and Fall of the Great Powers (Kennedy), 384
Rise-and-fall theories of social change, 384–385
Ritzer, George, 89
Robinson, Jackie, 230, 231, 386–387
Robots, 370–372
as employees, 344–345
Rodriguez, Alex, 172
Role-taking, 101
Rolfe, Frank, 193
Roosevelt, Theodore, 77
Rosenthal, R., 350
Rosser, Phyllis, 277
Rostow, Walt, 219–220
Rothschild-Whitt, Joyce, 147
Rousseau, Jean-Jacques, 10, 287
Rules
bureaucracies and written, 142–143
unwritten, 100
Rumors, 391
Ruppanner, L., 276
Rutledge, Pamela, 96
Rwandan genocide, 259, 260

Sadker, David, 274
Sadker, Myra, 274
Saez, Emmanuel, 200
Salinas, Elaine J., 250
Same-sex marriage
legalization of, 68, 318
millennials and, 271
social desirability bias and, 48–49
Sample, 45–46
defined, 45
Sampling
convenience, 46
random, 46
snowball, 46
stratified, 46
technology and, 52
Sapir, Edward, 76
Sapir-Whorf hypothesis, 76
SAT mathematics scores, gender and, 276–277
Saving for Change, 299, 301
Sawyer, Diane, 269
Scapegoating, 262
Scheff, T. J., 118
School busing, 355
Schooling in Capitalist America (Bowles & Gintis), 349
Schools
American Indian, 352–353, 356
cyberbullying and, 144–145
gender in high school, 276–277
gender socialization and, 273–274
homework, 117–118
school to prison pipeline, 179–180
socialization and, 105–107, 348
School segregation, 354–356
Schulhofer, Stephen J., 83
Schuppe, Jon, 158
Schwarz, Ori, 97
Scientific, defined, 2
Scientific management, 364
Scientific method, 39–44
defined, 37
Scientific research, objectivity in, 44
Scientific revolution, 9–10
Scientific theories, 39–40
Scott, Hunter, 225
Scott, Keith Lamont, 177
Screen time, number of hours per week, 110, 112, 272
Scythian-Sarmatian burials, 74
Secondary deviance, 168
Secondary groups, 100, 129
characteristics of, 130
Second shift, 276
Segregation, 233–237, 239
de facto, 356
defined, 233
occupational segregation by gender, 282–286
school, 346, 354–356
Selassie, Haile, 385
Self
looking-glass, 100, 130
presentation of, 119
Self-driving cares, 370–371, 372
Self-fulfilling prophecy, 350
Self-help groups, 389
Selfies, 96–97
Sellin, Thorsten, 166
Semiperipheral states, 221
Sennett, Richard, 199
September 11, 2001, Arab Americans and, 253
Serial monogamy, 310
Seri language, 76–77
Service economy
automation and, 366
emotional labor and, 367, 369
growth in, 203, 206
overview, 367
Services, defined, 361, 363
Sex
defined, 267
as dynamic concept, 268
Sex category, 274–275
Sex in Education (Clarke), 278
Sexism, 290
Sex ratio
in China and India, 336–337
in United States, 317
Sex-role differences, Parsons on, 25, 27, 287, 291, 312
Sex selection, 336
Sextortion, 296
Sex trafficking, 297–298
Sexual abuse, child, 326
Sexual assault, 84, 295
Sexual deviance, 171
Sexual division of labor in modern societies, 312
Sexual harassment, 295
Sexuality
defined, 268
seniors', 114–115
Sexual orientation, college completion and, 281
Sexuoeconomic relation, marriage as, 287
Shakespeare, William, 79, 82
Shaw, M., 260
Shipler, David, 196
Significant others, 101
Silk Road, 164
Simmel, Georg, 130–131, 390
Sinclair, Upton, 373
Single-parent homes, 330–331
Size, effects of group, 130–134
Skinner, B. F., 99
Slavery, 193–194, 238–239, 249
Sleep, grades and, 41–42, 43
Slumdog Millionaire (film), 87, 89
Smartphone apps, addressing gender wage gap, 284
Smelser, Neil, 389
Smith, Anthony Lamar, 241
Smith, Dorothy, 292
Smith, Jada Pickett, 247
Smith, Roger W., 257
Smith, S., 273
Smith, Shantana, 242–243
Smith, Tommie, 230–231
Smith, Will, 247
Snapchat, 96, 370

Snowball sampling, 46
Social and community service manager, 339
Social behaviorism, 99–100
Social bonds, 165
Social capital
groups and, 138–139
social media and, 97
Social categories, 194–195
Social change
careers in, 405–406
defined, 381
dystopia and, 404
online social activism, 392
sociological perspectives on, 381–385
sources of, 385–391
sports and, 386–387
student activism, 380–381
Social class
academic performance and, 39
child-rearing practices and, 105, 106–107, 326–329
culture, inequality, and, 85–86
family and, 326–333
in industrial capitalism, 364–365
mealtimes and, 113
schools and, 346
Social class and inequality. *See also* Global inequality
income inequality, 199–201
inequalities in health care, health, and access to consumer goods, 202–205
neighborhood poverty, 208–211
persistence of stratification and poverty, 211–213
poverty and prosperity in the United States, 192–193, 207–208
reasons for growth in inequality, 205–207
reasons to study, 224
sociological building blocks of social class, 194–199
stratification in traditional and modern societies, 193–194
wealth inequality, 201–202
Social class reproduction, 85–86
Social closure, 134
Social computing, 204
Social conflict explanation of persistence of stratification and poverty, 212–213
Social conflict paradigm, 27–29
Social conflict theory, 23, 27–29. *See also* Conflict perspectives
Social constraints, in development, 103–104
Social construction of race and ethnicity, 231–232
Social control
defined, 178
of deviance, 170, 178–185
formal, 178
informal, 178
Social desirability bias, 48–49
Social distance, 118
Social diversity, defined, 30
Social dynamics, 11
Social embeddedness, 3
Social entrepreneur, 375
Social epidemiology, 246
Social facts, 12–13, 335
Social inequality, schools and, 348
Social integration, language and, 77–78
Social interaction, 116–122
ethnomethodology and conversation analysis, 120–122
reasons to study, 122
studies of, 118–119
Socialism and Sexualism (Valette), 21
Social isolation, lack of socialization and, 98–99
Socialist feminism, 291
Socialization
agents of, 97–98, 104–114
aging and, 114–115
anticipatory, 108, 114
behaviorism, 99–100
biological needs *vs.* social constraints, 103–104
defined, 97
family and, 104–105, 106–107
mass media and social media and, 110–111
nature *vs.* nurture debate, 98
organized sports and, 109
peers and, 107–108
reasons to study, 122
religion and, 109–110
social interaction, 116–122
social learning, 99
stage of development, 102–103
symbolic interaction and, 100–102
teachers and schools and, 105–107, 348
total institutions and resocialization, 115–116
work and, 111–112
Social learning, 99
Social learning theory, 99
Social media
as agent of socialization, 110–111
body shaming on, 71
building social movements and, 402
charity organizations and, 140
crowdsourcing, 395
effect on studying time, 54–55
netizens and, 151
seniors and, 115
social activism and, 381
social movements and social change and, 392
Twitter, 18–19
young adult use of, 96–97
Social media coordinator, 405–406
Social Media Today, 19
Social mobility, 195
agency, structure and, 6
education and, 39
Social movement organizations (SMOs), 399–400
Social movements, 391–403
defined, 393
micromobilization contexts for building, 402
new, 393, 402–403
online, 392
reactionary, 393, 397
reasons for, 398–402
rebellions, 393, 396–397
reformist, 36, 393, 394
revolutionary, 393, 396
types of, 393, 394–398
utopian, 393, 397–398
Social Opportunity Survey, 45
Social power, 178
Social science research assistant, 262
Social sciences, 3
Social self, birth of, 97–104
Social solidarity, 13
deviance and, 162
education and, 347
Social statics, 11
Social stratification, 193–194
characteristics of, 194–195
defined, 193
persistence of, 211–213
Social welfare, political party affiliation and support for, 68
Societal reaction theory, 168
Societies, 381
Society in America (Martineau), 12
Socioeconomic status, educational attainment and, 349, 350, 351
Sociological debates, 9

Sociological imagination, 3–6, 21
  defined, 3–4
  new social movements and, 403
Sociological research
  conducting, 45–53
  reasons to learn how to do, 58
  scientific method and, 39–44
  sociology and common sense, 37–39
  student's guide to, 53–58
Sociological theories, 22–29. *See also* Social conflict theory; Structural functionalism; Symbolic interactionism
  defined, 22
Sociological thinking, development of, 9–22
  birth of sociology, 9–11
  19th-century founders, 11–17
  significant founding ideas in U.S. sociology, 17–21
  women in early sociology, 21–22
Sociology
  defined, 2, 3
  feminist perspectives on doing, 292–293
  goals of, 2–3
  reasons to study, 30–31
Sociology of masculinities, 293–295
Sommers, Christina Hoff, 277
Sons, preference for, 336–337
Sorokin, Pitirim, 384, 385
Southern Christian Leadership Conference, 399
Spacey, Kevin, 285
Spanking, 105, 106–107
Spatial organization of society, social movements and, 400–401
Specialized offices, bureaucracies and, 142
Spencer, Herbert, 381
Sports, social change and, 230–231, 386–387
Spurious relationship, 41
Standpoint epistemology, 292–293
Standpoint theory, 292
Stanford prison experiment, 56, 57, 136–137
Stanton, Elizabeth Cady, 290, 382, 383, 394
Starbucks, 212
State crimes, 178
Statistical data, 51
Statistical software, 59
Statistician, 59
Status, 198
Stelle, Claude, 115
Stereotypes
  about minority students in the classroom, 350–351
  gender occupational segregation and, 283–284
Stereotype threat, 277
Stereotyping, defined, 240–241
Sterling, Eric, 158
Stiglitz, Joseph, 200
Stigma, 240
Stigmatization, 168
Stone, Biz, 18
Stowe, Harriet Beecher, 20
Stowe, Isabella Beecher, 20
Strain theory, 163
Stratified sampling, 46
Structural contradiction theory, 167
Structural functionalism, 23–27. *See also* Functionalist perspectives
  on crime and deviance, 28–29
  values and, 70
Structuralism, 138–139
Structural strain, 163
Structure, 5–6
  defined, 5
Student debt, 317, 357, 360
Student protest movement, 380–381
Student's guide to doing research, 53–58
  conducting literature review, 55
  data collection and analysis, 56
  framing research questions, 53
  research formula, 55
  selecting research method, 55
  sharing results, 56, 58
  weighing ethical implications, 56
Studying, technology effects on, 54–55
Sturgeon, Sam, 308
Stuttering, stigmatization and, 168
Subcultural theories, 166
Subcultures, 75–76
  deviance and, 166
Suburbanization, family and, 315–316
Suicide, anomie and, 162
Sumner, William Graham, 67
Superego, 103–104
Surma people, 270
Survey research, 45–47
  factors affecting responses, 48–49
  truthfulness of respondents, 44
Survey statistician, 59
Suspension, in schools, 179–180
Sutherland, E. H., 169, 177
Swarup, Vikas, 87
Symbolic analysts, 366–367
Symbolic interaction, socialization as, 100–102
Symbolic interactionism, 23, 29
  on education, 350–351
  on ethnicity, racism, and minority status, 239–240
Symbols, 29

Taboos, 68
  characteristics of, 66
Taco Bell, 212
Takeoff stage of development, 220
Taliban, 86–87
Tandan, Loveleen, 87
Taslitz, A. E., 83–84
Taylor, Frederick Winslow, 364
Taylorism, 364
Teachers and schools, as agents of socialization, 105–107, 348
Tea Party political movement, 389, 401
Technological change, social change and, 403, 404
Technologies of discrimination, 246
Technology
  dystopia and, 404
  effects on studying, 54–55
  future of work and revolution in, 369–372
  sampling and, 52
Television
  as agent of socialization, 110
  Kellner on, 81
  reinforcing gender identities, 272
Temporal flexibility, 286
Theories, testing, 42–43
THINX underwear, 375
Third-wave feminism, 291–292
Thomas, D. S., 66
Thomas, Dorothy, 231
Thomas, W. I., 66, 231
Thompson, K. M., 273
"Three strikes" laws, 181
Thrifty food basket, 209
Throwbacks, 162
Tiananmen Square protests, 400, 404
Tibetan sky burial, 75
Title IX, 271, 278, 386
Tocqueville, Alexis de, 199
TOMS Shoes, 375
Torres, Lisa, 139
Total fertility rate (TFR), 217
Total institutions, 141
  resocialization and, 115–116

Toys, gender socialization and, 271
Traditional stage of development, 219
Trafficking, 165
Trafficking in Persons Report, 297
Trailer park industry, 192–193
Trained incapacity, bureaucracies and, 145
Training and development specialist, 152
Transactional leader, 134–135
Transformational leader, 134
Transgender, 268–269
  defined, 268
Transnational nature of immigrant families, 321
Transparency International, 222
Transportation, poverty and, 218–219
Transsexual, defined, 268
Triad, 131, 133
Trimble, L. B., 139
Tristan, Flora, 21
The Truly Disadvantaged (Wilson), 329–330
Truman, Harry S., 52, 143, 386
Trump, Donald, 52, 300
Tumin, Melvin, 211, 224
Turner, J. S., 272
Turner, Nat, 397
Turner, Ralph H., 389
Turn taking, 122
Twitter, 18–19, 96, 151, 402

Uchitelle, Louis, 333–334
Ulbricht, Ross, 164
Underclass, 195–196
Underemployment, 368–369
Unemployed, 368
Unemployment
  of college graduates by gender, 4–5
  educational attainment and, 359–361
  in United States, 368–369
Uniform Crime Reports (UCR), 172–173, 174–175
Unions, 365, 396
United Nations, 147, 149
  Convention on the Prevention and Punishment of the Crime of Genocide, 256–257
  data from, 51
  Development Programme, 222
  Development Project, 296
  on global hunger, 215
  High Commissioner for Refugees, 233
  Population Fund, 295
  on refugees, 258
  Security Council, 150
United States
  American Indian reservations in, 233
  changes in group affiliation in, 151
  child care in, 319–321
  class and inequality in, 199–208
  class structure in, 196
  correlation between education and median earnings, 41
  crime statistics in, 174–175
  culture of thinness in, 72–73
  death penalty in, 183–185
  English-only movement in, 77–78
  eviction in, 36–37
  food deserts in, 203, 204–205
  foreign-born Hispanics in, 251
  growth of inequality in, 205–207
  hate crimes in, 234–235
  ideal and real culture in, 70–74
  imprisonment in, 180–183
  local consumption, global production and, 26–27
  marriage and divorce in, 14, 316–319
  percentage of population speaking language other than English at home, 78
  population by race and Hispanic origin, 247
  poverty in, 24, 207–208, 209
  racial and ethnic groups in, 247–256
  refugees and, 258
  segregation on basis of race in, 235–236
  state and federal prison population, 1925–2015, 159
  top feeder countries for migration to, 322
  top 10 largest immigrant groups, 322
  unemployment, employment, and underemployment in, 368–369
  violent and property crime in, 172–173
  wealth inequality in, 24–25
U.S. Air Force Academy study, 132–133
U.S. Bureau of Justice Statistics, 51, 234
U.S. Bureau of Labor Statistics, 282
U.S. Census Bureau, 45, 51, 59, 192, 199, 208, 283
  race, ethnicity, and Hispanic origin questions, 255–256
U.S. Department of Commerce, 284
U.S. Geological Survey, 19
U.S. Holocaust Memorial Museum, 259
U.S. sociology, significant founding ideas in, 17–21
USAID, 149
University of Chicago, 19
University of Kansas, 19
Unwritten rules, 100
Upper class, 196
Upper-class families, child rearing and, 326, 328
Upper middle class, 196
Upper middle-income countries, 213, 215
Urban and regional planner, 303
Urbanization, 10–11, 315
Urban riots, 390
Use of existing information in research, 46, 50–51
Utilitarian organizations, 140–141
Utopian movements, 393, 397–398

Valette, Aline, 21
Validity, 43–44
Value-added theory, 389
Value neutrality, 44
Values, 69–70
  characteristics of, 66
  defined, 69
Vanilla Ice, 172
Van Wees, Hans, 257
Variables
  defined, 40
  dependent, 50, 57
  experimental, 50
  independent, 50, 57
  qualitative, 41
  quantitative, 40–41
  relationships between, 40–42
Veblen, Thorstein, 145
Verstehen, 16
Video games
  engagement with, 88
  gender stereotypes in, 272–273
  hours per day engaged in, 404
  violence in, 50, 84
Vietnam War protests, 380, 391, 399
A Vindication of the Rights of Women (Wollstonecraft), 21
Violence
  domestic, 118
  effects of media, 88–89
  family, 325–326
  media, culture, and, 83–84
  normalizing, 84
Violent crime, 172–173
Violent masculinity, 84

Volkswagen AG, 176
Voltaire, 10
Voluntary associations, 141
Voter turnout, social desirability bias and, 48
Voting rights, ex-offenders and, 182, 244

Wages. *See also* Earnings
federal minimum, 362
gender wage gap, 281–282, 284–285
Wagner, W. E., 109
Waite, L. J., 276
The Walking Dead (television program), 64, 65
Wallace, David Foster, 18
Wallace, George, 355
Wallerstein, Immanuel, 221
Wallis, C., 272
Wall Street Journal, 285
Walmart, 212
War, rape in, 298–299
War of the Worlds (radio broadcast), 390
"War on drugs," increased prison population and, 181
War on Poverty, 207
Washington, Booker T., 20
Waste, bureaucracies and, 145
Watanabe, T., 323
Watson, John, 99
Watson, Wendy K., 115
Wealth, 197–198
Wealth inequality, 201–202
in United States, 24–25
Weathering, 245
Weber, Max, 16–17
bureaucracies and, 129, 141–142, 145, 146
critical thinking and, 6
on formal organizations, 139
grobalization and, 89
historical research and, 51
on social change, 384–385
social closure and, 134
symbolic interactionism and, 23
value neutrality and, 44
Wedding ceremony, norms surrounding, 67–69
Wedding industrial complex, 67
Weinreich, Max, 250
Weissman, Dan, 192–193
Weiss-Wendt, Anton, 260
Welles, Orson, 390
West, Candace, 274
WhatsApp, 370
White, Betty, 112
White-collar crime, 29, 173, 175–176
White-collar occupations, 198
White ethnic Americans, 254–255
White flight, 314
"White Privilege" (McIntosh), 254–255
Whorf, Benjamin, 76
Wiig, Kristin, 288, 289
"Wild boy" (Victor), 98
Williams, Christine, 286
Williams, Evan, 18
Williams, Robert M., Jr., 69
Willis, Paul, 351
Wilson, William Julius, 196, 329–330, 331
Wingfield, A. H., 286
Wirth, Louis, 239–240
Witchcraft, beliefs and, 66
Wittstock, Laura Waterman, 250
Wizard of Oz (film), 120
Wolf, M., 354
Wollstonecraft, Mary, 21
Women. *See also* Gender; Girls
access to transportation and, 218–219
conversation with men, 121
disregard for, 297
in early sociology, 21–22
educational level and divorce, 14–15
education and child health outcomes, 217, 219
education and health and, 295
empowerment of, 299–302
global woman, 334–335
incarceration rates for, 181, 183
lack of rural health systems for, 295–297
maternal mortality, 295–297
networking and, 139
in political office, 300–301
popular culture and violence against, 84
rape in war and, 298–299
service jobs and, 206
sextortion and, 296
sexual exploitation and sex trafficking, 297–298
violence against, 84, 118
workplace socialization and, 112
Women and Economics (Gilman), 20
Women's March, 395
Woodhull, Victoria, 394
Word poverty, adult illiteracy and, 353–354
Work, as agent of socialization, 111–112. *See also* Employment
Working class, 196
decline of marriage among, 30–31
Working-class families
child rearing and, 326–329
globalization and, 334
Working poor, 196
Working with existing information, 46, 50–51
Work-life balance, among middle-class families, 331, 333
Workman, J. E., 84
World Bank, 51, 213, 218
World systems theory, 221
Wright, Erik Olin, 196
Wright, Robin, 284–285
Written communication skills, careers using, 186–187
WuDunn, S., 295–296, 298
Wuthnow, Robert, 64

Xia, Jenny, 262
X Men: Apocalypse (film), 84
Xodus, Voltaire, 375

The Yellow Wallpaper (Gilman), 20
Y2K problem, 390
Youth, social media use and, 96–97
Yugoslavia, former, rape in war and, 299

Zamoff, Richard, 386
Zappos, 147
Zell, Sam, 192
Zero tolerance policies, 179
Zimbardo, Philip, 56, 57
Zimmerman, Don, 274
Zombie phenomenon, 64–65